FALLINGWATER   RISING

F A L L I N G W A

FALLINGWATER, THE KAUFMANN HOUSE, 1934–37, NEAR PITTSBURGH, PENNSYLVANIA. BILL HEDRICH'S FAMOUS VIEW, NOVEMBER 1937.

ER RISING

FRANK LLOYD WRIGHT,

E. J. KAUFMANN,

AND AMERICA'S MOST EXTRAORDINARY HOUSE

FRANKLIN TOKER

ALFRED A. KNOPF   NEW YORK   2003

THIS IS A BORZOI BOOK PUBLISHED BY ALFRED A. KNOPF

Copyright © 2003 by Franklin K. Toker

www.aaknopf.com

Library of Congress Cataloging-in-Publication Data

Toker, Franklin
Fallingwater Rising : Frank Lloyd Wright, E.J. Kaufmann, and America's Most Extraordinary House / Franklin Toker.
p. cm.
Includes index.
ISBN 1-4000-4026-4 (hc : alk. paper)
1. Wright, Frank Lloyd, 1867–1859—Criticism and Interpretation. 2. Kaufmann, Edgar J., 1885–1955—Homes and Haunts—Pennsylvania. 3. Fallingwater (PA) I. Title

NA737.W7165 2003
728'.372'092—dc21
2003056181

Remembering Ethel

I conceived a love of you quite beyond the ordinary relationship of client and Architect. That love gave you Fallingwater.
You will never have anything more in your life like it.

—FRANK LLOYD WRIGHT to Edgar Kaufmann

Make something, and die.　　　—IAN McEWAN, *Amsterdam*

CONTENTS

1909 E. J. Kaufmann discovers Bear Run; marries his cousin Liliane the same year.

1910 Kaufmann takes control of family department store in Pittsburgh; his son Edgar Junior born.

1916 Kaufmann rents Bear Run as a camp for his employees.

1926 Kaufmann's Department Store buys the 1,600 acres at Bear Run.

1933 Kaufmann seeks CCC status for Bear Run; when that fails, he buys the property in Liliane's name.

1934 E. J. proposes huge jobs in Pittsburgh to Frank Lloyd Wright; Edgar Junior goes to study with Wright at Taliesin; E. J. and Liliane follow; Kaufmann commissions Wright to build Fallingwater December 18.

1935 Edgar Junior leaves Wright; Wright conceives Fallingwater in July, draws it out September 22, presents drawings to family in Pittsburgh in October.

1936 Engineers caution Kaufmann not to build Fallingwater; working drawings ready by May; construction begins in June; Walter Hall joins as builder in July; cantilevers begin to crack.

1937 *Architectural Forum* offers to publish Wright's new work; Bill Hedrich photographs Fallingwater in November; Kaufmanns occupy Fallingwater in December.

1938 Fallingwater featured at MoMA, in *Architectural Forum, Time,* and *Life,* in hundreds of newspapers and periodicals worldwide.

1939 Guesthouse added.

1952 Liliane dies; her tomb begins to rise at Bear Run the next year.

1955 E. J. Kaufmann dies.

1963 Edgar Kaufmann Jr. gives Fallingwater to Western Pennsylvania Conservancy.

1989 Edgar Kaufmann Jr. dies.

1997 Engineers detect failure in the cantilevers; Fallingwater shored with steel girders.

2002 Post-tensioning restores cantilevers to health.

Fallingwater, with its approach bridge and the guesthouse further uphill

APPROACHING FALLINGWATER

These two houses [Fallingwater and the Willey house] show Frank Lloyd Wright at the top of his powers, undoubtedly the world's greatest living architect.

—LEWIS MUMFORD, *The New Yorker,* 1938

Frank Lloyd Wright, the greatest architect of the 20th Century.

—*Time,* 1938

There are two ways of seeing," the seventeenth-century French painter Nicolas Poussin would always insist, "with the eye *and* with the mind." We will need both those powerful instruments as we approach Frank Lloyd Wright's Fallingwater. Actually, you are already approaching Fallingwater in your mind. You probably recognize Wright's name, and quite possibly you have heard of Fallingwater, or would recognize it when shown a picture of a house perched over a waterfall. You may have encountered the description often applied to Fallingwater: "unquestionably the most famous private residence ever built."

A monument of such fame beckons us to make a pilgrimage, which itself is a journey of the eye and of the mind. A pilgrim dreams half his life about visiting a site, then moves heaven and earth to get there. So even before setting out to western Pennsylvania, we can picture ourselves alongside the waterfall on the Bear Run stream. But we cannot flutter to Fallingwater like Tinkerbell: to begin with, there is no public transportation, which obliged one German student to hike the twenty-three miles from the nearest bus stop at Uniontown.

There is a second problem if we go by car, and that is aesthetic. Both the hour-long car trip from Pittsburgh and the passage of several hours from Washington, D.C., feature soothing hills but not much else to cheer about visually. A New Yorker may feel momentarily at home on seeing IRWIN GREENSBURG as the first Pennsylvania Turnpike exit east of Pittsburgh, but the sign proves to be shorthand for the two Revolutionary-era communities nearby: one founded by Colonel John Irwin, the other named for General Nathanael Greene. Southwestern Pennsylvania looks little changed from the hardscrabble country it was in the eighteenth century. Except for the Mellon holdings at Ligonier, this is deer-hunting country, not the foxhunting estates of old Virginia.

The honky-tonk that greets us at the turnpike's Donegal exit, nineteen miles north of Fallingwater, offers cultural dislocation of another sort. The first half-mile of local roadway brings us Exxon, Sunoco, BP, Hardee's, Pizza Hut, Days Inn, Caddie Shak, vegetable stands, an artificial waterfall selling something, Eclipse Exotic Dancer's (as the sign says), go-karts, astrologers, bingo, and Holistic Physical Therapy. The ammunition shops, ski rental huts, and chiropractic services lining our route arrange themselves in a near-perfect 1:1:1 ratio. The billboard-heralded Mountain Pines Resort turns out to be a vast and soggy trailer park, as we should have guessed.

Farther south, Routes 711 and 381 take us through a Pennsylvania Bible Belt: Baptist, United Methodist, Assembly of God, Church of God congregations, the County Line Church of the Brethren, and Stepping Stones Christian Bookstore, followed by the Normalville Rod & Gun

Club. The billboards drop away somewhat when we reach the village of Mill Run, which serves as a gateway to Fallingwater. After a final pitch for Yogi Bear's Jellystone Park, a GO IN PEACE sign sounds the first hopeful note in miles, and we get some decent views of nature on the margins of the Youghiogheny River valley. Fields look better tended here. Two more churches, then the woods thicken and the road dips down to a dwarf bridge that carries us over the stream called Bear Run. Signs discreetly inform us that it is time to turn for Fallingwater.

Fallingwater and other buildings at the Kaufmann estate of Bear Run

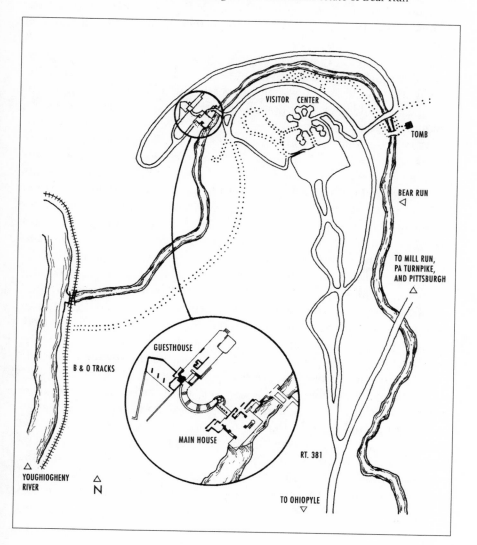

We enter darkly wooded grounds, drive a moment, halt at a ticket kiosk in the witty disguise of a Victorian outhouse, park the car, and park any children under the age of six at child care in the visitor center. For a minute or so we descend through a thicket of rhododendron via a stately wooden ramp into the perfect quiet of a lush glen. Alongside the ramp is the exposed sandstone wall of the ravine, its ledges recalling the photographs of Fallingwater's walls that hang in the visitor center. On the valley floor we encounter a forest of such virginal purity that we walk through it as though enchanted. Now the sound of Bear Run reaches us with almost oceanic intensity. A clearing in the woods reveals the stream, a concrete bridge, and a corner of Fallingwater.

In the old pilgrimage to Santiago de Compostela, the bedraggled faithful coming over the last Spanish hill would jostle one another to see who first could shout "I see the towers!" But our brother-pilgrims to Fallingwater hold back. Our first glimpse of the house brings us to a stop, and total silence.

Why the silence? Confusion, for one thing. This is not the mighty fortress of the famous photographs, but something else that stands whisper-quiet, even vulnerable, beyond the roar of the stream. The house presents itself not proud but modest and abased before us (the pious might think of Mary before Gabriel). There is no chance to ascend to Fallingwater because the house spreads itself at eye level, or below us. More confusion. We can hardly remember when we *descended* to view a famous building: such monuments normally tower over us. It does not help, either, that Fallingwater gives no hint of an entryway: are we not to enter the house at all? More confusion is spawned by the materials in and around the house. Fallingwater is not merely *in* the woods, it *enwraps* itself in a rich verdant shroud like no building we have ever experienced. We look for correspondingly soft, rich materials in Fallingwater (wasn't Wright famous for organic architecture?), but its dun-colored concrete balconies give it all the grace of a battleship.

The concrete bridge, a smaller version of the balconies staring us in the face, bids us approach, and a guide urges us to step lively. We gather on the bridge and discover that its job is not just to get us over the water now thundering under our feet: its primary function is to serve as a viewing platform. It reveals the house visually and nature aurally, just like the ancient Chinese and Japanese viewing platforms that took advantage of both sublime views and the affecting sounds of nature. The bridge presents the balcony corners at Fallingwater canted at a 45-degree angle, so the house seems to dissolve into an endless battle of crisscrossing axes. Somebody behind us murmurs, "Cubism," and we realize that the makeup of the house is far more complex than we had bargained for.

Our confusion is not over. Forget the missing front door: how does Fallingwater hold itself up? The main balcony stretches in front of us with nothing (so far as we can see) supporting it from below. But the strain imposed on this marvel ("Cantilever technology," babbles the guide) is soon evident: the balcony nearest us looks half a foot lower at its corners than at its middle. The resulting curvature makes Fallingwater look a little more "organic" than even Wright expected, but all the other clichés about the perfect fit between the house and its natural setting seem to hold true. None of us has ever seen a structure built so daringly close to water. The staircase leading down from the living room stops just inches over the brook. "Wright never heard of a once-a-century flood?" grumbles the engineer from Baltimore.

It takes a while to realize that we really are standing at Bear Run, gazing at something that millions have heard about but few get to see. Then it hits us. Visiting Fallingwater has only a little to do with architecture and engineering: the quality we perceive here is essentially spiritual. Nearly everyone falls under the spell of the house, recognizing in it the most serene building we will ever encounter. We see now why more than a few visitors speak of their pilgrimage to Fallingwater as a turning point in their lives.

The concrete bridge invites us to move toward the house, but visitors who are exploring Bear Run on their own almost never do. Instead they feel compelled to find "the view"—to picture Fallingwater as the photographers of the past immortalized it. Some make for the stone steps that lead down to the water. (These steps are now marked off-limits as too hazardous, but another good outlook is provided downstream.) The flat stone bed of Bear Run and the little hill downstream provide new viewing platforms, and our confusion over Fallingwater begins to clear up. We realize when we see the brooding concrete masses alternating with the hand-hewn stone walls that it is not the modernity but the antiquity—even the eternality—of Fallingwater that enthralls us. The rocks that are so much a part of the house will be here forever. The water that animates it will never stop flowing. And despite its daredevil engineering, Fallingwater will never fall down—although it threatened to, a few years back.

Now we maneuver over the rocks in the stream until the concrete balconies hover in space over us. We have finally stepped right into Bill Hedrich's 1937 photograph that immortalized the building when it was brand-new. Here is one of the most photogenic buildings in creation. So is the Taj Mahal, but the two work so differently: the Taj Mahal so perfect in its balance, Fallingwater so restless that it looks like a living thing sprouting out of the rocks.

We will have occasion to see Fallingwater like this, "with the eye," many times in these pages. But when we turn to seeing Fallingwater in Poussin's second way, "with the mind," our vision of the house is beclouded by four myths that have gone unchallenged for the better part of a century. So long as these myths are in our way, when we look at the most famous private house in the world with our minds, we are unable to see straight.

An unending cascade of Fallingwater publications and videos retells the four myths along these lines:

- The man responsible for Fallingwater was Edgar J. Kaufmann Jr., scion of a Pittsburgh department-store dynasty, who in 1934 became an apprentice to the architect Frank Lloyd Wright. It was Kaufmann Jr. who convinced his father, Edgar Kaufmann Sr., to commission Wright to design a family retreat in the virgin forest of Bear Run, forty-five miles southeast of Pittsburgh.
- Once Wright got the commission, he did nothing with it for nine months, until he took blank tracing paper on September 22, 1935, and in two hours drew up complete plans for the house he called "Fallingwater."
- In the construction of Fallingwater over the next two years, Wright demonstrated a grasp of engineering that was as strong as his artistic sense. To show his confidence in his daringly cantilevered balconies, he risked his life by standing below them when the supporting wooden posts were removed.*

---

*As Edgar Kaufmann Jr. recalled it: "The contractor was frightened beyond measure (perhaps remembering some of his poor workmanship) and refused to strike away [the] last timber rising from the falls to the big cantilever. Wright, disgusted, stood next to a workman who struck the post out—and the house stood firm." Wright's apprentice Donald Hoppen made the story even juicier, insisting that it was the architect himself who "demonstrated his faith in his design by grabbing a sledgehammer and knocking out the post."

The problem is that none of this ever happened, since we have no evidence that Wright attended the removal of the scaffolding. Kaufmann Jr. either derived this myth from something the architect Howard Roark might have done in Ayn Rand's 1943 novel *The Fountainhead* (Roark does the opposite, actually, blowing up one of his own buildings after it had been disfigured by other designers), or from Henrik Ibsen's *Master Builder,* in which a designer loses his life in a similar display of bravado.

- After Fallingwater's completion in January 1938, public opinion in the United States and around the world spontaneously acclaimed it the crowning achievement of modern architecture.

These are great stories, but each is too good to be true. There are some remarkable coincidences in Fallingwater's history, but these near miracles are such whoppers that they threaten to turn the entire history of Fallingwater into a fabrication. Start with September 22, 1935, the day Wright is alleged to have drawn up the Fallingwater plans from scratch in a couple of hours. It defies rationality to think that the most complex house of the twentieth century blazed forth from blank sheets so fast. The myth is disproven anyway by the few drawings that survive from that day. Anyone who examines these drawings with a magnifying glass can spot the erasures that disprove the notion that Fallingwater emerged perfect from Wright's mind, like Athena popping full-grown from the brow of Zeus.

Now proceed to the engineering of Fallingwater, which was anything but flawless. The cantilevered balconies started cracking, heaving, and sagging even before the Kaufmanns moved in. The house might have collapsed in months had Kaufmann Sr. and Wright's apprentices not furtively added more steel than was called for in Wright's drawings.

Then, the acclaim that greeted the house in 1938. It certainly looked spontaneous, but in reality Fallingwater was "puffed" by such masters of publicity as Kaufmann Sr. and Wright himself, Henry R. Luce, William Randolph Hearst, the public relations division of the Museum of Modern Art (MoMA), and, later, the novelist Ayn Rand. Without these interventions, how likely was it that a house in a remote forest eighteen miles from the Mason-Dixon line would become the poster child for modern architecture worldwide?

About that forest of Bear Run: it is as virginal as Mae West, since the Kaufmanns reclaimed it from an industrial domain. Critical Theory tells us that erasure of the past is a prime characteristic of modernism, which makes Bear Run the most modern forest on earth. Since the Kaufmanns' revirginized forest colors all our impressions of the house over a waterfall, its story demands an accurate retelling, too.

But of all the inaccuracies or omissions in the old myth-strewn history of Fallingwater, it is the role of E. J. Kaufmann Sr. that is most in need of reexamination. Granted, the sometimes outrageous E. J. is hard to picture as a leading patron of architecture, especially when Edgar Jr. tells us that his father never really grasped what modern architecture was. It *is* baffling that in the space of fifteen years Kaufmann Sr. switched from building traditional Georgian palaces to the modernistic style, then jumped from modernistic to Wright, and finally overthrew Wright for Bauhaus modern. I acknowledge these eccentric jumps in style, but I interpret them to mean only that Kaufmann Sr.—unlike his son—was no architectural ideologue. He was a merchant, and that is what merchants do: jump from style to style as the market demands.

Previous books and articles on Wright acknowledged Kaufmann Sr. as the "client of record" at Fallingwater, and mention was sometimes made of his personal creativity, but these studies typically presented him as a rich man whose main artistic activity was the signing of checks. Creating an accurate portrait of E. J. Kaufmann is encumbered by the disappearance of virtually all his business and personal papers and by the absence of any memoir by or about him. So sparse a record would not be a problem were we dealing with an ordinary client, but it greatly hinders our understanding of the patron of Fallingwater. Without Kaufmann to back it, Frank Lloyd Wright's house over a waterfall would have remained an exciting drawing, nothing more. In the middle of the Depression, Wright was going to find few E. J. Kaufmanns to bring his drawing to life.

I see Kaufmann not only as someone who assumed considerable financial risk to put up his fabled weekend house, but almost—I stress "almost"—as Fallingwater's coarchitect. He certainly knew something about both architecture and engineering, having studied engineering at Yale. Less clear, but far from negligible, was Kaufmann's role in the artistic design of Fallingwater. All in all, E. J. strikes me today as one of the most creative patrons of architecture since Shah Jahan emptied his treasury to put up the Taj Mahal.

In my research I could not fail to note that E. J. always came off worst in the Fallingwater studies published by Kaufmann Jr., who had enjoyed a distinguished career as curator of design at MoMA and as professor of architectural history at Columbia University. Junior several times alleged in print that his father contributed little to the house, and that he had meddled in its construction to the point of harming it. With the father long dead and little remembered, it was natural for journalists to tag Junior rather than E. J. as the significant architectural client in the Kaufmann family.

It took me years to determine how Fallingwater was born. My first steps came in the mid-1980s, when research for my book *Pittsburgh: An Urban Portrait* opened my eyes to the fact that E. J. Kaufmann had been a sophisticated architectural patron decades before Fallingwater went up. In 1986, I gave a lecture at Columbia University that proposed E. J. as a

major force—maybe *the* major force—behind Fallingwater. Kaufmann Jr.,
who sponsored the lecture, was annoyed at my revisionist reading of his
father, and he soon cut off communication between us. I had unknow-
ingly stepped into a scholarly minefield, particularly when my proposed
1989 article (for the *Art Bulletin*) on the origins of Fallingwater was blackballed by a Kaufmann Jr. loyalist.

Then, one by one, research barriers came tumbling down. In 1987,
Columbia University's Avery Architectural and Fine Arts Library had
dropped the restrictions that Kaufmann Jr. had imposed on the Fallingwater drawings and documents he had deposited there. The next year,
the Getty Foundation made publicly available reproductions of 24,000
Wright drawings and 103,000 items of his correspondence that had been
previously accessible only with difficulty at Wright's Taliesin West compound in Arizona. Now I could examine for myself just what Kaufmann
and Wright had said to each other, and the results were unexpected.

More barriers came down in 1992: E. J.'s niece donated hundreds of
family documents to Fallingwater and to a Pittsburgh history center. This
donation allowed me to be the first scholar to survey the Kaufmann
dynasty in both the United States and Germany. To my surprise (I had
always regarded them as nouveaux riches), they turned out to be an
ancient family, whose bloodlines I could trace back nearly five hundred
years. Kaufmann's Department Store also made available its fragmentary
but valuable archive on E. J. as a business promoter. By the end of the
decade I was ploughing through archives at MoMA in New York and at
the Getty Center and UCLA in Los Angeles, where I found materials that
linked Wright, Kaufmann, Fallingwater, and California modernism in
ways never considered before.

The newly available documents made Junior's account of the origins
of Fallingwater look highly suspect. It was as though Junior (who published nothing on Fallingwater until both E. J. and Wright were dead) was
struggling with his father to see who would get credit for the house.

Consider, for example, the historic first meeting of client(s) and
architect at Bear Run on December 18, 1934. In his first publication on
Fallingwater, a 1962 memoir in the Italian magazine *L'Architettura*, Kaufmann Jr. wrote that four people had been present: Wright, E. J. and his
wife, Liliane, and Junior himself. In his 1986 coffee-table book *Fallingwater: A Frank Lloyd Wright Country House*, Kaufmann eradicated his
mother and declared instead: "Father and Wright drove to the mountain
property to consider a site; I went along." But he didn't! One of the letters
at the Getty revealed that Junior was in Wisconsin that day: Wright and
E. J. had met without him. Junior's recollections contained a dead give-
away in any case, when he reported that the Bear Run rhododendron

were in full bloom at the time of the meeting. On a December day in western Pennsylvania those blooms would have been miraculous for sure.

These terminological inexactitudes (I follow Winston Churchill in carefully avoiding the word "lie") made me question the rest of Junior's litany. Take his enrollment as an apprentice to Wright at the architect's Taliesin East estate in Wisconsin, which historians had always adjudged the spark that flamed into Fallingwater. Kaufmann summarized it in 1982 in a film interview that became the core of the 1994 documentary *Fallingwater: A Conversation with Edgar J. Kaufmann, Jr.*, in which he says:

> In 1934, I came back from a long stay in Europe, because money was short. And I found myself wanting to continue to try to be a painter, as I had been attempting to do in Europe. I had a friend who worked in a New York art gallery, and she told me that she had read a very interesting book, which was the *Autobiography* of Frank Lloyd Wright. I had heard his name, but I really had no image of what he stood for or what his work was like at all. But I read the *Autobiography*, and I must say it really bowled me over, thoroughly. The first thing that I did was to go out and call on Mr. Wright, and say that if he were willing, I would like to spend time working under him, with the other people.

Junior shades the truth in each of the four main points in his statement: the date of his return from Europe, the reason he returned, the birth of his interest in Wright, and the form and content of his pledge to Wright. Junior held to 1934 as the date of his return from Europe even after one of his own protégés reminded him that the year was 1933 (details in chapter 12). This is a crucial point, since 1934 was the year Fallingwater was born. There was a parallel dissimulation in Junior's claim that he had to come back because "money was short." Many an American family discovered money to be "short" during the Depression, but not the Kaufmanns: 1933 was the year E. J. showered his mistress with the equivalent of a quarter of a million dollars in diamond and platinum jewels. No, what made Junior return from Europe in 1933 was the rise of Hitler, which affected him as a Jew living in Austria and Italy. I learned this in 1989 when I located the woman who shared Junior's table during his voyage home on the SS *Champlain*. She well remembered the young man who talked of little else.

What of the unnamed woman friend in a New York art gallery who changed the history of architecture by enlightening Junior about Wright? When quizzed about her in later years, Junior equivocated on both her name and her gender, which raises the possibility that both she and the episode were fictional. The little declaration to Wright that Junior paraphrases in the film can't be verified, either: when Kaufmann came calling on the Master of Taliesin, Wright was not at home.

Junior did eventually serve a shadowy apprenticeship with Wright, but we can't fully reconstruct it, since he elaborated neither on what brought him to Taliesin nor on what took him away. Kaufmann's 1986 book contained his first acknowledgment that he had worked no more than a few months with Wright, and that he had left before the Fallingwater drawings emerged in September 1935. (Before 1986 it was unclear whether or not Kaufmann had stuck it out until the Great Moment.) Junior's refusal to explain his flight from Taliesin gave widespread credence to Brendan Gill's clamorous declaration in the March 1990 *Architectural Digest* that Wright had expelled him for homosexual activity.

As to what brought Junior to Taliesin, it turns out that it was not the son who first got in touch with Wright, but the father. Junior always represented his father's first encounter with Wright, in November 1934, as an accidental by-product of visiting day at Camp Taliesin. But this, too, was dissimulation, because the surviving telegrams show that the meeting of Wright and Kaufmann Sr. was planned with not much less care than the Normandy landings. I now doubt whether Junior guided his father to Wright at all; if anything, the reverse was true. One document implies that Kaufmann Sr. *made* his son study with Wright.

Put this book down now if you can't live without the old myths about Fallingwater. But take comfort in the fact that a Fallingwater history shorn of miracles can still be thrilling. The story of the house goes beyond architecture to encompass George Washington battling the French near Bear Run; E. J. and his spouse-cousin, Liliane, caught up in a Jazz Age glitter straight out of *The Great Gatsby;* and a Depression-wracked America that was enchanted by Fallingwater in 1938 the way it would be by *The Wizard of Oz* the year following. (The connection between the two was not irrelevant, as we will learn: L. Frank Baum, who wrote *Oz,* was in private life the guru who taught merchandisers like E. J. Kaufmann how to entice customers into their stores.)

The story of Fallingwater even contains a few titillating details: E. J. Kaufmann's mistresses and a daughter born out of wedlock; Liliane's X-rated portrait, her own lovers, and an alleged suicide; and the intricacies of Kaufmann Jr.'s life as well. I researched these sidelines also— maybe not as energetically as some readers would like—because you can't understand Fallingwater without them. What made the house so radical, I believe, was the urgent need of its designer and of its patron to redress the wrongs the world had done them. For Wright, this meant the mockery of the German modernists who had outflanked him; for Kaufmann, it meant the anti-Jewish snobbery of Pittsburgh.

Happily, we can leave intact large chunks of the old history of Fallingwater. The tale that the once-famous Frank Lloyd Wright had hit rock bottom before Kaufmann saved his professional life: that's entirely true. And all the accolades bestowed on Fallingwater over the years—there is no reason to abandon them, either. The fabled timelessness of Fallingwater, its special appeal to us among all of Wright's creations: these still hold true. Fallingwater merits the praise traditionally showered on it, and justly bears its designation as a great house—possibly the greatest house—of modern architecture, and a reasonable claimant, at least, to the title of greatest house on earth.

Opposite: Frank Lloyd Wright a few years after he designed Fallingwater

ONE

THE DEAD MAN OF
MODERN ARCHITECTURE
PLANS A COMEBACK

Nothing is so dangerous as being too modern. One is apt to grow old-fashioned quite suddenly.

—OSCAR WILDE

Ahistory of Fallingwater must begin with Frank Lloyd Wright, because he conceived a house sailing over the waterfall on Bear Run long before E. J. Kaufmann dared contemplate building it. But the Wright of our story is not the bombastic "greatest architect in history" that he became. Rather he is a Depression-era edition, a chastened architect who would draw life from his most famous building fully as much as it drew life from him.

When he died in 1959, still active at the age of ninety-one, Wright was the most famous architect in the world, literally. He had by then been practicing his craft for more than seventy years, during which he completed over four hundred buildings and worked on twice that many projects that were left unbuilt. His career is without parallel in the history of architecture. Painters can finish a thousand times more works than architects because a canvas demands little time and less money. Architects by contrast devote endless amounts of their energy and their clients' dollars to produce a significant body of work.

Because Wright lived so long, we think of his career as unidirectional, always going up. But what is fascinating about the career are not the heights of success but the fallows during which he produced few buildings but incubated the ideas he would use to brilliant effect later. The longest of these droughts stretched from the completion of the Imperial Hotel in Tokyo in 1922 to the design of Fallingwater in 1935. Particularly galling to Wright was the second half of the drought, during which he completed just two buildings: a house for his cousin Richard Lloyd Jones in Tulsa in 1929, and another for Malcolm Willey in Minneapolis four years later.

While Wright served as the model for the architect Howard Roark in Ayn Rand's *The Fountainhead,* in the 1930s his difficulties were far greater than those facing his fictional counterpart. Roark had enemies, but he was still young and had fine prospects before him. Not so Wright. By the mid-1930s Wright was nearing seventy (he was born in 1867, although he claimed 1869), and his promise was as spent as his youth. He retained a certain notoriety among architects and laypersons, but that was mainly as an outrageous character who was good for quotes on a slow news day, not as the trailblazer of modern architecture he had been decades earlier.

John Cushman Fistere, writing in the December 1931 *Vanity Fair,* was typical of the critics who saw Wright as finished:

Nevertheless there are many who believe that Mr. Wright is more genius than architect, and who justify their opinion by pointing to his characteristic idiosyncrasies, and to the still more significant fact that he has designed comparatively few buildings to support his manifold theories. Even his most zealous disciples have difficulty in listing his actual achievements: the Larkin factory, "that hotel in Japan," and the glass and steel apartment house for New York that has never been built. As an architectural *theorist,* Mr. Wright has no superior; but as an architect he has little to contribute for comparison.*

By the 1930s even many of Wright's admirers were resigned to his disappearance from the central stage of modernism. In 1936 the New York architect Harold Sterner was forced to admit:

> In Europe the names of Sullivan and Wright are famous and respected, but both of these men were given relatively few opportunities to practice their genius, and now Sullivan is long since dead and Frank Lloyd Wright [is] approaching the end of his career.

Nothing irked Wright so much as the way historians and critics praised his early work but ignored what he had built later. To the critic Fiske Kimball, who refused to put Wright's recent work in his *American Architecture* survey, Wright wrote in 1928: "I have been reading my obituaries to a considerable extent over the past year or two, and think, with Mark Twain, the reports of my death greatly exaggerated."

Wright's troubles in the 1920s and 1930s constituted what seemed like a tragic end for the man who thirty years earlier had been acknowledged as the world's leading modern architect. But what did it mean to be "modern" in those early days? The pioneers of modern architecture had not consciously sought to invent a new style any more than the engineers of the twelfth century intended to invent Gothic. Modern and Gothic both started as technical innovations that were later fleshed out into systems of design. Creating the early structural triumphs of modernism was comparatively easy: London's Crystal Palace of 1851 and the thousand-foot-high Eiffel Tower of 1889 in Paris showed architects how to exploit iron and glass. Tempering iron into steel, using steel to reinforce concrete, achieving transparency through glass, applying prefabrication and the interchangeability of parts to architecture—these adjustments to building technology would soon follow, and so, eventually, did a matching aesthetic.

---

*Copying out this statement in 1937 as part of her preparation for *The Fountainhead,* Ayn Rand snarled in her journal: "May I be forgiven for copying this! This is Toohey [the mealymouthed architecture critic of her novel] par excellence—god damn him!"

But the core problem of modern architecture was neither technological nor aesthetic; it was how to harness the new materials to create a humane environment. Here lay the special achievements of Wright and his master, Louis Henry Sullivan. Both Wright and Sullivan sought to reconcile the two most influential architecture theorists of the nineteenth century: John Ruskin, with his plea for a sensuous, tactile, emotion-based architecture, and Eugène-Emmanuel Viollet-le-Duc, with his vision of architecture as structural rationalism. Having dropped out of engineering after two terms at the University of Wisconsin, Wright jump-started his career in 1887 as head draftsman to Sullivan and Dankmar Adler in Chicago. Sullivan's severely rational but richly decorative Wainwright skyscraper of 1890 in St. Louis (with Wright assisting) achieved an ingenious synthesis of the opposing philosophies of Ruskin and Viollet-le-Duc. Sullivan's later Carson Pirie Scott Department Store in Chicago drank more deeply of the decorative Art Nouveau, but even there, in contrast to the Europeans, Sullivan insisted on obeying and not subverting the logic of his industrial building components.

In 1892, Wright emerged from Sullivan's shadow and began working on his own. In the first decade of the new century he produced a trio of works so singular that they would have assured him lasting fame had he put up nothing else. The 1903 Larkin Administration Building in Buffalo was a radical restatement of the form and social environment of the office tower; Unity Temple of 1904 in the Chicago suburb of Oak Park marked a no less radical change in the concept of sacred space; while the Frederick Robie house of 1909, in Chicago, is the ancestor (directly, or via Fallingwater) of half the postwar suburban houses in the United States. Wright

Louis Henry Sullivan: Carson Pirie
Scott Department Store, Chicago, 1899
and later

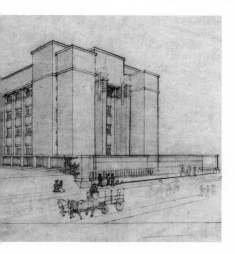 

Above left: Wright's Larkin Administration Building in Buffalo, in his original drawing of 1903
Above right: Wright's apprentices redrew the Larkin Building in Bauhaus style around
1930 to emphasize the debt that German modernism owed their master

capped the decade with a stunning publicity triumph in the publication in Germany of two sumptuous portfolios of his buildings and projects, the *Ausgeführte Bauten und Entwürfe von Frank Lloyd Wright* (Executed Buildings and Studies by Frank Lloyd Wright). Wright always claimed that everything significant in modern architecture had come from him. Allowing for his usual boastfulness, there is no question that Wright's two volumes hit European architecture like a shock wave. As late as the 1920s, Dutch and German architects were still improvising on themes that first came to light in the pages of the *Ausgeführte Bauten*.

Below left: Wright's Unity Temple, Chicago, 1904
Below right: Wright's Robie house, Chicago, 1909

But then, just as the modern movement began to flex its muscles in Europe, Wright fell into a tailspin at home. In 1909 he entered a radicalized lifestyle and ran off to Europe with a client's wife, then lived openly with her at his beloved Taliesin estate until her death five years later. These scandals not only cut Wright off from potential clients, they brought disorder to his life as an artist. In the 1920s this disorder seemed to seriously affect his artistic focus. His Imperial Hotel in Tokyo and the four Mayan-style homes he built in the twenties in Los Angeles were so decorative and neohistoricist that critics could reasonably ask if Wright was still a modernist at all.

Like many an artist and many a politician of the 1920s, Wright felt squeezed by forces both to his right and to his left. To his right was the post–World War I "return to order" (*retour à l'ordre*) that gave a severe and conservative cast to a good deal of the art produced in the 1920s. Picasso's post-Cubist work of the 1920s, for example, marked a significant backsliding from his earlier radicalism. This artistic conservatism of the 1920s soon proved part of a wider European shift to political conservatism that culminated in the 1930s in the art and politics of Fascism, Nazism, and Stalinism. In the 1920s Europe managed to foster both an artistic left and an artistic right, but America tilted decisively to the right. As more than one scholar has observed, the Great War made European architecture take refuge in the future, while architecture in America took refuge in the past. This swing to architectural conservatism was made obvious in the 1922 competition for the Chicago Tribune Tower. Of 263 entries from twenty-three countries, only those from Europe kept alive the functionalism and minimal decoration that were the hallmarks of the Chicago School in the 1890s. All but a handful of the Americans—neither Wright nor Sullivan entered—wrapped their steel skeletons in the historicist dress of the Classical, Gothic, Renaissance, Baroque, or Georgian styles. John Howells and Raymond Hood won the competition with a so-called modern Gothic takeoff on Rouen Cathedral.

Conservative architects (we could equally well call them traditionalists, academicists, or historicists) would dominate the profession in the United States from the 1893 World's Fair in Chicago right through the early 1950s. The huge new buildings created for Franklin Roosevelt's Depression-era Washington, D.C., in the 1930s showed how much power the conservatives still had. The traditionalist John Russell Pope got rich plums like the National Gallery and the Jefferson Memorial, both finished in 1937, the same year as Fallingwater. The new Supreme Court of

Cass Gilbert: U.S. Supreme Court,
Washington D.C., 1935

1935 presented itself as a Greek temple of such unabashed classicism that
except for its electrical wiring it could have carried the date of 1835 or 435
B.C. It staggers the mind that troglodytes like these were contemporaries
of Fallingwater.

Certain government buildings had at least a dim awareness of modernism. Washington's Folger Library is a little more lively than the neighboring Supreme Court, but it is no less hostile to the informal planning
and ahistorical styling of the modernists. "Classical modern" behemoths

Julia Morgan: William Randolph
Hearst's castle at San Simeon,
California, 1919–37

such as the Rayburn House Building kept going up even after World War II, and some get built even today if the budget will bear it. Conservatives equally dominated the building of America's churches and colleges until the eve of World War II, though here Gothic rather than Classical style was king. American Gothic is not entirely dead even today, although its last real hurrah was Princeton's Firestone Library, completed in 1946.

Conservative taste held sway even longer in the design of America's houses. William Randolph Hearst kept adding to his castle at San Simeon in California until his cash flow gave out in 1937. The big Newport-style Renaissance palaces never went out of fashion, either, though there was less call for them during the Depression. Traditionalists kept building neo-This and neo-That suburban estates even in the postwar years, and such mansions made a comeback a generation later in the wave called postmodernism. Except for the immediate postwar years, designers of modern homes generally got only scraps from this architectural feast. So secure was traditionalism in the 1920s and 1930s that some municipalities prohibited the construction of homes in the modern style, and banks were notorious in refusing to finance them.

But caution: the traditionalist architects were never the doddering oafs Wright ridiculed in his speeches, nor the fools Ayn Rand made them out to be in *The Fountainhead*. Many were brilliant designers. Certainly the adjective fits Addison Mizner and his neo-Spanish buildings in Boca Raton and Palm Beach in Florida; Julia Morgan, Hearst's architect at San Simeon; and Philadelphia's George Howe, who was better as an academicist than as the modernist he became after a surprise conversion in the late 1920s.

The traditionalists' agenda overlapped at many points with that of the progressives: a concern for aesthetics, for harmonious use of the building site, solid building materials, good functional layouts, and—for some—linkage with the vernacular tradition. The distinction between the two camps lost some of its sharpness in the interwar years. Real progressives like Wright were blindsided by pseudo-progressives who thought of modernism only in terms of advanced building technology. Certainly they knew as much as Wright about the improved mechanical systems (heating, ventilating, cooling) and the handling of glass, steel, and reinforced concrete.

The leading pseudo-progressive was Wright's friend Raymond Hood, who jumped with ease from style to style. After Hood vaulted to the top of the profession with his suavely Gothic Chicago Tribune Tower, he switched to "modernistic" skyscrapers like the 1931 McGraw-Hill Building in New York. Modernistic was not the severe modern style popularized

Wright's Johnson's Wax Administration Building in Racine, Wisconsin, constructed in the same years as Fallingwater

in the United States in the 1950s by Mies van der Rohe, but a Jazz Age variant of the old classicism that turned up in Miami Beach hotels, in the decorative parts of Rockefeller Center, and in the fantastic spire atop the Chrysler Building. A MoMA architecture guide of 1940 severely admonished its readers that " 'Modernistic' means pseudo-modern, and applies to works which specifically imitated the forms of modern art, reducing them to decorative mannerisms, as in Shoe Shoppes, The Chicago Fair [1933], and, alas, too much of the New York World's Fair [1939]."

The core of the modernistic camp in the United States were the practitioners of the style known today as Art Deco. This group was large but ideologically unfocused, and included such superficial fellow travelers on the road to modernism as Hood and the Chrysler Building's William Van Alen. Today we regard Art Deco buildings like the hotels in Miami Beach as a delight, and it seems a puzzle why MoMA took so snobbish a disdain for the style. The reason is that the Art Deco architects were essentially crowd-pleasers, not designers with the intense drive for originality and philosophic balance that characterized Wright and the other giants of modernism. Certainly, the modernistic designers were not lacking in creativity. The best of the Americans was the Vienna-born Joseph Urban, whose New School for Social Research remains one of the glories of Manhattan. The style ultimately found its most exuberant expression in the "streamlined" cars and radios of the 1930s and in Radio City Music Hall. Wright himself was not immune to its charms, as he showed in the late 1930s in some of the streamlined details in the interiors of his Johnson's Wax Building and at Fallingwater itself.

. . .

Just as Gothic ended up in a fantastic variant called Flamboyant, so modernism inevitably gave birth to what journalists of the 1930s loved to call ultramodernism. Wright soon perceived that his major artistic threat came not from the conservatives to his right but from the radical modernists to his left. This should have been predictable, because from the first there had been other varieties of modernism besides the one practiced in Chicago. In the 1890s, architects in France and the Low Countries perfected the florid Art Nouveau, while Charles Rennie Mackintosh in Glasgow and Antoni Gaudí in Barcelona sought a middle ground between that style's seductive curves and traditional structure and decoration. In Vienna a bit later, Otto Wagner and Adolf Loos devised their own minimally decorated aesthetic, while the Berlin architect Peter Behrens experimented with the application of industrial components not only to factory design but to commercial and even domestic architecture. In 1910, Behrens had three of the world's most promising young architects working for him: Walter Gropius, Ludwig Mies (he would add the "van der Rohe" a decade later), and the Swiss-French designer Charles-Édouard Jeanneret, who would soon call himself Le Corbusier.

Gropius began appropriating Wright's strong horizontals and overhangs into his buildings almost as soon as he saw them in the *Ausgeführte Bauten* portfolios after 1910, but by the time he built the factorylike Bauhaus art school at Dessau in 1925, he had hammered out a personal aesthetic. Wright was radical in his own way, but his cultural mind-set resisted the embrace of industrialism that swept over Germany and France after World War I. Wright could not force himself to design a school that looked like a factory, and he was not amused by the sheer walls of glass at the Bauhaus, either: they subverted his philosophy of a structure-based aesthetic. Looking at a wall of glass, a viewer has no idea how the structure supports itself. The glass walls at the Bauhaus were made practical through the principle of the cantilever, which extends a structure horizontally beyond its vertical supports. Since there are no structural demands on the glass itself, Gropius dematerialized the whole wall into one immense window.

But the transatlantic borrowings of modern architecture went beyond the one-way contributions of Wright, into something both reciprocal and convoluted. Gropius could not have mastered the cantilever without the precedent of earlier work in America. Already in 1908, Louis Curtiss had incorporated a wall of glass in his Boley Building in Kansas City, Missouri, and Willis Polk erected an even slicker glass facade for San Francisco's Hallidie Building in 1917. Nonetheless, most American designers

Walter Gropius and Adolf Meyer: the Bauhaus, Dessau, Germany, 1925

thought of the cantilever as a structural feature, not as a stylistic element. (As late as 1931, the progressive industrial architect Albert Kahn specifically mocked the striving for novelty in the European modernists and their few American followers.) In the main, the Americans found Gropius's showy use of glass illegitimate, forgetting where he had learned it. What Gropius got out of his famous glass wall was the shimmer of reflections during the day and the exaltation of light pouring outward from the building at night. In the 1920s, Wright found those effects too showy, but ten years later he would use the dramatic cantilever, the sheer wall of glass, and the outward-pouring evening light in much the same fashion at Fallingwater. Now who was influencing whom?

In 1925, Gropius published a book with the title *International Architecture,* in which he argued for an architecture that was not confined to any specific place. He urged architects to build free from restrictions of site, climate, regional vernaculars, and historical traditions that might undermine design as a strictly rational process. The globalization implied by the International Style was serious enough that the amateur architect Adolf Hitler banned it from Germany. The Nazis even threatened to clap a pitched roof on the Bauhaus to make it conform to traditional German style.

The International Style principles of design, which stressed an open plan with a central core, broad bands of windows, severe asymmetrical

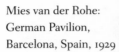

Mies van der Rohe:
German Pavilion,
Barcelona, Spain, 1929

facades, and avoidance of applied decoration, were by no means foreign to Wright's work. Far from it: Gropius's pinwheel plan with central core at the Bauhaus, for example, originated in the house plans he had studied in Wright's *Ausgeführte Bauten*. But Wright's imprint was missing from the mechanistic severity of the new buildings by Gropius, Mies, and Le Corbusier. By 1930 each of these young men had produced one world-famed building: Gropius the Bauhaus, Mies the 1929 German Pavilion for a world's fair in Barcelona, and Le Corbusier the 1929 Villa Savoye, outside Paris.

As was true of the traditionalists he battled in the United States, Wright had more in common with the International Style practitioners than either he or they would admit. Even Mies, the most cerebral of the

Le Corbusier:
Villa Savoye, near
Paris, 1929

European modernists, was sufficiently taken by Wright's sanctified watchword "organic" to use it at least once to describe his own design philosophy. He also adapted the asymmetrical plan of one of Wright's early houses for his 1923 project for a brick-walled country villa, although his adaptation was so radical that the plan gave barely a clue that it was meant for human habitation.

Wright had the option of taking pleasure or taking umbrage at the Europeans' interpretation of his early work, and he chose the latter. All he could see in their hard-edge austerity was a rejection of his warm and decorative designs. One glance at Le Corbusier's Villa Savoye shows the contrast between its sleek skin and the rugged stone walls of Fallingwater. For Wright, it was vital that his homes hugged the ground and were at one with it. Villa Savoye, by contrast, was elevated from the ground on metal stilts, like a rocket ship.

The International Style's mechanized vision of the future, famously expressed by Le Corbusier's dictum that "a house is a machine for living in," was in blunt contrast to Wright's belief that architecture was obliged to exalt and imitate nature alone. (Wright was being inconsistent here, since in 1901 he gave a celebrated speech, "The Art and Craft of the Machine," which pointed in the direction the Europeans later took.) Wright found the "Internationalists"—his mocking term—so obsessed with functionalism and abstraction that they were a worse menace than the traditionalists. He aggrandized his battle with the European moderns into a personal crusade. An apprentice confirmed for me that whenever Wright swatted flies at Taliesin he would gleefully announce the window-kill as "Got Gropius . . . got Mies . . . got Le Corbusier."

Wright could posture all he liked, but we can tell from one significant episode how much he feared being swept away by the International Style. Around 1929 or 1930 he either allowed or encouraged his draftsmen to transform a half-dozen of his early renderings by imitating the electrifying slickness in the perspectives of Erich Mendelsohn, a German modernist who had visited Wright a few years before. As reworked, the sketches for the old Larkin Building, Unity Temple, the Robie house, and other works from the years 1902 to 1909 reemerged twenty-odd years later as more Miesian than Mies. The drawings were not updates but outright falsifications—several now bearing feigned early dates—that were made to remind the world that Wright was the source for German modernism. Nor were these drawings just in-house jokes, though they may have begun that way. Wright placed a newly slick perspective of Unity Temple in his *Autobiography* of 1932, and he submitted a falsified perspective of the Larkin Building to accompany the chapter on him in Thomas Craven's 1934 survey *Modern Art: The Men, the Movements, the Meaning.* Not a few people were taken in—and continue to be taken in—by the deception. Buckingham Palace would just as easily resemble Mies's Barcelona Pavilion if we could rework the original drawings to make it look that way.

Wright correctly saw his greatest challenge as coming from Europe, but paradoxically his fame continued to rise there while it sputtered at home. In the late 1920s three new monographs celebrating Wright were published in France, Germany, and the Netherlands, but no comparable recognition came from the United States. Bruno Taut was startled to find that an architect esteemed in Europe "is by no means held in such esteem in the United States." Many Americans increasingly regarded him as no more than a starting point for the European moderns, not as their equal. In 1932, the critic Ralph Flint could write in the *Art News:* "After continued contemplation of the new [European] modes, even the work of such moderns as Frank Lloyd Wright begins to look overloaded and fussy."

As long as an ocean lay between Wright and the European modernists, his perceived enemies were an annoyance but not a threat. Soon, however, the Europeans were drawn to America, a trend that had begun with a visit by the Viennese Adolf Loos in 1899. Typical was Mendelsohn, who in 1924 prominently featured a photo of the Larkin Building in his influential *Wie Baut Amerika?* The irony was perfect: the Europeans were coming to the United States in order to see Wright's early works.

It was only a matter of time before the "Internationalists" invaded the United States as permanent residents. The first of these were the Austrian modernists Rudolf M. Schindler and Richard Neutra. Schindler came first, in 1914. He was at first deferential to Wright, who employed him in the 1920s to superintend several of his Los Angeles houses. When he remodeled one of these houses a few years later, Schindler predictably soured his relationship with Wright. Neutra came to the United States in 1923 and worked half a year for Wright; his devotion was such that he named one son Frank L. Neutra. But Neutra soon detached himself from Wright, too, and he and Schindler began hanging cool white Bauhaus-style concrete boxes on the hills of California.

Other European modernists began to influence architectural design in the United States without leaving home. The few modern projects for the 1922 Chicago Tribune Tower competition gave inspiration to the tiny camp of American architectural modernists that now took its place along-

Above left: William Lescaze and George Howe:
Philadelphia Savings Fund Society tower (PSFS), Philadelphia, 1929–32
Above right: Mies van der Rohe: Seagram Building, New York, 1958

side the earlier camps of traditionalists, progressives, and modernistics. Bit by bit, America got a few examples of authentic modern architecture. In commercial architecture there arose the elegant Philadelphia Savings Fund Society (PSFS) tower of 1929–32. Its architects were the Swiss immigrant William Lescaze and the modernist convert George Howe. Albert Frey, another Swiss immigrant, made a momentous debut in 1931 with his sleek all-metal Aluminaire House. Frey (joined by A. Lawrence Kocher) designed this thrilling little structure in homage to Le Corbusier's Villa Savoye, on which he himself had worked a year or two earlier. Frey then went west to spend a half-century building highly creative homes in California.

Still, there was strong resistance to modern architecture in the United States until the later 1930s. New York City, for example, had no uncompromisingly modern work until the MoMA headquarters opened in 1939. What inhibited the growth of modernism was a native American resistance to the show-off "mannerisms" in modern European work—the

Wright's Guggenheim Museum in New York was planned in the 1940s but not built until 1956–59

same charge MoMA made against the modernistic architecture at the New York World's Fair. One of the most derided of the Europeans' mannerisms was the corner window, which put a void where one expects a strong support; another was the extreme overhang that exploited cantilever technology. By the time Wright used these and other European design elements at Fallingwater, Americans had warmed up to European modernism, but what they never grasped was its ideological basis. The Europeans invested modern architecture with an intense idealism, seeing in it a salve to heal a world torn asunder by nationalism. Americans saw it instead as just the latest fashion in a long line of architectural styles.

The International Style got a huge boost in the United States when Hitler pushed numerous modern architects toward its shores. Gropius immigrated in 1937; Mies came over in 1937 and settled permanently in 1938. The first became dean of architecture at Harvard; the second took over the architecture school at what is now the Illinois Institute of Technology in Chicago. Le Corbusier visited but did not stay; he recorded his impressions of America in *When the Cathedrals Were White* (1935). A score of other German and Austrian modernists entered American commercial practice in the late 1930s, including Mendelsohn and the shopping-mall pioneer Victor Gruen. Some Bauhaus instructors found jobs as teachers in the New Bauhaus school in Chicago or at Black Mountain College in North Carolina.

Wright would eventually lose out to the International Style as the dominant architectural idiom in America when Mies's elegant glass towers, particularly the Seagram Building of 1958, attracted a huge following in the postwar years. But he and his surrogates continued to challenge the Miesian camp. One of those surrogates was *House Beautiful* editor Elizabeth Gordon, whose editorial, "The Threat to the Next America," in the April 1953 *House Beautiful,* warned against the cultural dictatorship of "a self-chosen elite who are trying to tell us what we should like and how we should live."

By the postwar years, Wright was at least secure in his own niche, but when the foundations for the Miesian triumph were being laid in the 1930s, he could count on no such support. Wright in fact lost his first two skirmishes against the International Style. In 1931, Rudolph Schindler's wife, Pauline, mounted a photographic display at UCLA of the work of a half-dozen California architects. Wright's Los Angeles houses were shown between panels devoted to Neutra and Schindler, which led Wright to grouse that he was another Christ at Golgotha, crucified between two thieves. But the witticism only half-worked: it was Schindler and Neutra who had struck critical and financial success, and Wright who had hit rock-bottom. Wright stayed cordial with Neutra in the early stages of the younger man's career, but when Neutra surpassed him in success, Wright turned against him with fury. Even Wright's friend, the modernist scholar Henry-Russell Hitchcock, intoned: "We are forced

Wright's Marin County
Civic Center, California:
1962 and later

to interpret your opposition to this man who has frequently expressed his indebtedness to you as due to a jealousy at once meaningless and undignified."

How could the father of modern architecture lag so far behind his sons? The answers are varied. As a dedicated modernist, Wright's fortunes rose and fell with the modern movement in general. His first triumphs, between 1890 and 1910, came when American modernism was enjoying its first strength. Wright's popularity fell when attention shifted to European experiments in the 1920s, then rose again when modernism reemerged triumphant in the United States in the postwar years. Another problem was that the public linked Wright with his acerbic personality, not with his obscure philosophy of organicism. Wright's organic concept put him at another disadvantage. Unlike Mies, he crafted a unique-looking building for each site, which meant that the architectural product coming out of Taliesin was less easy to market than Bauhaus work, which carried a far more predictable style.

Something else made Wright the odd man out of American modernism between the wars. The best buildings of those years tended to look like the Philadelphia Savings Fund Society tower: self-effacing, modest, anonymous, and international. Imposing a heroic image on an architectural design—what critics used to call "form-giving"—was largely out of favor at the time. As a form-giver to the core, Wright could never look anonymous. When form-giving came back in popularity in the 1940s and '50s, Wright's popularity rose with it. The public loved his futuristic Johnson's Wax Building, the neo-Babylonian Guggenheim Museum, and the mall-like Marin County Civic Center in California. But in the 1920s and early 1930s Wright's form-giving found few takers.

By 1932, Wright was truly caught in a drought: three years without a single new building. To save what he could of his flamboyant lifestyle, he came up with two financial initiatives. The first was writing *An Autobiography*, which came out in 1932 and was successful both in the self-validation it provided and the money it brought in. The second also came that year, when Wright charged a dozen young architects $675 a year (hiked in 1933 to $1,100) to work with him at Taliesin. That was high tuition in those days, more than live-in students paid at either Harvard or Yale. The young men and women who responded to Wright's offer agreed to plant the crops, tend the livestock, cook and bake their meals, wash their laundry (Wright's, too)", and hew wood to heat the place. Those who could were expected to play Bach and Beethoven on Saturday nights.

The *Autobiography* and the Taliesin Fellowship kept the wolf from the door financially, though Wright made no secret of his penury; he wrote the architect Joseph Urban in 1931: "We are desperate here, Joe." But schemes alone could not restart his career. In 1931, Wright was excluded from the list of potential architects for the 1933 World's Fair in Chicago, a treatment even shabbier than Sullivan's in the Chicago fair of 1893, where the older architect was allowed only minimal participation.

Worse was to come. In 1931, Wright was also blackballed from the most influential exhibition of architecture ever held, which was MoMA's "Modern Architecture: International Exhibition," mounted the following year. The promoters were Henry-Russell Hitchcock and MoMA's curator of architecture, Philip Johnson, who years later made his own comeback as the Andy Warhol of American architecture. The show recognized the Bauhaus claim to be the only legitimate line of modern architecture, excluding other claimants such as the increasingly quaint-looking Frank Lloyd Wright. Only backroom politics—the MoMA trustees demanded some token American representation—got Wright a grudging invitation to participate.

Though Wright made it into the MoMA show, barely, it was a source of irritation rather than satisfaction for him. He designed a luminescent German-style "House on the Mesa" especially for the show, but the exhibition catalogue, *The International Style: Architecture Since 1922,* all but ignored it. In this and in a second book, Hitchcock and Johnson praised Wright's early works, as usual, but refused to rank him among the sixty-five leaders of contemporary architecture around the world. Like many a prominent figure in the 1930s, he was punished for departing from the prevailing ideology.

Wright always gave as good as he got, and he reserved plenty of mockery for the MoMA show. "Architecture was made for man," he wrote (the self-identification with Christ again), "not man for architecture. And since when has the man sunk so low, even by way of the machine, that a self-elected group of formalizers could predetermine his literature, his music, or his architecture for him?" But Wright knew how precarious his standing had become when Hitchcock characterized him as irrelevant to the progress of modernism: "Wright belongs to the international style no more than Behrens or Perret or Van de Velde. . . . They are more akin to the men of a hundred years ago than to the generation which has come to the fore since the War." This made Wright howl back:

I warn Henry-Russell Hitchcock right here and now that, having a good start, not only do I fully intend to be the greatest architect who has yet lived, but the greatest who will ever live. Yes, I intend to be the greatest architect of all time. And I do hereunto affix "the red square" [Wright's logo] and sign my name to this warning.

To Philip Johnson, who had tried to block Wright from the MoMA show, Wright wrote in 1932:

I find myself a man without a country, architecturally speaking, at the present time. If I keep on working another five years, I shall be at home again, I feel sure.

Did ever a prophet speak with greater accuracy? Wright's comeback required exactly the five years that he foretold: 1937 was the year the Kaufmanns moved into Fallingwater.

Opposite: E. J. Kaufmann reads blueprints in his Wright-designed office in downtown Pittsburgh, about 1940

TWO

E. J. KAUFMANN
OF PITTSBURGH SUFFERS
HUMILIATION OF ANOTHER SORT

You stick to your side, I'll stick to mine! A strange denial of the common pulse of humanity.

—D. H. LAWRENCE, *Lady Chatterly's Lover*

In democracies there is nothing greater nor more brilliant than commerce; it is what attracts the regard of the public and fills the imagination of the crowd; all energetic passions are directed toward it. . . . The rich in democracies therefore throw themselves into commerce on all sides; . . . those who live amid democratic instability constantly have the image of chance before their eyes, and in the end they love all undertakings in which chance plays a role.

They are therefore all brought into commerce, not only because of the gain it promises them, but for love of the emotions that it gives them.

—ALEXIS DE TOCQUEVILLE, *Democracy in America*

Pittsburgh's supercilious *Bulletin Index* gave its readers a special treat in its issue of September 28, 1933: full coverage of the court battle that had raged all summer between E. J. Kaufmann of Kaufmann's Department Store and the management of the rival Horne's store. Horne's refused to take back six diamond and platinum bracelets costing $20,000 (about a quarter of a million of today's dollars) that Kaufmann, the Merchant Prince of Pittsburgh, had repossessed from his mistress of the moment, one Josephine Bennett Waxman. The article branded Kaufmann with the usual code words reserved for Jewish businessmen in the 1930s: "sharp . . . hard featured . . . socially, politically and financially ambitious."

Were the major histories of architecture published in Pittsburgh rather than in New York, the house on Bear Run would be known today as "E. J. Kaufmann's Fallingwater" not as "Frank Lloyd Wright's Fallingwater." Outside of Pittsburgh and some footnotes in Wright studies, however, Kaufmann is a forgotten man today. Worse, what is said about him tends to the trivial. The chapter on Kaufmann in Leon Harris's *Merchant Princes,* for example, harps for thirteen of its twenty-one pages on the man's creative sex life.

The most constructive approach we can take to Kaufmann is the one that has proved most productive with Wright: as part of a dynasty. Just as Wright was the product of a Welsh clan that had taken root in the fields of Wisconsin, so Kaufmann was part of an impressive dynasty shaped by the industrial might of Pittsburgh. We can trace the Kaufmanns back to medieval Germany. Their first documented ancestor was Rabbi Eliezer the Levite, who was born eleven generations back, around 1620. Eliezer's name used the traditional "son of" Hebrew format, as did the names of the four generations who followed him, but in the eighteenth century the clan chose, or was assigned, the permanent surname of Kaufmann— German for "merchant." By then they had lived as horse and cattle dealers in the Rhineland village of Viernheim for close to five hundred years. They were a strictly rural clan, having nothing to do with the brilliant cultural and commercial achievements of German-speaking Jews like the Mendelssohns, the Rothschilds, Heinrich Heine, Freud, or Einstein.

Abraham Kaufmann, the patriarch of the seventh documented generation, saw his oldest sons Jacob and Isaac set sail for America around 1867. The two brothers started by peddling clothes southeast of Pittsburgh, through the farms, villages, and coalfields of the Youghiogheny River valley. The route took them sixty miles along the new Baltimore & Ohio Railroad tracks on the riverbank as far as Connellsville, which

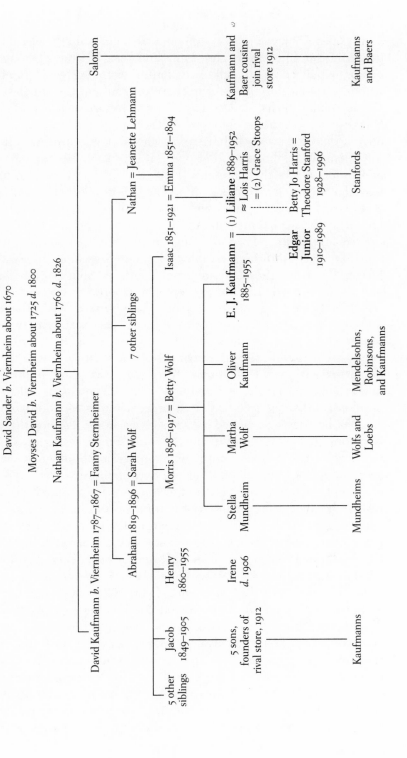

Henry Clay Frick was at that moment developing into the world capital of coke (the burning kind). The Kaufmanns would trudge through Frick's company-policed coal-patch towns until they found Jewish families with whom to spend the night, for in those days all but the smallest western Pennsylvania towns had a few Jews. The synagogues of Clairton, Brownsville, Jeannette, Monessen, Donora, and Connellsville (where once even the mayor was Jewish) are closed now, but others cling to life in Greensburg, Johnstown, Latrobe, Mt. Pleasant, Uniontown, Oil City, and Braddock. In their rambles, Jacob and Isaac would also have canvassed a small but vigorous commercial depot that had grown up by the B & O tracks east of Connellsville, about halfway between the hamlets of Ohiopyle and Mill Run. This stop was called Bear Run, for the name of the stream that joined the Youghiogheny River at that point.

In 1871 the brothers established a tailoring shop on East Carson Street, the main thoroughfare of Pittsburgh's South Side. Their customers were mostly the ironworkers who labored nearby at the Jones & Laughlin hot rolling mill or at James Laughlin's Eliza Furnace on the opposite bank of the Monongahela River. The next year two younger Kaufmann brothers, Morris and Henry, also immigrated and joined the enterprise. (So did their sister Dina, but she died soon after, apparently unmarried.) In 1877, J. Kaufmann & Brothers moved to Smithfield Street in the Golden Triangle, as Pittsburgh's downtown is still called. A block north stood the cast-iron bank that Judge Thomas Mellon had built four years earlier, having resigned from the bench in 1870, saying that any man who could not get rich in Pittsburgh within ten years was a fool.

In 1885 the renamed Kaufmann Brothers firm built a new wing at the prize corner of the Golden Triangle: Smithfield Street at Fifth Avenue. Conscious of their triumph, the brothers erected a miniature Statue of Liberty holding a blazing torch of natural gas on the corner, beating the real thing in New York by a year. When E. J. later put a clock at the corner, the most-used geographic designator in Pittsburgh became "Meet me under Kaufmann's clock." Close to a hundred years later, it still is.

The Kaufmanns had selected one of the richest commercial districts in the United States for their store. Every Saturday 100,000 Pittsburgh millworkers got their pay in cash, and not only the bars and brothels but the city's retail zones would so engorge with customers that you had to fight for room on the sidewalks. Marvelous to behold, the whole of Allegheny County seemed to funnel itself to Kaufmann's. The newly electrified trolley lines stretched octopuslike from Smithfield Street out to all the mill towns: north and east to the glass and aluminum plants up the Allegheny River valley, south to the steel towns and electric plants along the Monongahela, and northwest to the gigantic new mill that Jones &

The four Kaufmann brothers from Viernheim, in Pittsburgh, around 1890. *Left to right:* Jacob and Augusta; Henry and Theresa; Morris and Betty (Edgar's parents); and Isaac and Emma (Liliane's parents).

Laughlin was putting up downstream on the Ohio, at Aliquippa. Kaufmann's had to double its capacity in 1898 with a new nine-story wing along Smithfield; another wing followed on Forbes Avenue (Diamond then) in 1904. "The Pittsburgh district spends more per capita in its department stores than any other city in the world," claimed an article from the 1920s, and Kaufmann's made the most of the situation. By 1910 the brothers had 3,000 employees, including interpreters working in ten languages, and sales were $10 million a year. With close to a million square feet of display and office space, Kaufmann's ranked among the ten largest department stores on earth in 1925. The downtown store is considerably bigger today than it was in 1925, and probably qualifies for that ranking still.

Besides the perfect configuration of the trolley tracks, what brought the crowds to Kaufmann's were service, novelty, its flair for publicity, and its alluring architecture. The store claims to have been the first retailer in America to take out full-page newspaper ads. Before electricity came to Smithfield Street in the 1890s, employees would take turns in the basement hand-cranking the mannequins so they would gyrate on pedestals in the store windows. Like many a commercial enterprise during America's Gilded Age, Kaufmann's also put great stress on cutting-edge architec-

Pittsburgh's Grant Street, a block from the Kaufmann store, was enhanced in 1888
by the addition of H. H. Richardson's world-famed Allegheny County Courthouse
and Jail. Henry Clay Frick built the row of skyscrapers opposite the courthouse;
a fragment of a late addition to Kaufmann's appears at upper right.

ture. The store was fortunate that in the twenty years between 1885 and
1905 some of the best commercial and government buildings in the land
were rising around it. The crown architectural jewel of Pittsburgh in
those years was also the most praised new building in the United States:
H. H. Richardson's Allegheny County Courthouse and Jail of 1884–88,
which stands on Grant Street, just a block from Kaufmann's. Richardson's courthouse became a national and international sensation; next to
Philadelphia's Independence Hall, it was the most frequently imitated
building in the country.

The Kaufmanns exploited their proximity to the courthouse both in
their advertising, which showed the two structures together, and in the
design of their 1885 wing, which was in similar Romanesque Revival style.
For the 1898 and 1904 wings, however, they got their architect, Charles
Bickel, to employ certain features of the Chicago School, the way Louis
Sullivan did in the same years for the merchants Leopold Schlesinger and
Daniel Mayer in Chicago (the Carson Pirie Scott store today). Elements
of the Chicago School also showed up in the skyscraper headquarters for
Andrew Carnegie's steel empire, which blossomed next door to the Kauf-
mann block in 1892. In 1901 and 1906 the architectural flowering of the

block was rounded out with two gleaming skyscrapers that Chicago's Daniel Burnham built for Henry Clay Frick. With the Mellons, Carnegie, and Frick as corporate neighbors, the Kaufmanns stood cheek-by-jowl with some of the most important commercial names in the world.

Such was the dynasty into which Edgar Jonas Kaufmann was born on November 1, 1885, as the second child and first son of Morris and Betty Wolf Kaufmann. Almost as a presentiment, his birth coincided with construction of his family's Statue of Liberty wing at the store. The store would be everything in Kaufmann's life. At thirteen he watched Charles Bickel's 1898 wing go up; at nineteen he observed the construction of Bickel's second wing. E. J. would himself add four wings and two parking garages to the store, and it would be a rare moment when he was not found selling his merchandise, his city, and himself.

By the time E. J. was born, his father and uncles had acquired a rich taste in architecture both at the office and at home. When Kaufmann's was on the South Side, Morris or another brother had to sleep inside every night for security; when the store moved downtown in 1877, the brothers still felt obliged to live nearby. But by 1885 the Kaufmanns were wealthy enough to take up residence in the Manchester section of Pittsburgh's North Side, specifically in a nouveau riche district of elaborate Queen Anne townhouses that the neighbors called North Jerusalem because it had attracted so many Jewish families. Superficially, those streets look almost unchanged today. After a long slump, the neighborhood has returned in glory, and the refurbished townhouses on Liverpool and Sheffield streets—along with some solar-powered neighbors—would be the envy of any city on the continent.

But late-Victorian Pittsburgh was not all work and wealth. It was rich in culture, too. A small example: James Laughlin named his Eliza blast furnace on the Monongahela River in honor of his daughter Eliza Laughlin Phillips. Eliza's son Duncan Phillips was one of the most astute collectors of modern art in the nation. His cousin James Laughlin IV became a pioneer editor and publisher of modern literature.

The core of Pittsburgh's cultural life was right where the Kaufmanns lived, on the North Side, which until 1907 was the independent town of Allegheny. In 1874 the writer Gertrude Stein was born there, to a family in the same German-Jewish milieu as E. J.'s. "I was firmly born in Allegheny, Pennsylvania," Stein wrote, and her home still stands on Beech Avenue, a few blocks from North Jerusalem. Other luminaries in Kaufmann's neighborhood over the years were the industrialists Carnegie and H. J. Heinz, the composer Stephen Foster, the scientists John Brashear and Samuel

Pierpont Langley, the painter Mary Cassatt, the poet Robinson Jeffers, the novelist Mary Roberts Rinehart, and the modern dance pioneer Martha Graham. Willa Cather, just arrived from Nebraska, taught English at the local high school. Excepting Greenwich Village, not many square miles in America were ever blessed with more creativity.

Since the Kaufmanns were neither writers nor painters, they found their prime cultural expression in architecture, the art form most congenial to merchants. The store always came first, but the four brothers left their architectural mark in houses and charitable foundations, too. We'll look at the houses first. Late in the nineteenth century, the Kaufmanns were on the move again, this time leapfrogging over the Golden Triangle to the residential neighborhoods of Pittsburgh's East End. In 1894, when E. J. was nine, his father built the family a mansion in Squirrel Hill, a hilltop that over the next few decades would be divided into estates for the Mellons and such future socialites as Perle Mesta, Marjorie Merriweather Post, and Martha Crawford—the future Sunny von Bülow. Morris's brick and stone house still stands at 5538 Forbes Avenue, a conventional mix of the Romanesque Revival and Queen Anne styles, but cavernous enough to yield twelve apartments today. The architect was James Steen, a favorite house designer for the Mellons and creator of the brand-new campus for the University of Pittsburgh. Morris—or Steen—got the house a brief notice in the *Inland Architect and News Record:* it was the first of scores of thousands of clippings that three generations of Kaufmanns would amass as patrons of architecture.

Below left: Morris Kaufmann's new home was published in 1905 as one of the great
mansions of Pittsburgh. His son E. J. lived there a year or two.
Below right: Henry Hornbostel's Rodef Shalom Temple, 1907, was one of the
Kaufmanns' most successful attempts at monumental architecture
outside their homes and their store.

In 1905, when E. J. was twenty, his parents took over the Frauenheim house, which exceeded in bulk even the Mellon castles that set the tone for Squirrel Hill. A half-dozen houses from the twenties still mark the footprint on Beacon Street where this leviathan once stood. The rest of the clan clustered nearby in lesser mansions, except for Uncle Isaac, who lived in the Oakland area across from the little hill (now flattened for the Carnegie Mellon campus) on which stood the residence of A. W. Mellon, the richest man in the United States.

The Kaufmann brothers skillfully propagated their image as merchant princes through public architecture as well. When his wife died in 1895, Isaac immortalized her with a community health service at what later became the University of Pittsburgh's medical school, and with an endowed professor's chair. The school pulled up stakes decades ago, but gold letters yet proclaim EMMA KAVFMANN CLINIC on Isaac's large and bounteous structure, still looming over Polish Hill. Morris followed in 1906 as an equally lavish donor to Pittsburgh's new Jewish hospital in an adjacent immigrant district called the Hill.

In 1901 the brothers used their store architect Bickel to rebuild their downtown synagogue, but a shifting Jewish population and frequent flooding from the nearby Allegheny River led the temple to rebuild just six years later. The pompous Rodef Shalom Temple went up in Oakland, alongside Pittsburgh's other new civic monuments. The Kaufmanns were the only named donors in the financing of what was and remains one of America's distinguished houses of worship. Henry Hornbostel, a dazzling French-trained protégé of Stanford White, here synthesized the Beaux-Arts style of Paris with the common yellow brick of Pittsburgh's industrial architecture. This was the formula that Hornbostel also used with success in the college campus he was building for Andrew Carnegie a block away. Here was one more architectural success for the Kaufmanns: not only did their buildings stand daringly close to those of the supreme lords of Pittsburgh, but they themselves shared architects with those august persons as well.

Isaac was the first Kaufmann to stamp a public building with the family name; then in 1910, Henry did, too, and won the clan considerable national attention. Henry's Irene Kaufmann Settlement opened on the Hill to provide immigrants with a dozen classrooms, a library, a gymnasium, an auditorium, an infirmary, a public laundry, and public baths. With sixty-seven rooms, the IKS was rated one of the most advanced settlement houses in the country. The Kaufmann Settlement house also brought the family two special marks of local distinction. It linked them directly to the industrial aristocrats Henry Clay Frick, who donated $3,000, and Andrew Carnegie, who donated $10,000. And the public baths in the complex carried a particularly gratifying symbolism, for until then custom dictated that public baths be erected only by super rich Pittsburghers like Carnegie, his partners Henry Phipps and Henry Oliver, H. J. Heinz, and George Westinghouse. Henry Kaufmann's architectural benefaction had unwittingly bumped the family into a truly exclusive group.

In 1913, it was Morris's turn to build. Morris was president of the Concordia Club, which he moved to Oakland from the North Side, where it had stood since 1874 (a year after the Duquesne Club was founded to the exclusion of Jews). The Beaux-Arts structure uses the same factory brick that Hornbostel designated for the Kaufmanns' temple, but it has a double-ramp staircase inside that gives it a nice touch of Versailles. E. J. Kaufmann, by then the power behind the family store, would have followed both these high-profile building operations with interest, and he surely offered his father and uncle advice of his own.

By now the Kaufmanns could be classed as capable and even prolific builders. Apart from the Golden Triangle store, the name Kaufmann was emblazoned on buildings on the South Side, the North Side, the Hill and Polish Hill, in Oakland and Squirrel Hill, and on the store's new stables and warehouse in Uptown. E. J. Kaufmann returned to the North Side around 1920 with a huge reinforced-concrete warehouse that now lies buried beneath the Steelers' stadium at Heinz Field. He moved farther upriver on the Allegheny a few years after that, and took up residence in the suburb of Fox Chapel. By World War I, there was almost nowhere you could go in Pittsburgh without encountering one of the Kaufmanns' mansions or their dozen commercial and public buildings. The Medici put their stamp on Renaissance Florence with not half this many monuments.

As the Kaufmanns advanced from well-off to seriously rich, young E. J. was sent to Shady Side Academy as one of the few Jews allowed to rub shoulders with Pittsburgh's upper crust. Upon graduation in 1903 he enrolled at the Sheffield Scientific School at Yale. What Kaufmann sought at Sheffield is unclear, since he quit after one year. The heart of Sheffield was its three-year engineering curriculum, but it also prepared students for medical school, and E. J. later insisted that his first ambition was to be a surgeon. The surgeon talk may have been no more than a topos, however. Such Pittsburgh Jewish dynasties as the Franks and the Lehmans had done well in engineering, and

E. J. may have thought to take his chances at it. Additionally, if his grades at Shady Side were poor (they disappeared long ago), Kaufmann would have found Sheffield fairly easy to get into. Not being truly "Yale," it held Jews to a less stringent quota than did the College proper.

Future doctor or future engineer, Kaufmann was smart not to bank on a career at the family store, because in 1903 his prospects of rising to the top were poor. The Kaufmann clan was both sizable and fractious. As the second child of the third Kaufmann brother, E. J. was no better than fifth in the line of succession to manage the store; to control the firm outright he would have had to buy out nearly a dozen Kaufmanns. In his own branch he needed to gain control of the shares held by his father, Morris, by his younger brother Oliver, and by his sisters Stella Mundheim and Martha Wolf. From the three other branches Kaufmann needed the shares of Uncle Jacob and his five sons; the shares held by Uncle Henry and his daughter, Irene; and those of Uncle Isaac and his daughter, Lillian. He also had to vanquish a host of other cousins descended from his great-uncle Salomon Kaufmann: attracted by tales of their rich kin, they had come over from Germany, too. Distant cousin Morris Baer had also immigrated to Pittsburgh and had won appointment as general manager of the store. He installed another half-dozen Baer cousins behind the counters.

The world never got E. J. Kaufmann the surgeon or engineer, because within a few years he effected the impossible and captured the store. The takeover began with two strokes of macabre luck. In 1905, Uncle Jacob died, which put into motion a preexisting family compact—technically called a tontine—that forced his five sons to sell their 25 percent interest in the store to their three surviving uncles. For eight years the disenfranchised Kaufmann cousins fought to break that compact, but in 1913 the Pennsylvania Supreme Court upheld it, in a judgment that set a significant precedent in partnership law. The year 1906 brought more strange luck in the suicide of his cousin Irene, which led her brokenhearted father, Henry, to retire from the store. The deaths of his uncle and cousin so improved his prospects that after 1906 E. J. seems to have cast aside thoughts of anything but a career in retailing.

E. J. had whiled away the year 1904 in Europe, as he reported to his ex-classmates at Yale; now he spent 1907 and 1908 in apprenticeship at the Marshall Field store in Chicago, at Les Galeries Lafayette in Paris, and at the Karstadt store in Hamburg. He returned from Europe in 1908, but not to Pittsburgh. Instead, he bought and operated a general store in Connellsville—the same town in which his uncles had peddled clothes forty years earlier. This was a peculiar choice for a young man straight out of Hamburg and Paris. My suspicion is that E. J. saw Connellsville as a shelter in which to wait out the power struggle raging within the clan. The various deaths, forfeitures, and departures now left just one heir to the business outside Edgar's branch. This was Uncle Isaac's vivacious daughter, Lillian. In the most momentous decision of his life—until Fallingwater—E. J. now asked for her hand in marriage.*

Edgar and Lillian wed on June 22, 1909, in New York, since Pennsylvania did not, and does not, countenance unions of first cousins. Within seventeen months of the marriage, E. J. had control of the store and also the beginnings of his own dynasty, with the birth of Edgar J. Kaufmann Jr. late in 1910. The retreat to Connellsville was providential in another way, too. Twelve miles upstream on the Youghiogheny, E. J. discovered a forest full of rhododendron along Bear Run. The lure of those woods was heightened by the widespread belief that George Washington had been their first landholder. Here, a quarter of a century later, E. J. would build Fallingwater.

Before Fallingwater, however, Kaufmann put up many other buildings. He turned to architecture the first time not for pleasure but to resolve a matter of fiscal life and death. Pittsburghers of a great age still recall when Kaufmann's was called "the Big Store." The nickname (appropriated from New York's Siegel, Cooper & Company) was occasionally bandied about in Kaufmann's early days, but it was regularly hyped only after 1913. The nickname sounded grand, but its practical function was to distinguish the original Kaufmann's from the upstart Kaufmann & Baer store that aimed to sink it. The rival store was the revenge of E. J.'s five disenfranchised first cousins plus the more distant Kaufmann and Baer kin. The disgruntled cousins bolted from the original store with half the clerks in tow, and in 1912 the rebels started building a striking thirteen-story skyscraper just two blocks from the original Kaufmann's. Wrapped in creamy terra-cotta, it promised to be the retail sensation of Pittsburgh. The cousins hired the New York firm of Starrett & Van Vleck as their architects—the same designers Uncle Henry had just used for the Kaufmann Settlement house on the Hill. The threat of the new store impelled E. J. to outshine whatever his cousins were building, and he did. In 1913 he tore down the Statue of Liberty end of the store (it was less than thirty years old), and replaced it with a thirteen-story terra-cotta wing by the up-and-coming society architect Benno Janssen. E. J.'s new wing was bland

---

*Lillian—she Frenchified herself into Liliane in the 1920s—would have found it natural to marry a first cousin because her parents Isaac and Emma were themselves first cousins. That means that if Edgar Kaufmann Jr. had chosen to settle in his beloved Mexico he had the theoretical right to style himself Edgardo Kaufmann y Kaufmann y Kaufmann.

Kaufmann's Department
Store after E. J. enlarged
it in 1913 and 1922; the
Carnegie and Frick
buildings rise at the left

in style, but it outraced the rival cousins' store by a full year, which was all that mattered.

His first building taught E. J. Kaufmann a lesson that every pharaoh and emperor knew by instinct: apart from military victory, nothing outshines architecture as propaganda. The new wing at Kaufmann's took the wind from the cousins' sails, and Kaufmann & Baer's was later forced to sell out to Gimbels. (The rival store on Smithfield Street survives today as the North American headquarters for the H. J. Heinz Company.) In 1913, E. J. put his mark on the finances of the store, too. He took over the shares of his uncle and father-in-law, Isaac, while his father, Morris, bought out brother Henry's shares. This yielded $10 million for Henry, who moved to New York and over the next forty years gave the money away to charity. E. J. and Morris then reincorporated the business with $10 million in stock. By the early 1920s, sales had trebled to $30 million. These figures drooped during the Depression, but they were back to $27 million by 1940 and much higher thereafter. By 1940, Kaufmann's carried 100,000 items and was visited by 10,000 people every Saturday—exceptional figures for a single store in a relatively small city.

His ebullient personality made it appear that E. J. had the run of the store, but this was a mirage. E. J. never owned more than 45 percent of the voting stock, and the more prudent members of his clan, who owned another 25 percent, tried to rein him in. Liliane retained a few of her father's shares, and she reigned supreme over Vendôme, a moneymaking haute couture and antiques boutique she had created within the store. E. J. also had to share governance of the firm with his brother Oliver and assorted relatives. E. J. jettisoned his brother-in-law Samuel Mundheim as chief executive around 1920, but the clan retaliated by replacing Mundheim with sister Martha's husband, the Arkansas cotton broker Irwin D. Wolf. A retailing powerhouse himself, Wolf remained the hands-on manager of the store for the rest of E. J.'s life. Unlike Frank Lloyd Wright, who slipped free of his family by abandoning his wife and six children, Kaufmann would never be able to give his clan the slip anywhere but at Fallingwater.

N ear the end of his life Kaufmann declared: "I love my city, my country, and my religion—in that order." Here was a characteristic if imperfect snapshot of a man who had momentarily forgotten that he also loved his family and his business, but otherwise the

Pittsburgh in 1947, when Kaufmann and Wright made their second attempt to improve it

Kaufmann (*third from left in this 1945 photograph*) was a prominent planner of the Pittsburgh Renaissance, along with Mayor-Elect David Lawrence (*third from right*) and Kaufmann's only close associate in the Pittsburgh establishment, H. J. Heinz II (*left*)

order of loyalties in Kaufmann's aphorism was correct: Pittsburgh meant more to him than did the United States.

There were four basic elements in E. J.'s persona: the civic leader, the merchant, the Jew, and the family man. Kaufmann was hardly ignorant of the world outside Pittsburgh: he was at Yale in 1903; in Europe for much of 1904; in Chicago, Paris, and Hamburg in 1907–08; and in Berlin for the winters of 1910–11 and 1920–21. He was in Washington, D.C., for much of World War II, and maintained a second home in California from 1947 to 1955. Nonetheless, Pittsburgh always came first, because it was his perfect theater of operations. No one could be king of Pennsylvania or king of America, but Kaufmann could aspire to be king of Pittsburgh. His reign over Pittsburgh was special in its intensity, but the leading merchant in every American city was expected to be tireless in promoting his hometown. The Marcuses, the Magnins, the Riches, and the Goldwaters tried to do for Dallas, San Francisco, Atlanta, and Phoenix just what E. J. did for Pittsburgh.

E. J. worked hard at being Mr. Pittsburgh: a first lieutenant in the Army in World War I, president of Kaufmann's Department Store for forty-two years, president of the Young Men's Hebrew Association for eight, founder and president of the Pittsburgh Civic Light Opera, delegate to the 1952 Republican National Convention, founding member of both the Allegheny Conference on Community Development and Pittsburgh's Urban Redevelopment Authority, holder of an honorary doctorate from the University of Pittsburgh, director of Allegheny General and Montefiore hospitals, and director also of the Pittsburgh Horticultural

Society, the Emma Farm Association, and the Salvation Army. Kaufmann's earnest efforts at civic betterment endeared him to a citizenry that
regarded him with affection and bid him farewell in 1955 with the most
striking funeral in the history of Pittsburgh.

His city and his store were as one to E. J. He made Kaufmann's the
nerve center of the metropolis, as *Fortune* wittily delineated in a feature
on him in 1944. Conversely, he sought to improve Pittsburgh as he had so
resoundingly improved the store. In the proposals he would set before
Wright in 1934 for a planetarium, public housing, multiple bridges, highways, tunnels, and riverfront improvements for Pittsburgh, Kaufmann
conceptualized all by himself what became the Pittsburgh Renaissance
twenty years later. When the Renaissance finally retrieved the city from
decay, it was Mayor David Lawrence and financier Richard King Mellon
who got the credit, but insiders knew that Kaufmann was the real brains
behind it. Kaufmann's finest hour came when he pushed for the creation
of downtown Pittsburgh's Point State Park, even though the project was
an enormous benefit to Horne's Department Store next door, but meant
nothing to Kaufmann's, several blocks away. A central player in that urban
transformation said of E. J.:

> There's only one Edgar Kaufmann. . . . In his prime [he] was the most
> brilliant mind in Pittsburgh . . . an idea man. . . . very forward look-
> ing . . . extremely generous. . . . In addition to his own ability and his
> own very keen mind and his courage—he had courage—he had money,
> and when you put that combination together you've really got some-
> thing. . . . I can only say Edgar was the type of man who comes along
> once in two, three generations as far as a city's concerned. I think he
> was a really brilliant man.

We must nonetheless be careful not to imagine Kaufmann as some
colossus striding across the United States, for he was nothing of the sort.
His long reign at the store gave him regional distinction as a civic leader
and as a socially responsible retailer, but he attained national and international status only with Fallingwater. E. J. got the store to pay him an
impressive salary ($85,000 in 1935), but he was still not especially rich:
like Wright, he *lived* rich. The Kaufmann wealth could not begin to
match the ten or twenty fortunes that Pittsburgh families had stockpiled
from oil, steel, coke, ketchup, glass, railroading, electricity, aluminum,
and aerospace. The family could not touch the wealth of the German-
Jewish merchants and bankers of New York, either. Nor were they even
the wealthiest Jews in Pittsburgh: E. J. always said he was not worth one-
tenth as much as his friend A. C. Speyer.

In 1944, *Fortune* featured Kaufmann's eccentric counters on the sixth floor,
for which E. J. claimed authorship

.   .   .

If Kaufmann's image seems so much bigger to us today, we need to
remember that he was not the only merchant to get a formidable publicity boost from a store. The department store was a major force in shaping
popular culture all over America from the 1890s until the 1930s, when
Hollywood and the other mass media supplanted it. In those forty years it
was a merchant culture and a merchant aesthetic that shaped the core
American social experience, both in the cities and on the farms. (Rural
America shopped at the same stores by mail order.) The lights, the colors,
the glass, the escalators and the elevators in the department stores gave
an excitement to American life that was a foretaste of radio and the
movies later on.

One of the prime attractions of the department store in its glory days
was its function as a museum. Modern art, for example, entered American
life in large part through the department store. The first exhibit of modern
art in the United States, the so-called Armory Show of Cubist art in New
York in 1913, later circulated around the country at Gimbel Brothers stores
in Milwaukee, Cleveland, New York, and Philadelphia. Pittsburgh had no
Gimbels at the time, and the Kaufmann store was undergoing reconstruction, so the exhibit showed instead at the Boggs & Buhl store on the North

Side. Once E. J. put up the new auditorium on the eleventh floor, Kaufmann's was tireless in hosting such exhibits. In 1926, E. J. put on an elaborate "International Exposition of Arts and Industries" as a counterpart to
the similarly named fair in Paris the year before.

After its founding in 1929, the Museum of Modern Art sent its traveling exhibits to department stores as well as to museums all over the country. Its International Architecture show of 1932, for example, toured the
United States for several years after leaving Manhattan. It was installed
in museums in Pittsburgh, Philadelphia, Hartford, Buffalo, Milwaukee,
and Cleveland, among other cities, but when it got to Los Angeles, its
venue was the new Bullock's Wilshire Department Store. In 1933,
MoMA's Philip Johnson was assiduous in trying to get E. J. to house an
exhibit on modern housing at his store.

Kaufmann saw his entire store as a gallery of good design, and he
sometimes got directly involved in its interior architecture. Around 1925
he redesigned the counters of the main floors as radiating spokes, and in
1944 he reconfigured the sixth-floor counters in a curvilinear sequence, as
we learn from another illustration in *Fortune*. There is no evidence that
these innovations drummed up business, however: their main value
seems to have been as outlets for Kaufmann's artistic imagination.

Kaufmann's real calling lay in publicity. In an era in which the
Lazarus, Neiman Marcus, and Filene stores kept public relations pioneers
like Ben Sonnenberg and Edward Bernays on exorbitant retainers, E. J.
may also have employed a national publicity firm. But he did not need PR
professionals when he himself had such a subtle grasp of publicity. He
brought the store outstanding PR in 1930 by convincing Henry R. Luce to
carry a Kaufmann's-sponsored essay contest on the subject of arts and
industry in his brand-new *Fortune* magazine. The contest gave national
publicity to the remodeling of Kaufmann's ground floor. (The winner was
Catherine Bauer, who used her essay on modern German housing as a
springboard to a distinguished career of writing on architecture.)

Whether instructed or intuitive, Kaufmann was able to pull off one
publicity triumph after another. In 1910 the store profited from its ability
to fit President Taft's mammoth bulk with a new pair of trousers right off
the rack. In the next decade Kaufmann's sponsored the first radio news
broadcasts in Pittsburgh, and in 1927, E. J. capitalized on Lindbergh's
flight to Paris by placing the first Pittsburgh-to-Paris telephone call. The
next year he exploited Lindbergh's popularity again by assembling a complete airplane on his ground floor. Most Pittsburghers had never seen a
plane, and 50,000 extra shoppers took the bait.

The Kaufmann art department had a building all to itself, and it was
legendary for its speed and creativity. On D-Day, the entire store was fes-

Kaufmann (*second from left*) played host to Albert Einstein during his visit to Pittsburgh in December 1934

tooned by 10 A.M. with banners vouchsafing victory to the Allied troops. The Christmastime angels in Kaufmann's windows were so alluring that the Catholic diocese asked the store for extras that they could use in their churches. The merchandise Kaufmann picked up in Europe or through his twenty-seven buying offices from New York to Shanghai was always novel and fetching, but in showcasing his goods E. J. did even better. Kaufmann came to power at his store just when merchandise display had become a science. The Newton of showcasing theory was L. Frank Baum. Baum had come to national prominence in 1900 as the author of *The Wonderful Wizard of Oz,* often called the only American fairy tale, but E. J. and his cohorts knew him as the editor of *The Show Window* (now *Visual Merchandising and Store Design*). Baum's two claims to fame were less diverse than might appear, because he taught America's retailers how to make their counter and window layouts as seductive as the yellow brick road that led Dorothy and her friends to Oz.

Kaufmann could spot emerging trends in merchandise and display because he was top dog in a fraternity of hundreds of retailers around the country, and he liberally copied what the others did. When Stanley Marcus began placing full-page ads for Neiman Marcus in *Vogue, Harper's Bazaar,* and *Vanity Fair* in the 1930s, Kaufmann followed suit. When New Yorkers said "Meet me at the fountain" in the Siegel, Cooper store, Kaufmann got the same free advertising by directing Pittsburghers to meet under his clock. New York's B. Altman store was probably the model for

Kaufmann's elegant home-delivery carts, for its shortened work week, and for its subsidized employee cafeteria. Kaufmann himself decided to clone the *Saksagram* newsletter for Saks employees into the *Storagram* for his clerks. Kaufmann's interpreters in ten languages aped the interpreters at Gimbels, who spoke a still more remarkable twenty-five.

The quick transmission of ideas among retailers like E. J. was encouraged by a special circumstance: there were national chains among the mail-order houses and the five-and-ten-cent stores, but there were only a few chains among the quality department stores in those years, notably Gimbels and the May Company. Merchants had neither motive nor mechanism to trespass on one another's territory; rivals they certainly were in the boasting department, but they kept up a free exchange of ideas. The one field in which Kaufmann seemed to be ahead of the curve as a retailer was in the application of new technology. This I attribute to his three long stays in Germany. Kaufmann's German was serviceable enough to allow him to act as interpreter when Albert Einstein came to town in 1934, and some of his German and Austrian contacts wrote him without bothering with translations. We can see for ourselves that Liliane's German was letter-perfect: a handwritten letter of hers in German survives from 1927 in the Library of Congress.

In Berlin, E. J. could observe and make contact with the world leaders in lighting and other electrical applications, in broadcasting, and in the production of movies and records, well before that technological lead passed to New York and Hollywood. Stanley Marcus spoke admiringly of E. J.'s experiments with an inventory control system that was half a century ahead of computer databases. Just as Marcus recalled, you can see primitive but elaborate punch-card tabulators in the 1933 newsreel *The Pittsburgh Plan: E. J. Kaufmann Explains Plan for Worker Relief . . . to President Roosevelt*. Marcus himself was probably Kaufmann's only serious rival for recognition as the most creative American retailer of the 1930s, though he insisted otherwise. "You can't compare me to E. J. Kaufmann," Marcus told me. "E. J. was the top retailer in the U.S."

For all its prodigious monetary harvest, the Kaufmann store was a remarkably pleasant environment in which to work. The Kaufmanns themselves participated in the annual employee "follies," which got so elaborate they had to leave the store auditorium for a downtown theater. Anyone going through the store's archives today would think that running Kaufmann's in the 1920s was a constant party. The secret, I believe, was the way E. J. acted as the personal embodiment of the store. This was certainly true of businessmen like Elbert Hubbard, of whom it was said that

"Hubbard's life was an advertisement." The 1933 *Bulletin Index* profile of Kaufmann (the one that mocked him for his bracelets and his mistress) summed him up nicely as a merchant who sold his life and not merely his wares: "Smart store-man, Edgar Kaufmann has realized the value of publicity. . . . Art-lover, he has used art to publicize his store. . . . His private collections in his Fox Chapel home are choice, hand-picked. . . . He used art to good advertising advantage when he opened his remodeled first floor in 1930." In another city it might have seemed odd for Albert Einstein to stay for three days with a merchant, but in Pittsburgh it made perfect sense. The 1944 *Fortune* article on Kaufmann also put a high price tag on E. J.'s carefully cultivated public profile.

The cost and care that Kaufmann lavished on building his three houses—we will meet them in detail later—shows that, like his Medici predecessors, he knew that a merchant could rely on no more effective advertising than a glamorous lifestyle. In the 1930s the patrician John Nicholas Brown refused *Life* magazine's request to publish his modern house, but Kaufmann accommodated everyone who wanted to write on Fallingwater. His homes were not merely opulent: each was a perfect definition of high style at the moment. Kaufmann's suburban Pittsburgh estate perfectly expressed the lavishness of the nineteen-twenties, Fallingwater the search for American roots in the Depression thirties, and his California house the technological beguilement of the postwar forties and fifties.

Frank Lloyd Wright was on target when he nicknamed Kaufmann the Shopper, though more charitably we should call E. J. a merchant of culture. In selling culture Kaufmann ranked just a notch below Hollywood's movie moguls and the press lords like Luce and Hearst. The first group defined the country on the silver screen, the second on the printed page. But screen and newsprint gave the average citizen only transitory images, not something he could possess. What Kaufmann sold was less glamorous but more tangible: wonderful things that his customers could buy and take home.

If Kaufmann excelled as merchant and civic leader, he defaulted on the two other social roles he had to play: he was miscast as a family man and adrift as a Jew. The latter deficiency was endemic to an era in which America's Jews had lost their traditional self-definition. (The Fallingwater archives has a poignant illustration of this drift: an inscribed photograph of around 1905 to Lillian Kaufmann from Rabbi Leonard Levy, dressed exactly like an Episcopal priest.) By an odd twist of fate, America's Jews chose the exact time and place of Kaufmann's birth for their most decisive break with traditional Judaism. In November 1885, a dozen Reform rabbis met in the Concordia Club on Pittsburgh's North Side to craft the "Pittsburgh Platform," which emancipated their fellow Jews from all ritual regulations in the Bible. The Kaufmanns had made already their own break with ritual: in Germany the family was so devout that they maintained their own ritual bath (*mikveh*) on the farm outside Viernheim, but after ten years in America they were rampant assimilationists.

This process of forgetting their roots was not peculiar to the Kaufmanns. In New York, the Strauses, the Lehmans, and even mavericks like Olga Guggenheim felt obliged to fill their dim apartments with Renaissance Madonnas and altarpieces. The Kaufmanns were rustics compared to these grand members of "Our Crowd." When, years later, the *Encyclopedia Judaica* covered hundreds of families of German-American Jews, it saw no need to devote even a line to them. Still, E. J. and Liliane knew how to copy their Manhattan betters. Around 1926 they picked up the six Old Master paintings that one sees hanging on their walls in photographs of the 1930s and '40s. The paintings cost $159,000—about what they paid for Fallingwater a decade later. The works were not so much fakes as "school of" Botticelli, Luini, El Greco, Bronzino, and Titian, with a possible Cranach added later. Nearly all were explicitly Christian in subject matter, starting with four Madonnas.

It is hard to know what part of the Kaufmanns' aping of Christianity was meaningful and what part merely arriviste. Judaism was still a vital faith to Jacob Schiff, to the Warburgs, and to other New York Jews who were leagues ahead of the Kaufmanns in worldliness and wealth. E. J. intermittently saw himself as Jewish when it suited him: in 1917 he earnestly solicited votes from Pittsburgh's Jews to send him as a delegate to the American Jewish Congress. Thirty years later he again felt Jewish enough to join Temple Isaiah in Palm Springs, California, when some bigots tried to strangle the synagogue at birth. Kaufmann may well have understood the danger of someone in the public spotlight abandoning Judaism: the half-Jew Joseph Pulitzer was regularly raked over the coals by the *New York Evening Sun* for being a "renegade Jew" and "a Jew who does not want to be a Jew."

By the 1920s, though, we could say that the Kaufmanns had largely divorced themselves from anything spiritually Jewish. Here again New York may have set the pattern, because E. J. in the 1920s looked like a carbon copy of the Wall Street banker Otto Kahn. Kahn's wealth, bonhomie, and stable of mistresses made him the king of twenties New York, but he was personally rootless and lonely. More cultured than Kaufmann, Kahn single-mindedly championed the Metropolitan Opera while E. J. ogled the girls at the Ziegfeld Follies. Like some of the Guggenheims, Kahn was

Kaufmann
foxhunting, 1920s

by then more drawn to church than temple, and only the rise of Hitler deterred him from turning Christian. Many Jews flirted with Christianity in the interwar years, among them the Hollywood producers Louis B. Mayer and Harry Cohn. We might call Kaufmann a parallel case, since he commissioned the artist Samuel Yellin to shape a wrought-iron crucifix for his bed. Liliane's friends Cecilia Frank and Vivian Lehman crossed over to Episcopalianism around this time, and Liliane herself seems to have explored Catholicism during her volunteer nursing with the Sisters of Mercy during World War II.

People who knew E. J. Kaufmann reacted with vehemence when I asked them whether he was a social climber. They found it repugnant to think of him as a sherry-sipping toady, worrying whether he was picking up the right fork. But the question is not irrelevant. Kaufmann's brother, Oliver, was a classic social climber, and the 1933 *Bulletin Index* attack accused E. J. of being one, too. But not all social climbers are of the same stripe. We should perhaps call Kaufmann a social vaulter, because his wish was not to measure up to social norms but to jump over them. All the same, the man took great care to join the right clubs, live in the right neighborhoods, and do the right things in his spare time. In 1918, Kaufmann was still new at this game: the club memberships he listed in Pittsburgh, New York, Cleveland, Chicago, and Detroit were all low-status groups, either of Jews or merchants. No better was the early published résumé in which Kaufmann included his membership in the Loyal Order of Moose. Kaufmann later claimed in print to belong to one fancy Pittsburgh club, where he had never been more than a guest.

Kaufmann's passion for horses was upscale, too. He knew horses from hanging around the department-store stables as a boy, and by iron willpower he made himself into a decent rider: family movies show a grimly determined E. J. jumping dozens of hurdles at an indoor track. Kaufmann attained some national prominence as a stable-owner as well: in the 1920s, the French-bred steeplechase horses of his Fox Chapel Stud competed against steeds owned by bluebloods like John Hay Whitney and Colonel Robert McCormick.

Liliane's favorite social venues were the dog shows where she showed off the long-haired dachshunds she bred. In interwar America, raising dogs was even more socially exclusive than racing horses. Nothing dominated issues of William Randolph Hearst's *Town & Country* like dog shows—some months gobbling up a quarter of the magazine. But Liliane's interest in the sport had to be contrived, or at least conflicted: the March 1938 *Town & Country* followed its dog news with an ad for German tourism that showed swastika pennants gaily waving on a beach. Its June issue that same year featured an otherwise amusing story by Ludwig Bemelmans that taunted "corpulent businessman" Stanley Cohen. Was that really Liliane's crowd? It is hard not to surmise that the horse-riding, dog-breeding Kaufmanns were striving for entry into the winner's circle not just in sports but in the whole of high society.

Happily, it is nearly impossible today to imagine the viciousness of race prejudice in the United States in the 1920s and '30s. Any student of sports history knows that Adolf Hitler refused to shake hands with the great African-American runner Jesse Owens after his triumph at the 1936 Berlin Olympics, but Franklin D. Roosevelt managed to avoid Owens's handshake also. Prejudice against Jews was less intense but not much less pervasive than that against African-Americans. Abby Aldrich Rockefeller put the two together when she wrote her sons about prejudice in 1923: "It is to the disgrace of America that horrible lynchings and race riots frequently occur in our midst. The social ostracism of the Jews is less barbaric and brutal, and yet it often causes cruel injustice and must engender in the Jews a smouldering fire of resentment."

Between the First and Second World Wars, American bigots felt unusually free to mock, belittle, and occasionally lynch Jews. Harvard president A. Lawrence Lowell offered his spirited defense of university quotas against Jews on the front page of the *New York Times* in 1922. Pittsburgh was no more liberal in these quotas than other American cities, and generally less so. The University of Pittsburgh medical school kept its 10 percent Jewish quota until the 1950s. The quota could be pretty literal:

one class had 5 Jews out of 55; another had a mathematically perfect 9.5 Jews in a class of 95.

Wealthy Jews like the Kaufmanns were the particular target of Henry Ford's *Dearborn Independent,* which reproduced whole chapters of the forged *Protocols of the Learned Elders of Zion* on a supposed Jewish plot to dominate the world. Every week Father Charles Coughlin's vitriolic anti-Jewish diatribes reached an immense radio audience. Glamorous Jews fared no better: the Jewish girls in Ziegfeld's chorus line either passed as Christian, which turned Marian Levy into Paulette Goddard, or they were put on stage as self-mocking, Yiddish-spouting Jews like Fanny Brice.

With no more than some highly elliptical allusions by Edgar Jr. to go by, we cannot calibrate precisely how much the Kaufmanns suffered from snobbery and discrimination, but it must have been plenty. We can still read how E. J. was subject to mockery both in the *Bulletin Index* and in a novel in which two Christians spot him—alias Pittsburgh department-store mogul "Warren Kamen"—when they scrutinize a 1930s Jewish country club as though visiting a zoo. We know the Strauses and the Guggenheims were routinely excluded from hotels, and even Jewish refugees commonly said that prejudice in the United States exceeded anything they had experienced in pre-Nazi Germany. In 1935, Frank Lloyd Wright's patron Alexander Chandler initially refused to allow either E. J. or Stanley Marcus to stay at his Arizona hotel, and Wright got Marcus into the Arizona Biltmore only because his wife, Billie, was Christian. E. J. and Liliane made do with a room at an abandoned motel where Wright and the apprentices were working—a latter-day Joseph and Mary.

Discrimination was almost literally in Kaufmann's face in his relationship with the Mellons, whose dislike of Jews was notably keen. In various forms the Kaufmann store and Mellon Bank have faced each other for 125 years, and the two did business together: in 1929 the Mellons' Union Trust lent the Kaufmann store $3,500,000. Richard King Mellon would occasionally invite Kaufmann to lunch at the bank, but not at the Duquesne Club. For almost four decades the men were equally frosty neighbors in the country, since the Mellon estate at Ligonier lies not far from Bear Run. Until the Pennsylvania Turnpike cut through in 1940, Kaufmann had to drive to Ligonier before he could turn off for his own estate. Clippings record E. J. at the occasional horse race at Mellon's private Rolling Rock Club, but according to the lawyer who worked for both men, R. K. Mellon wanted no Jews inside his club, even for lunch.

The trick for Jews like the Kaufmanns was how to retain their dignity despite the "smouldering fire of resentment" that Abby Aldrich Rockefeller saw was burning inside them. Some Jews turned more insistently Jewish in response to prejudice; some, like Liliane's two friends, turned

Christian; and some became masochists who asked their tormentors for more. Budd Schulberg's 1941 novel *What Makes Sammy Run?* captured all three of these responses. E. J. was no masochist, but he certainly bent over backward to suit the majority culture of his day. In the face of Mellon prejudice he funded a retail fellowship at Pittsburgh's Mellon Institute in 1932, although the institute was otherwise entirely dedicated to serving Mellon-controlled companies. He made Rolling Rock habitués Frank Denton, James Beal, and Ralph Demmler his closest financial and legal agents, and, later, he appointed them the sole nonfamily directors in the Kaufmann charitable trust. These overtures made no more sense than Lessing Rosenwald's choice of Robert Wood to run Sears, Roebuck despite Wood's notorious anti-Jewish prejudice and leadership of the isolationist America Firsters.*

Sociologists call people like Kaufmann *déraciné*, rootless, because he was spurned by Christians and regarded as borderline within the Jewish community, too. Some Jews shunned him for both his mistresses and his merchandising. Merchants formed the core of Jewish society in New York, but the top Jews in Pittsburgh were industrialists: the Speyers in coal, the Falks and Levinsons in steel, the Kaplans in copper alloys, the Lehmans and the Blaus in concrete, the Franks in engineering and glass. Kaufmann was a man of a thousand friends but no community.

The ironic title of Merchant Prince was a perfect fit for E. J. Kaufmann. This prince would not be king, because Pittsburgh society would not allow him to escape his caste. The philanthropist Paul Mellon, growing up in Squirrel Hill and attending Shady Side Academy a dozen years after E. J., remembered life in his Calvinist birthplace: "In those days no one in Pittsburgh ever pulled his or her living room or dining room blinds down in the evening. As you walked along the street, you could look into each house, where the lights burned brightly and where you could see the families reading the newspapers, having dinner, or talking after dinner. They seemed to be mortally afraid of privacy." It was also a town of remarkable social backwardness, where magnates like Henry Clay Frick rode in elevators reserved for them alone, where a man could not appear in public with a married woman, where women dared not enter the Duquesne Club except by the side door, and Jews dared not enter.

This social isolation brought out the roué in Kaufmann, whose impeccable credentials on paper gave no clue to his libidinous and unfettered private life. Kaufmann loved to flout authority in religion, in sexual

---

*Sometimes E. J. just had to laugh. When he was building his Palm Springs house in 1946, he required the services of his junior store manager, Roy Oliver, in Los Angeles. Kaufmann booked Oliver into the then restricted Jonathan Club, where he himself could not set foot.

A home movie
captured Kaufmann
and his daughter,
Betty Jo Harris,
in 1932

morality, and—after he met Wright—in architectural style. Like Wright, Kaufmann needed to live life at the edge: both men did best when they had stringent rules to break. (One story has E. J. insisting that his chauffeur wait at the curb while he carried on a certain dalliance, rather than having the limousine hide one block over.) He could complain that Edgar Jr. "refused to be a son," but he himself refused to be a dutiful husband and father. He was fastidious in his attentions to his mother, Betty, right until her death in 1942, but his infidelities to Liliane were almost beyond counting. Kaufmann's attraction to the chorus-line beauties in the Ziegfeld Follies was notorious: he once hijacked the whole troupe for a weekend at Atlantic City. In 1928 he fathered a girl in a liaison with the store model Lois Harris, but far from making a secret of her existence, Kaufmann named her Betty Jo in honor of his mother, then engaged what seemed like half the bankers and lawyers of Pittsburgh to set up the trust fund that still helps to support his four grandchildren today. In 1931 the *Pittsburgh Press* printed a gossip item, in code, that said Liliane was on her way to Reno, Nevada, to divorce E. J. That never happened, but the mistresses continued to be so numerous that Kaufmann's Department Store issued them distinctive charge plates they could use for free.

Kaufmann's behavior was less eccentric for his day than for ours. The Pittsburgh steelmen typically had mistresses: Henry Clay Frick kept his in a Paris hotel. When he died, she married a proper businessman and became an arts patron in San Francisco. A. W. Mellon may or may not have been "proper," but his wife, Nora, evidently was not: rumors of Paul Mellon's illegitimate birth were circulated freely enough that one of his uncles could tease him about it. Pittsburgh was in general ill suited for the libidinous life, but New York was close at hand, and once a year or so

E. J. would revisit Europe. The Kaufmanns spent close to a year in twenties Berlin when it was the sex capital of the world.

Another place where E. J. could escape the strictures of Pittsburgh was California. California cared nothing for Pittsburgh, but the reverse was not true. As early as 1905 one Pittsburgh suburb consciously imitated the bungalows in the Los Angeles suburb of Pasadena, and it was unlikely to have been a coincidence that the name given the brand-new street developed by the Kaufmanns in 1925 was Pasadena Drive. The society pages of Pittsburgh's *Jewish Criterion* attest to a Kaufmann presence in California at least as early as 1915, and an office memo from 1928 survives to document E. J.'s ties to numerous Californians in San Francisco and Chula Vista. Kaufmann's nieces and nephews speak of Liliane and E. J. as "constantly" going to California in the 1920s and '30s. They typically began in Los Angeles, which they reached first by train but after 1935 by airplane. Then they proceeded by rail or air to their main pilgrimage, the California desert town of Palm Springs. Betty Kaufmann was a Palm Springs regular by 1930, and E. J.'s cactus gardener, Patricia Moorten, recalled for me that Kaufmann would come out every winter to be with his mother. He spent increasingly long stays in Palm Springs, and finally built a second home there in 1946.

The dry warmth of Palm Springs was good for Kaufmann's arthritis, but a bigger attraction was California's open lifestyle. The Kaufmanns were relatively more free to join the social scene there than they were in Pittsburgh, but it is instructive to learn what "relatively" meant. The Chamber of Commerce view propagated in Palm Springs today is that the fledgling town (it incorporated only in 1938) was open to anyone with money, but that is false. Jack Benny could not join the Thunderbird Country Club because he was a Jew, and civic leader Ruth Hardy kept her Ingleside Inn slammed shut against Jews as well. The El Mirador Hotel, where Betty, E. J., and Liliane Kaufmann stayed, discriminated like clockwork: Jews could stay in November, December, and January, but not during the top months of February, March, and April. Frank Bogert, publicist at El Mirador and twice mayor of Palm Springs, told me that rich and prominent Jews like the Lilienthals of San Francisco or the Kaufmanns of Pittsburgh (whom he remembered) might get around those regulations a bit, but never "the kikes from Hollywood."*

---

*How in this restricted context did Albert Einstein get to be El Mirador's most famous guest? Early in 1933 he was staying with the lawyer Samuel Untermyer when the Mirador invited him to lodge there for a month, all expenses paid. This publicity stunt was worth every penny to the hotel, even though, as Bogert told me, "Einstein was a little bit Jewish himself." The scientist-celebrity only stayed a few days.

The embodiment of the California lifestyle in those days was the publishing king William Randolph Hearst, whose life intersected Kaufmann's in numerous ways. In 1927, Hearst bought the *Pittsburgh Sun-Telegraph,* in which E. J. became the biggest advertiser. At the same time, Kaufmann was the dominant sponsor of news broadcasts on the two radio stations Hearst created in Pittsburgh, among his first. Kaufmann similarly advertised his store nationally in Hearst's *Harper's Bazaar,* and in 1933 he used Pathé, which had been making newsreels in association with Hearst since 1913, to film *The Pittsburgh Plan,* his slick newsreel-style documentary on combating unemployment. That meant that Kaufmann used all four of Hearst's media: newspapers, magazines, radio, and films. The two men would have met in three cities: occasionally, when business brought Hearst to Pittsburgh; more frequently when they both wintered in Palm Springs; and most often in the second row of the Ziegfeld Follies in New York, where Hearst, Kaufmann, and their mutual friend Paul Block (owner of the *Pittsburgh Post-Gazette*) were regulars. We know that Block and Hearst shared the Ziegfeld showgirl Marion Davies, who started out as mistress to the first before she switched to the second. All three men, Block, Hearst, and Kaufmann, gave employment of another sort to Joseph Urban, Frank Lloyd Wright's friend and the designer of the Ziegfeld Theater. Block used Urban as a decorator in New York; Kaufmann for two or three architectural commissions in Pittsburgh; and Hearst for a house in Florida, an office building in New York, and for movie sets at his Cosmopolitan Pictures in Hollywood.

At home Kaufmann, like Hearst, was a partner in a hollow marriage. We should not read too much into the Kaufmanns' separate bedrooms at Fallingwater, since this was a standard feature for rich young couples in the twenties and thirties: Grete and Fritz Tugendhat asked Mies for separate bedrooms in the famous house he designed for them in Czechoslovakia in the same years. But at times Liliane even lived apart from E. J. in her own hideaway apartment. The general impression in her circle was that, despite the monetary basis of their marriage, Liliane adored her husband; but he treated her coolly and at some point she found lovers of her own.

Because of Liliane's artistic nature and the absence of solid documentation on her role at Fallingwater, some scholars have imagined that she was its true motivating force, rather than her husband or son. This seems like overcompensation to me. No one disputes the importance of Liliane's role in decorating Fallingwater, but nothing indicates that she felt the need to put her own stamp on a building until the very last years of her life. Liliane shared her husband's and son's unconventionality in other ways, however. This is suggested not only by her lovers but by her nude oil portrait by Victor Hammer, a borderline Surrealist painter whom the Kaufmanns got to know in Vienna in the 1920s. (The strips flanking the portrait were probably meant to carry shutters, for privacy.) Liliane was forty-three when she sat for Hammer in Florence in 1932, still strikingly beautiful although the portrait head alone was hers—the breasts belonged to a model in Vienna. The portrait hints at the sensual aura that made one niece recall (in a positive way): "I can still smell her." But in practical affairs Liliane was no less capable a manager than E. J. In 1929 she went to Europe to buy decorations for the new thirteen-story Montefiore Hospital, and from 1934 to 1943 she ran Montefiore as the only woman to serve as its president. At the store she personally selected the clothes, art, and antiques for her Vendôme boutique. Vendôme gave a big boost to Kaufmann's profits and public relations: it was Liliane's part of the store, for example, not E. J.'s, that was carried in the advertisements in *Harper's Bazaar* and *Vogue*.

Architecture was the perfect mediator between the Republican businessman at one end of Kaufmann's personality and the libertine at the other. It gave Kaufmann the high public profile he sought and redressed the social isolation that fate and Pittsburgh society had assigned him. If he previously seemed lucky rather than astute in his architectural patronage, it was only because no study on Fallingwater gave serious consideration to his early buildings. Unlike such movers in capitalist urbanization as the Earl of Bedford in London, the Levitts in their Levittowns, or the Zeckendorfs in Manhattan, Kaufmann had no professional involvement in the building industry—save, perhaps, for one trial balloon in the 1920s. Yet he had a masterly command of the numerous buildings he created, bought, or rented. Kaufmann also mastered the use of architects. He built with or negotiated with nearly a dozen: four or more before he met Wright, and at least six after him.

Even discounting certain minor projects at Bear Run and philanthropic buildings that demanded little personal attention, Kaufmann produced an exceptional group of several dozen buildings; these are detailed in the Source Notes. Fallingwater was notable enough, but in addition Kaufmann's earlier home in Pittsburgh was published and admired across the country; his Civic Arena was a marvel of postwar engineering; and his 1940s winter home at Palm Springs is—along with Fallingwater—one of the most frequently illustrated houses in the world.

It is curious that Kaufmann's early buildings have not previously been perceived as the trail that led to Bear Run. True, they were as dissimilar to

Fallingwater as they were to each other, with the store Beaux-Arts, the rented houses early American, the YMHA neo-Georgian, and the suburban house fake-Norman. None seemed to point to Fallingwater, but if we ask not what Kaufmann's buildings looked like but what he got out of them, then his move from conservatism to modernism becomes perfectly consistent. It was irrelevant to Kaufmann whether his buildings were conservative or radical in terms of style, because what he sought was impact, not aesthetics. Fallingwater served Kaufmann no differently than did his earlier buildings: only the architectural fashion changed, and the amount of propaganda he could harvest from it.

The key to the early structures was their architect, Benno Janssen. For twenty years Janssen served E. J. as confidant, court architect, and architectural mentor—the three roles Frank Lloyd Wright would take over in 1934. Janssen, seven years younger than Wright but much more conservative, represented everything Wright despised. He trained in architecture schools in the Midwest and at MIT (Wright had quit college); he studied from 1902 to 1904 at the École des Beaux-Arts in Paris (Wright had rejected Daniel Burnham's offer to sponsor him there); and he apprenticed with Shepley, Rutan & Coolidge in Boston, who were top purveyors of the revival architecture that Wright ridiculed.

Janssen was one of America's best academic designers, on a par with Carrère & Hastings in New York, Trumbauer or Eyre in Philadelphia, or Mizner in Florida. From 1905 to 1938 he created magnificent settings for Pittsburgh's Twentieth Century and Longue Vue clubs, the Pittsburgh Athletic Association, and a stunning garden patio for the Duquesne Club. Janssen's client list included the Mellons (stables and kennels at Rolling Rock and the lavish Mellon Institute), George Westinghouse (a library and a huge office block), and the aluminum-rich Hunts (domestic, commercial, and industrial work). Henry Clay Frick employed Janssen, too, for his high-society William Penn Hotel and for a vast but unexecuted apartment house complex in Pittsburgh's Oakland civic center.

Benno Janssen was crucial for Kaufmann's success at architectural politics in several ways, but the most obvious was that he gave Kaufmann links to Pittsburgh high society that he could have gained in no other way. Other Pittsburgh Jews also understood the game of architectural politics but played it less well. Maurice and Leon Falk used Janssen in 1932 when they donated the Falk School to the University of Pittsburgh. In 1930 they had dared even higher, employing E. P. Mellon (nephew and in-house architect to his uncles A. W. and R. B. Mellon) to design the Falk Clinic. The results were not memorable, though, because Janssen possessed talent but Mellon did not.

Kaufmann gave Janssen more commissions than anyone, and without

Pittsburgh's civic center in Oakland features monumental buildings financed by Andrew
Carnegie, the Mellons, the Fricks, and the Heinzes. Kaufmann's YMHA (the middle of
the three trapezoid structures) stands proudly among them.

doubt he had tighter emotional and professional bonds with him than did
any other client. But the bonding of the two men had its dark side: E. J.
and Liliane were forbidden to join any of the clubs that Janssen had
designed. Through Janssen, Kaufmann became a voyeur of the city's rul-
ing class. (Kaufmann's sole high-society friend in Pittsburgh was the like-
minded H. J. Heinz II, who maintained twelve houses around the globe.)
The world Janssen designed for Kaufmann served as a simulacrum, or virtual reality, of the world to which he was denied access. So near yet so far:
Kaufmann must have seen himself trapped in an architectural apartheid.

Janssen's first service to Kaufmann was his lightning-fast erection of
the big new wing for the store in 1913, the one that quashed the cousins'
revolt. That same year, Kaufmann moved into the first of his three
Janssen-designed houses, an elegant Anglo-Norman home in Squirrel
Hill a few blocks from the huge house in which E. J.'s parents then lived.
His new home was at the height of his social reach: on one side lived
Janssen's socially prominent partner, Franklin Abbott, while his backyard
neighbor was William Larimer Mellon, the founder of Gulf Oil. In 1920,

Kaufmann left this house for a rich Federal-style villa that the architect had built for himself a block away. In the second house Janssen was E. J.'s landlord, in a peculiar turnabout of the usual architect-client roles.

Kaufmann and Janssen achieved stunning results together in the Young Men's Hebrew Association building of 1924–26, now the University of Pittsburgh's Bellefield Hall. Kaufmann micromanaged every part of the project, I was told by old-timer Alexander Lowenthal, and he named the auditorium for his father. The YMHA constitutes a kind of academic dream world, in which a fifteenth-century papal palace in Renaissance Siena is fused with Stratford, the eighteenth-century Lee mansion in Virginia. One gets the sense of a building trying hard to pass for Christian, the way Liliane's friends had. It is instructive that Pittsburgh's Jewish leaders sold the YMHA the moment they gained admittance into Janssen's Christian clubhouses a few blocks away.

Good as the YMHA is as architecture, it is even better as urban symbolism. In setting it among its high-society neighbors in the heart of Oakland, Kaufmann took advantage of a loophole in Pittsburgh's harsh social code. That code was inflexibly segregationist for social intercourse and entry to clubs, but it was topographically lax: anyone could build wherever they pleased. Tongues must have wagged nonetheless when Kaufmann put the YMHA next to the Frick-funded Board of Education building and a half-block from Andrew Carnegie's palatial museum and library. The YMHA faced "Frick Acres," for which Janssen had devised his palatial but unbuilt apartments for Frick eight years earlier. In 1920, the brothers A. W. and R. B. Mellon purchased those acres for construction of the University of Pittsburgh's skyscraper-Gothic Cathedral of Learning. Soon afterward, the Mellons erected Mellon Institute on the far side of the YMHA and the Heinzes positioned Heinz Chapel in front of it. When all was complete in 1937, Kaufmann had the Heinzes and Mellons facing and to the left of his building, Frick to the right, and Carnegie down the block. Here were the architectural peacocks of Pittsburgh, and Kaufmann's YMHA strutted at the center of them all.

It was no surprise to find Kaufmann and Mellon buildings cheek-by-jowl in Oakland, since that was already the pattern established downtown, in Squirrel Hill, and in the nearness of the two families' weekend escapes. Additionally, in the heat of the summer, Kaufmann, William Larimer Mellon, and numerous members of the Duquesne Club went up to central Ontario to reach their cottages around Georgian Bay: Kaufmann at McGregor Bay, Mellon on Muskoka Lake, the others at a hunting and fishing lodge maintained by the Duquesne Club. These architectural conjunctions were numerous enough to suggest that Kaufmann had gone from copying the Mellons to deliberately squaring off his buildings against theirs.

Kaufmann could learn about architectural patronage from other skilled mentors besides Janssen. Two of America's best were right in Pittsburgh, in Carnegie and Frick. Carnegie adroitly used architecture to overcome the public relations nightmare of death and deceit after a bloody clash at his Homestead steelworks in 1892. By the 1920s, when Kaufmann was in his second decade as a serious patron of architecture, there was nowhere one could turn in Pittsburgh without spotting a Carnegie Library. (Carnegie's 3,500 libraries blanketed the whole United States and much of the world, of course, but the blanket was nowhere so thick as at home.) One of the earliest and most elaborate of the libraries, complete with the original Carnegie Music Hall, opened right in Kaufmann's North Side neighborhood when he was five. Later, Kaufmann could not visit his family synagogue or Uncle Isaac's house in Oakland without passing the fortresslike Carnegie Institute and the campus of Carnegie Tech. Both stretched Smithsonian-like for acres, rivaling in impressiveness the immense steel mills that Carnegie and the other moguls controlled around the city.

Frick's buildings were more subtle than Carnegie's. Everyone in town knew how Frick had challenged Carnegie to architectural battles in three different Pittsburgh neighborhoods before the two men fought over bragging rights for the most palatial house in New York. E. J. was not likely to have had extensive contact with Carnegie, but we can have no doubt that he personally knew Frick. Frick came from the hamlet of West Overton,

Below left: Benno Janssen designed La Tourelle around 1925
for E. J.'s move to a fashionable Pittsburgh suburb
Below right: Wright and Kaufmann discussed Fallingwater
in the stylistically backward living room of La Tourelle

just a half hour's drive from Fallingwater, where his birthplace still stands. The nearby town of Connellsville was the epicenter of Frick's coke empire: when Kaufmann ran his store there, he would have heard the name Frick about as often as a student at the University of Virginia catches the name Jefferson.

Like Carnegie, Frick craved an improved public image after he crushed the 1892 strike at the Homestead steelworks. Like Carnegie, too, he ploughed his money into buildings, though with a commercial rather than a philanthropic emphasis. Even when he decamped for New York in 1905, Frick stepped up his building operations in downtown Pittsburgh, and when both he and Carnegie died in 1919, he left behind four palatial skyscrapers in the Golden Triangle. Two were the office towers that rose right behind the Kaufmann store, one was a shopping arcade next door, and the fourth was the Janssen-designed William Penn Hotel where Kaufmann later lived. The Frick Building of 1901 was—is—a virtual sanctuary for the cult of Henry Clay Frick. Besides the bare-breasted nymph who exhaled the perpetual fire by which Frick's cronies lit their cigars, the lobby still vaunts a stained-glass window by John La Farge, two lions by the sculptor whose beasts also guard the New York Public Library, and a marble bust of Frick that used to be reverently hooded in velvet every night. Near the end of his life Kaufmann came full circle with his putative mentor when, in 1948, he took over Frick's second office tower as an annex to the store. In 1953 he tore down the Carnegie Building and replaced it with a new wing for Kaufmann's.

In 1924, Janssen and Kaufmann planned their masterpiece, the suburban house called La Tourelle. In the mid-1920s, both Oliver and Edgar turned to Janssen for new houses. For the conservative Oliver, who was mad for horses, Janssen constructed a faux Virginia plantation in Squirrel Hill. E. J. instead abandoned Squirrel Hill for suburban Fox Chapel, where he planted five homes on a sixty-acre hilltop on which H. J. Heinz had formerly grown tomatoes. E. J. invaded Fox Chapel in a kind of phalanx, designating the homes for three Christian associates, his sister Martha Wolf, and himself. Later E. J. permitted his friend Irvin F. Lehman to add another large house on a corner of his land.

For Kaufmann's La Tourelle, Janssen contrived a cunning composition of an Anglo-Norman entrance tower (the *tourelle* of the estate's name) and five separate building fragments. With eighteen fireplaces and a fortune in Samuel Yellin's ironwork, La Tourelle cost Kaufmann about $250,000 (millions of dollars today), which was far more than he later paid for Fallingwater. In its fragmented volumes and high-pitched roofline, the pseudo-antiquity of its handmade bricks and hand-hewn Vermont slate shingles, and the picturesque layout of its numerous outbuildings, we can see La Tourelle as a fraternal twin to the Longue Vue clubhouse that Janssen was building on the opposite bank of the Allegheny River. The July 1930 *Architectural Record* published La Tourelle and Longue Vue on the same page, as though there was no functional distinction between them. La Tourelle *was* effectively a clubhouse, its membership restricted to E. J. Kaufmann alone.

The stuffy interiors of La Tourelle perfectly represented the bland conventions of American architecture that Fallingwater would shatter eight years later. Finished around 1928, it was the darling of the architectural conservatives, who promoted it in numerous articles in national magazines. Several of the articles carried an aerial view of the estate, which in the 1920s was a gesture reserved for top houses alone.

La Tourelle, with its twenty-three-acre grounds, its stables, kennels, greenhouses, cow barns, and servant housing, was the most costly estate ever to go up in Fox Chapel. But the natives never warmed up to Kaufmann, and he left the house just twelve years later to live downtown. This short tenure suggests that the real function of La Tourelle was to be another of Kaufmann's battering rams into Christian society. There was in truth something ludicrous in the Kaufmanns' posing as lords of the manor, with their wrought-iron crucifix and their Renaissance Madonnas on the walls, as though they had arrived in Fox Chapel with William the Conqueror in 1066.

Janssen left behind no notes, but we can tell from one commission that he seems to have found Kaufmann's jousting of architecture and ethnicity a little risible. The stables and kennels he produced for the Mellons at Rolling Rock reproduced the main lines of La Tourelle in the heart of enemy territory. Rolling Rock's squat *tourelle,* its fragmented volumes, and its rough textures echo what Janssen had designed for the Kaufmanns a year or two earlier, in a fashion too literal to be coincidence. The *tourelle* at Ligonier is no marginal feature, either: as the trophy room, it was the Holy of Holies of the Mellon clubhouse. Janssen had superimposed Kaufmann's image on a club that would not let the man in for lunch.

With his penchant for innovation and novelty, Kaufmann hardly fit the picture of an architectural conservative, but promoting stylistically backward architecture netted him big publicity gains. In May 1930, for example, he served with the chancellor of the University of Pittsburgh and the Pittsburgh bluebloods Howard Heinz, J. H. Hillman Jr., and R. B. Mellon on an honorary jury to vote on the best of recent local architecture. Janssen captured all but two of nine prizes in the popular vote, including "best house" for Kaufmann's La Tourelle. E. J. may have had his doubts about the architectural horse race on which he had embarked, but he had at least bet on the right horse.

May 1930 marked Kaufmann's embarcation on a different architectural journey: the makeover of his store's ground floor in Art Deco style. This move to near-modernism was less radical than his later switch to the uncompromising modernism of Fallingwater, but it was still significant. It poses three related questions: Why had Kaufmann been so conservative in his architecture before 1930? Why did he move to modernism? And how could he enjoy two contradictory architectural styles at the same time?

The third of these questions answers itself most readily. The cultural historian William Leach calls people like Kaufmann the "brokering class." Members of this class have no set loyalties themselves but are astute at "repressing one's own convictions and withholding judgment in the interests of forging profitable relationships." This was the mark of social modernism, to have no specific stylistic loyalty but to jump from style to style as the market demanded. Those jumps were bewildering only to ideologues who were fixed in their loyalty to a particular architectural camp.

The surprise is not that Kaufmann started out as an architectural conservative, but that he eventually moved to modernism. Conventional wisdom says that Jews support the avant-garde, and we cannot discount the fact that by 1930 four of the five most radical houses in the world were lived in by Jews: Philip and Leah Lovell in their homes by Schindler and Neutra in Los Angeles, Fritz and Grete Tugendhat in their home by Mies in Brno in Czechoslovakia, and Michael and Sarah Stein in their villa by Le Corbusier at Garches (the fifth house was Le Corbusier's Villa Savoye). A visitor to the Guggenheim or Hirshhorn museums or to the Cone sisters' Matisse collection in Baltimore could argue the same position. But it is easy to find as many counterexamples. In 1933, the year before Kaufmann commissioned Fallingwater, the Hollywood producer David O. Selznick put up an elaborate Colonial Revival house in Beverly Hills. Sociologically, Selznick's mansion made more sense than Fallingwater, because outsiders generally support insider culture, rather than tear it down.

Liliane reacted to prejudice in the same way, joining the high-society world of horses, dogs, and Renaissance Madonnas, and E. J.'s conservative architecture did the expected thing, too. It was his move to modernism in the 1930s that was unexpected, because before World War II, America's dominant class was almost totally against modernism. Of the hundreds of city and country homes illustrated or cited in Augusta Owen Patterson's 1924 *American Homes of To-day*, not a single one was modern. Patterson's book also functioned as an illustrated social register, since nearly all her home-owners were upper-class. Books like Patterson's were nearly as segregated as the clubs their owners belonged to.

Kaufmann's slow conversion to architectural modernism went apace with the snail's progress that the movement was making in the United States overall. Typical of the reactionary cast of American buildings after World War I were three major projects of John D. Rockefeller Jr. in the late 1920s. His Riverside Church of 1927 near Columbia University was Gothic; the Cloisters (1928) in upper Manhattan was Romanesque; and his pseudo-reconstruction of Williamsburg (1929–34) was Colonial. William Randolph Hearst patronized the same revivalism in his castle at San Simeon, with its acres of imported European loot. Those were the years in which Kaufmann grabbed some architectural loot himself, in the fragment of an Austrian Rococo monastery that he rebuilt as the store's executive conference room.

Aside from certain industrial buildings, Pittsburgh was one of the last American cities to move to modern architecture. The city's social and corporate élite housed itself behind traditional facades not only after World War I but well past World War II. The Mellons, for example, shunned modernism utterly: every one of their Pittsburgh buildings dwelt in the architectural past. Paul Mellon stuck with conservative corporate architecture as late as 1952, when he and his cousin Richard King Mellon used an old partner of Janssen's to tone down the slight modernism of Harrison and Abramovitz's skyscraper addition to the Mellon Bank. Mellon's homes were even more backward: he never occupied a modern house in his life.

We could think of Kaufmann's education in modern architecture as a class that covered two semesters: the 1920s exposed him to modernistic, and the 1930s to more radical modernism. Where E. J. acquired this architectural education is nowhere recorded, not even in family stories. I link his move to radical modernism with his discovery of the advanced architecture of the 1930s in Los Angeles and southern California, which is a tale for later. His exposure to modernistic architecture in the 1920s seems to me to have come not at home but abroad, especially in Mexico, Austria, and Germany. Kaufmann probably encountered Mexico during his trip to Panama in 1912. In those years the country held a double fascination for Americans. One was its primitivism, but the other was the opposite: Mexico was light-years ahead of the United States in its embrace of modernism. Kaufmann liked the mural painters he met in Mexico so much that he later brought Juan O'Gorman to Pittsburgh to decorate the Oakland YMHA. Two watercolors by Diego Rivera hang at Fallingwater today, and Rivera himself came to the house as a guest.

Kaufmann's involvement with the Mexican painters led to his most important art commission outside of architecture. This was his 1927 contract with Boardman Robinson (an important name then, though close to forgotten now) for a set of murals for the remodeled ground floor of the store. The murals, constituting a history of commerce, excited much interest when exhibited at the Art Students League in New York in December 1929 and again when unveiled at Kaufmann's in May 1930. The Architectural League of New York rushed to award Robinson its Gold Medal for 1930 for his accomplishment.

Both in form and content, Robinson's works for Kaufmann were the first modern murals in the United States—strikingly different from the "American Renaissance" murals of the pre–World War I generation. The Bullock's Wilshire Department Store in Los Angeles had hired Howard Sachs to paint large panels for its opening in 1929, but Kaufmann's commission was earlier and more important. Technically, at least, it was the forerunner of the thousands of school and post office murals by the WPA artists of the 1930s.

The Mexican artist who intrigued the Kaufmanns the most was Frida Kahlo, from whom they bought *My Birth* and *Remembrance of an Open Wound*. The first painting dates from 1932 and was purchased by the Kaufmanns from the Julien Levy Gallery in 1938. A Kahlo scholar comments that the painting "shows a fairly bizarre taste in art and gift-giving in the Kaufmann family." Kahlo painted the equally gory *Remembrance of an Open Wound* in 1938; it was exhibited at the Julien Levy Gallery that year, and came to E. J. in 1940.

A second important point of entry for the Kaufmanns' exploration of modernism was Austria, beginning with their friendship with the painter Victor Hammer. Hammer's reputation is undeservedly minor today. He was an important member of a group of Neue Sachlichkeit ("New Objectivity") portraitists of the 1920s and 1930s who sought alternatives to expressionism and abstraction. Besides his 1932 nude portrait of Liliane, Hammer made a pencil sketch of her in 1926, one of Junior around the same time, and in 1929 he painted the large portrait of E. J. as a hiker that now hangs at Fallingwater. Hammer several times came to Pittsburgh as a guest of the Kaufmanns; they rank as the great patrons of his career. The Kaufmanns' paintings and prints by Hammer are now divided among the National Portrait Gallery in Washington, the art museum of the University of Kentucky in Lexington, and diverse public and private collections.

Hammer is the earliest documented link between the Kaufmanns and a large group of Austrian modernists. Other members of this group were the architects Joseph Urban, Bernard Rudofsky, and Richard Neutra; the designers Laszlo Gabor, Paul Theodore Frankl, Walter Sobotka, and Josef Frank; and the architectural theorist Hans Vetter. E. J. and Liliane were patrons to so many Austrian artists and designers that Pittsburgh followed right behind New York as their key American destination when they were obliged to emigrate in the 1930s.

Joseph Urban: 1928 project for remodeling Kaufmann's Department Store

The Budapest-born Gabor was the Austrian designer the Kaufmanns knew best. He met Kaufmann Jr. in Vienna around 1928, then came to Pittsburgh in 1935 as chief art designer for the store. His window treatments were renowned in American retailing circles. The Kaufmanns later got him a job as critic in the architecture school at Carnegie Mellon University, which led to a similar post for his friend Vetter. The graphic and furniture designer Paul Theodore Frankl was also close to the Kaufmanns. He gave at least one public lecture on modern design at the Kaufmann store, in 1929, and Kaufmann Jr. always called him an early teacher and important influence.

A key element in the Pittsburgh-Vienna axis was the Wiener Werkstätte, the industrial arts or applied arts consortium that was part of the transatlantic movement generically called "art and industry"—exactly the subject of E. J.'s essay contest in *Fortune*. This movement attracted the Kaufmanns both artistically and commercially, and led Kaufmann Jr. to study applied art in Vienna at the end of the decade. The Werkstätte outpost in New York was run by Joseph Urban. Urban came to New York in 1914, and had a high profile among American architects until his premature death in 1933. He was particularly important as one of the first architects to make his personality a selling tool: his profile in *The New Yorker*, for example, was the first in those pages devoted to an architect. These marketing devices were not lost on Urban's friends Kaufmann and Wright.

Urban transposed his skill at scenography into San Simeon–like country houses, such as his Mar-a-Lago of 1927 for Marjorie Merriweather Post and her then husband, stockbroker Edward F. Hutton. The Florida estate was a great boost to Urban's career, bringing him noted clients such as Hearst and the socially impeccable A. J. Drexel Biddle. (An unexecuted office building project of 1928 for Hearst popped up more than a decade later as the "Wynand Building" in Ayn Rand's *Fountainhead*.) Although Urban beat out Frank Lloyd Wright for the New School for Social Research commission in 1928, the two men remained close and affectionate, as their numerous letters show.

What drew Kaufmann to Urban was probably Urban's high-status clientele and his fetchingly elegant brand of modernism. Urban's first work for Kaufmann seems to have been the apartment that Liliane maintained in town. He then worked with Benno Janssen on the new wing of the William Penn Hotel, a collaboration almost surely brokered by Kaufmann. Urban's ravishing Art Deco ballroom at the hotel survives as an outstanding exemplar of the style in this country. In July 1928, Urban created an elaborate scheme for rebuilding Kaufmann's ground floor, also in Art Deco. Kaufmann doubtless knew of the design, since Urban needed plans of the store on which to base it, but no correspondence survives to document it. Urban's zoomorphic lights growing from the piers into the ceiling would have made Kaufmann's an unforgettable piece of Art Deco commercial work. But the design was impractical, and Kaufmann did not touch it. Instead he employed Urban in 1928–1929 for an opulent Art Deco swimming pool at the Kaufmann Settlement house, which stood incongruously behind a Georgian facade by the local traditionalists Edward and Charles Stotz. This inside-outside mishmash suggests that Kaufmann was still hedging his architectural bets.

Sooner or later, E. J. *had* to turn to modernism, because by the late twenties the concept had become a national fixation, particularly among women consumers. As an advertisement in the January 1929 *Vogue* put it: "MODERNISM is sweeping the intelligent world. You find it in music, in the arts, in literature. You can't just ignore it. Yet, what do you know about it? What do you think of it?"

Merchants were quick to discover that modernism was good for business. This message was strongly underlined by the merchants of the first country in which Kaufmann encountered modernism: Germany. E. J. and Liliane's ties to Germany were intense. Their long stays in Berlin in 1910–11 and 1920–21, their annual or biannual visits thereafter, and the excellence of their spoken and written German leave no doubt on this.

Erich Mendelsohn's Schocken Department Store in Stuttgart, begun in 1926, was the outstanding commercial work of its decade. Based on Sullivan's Carson Pirie Scott store in Chicago, ironically, it showed that German merchants and frequent visitors to Germany like the Kaufmanns were years ahead of most Americans in their understanding of modernism and its business applications.

What we cannot so simply determine is what they got out of those ties. The links to Germany were not in themselves exceptional. Contrary to all the other immigrant groups that quickly dropped the old mother tongue, America's German-origin Jews used German in private gatherings and in worship right up to World War I. (They were not alone in this: so did much of the British royal family, and élites in other countries.) A few German-Jewish families like the Warburgs kept up massive economic activity between Germany and the United States until the rise of the Nazis, but E. J. and Liliane were not merchant bankers and, again unlike the Warburgs, they themselves had not been born in Germany. By the early twentieth century, and certainly by 1918, the vast majority of American-born Jews like the Kaufmanns had severed their ties to Germany. Within the Kaufmann clan itself, the visits back to Germany came to a dead stop after World War I. Here, however, E. J. and Liliane decisively broke with their clan. They carefully refurbished their links with Germany each year, but their motive, I believe, was commercial rather than sentimental. With the exception of E. J.'s Heidelberg dueling scar—probably a fake story to begin with—there is no instance of their treating Germany as an "old country" remembered in gastronomy and mumbled song. It was for them a vibrantly new country, where the universities, technology, business administration, and German *Kultur* in general were markedly superior to their American counterparts. Jews participated in business and culture in Germany even more intensely than they did in America. Here was a cultural and commercial well from which Liliane and E. J. would not cease to draw until Hitler plugged it shut.

One of the outstanding lessons that Germany taught E. J. was the commercial exploitation of architecture. Kaufmann's three stays in Germany exposed him to innovative commercial architecture far earlier than most Americans of his generation. Nor was this art for art's sake: German merchants saw early on that contemporary architecture enhanced consumer spending. By the time Kaufmann apprenticed at Karstadt's in Hamburg, that store was the largest in northern Germany and claimed to be the largest in Europe. (The chain is among the largest retailers in the world today. Its 2001 sales were $15 billion, while the Kaufmann chain sold just a respectable $1.55 billion that year.) In 1912 Karstadt's main block was rebuilt as a fantasy in the Vienna *Sezession* style. Kaufmann would have kept himself well informed on these commercial marvels on his frequent visits to Germany.

When E. J. resumed his trips to Germany after World War I, he stepped into the largest body of advanced commercial architecture in the world. He had easy access to the patrons and architects responsible for this development, many of whom were Jewish. This was true, for example, of the Mosse family's rebuilding of their *Berliner Tageblatt* publishing plant in Berlin in 1921, for which the designers were Erich Mendelsohn and Richard Neutra. Mendelsohn's Columbushaus of 1930–32 in Berlin and his numerous department stores for Schocken and other Jewish chains in the late 1920s gave birth to a whole new image for retail stores. Their ribbon windows, huge lettering, and sleek entrances delighted the public and reinforced Kaufmann's contention that the prime merchandise to pull shoppers into a store was the store itself.

The first semester of Kaufmann's own education in progressive architecture ended in 1927 with his decision to rebuild the ground floor of his store, which now covered a full city block. The effect had to be sleek but rich, more the elegance of the SS *Normandie* that took Kaufmann to Europe than the harsh "ultramodernism" of Gropius and Mies. By 1928, Boardman Robinson was hard at work on his murals and Benno Janssen was ordering acres of black carrara glass from Pittsburgh Plate Glass in which to encase the store's old classical columns. Kaufmann's engineers set what was claimed to be the new world standard for elevators, incandescent lighting, and air-conditioning. The grand reopening of the store was the happiest moment Pittsburgh would enjoy in 1930 and the harsh decade to follow.

E. J. won national acclaim for this achievement, thanks to the twenty-four-page color brochure that Hearst's *Sun-Telegraph* printed for him and the way he tied the redecoration to the contest he ran in Luce's *Fortune. Harper's* proclaimed: "Edgar Kaufmann, son of a Jewish peddler, has just completed what is perhaps the most beautiful department store in the United States, if not in the world." Getting credit for the most beautiful store in the world would satisfy most people, but was it enough to assuage the humiliations that E. J. Kaufmann carried in his heart? If not, perhaps there was another kind of architectural monument that would.

Opposite: The waterfall before Fallingwater: employees of
Kaufmann's Department Store at Bear Run in the 1920s

THREE

BEAR RUN:
THE LAND AWAITING

When we try to pick out anything by itself, we find it hitched to everything else in the universe.

—JOHN MUIR, *My First Summer in the Sierra*

Blessed be light and darkness; ebb and flow, cold and heat; these restless pulsations of nature which by and by will throb no more.

—RALPH WALDO EMERSON

For every visitor who enters the forest of Bear Run for the first time, the house is important but the stream is everything. Bear Run—a "run" being the Scots-Irish term for any small watercourse—starts in some two dozen tiny springs or microswamps (geographers call them seeps) in the woods on the opposite side of Route 381 from Fallingwater. The woods grow on the gentle west slope of Laurel Ridge (Laurel Hill). The land is shaped like a scoop, the better to function as a drainage or catchment basin for Bear Run. The basin measures about a mile in length along its east-west crease, which fixes the basic axis of the stream, and its width from north to south is roughly twice that. The waters that gather in this basin drain into Bear Run, then rush with increasing speed as they move west under the highway, tumble 30 feet in the main waterfall under Fallingwater's balconies, drop another 7 feet in a second falls a short way downstream, then join the Youghiogheny River a quarter-mile farther west. The river goes by its nickname of the Yough, as in "yawk" or "yuk," though everyone regards it with affection.

These topographic details are lost on the majority of tourists to Fallingwater, who generally see only a few of the 1,600 acres on the Kaufmann estate, and catch only a glimpse of the 3,500 acres that the Western Pennsylvania Conservancy (WPC) later added to it. But hikers also come to the Kaufmann Conservation on Bear Run by the thousands, and a short hiking excursion up Laurel Ridge allows us to trace the general outlines of the Bear Run catchment basin as well as the watersheds for neighboring runs to the north and south. The runs to the south spill directly into the Youghiogheny near the village of Ohiopyle, seven miles distant. Immediately north of the Kaufmann lands lie the catchment basins for Laurel Run and Mill Run. The latter stream drains first into the Mill Run Reservoir (Indian Creek Reservoir on some maps), then into the Youghiogheny. The reservoir looks like the kind of lake that nature takes eons to form, but it is an industrial artifact that dates only from 1904. It was created by the Pennsylvania Railroad to feed water troughs that were strategically placed on its main track, near Greensburg. Steam locomotives would plough through the troughs with their intake valves open and so replenish themselves with water without wasting time at a stationary refill. The industrial origin of the Mill Run Reservoir is our first signal that at Bear Run nothing is quite what it seems.

The geographical coordinates of Fallingwater are 39° 55′ 18″ north, 79° 31′ west. We can make some sense of this abstraction if we follow the Bear Run watercourse as it wends its way through Stewart Township and Fayette County, then through western Pennsylvania and a good slice of

North America. We can "see" the watercourse with special clarity, because Bear Run lies on the edge of a continental divide. A continental divide is not something visible like a mountain peak; rather it is a demarcator of two major watersheds—in this case, those of Chesapeake Bay and the Ohio and Mississippi river valleys. Geographers have fixed the precise line of demarcation between the two along Maryland's Backbone Mountain, some forty miles south of Fallingwater. But old-timers in Cresson, to the northeast, always claimed that the continental divide passed through their town instead. In fact, they fantasized that the continental divide ran through a specific house, which had two gables. The water runoff from one gable, they said, drained into the Gulf of Mexico; the runoff from the other drained into the Atlantic Ocean.

If the old-timers in Cresson can get away with a little fantasy about the continental divide, so can we. Suppose we drive north on Route 381 until we are a mile from Fallingwater, then turn east, opposite Indian Creek Baptist Church, until we reach Fairmont and Turkeyfoot roads. As we follow the second road to its peak, we find ourselves about two miles east of Fallingwater. At this point we are standing on one of the sharp-edged ridges of Laurel Ridge, with the land sloping away on both sides of the roadway. If we could view ourselves from a hot-air balloon, we would see that Laurel Ridge demarcates Fayette County on the west from Somerset County to the east. Going up higher in the balloon, we would see that Laurel is the middle of three ridges, with Chestnut Ridge eleven miles to the west and Allegheny Mountain to the east. We can spot Fallingwater in the saddle between Chestnut and Laurel ridges.

To concretize how the continental divide works, let us call forth two glasses of metaphysical Gatorade. If we pour the first glass on the west side of Turkeyfoot Road, into the catchment basin that slopes toward Fallingwater, it gets absorbed into one of the springs that feed Bear Run. The Gatorade will roar through Bear Run, pass alongside Fallingwater, join the Youghiogheny, flow with that river as it cuts through Chestnut Ridge at Connellsville, flow another 50 miles to McKeesport, and there join the Monongahela River coming up from West Virginia. The Mon—once putrid, now clean—will dawdle as it passes 20 miles of rusting steel mills on its way north to Pittsburgh. At Pittsburgh our Gatorade enters the headwaters of the Ohio River (what the eighteenth century called the "Forks of the Ohio"), and flows another 975.5 miles to Cairo, Illinois. At Cairo it joins the Mississippi for an additional journey of 964 miles to New Orleans, where it enters the Gulf of Mexico.

That itinerary—which also shows how a barge could get from Fallingwater to Rotterdam or Yokohama—is strikingly different from the itinerary of our second glass of metaphysical Gatorade, which we now pour on the eastern side of Turkeyfoot Road. That Gatorade gets absorbed into a totally different watershed that drains southeast about 30 miles until it joins the Potomac River at Cumberland, Maryland (this is the part of our experiment that requires a little willing suspension of disbelief). Once in the Potomac, the Gatorade continues its flow east another 250 miles through Washington, D.C., and into Chesapeake Bay. The two glasses of Gatorade would end up at least 800 miles apart.

There may be more dramatic continental divides in North America in geographic terms, but there are none that are more significant politically. For what was North America in the middle of the eighteenth century if not one continent carved into two geopolitical entities? The French (our first glass of Gatorade) held control of the 2,500-mile length of the mid-continental waterways from Canada to the Gulf of Mexico—a system that drains water from thirty-one states and two provinces of Canada today. The British (our second glass) planted their thirteen colonies instead between the east slopes of the Appalachians and the Atlantic shore.

Nor is the pedagogical usefulness of our two-glass experiment over. It shows, first, that any clash over control of the continental heartland would necessarily involve western Pennsylvania—which is just what happened, starting with George Washington's ambush of the French in 1754, ten miles from Fallingwater. It shows, second, that a city built on the cusp that was common to both the continental waterways and to the Appalachian chain would grow immensely rich, which is what nineteenth-century Pittsburgh did.

But why a waterfall on Bear Run? North America must have a million rivers, streams, and creeks that do not feature a waterfall. Why did the waters of Bear Run not adopt one of those placid forms instead of rushing toward the Yough over two waterfalls?

The answer involves three factors. The simple one is a notable difference in heights: the high point of Laurel Ridge stands at 2,900 feet above sea level, while the water level of the Yough, just four miles to the west, rises to only 1,200 feet. This dramatic drop also provides a rough measure of the depth of the gorge that the Youghiogheny cut through the Laurel and Chestnut ridges over millions of years. And the falls on Bear Run are just a warm-up for the falls on the Youghiogheny at Ohiopyle: there the Yough plunges about 90 feet as it flows roughly two miles around Ferncliff Peninsula. (Youghiogheny means "stream flowing in a round-about course" in the Delaware and Lenni-Lenape tongues; *Ohiopehhl* means "white, frothy water.") Little wonder that the Yough provides the best white-water rafting in the eastern half of the United States. But nature will not be mocked: every year one or two rafters drown when the Yough overturns a craft and pins the body underwater—once for four days. Dimple Rock, the most treacherous hazard of all, lies just downriver from Fallingwater.

The second factor creating the falls on Bear Run is the slanting of the landforms on the west face of Laurel Ridge, which tilts any water collected there and impels it faster and faster toward the Youghiogheny. The third factor is erosion: the two waterfalls on Bear Run were created by the deterioration of softer layers in the main strata of Pottsville sandstone, a widely found sandstone that is named for one of its main find-spots at Pottsville, Pennsylvania. This is not your classic erosion by grinding away: the Pottsville sandstone shows very little of this effect. Rather than grinding away, the lower layers crack away by the action of ice and frost in winter. These softer layers of sandstone undermine the harder layers overhead, which then break off, and voilà: a waterfall. Over the last few eons, ice and frost have fractured the stone to the point that the falls initially located at the meeting of Bear Run and the Youghiogheny have retreated a quarter of a mile—halting for the moment right where the Kaufmanns built their house.

But what made the Pottsville stone itself? The sandstone is an indirect remnant of a primordial Rocky Mountains that once existed in eastern Pennsylvania. As these mountains eroded, the outwash flushed into central and western Pennsylvania and gelled about half a billion years ago into the bed of a mighty inland sea. That sea stretched from its eastern rim, close to Philadelphia, all the way west to Indiana. At its western end, the sea left Indiana richly endowed with some of the world's deepest strata of limestone. At its eastern end, lush vegetation compressed in warmer epochs into the Pittsburgh and West Virginia coal seam, and at cooler times into sandstone. The layers that became Pottsville sandstone could be regarded as part of a beach of sand to which enormous pressure was applied by the upper layers. Certain stones in Fallingwater's walls—the window sills in the guesthouse particularly—still show the rough texture of a beach.

About 400 million years ago the inland sea drained, and its bed was subjected to pressure that pushed the land up into what geologists call the Allegheny Plateau (to locals it's the Pittsburgh Plateau). The plateau has been deeply eroded, which makes Pittsburgh and its environs look hilly, even though in geological terms the land is flat. The plateau starts on the west side of Chestnut Ridge at Connellsville, about ten miles west of Bear Run as the crow flies. If you drive west from Connellsville it will be a thousand miles before you see another mountain, at the foothills of the Rockies at Denver. This geopolitical peculiarity so impressed Alexis de Tocqueville when he toured North America in 1830–31 that he stated it on the first page of the main text of his *Democracy in America*. (As a Frenchman, de Tocqueville would have found this observation somewhat melancholy, for it was this feature that was the key to the strategy by which France had hoped to dominate North America, and lost.)

Now things got dramatic. The world's continents were ill formed until 300 million years ago; they resembled the biblical account in Genesis, a world created but amorphous. What is now western Pennsylvania found itself south of the Equator, drifting north, when a fringe of the flat plateau was turned into one of the earliest mountain ranges on the planet. This happened because the tectonic plate that carries the eastern edge of North America locked against the tectonic plate that undergirds the Atlantic Ocean. Effectively, what was becoming North America slammed into what was becoming Africa, and the resulting pressure pushed the Pittsburgh Plateau a mile high—not on the Atlantic coast, where the clash took place, but hundreds of miles inland, where the new continent's crust was softest.

For 50 million years the Appalachians buckled into furrows like a gigantic washboard, from Scranton and Wilkes-Barre in the northeast down to Kentucky and Tennessee to the southwest. Bear Run found itself reformed into a trough between Chestnut and Laurel ridges. Geologists call this trough the Ligonier syncline: to the Kaufmanns, the Mellons, and the other families vacationing here, it was simply the Ligonier Valley.

The same pressure split the various flat strata of Pottsville sandstone at Fallingwater into a V-shaped formation, as though a karate champion had cracked it in two. That explains why nearly all the rock around Fallingwater is sandstone, from the top of Laurel Ridge to the bottom of the V-formation. At the bottom of the V snakes the Youghiogheny and its tributaries, now themselves furrowed into rapids and falls.

Bear Run is one of a score of tributaries that flow into the Youghiogheny from east and west. The particular point at which Bear Run meets the Youghiogheny is called Swimmers Rapids or Swimmers Falls. Since 1872 it has been impossible to see the actual meeting point of stream and river because the B & O Railroad piled up thirty or forty feet of fill on the Yough's east bank to make a level bed for their tracks. For over a century Bear Run's waters have been forced to pass through a man-made conduit in order to join the Yough.

Despite this intrusion, the view of Bear Run where it meets the Youghiogheny is well worth a visit. One gets to it most easily with a ten-minute walk down the south slope of the Bear Run valley from the

Fallingwater visitor center. A still more dramatic "aerial" view is provided at an overlook on the opposite north slope of the Bear Run valley. The overlook is reached by starting at the staff parking lot uphill from the Fallingwater guesthouse and following an unnamed trail west for a few minutes. (Some caution is called for: snakes love to bask on the overlook's flat rocks.) The Bear Run valley is hundreds of feet wide and exceptionally steep as it opens out perpendicular to the Youghiogheny gorge, since the undercutting of less resistant rocks below the top layer of sandstone has left the valley almost vertical-walled. The effect of the two gorges together—Bear Run and the Youghiogheny—is hauntingly picturesque. Two sensations dominate: we seem to be outside conventional space as the Youghiogheny viscerally cuts its way a thousand feet or more through the Allegheny ridges. And we seem to be outside conventional time: the land before us looks more like a nineteenth-century American landscape painting than the real thing.

As the Yough carved its way north and west through the ridges of western Pennsylvania for several million years, it brought rich plant life with it. The whole Ligonier Valley became exceptionally fertile, protected by its high walls from inhospitable cold blasts. The deep, swift-flowing Yough became and remains a notably warmer miniclimate than the land on both sides of it. As it winds its way from its source, near the town of Oakland, Maryland, it carries with it spores and seeds brought from the south, which germinate on the Yough's protected riverbanks. Botanists flock to Ferncliff Peninsula, a few miles south of Fallingwater, because they regard these southern plants flourishing on northern soil as one of the singular phenomena in the floral makeup of North America. We could term this a botanical divide, as a counterpoint to the geographical divide of the watersheds.

Such a hospitable land naturally attracted animals. Naturalists have found heron and ruffed grouse (the state bird) and more than 150 other species of birds at Bear Run. Species of mammals include seven of shrew, two of mole, four of bat, two of rabbit, six of squirrel, ten species of mice, rats, or voles, and both the red and the gray fox. Mammals of single species include the Virginia opossum, woodchuck, beaver, muskrat, coyote, raccoon, weasel, skunk, mink, muskrat, bobcat, beaver, mountain lion, and the white-tailed deer—534 species of wildlife in all. The waters of Bear Run are also notably rich in trout: back in 1880 one fisherman claimed to have caught 153 in a single day—equaling St. Peter's miraculous draught of fishes on the Sea of Galilee. Finally, in the summer of

1999, one enterprising Fallingwater guide made a plaster cast of bear tracks on the banks of Bear Run near Highway 381. After a wait of a century or more, Bear Run once again lives up to its name.

Now it was time for people, and roads. The latter preceded the former, oddly enough, because the first road-builders in the district were the eastern woods buffalo. It was they who discovered where the spine of the hills lay, where the firmest and driest land was, where they could ford rivers at their shortest and shallowest points, which salt licks were richest, and where the water was best to drink. Humans later hunted the buffalo to extinction along these trails, but not before they picked up these vital forest secrets.

We are, and will probably remain, deficient in our knowledge of the Native American occupation of southwestern Pennsylvania, because the traditional tribal districts were drastically changed by upheavals among the Indians just before the European contact period. The main tribes that figure in the notebooks of Lieutenant Colonel George Washington are the western Delaware, the Shawnee, and the Seneca. A few Native American artifacts have been found at Bear Run over the years, but we have no way of knowing if Indians settled there. Indian Creek, near Fallingwater, got its name in 1758 not from any live Indians the British troops encountered but from the vestiges they discerned of a deserted village.

About a dozen miles south of Fallingwater, on that portion of Route 40 that lies between the hamlet of Farmington and the intersection of Pennsylvania Route 381, there stands a circular wooden palisade called Fort Necessity. Large signs invite tourists to visit the fort, but few do; a pity, because there is no more evocative site for the early life of George Washington.

Washington knew southwestern Pennsylvania better than any part of the thirteen colonies save his own Virginia. Actually, southwestern Pennsylvania *was* Virginia in Washington's mind, since the Old Dominion claimed possession of all land west of the Youghiogheny, the Monongahela, and the Ohio. It was to clarify these conflicts among the colonies that King George III had the Mason-Dixon line surveyed from 1763 to 1767 between Pennsylvania on the north and Maryland and Virginia (West Virginia since the Civil War) on the south. The line passes about eighteen miles south of Fallingwater. At the west end of the Mason-Dixon line, some sixty-five miles from Fallingwater, the real wilderness began. Had Virginia's claim not been denied in federal court around 1780,

Fallingwater would still stand in Pennsylvania but the opposite bank of the Youghiogheny would be in Virginia.

During his second trip to the region in 1754, Washington tried to descend the Youghiogheny in hopes of effecting a water bridge between the Potomac and Monongahela rivers, and thence to the Ohio Valley. His notebook locates him "ten miles below Turkeyfoot"—the three-pronged junction of Laurel Hill Creek, Casselman Creek, and the Youghiogheny that is now Confluence, Pennsylvania. But Washington saw that the falls of the Youghiogheny were impassable even to rafts. He then walked north with his Indian guide along the Youghiogheny, which makes it likely that he at least momentarily paused at Bear Run.

The various links between Washington and the Youghiogheny gave plausibility to the Kaufmanns' claim that Washington once owned Bear Run, too, but none of his ownership records appear to correspond. Kaufmann Jr. nonetheless published the speculation as fact and taught it to the guides at Fallingwater. For years they featured this harmless fiction at the start of every tour.

Following the Revolution, the Commonwealth of Pennsylvania gave the land in the Ligonier Valley free or at minimum cost to any settlers who cultivated and improved it, which gave permanence to the settlements along Mill Run and Bear Run creeks. (Pennsylvania today has several unrelated Bear Runs, plus Bear Creek, Bear Gap, Bear Lake, Bear Rocks, Bear Swamp, Bear Valley, Bears Crossroads, Beartown, and Bearville.) The settlers on both creeks were Scots-Irish families who reached a population spike in 1904, when they erected the one-room Bear Run School that still stands on 381, at the edge of Fallingwater's forest. In the 1960s the school was sold to Fallingwater, which uses it to house overflow inventory for its gift shop, but the Church of the Brethren that went up next door in 1921 is still in use.

Without the Alleghenies, western Pennsylvania would have been dominated by Philadelphia and the eastern half of the state, but with that mountain shield in place, hamlets like Mill Run became the nucleus of a highly distinctive Scots-Irish culture. At Bear Run, nine land grants made up the 1,600 acres the Kaufmanns would later buy. At least some of the local farmers got prosperous, to judge from the elaborate farmhouse Ross Tissue put up on 381 shortly after the Civil War. (E. J. Kaufmann later bought the house and its barn: both are now key parts of WPC's education programs at Fallingwater.) Soon, though, farming took a back seat to more profitable industrial activities around Bear Run. From earliest times the Laurel Highlands were marked by a keen interest in the application of technology. The massive bulk of the Alleghenies had proved effective in indirectly promoting a local culture, but it blocked farmers from getting their corn and wheat to the Philadelphia market before it spoiled. The farmers brought their grains instead to local mills such as George Washington's at Perryopolis, and refined it in a hundred illegal stills into whiskey. (Washington's mill has the most elaborate of the surviving stills, but it probably postdates the Founding Father.) Whiskey demanded bottles, which became Pittsburgh's first industrial product. Glassmaking demanded cheap fuel, which led to the exploitation of the coal seam that passes through Connellsville and Bear Run. The same coal attracted ironmaking to the Laurel Highlands, at first using local ores and later imported supplies. Big Steel in Pittsburgh would ultimately descend from these pioneer ventures.

Ross Tissue, builder of that elegant farmhouse, was himself as much industrialist as farmer: he ran a slaughter shop at the mouth of Bear Run, while his son Charles ran a blacksmith shop just about where Fallingwater now stands. Some of these nonfarming ventures lasted long enough for the Kaufmanns to take them over. One was the sale of ice, which was cut from a pond adjacent to Bear Run and stored in a double-walled icehouse for sale to the community at a dollar a pound. It survived into the 1920s, at which point its proprietor was listed as E. J. Kaufmann.

Larger-scale industrialization was taking place at Ohiopyle, south of Bear Run. There was an abortive attempt to derive waterpower from the falls in 1842, but a few years later, success came with a profitable sawmill. Grist and planing mills followed, then a new sawmill in 1870. Other entrepreneurs ran a tannery and factories that produced wooden wheels and barrel parts. A dam and a raceway were constructed above the falls to generate waterpower, which led to a hydroelectric plant that brought electricity to Fayette County in 1906. Thus did a bucolic natural site turn itself into a mini-Pittsburgh. When Kaufmann brought Wright to Bear Run in 1934, Ohiopyle's power dam and sawmill still dominated the town.

Bear Run's commercial enterprises were more modest than those at Ohiopyle. Hunters shot and sold its deer, grouse, squirrel, and wild turkey. Fishing continued to be profitable, and the Commonwealth of Pennsylvania promoted trapping. Beavers, for example, had become virtually extinct in the state by the early twentieth century, but by 1934 they had replenished themselves to the point that they could be legally trapped. The Kaufmanns supported the local trappers, who appear in their home movies waving various pelts at the camera. Bear Run's fox, muskrat, mink, weasel, and skunk were on sale until the mid-1930s, and locally trapped muskrat and raccoon skins still brighten Fallingwater's living-room couches.

The railroad stop at Bear Run
in the 1890s

Trapping was the exotic commercial activity on Bear Run, but logging
was the cash crop. There was high demand for wood in southwestern
Pennsylvania, some for building and heating homes but most as the prime
fuel for iron smelting before coke replaced it later in the nineteenth century. (Tellingly, the locals called land that was good only for growing trees
"iron plantations.") Bear Run was logged from earliest settlement times,
but its major industrialization dated from 1861, the year John Williamson
declared in a legal note that he had built a mill "on the waters of Bear
Run." Adam and Jud Wolfe followed with a steam-powered sawmill in the
1870s, established near Bear Run's confluence with the Youghiogheny. By
1900 two tramroads (small railways with cars and trucks for hauling lumber and other goods) were running at Bear Run.

Industrial activity at Bear Run much intensified when railroads were
laid on either side of the Youghiogheny. Until World War I, the Baltimore
& Ohio trains stopped twice a day at Bear Run, which induced George
Stickel to set up a general store by the depot. The depot looms large in a
photograph of the B & O stop in the 1890s, but the same image also
shows the price Bear Run paid for this industrial prosperity: the mournful
hill behind the depot carries not a single decent-sized tree.

The Western Maryland Railroad later constructed a parallel track on
the west bank of the Youghiogheny, which was in service from 1924 to
1975. Until the 1930s the Kaufmanns could get the B & O trains to stop
at the Bear Run depot (rechristened "Kaufmann") by special arrangement. The commercial and railroad buildings at "Kaufmann" are gone
now, but Amtrak and Chessie System trains regularly use the tracks. The
last time a B & O train stopped near "Kaufmann" was in 1986, when
Richard Mellon Scaife hired a train to bring guests to a Fallingwater benefit party.

Rail access greatly intensified logging and mining operations at Bear Run. The easiest minerals to mine were coal and clay, whose surface deposits the Soisson clan had been removing for decades. Also easy to reach were the sandstone outcrops along the stream: these were shaved off and ground up for the production of glass or broken up and used as ganister rock in making brick kilns or refractory products such as silica brick. A bit lower in Fayette County's soil were the sandstone layers that were almost as easily quarried either for country villas such as Fallingwater or for the beehive ovens that roasted coal into coke. Still lower down were the minerals that the small-time ironmasters around Bear Run needed to launch their industrial enterprises.

A turbulent stream like Bear Run was itself a commercial asset: it could run the trip-hammers that banged reheated iron ingots into the pots, stoves, and wrought-iron beams that were eagerly snatched up by the farmers and city folk of the early republic. The Virginian Isaac Meason barely needed to leave his plantation near Uniontown to turn himself into a wealthy ironmaster. By 1802, Meason was rich enough to import the British architect Adam Wilson to design his sumptuous late-Georgian mansion, which he called Mt. Braddock. That cut-stone marvel still stands off Route 119, halfway between Connellsville and Uniontown, about eight crow-miles from Fallingwater.

The production of coal and coke brought some occasional violence to life around Bear Run. In 1891, 109 men died in an explosion at Henry Clay Frick's nearby coke works; nine more were shot to death the same year when company police broke up a strike. The local newspapers commended the police for dispersing these "Hunkies" and "riotous Huns."

Deep coal mining near Bear Run ceased in 1966, but plenty of barely cosmeticized strip mines still operate nearby. There is no record of strip mining at Bear Run itself, but geologists have detected numerous "drift mines" in the area—minor points where coal seams were exposed. As late as 1955, some of the Kaufmanns' immediate neighbors signed ten-year leases for drilling rights for oil and gas on their land, and the area remains deeply committed to energy production. Natural gas is still being pumped from several minor gas wells in Mill Run and from the major gas well near Confluence, just over the border in Somerset County.

The loggers' tramroads disappeared from Bear Run long ago, though logging remains an important commercial activity elsewhere in Springfield and Stewart townships. Ice-cutting, commercial hunting and trapping, railroading, and mining have just about ceased in the area, which is now sparsely populated. Deindustrialization has hit the whole of Fayette County hard. Today it is the second-poorest county in the state, its population much reduced from the 200,000 souls it had in 1935, and its per capita income just $9,791. A recent census characterized a quarter of its inhabitants as functional illiterates, the highest rate in Pennsylvania. Fayette continues to be a tough county to govern: as recently as 2002, a former county commissioner was jailed for promoting prostitution.

In an unexpected turnabout, after the Civil War the sullen industrialized countryside of Fayette County developed a reputation as an admirable vacation spot. This saving grace appeared when least expected: the railroads that were made to export raw materials began to import vacationing families as well. The epicenter of this resort boom turned out to be Ohiopyle. With daily tourist excursion trains from Pittsburgh, a half-dozen hotels in town and three more on Ferncliff Peninsula, it became the second-most-popular resort destination in Pennsylvania, after the Pocono Mountains.

Mill Run was not blind to the lure of tourist dollars, either. In 1906, Charles Hood, president of the Indian Creek Valley Railroad Company, endowed Killarney Park with a "dance hall, picnic area, two lakes for boating, and overnight accommodations" in a bid to attract weekending Pittsburghers. One year the special rail excursions brought in thirteen coaches full of tourists, who proceeded to consume 3,000 servings of homemade ice cream. In 1926 the B & O line leased Killarney Park to a Jewish agency from Baltimore, which ran it over the years as Camp Red Feather and Penn Mountains Camp. A church group in Somerset County purchased the camp in 1942, and emphatically renamed it "Camp Christian." It's still there today.

Why the sudden rush to vacation in Fayette County? The question finds various answers. Ease of rail access is one; a prosperous Pittsburgh middle class is another. The prime early American playground for the rich was Newport, Rhode Island, followed by the Adirondacks, the New Jersey shore, and Palm Beach. The Laurel Highlands were never in that league, yet improbably for such a poor area, Fayette and the neighboring Westmoreland, Somerset, and Cambria counties had a long history of luxury houses that would make the district attractive to the rich.

Carnegie, Frick, and a score of Pittsburgh's Gilded Age steel barons acclaimed the western Pennsylvania hinterland for some of the best hunting and fishing in the eastern United States. Carnegie discovered the Laurel Highlands early, since the Pennsylvania Railroad main line for which he worked as a telegrapher cut straight through them. He began to summer at Cresson after the Civil War, joining other Pittsburgh families in the rambling Mountain House. Carnegie, Frick, and the steelmaker B. F. Jones took turns using a luxurious wooden castle that still stands at

Cresson under the name of Carnegie Cottage. A score of Pittsburgh industrialists then put up the South Fork Fishing and Hunting Club, creating for themselves what was advertised as the world's largest artificial lake. Foolishly, and probably arrogantly, the club held the lake back with nothing more than an earthen dam. When the dam gave way in 1889, it took only a few minutes to kill 2,209 residents in nearby Johnstown.

The reigning nobility of the Laurel Highlands for generations were the Mellons. They farmed here after they immigrated from Ireland around 1807, and Judge Thomas Mellon was born here. Business brought him back to the Laurel Highlands around 1870, when he came to inspect a bankrupt railroad as a possible investment. One of the judge's sons, Richard Beatty Mellon, loved the hills east of General Forbes's old Fort Ligonier, an area that has been the family stronghold ever since. The Mellons eventually acquired 6,000 acres here, which they remade into the best foxhunting country in North America—in the world, actually, since riding experts say England has nothing like it.

By the early twentieth century the Laurel Highlands catered to numerous summer and weekend visitors. The Summit Inn, still in operation near Fallingwater, opened in 1907 for the convenience of such notables as Thomas Edison, Henry Ford, Harvey Firestone, and a succession of presidents. Decades later, the Rockwells, a Pittsburgh clan that pioneered in electronics and space flight, created their own private lodge called Nemacolin on 3,000 acres along Route 40, south of Bear Run. The Rockwells sold the estate to the Mellon heiress Cordelia Scaife May, and it later passed to the lumber baron Joe Hardy, who made it into the sybaritic Nemacolin Woodlands Resort and Spa. As with the Mellons, Anglophilia reigned in polo matches and pageants every time Hardy bought himself another minor title of British nobility. Then in the 1990s a real British nobleman came to roost a few hills over, when Lord Peter Palumbo of Walbrook bought the nearby Wright house called Kentuck Knob.

The presence of high society effected a significant cultural shift in the Laurel Highlands. In the 1870s, a school of Pittsburgh painters began to capture the local creeks and forests in canvases reminiscent of the Barbizon style in France. These half-dozen painters called themselves the Scalp Level group, from the name of their camp, and were led by the Alsatian immigrant George Hetzel. Hetzel started off painting imaginary landscapes in his studio—highly romanticized views with little correspondence to the rough landscapes before his eyes. By the late 1870s, though, he was hauling his canvases and easels into the woods, painting in true *plein air.* The creeks, gorges, rocks, and falls at Scalp Level are visually identical to those at Bear Run, so it comes as no surprise how much Hetzel's paintings of the 1870s look like photographs of Bear Run in the 1930s, or even today.

The nineteenth-century paintings had a certain resemblance to the Depression-era photographs of the area because both periods reacted against the Industrial Revolution by exalting nature. As if by herd instinct, the industrial moguls of post–Civil War America turned for solace from their labors to the thrilling paintings of Niagara Falls by Frederick Church, the Rocky Mountain views of Albert Bierstadt, or the photographs of the West by William Henry Jackson and Solomon Carvalho. For the Pittsburgh steelmen, starting in 1881 with Henry Clay Frick's purchase of a Hetzel as the cornerstone of a collection that later took in Holbein, Vermeer, and Rembrandt, buying views of the Laurel Highlands allowed them to appreciate nature without the uncomfortable reminder that nothing was polluting Pennsylvania like their own satanic mills.

The synergy between the industrialists and the painters of late-Victorian Pittsburgh took another form, too. Nearly all these artists understood that there was aesthetic potential in depicting industry as well as nature. The same George Hetzel and such colleagues as the Kings and the Walls, and later the painters Aaron Gorson and Johanna Hailman, all worked in a new genre of factoryscapes that aestheticized the clouds of pollution over Pittsburgh into thrilling patterns of formal sensibility. The movement never received a name, so we are free to call it Industrial Impressionism. The epicenter of this artistic cult was the marbled lobby of Pittsburgh's Carnegie Museum of Art, where the locally born Beaux-Arts muralist John White Alexander fulfilled a commission from Andrew Carnegie for a dozen scenes that show a smoke-besotted humanity attaining enlightenment through steelmaking.

We could call Frank Lloyd Wright a nature painter akin to George Hetzel, because he saw better than anyone the aesthetic potential of the falls on Bear Run—better, but not earlier, because half a century before Wright, budget vacationers had already discovered the thrill of this finest of Laurel Highland landscapes. Then, a thunderbolt. In 1890 a group of Masons from Pittsburgh began buying parcels of land at Bear Run on both sides of what is now Route 381, including the parcel where Fallingwater stands. The men soon assembled 1,598 acres and opened their new hotel and a dozen outbuildings as the Bear Run Country Club in 1895. The waterfall proved an insufficient attraction, however, and the club went bankrupt in 1906.

Now Bear Run began its link with the Kaufmanns and, eventually, Fallingwater. Which Kaufmann saw Bear Run first we don't know, but it was more probably the peddlers Jacob and Isaac than their nephew E. J. The Laurel Highlands would have held little aesthetic appeal for them, because peddlers do not travel to amuse themselves. But his uncles' stories of Fayette County evidently resonated with E. J. when he launched his retail career in Connellsville years later. That put him ten miles from Bear Run as the crow flies, about seventeen miles by car.

Kaufmann had a stock tale of how he discovered Bear Run: he was on horseback, taking time off from a slow day at his store in 1909. It's a good story, but totally inconsistent for a man who never went on aimless excursions, on horseback or not. More likely, E. J. had heard that the Masonic syndicate had gone belly-up, and he wanted to make a low-key inspection of the property that was for sale. E. J. was possibly a Mason himself (a high-ranking Mason writing to Fallingwater in later years hailed him as "Bro. Kaufmann"), but even if he was not, everyone in Connellsville knew people connected to the bankrupt club. The Connellsville retailer J. Fred Kurtz, for example, was an officer and later a co-owner of the Bear Run Country Club: he was perfectly placed to induce Kaufmann to buy it.

E. J. possibly bid on the Masons' land right when he saw it, but if so he was either too low or too late: the club reopened in 1910 under the name of the Syria Country Club ("Syria" being the main Masonic lodge in Pittsburgh). The centerpiece was a new U-shaped hotel of wood-frame construction, three stories tall, with a nearby bowling alley and swimming pool. Back in the woods were secondary cottages with names like Spray Rock, Stone, Arbutus, Back-to-Nature, Mountain Laurel, and Oaks. When the Syria Country Club followed its predecessor into bankruptcy, in 1913, Kaufmann got a second chance to bid on it. His offer to rent the camp seems not to have gone through (the paper trail is ambiguous), but he finally consummated a three-year lease with the Masons in 1916, and Camp Kaufmann launched its first season as a summer resort for his employees that June.

Camp Kaufmann was a success from day one, since, like so much of the store, it was a creative adaptation of someone else's idea rather than E. J.'s personal innovation. In the early twentieth century many American and European companies had budget-rate camps for their employees. One of the oldest and best belonged to Wright's future clients at Johnson's Wax: it still flourishes today. Two such corporate camps existed near Pittsburgh: one run by Heinz foods, the other by Horne's Department Store.

About a third of Kaufmann's 3,000 employees frolicked at Camp

E. J. Kaufmann (*lower right*) and some of his employees enjoying Camp Kaufmann, 1920s

Kaufmann every summer—a high percentage for this kind of operation. The camp was the glue that held employee morale together the rest of the year: if Kaufmann's operated like a family—and it did—then the resort on Bear Run was the kitchen in which everybody let their hair down. The main clubhouse held seventy women; the men's club accommodated thirty men; there were also five family cottages and two new "back to nature" cottages. The cost to workers was $7 a week; store executives, their families, and their friends paid $15.

Camp Kaufmann had two distinctions: the beauty of the site and the simplicity of getting there. The 1927 *Storagram* reported: "Every train that stops at the little station in the mountains, called Kaufmann, Pa., will unload a jolly crowd of Kaufmann fellow workers." Motoring was easy, too. One store clerk related in 1921 that the Penn-Lincoln Highway to Bear Run was "smooth as silk" until the turn-off for Route 381, unpaved in those days. The most marvelous thing about the camp, said every report in the *Storagram,* was the Bear Run brook itself. All agreed there was no better employee camp in the United States.

The 1920s changed Camp Kaufmann in two important ways, one fiscal and one social. The Kaufmann store finally bought the camp from the Masons in 1926, listing the "Kaufmann Beneficial and Protective Association" as buyer of record. This sounds like an employee credit union, but events later showed that it was part and parcel of the store itself. The social change was no less momentous: the boss began to spend summers with his employees. As late as 1920, E. J. was only a day visitor at the camp. The *Storagram* for that season featured a photograph of Liliane and her godlike husband. "Mr. and Mrs. Kaufmann spent a whole day at the camp during the past season," the report ran, "and participated in all the sports and fun offered. A swim in the morning, a lunch, tennis and tramping in the afternoon, and a delightful motor ride to the city in the evening." It was as though the employees were extending their graciousness to the boss, not vice versa.

Kaufmann never explained why he decided to join his employees in their paradise, but by the early 1920s the teenaged Junior may have been resisting the long trek to the family fishing lodge in Ontario.* Possibly it just tickled E. J.'s ego to think that he could live in such intimacy with his staff. By moving to Bear Run, E. J. truly made himself into a kind of god living among his subjects. The move could only have enhanced the employees' pleasure in coming to the camp, and did him no harm as boss of the whole show.

The cabin that Kaufmann put up around 1921 overlooked the unpaved 381 road, and stood near the employee clubhouse. The tone of Kaufmann's rural hideaway was set by his need not to lord it over his clerks, which certainly proved to be the case. Postcards of "Mr. Kaufmann's Cabin" show a prefabricated structure a good deal more primitive than the employee accommodations. Except for a stone chimney, E. J.'s cabin was all wood, and it lacked the electricity, the heating, the running water, and the indoor plumbing that the employees enjoyed just down the road. Because it tottered on a ridge, everybody called it "The Hangover," with emphasis on the double entendre.

The simplicity of The Hangover suggests that Kaufmann was unconcerned, at least at first, with the elegant architectural posturing of the earlier lords of the Laurel Highlands. But a country house turns every man into a bit of a country squire. That Kaufmann shared his retreat with a hundred employees changed nothing: Thomas Jefferson shared Monticello with a good many "employees," too.

Now the nagging question: did E. J. Kaufmann really like the country? In home movies he seems to be enjoying himself, although he began to wear lederhosen only after 1935, when his art director, Laszlo Gabor, bought him some. We know that E. J. hiked a bit with the Wrights in Arizona and later he liked to walk in the San Jacinto Mountains in back of Palm Springs, but his taste for hiking may have been another cultural

---

*The Kaufmanns retained ownership of the Ontario fishing lodge until 1960; spotty references in the Wright-Kaufmann correspondence show that both E. J. and Liliane fished there as late as the 1940s. The construction of their Bear Run cabin evidently cut down their trips to Ontario because at one point they did not go to McGregor Bay for eleven years. This we know from one of the stranger Kaufmann episodes: the proprietor of the local laundry asked a Pittsburgh friend of theirs when E. J. and Liliane were coming back, since their clean clothes had been waiting on his shelves for eleven years.

influence from Germany or Austria. It was in Vienna that Victor Hammer painted Kaufmann's 1929 portrait as a hiker, with walking stick but no lederhosen. Kaufmann may indeed have enjoyed nature, but he was pure city boy, and his country inflection may have been just one of the roles he had taught himself to play.

But we must not jump to conclusions. Go back just one generation and we find that the old-country Kaufmanns were authentic country folk. Certain German Jews like the Kaufmanns had specialized in horse-trading and cattle-dealing for centuries, and E. J.'s ancestors, including his grandfather Abraham, lived all their lives on the family farm or in peasant villages the size of Mill Run. Now we have E. J., the first city-born Kaufmann in half a millennium, "going country" with a fake country estate in Fox Chapel and fake-rustic cabins in the Ontario and Pennsylvania woods.

Then, suddenly, the employees stopped coming to Bear Run, their paradise forsaken. The demise of Camp Kaufmann around 1930 remains unexplained because no employee newsletters survive from those years—the store apparently suspended the *Storagram* as a Depression economy. Either Kaufmann's employees could no longer find $7 a week for their vacations, or they could no longer imagine vacationing at all. Even if they had the money, it did not help that the direct train service to Bear Run had been cut back as part of the B & O's own retrenchment, and few Kaufmann employees owned cars. Some women employees had a beef with management, too: they resented not being allowed to bring their noncompany boyfriends to the camp. There was a souring of employee-management relations in general, with an unprecedented strike in 1932 that would have made it awkward to go camping with the boss. For this mix of reasons, Kaufmann's Department Store got out of the employee camp business overnight.

The Kaufmanns now had Bear Run to themselves, which soon papered over any regrets about the departure of the employees. There were certainly enough Kaufmanns to animate the place: brother Oliver built a stone lodge for his family of five; sister Martha and I. D. Wolf and their three children had another cottage; and I. D.'s siblings occupied still other cottages when they came north to escape the heat of the Arkansas summer. Liliane's Bachman cousins were regulars in another cabin, close friends Alexander and Tillie Speyer and their four rambunctious children had another, and two trusted employees named Schlosser had a third.

E. J. enlarged The Hangover around 1931, which seems to have marked the outer limit of his architectural ambitions at Bear Run at the time: a persistent family tradition insists that he always preferred the scruffy Hangover to Fallingwater. But other dynamics were at work. The paving of Route 381 in the early 1930s as a public works project exposed the Kaufmanns' highway perch to view by high-speed and sometimes drunken strangers, not the passing farmers or hiking employees of yore. The departure of the employees and the arrival of the drunken drivers now appear to us as milestones on a road that inexorably led to Fallingwater, and they were—but the road took a curious detour first.

In 1933, Kaufmann had different options for Bear Run: soundproof The Hangover, build a new house with greater privacy, or find a new estate altogether. He took none of these paths, but hatched instead a scheme whereby the federal government would improve the place for free. It was Franklin D. Roosevelt who came up with the perfect way to upgrade Camp Kaufmann into a fancy estate. This was the Civilian Conservation Corps (CCC), which historians often cite as Roosevelt's most widely praised creation. The kernel of the idea was already in Roosevelt's first inaugural address of March 4, 1933. Within five days Roosevelt had on his desk an outline of the proposed conservation relief measure, and on March 21 he sent Congress an Emergency Conservation Work bill. This envisioned a quarter of a million men working in the CCC (eventually there were over 2 million) on federal and state-owned land for "the prevention of forest fires, floods, and soil erosion, plant, pest and disease control." On March 31 the bill became law. A prototype Camp Roosevelt was assembled at breakneck speed in Virginia and began operations on April 17, 1933.

Pennsylvania lost no time entreating the federal government for its share of the bounty. The *Pittsburgh Post-Gazette* told its readers the next day, April 18, that the Commonwealth had been granted funding for fifty-nine forest camps, five on federal land, the rest on state land. But E. J. Kaufmann was well ahead of the *Post-Gazette*. Already in the first week of April, immediately after the CCC bill passed but before the agency was legally incorporated, he dispatched Nathan Jacobs of the Knowles engineering firm to meet in Washington with Louis Staley, secretary of Pennsylvania's Department of Forests and Waters. Jacobs alerted Staley that Kaufmann wanted Harrisburg to certify Bear Run as an auxiliary forest reserve for the CCC. On April 7, Kaufmann's staff member D. Tynberg wrote the chief U.S. forester, R. Y. Stuart, extolling the advantages of the property at Bear Run. "This equipment includes beds, mattresses, kitchenware and large comfortable club house in good repair, that can easily accommodate the two hundred workmen needed for the various forestry works on this property. This work includes forestation, clear dead and undesirable trees, plant new trees, developing a game reserve, which includes a picket fence surrounding the property, clearing slopes for grazing lands, damming the stream for bathing and water places, and the installation of winter feeding places, fire lanes and fire roads." How two hundred burly CCC workers were to fit in the clubhouse that had a capacity of seventy countergirls was anybody's guess.

Though Knowles moved heaven and earth to meet the April 17 deadline, they missed it by a day, and Kaufmann's CCC application was rejected. But timeliness was the least of the application's problems. As an active Republican, Kaufmann was naïve to expect the Democrats in Washington to grant special pork-barrel status to Bear Run. Private property required a special CCC status that only the president of the United States could approve, and FDR would have guffawed at the hubris of a Pittsburgh millionaire who expected the taxpayers to give a free touch-up to his lordly domain.

Back to the drawing board. We can suppose that E. J.'s interest in the CCC itself was minimal: what he wanted at Bear Run was not a work camp but the resulting fine estate on which he could erect a showpiece weekend house. That makes April 1933, the month of his CCC application, Fallingwater's conceptual date of birth.

One of the reasons Kaufmann grew more interested in Bear Run around 1933 was its newly increased accessibility. First came the paving of Route 381, which created some inconvenience but provided a new road that was a godsend compared to the dusty old one. Then the Westinghouse Bridge was inaugurated at the Pittsburgh end of Route 30, with another dramatic increase in speed and convenience. At about the same time, the first rumors emerged from Harrisburg of an extraordinary new highway that would link Philadelphia and Pittsburgh by means of the first statewide expressway in the United States. This promised to get Kaufmann home from Bear Run in little over an hour. The Pennsylvania Turnpike's opening was delayed until 1940, but E. J. knew its intended route years before: he was close enough to the project that he was later asked to serve as a turnpike commissioner, and any turnpike questions could be answered by his neighbor R. K. Mellon, who financed the western extension of the project. A cynic might even see the placement of the turnpike's Donegal interchange at such flawless equidistance between Bear Run and Ligonier as evidence that Kaufmann and Mellon had rigged the route.

Kaufmann was now moving fast on Bear Run: April 1933 was the month of both his CCC application and the transfer of the property's title from the shadowy Kaufmann Beneficial and Protective Association to the even more tenebrous Investment Land Company, a holding company for a variety of Kaufmann family interests. Then just months later, on July 28, 1933, E. J. transferred title to Bear Run a second time, now to Liliane S. Kaufmann, at the long-ago price of $30,000. That took place only a day or two before Kaufmann Jr. returned to Pittsburgh after his years in Europe. Listing the 1,600 acres at Bear Run as Liliane's meant that she and E. J. would now have to pay taxes on the property, rather than fobbing them off on the store. On the other hand, they got a splendid estate at a bargain rate.

Though the CCC application was a scam to get the improvements that the Knowles engineers told E. J. he needed to undertake at Bear Run, it also showed Kaufmann's sensitivity for the land as no ordinary commercial property. This was land that needed to be nursed back to health. Kaufmann's concern for the acreage emerged in the letter that his assistant Tynberg had written the head of the U.S. Forest Service. Terms such as "forestation . . . plant new trees . . . game reserve . . . grazing lands . . . winter feeding places" show that beyond the usual CCC make-work, Kaufmann understood that stringent measures were needed to turn the worked-over hills and the polluted stream at Bear Run into a flora and fauna paradise. The only change occasioned by the CCC rejection was that E. J. would have to do this work himself.

Kaufmann had already taken some steps toward healing the land in 1932, when he contacted Pennsylvania's Department of Forests and Waters for advice. The department's district forester, V. M. Bearer, visited Bear Run and told E. J. to clear away the distressed chestnut trees on the grounds (they had died by the hundreds in an epidemic around 1920) and to plant thousands of spruce. By the time Frank Lloyd Wright saw it in 1934, Kaufmann's stunning transformation of Bear Run was well begun. All through the 1930s he was vigilant in revitalizing its game and fish life, as well as reforesting its plants and trees. When forester Bearer returned to Bear Run in 1940, he praised Kaufmann's efforts to the skies: "The area is well stocked with mixed hardwoods, laurel, rhododendron, hemlock and many shrubs. The clear, cold water of the swift and rocky Bear Run . . . helps make this one of the finest areas in Pennsylvania."

Whatever his motives, E. J. was an early and generally effective conservationist. How he might have treated Bear Run in his "academic" years of association with Benno Janssen, we can't tell. But ten years of living in his modest cabin close to the land had opened his eyes to the needs of the environment. He had outgrown the Kaufmann of La Tourelle. Not for him—any longer—were buildings that dominated the land the way La Tourelle and Janssen's golf clubs did. Kaufmann now put land before architecture, which meant that whatever the makeup of his future weekend house on Bear Run, it would be a forest lodge quite unlike the castles of such Laurel Highlands plutocrats as Albert Gallatin at Friendship Hill, Isaac Meason at Mt. Braddock, Abraham Overholt (Henry Clay Frick's grandfather) at West Overton, Carnegie and Frick at Cresson, Carnegie's partner Charles Schwab at Loretto, and the Mellons at Ligonier. The manor houses of those earlier lords of Fayette and Westmoreland counties all dominated their clipped and manicured grounds in traditional architecture and landscaping.

It was not just its modernism that made Fallingwater turn out to be so different from the houses of those other rich men. Kaufmann rejected the whole pompous architectural image of the country house: his lodge would stand unembellished before nature. That vision makes E. J. a kind of protoarchitect of Fallingwater, because all later design decisions on the house had to conform to his fundamental objective—to live in concert with nature.

The year 1933 had brought Kaufmann many problems. He was wrestling with a Depression-sized drop in revenue at the store, a vagabond son back from Europe, a breakup with his mistress, a messy court fight with Horne's, a furious Liliane at home, and now Hitler a menace to the Kaufmann uncles and cousins in Germany. It was not obvious who would be the architect for his new house at Bear Run. Joe Urban died in July 1933, and Benno Janssen was rich but exhausted from building the gargantuan Mellon Institute. For respite from his larger cares, E. J. might have glanced at a plan drawn up of Camp Kaufmann in 1920. The fourteen buildings depicted on the plan bore names derived from nature or from families that had once lived there. One of the outlying cottages offered a mystic prefiguration of the architect Kaufmann would eventually get for Bear Run. It was a small cottage, but its name had a good ring to it. That name was Wright.

Opposite: Kaufmann and Wright at Taliesin West, 1940s

FOUR

FRANK LLOYD WRIGHT SEEKS A CLIENT, GETS A PATRON

Definition of a client: a timid sheep always in a huddle, looking for a shepherd.

—WRIGHT to Kaufmann

I don't know what kind of clients you are familiar with, but apparently they are not the kind I think I am.

—KAUFMANN to Wright

He works his work, I mine." Tennyson's line from "Ulysses" describes Ulysses and Telemachus at their separate yet conjoined tasks, but it could equally well apply to the architect and his or her client: two people at separate tasks, but the one reinforcing the other. It is a truism that an architect needs a client more than does any other artist, since an architect without a client can produce nothing. But the architectural client will always be special because she or he has a real need for a house or an office tower, not merely the intellectual interest a patron might take in a painting.

It is a shock to realize that until well past the Renaissance the client counted for 90 percent of a building project and the architect-technician handled the other 10 percent. This was certainly true around 1140, when Abbot Suger put up the Gothic portions of the Abbey of St.-Denis outside Paris. Suger's chronicle of this breakthrough work suppressed the name of the architect, which reminds us that architect and client are rarely equals: one invariably trumps the other.

Over a period of twenty years E. J. Kaufmann and Frank Lloyd Wright seduced each other, loved each other, hated each other, and betrayed each other, now with the one getting the upper hand and now the other. It is hard to imagine the often-buffoonish Kaufmann as the prime client of Frank Lloyd Wright's career, and still harder to take in what Kaufmann's support did to launch Wright on one of the great comebacks in art history. That comeback was remarkable not only for its chronological precision—exactly the five years that Wright prophesied from his humiliation at MoMA in 1932 to his triumph at Fallingwater—but even more for its completeness. The 1938 reviews of Fallingwater in *Time, The New Yorker,* and elsewhere conceded to Wright nothing less than the title of greatest architect of the century. After Fallingwater it was just a matter of time before Wright got the status he felt he deserved: greatest architect of all time.[*]

Architects cannot stage their comebacks alone; what Wright needed was neither cash nor an adoring public but a courageous patron. The worst part of his decline in the 1920s and early 1930s was the loss of clients to death, the Depression, or disagreement. He was abandoned

---

[*]Nothing less than "greatest architect ever" would do for Wright. Once, when Olgivanna reproved him for declaring in court that he was the world's greatest living architect, he replied: "You forget, Olgivanna, I was under oath." With a preacher father and a deeply religious family background, including a good sense of medieval culture (his mother hung views of English Gothic cathedrals about the house), Wright was well placed to have known some of the numerous medieval manuscript illustrations that depicted the Lord God as *architectus mundi*—the architect of the universe, complete with medieval drafting tools. Was this the "greatest architect of all time" to whom Wright was comparing himself?

first by Albert Johnson, for whom he had designed a desert compound and the inventive but aborted 1924 National Life Insurance Building for Chicago. (Wright later called Johnson "intensely interested in ideas, though not himself the kind of man inclined to build much. He seemed rather of the type, called conservative, who, tempted, will sneak up behind an idea, pinch its behind and invariably turn and run.") Next to disappoint was Gordon Strong, for whom Wright had projected a combination planetarium and parking garage in Maryland in 1927. In 1929, Elizabeth Noble canceled an apartment project for Los Angeles, as did Aline Barnsdall for her theater project there. In New York, the Episcopal priest Norman Guthrie withdrew his support for two visionary buildings, the 1926 Steel Cathedral and the brilliantly Cubist St. Mark's-in-the-Bouwerie apartment towers of 1929. The crash of the stock market sunk another half-dozen prospective clients, starting with the Arizona developer Alexander Chandler. Just as jarring was the loss of Wright's loyal client Darwin Martin (he of the 1903 Larkin Building), who died in December 1932 after giving Wright thirty years of moral and financial support. With Martin's death Wright entered 1933 with hardly a client, old or new, to stand by him.

The odds of finding a major client were stacked against him. In those years not one American businessman in ten would have commissioned a house in modern style; not one in a hundred would have associated with Frank Lloyd Wright; and not one in a thousand would have agreed to live over a waterfall. But if he could get just *one* client to accept a radical architectural solution, Wright could restart his career. E. J. Kaufmann did not create Fallingwater, but it speaks volumes for his courage and shrewdness that when Fate gave him a chance to sponsor an architectural wonder, he seized it.

Within a year of entering Wright's universe as a blinding nova, in 1934, Kaufmann had snapped Wright out of a decade of financial, artistic, and personal depression with his combination of talk and action on a house at Bear Run, an office at Kaufmann's Department Store, a planetarium and civic improvements for Pittsburgh's Golden Triangle, the projected publication of Wright's work in architecture, and the model of Wright's suburban-utopian Broadacre City. This last had its world premiere in April 1935 at Rockefeller Center and its second showing at Kaufmann's Department Store.

This work was a godsend to Wright in financial terms, but it represented far more than that for his career: in the commission for Fallingwater, Kaufmann gave Wright his first chance in thirty years to speak directly to the American people. This Wright did via the torrent of publicity that made Fallingwater the house of the century. Energized by his success at Fallingwater, Wright entered the longest and most fertile part of his career. Within five years he designed the Johnson's Wax Administration Building of 1936–1939, the epochal low-budget Herbert Jacobs house, the innovative Hanna "honeycomb" house in California, and the first form of the Guggenheim Museum. Wright continued that pace right until his death in 1959, completing the Guggenheim and Beth Sholom Synagogue in Philadelphia that same year. The sprawling Marin County Civic Center in California, which opened in 1962, ought to be listed as Wright's last work, but his creativity was so fierce that after his death a dozen buildings went up from drawings he left behind. It was not before Fallingwater but after it—and because of it—that Frank Lloyd Wright became the prophetic voice of American architecture.

The partnership of Wright and Kaufmann was brilliant but weird. Kaufmann steadied Wright with his sure grasp of popular culture, since it was he and not Wright who had the unfailing intuition of how architecture made a client appear. When, in the middle of the Depression, Wright proposed to gild Fallingwater's balconies, he was thinking of the inspiring formal effect that would result, but Kaufmann saw what a public relations disaster a gold-leafed house would be. It was one of Wright's strengths that he could be bullheaded in quest of his vision, but when he followed that vision without counterbalance, as in his strange neo-Mayan houses of the 1920s in California, he risked alienation from popular culture. At Fallingwater, Kaufmann mainstreamed a Wrightian vision that had grown too eccentric for American taste.

It is hard to comprehend how Kaufmann could have been Wright's most important supporter and simultaneously the least loyal of his clients, but the answer lies in their differing personalities. Loyalty—obedience, really—was the prime expectation Wright had of his clients. Kaufmann, however, was one client who would not be bullied. Liliane was worshipful toward Wright, and once wrote him: "Living in a house built by you has been my one education—and for that and for the privilege of knowing you, I will always be grateful." But her role at Fallingwater was minor: her husband approved the design without bothering to consult either his wife or his son. Kaufmann himself was anything but worshipful; after Fallingwater he gave a half-dozen commissions to other architects even when Wright hungered for them himself. In fact, although Wright and Kaufmann completed two projects together, they failed to consummate two dozen more. How could the partnership that produced Fallingwater never recapture its teamwork again? The list of their architectural abortions is so long that it needs to be divided into the pre-Fallingwater, Fallingwater, and post-Fallingwater phases. The abortions began almost as soon as Wright and Kaufmann met: not a single thing panned out of the multimillion-dollar commissions that Kaufmann dangled before Wright's eyes in 1934. To these unbuilt works should be added Kaufmann's failed promise in 1935 to publish a book of Wright's drawings, and in 1938–39 his failed mass-marketing of Wright's line of "Usonian" homes—low-budget standardized houses whose name derived from U.S. of North America.

There were numerous architectural abortions at Bear Run itself. The only executed commissions were for the house (1934–37) and guesthouse (1938–40). The phantom projects for Bear Run include a farmhouse and gate lodge, a dining-room extension, revision of the garage and servants' quarters, and a chapel. Kaufmann Jr. added to his father's list with his own aborted projects for a gate lodge in 1956 and 1957.

Then there were the post-Fallingwater flops: eleven public projects for Pittsburgh that Kaufmann and Wright worked out between 1947 and Kaufmann's death in 1955. Kaufmann's payment of $10,000 as Wright's fee for Fallingwater was eclipsed twentyfold by his outlay for concept drawings and (in one case) fully detailed plans of these projects, which included a huge structure for the Point (the confluence of the Monongahela, the Allegheny, and the Ohio rivers at Pittsburgh); the Point View apartment tower astride Mt. Washington; and a helical suspension parking garage for the Kaufmann store. Not one of these wondrous projects saw the light of day.

Unbuilt projects constituted only part of the grief that Kaufmann caused Wright. Worse were the occasions on which he gave commissions to other architects. No other Wright client comes to mind who would have hurt the old man as much as E. J. did when he hired the despised Richard Neutra—one of Wright's "two thieves" from 1931—to design his house in Palm Springs. More than anything else, it was Kaufmann's jump from Wright's organic design to the sleek lines of Neutra and the high tech of Pittsburgh's Civic Arena that caused orthodox Wrightians such as his son to regard E. J. as a superficial dabbler in architecture. Wright, in a 1950 letter to Kaufmann Jr., slyly linked E. J.'s promiscuity with women to his promiscuity with architects: "Father seems to be with architects as he is with women."

The Kaufmann father and son had very different relationships with Wright. The son was articulate, supportive, deferential, and deeply caring. The father was the man with the checkbook: capricious, powerful, sympathetic to Wright the person but much less kind to Wright the artist.

This capriciousness seems to validate the charge that Kaufmann had not really understood Wright in 1934 (E. J. "did not deserve Fallingwater," as Wright put it). But as part of the "brokering class," Kaufmann was simply following his instinct that modernism rather than traditionalism would give him entrée to a world far bigger than Pittsburgh. He had already essayed progressive architecture in the Art Deco restyling of his store; now by hiring Wright he would move from pseudo-modernism to the real thing. A decade later he moved to Neutra, when it was his work that Kaufmann saw as leading-edge.

"Henceforth you will never, as a Patron of the Arts, be in a position to help me with one hand and hurt me with the other, because I shall never trust my work to you again," growled Wright after he learned of E. J.'s commission to Neutra in 1946. But Kaufmann saw that it was the technology-based Bauhaus style that was going to sell in postwar America, not Wright's earthbound, custom-made fantasies. Many years later, Wright himself changed his style into something much sleeker than Fallingwater, ending up with the motel-modern of the Marin County Civic Center in California. Given his own penchant for stylistic evolution, it was hypocritical for Wright to accuse Kaufmann of having fickle taste. Moreover, it was pointless. For E. J., buildings were not questions of taste: they were merchandise.

"All right, then, how do you get your houses built? By telling the owner what he's got to do? Or do you hypnotize him?"

"Yes, I hypnotize him. There is nothing so hypnotic as the truth. I show him the truth about the thing he wants to do . . . the client will see it and take it, I have found."

"But suppose he *wouldn't* take it?"

"But, by God, Ray, he *would* take it."

Frank Lloyd Wright found this made-up dialogue with Raymond Hood amusing enough to include it in his 1932 *Autobiography*. Since he had no clients, it could do him no harm, but when Wright revised the *Autobiography* in 1943, he had numerous clients, and the potentially offensive passage had to go. Not that Wright ever gave up trying to find clients to hypnotize. "I would like a guy like you for a client and I would take pride and pleasure in getting your house built for you," he wrote a certain William Kittredge in 1932. He used almost the identical phrasing on Stanley Marcus and E. J. Kaufmann, his two potential clients of 1934. But Kittredge, Marcus, and a hundred other prospects withered away, while Kaufmann stuck by him for twenty-one years

(1934–55). That was the identical time span as Norman Guthrie's association with Wright (1908–29), but Guthrie and Wright never produced a single building together. This left Kaufmann as both the most steadfast and the most disputatious of Wright's clients.

But shall we call Kaufmann a Wright client or a Wright patron? Both clients and patrons of architecture have fat wallets as their main attributes, but there the similarity ends. A client just pays for a building, but a patron normally invests himself or herself in the design process. There is an important distinction in social terms, too: the patron lords it over the architect, but the client—think of poor Blandings in the 1940s novel *Mr. Blandings Builds His Dream House*—is more often at the mercy of his architect.

E. J.'s boisterousness sometimes makes it difficult to take him seriously, but the number and importance of his buildings mark him as a significant architectural patron, and so does the way in which he controlled his architects more than they controlled him. But there are fundamental problems in seeing E. J. as a patron of art and architecture. One is the way he jumped from style to style. For a quarter of a century he had put up houses, stores, and charitable foundations in a virtual parade of academic clichés. Why suddenly did he wish to build a masterpiece of modernism?

Wright had some justification in mocking Kaufmann as "the Shopper," but E. J.'s architectural style-hopping strikes me as no more than changing tactics in a war: his fixed strategy was to use architecture to raise his social status. But a second fundamental problem is that Kaufmann resists categorization as a patron. Architectural patrons generally come in four categories. In the first of these is the patron who is his or her own architect, imbuing the building with all its ideological, formal, and technical qualities. Thomas Jefferson trudging on horseback at the age of eighty to superintend progress at the University of Virginia is the perfect example. The Roman emperor Hadrian represents a second kind of patron: one who has real design skills (Hadrian seems to have had personal involvement in shaping the Pantheon and his villa at Tivoli) but who needs a professional designer like Apollodorus of Damascus to make the building "work." Lorenzo de' Medici represents a third category: the patron who supplies the intellectual basis for a design but lacks the formal and technical training that is needed to turn a dilettante's concept into a practical solution. Prince Albert as the catalyst behind London's Crystal Palace represents a fourth type of patron: one who neither builds, nor designs, nor conceptualizes, nor even conceives of a physical solution at all, but who by force of will gives concrete form to the project of a professional designer. The Pharaoh-Queen Hatshepsut was probably such a patron at her precedent-shattering tomb at Deir-el-Bahari, and so were the emperors Trajan and Charlemagne, Abbot Suger with his break-through Gothic abbey at St.-Denis, and Shah Jahan at the Taj Mahal.

Kaufmann qualifies as patron of Fallingwater in that sense, because he provided the inspiration, the funding, and the force that made it possi-ble. (Wright acknowledged this when he saluted Kaufmann in 1948: "Dear Edgar: As an 'Idea Man' you would soon fashion a new-world, with my help.") If we still quibble with his patron status it could only be in the intellectual realm, for we have no idea what Kaufmann knew or under-stood about modern architecture. Not that all patrons of architecture have to be learned, but you can generally size them up by analyzing the books in their library. In the sixteenth century, for example, Sir Francis Willoughby assembled thirty books on architecture—a high percentage of all the architecture books then in existence—to guide him in building Wollaston Hall. William Byrd owned more architectural books than any man in the thirteen colonies, and his elegant plantation house at West-over, Virginia, shows how well he read them. (Jefferson borrowed Byrd's architecture books until he could purchase his own.) But this biblio-graphic approach to patronage fails utterly with Kaufmann. E. J. seems not to have owned a single book on architecture, nor can any family mem-ber recall him in the act of reading.

Another problem: what kind of architectural patron would accept the design of a house cantilevered over a waterfall without asking for a single change? We can contrast Kaufmann's seeming passivity with John Nicholas Brown's interaction with Richard Neutra on Windshield, the Browns' 1930s International Style mansion on Fisher's Island in Long Island Sound (after a hurricane, Anne Brown called it Won't Shield). The clients' son, John Carter Brown, recalled that it took three years and scores of calls and memos until the Browns were satisfied with their design. E. J. involved himself in the execution of Fallingwater but not in the design—a big difference. He was an active player in finding the right paint for the balconies, the right cork for the bathroom floors, and even the right amount of steel in the cantilevers, but the changes he proposed to the architectural design were minimal.

Some architectural patrons meddle and some don't. William Ran-dolph Hearst ordered a certain garden wall at San Simeon rebuilt six times, but Kaufmann was generally hands-off, more like Pope Julius II, who chose top artists like Raphael, Bramante, and Michelangelo, encour-aged them to think big, then gave them the freedom and support to do it. As someone who dealt with a thousand suppliers at the store, E. J. had learned to engage the best people, then let them work unhindered. We should see Kaufmann's deference to Wright as a sign of strength, not of weakness. Great patrons get great results from their architects without meddling, not because they are weak but because they are strong. What was crucial was that neither Wright nor Kaufmann feared the other.

E. J. Kaufmann made three separate decisions on the road to Fallingwater: one was to build a weekend house, the second that it be modern in style (the two issues were linked but not bound), and third, that it be designed by Wright.

Insisting that Fallingwater be called a weekend house rather than a summer or country house is not pedantic, because the three similar building types have important functional differences, the way jails are not the same as prisons even though both building types put bars on their windows. The weekend house was a specific American invention of the 1920s and 1930s. It was part of a tendency to increasingly specialized homes, and could not have existed before the widespread use of automobiles. The weekend house could be in any style of architecture, or none, but since it was a new mode and tied to the newly popular automobile, it often made its appearance on Long Island or on the fringes of Los Angeles in modern style.

The Depression popularized weekend homes as "houses of the future" and "houses of tomorrow" to an American public that was only too tired of the present. Department stores were the main force promoting these future-based homes, which seem to have been highly important in conditioning Kaufmann's thinking about a new house for Bear Run. The year Kaufmann commissioned Fallingwater, 1934, was the year in which the mania for "houses of tomorrow" reached its peak. Houses had been a regular, if oversize, item of merchandise in American department stores ever since Sears, Roebuck began selling bungalow kits around 1908. It was a Chicago department store, for example, that gave Buckminster Fuller the first showing of his futuristic Dymaxion house after he invented it in 1927. In the 1930s the New York department stores took the lead in presenting "tomorrow" houses to the public. Macy's, collaborating with *Architectural Forum,* put up a full-size "modern" house inside its store in 1933, and in May 1934, Lord & Taylor paired with Hearst's *House Beautiful* magazine to put a weekend house on view at Rockefeller Center. Thousands of visitors poured in to see what was in function, if not in style, a preview of Fallingwater. In November 1934, even closer to the moment at which Kaufmann asked Wright for a house on Bear Run, an experimental house was erected on Park Avenue that attracted 10,000 visitors in a few days. Home furnishings were a major component of E. J.'s sales, and it is reasonable to suppose that he saw at least a few of these

Albert Frey's Aluminaire House attracted 100,000 visitors to a New York trade show in 1931. It is likely that E. J. Kaufmann was among them. (The house now stands in Central Islip, Long Island.)

model homes on his monthly visits to New York (the family store had its legal headquarters not in Pittsburgh but in Manhattan). We need to remember, however, that while these model houses were invariably leading-edge in technology—*Town & Country* used the term "ultramodern" as a synonym for "packed with gadgetry"—in architectural style most of them were houses for yesterday rather than tomorrow. The Park Avenue "ultramodern" house was typical in hiding behind a fake-Georgian façade.

The homes of the future at other venues, however, were authentically future-looking. Albert Frey unveiled his avant-garde Aluminaire House at the 1931 Allied Arts and Building Products Exhibition in New York, where 100,000 visitors saw it in a week. Apart from the business and pleasure that regularly brought him to New York, E. J. had a special reason to attend that show, since Benno Janssen was in the adjoining exhibit of the Architectural League of New York, probably showcasing his new ground floor at Kaufmann's. (Years later, Kaufmann's answered the Aluminaire House with its own Steelaire House, mounted on the specially strengthened roof of the last store expansion that E. J. supervised. Kaufmann's anticipated 250,000 visitors.) The next year, 1932, brought another revolutionary "House of the Future" in the pages of Norman Bel Geddes's new book, *Horizons*. Bel Geddes, a pioneer of streamlining, was by then a close Kaufmann associate: he had joined E. J. and Joseph Urban the previous year as a judge for the essays in Kaufmann's 1930 "Arts and Industry" contest in *Fortune*. We can also document that the Kaufmanns were among the 39 million visitors to the "Century of Progress" fair in Chicago in 1933 and 1934, which offered fourteen model homes, including George Keck's radical "House of Tomorrow." It was at the Chicago fair that ordinary Americans encountered home air-conditioning and dishwashers for the first time. With his special connections in Germany, E. J. might even have seen the striking full-scale homes of the future that Mies van der Rohe and others created for the "Dwellings of Our Time" trade show in Berlin in 1931.

Nor was E. J. just a passive viewer of model homes; under his leadership, Kaufmann's Department Store itself entered the business of selling and furnishing such houses. Though details are inconclusive, E. J. undertook commercial house-building in 1925 with a prototype home that still stands east of Pittsburgh, in Johnstown. A half-dozen references also survive from the years 1935 to 1939 to show that Kaufmann was pressuring Wright into creating a model house that his store could put on sale, and in 1938 Kaufmann's was part of a joint venture with *Life* magazine to the same end. Fallingwater was too expensive to be a prototype tract house, but in thinking about what to build on Bear Run, E. J. was not just dreaming about a forest retreat for his personal delight: he was contemplating an enterprise with definite commercial possibilities.

The "houses of tomorrow" at the Chicago fair and in the New York department stores were not the only modern houses going up in America in the 1930s. At the beginning of the decade, the architect Wallace K. Harrison built himself a modern house on his estate on Long Island, and a year or two later he reconstructed Frey's Aluminaire House there. The high-society black sheep Frederick Vanderbilt Field erected a much-publicized International Style house in 1931 at New Hartford, Connecticut, using William Lescaze as his architect. Two years later, Edward Durell Stone built the sleek Mandel house in Mount Kisco, New York—after which the town joined the numerous municipalities that banned modern houses. In 1934, Lescaze's partner George Howe put up the Wasserman house near Philadelphia as the first modern house in the U.S. to rival the academic-style estates in size. *Fortune* magazine lavishly praised both homes in its October 1935 issue.

Whereas Augusta Owen Patterson's 1924 book on new houses had not admitted a single one in modern style, these were common enough by 1940 that James and Katherine Ford devoted a whole book to *The Modern House in America*. The Fords' book and the architectural magazines of the 1930s and 1940s show that modernism was making its greatest inroads on the West Coast but dragging in the East and South. Women patrons of

modernism were represented disproportionately to men, Jews disproportionately to Christians, and self-made patrons disproportionately to those
of inherited wealth. By 1938 the same Augusta Owen Patterson who could
not understand the term "modernism" in 1924 would be obliged to admit
Fallingwater as the first modern house between the covers of *Town &
Country.*

Ordinary Americans were finally getting better educated about architectural modernism. When the George Washington Bridge approached
completion in New York in 1931, there was an outcry when the engineer's
steel_endpiers were nearly hidden under classical-style abutments by the
traditionalist Cass Gilbert. The public demanded that the steel show
through for a more honest and dramatic effect.

The crucial year in the growing appreciation of architectural modernism in the country was 1932. That year saw the MoMA International
Style show, the appearance of Wright's *Autobiography,* and the unveiling
of Howe and Lescaze's Philadelphia Savings Fund Society tower as the
breakthrough American exemplar of the International Style. In 1934,
Hartford's Wadsworth Athenaeum became the the first cultural building
in the country to adopt the same severe idiom, for its Avery Court.

Kaufmann might have ignored the *Autobiography,* but he could not
have ignored the skyscraper in Philadelphia or MoMA's International
Style show in New York. E. J. had to sound at least conversant on modern
architecture after the essay on contemporary German housing won his
"Arts and Industry" contest in *Fortune.* The International Style show was
still hanging at MoMA when its curator, Philip Johnson, began to pressure E. J. to sponsor an exhibit on modern housing. It would have been no
more than prudent for E. J. to check out the MoMA show, either in New
York or when it came to Pittsburgh a few months later.

Modern architecture was finally showing up at home, too. Starting in
1902, the Pittsburgh Architectural Club brought drawings by European
and American progressives to the walls of the Carnegie Museum of Art—
including some by Wright in 1907 and 1913. Wright also had attentive
followers in Pittsburgh. The Pittsburgh architect Frank Ullom asked to
buy his luxurious German portfolios immediately after their publication,
and the progressives Frederick Scheibler and the firm of Richard Kiehnel
and John Elliott selectively inserted Wrightian features in their local
buildings.

Pittsburgh industry had a long tradition of adopting technological
innovations in its architecture. Around 1905 the nearby milltown of
McKees Rocks got one of the pioneer reinforced concrete factories in the
world, the work of an engineer who had learned the technique in his
native England. In the 1920s Pittsburgh's Strip district got a similarly pro-

gressive warehouse, whose glass walls gave a hint that their designer was at least cognizant of the International Style. Kaufmann himself adopted advanced technology around 1920 in the reinforced-concrete warehouse he built for the store, and he was involved a few years later in putting up a skyscraper for Allegheny General Hospital, where he was a board member.

Then, in 1934, another local breakthrough for modernism. The pioneer tract-housing complex in modern style in the United States began to go up at Swan Acres, a few miles from Kaufmann's home in Fox Chapel. We can be certain Kaufmann knew this grouping of Wrightian and Corbusian knockoffs, because an early photograph of the development survives among his papers at Fallingwater.

Above all the various American regions experimenting in modernism stood California. If, as I proposed earlier, Kaufmann's architectural education was a two-part class, with the first semester devoted to "modernistic" work of the 1920s, then the second semester was his exposure to radical modern architecture in the 1930s. Normally, the second leg of his education, like the first, would have taken E. J. to Germany and Austria, but this route was blocked when the Nazis came to power in 1933. Kaufmann shut down his buying office in Berlin, and he closed or lost his buying office in Vienna some years later. E. J. never reconnected with Germany again, but in architectural terms he did not need to: his new style mecca was Southern California.

By the time the International Style made its tepid entry on the East Coast, it had already conquered California, where by the early 1930s Schindler, Neutra, Frey, and others had completed a score of radical modern houses. Neutra, in particular, had blossomed into a world figure who lectured widely all over the United States, served as a critic at the Bauhaus, and represented his adopted country at the International Congress of Modern Architects in 1931. Neutra's Lovell house in Los Angeles was arguably the most famous house in the world at that moment: it lured 10,000 visitors on its opening weekend in 1929, in a publicity blast worthy of E. J. Kaufmann. The *Los Angeles Times Sunday Magazine* carried a long column by Philip Lovell on the glories of his new house, and the *Hollywood Daily Citizen* for December 15, 1929, featured a huge photograph of it, stating: "The [Lovell] Healthhouse stands complete and is open for inspection today. Executed to one-tenth of an inch in exactness . . . the result of two years' careful research and design by Richard J. Neutra, foremost leader of the international movement for new architecture."

Suddenly, it was not Berlin but Los Angeles that was the primary home of modern architecture, and E. J. came running to see it. He had to stop in Los Angeles to get to Palm Springs in any case, but his interest in the buildings of Los Angeles was surely intense. Kaufmann was obliged, for example, to inspect Bullock's Wilshire after it emerged as America's most flamboyant department store in 1929. And after commissioning his house from Wright, he would have wanted to inspect Wright's Los Angeles houses. This is no speculation, because we *see* Kaufmann in Los Angeles in 1935 through his home movies, now in the Fallingwater archives. In these movies E. J. attentively filmed Wright's house for Aline Barnsdall on Olive Hill, which even today can be reached by car in minutes from Bullock's Wilshire, straight up Vermont Avenue. Olive Hill rises mesalike above the eastern Hollywood plain, and affords a perfect view of the glistening white Lovell house directly to the north. You cannot miss seeing the Lovell house from this vantage point today; with the minimal vegetation in Griffith Park in 1935, Neutra's masterpiece would have displayed itself to Kaufmann like a rocket burst (page 177).

Two additional buildings would have lured Kaufmann to the Hollywood Hills. One was the just-completed planetarium wing at Griffith Observatory. E. J. was still engaged with Wright in their planetarium project, and he would not have failed to inspect such an important precedent. From the Griffith promenade Kaufmann would have had a second fine vista of the Lovell house, as any visitor still does. The third architectural monument you could not miss from Olive Hill was Wright's huge mansion for Charles and Mabel Ennis. E. J. might have gotten Mabel Ennis's name (Charles was dead) from Wright, but he probably knew her personally because—small world—the Ennises had once been in the men's clothing business in Pittsburgh. The side terrace of the Ennis house offers a third and still more splendid view of the Lovell house.

It is a safe bet that E. J. knew the Lovell house not just from gazing at it from these three vantage points but close-up as well. Philip and Leah Lovell were exactly like the Kaufmanns: worldly, affluent, sociable, *arriviste,* and Jewish. A magnetic personality and publicity hound, Philip Lovell was among the best-known citizens of Los Angeles, where his weekly column "The Care of the Body" (Lovell was a naturopath) had the highest readership of any feature in the *Los Angeles Times.* It would have been simple for Kaufmann to get in touch with him.

Imagining the Kaufmanns and the Lovells together is speculative but low-risk. E. J. and Liliane's primary entrée to progressive architectural circles in Los Angeles came through Wright and through his son Lloyd (by then a better-known West Coast architect than his father, and in touch with the Kaufmanns independently). But E. J. and Liliane also had multiple Los Angeles contacts via Pittsburgh. By the time the Kaufmanns paid their visit to Olive Hill, Wright's dynamite client Aline Barnsdall had given her mansion away to the city's art commission and no longer lived there. But the Kaufmanns may well have contacted Barnsdall anyway, because chances are excellent that they already knew her from home. Barnsdall was Pittsburgh-born and -bred: her father was a splashy oil millionaire who used the Kaufmanns' city as his base. Norman Bel Geddes, one of Barnsdall's main collaborators on Olive Hill, was also well known to E. J. from their work together on the essay contest in *Fortune*.

E. J. and Liliane would thus have known several key patrons of modern art and architecture in Los Angeles: besides Barnsdall and the Ennises, the Dada patrons Walter and Louise Arensberg were Pittsburghers, too; they had lived for years on Olive Hill next to their friend Barnsdall. Leah Lovell and Pauline Schindler were also habituées of Olive Hill, since for years they had run Barnsdall's school there. Pauline's husband, Rudolph, built three homes for the Lovells: one that is still in family hands today at Newport Beach and two others inland. This important group of art and architectural patrons was extended by blood ties, since Leah Press Lovell and Harriet Press Freeman were sisters (Harriet and her jeweler husband, Sam, had used Wright for their important house in West Hollywood). Had Aline Barnsdall laid out tea or drinks for the visiting Kaufmanns—and this *is* pure speculation—her possible guests could have been the Lovells, the Freemans, the Schindlers or the Neutras (the two architects were no longer on speaking terms), Mabel Ennis, the Arensbergs, the Bel Geddeses, Lloyd Wright, and, if he happened to be in town, Frank Lloyd Wright.

We can document another critical tie between Kaufmann and the Los Angeles avant-garde. E. J. and Richard Neutra were made at least minimally conscious of each other thanks to the Spring 1930 building supplement issue to the *Literary Digest,* which published projects dear to each man. The cover of the issue carried a superb color reproduction of one of Kaufmann's new Boardman Robinson murals, while inside was a photograph of Neutra's Lovell house with a long caption. Kaufmann and Neutra did not collaborate on E. J.'s Palm Springs house until 1944, but they might have met years before. At the least, each would have read about the other in the *Literary Digest*. Additionally, Neutra would have spotted Kaufmann's appearances in *Fortune* and *Harper's Magazine,* and E. J. would have remembered Neutra from his prominence in the 1932 MoMA show. Neutra was notoriously aggressive at seeking clients, which was why Schindler no longer spoke to him. When, in 1934, Wright expressed his fear that Kaufmann would fall into the arms of one of the "popular architects," Neutra would be the first to come to mind.

But Kaufmann did not build Fallingwater with Neutra, nor with any other Californian, nor with any of the refugees by then streaming to the United States: he built it with Wright. "My parents knew [of] Wright and admired his work [before contacting him for Fallingwater]," said Kaufmann Jr. in his 1982 film interview. But this was unremarkable: any American of reasonable cultural breadth knew of Wright by the 1920s. The Kaufmanns' friend Dorothy Blumenthal was well aware of Wright by then, and Caroline Wagner, an acquaintance of Junior's, stayed at Wright's Imperial Hotel in Tokyo when it was brand-new. Long profiles of Wright appeared in *The New Yorker* and *Reader's Digest* in 1930, and in the *New York Times Magazine* in 1932—hardly obscure venues. Wright's *Autobiography* was widely reviewed when it came out in 1932, and he also spoke about it by nationwide radio hookup. In 1933, Wright accepted the invitation of Stanley Marcus to lecture on his work in Dallas, and we can take for granted that the Kaufmanns knew of Wright ahead of people in Texas.

Like most important things in life, Kaufmann's choice of Wright for Fallingwater was probably part intentional and part accidental. When an associate told Wright in 1934 that he and Kaufmann knew many people in common, this was no exaggeration. Joseph Urban could have brought his friends Wright and Kaufmann together at any time. If not, a score of other intermediaries could have made the introduction: Stanley Marcus, Aline Barnsdall, Benno Janssen, or the designers Paul Frankl, Josef Frank, and Norman Bel Geddes. By 1931, Kaufmann's protégé Catherine Bauer was also in close touch with Wright. Nor was Wright shy at hunting for clients by himself: he might have been tracking E. J. ever since the write-ups about him in *Fortune* and *Harper's*.

I n the 1987 video *The House on the Waterfall,* a questioner asks Edgar Kaufmann Jr.: "How was it that your father and Frank Lloyd Wright got together?" and Kaufmann answers with a single word: "Me!" The truth is longer but more interesting than that, because one of the great collaborations in architectural history was based on mutual seduction.

On January 2, 1934, E. J.'s secretary Ethel Clinton wrote this brief note to Taliesin:

Dear Mr. Wright: Mr. Kaufmann has had the request from one of the Pittsburgh newspapers for a photograph of yourself,—the Sun Telegraph. The only one they have is very old—hair in abundance and very black. They would like this photograph in their files so that if they should need it in the near future they will have it at hand.

If you wish, you may send it to me and I will be very glad to deliver it to the paper, or you may send it direct to Mr. W. M. Jacoby, Publisher of the paper.

> Wishing you and your family a very Happy New Year, remain,
> Sincerely,
> E. Clinton
> Secretary to Mr. Edgar J. Kaufmann

A note of no great import, but just the tip of an iceberg, because a close reading of the text tells us that this was not the earliest letter between Kaufmann and Wright: it is merely the earliest *surviving* letter. Consider that Clinton had Wright's address in Spring Green, Wisconsin, which suggests a prior point of contact. Her letter starts right off with "Mr. Kaufmann has had the request . . . ," but a first letter would have defined who Mr. Kaufmann was. And why would the *Sun-Telegraph* ask Kaufmann for a recent photo of Wright unless it was common knowledge in Pittsburgh that the two men were associated? Clinton says the photograph in the *Sun-Telegraph* files is "very old—hair in abundance and very black." How would Clinton—a bright but provincial person—know that Wright's hair had thinned and greyed unless she had set eyes on him? Clinton's jocular tone suggests the same thing: you don't tell a famous figure how much he has aged without some basis of familiarity.

And why did the *Sun-Telegraph* expect to run Wright's photograph "in the near future"? Had Kaufmann alerted it to some major project that would involve Wright? Finally, wishing Wright a Happy New Year was unexceptional for a letter dated January 2, but saluting "you *and your family*" constitutes a second Clinton familiarity. She appears to have met Wright personally or via correspondence before.

This detailed parsing is not overkill, because the received tradition is that Kaufmann and Wright met only in November 1934. Kaufmann Jr. never explicitly said otherwise, but as the reputed matchmaker who brought the two men together, he always focused on how they got along in the meetings he knew about. But we will learn that there was much about the relationship of his father and Wright of which Junior knew nothing.

The requested photograph was sent from Taliesin on January 9, not to the *Sun-Telegraph* but to the Kaufmann store. In his cover letter, Wright's secretary Eugene Masselink got Clinton's gender wrong, but he was new on the job, and gender confusion was common in Taliesin correspondence (Baroness Rebay of the Guggenheim collection and Ayn Rand were initially addressed as men, while professor Baker Brownell was taken for a woman). Clinton acknowledged receipt of the photograph on January 11.

Then, silence. Nothing. But suddenly—or suddenly *to the best of our knowledge,* since other letters are cited that no longer survive—on August 16, Kaufmann wrote Wright that he had "a very interesting matter" to discuss next time the architect was in Pittsburgh or New York.

The unspecified "interesting matter" becomes clear from later context. In the winter of 1933–34 the Public Works Administration released a flood of money for bridges, highways, harbors, tunnels, and riverfront improvements to any city or state that proved its need of them. This subset of the PWA was called the Civil Works Administration (CWA in the abbreviation-mad Roosevelt administration), and by January 1934—the month of the *Sun-Telegraph's* photo request—it had 4 million workers on its payroll. Pittsburgh set up the Allegheny County Authority to capture $24,000,000 of the special CWA windfall or the regular PWA funds. The authority head was the academic architect Press C. Dowler. As a Republican in a sea of Democrats, Kaufmann had little chance of getting a seat on the authority board, but he could play éminence grise if the board would accept an architect of his choosing.

Kaufmann did not have to specify the "interesting matter" to Wright, because the lord of Taliesin already suspected what it was. To learn more, Wright dispatched a spy to Pittsburgh. This was his former secretary, the Danish-born Karl Jensen, a man somewhat older than Wright. Jensen reported in early September:

Dear Mr. Wright:

Herewith some of the essentials concerning Kaufmann: He owns one of the largest Department Stores in Pittsburgh, in the very heart. 13 stories covering an entire block—employing a total of 2800 people.

He also owns the site opposite the store now used for parking purposes—size 100′ × 240′ with a slope on the 240′ side having a pitch of ab. 15 feet. It is for this site the planetarium is considered. I am coming to that.

Kaufmann is jewish, about 50, a very charming, and very intelligent and dynamic personality. He has one son (25, dappling [*sic*] with painting) intelligent but not the father's strong character. However he has been responsible to some extent in making his father acquainted with you. I stayed overnight at Mr. Kaufmanns home and this is about the proposition he is making:

The county of Pittsburgh (which really means the actual environs of the city itself) has received 25 million dollars from the c.w.a. for various building—notably several tunnels, a large river-front retaining wall, a pump station, a childrens detention home etc. The Federal government must approve the plans the county makes but have no power of veto— so that eliminates a good deal of red tape. The spending of this money (which will begin very soon) rests with two commissions each made up of three men. Kaufmann is quite sure he has two men with him in anything he decides on one commission and one man on the second. Kaufmann wants to see that besides engineering they will get architecture and although (because of politics and the nature of the work) it will likely be built out of the citys own engineering facilities—your directions would prevent stupidities and give Pittsburgh something fine instead. I presume in this capacity a yearly retaining fee would be the manner chosen for payment. One of the men present mentioned 25000 to 50000 a year depending on the scope of your activities. Kaufman was not sure if you would work on some such basis—and neither am I although I did not say so. But since it would all be built by engineers with you as the only architect and only your word carrying the weight in matters of design I would be at a loss to understand if you turned it down. Especially since it does not add to the congestion but will be material in breaking up this condition.

Kaufmann is rounding up the members of the commission this week and there is hardly a question but that he will succeed both because of his position in civic affairs, and for the reason that he has on several other occasions been responsible for the change of design in city structures . . . the last major instance being when he went to Mellon and had him change the design of the new postoffice (a huge building not finished yet). This building is not particularly good but better than the first design and K. is perfectly aware of his limitations of judgement in design. That is why he's looking for your co-operation. If you believe you can extend this <u>will you wire or write Kaufmann to this effect now?</u>

I told him you would do so as soon as I had acquainted you with the nature of the work. He should know <u>at once</u> or he cannot take a stand in your behalf with the commissions. After he has this assurance from you he will want you to come for a meeting with the men and send you expenses for this purpose. I understand this will culminate within two weeks so there's no time to lose.

Second: Kaufmann wants to build a planetarium, surrounded by a small park on the lot opposite the store as a gift to the city. This problem I understand will also include tunnel approaches under the street from the store and probably some car-parking facilities also. He wants to know on what basis will you study this problem and draw plans? I explained the customary procedure of retainers but mentioned no sums. Please deal also with this in your reply to K. If terms are arranged this would start immediately. There may be some connection between the two propositions that would work in K. favor—but I don't believe he is a shopper for plans and he is definitely not another Goldsmith. In either direction, or both, I am hopeful it will mean work. The stabilizing effects of this will be astonishing in the affairs of the Fellowship. Please inform me how it comes out.

It is hard to imagine a more thorough analysis of an architectural client in any language. It spells out the two jobs Kaufmann was offering: the combined planetarium and parking garage for the store, and federally funded public works for Pittsburgh. Jensen's report—previously unknown in Wright scholarship—also tells us about Kaufmann Jr. "[H]e has been responsible to some extent in making his father acquainted with you" is hardly a ringing endorsement of Junior's later claims to have delivered his father to Wright. What it sounds like—given other indications that E. J. took the initiative in sending Junior to Taliesin—is that Kaufmann discovered Wright on his own, but asked Junior to check him out with friends in New York or elsewhere.

Extraordinary is the attestation that Kaufmann successfully pressured Secretary of the Treasury A. W. Mellon to improve the design of the new federal courthouse and post office in Pittsburgh. Characteristically, Mellon ran the construction of this public building as though it were one of his branch banks. He used Trowbridge & Livingstone, the firm that had put up the Mellon banking hall opposite Kaufmann's, plus his nephew E. P. Mellon as supervising architect. The mammoth federal courthouse still stands a few blocks from the Kaufmann store, its style either fascist or classical modern depending on your architectural politics. It is hard to imagine it as an improvement over anything, harder still to think of E. J. and A. W. in a tête-à-tête for more than thirty seconds, but if Kaufmann pushed Mellon to improve something that could have been even worse, God bless him.

Jensen's report has numerous other points of interest. The obvious one is that Kaufmann's job involved not a house but a combination planetarium–parking garage. This explains why Kaufmann had chosen Wright: someone must have alerted him to Wright's project of a combination of planetarium and garage for Gordon Strong in Maryland seven years earlier.

Kaufmann was eventually forced to abandon the planetarium concept because such a building was soon put up instead by the Boggs & Buhl Department Store on the North Side, almost as though they had been reading E. J.'s mind. Jensen's report to Wright on the public works projects was generally accurate, but he left out the detail that the architect heading the Allegheny County Authority was a conservative diehard.

With Jensen's report to hand, Wright was finally ready to respond to Kaufmann's note of the month before. On September 18 he wrote E. J. that he had no funds to come east at that time, but he would come to Pittsburgh if Kaufmann paid him to. "As you know there has been no building to speak of these past years and architects, good and bad, have been severely hit by the depression for this reason to say the least. Probably wiped out." He enclosed "a little folder showing you what keeps me tied up here at present." In 1934, Wright had no promotional flyer on his architectural work, so the folder must have been the one on the Taliesin Fellowship. Was this the first snare to capture Kaufmann Jr. for Taliesin?

Telegrams and calls flew between New York, Pittsburgh, and Wisconsin for another ten days, when a second meeting was scheduled for New York, with Jensen again standing in for Wright. On Friday, September 28, Jensen dined for three hours with Edgar and Oliver Kaufmann in the Central Park Casino, which Joseph Urban had built a few years before. He then dashed off a seven-page memo to Wright. Jensen guaranteed Wright that he would get to build Kaufmann's planetarium ("Kaufmann is a firm believer in the stars and in Horoscopes. There are many people you know in common"). He assured Wright a second time that he would get major jobs from Allegheny County, since Kaufmann had power over the main commissioner on the three-man board. Kaufmann now had a second job for Wright, Jensen reported, not just the planetarium but an executive office in the store. Jensen then moved to strategies for securing Kaufmann as a client:

> Kaufmann's son was at Taliesin Tuesday [Wright was away from Taliesin at the time]. His father wants him to go there. Jr. reports he is "impressed." But to be frank I suspect the advisability until things become more lively—which should not take long. What do you think? I will see the boy in N.Y. this week. This week Tom Maloney will phone you from Chicago to ask you if you consent to be on the jury of the great industrial arts exhibit opening in April. It will include everything from airplanes and pre-fabricated houses to water pitchers. Here is the "jury":
>
> > Frank Lloyd Wright (?)
> > Lewis Mumford
> > Walter Chrysler
> > A. Sloan
> > Chas. Kettering (G.M.)
> > Edsel Ford
> > Nelson Rockefeller
> > Walter Teague
> > Malcolm Muir
> > Hugh Bennett (Toledo Scale)
> > Lessing Rosenwald
> > Tom Gertler
> > Edgar Kaufmann
>
> I had Maloney include K. because he will be flattered by the company. You won't be, I know, but Maloney wants you so bad because he expects you will be the only one (except Mumford perhaps) who will get

up at the dinner of the occasion and say what you think about the whole works. It will be a grand chance for a slam and some concrete pointers I don't hope you will forego. . . . What has happened up to now has been a preliminary skirmish. The work is still ahead. There is therefore nothing more important than that you relax and do not allow the present details to wear you out.

If historians ever establish an archive of architectural seduction, this Machiavellian letter will serve as exhibit A. Jensen's manipulation of Kaufmann counted on two separate lures to reel E. J. in: one was his son, the other his ego. Let's consider the ego first. Jensen informed Kaufmann that he would be a juror for "the great industrial arts exhibit opening in April," by which he evidently meant the second Industrial Arts Exposition of the National Alliance of Art and Industry that was planned for April 1935 in New York. The man mentioned in this context as "Maloney" was Thomas J. Maloney, a journalist, publicist, and later editor of *Photo World,* who in the 1930s promoted Wright in the "Arts and Industry" constituency in New York. Kaufmann's dozen cojurors included the top automobile executives Walter Chrysler, Edsel Ford, and Alfred Sloan and Charles Kettering of General Motors; the Sears, Roebuck chairman Lessing Rosenwald; *Newsweek's* publisher Malcolm Muir; the Toledo Scale president Hugh Bennett; and oilman, builder, and philanthropist Nelson Rockefeller. There were, in addition, Wright, the critic Lewis Mumford, and the industrial designer Walter Teague (I cannot yet identify Tom Gertler). No wonder Jensen was so sure Kaufmann would do Wright's bidding: his connection with Wright would allow E. J. to fraternize with a dozen of the most important businessmen on the planet.

The Industrial Arts Exposition and the National Alliance of Art and Industry both sought to interest American businessmen in progressive product design. Their first show had taken place in April 1934 in the RCA Building in Rockefeller Center: that was the one made memorable by Macy's model weekend house. The second show opened at Rockefeller Center in April 1935. Its star was a model of Wright's Broadacre City, and in the end E. J. Kaufmann was its sole sponsor.

The second lure was "the boy"—though Kaufmann Jr. was twenty-four! Piecing together the relevant telegrams, letters, and references to other letters since lost, it appears that Kaufmann Sr. and Wright cooked up the idea of Junior's apprenticeship by themselves. Jensen hammered on the idea because he had a pecuniary interest in doing so: Wright had guaranteed him a bounty of 10 percent of the tuition for every apprentice he enrolled. In 1934, you could live for months on $110.

Jensen advised Wright not to admit Junior until the father was firmly on the hook, and that is essentially what happened. Junior entered Taliesin on October 15 and Senior was hooked by October 20, when he offered Wright the definitive commissions for his office and the store planetarium, in addition to the $24 million in civic improvements Wright could expect to build in Pittsburgh. These Kaufmann now described as "eight or nine bridges, a tunnel, a retaining wall and wharf improvements, and various highway projects." But the list proved a mirage until the late 1940s, and in the end Wright would never get to poke his finger into this delectable pie.

In November, Wright proffered a third lure to Kaufmann, which played on his rivalry with the other man regarded as the smartest merchandiser in the country: Stanley Marcus. Marcus, we saw, brought Wright to speak in Dallas in 1933 as part of his attempt to import culture to Texas. Now, on November 6, 1934, a fortnight after Kaufmann offered Wright his various public and commercial commissions, Marcus asked Wright to build him a house. The Marcus house was never built, because the cost was high and he and Wright proved inflexible in negotiations. While it lasted, though, Wright used the house project as a pawn in fostering an artistic rivalry between Marcus and Kaufmann. Wright now had the country's two best retailers on the line at once—no wonder he habitually treated them as two halves of the same person. At one point, when Wright wrote Marcus and Kaufmann on the same day, his frugal secretary typed the carbon copies of both letters back-to-back, so today Wright's twin letters to his two Jewish prospects bleed into each other as though one.

Sunday, November 18, 1934, was a Fallingwater milestone: the day Wright and Kaufmann tested each other out. Like all their visits, this one was preceded by a flurry of telegrams and letters between the faithful Masselink at Taliesin and the faithful Clinton in Pittsburgh. Though Junior for decades feigned otherwise, the telegrams make clear that his parents were *not* driving through the cusp of a Wisconsin winter just to see him. Wright wrote Jensen on November 9: "I've written Kaufmann a note [this does not survive] and he is coming to Taliesin with Mrs. Kaufmann next weekend. But I cannot combat the pretenses and lies of any popular architects [this is the nonsyntactic line that evidently referred to Neutra or another competing designer]. So I have very little hope of anything where they are concerned." The surviving scraps of information characterize the meeting as urgent, but lacking the telephone logs and memos that fleshed it out, we cannot say why. Wright dearly wanted the commissions for the planetarium and office, but nothing was "urgent" about them. The public works for Pittsburgh would require months to go through channels, so they were not literally urgent, either.

That leaves just one other possible point of urgency for the meeting: Wright's Broadacre City project. Wright had cited or described this exurban utopia in three different venues in 1932: in his *Disappearing City* book, in his *Autobiography,* and in the *New York Times Magazine.* But to convince the public, he required a visualization and not a theory: Broadacre City had to be rendered in a three-dimensional model. In 1934 the Federal Housing Authority had just been constituted, and the Taliesin community hoped the government would fund Broadacre City as a demonstration piece. That, too, would demand a detailed model, and Karl Jensen was sure that in E. J. Kaufmann he had found the pigeon who would pay for it. Around November 1, without consulting Wright, Jensen asked E. J. for funds to build a centerpiece for the Industrial Arts Exposition in April 1935. He justified his action to Wright several weeks later: "No more appropriate exhibit for the industrial arts show in April would be possible than a model of 'the broadacre city' as you would visualize the pattern. Surrounding it would be large scale photographs showing old city-patterns and congestion."

In that short time frame, getting funding for a Broadacre City model was indeed urgent to Jensen and Wright, though not to Kaufmann. Perhaps, though, Wright could make Broadacre City seem urgent to E. J. if he conveyed the right message through the right messenger. The messenger would be Junior, who had been living at Taliesin just under a month. The message would be peripherally about Broadacre City but mainly about Stanley Marcus's request for a house from Wright, which had just arrived in the mail. Properly rehearsed, Junior would summon his father to Taliesin and egg him on to eclipse his Dallas rival by counteracting the Marcus house commission with one of his own.

No one buttered up prospective clients better than Frank Lloyd Wright. Alistair Cooke recalled his old friend's "delicate and warmly modulated" voice, which had "for fifty years seduced wax manufacturers, oil tycoons, bishops, university boards of trustees and at least one emperor of Japan." Meryle Secrest adduced one example of this. Wright and Herbert "Hib" Johnson "became enormously fond of each other," but Johnson once appealed to Wright: "Please, Frank, don't scold me in front of my board of directors." All Wright's powers of seduction were in high gear when the Kaufmanns arrived at Taliesin on November 18. Wright himself, rather than the usual acolyte, reported on their visit in the weekly "At Taliesin" column that ran in a number of Wisconsin newspapers. He flattered the Kaufmanns as the "merchant prince and princess of Pittsburgh," and emphasized the importance of their thirteen-story department store and its 2,500 employees. Kaufmann spoke to the apprentices himself—another departure from the usual Taliesin script—

and gave an eloquent talk (Wright said) on the theme of arts and industry. This Wright also summarized at length in his newspaper account. Here again it is clear that this royal visit was no casual drop-in on Junior. "Mr. Kaufmann [Wright continues] gave us the most encouraging view we have had of the hand the enlightened merchant is taking in improving the product he sells. The merchant is naturally the anterunae [this was either a typographical error or Wright-speak for partner or forerunner] of the maker but, more than that, now under leadership like Edgar Kaufmann's, he is banding together to make actual experiments to improve the maker's output." Wright was unstinting in his flattery of the enlightened Kaufmann and how much he had done for Pittsburgh.

Wright naturally showed off Taliesin for the Kaufmanns, who slept in the main guest bedroom. The bedroom's balcony, then as now, overlooked a dammed-up millpond. Like Rubens selling himself to clients with his elaborate home and studio in Antwerp, Wright was selling himself to the Kaufmanns through Taliesin, which was probably the first Wright house they had seen. This was a prophetic foreshadowing, because in many ways Fallingwater was to replicate Taliesin.

At dinner Sunday night Wright spoke of his Broadacre City project, and Kaufmann spontaneously offered $1,000 to finance construction of a model. But this was a charade: the script worked out with Jensen and Maloney called for Kaufmann to make the offer for exactly that amount. E. J. played his part so adroitly that even a bright apprentice like Edgar Tafel mistook the spontaneity as authentic. But isn't every royal visit almost by definition a charade?

The short-term importance of the love feast of November 18 is that it launched the Broadacre City model, an important element in rehabilitat-

February 1935: Wright and apprentices Bill Bernoudy and Edgar Kaufman Jr. (*left*), with part of the Broadacre City model then under construction in Arizona

ing Wright's reputation. Within days of Kaufmann's making his subsidy offer, Jensen and Maloney had plans showing just where the model would fit in Rockefeller Center's exhibition floor the next April. Before the month was up, Maloney was flattering Kaufmann aplenty: "You have a way of doing things in a big and decisive manner which is most agreeable to me," and promising to make the awards at the forthcoming industrial arts show out of aluminum or something else "symbolical of Pittsburgh and your own surroundings." There was talk of sending the model on a national tour.

What was the long-term significance of November 18 for Fallingwater? Its prime importance was that it bonded Wright, Kaufmann, and their wives into a partnership strong enough to withstand the vicissitudes of so radical a project. Whether a weekend house was discussed before, during, or immediately after November 18, we don't know.

The house project soon came into focus. Two weeks after the Taliesin visit Kaufmann wrote Wright: "Had luncheon with the three Allegheny County Authority men today and it was a triumphant luncheon. . . . It is time for you to appear on the scene." Kaufmann got Wright's attention with an enclosed check for half the promised $1,000 on the Broadacre City model. Wright replied that he would appear in Pittsburgh on December 14, which he later postponed by a few days. "Kaufmann has sent for me to come to Pittsburgh," Wright wrote Jensen. He knew what it was to be summoned to an imperial presence: when Wright lived in Tokyo, an emissary of the Mikado had more than once banged on his door.

The overnight train from Chicago pulls into Pittsburgh's Penn Station at 8:00 A.M. these days, but the morning of Tuesday, December 18, 1934, it arrived at 9:45, and Frank Lloyd Wright was on it. Kaufmann had ostensibly summoned him about the big public works that were still on the agenda, but the schedule was suspiciously light. Shouldn't Wright have been penciled in to meet with the three Allegheny County commissioners, the mayor of Pittsburgh, some councilmen, the public works director, and the two separate boards of the Allegheny County Authority? Instead, E. J. prepared nothing more than supper with the authority head, Press Dowler, and one or two other men. Wright's postmortem letter of December 26 was vitriolic about Dowler, which suggests the meeting went nowhere. Kaufmann's efforts to mobilize the city's movers and shakers behind Wright were so minimal that both men seem to have recognized that the public works horse was dead before Wright would get to ride it.

Now—and here he *was* operating just like the Mikado—Kaufmann revealed his true reason for summoning Wright. They were driving direct from Penn Station to his land at Bear Run, where Kaufmann wanted Wright to design a weekend house. They would spend Wednesday morning at the Kaufmann store, so on Tuesday they would largely bypass the Golden Triangle, except for H. H. Richardson's Allegheny County Courthouse and Jail, which Wright praised in print a few weeks later. Kaufmann and Wright rode out of town on the Penn-Lincoln Highway, with the architect surely both awed and dismayed by the industrial might of the city he could glimpse from the new George Westinghouse Bridge.

About two hours later Kaufmann and Wright reached Bear Run. Liliane had no interest in construction, and did not go along. Junior always wished he had been present, and for half a century he claimed he had been, but we know he stayed at Taliesin until just before Christmas. That left just Wright and E. J., and probably a chauffeur, to tramp the Bear Run grounds, see The Hangover, and press on to the waterfall they could hear long before they saw it.

We can imagine that E. J. told Wright something of the geography of Appalachia, and he may have summarized the history of Bear Run. Taliesin lore says he told Wright that Indians had once made their campfires on the big boulder north of the waterfall, and we can surmise that Kaufmann told his visitor that the property had once belonged to George Washington. Wright asked Kaufmann to mail a good topographic map of the site to Taliesin.

The two men motored back to Pittsburgh for a profitless dinner with Press Dowler that evening and (if Wright had the energy) perhaps a visit to one of E. J.'s favorite strip joints. Three years later, Bill Hedrich, come to photograph Fallingwater for *Architectural Forum,* was bug-eyed when Kaufmann lent him his entry card to one of those fleshpots.

Wright spent the next morning at the store, looking over Kaufmann's executive office suite in preparation for the transformation that E. J. wanted from him. He asked for and later got a blueprint of the tenth floor, then took off like any other shopper let loose in one of America's most glittering emporia. He bought two hand mirrors for $75, which he grandly put on credit; left another order for $500 in music instruments with E. J.; and sent Ethel Clinton scurrying around Pittsburgh in search of a harp (daughter Iovanna was just beginning to play it: one stands in the background at Wright's Arizona compound of Taliesin West in the photograph showing him with E. J. there). Wright then left for two days in New York and returned before Christmas on the Twentieth Century Limited to Chicago with a friend, the Round Table writer and wit Alexander Woollcott.

It had been a momentous year for Kaufmann, starting with Wright as a photographic image and ending with the architect himself by his side at the Bear Run waterfall. But 1934 held one more indelible moment for E. J. Ten days after Frank Lloyd Wright slept in La Tourelle's guestroom (Junior's suite, actually), the same bed was taken over by Albert Einstein. The annual meeting of the American Association for the Advancement of Science came to Pittsburgh that last weekend of December, and it had a sensational catch: Professor Einstein's first scientific lecture in America since escaping from Nazi Germany. Einstein spoke on the mass-energy theory to scientists in the sumptuous Little Theater on the Carnegie Tech campus, then went to the nearby estate of E. J.'s friend Nathaniel Spear to take questions from newspapermen. E. J. hovered by Einstein's side at every moment: a much-reproduced *New York Times* photograph (page 51) shows him standing guard as the Great Man met with journalists.

Now that they had finally had several hours of contact, what did Kaufmann and Wright see in each other? Kaufmann must have been appalled at the fiscal disorder he glimpsed at Taliesin in November, and Wright would have had no more stomach for the aesthetic disorder he discerned in the fake-medieval living room in Fox Chapel in December. How could Kaufmann live like that? Stranger still, after Wright created the futuristic Fallingwater for E. J., how could Kaufmann have loved both it *and* his backward house in Pittsburgh, seemingly oblivious to the immense stylistic and cultural gap between them?

The partnership held—at first—because there was genuine fondness between the two men, and Kaufmann and Wright were also linked by their parallel roles as fathers to Kaufmann Jr., one biological, the other artistic. There is also something about architecture that bonds male designers to male clients but leaves them unaffected by females. That was true of Wright, at least, and Wright was little different from Sullivan, who lived entirely among males before, during, and after his brief marriage. Sullivan in turn differed little from H. H. Richardson, a "man's man," of whom his client Frances Glessner said "aside from his profession . . . not what I should call an interesting man."

Of the two, it was Wright who was affectionate, even mawkish with Kaufmann, once declaring, "I would deny you nothing I had to give, short of suicide" and later reminiscing: "I conceived a love of you quite beyond the ordinary relationship of client and Architect." It must have galled Wright that his love was not reciprocated. Even at his most affectionate, Kaufmann was the conventional businessman in his letters. "With kind personal regards I remain . . ." was as homoerotic as he got.

The letters make clear that Wright was both attracted to Kaufmann and repelled by him. Wright enjoyed Kaufmann's handsomeness, his virility, and his enthusiasm for nature (they once contemplated a swap between their Pennsylvania and Wisconsin cow herds). They shared a taste for fast cars—one of which Kaufmann presented to Wright for Christmas. Both men lived in their own moral universe and had chosen eccentric and self-indulgent lifestyles that allowed them to break society's rules, including those involving sexual conduct. Both men were master merchandisers who knew how to seduce clients, sell new products, and generate demand for more. Their friendship, carried out in scores of visits and letters, was always lively and often touching, and it ultimately survived the blasts hurled from both sides. It ended with the report that Wright was at Kaufmann's side the night he died.

Despite their mutual sympathies, there was much the two men did not understand about each other. The problem lay in their transactions, both fiscal and artistic. Wright's apprentice Edgar Tafel recalled that his boss was dilatory and disorganized in billing clients, then was hurt when the client did not pay without being asked. That would drive a businessman like Kaufmann crazy in practical terms, but it suggests at a deeper level that their relationship would ultimately fail because so many cultural issues kept them apart. It is a miracle they achieved anything at all together. It must have been quite a relationship: the city man teamed with an agrarian populist, the Jew yoked with a midwestern isolationist who habitually called Jews kikes. It makes you think of those movies in which two escaped prisoners, handcuffed together but hating each other, are forced to work together to make a successful getaway.

Wright's regional, racial, ethnic, and sexual-orientation prejudices were both numerous and inconsistent, but the most important thing he never understood about E. J. Kaufmann was the worldview of the merchant. Wright could flatter Kaufmann as "enlightened" all week long, but the agrarian populist could never get over his discomfort with merchants. Not that Wright was a stranger to the mechanics of commerce, for he was a legendary skinflint and conniver. Tafel recalled an occasion in which Wright attempted his usual bargaining in a Jewish-owned store in Wisconsin. "He can lie in hell," grumbled one of the Yiddish-speaking merchants to the other, unaware that Tafel was drinking it all in.

In his conflict with merchants Wright was also in conflict with himself. The prime discovery in Wright scholarship in recent years was not about the man's buildings but about his colossal traffic in Japanese prints—much of it unethical. Wright's sale of thousands of prints to the

Metropolitan Museum in New York—four hundred in the year 1918 alone—netted him not less than $300,000, or the cost of two Fallingwaters. For many years Wright covered his expenses by selling prints rather than building designs. And he insisted that the Metropolitan recognize him not as a collector but as a merchant. In one letter of 1922 he grumbled: "In this matter I am a merchant and expect to be treated like one." Kaufmann, the merchant with one year's exposure to engineering, meet Wright the architect making a fortune in commerce. Is it any wonder that two men with so much overlap in their expertise were destined to clash?

Then there is the fundamental difference between the culture of wrights and *Kaufmänner* (merchants). Like all artificers, wrights deal in material substances, while merchants deal in images. Together at Fallingwater, and later apart, both Wright and Kaufmann held true to their names and their roles in life. Kaufmann was aware of this when he presented himself in mock modesty before Wright: "We are only trades people and cannot see as clearly as others." Wright also recognized the divide between their two cultures: he pointed out the distinction between makers and merchants in his published comments about his first meeting with Kaufmann at Taliesin.

Both Wright and the academic architects of Pittsburgh mistakenly assumed that in working with them Kaufmann had made a permanent commitment to their brand of architecture. In commerce, however, brand loyalty is short-term, not permanent. Alexis de Tocqueville would have found nothing surprising in Kaufmann's shifts of taste. That was just what he meant when he wrote of the "constant excitement" of the world of commerce.

Then there was the ethnic distinction. Wright's new client was a Jew, only the third member of that small tribe with whom he had built until then. Either Wright was a world-class hypocrite or he had tremendous capacity for compartmentalization, because he certainly was ambivalent about Jews. Nor was he shy about letting the world know it. His 1932 *Autobiography* goes on for pages about his battles with Jews when he got to Chicago in the 1880s, though he was forced to admit the generous treatment he had received from Dankmar Adler. Wright's account of his first day in Adler and Sullivan's drafting room bears enough paranoia to make good Nazi propaganda:

> Next table to mine Jean Agnas, a clean-faced Norseman. To the right Eisendrath—apparently stupid. Jewish. Behind me to the left Ottenheimer—alert, apparently bright. Jew too. Turned around to survey the

group. Isbell, Jew? Gaylord, no—not. Weydert, Jew undoubtedly. Directly behind, Weatherwax. Couldn't make him out. In the corner Andresen—Swedish. Several more Jewish faces. Of course—I thought, because Mr. Adler himself must be a Jew.

Wright then takes to a boxing ring and defeats some of the draftsmen he works with.

Then and there I made up my mind to stay in that office till I could fire every one of the gang, and said so. Ottenheimer, the ringleader, an active, intelligent, little Jew was not present. He got the report from the gang next day and I heard him say, "Ooi, the god-damn son of a bitch! Leave him to me."

Back in the drafting room some weeks later, Wright physically attacked Ottenheimer, the "heavy-bodied, short-legged, pompadoured, conceited, red-faced Jew" who was trying to study for his entry exams to the École des Beaux-Arts in Paris. Ottenheimer picked up a draftsman's edging knife and eleven times stabbed Wright to the bone, with Wright fighting him off with a T-square. Wright insisted on retaining the detailed account in later editions of the *Autobiography* even while dropping other inappropriate passages. He evidently regarded this drafting-hall fight as a presentiment of the many battles he would encounter in his profession: Ottenheimer the Beaux-Arts academician versus Wright the progressive, trying to kill each other with architectural drafting tools.

City life did little to blunt Wright's anti-Jewish invective. In 1926, when hounded by charges of adultery, Wright lashed out against the "photographers, lawyers, Kikes and shysters who played upon an outraged father." Wright expressed anti-Jewish sentiments in at least a score of his letters: he tormented apprentice Abe Dombar for being too Jewish; chastised Kaufmann for some mild support of Zionism; stridently supported Lindbergh, isolationism, and America First; and demonized his renegade protégés Neutra and Schindler as Jews. Wright's friend Henry Churchill also took pains to single out Walter Gropius and the Dutch modernist J. J. P. Oud as Jews (we have no evidence that they were), as though that explained why they were dangerous to Wright.

We could call Wright more a cultural than a political isolationist, since he spent most of his life isolated in a Wisconsin valley or the Arizona desert (just how isolated Taliesin East is I learned for myself when I stayed nearby: my motel radio would not bring in even one station without static). In the 1930s, though, he increasingly associated with outright fascists. In the September 1941 issue of *Scribner's Commentator,* a Nazi propaganda pipeline that had been purchased outright by the German government, Wright attacked the private bankers in London and New York: i.e., the Jews. Another of his articles, in the July 1941 issue of the far-rightist *Money* magazine, brought him a warm commendation from the California fascist Edward Arps. Arps favored Wright with a carbon copy of his all-out Nazi exhortation to the American fascist Jesse Howell, in which Arps prayed for "divine protection" for Adolf Hitler, "the product of the divine prayer of the German people, where the Jew after the war had enthroned himself and completely enslaved them." The letter looked forward to Nazi control of Europe. Arps would not have written thus unless he expected the architect to share his sentiments. Whether Wright did or did not, we can't say, but he carefully retained the letter all his life.

What is wonderful to behold is Wright simultaneously intoning the perennial cliché that "my best friends are Jews." And something still more wonderful: the claim was far from false. Jews like E. J. Kaufmann and Solomon Guggenheim represented a big chunk of Wright's clientele, in the postwar years accounting for nearly a third of his commissions. Many of Wright's apprentices were Jews, and among them none were more loyal than Tafel and Aaron Green, who got him the huge Marin County commission. Wright treated his engineer Mendel Glickman like a son: no—far better than he treated his own sons. He honored the builder George Cohen as his joint creator at the Guggenheim; warmheartedly corresponded with three rabbis; and at the end of his life he found himself spiritually recharged in the creation of his Beth Sholom Synagogue.

Perhaps the answer to the riddle is that like many a nonconformist, Wright hated nonconformity in anyone else. It must have required considerable shifting of gears when, just two years after writing the *Autobiography,* Wright got the chance of his lifetime from exactly the kind of person who irritated him so much: a "rootless" urban Jew.

At Fallingwater, Wright and Kaufmann worked together like angels, but they never created a work of genius together again, probably because Fallingwater would change both men too much. It made Wright famous again, although Kaufmann would always remember him as the unemployed architect he had been in 1934. It transformed Kaufmann himself into a well-known patron of the arts, although Wright kept belittling him as the provincial merchant he had been in 1934. But Kaufmann was no longer that, either. Soon he would become the man who built Fallingwater.

Opposite: Wright and apprentices Bob Mosher, Edgar Tafel, and Wes Peters,
in the Taliesin office in which Fallingwater was given birth

FIVE

THE DESIGN OF FALLINGWATER STRUGGLES NINE MONTHS TO BE BORN

Fallingwater is a great blessing—one of the great blessings to be experienced here on earth. I think nothing yet ever equalled the coordination, sympathetic expression of the great principle of repose where forest and stream and rock and all the elements of structure are combined so quietly that really you listen not to any noise whatsoever although the music of the stream is there. But you listen to Fallingwater the way you listen to the quiet of the country.

—FRANK LLOYD WRIGHT

Few passages in English capture the dread and exultation of an architect engaged in designing a building better than one from *The Fountainhead,* in which client Austen Heller confronts architect Howard Roark: "You're completely natural only when you're one inch from bursting into pieces. What in hell are you really made of, Howard? After all, it's only a building. It's not the combination of holy sacrament, Indian torture, and sexual ecstasy that you seem to make of it."

To which Roark replies: "Isn't it?"

To hear Frank Lloyd Wright tell it, designing the most complex house of modern architecture was no more complicated than selecting bananas at the supermarket. "There in a beautiful forest was a solid, high rock-ledge rising beside a waterfall and the natural thing seemed to be to cantilever the house from that rock-bank over the falling water. . . . Then came (of course) Mr. Kaufmann's love for the beautiful site. He loved the site where the house was built and liked to listen to the waterfall. So that was a prime motive in the design. I think you can hear the waterfall when you look at the design." But the task was evidently not as simple as that, since Wright took nine months to put Fallingwater on paper.

Architectural design presents a paradox. On the one hand, the *utilitas-firmitas-venustas* formula laid down by the Roman architect Vitruvius two thousand years ago looks simple: make the building functional, structurally sound, and good-looking. On the other hand, architects speak of the design process as though it were a branch of neuroscience—and to some degree it is that, too. We may make some progress in resolving the paradox if, before looking at how Wright designed the whole of Fallingwater, we examine only how he conceived the stairs that lead from the terrace outside E. J.'s second-floor bedroom to Junior's bedroom in the third-floor penthouse. These penthouse steps are among the most melodious stairs in modern architecture, but they present a Vitruvian difficulty right away, because they have no essential function. The practical way to get to the penthouse is to use the regular steps inside Fallingwater, not the steps outside. And when would the Kaufmanns ever have occasion to use those steps? Chances are zero that Kaufmann Jr. ever dropped down to E. J.'s bedroom for some fatherly advice, or that E. J. walked up to Junior's bedroom very often to discourse on his philosophy on life. So much for form following function.*

But the *metaphorical* function of the stairs is great: they forge a sym-

*The back steps might, however, have been put in for a *non*-family function. If E. J. expected thousands of visitors to pour through his experimental house the way they already had for the radically modern houses put on view in New York and Los Angeles, then back steps were a necessity. Today's Fallingwater guides depend on the external penthouse steps to keep tourists moving through the house.

The adobe-style steps
from E. J.'s terrace up
to Junior's penthouse

bolic architectural bond between a father and a son who lacked any other kind of bond. Wright doubtless saw that the two male Kaufmanns had even less of an emotional relationship than he had with his own sons. The staircase possibly offers the hope that this alienation would not always be so. Those hopes were soon dashed, though, when Junior moved out of his tower bedroom, as though even the thought of the nearby father-son staircase repelled him.

Second difficulty: the steps are structural parasites. They do nothing to hold up the house, and their weight puts needless stress on the terrace

Adobe steps lead to the
old kiva at Pueblo San
Ildefonso, New Mexico

below. At best they have the minimum structural integrity needed to keep themselves from falling down.

A third anomaly: the penthouse steps are strikingly fat. We can see in spots where they have weathered that Wright's construction crew added a hand-applied concrete wrap over a poured-concrete core. That makes the steps not only structurally ineffectual but irrational, or at least hard to reconcile with Wright's philosophy of using materials with honesty and economy. So much for organic architecture.

Why did Wright fatten the steps? I believe it was to make them resemble adobe (sun-dried mud or bricks), which is concrete's prehistoric ancestor. Wright had originally designed Fallingwater's balconies and steps as straight-edged: they show up that way in the early drawings. A month or two later he switched them to rounded. Fat and rounded, the balconies and the steps now took on the subliminal image of adobe, as though Fallingwater had been built by Native Americans seventeen hundred miles to the southwest. Kaufmann Jr.'s steps particularly resemble the steps leading into the kiva (underground religious chamber) at New Mexico's Pueblo San Ildefonso, north of Santa Fe, although hundreds of other adobe staircases survive as possible models, too. Wright knew and admired both pueblos and kivas: he used the form and even the name "kiva" for the darkened room he designed for showing movies at Taliesin West.

When the Wrights and the Kaufmanns vacationed together in February 1935 in the Phoenix suburb of Chandler, Arizona, it would have been easy, and typical of Wright, to have driven his guests to San Ildefonso or some other ancient site. It takes only a half-hour today to drive from Chandler to the Hohokam fortress at Casa Grande Ruins National Monument, which offers another vivid demonstration of adobe technique. There you can also see the slit windows that Wright used above and beneath the penthouse steps. They, too, are hallmarks of both the adobe and cut-stone Native American monuments of the Southwest.

Art historians would say that the penthouse steps have an iconographic role: by recollecting the adobe steps of the Southwest they set this house firmly and uniquely in the United States of America. The connection is far from obvious, since Pennsylvania is remote from the Southwest, but Wright knew of no monumental architecture of the eastern woodland Indians that he could quote in this manner, so he turned to a region that is rich in surviving Indian buildings. He gloried in the regional idiom of the Southwest, and he knew E. J. and Liliane would appreciate it once they saw it, too. Wright dared not make Fallingwater's steps out of true adobe—in that cold, wet environment they would have cracked into smithereens in a matter of months. In making the steps out of concrete Wright used a modern derivative to praise the great builders of ancient America. Even visitors to Fallingwater who know nothing of concrete can intuit that the steps represent an ancient and noble chapter in the history of engineering.

The steps may also have held a totemic meaning for Wright and the Kaufmanns. Wright spent the last quarter-century of his life in the Southwest, which became even more precious to him than Wisconsin, given the added enchantment of its ancient structures. The stairs commemorate the happy and productive times of the first winter he spent with the Taliesin Fellows in Arizona, all the better that he shared some of the time with E. J. and Liliane. Those good times cemented the special bond between the architect and his clients, and served as an augury for the successful completion of the Kaufmanns' new home. In adding this Southwestern-style staircase to Fallingwater, Wright inserted a talisman into the house, binding him forever with his clients. The staircase held a second set of happy memories for the Kaufmanns, too: the El Mirador Hotel in Palm Springs (later burned, today in part rebuilt) had two of this sort, which E. J. and Liliane would have recollected through this replica.

As spectators, we can attribute meaning to the penthouse steps even without knowing what the meaning is, and one of the prime meanings we intuit from them is the act of structure itself. The steps and the landing are cantilevered out to remind us of the technology that makes the entire house possible. By making the staircase base hollow rather than solid, Wright also makes sure we do not misread the material as authentic adobe, which is structurally so weak that it would demand a solid base. This in turn tells us that the steps must be made with something stronger buried inside the concrete, which we can guess is steel. Louis Henry Sullivan did something similar in his skyscrapers: whenever he resorted to dishonest effects, he made sure you *knew* they were dishonest. Wright had a practical requirement for a hollowed-out base, too, since he placed two windows below the stairs. Had Wright filled in the base, E. J.'s bedroom would have been much darker.

Wright's placement of these steps at the top of Fallingwater makes us think a second time of the architecture of the Southwest. They make Fallingwater resemble a pueblo, a house type normally entered from the top. Wright was not being literal here, because Fallingwater has other entrances, but why else did he make this point of entry the most elaborate? He invites a visitor to use these steps to climb to the top of the house, then descend three floors to the bowels of the earth. Being top-entered and nearly pitch-dark inside, the old pueblos were closely related to the sacred kivas, and must have imparted a degree of kivalike sacredness to their inhabitants. These pueblolike steps at the top of a pueblolike house make Fallingwater partake of the sacred, too.

A visitor who knows nothing of adobe and pueblos will still enjoy the expressive impact of these stairs. The zigzags created by the six jogs on the stair wall bespeak "steppedness" far more than would a standard diagonal railing. In a wider sense, these steps and the stepped canopy up to the guesthouse express the steppedness of the whole house as it steps down a hillside to meet the water.

Some purists may complain that copying steps from a New Mexico pueblo manifests a lack of originality in Wright, but this was no crime by his standards. Every age but ours has regarded an architectural copy as an act of devotion. In Japan each generation copies the archaic shrine at Ise as an act of the highest veneration—as Wright knew firsthand. In the West the ancients esteemed architectural copying, too: Emperor Hadrian re-created a dozen of his favorite buildings at Tivoli, outside Rome. For close to two millennia, Christians have thrilled to copies of the Holy Sepulcher in Jerusalem, no matter how approximate most of the copies are. So, too, Wright's copies: they give spiritual strength to a structure, as though the original building is blessing its offshoot.

The penthouse steps have taught us much about Wright as a designer. We see him separating himself from mainstream modernism in being unafraid to incorporate symbolism, iconography, and even irrationality in his buildings. The typical modern use of concrete in the 1920s and '30s was mechanistic, but Wright used concrete for lyrical and even humanistic effects. This house so rich in materials and meaning goes beyond the function-structure-beauty formula of Vitruvius. Wright gives us a house that is not only good-looking but good-*feeling,* because it has intellectual richness. By using steps to make us reflect on the natural contours of his site and its waterfall, he further imbues Fallingwater with contextual richness. Finally, the numerous links Wright establishes with nature, the way his materials evoke the antiquity of Native America, and the way the steps reflect the Kaufmanns as a family—these all give Fallingwater an additional richness that we can best term spiritual. When visitors call Fallingwater emotionally or spiritually affecting, as they so often do, they intend by that the layer upon layer of meaning that they intuit in the house. Certainly, Wright squeezed meaning out of every part of Fallingwater—the plan, the structure, the interior sequences, and the afterimages we take away from it. We could think of Wright running Fallingwater the way Wagner did his operas, controlling not just the music but also the words and the staging. The architect was master of everything.

Now for the Fallingwater design process overall. The design had its conception by the waters of Bear Run on Tuesday, December 18, 1934, and its birth at Taliesin on Sunday, September 22, 1935, nine months and four days later. The exact same months saw the gestation of an equally important icon in American music: George Gershwin began to orchestrate the opera *Porgy and Bess* in late 1934, and he completed the score in September 1935.

Fallingwater's design presents four questions: Why did it take Wright so long to create the design? What mental image did he form of the house during that time? By what process did he fine-tune this mental image? And when and how did he finally get his mental image of Fallingwater on paper?

Much has been written on writer's block, but next to nothing about architect's block, so we can only guess what concerns haunted Wright during the longest wait to deliver on a job in his career. Nearing seventy, with creditors hammering at Taliesin's door and clients nowhere in sight, Wright surely found those months torture. He never explained why he took so long to produce his plans for Fallingwater. A psychohistorian might propose that he stalled because his personality demanded that he live life on the edge. The Master seemed to jinx himself whenever he came too close to success, most spectacularly when he ran off with his client's wife in 1909.

As a practical matter, Wright may have felt the need to test the steadfastness of client Kaufmann. Kaufmann's lavish promises of millions of dollars of work in 1934 had proved phony. Holding back on Fallingwater gave Wright a nine-month test of Kaufmann's steadfastness as a patron. Only after testing St. Peter could Christ say: "Thou art Peter, and upon this rock I will build my church" (Matt. 16:18). Wright needed to be sure that Kaufmann was as strong as the boulders on which he would anchor Fallingwater. On those two rocks would he rebuild his career.

The instant he saw Bear Run, Frank Lloyd Wright seems to have grasped how to place by the falls a house that would flow as effortlessly as the waterfall itself. He wrote Kaufmann on December 26, 1934, eight days after his visit:

> Visit to the waterfall in the woods stays with me and a domicile has taken vague shape in my mind to the music of the stream. When contours come you will see it.
>
> Meantime, to you my affection.

Wright had prodigious powers of observation, but he was not superhuman. He was able to fit Fallingwater so perfectly over Bear Run only after making several visits to the site, and giving intense study to its detailed contour maps. His request for those maps should have been simple for E. J. to satisfy because the Morris Knowles firm had already furnished him such a plan back in 1920 (Kaufmann's copy survives in Avery Libary). If Kaufmann had temporarily misplaced his copy, fifteen minutes would have sufficed for an office boy at Knowles to print a new one and run it across Smithfield Street. Wright was obliged to ask for the plans a second time on January 10, 1935, but again E. J. dragged his feet.

Kaufmann's delay in sending Wright the estate plans may have reflected uncertainty about pursuing the project, but we can also call it the first of many passive-aggressive jabs that Kaufmann would administer to Wright over the next twenty years. On February 20, Wright demanded the site surveys a third time, at which point Kaufmann finally ordered the Knowles firm to chart the topographic features around the falls at Bear Run. The Knowles plan, an update of their earlier survey, showed the trees species by species, the boulders, the rock ledges, the stream, the bridge upstream from the falls, and the Shady Lane driveway that led up the hillslope. The survey was finished on March 9, 1935, and reached Wright a week later.

Kaufmann expected construction on his house to begin right away, but Wright needed time to reflect. One of the myths of Fallingwater is that during his nine-month wait Wright gave Kaufmann no hint of his design ideas, then ambushed him with a surprise placement of Fallingwater over rather than opposite the waterfall. This ignores letters and other accounts that show otherwise. On April 27, 1935, for example, Wright told Kaufmann: "We are ready to go to work on the waterfall cottage at Bear Run." The descriptor "waterfall cottage" should have forewarned E. J. that his house would embrace the falls and not view them from afar.

In June came more hints about the house. Wright wrote Kaufmann: "We are starting on the Home at 'Bear Run,' a specially difficult project, but on which we will charge you the usual ten percent fee only." Wright was in the Kaufmann store twice that month to install and dismantle the Broadacre City exhibition. He came to Pittsburgh five times before he was ready to draw up Fallingwater: December 18, 1934; May 18, June 13, June 29, and July 3, 1935. We know that three of the trips, maybe four, brought him back to Bear Run.

The key visit was the one on July 3, 1935, by which point Wright had a full vision of the house. His apprentice Cornelia Brierly (Berndtson) told me that Wright took her down the gorge to the foot of the main waterfall that day, pointed to the spot alongside the falls where he intended the house to go, and said: "Well, Cornelia, [with this house] we are going to beat the Internationalists at their own game." The phrase shows that Wright had by then chosen the spot, the overall character, and the most photogenic viewpoint for the house. His hint to Brierly about the "Internationalists" meant that Fallingwater would itself carry the hallmarks of the International Style. You can't beat your enemy at his own game without playing it yourself.

Apprentice Blaine Drake was Wright's chauffeur to Bear Run on July 3, and backed up Brierly's recollection: "[Wright] was able to describe so completely his concept of the ultimate design. . . . The finished design was as I visualized it when he was talking to the Kaufmanns. I remember E. J. being quite surprised that the house would be above the falls." So Kaufmann knew by early July—not late September—that he would be living over a waterfall. Letters confirm that on July 3 architect and client discussed a construction budget in the range of $20,000 to $30,000 (later bumped up by Wright to $35,000). They could have done this only if Wright had brought considerable specificity to his design.

July 3 was the first design meeting to include Kaufmann Jr., who recorded that "sun, rain and hail alternated; the masses of native rhododendron were in bloom; the run was full and the falls, thundering." E. J. evidently had told Junior little or nothing about his earlier meetings with Wright, and Wright practiced a parallel deception on Blaine Drake. Drake recorded: "He never mentioned [his earlier visits] to me . . . and it was his nature to talk freely most of the time when we were driving." When we couple these deceptions with the charade about Kaufmann's "spontaneous" decision to fund the Broadacre City model and Wright's "spontaneous" creation of the Fallingwater plans the following September, it looks as though Wright and E. J. shared their architectural intentions with no one but themselves.

Wright and Kaufmann decided to resolve the problem of E. J.'s downtown Pittsburgh office first, and by mid-August 1935 that project reached the stage of construction drawings. Now both men could concentrate full-time on the house, but the legend that presents an imperious Kaufmann descending without warning on Taliesin is way off-base. Kaufmann's store manager, I. D. Wolf, had informed Wright by August 20 that he and E. J. would be in Milwaukee in September, and that they intended to motor over to Spring Green. Wright echoed these travel plans in writing, and added the cheery but vague phrases: "We're working [on the house plans]. You'll have some results soon." On the eve of the visit, Wright would once again confirm the expected arrival of the two men, though in the end only Kaufmann came.

Wright now gave Kaufmann a third assurance that the house plans were aborning. He directed his apprentice Edgar Tafel to write the Kaufmanns that Fallingwater had started to emerge on paper, which the family took at face value. "Dear Mr. Wright [wrote Junior in late August], we were all delighted when a note from Edgar said the office & house were both to some extent on paper." Kaufmann Senior reacted in a practical manner, sending Wright $250 on August 22 as a retainer for the production of more sketches. There was still a month before Wright had to face E. J. in September.

Tafel was equivocating, to put it mildly, when he told E. J. that plans for the house were under way by August. Something *was* on paper, but it was probably no more than a redrawing of the Knowles site plan of Bear Run. Wright was famous for not putting his designs on paper until the last minute, but this does not mean he ignored Fallingwater for nine months—just the opposite. In the movies an architect suddenly blurts out "Eureka" and grabs for a napkin on which to make a tiny sketch. It is unclear whether Wright ever did that, but we know other architects did. H. H. Richardson began drawing plans for Trinity Church in Boston right on the letter announcing the competition for the church, probably within ten minutes of opening his mail. And he put other marvelous sketches on whatever scraps of paper were within reach when inspiration struck; one or two might well have been on napkins.

Wright's procedure in firming up a design was the opposite of Richardson's. He warned his disciples that the last thing they wanted was to fix a design on paper too early:

> One must be able to walk around and inside the structure, know every detail, before putting pencil to paper. . . . I never sit down to a drawing board—and this has been a lifelong practice of mine—until I have the whole thing in my mind. I may alter it substantially, I may throw it away, I may find I'm up a blind alley; but unless I have the idea of the thing pretty well in shape, you won't see me at a drawing board with it. But all the time I have it it's germinating, between three o'clock and four o'clock in the morning. . . .

To the profession as a whole, he wrote:

> Conceive the building in the imagination, not on paper but in the mind, thoroughly—before touching paper. Let it live there—gradually taking more definite form before committing it to the draughting board. When the thing lives for you—start to plan it with tools. Not before. . . . Work-

ing on it with triangle and T-square should modify or extend or intensify or test the conception—complete the harmonious adjustment of its parts.

Why was Wright so insistent that the act of drawing come at the end and not at the beginning of the design process? A major defect of the second method was its association with the Paris-based École des Beaux-Arts. Wright was one of those people for whom positive motivations are not enough: they need to invent some malevolent force that wants to do them ill. For years Wright needed to feel persecuted by the "Beaux-Arts," until the Bauhaus and MoMA took over as the villains in this important but fictional role.

Nearly all the eminent Victorian architects of America studied in Paris, beginning with Richard Morris Hunt and Richardson in the 1850s and 1860s. Wright's master, Sullivan, attended the École in the 1870s but quit in opposition to it. Wright adopted Sullivan's contempt for the École: we saw earlier that he literally bloodied himself in battle with its adherents, and spurned Daniel Burnham's subsidy to go there. Wright posed as the sworn enemy of the Beaux-Arts and the architectural establishment throughout his career.

Sullivan and others have described the École's key ritual in detail. In the *concours* (exams) a surprise design problem—say a customs house or a residence for the governor of Algiers—would be assigned. The student had twelve hours in which to solve it, during which time he was locked up in a *loge,* or compartment. At the conclusion of the twelve hours the student turned in not a detailed plan but an *esquisse*—a sketch that combined a plan and elevation (front view) of the future building. He also made a tracing of the *esquisse* for himself, then had two months in which to tease it into elaborate plans and elevations. If, however, the jury felt the final plans departed too much from the initial *esquisse,* the student got zero for his pains.

The Beaux-Arts method was brought to the United States in the 1870s, where even the *loges* were replicated (among the last were the dozen that Henry Hornbostel inserted in the attic of his College of Fine Arts at the Carnegie Technical Schools in Pittsburgh). American cities put up thousands of "bozarts" buildings that copied earlier masterpieces of the style such as the Paris Opera House. Wright and other progressives mocked these copies for their flowery exteriors and for their structural dishonesty, since they were often masonry outside but steel skeletons inside. If one looked behind the external clichés of its columns and pediments, though, Beaux-Arts was a strong and helpful design methodology, because it fixed the image, the function, and the essential plan of a build-

Claude-Nicolas LeDoux's project for an Inspector's house at the source of the Loue River, around 1790

ing right at the beginning of the design process. Louis Kahn, for example, used the method brilliantly for his thoroughly modern museums and his Salk Institute in California. The *esquisse* encapsulated the two most important elements of the Beaux-Arts curriculum, which were *parti* and program. The *parti* is the essential design element of a building, the simplest image to which the building can be reduced. *Parti* (from the French *parti pris,* meaning "option taken") prods the architect into selecting a single design from thousands of alternatives.

The *parti* gives a building a memorable external image, while the program invests it with a functional interior. That is true of such Beaux-Arts masterpieces as the main New York and Boston libraries: they combine monumental exteriors with a clarity of plan inside that works perfectly for both the user and the books. Among the unforgettable *parti*'s in architecture are Claude-Nicolas LeDoux's Loue River project of a building perforated by a river, and the Gateway Arch that Eero Saarinen put up in St. Louis in the 1960s. But in these simplified designs (the first a theoretical project only, the second more a diagram than a building), neither LeDoux nor Saarinen had to wrestle with the second Beaux-Arts demand, which was to satisfy the "program"—the itemized functional needs of a building.

We can clarify the interface of *parti* and program with the example of the Capitol in Washington. The *parti* of the east side of the Capitol is a long building with a huge dome and a triangular pediment at the center, then smaller pediments at each end. The program for the Capitol meshes perfectly with that: the Senate and the House of Representatives meet separately at the two ends, then come together in an ornate lobby for events of symbolic importance such as presidential inaugurations (before they moved outside) and funerals. A diagram of the legislative branch of the U.S. government looks almost the same: the Senate and the House equal but opposite, and "coming together" in a resolution process that creates a bill for the president's signature. An *esquisse* of the Capitol would synthesize *parti* and program into an ideogram that allows you to grasp not just its rooms but its functions.

It was his command of the Beaux-Arts method that allowed H. H. Richardson to win a host of design competitions in the 1870s and 1880s. What distinguishes Richardson's buildings is the swiftness with which visitors grasp their organization. That is supremely true of his Pittsburgh Courthouse (page 38), widely praised as the great building of nineteenth-century America (a judgment that Wright ratified in print in 1935). Like the best of Beaux-Arts designs, you can read the courthouse externally, before you get in the door. Anyone standing on Grant Street can under-stand not only its plan but how the courthouse works as a dispenser of justice. The judges' chambers and the jury rooms, for example, bulge out from between the courtrooms, as literal and metaphorical buttresses to the judicial process. The exterior of the courthouse is a virtual diagram of both the building and the workings of the institution itself.

Sullivan adopted much of the Beaux-Arts outlook, since he ingested the essence of the method and rejected only its frills. His essay "The Tall Office Building Artistically Considered" instructed architects to tell the viewer on the street how the plan of the building works, how structure holds it up, and what human functions take place inside—all before he or she walks in the door.

We could say that Wright, like Sullivan, was as much attracted to as repelled by the Beaux-Arts method: indeed, he crafted a perfect Beaux-Arts design for a library in Milwaukee in 1895. But even after he repudi-ated the Parisian frills, he continued to use a similar method—whatever he wished to call it—to organize complex public buildings right through his career. His early institutional buildings such as Unity Temple and the Larkin Building emulated Beaux-Arts plans to help in their organization. The plan of his Imperial Hotel in Tokyo was a documented "steal" from the Beaux-Arts Grand Prix winner of 1864.

No such theft appears in the plans for Wright's later Guggenheim Museum and Marin County Civic Center, but these buildings reveal their form and function in another way. Anyone standing outside the Guggenheim can read its interior workings perfectly, as though with X-ray vision. Standing outside Wright's Beth Sholom Synagogue in Philadelphia, you don't even need the X-ray: the huge wire-glass roof is only translucent, not transparent, but the building is so well structured in terms of function that you seem to be able to look right into it.

Organizing houses is a different matter. Houses are relatively small and uncomplicated, and families can only loosely be called institutions. Sullivan's houses were few and undistinguished, while Richardson's were so large and complex that they read like his churches, courthouses, and libraries. Wright sought to organize his houses without stultifying the lives that unfolded inside. He could do this with his early houses because of their symmetry; for his later Prairie Style residences he dropped such formality but still gave his homes a crystalline compartmentalization worthy of a honeycomb.

The one element in the Beaux-Arts design method that Wright could never countenance was rigid adherence to the preliminary plan. Wright not only avoided committing himself on paper; he liked to change details on his projects right to the moment in which bricks and mortar made them immutable. David Dodge, a highly trusted apprentice from the 1950s, told me that when the Guggenheim was going up, Wright tore into one of the plans and, theoretically, demolished an entire wall. When Dodge warned, "Mr. Wright, that wall has already been built in New York City!" Wright had to accept this as one change he could not make. Dodge then reworked the drawing to rescind Wright's impetuous changes.

M any architects would have drawn a tiny sketch of a waterfall cottage the moment they saw Bear Run, but not Wright. His first *esquisse* existed just where he said it was: not on paper but in his mind. Fallingwater would stay in his mind for nine months until he was ready to draw it. It was as though he were setting himself a *concours* at the École des Beaux-Arts, except that he required no paper and he took nine months, not two, to give practical form to his initial image.

Without drawings, we cannot be sure, but Wright seems to have determined a *parti* for the Kaufmann house rather quickly: two crisscrossed balconies sailing over a cliff. Wright's name "Fallingwater" conveys the ideogram of the building as house-as-waterfall. At some basic level the *parti* may even have been prefigured by the nickname the Kaufmanns gave their old cabin on Bear Run: The Hangover.

Fallingwater's *parti* is one of the most distinctive in architecture, but when he fixed it in his mind, Wright had only an image, not yet a building. To flesh an image into a home he needed to devise a functional solution, a structural solution, and a formal solution that would satisfy the old Vitruvian triad. Wright had other tasks before him as well: to engage with the history of architecture that had gone before, and to forge a perfect relationship between the building and its site. "Can you say," he would challenge his apprentices, "when your building is complete, that the landscape is more beautiful than it was before?"

To these design tasks Wright brought exceptional gifts, which I would number as seven:

- His powerful visual memory, which allowed him to assess the natural features of a site and envision a building that would improve on nature.
- His adroitness in composing buildings in his mind, the way Mozart is said to have been able to compose an entire symphony in his brain.
- The mathematical precision that allowed him to draw a building on paper in near-perfect scale. David Dodge and other Taliesin apprentices told me they watched Wright draw lines that were virtually perfect to scale without measuring them.
- Wright's exceptional accuracy in envisioning a building on paper just as it would appear in reality. Consider how perfectly his Fallingwater perspective of 1935 prefigured Hedrich's 1937 photograph.
- His capacity to mimic anything in the history of architecture. The man was a sponge: he could glance at a building, a drawing, or a photograph in a magazine and understand in the blink of an eye how that precedent could strengthen the design he was working on.
- His understanding of how to impart humanistic values and spiritual richness to his buildings.
- His tenacity: he never gave up on any essential design idea. Though half or two-thirds of his projects died on the drafting table, nearly all his core concepts got built at some point in his long life.

Wright would have applied these gifts to his design thinking on Fallingwater, focusing above all on the demands of the site and the needs of the Kaufmanns. Any architect can speak of marrying a building to its site, but Wright took this truism to near-literal status. He saw his own Taliesin, for example, as "a house that hill might marry and live happily with ever after." The Bear Run valley offered no obvious spot for the Kaufmann house, but Wright managed to place it so adroitly that the views we get from the bridge, from the streambed, and from the clearing in the trees downstream are exactly the ones he set up to yield the most dramatic mix of nature and engineering.

After satisfying his site, Wright had to satisfy the needs of his clients. The stereotype of Wright as someone high-handed and arbitrary in handling his clients is incorrect. Wright insulted his clients plenty, but he planned their houses with the closest possible attention to their needs—as many testified. Ayn Rand, for example, was thrilled with Wright's design for her house: "You designed exactly the house I hoped to have. The next time somebody accuses you of cruelty and inconsideration toward clients, refer them to me." Cornelia Brierly and other Wright apprentices told abundant stories of the old man's devotion to his clients and his wish to make them happy. Besides, if it were true that Wright disregarded the needs of his clients, why do no two of his hundreds of homes look the same?

> *Why hadn't I been consulted?*
> *Our home might have faced the falls,*
> *not hung out over them*
> *—like life catapulted to the edge.*

So poet Frances Balter imagines Liliane Kaufmann deploring her lack of input on the planning of Fallingwater, though the evidence is that Liliane voluntarily passed up her chance to influence the design, rather than being denied it.

Balter's poem points out a fundamental problem in architectural design: getting clients to articulate what they want. Wright had to size up not just the Kaufmanns' physical needs but also their psychic needs, as though he were both their architect and their analyst. It was easy to list the basic program: hiking, sunbathing, weekend entertaining; but what of the Kaufmanns' aspirations for the house? Measured by the clock, Wright's professional interaction with E. J. and Liliane was slight: there were no hours together over a sketch pad, as in *Mr. Blandings Builds His Dream House,* nor yet the scores of memos that the Browns dispatched to Richard Neutra during the planning of Windshield. Instead, Wright keenly observed his clients at work and play, first as their host in Wisconsin in November 1934, then as their guest in Pittsburgh a month later, and again in the same respective roles in Arizona in February and in Pittsburgh in the spring and summer of 1935. He also had the evaluation of the Kaufmanns from his scout Karl Jensen, and Junior would have added more details about his parents during the five months in which he lived with Wright.

Rumor holds that Sigmund Freud psychoanalyzed Junior during their overlapping years in Vienna, but what Freud—even better, Jung, who enthusiastically engaged in the psychospatial analysis of houses—really needed to analyze was Fallingwater. It would be hard to find a house plan that better charted the dynamics of a dysfunctional family.

When we put Fallingwater on the couch, we see E. J. and Liliane locked in their solitary bedrooms, Junior isolated in the penthouse, each one of them corralled into a separate terrace. There is something wry in the way Wright gave the master bedroom to Liliane and not to E. J. (Olgivanna already commanded the master bedroom at Taliesin). Liliane's balcony, not E. J.'s, was the external highlight of the house. Wright also "gendered" the house, much as Victorian architects designated the den and billiards room for men and the parlor and sewing room for ladies. As an apprentice, he had watched Sullivan balance male verticals with female horizontals at the Wainwright Building. Just so does Liliane's balcony give Fallingwater its horizontal strength, while the two Kaufmann men counterbalance this with the vertical strength of the stone tower that carries their bedrooms.

Wright's domestic arrangements at Fallingwater seem to mix optimism with pragmatism, as we saw earlier with his penthouse steps. Even while isolating the three Kaufmanns in noncommunicating bedrooms, he married their fireplaces into a single chimney stack. The three-in-one fireplaces had practical value, but they seem also to have reflected Wright's sad take on a tortured family. What should have been a single hearth to represent the unity of the family presents itself instead as fragmented: one fireplace for the living room but also three more in isolation above. These dispersed hearths may have reflected Wright's own domestic turbulence, too. In his early houses going back to the 1880s, the single hearth had been an important simile of the unity of the family. Perhaps as an adulterer and deserter to his wife, Catherine, and their six children, Wright had since learned differently.

Wright now had the data he needed on the site, the client, the program, and the budget. These helped outline his vision of Fallingwater, but the house could still have assumed any number of variants. In isolating a definitive shape, he used the same design process anyone uses for a needed artifact, whether a baby rattle or an after-dinner speech. He assembled a huge number of possibilities, then reduced them to a manageable number by subjecting them to decision points. Each time he arrived at one of these design crossroads he determined which route he wanted to pursue, and never looked back. After making his way through a few thousand of these crossroads, he could give Fallingwater the "inevitable" look it finally assumed.

Some of Wright's design decisions came early: length and width of the house, its compass orientation, choice of materials, type of structure, and whether the house would sit low in the Bear Run gorge or high up. Other decisions came later: Bedrooms on one floor or two? Closets 7 feet high or only 6 and a half? Liliane's bathroom to get a toilet at the far end or on the side? Steps down to the water at 9-inch intervals or only 7? The speed at which an experienced architect processes such decisions can make a calculator look plodding.

The key was to make every decision comply with the Kaufmanns' functional intentions for the house. E. J. and Liliane looked forward—at least initially—to hosting the same boisterous crew of friends and relatives in Fallingwater that they had in The Hangover. This ideally called for a breezy one-story California-type house, essentially an update of Wright's home for Aline Barnsdall in Los Angeles fifteen years before. But that was not practical at Bear Run: the Barnsdall house ("Hollyhock") encompasses several thousand square feet on one level. There was no way Wright could pack such an enormous architectural spread anywhere on the Kaufmann property without distorting either the house or its natural setting.

Fallingwater would have to be shaped unlike any house Wright had fashioned before. To get the scenic placement of the house over the falls, Wright had to anchor it on a narrow ledge between the valley hillside and the Bear Run stream. He then stacked it four levels high, until it reached a height of roughly 40 feet—one of just a handful of his domestic designs to grow that tall. Then he flung the house out horizontally on cantilevered balconies, so that Fallingwater would encompass just 2,885 square feet inside but an additional 2,445 square feet of balconies hanging in the air. He pointed the main balcony roughly south, with sidepieces facing west and east, and here he made the living room. He reserved the terrace above for Liliane, also pointing south; on the same level the private terrace for E. J. points west and a balcony for guests points east; higher up was the penthouse for Kaufmann Jr. That left just a tiny basement level for a boiler room, a wine cellar, a toilet for the servants, and a food pantry, all of which Wright tucked among the boulders at the base of the house. On that same level he needed structural supports to allow the rest of the house to float in the air: a stone buttress wall and four—later reduced to three—diagonal reinforced-concrete "bolsters" to support the main terrace from below. By floating half his building in the air, Wright could erect a house of considerable dimension, roughly 60 feet wide and 80 feet long, on a plot of land that was considerably smaller.

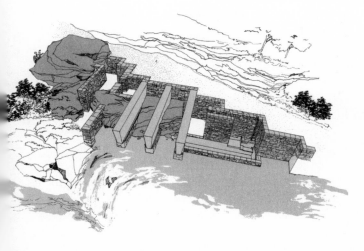

At the basement level, Fallingwater's "bolster" supports were laid in and over boulders

The cantilevered floors excluded any chance that Fallingwater would be built of wood, since only steel or reinforced concrete could carry them. Wright had employed cantilever technology several times, but just once before had he made it the structural key to a design. This was in his Imperial Hotel in Tokyo, made internationally famous when it survived the catastrophic 1923 earthquake there. Wright recalled the design process for the hotel in his *Autobiography*:

> Why not then carry the floors as a waiter carries his tray on upraised arm and fingers at the center—*balancing* the load? All supports centered under the floor slabs like that instead of resting the slabs on the walls at the edges as is usually the case? This meant the cantilever, as I had found by now. The cantilever is the most romantic, most free, of all principles of construction, and in this case it seemed the most sensible.

Fallingwater's main cantilever of reinforced concrete beams and joists extends the living room far into midair

Wright would make Fallingwater a structural twin of the Imperial Hotel, but with a key artistic difference. Since the hotel's cantilevers served a structural role only, they lay buried either in the mushy ground or at the core of the hotel's superstructure. No one could see them except where they extended out as balconies, and even there only the rare observer would have understood their structural function.

At Fallingwater, Wright used the cantilever not merely as a hidden structural device but as an expressive part of the architecture. Fallingwater would reveal its structure in the clearest and most dramatic way imaginable. (This was probably the main reason why Wright rejected a steel skeleton in favor of the newer technology of reinforced concrete for Fallingwater: steel is normally protected from fire and rust by being buried inside a building, while reinforced concrete would give the house a *visible* structure instead.) The waiter's diagonal fingers in Wright's analogy would become the diagonal bolsters emerging from the water, and the trays became Fallingwater's lyrical traylike balconies above. By means of these technical and artistic solutions, the *parti* of Fallingwater gained increased definition and ended as one of the sharpest in architecture. An amateur can draw the Taj Mahal from memory more easily than Fallingwater, but the visual complexity of the two buildings is not comparable. The basement and penthouse at Fallingwater recede from memory just as they literally recede from our vision. What remains indelibly are the thrusting balconies of the first and second floors, pulled out like drawers from a cabinet.

Wright anchored this "cabinet" just where nature would, wedging it among three large boulders lying north of the falls. He gave the prime structural role to the boulder that lies closest to the stream and is oriented east-west. He laid his concrete bolsters in and over this boulder. West of them he constructed the stone buttressing wall as a straight vertical rather than as a diagonal in profile; it carried the weight of the building's west wall. These four struts—three diagonal, one vertical—together sustain the four north-south beams that carry Fallingwater's main floor. What makes Fallingwater's main balcony a cantilever is the extension of the four beams far beyond the support-point of the bolsters.

Along with traditional Japanese architecture, Fallingwater was praised in every quarter as a supreme example of the integration of human work and nature. The early review of Fallingwater in *The New Masses,* for example, stressed that "never was nature more intimate. And this has been accomplished without freakishness, but rather as the logical fulfillment of the site and what it demanded." This delicate synthesis of nature and the built environment probably counts as the main reason why Fallingwater is such a well-loved work. The contouring of the house into cantilevered ledges responds so sympathetically to the rock strata of the stream banks that it *does* make Bear Run a more wondrous landscape than it had been before.

Nature had impact on Fallingwater's design in other ways, too. Wright often used nature as his structural exemplar, as in his treelike research tower for Johnson's Wax and the Price Tower at Bartlesville, Oklahoma. Were he ever asked to design a monumental building, Wright once said, he would go to the Grand Canyon to see how nature does it. Two instances of nature-as-structure particularly apply at Fallingwater. One is the analogy of the waiter's outstretched fingers with the diagonal bolsters; a second is the way the house follows nature in the selection of the invincible boulders for its foundations.

The engineers who later opposed Wright's design warned Kaufmann that the rock in the waterfall and in the hillside was unstable, which is why a cascade developed on Bear Run in the first place. This is true but irrelevant, since Wright used neither the waterfall nor the hillside for his foundation (though he gave the *illusion* that he had). He anchored the house exclusively in the boulders north of the falls, reasoning that they would have disappeared a hundred million years ago unless nature had certified their imperviousness to weathering.

When, however, Wright's apprentice Donald Hoppen praised his master's "uncanny sense of the *genius loci*" (the Roman "spirit of the place"), he meant it in more than a purely topographical sense. What Wright absorbed in his visits to Bear Run went beyond its waters, its trees, and its rock outcrops to encompass its animal life, the history and legends of the place, from George Washington to the Indians who supposedly had made campfires on the boulder where Wright would later set his fireplace. But we can imagine that nothing mesmerized him more than the waterfall. Most people today enjoy waterfalls, and they have been a favorite artistic subject for hundreds of years. The six nature scenes that George Washington commissioned for his dining room at Mount Vernon are not landscapes but waterscapes, half of them waterfalls.

What the eighteenth century saw in waterfalls was not something pleasurable but sublime. A post-Holocaust and post-Hiroshima age can never reconnect with the sublime as it was once perceived: as the untrammeled power of nature. The sublime excited our ancestors because, in a preindustrial world, nature was the most likely thing that would kill you. The falls of Bear Run are the primary natural force in these woods, but intimations of the sublime emanate also from the thick vegetation, the valley cliffs, the snakes you can still encounter, and the bears you hear about. Even the bridge upstream from the falls (concrete today, but wood when Wright first saw it) reminds us of the sublime, because crossing Bear Run would be a terrifying experience without it.

Wright was born so long ago and to a culture so distant that to him the sublime was not just a literary theory but a living emotion. This may explain why—exceptionally—he made not a single change to the physical environment of Bear Run. Certainly it was not from humility. Wright had no hesitation in improving on nature: at Taliesin he spent half a century moving roads, reconfiguring fields, and damming up the local stream. Yet he touched nothing at Bear Run, as though it was perfect for his purposes just as God had left it. The glen that looks admirable to us today would have seemed nearly miraculous to Wright in 1934, because it invited him to create something he had tried and failed to do a dozen times since the turn of the century, which was to cantilever a "waterfall cottage" over rushing water. Site and architect were just awaiting each other. We can document Wright's passion for the sublimity of waterfalls from his first trip to Japan in 1905. He returned from it with dozens of his own photographs and commercial postcards, a quarter of which were of waterfalls. On that trip or later, Wright purchased a colored woodblock view of Ono Falls by Hokusai, which juxtaposed a high waterfall with two cottages and a footbridge.

The first of Wright's dozen attempts to build in concert with water came in his 1908 project for the McCormick estate outside Chicago. Set high on a terrace overlooking Lake Michigan, this would have included an artificial waterfall plunging down into the lake. When Wright organized his own estate at Taliesin in 1911, he dammed up a creek to produce a pond and a spillway. The spillway was no raging torrent, but Wright maximized its effect by setting the main estate road on a bridge that made every visitor pass in front of the artificial waterfall, as they still do today (page 165). Around 1925, Wright harnessed the dam to a hydroelectric plant, which he housed in a tiny generator building that he cantilevered out next to the falls. The dam and cantilever were both previews of Fallingwater, and so was something else: Wright built rocks into the outer shell of the dam, which turned the spillway into a noisy splashing cascade of water. The dam was simplified after a flood in the 1930s and the "hydrohouse" was removed in the 1940s, but the sight and sound of falling water remains a joy to anyone approaching Taliesin today.

Bridge, cantilever, falling water, thundering noise—Wright had to contrive all these things at Taliesin, but a decade later he found them readymade at Bear Run. Finally, he could build something he had itched to do since his first trip to Japan. Here were a magnificent waterfall, an enchanting valley, and a client rich and courageous enough to pay for a house cantilevered over the falls. What Wright saw at Bear Run in December 1934 was not déjà vu but *jamais vu:* the nirvana he had dreamed of finding for half his life.

It is commonplace—though true—to note that the cascading profile of Fallingwater mimics the cascade of land down the steep gorge and the cascade of water over the falls. But the brilliant element in Fallingwater is that it does not merely overlook the falls, it *hovers* over them. Wright achieved this effect by observing that there are two waterfalls at Bear Run rather than just one. He then calculated the size and placement of the two main balconies to mimic nature. The first falls measure about 25 to 30 feet in height and the second some 7 to 10 feet, but the two fall lines are not parallel. The first waterfall cuts diagonally through the stream in a line roughly east-west, while the lip of the second cuts roughly northwest to southeast. This puts the two falls at a 45-degree angle of opposition to each other—an effect that Wright exaggerated into the 90-degree opposition of the two main balconies.

Any number of people today believe that water flows not merely alongside but *through* Fallingwater, as through a power dam. This illusion is much helped by the darkness at the bolster level, which makes it hard from a distance to determine the source of the water before it hits the falls. But the main reason why this cunning illusion works so well is the south-southeast orientation by which the house overlays the stream. The public was fooled by this illusion (the Latin *illudere* means "to fool") with the earliest published photographs of the house, as we learn from an early report that speculated on how E. J. could catch trout without having to get out of bed:

> First wild rumor was that a trout stream ran straight through the bedroom of the new Frank Lloyd Wright home at Bear Run, Pa so that Owner Edgar Kaufmann could hook himself a juicy breakfast of succulent fresh trout without getting out of bed. A little later news came that the furniture was carved out of solid rock. Next thing credulous Pittsburghers heard was that the house was gold-plated.

The illusion of water coursing through Fallingwater has implications for our reading of the house that go beyond E. J.'s breakfast. This illusion turns the house metaphorically into a power dam or a watermill set over the furious waters of a millrace. That industrial image may be one of the ways in which Wright conceived of Fallingwater, since it lies halfway between Mill Run (an industrial name to begin with) and Ohiopyle, where in 1934 Wright saw the falls still harnessed to industrial produc-

The dam and powerhouse at Ohiopyle as Wright saw them in 1934. Did this industrial image so close to Bear Run influence the industrial overlay he gave to Fallingwater?

tion. Do people who know Fallingwater only in photographs think turbines and flywheels are at work under the main balcony?

Once we read Fallingwater as a house of industry, then its association with Claude-Nicolas LeDoux's Inspector's house at the source of the Loue River becomes inescapable. The moment Fallingwater was finished, scholars pointed out its resemblance to LeDoux's much-published project drawing of around 1790. In his literal waterfall house, LeDoux proposed to run the river Loue through a building in the shape of a vertical, flattened doughnut. The image is so unforgettable that without hesitation we can declare that Wright knew it.* Nonetheless, how different the two waterfall houses are. LeDoux's has the coldness of a turbine, perverting nature into industrial service. Wright's house, extolling nature and hovering over it as a baldachin hovers over the Holy Eucharist, serves instead as a kind of blessing of nature.

The moment we perceive Fallingwater as an industrial image, we experience still another of its many layers of meaning, for Fallingwater does not solely emulate nature—it challenges it, too. Donald Hoffmann was poetic but accurate when he called the house "a great machine in the for-

---

*The United States came close to getting a waterfall building as its Capitol. Pierre-Charles L'Enfant intended to divert a tributary of the Potomac River so that water would gush from the basement of the Capitol and flow down the Washington Mall. That would surely have changed the image of the federal government forever.

est." Fallingwater looks most enchanting at night, when it detaches itself from nature and illuminates itself by electric light from within.

The concept of Fallingwater as "nature challenged" brings us back to Pittsburgh, which is the industrial environment that gives it text and context. E. J., as we have seen, spent his whole life wanting to erect something that would overshadow the buildings of his father and uncles, to say nothing of his more distant rivals Carnegie, Frick, and the Mellons. Fallingwater makes no sense in terms of Kaufmann's agenda unless we interpret it as both a dynastic monument and a civic monument of Pittsburgh. But how can it be the latter and still stand in thick woods forty-five miles away from the city? Wright's solution to E. J.'s needs, I believe, was to instill a second *genius loci* in the house, to make it reflect not just bucolic Bear Run but smoky old Pittsburgh. Had Wright literally meant the Kaufmann house to be a "waterfall cottage" it ought to have resembled the cozy bungalow in the waterfall view by Hokusai. Instead, the cottage grew in size, strength, and severity until it took on the industrial image that made it the perfect counterpart to the city that E. J. wanted to impress.

Would that explain the cognitive dissonance we feel when we stand before Fallingwater? The size and surface texture of the house make it cold and industrial; one could argue that had Wright and Kaufmann been truly respectful of Bear Run's environment they would not have imposed on it with so obtrusive a construction. Wright had crafted exquisite lodges of wood in his Lake Tahoe project of 1924: why did he not make the Kaufmanns' forest lodge out of wood rather than out of concrete, steel, and glass? Is it possible that (apart from practical reasons) Wright did this in compensation for the collapse of his hopes for the huge public works projects in Pittsburgh?

Wright himself suggested that Fallingwater was an alter ego to Pittsburgh in June 1935, the month in which he got the definitive rejection of his proposals for the Pittsburgh riverfront. In his fury he let loose a string of insults on the city: to a reporter asking how to improve the city he snarled: "It's cheaper to abandon it." But Wright also created a more constructive and even dreamy vision of Pittsburgh in a guest editorial in the *Sun-Telegraph*:

> Well—at this late day it isn't good medicine perhaps, to imagine (now) how the river might have been made into a beautiful feature by damming and pooling it into placid water and driving across the broad dams to the tune of waterfalls into and up to broad terraced levels picturesquely related to the water. . . .

How strikingly these terms, particularly the "tune of waterfalls," echoed Wright's thoughts after his first visit to Bear Run:

Visit to the waterfall in the woods stays with me and a domicile has taken vague shape in my mind to the music of the stream.

The river, the dams, the pool, the sight and sound of the waterfall, and the "broad terraced levels" that Wright had planned for Pittsburgh had fallen victim to the city's politicians and its jealous architects, but the same features all emerged three months later in Fallingwater.

This assessment of Fallingwater as Pittsburgh-on-Bear-Run makes it into a kind of industrial trophy, set in the bosom of nature and enhancing nature not by copying but by superimposing itself as a man-made nature—a literal *second* nature—over the real thing. It is unlikely to be coincidence that the nineteenth century saw Pittsburgh as just that—a "second nature" of industry that was as sublime in its terrifying way as nature itself. Visitors like Charles Dickens (in his *American Notes* of 1842) had long treated the city's smoke and fire, its audacious scale and complexity, as manifestations of the sublime. James Parton spelled this out in a memorable analysis of Pittsburgh in the January 1868 *Atlantic Monthly,* describing Pittsburgh as "Hell with the lid taken off," which Lincoln Steffens shortened in 1904 into his Pittsburgh aphorism of "Hell with the Lid Off." Parton did indeed say Pittsburgh looked like hell, but his text reveals how entranced he was by the city. Victorians like Parton recommended Niagara Falls and Pittsburgh as the two sights that best explained America to Europeans. The first conveyed the sublimity of nature in the New World; the second, the sublimity of American industry. Fallingwater gives us both.

The thrill of a man-made sublime was certainly not lost on Wright. He may have been a master interpreter of nature, but he responded to the expressive power of industry, too. All his life he recalled the view over Lake Michigan from Sullivan's penthouse in the Auditorium Building: "The red glare of the Bessemer steel converters to the south of Chicago would thrill me as the pages of the Arabian Nights used to with a sense of terror and romance."

By making Fallingwater a counterfoil to Pittsburgh, Wright plumbed an essential paradox of the city itself, because the twin glories of Pittsburgh have historically been nature and industry. Almost every visitor to the city since the pollution cleanup of the 1940s and '50s remarks on its enthralling natural setting, and many comment that San Francisco alone of American cities surpasses Pittsburgh in its memorable combination of water and hills. Wright's 1935 editorial makes clear that he could discern the potential beauty of Pittsburgh even through the industrial fog. Pittsburgh and Bear Run being geologically identical, they would also have been visually interchangeable until the eighteenth century, with a plenitude of water, steep green hillsides, and exposed strata of stone common to both. The hollows in Pittsburgh's Frick or Schenley parks would still look like Bear Run today except that their primordial torrents of water were diminished to mere creeks years ago. Today nature remains a strikingly visible component of Pittsburgh, while, conversely, industry remains a strikingly visible component of Bear Run.

The Kaufmanns used Fallingwater as a counterfoil to industry. Five days they would toil in the midst of Pittsburgh's pollution, then retire for two days in their unspoiled paradise. Pittsburgh had a long tradition of that kind of escape, beginning in 1851 with Evergreen Hamlet as one of the earliest commuter suburbs in the United States. If the squalor of industry heightens an appreciation of nature, then nobody in North America loved nature as much as the citizens of Pittsburgh. But industry can also aid our appreciation of nature, as in the railroad of 1852 that enabled the men of Evergreen Hamlet to commute between their hilltop homes and their offices in the city. Wright may have had a similar argument in industrializing Fallingwater. He seems to be saying that this was the modern way to lose oneself in nature.

Wright made still another discovery in his trips to Pittsburgh, which was the power of its architecture. His guest editorial in the *Sun-Telegraph,* quoted in part above, emphasized the striking architectural potential he found in the city. Wright did not merely tour Richardson's internationally famous courthouse, but also sought out the same architect's industrial-strength Emmanuel Episcopal Church, which few visitors bothered to see in those years. Wright talked about Pittsburgh when he gathered with his apprentices back home at Taliesin that same June, then repeated his praise of the city in several Wisconsin newspapers. His point was that Richardson's Pittsburgh buildings were great because they reflected the power of a great city. That would be his agenda for Fallingwater.

B y the spring of 1935, certainly by early summer, Wright had drawn numerous impressions from the site, his clients, and Pittsburgh, but these evidently had not yet cleared a path to a definitive house design in his mind. The terrain was obviously tricky, even for him: a boulder-strewn hillside, not a flat Midwest field. So was the engineering of what proved to be an intractable structural problem. It is hard to say what missing piece Wright needed to solve the puzzle, but it appears—from his buildings, not from his carefully self-censored writings—that at some point in nearly every design problem Wright forced himself to open up to outside influences, particularly from the past. He would begin by rethinking some relevant project he had wrestled with earlier in his career, then to consider certain historical buildings that had come to his attention. We could call this stage "lessons from history."

Wright was the most facile assimilationist in the history of art and architecture. "You cannot not know history," Wright's old antagonist Philip Johnson famously said (an echo, perhaps, of Abraham Lincoln's "We cannot escape history"). Wright occasionally cultivated the image of the antihistorical radical who owed nothing to earlier tradition, but this was pure posturing. Designing a palace for the Grand Canal in Venice in 1954, he made clear how attached he had always been to the earlier architectural traditions: "True modern architecture, like classical architecture, has no age. It is a continuation of all the architecture that has gone before, not a break with it." Wright could "not not know" and could not not be influenced by every building on earth once he had seen it, or a picture of it. As early as the 1920s critics recognized that his eclecticism actually exceeded that of the Beaux-Arts architects he ridiculed. Wright hid his copying better because he used so many sources: Roman, medieval, Renaissance, colonial English, colonial Spanish, seventeenth-century Italian, eighteenth-century French, Beaux-Arts, International Style, Mayan, Aztec, Japanese, and Native American.

The following story has been told in so many variations that at least some part of it must be true: a scholar visiting Taliesin West spots a book on Mayan architecture and says: "Why, Mr. Wright, this temple looks just like your Barnsdall house," whereupon Wright darts over, slams the book shut, and declares: "Never saw that book in my life!" Artists are notorious for never revealing their sources of inspiration: the painter Jim Dine once solemnly told me that the only painter he had ever looked at was the fifteenth-century Petrus Christus. But we can see that Wright got design ideas from old books and old buildings a hundred times. He transposed the ninth-century pagoda at Horiu-ji into his "tree" system for his 1929 St.-Mark's-in-the-Bouwerie towers, for example, and the Guggenheim echoes both Baroque churches and Mesopotamian ziggurats. Does that make Wright derivative? No: when the furnace of artistic energy burns as fiercely as it did for an artificer like Wright, the original contributions burn off, and only the new work is left.

Years ago the scholar Joseph Connors drew attention to the "brilliant and beautiful eclecticism of the [Fallingwater] design, the slightly shocking way in which elements from different visual worlds are combined." Now we can see that the external references at Fallingwater are even more numerous than Connors or anyone has heretofore guessed. As with all the literary allusions James Joyce was jamming into *Finnegans Wake* in the same years, we will never spot all these references, but a safe rule of thumb is that they fall into three categories: quotes from Wright's own works, references from the architectural past, and citations of Wright's contemporaries.

We'll start with Wright's own architectural backlog. By 1934, Wright had worked in architecture for half a century: his production by then amounted to about 250 completed buildings and twice that many unbuilt projects. Wright never constructed the same building twice, but scores of times a design that fate had aborted (in the form of a dead or bankrupt client) would come to life decades later. The ziggurat for the Gordon Strong planetarium that aborted in 1927 came to life in the 1950s as the Guggenheim. The rotated-axes tower of the St.-Mark's-in-the-Bouwerie project that failed in New York in 1929 rose in 1955 as the Price Tower in Oklahoma. The unbuilt Steel Cathedral of 1926 mutated several times— once as a failed chapel for the Kaufmanns—until it grew in the 1950s into Philadelphia's Beth Sholom Synagogue. The unbuilt circular Valley National Bank for Tucson was recycled a decade later into the Annunciation Greek Orthodox Church of Milwaukee; a dead project for an Oregon newspaper came to life as a headquarters for Johnson's Wax. Nearly everything that Wright could not build at first he got to build later—so long as there was a client to back him.

It was logical that Fallingwater should sum up so many of Wright's earlier built or unbuilt designs since it materialized at the end of his longest fallow period, when the host of projects that budded in his mind between 1928 and 1935 had germinated into only two buildings. This enforced idleness left him freer to dream than at any other moment of his career.

Irritated by accusations that Fallingwater copied the Europeans, Wright insisted that it was a strictly organic development from his early work. In 1957 he declared that "the Gale House built in wood and plaster in 1909 was the progenitor, as to general type, of Fallingwater, 1936." That declaration is accurate: the home for Laura (Mrs. Thomas) Gale in Oak Park *was* Wright's fundamental breakthrough toward Cubism in architecture from the exact year in which Braque and Picasso were working out Cubism in painting. Here we see prefigurations of Fallingwater's flat roofs, its massive chimney wall, four similar horizontal slab overhangs, and four cantilevered balconies (page 163). Fallingwater's debt to the Gale house would be even more obvious had the Gale balconies been rendered in reinforced concrete, as Wright apparently proposed. Even the corner windows and the ribbon windows at the Gale house are predecessors— less radical, to be sure—to the corresponding windows at Fallingwater. The Gale house lacks the drama of Fallingwater because its site is banal and its composition is predictable: its upper balcony pulls back from the lower, whereas at Bear Run the reverse is true.

What becomes evident only in a model or schematic drawing is the radical Cubist nature of the Gale house, which seems to have no core mass at all. The barely sustained equilibrium of horizontal and vertical spars that simultaneously push in and pull out from all sides forms a clear prototype for the crisscrossed balconies and overhangs of Fallingwater. No wonder European architects pointed to the Gale house as the start of an entirely new conception of architectural mass.

In 1916 the Dutch architect Robert van 't Hoff—who knew the Gale house from a visit with Wright—reproduced it in a concrete villa near Utrecht. Then came two even more interesting echoes. In 1923 the Dutch painter Theo van Doesburg and the De Stijl architect Cornelius van Eesteren exhibited in Paris a three-dimensional drawing that radicalized the Gale house into a free-floating Cubist maelstrom. (The early abstractionist painter Piet Mondrian was an important intermediary in this development.) Just months later that same year, Gerrit Rietveld produced his Schröder house in Utrecht, which seemed to blast the Gale house apart, then glue the bits and pieces together where they fell.

Lacking documentation, we have no basis on which to say whether Wright liked or loathed these three Dutch variants of his Gale house, although his track record would suggest the latter. What we *can* securely say is that Wright was aware of them, since van 't Hoff kept feeding Wright news of modern architecture in Europe right through the twenties.

Today, tourists to Oak Park ignore the Gale house or give it a perfunctory nod compared to the deep bow they render to the Robie house, which Wright finished in another Chicago neighborhood the same year. Ask these passersby which of the two houses most looks forward to Fallingwater, and nearly all would choose the slick Robie over the plodding Gale design. But the more perceptive observers would answer "both": Robie for form, Gale for intellectual content. Robie shares with Fallingwater the dramatic cantilevered overhangs, the cross-axiality of the main masses, and the counterbalance of its huge vertical chimney wall with its horizontal "trays," much as the stone tower of Fallingwater would counterbalance its balconies three decades later. The Robie house even "organizes" itself in a diagonal perspective view that prefigures the forced photogeneity of Fallingwater. But we can take the European modernists' word for it: the less well resolved Gale house was the more intellectually fertile of the two. Both these 1909 houses count as important milestones on Wright's road to Fallingwater, almost as though he yearned to recapture the phenomenal production he had achieved before scandal shunted him into a decades-long detour.

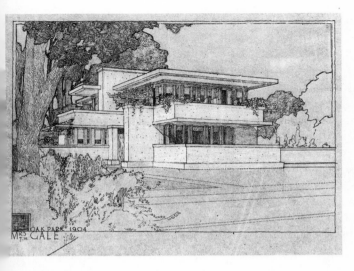

Wright's 1909 Laura Gale house in Oak Park was an early prototype for Fallingwater (the date 1904 was later added to the drawing in error)

The Gale and Robie houses were fine gems among the architect's early homes, but for Wright the jewel among his domestic designs was Taliesin. If Gale provided the analytical framework for Fallingwater and Robie the impetus for its form, then Taliesin endowed the new house with a heart. Just one look at Taliesin shows a dozen features that it shares with Fallingwater, from the rough horizontal stonework that Wright successfully recaptured at Bear Run to the gold-colored interior plastering that he tried—but failed—to upgrade to real gold on Fallingwater's balconies. Taliesin also looms largest among the models for Fallingwater because Liliane and E. J. Kaufmann enjoyed the house so much during their November 1934 stay.

But Taliesin also presents a significant problem as a source for Fallingwater. Suppose the Kaufmanns said to Wright in November or December 1934: "Frank, build us a home just like yours." Surely other

Gerrit Rietveld's Schröder house of 1923 in Utrecht "seemed to blast the Gale house apart, then glue the bits and pieces together where they fell"

prospective clients had asked Wright to copy his house, but none got their wish before the Kaufmanns. (Perhaps these other clients had not earned or deserved it, in Wright-speak.) Cloning Taliesin for the Kaufmanns, even though he would retain the original, meant intermingling his architectural gene pool with theirs: not merely a donation but symbiosis. True, having the Kaufmanns live just like him would give Wright a psychic power over them, but it would diminish him, too, since any replica lessens the original. (Fundamentalist cultures intuitively understood this when they opposed photography as taking away from their spirits.) Taliesin would never be exclusively Wright's again: henceforth, the Kaufmanns would own part of it, and part of him.

Were this a mere commercial enterprise Wright would have imitated his house as readily as Gilbert Stuart cranked out copies of his portrait of George Washington, but Taliesin was not merely Wright's house: it was his life. He had constructed it on ancestral land in 1911 as a love nest to share with Mamah Borthwick Cheney after he abandoned his home and family in Oak Park. Then, three years later, the tragedy of his life: a crazed servant murdered Cheney and her children, and torched the house. Wright reconstructed Taliesin after 1914 and again after a second fire in 1925. Now, in the 1930s, he was rebuilding parts of it once more, just as he was reviving a family life with his third wife, Olgivanna. In the end, Wright evidently decided it was worth reproducing Taliesin for the Kaufmanns, but the emotional demand of this act went to his very soul.

What exactly did Wright take from Taliesin for the Kaufmanns? We already saw their similarity in waterfalls, though Bear Run's is natural and Taliesin's synthetic. Wright, in addition, gave the Kaufmanns Taliesin's terraces, its overhangs, its rough stonework inside and out, its asymmetrical and informal plan, its diagonal bolsters, the similar way both houses descend a hillside toward water, and numerous minor connections. Among the smaller resemblances between the two houses are the square recessed cove ceiling in Wright's bedroom, which reappears, modified, in the Kaufmanns' living room; and Wright's private half-terrace/half-balcony at Taliesin, which at Fallingwater became E. J.'s private half-terrace/half-balcony. Even the carpets that festoon the parapets in Wright's perspective drawing of Fallingwater recall Taliesin, where you can still see them hanging over the loft-parapets in the living room and in Wright's office. The history of architecture presents many replicas, but Fallingwater is close to being Taliesin déjà vu—or *déjà entendu,* rather, since the two homes do not merely look alike: the waterfalls below their balconies make them sound alike, too.

· · ·

Wright's dam at Taliesin provided him with falling water, thundering noise, and a structure cantilevered over the falls—a decade before he saw Bear Run

If the list of houses that Wright recycled from his own *oeuvre* into Fallingwater turns out to be short—Gale, Robie, Taliesin—the list of buildings or styles he appropriated from history for the same task is long. Leaving his allusions to colonial New England kitchens for the discussion of Fallingwater's interior, the inventory starts with two or three Italian elements at Fallingwater—Italy and Japan being the only foreign countries in which he ever spent more than a week or two. Distinctly Italian in flavor are the four trellises in and around the house: one as part of the living-room ceiling, one immediately outside, one over Shady Lane, and one in the guesthouse. The stone tower that rises straight through the house has both the form and function of a Florentine or Sienese house tower, or *casa-torre*. Originally freestanding, these *casa-torri* survive by the hundreds in Tuscany, now embedded in horizontally disposed palaces that grew around them—effectively, just what we see at Fallingwater. The American who wrote more about Tuscan house towers than anyone was the historian Ferdinand Schevill, who Wright publicly called his closest friend. But Wright knew *casa-torri* even better than Schevill, because he had spent the whole year 1910 living in Florence.

Wright's Italian quotations at Fallingwater were in the vernacular or folk mode, not in the learned fashions of academic architects. This continued the tradition of the Italian-style farmhouse wing that Wright erected at Taliesin right after his return from Italy. Something else—very modest indeed—caught Wright's eye in Italy. Countless Italian tenements and even palaces that were built in pre-W.C. days now sport bathrooms that are typically cantilevered outside the main structural walls on wooden or steel beams. That exactly describes the bathrooms for E. J. and

Junior that Wright stuck out over Shady Lane, on the back wall of Fallingwater. By cantilevering the penthouse and second-floor bathrooms, Wright also obtained extra light for the dining area below.

Certain of Wright's historical references in Fallingwater are so conspicuous that there can be little doubt that he wanted us to catch them. We have already explored the probable historical context that lies behind the zigzag staircases on the west terrace. That pueblo-style staircase, like so much of Fallingwater, pays tribute to the Anasazi, Hohokam, and Pueblo Indian sites in the Southwest. The Cherokee red of the steel window frames, Fallingwater's freely asymmetrical plan, and the broad dun-colored terraces all link the house with the Southwest. Listen to what Friar Francisco Atanasio Dominguez wrote about the pueblo at Picuries around 1760:

> On this flat room [at the lowest level of the pueblo] there is another small ladder that rests on another flat room, and so another and another up to the top, the flat roof of one house being the terrace of another and serving as a landing between one ladder and the next.

Does this not capture the spatial experience of Fallingwater? The pueblo form had for years fascinated progressive architects like Irving Gill, a Wright acquaintance who began putting up pueblo-style houses in California early in the twentieth century. In those same years, Wright's future collaborator R. M. Schindler also saw the design possibilities inherent in the pueblo: his photo of Taos pueblo from 1915 still survives.

Wright was intrigued by the problem of incorporating external pueblo forms into Fallingwater, which he did in the balconies and the penthouse steps. But his main object was to exploit the visual and spiritual intensity of the spatial sequence inside a pueblo. This simulated pueblo experience was one of several ways by which he built into Fallingwater the timelessness that so many observers have found there. Most of the references Wright embedded in Fallingwater were culturally American, and so would have meant little to European modernists in the thirties, had they caught them. The practice of cultural grounding in architecture was in any case discouraged by the International Style, although more unconventional modernists like Alvar Aalto, and, sometimes, Le Corbusier, refused to abandon it.

But am I correct in hypothesizing that Wright knew—and cared—enough about the old pueblos and other Native American structures to incorporate them into Fallingwater? Written evidence is scant, but the chronology is perfect: Wright was living in the Southwest when he wrestled with the question of Fallingwater. Then we have the kiva that Wright himself designed as a pseudo-underground chamber at Taliesin West, which proves his knowledge of the originals. Third, we know Wright loved to visit the cliff dwellings of the Southwest. In March of 1935, Wright wrote E. J. from Arizona: "I wish you were both going to be with us Saturday and Sunday on the trip to the Cliffdwellers. I spoke of it to Junior but he thought 300 miles a long drive as no doubt it is."

Where was Wright going? Taking his "300 miles" as one-way distance from Chandler and Wright's specification of "the Cliffdwellers," then he was probably setting out for the famous cliff dwellings at Mesa Verde National Park in Colorado, some 320 miles distant. At other times Wright would have observed the cliff dwelling villages at Canyon de Chelly National Monument in Arizona and the ruins at Chaco Canyon National Monument in New Mexico (without cliff dwellings). We know that he also enjoyed visiting the so-called Montezuma Castle in Arizona, and then pushing on to the Grand Canyon and Las Vegas, but a weekend trip would not have allowed time for this.

Assuming from these parameters that it was the Mesa Verde that Wright studied in the midst of his thinking on Fallingwater, we need to pay special attention to the similarity of its three-story stone tower with the three-story central tower at Fallingwater. Fallingwater's masonry style may also derive from the excellent and highly colored masonry at the Mesa Verde or from the stunning stone-laying at other ancient sites like Pueblo Bonito and Chetro Ketl at Chaco Canyon. Scholars tell us that these walls were originally stuccoed over, but Wright would have taken them for what they were: the most lyrical stonework in North America— prior to Fallingwater.

But—you might reasonably object—how can Wright have taken inspiration from ancient towers in Italy and *also* from the American Southwest? That is just what Joseph Connors meant by the "brilliant and beautiful eclecticism" of Fallingwater: its ability to fuse two sources into one. Musical composers do this all the time: Mahler and Bizet gently and Charles Ives stridently, and so do architectural composers. The bridge that H. H. Richardson fashioned between his Pittsburgh courthouse and the corresponding jail synthesized the form of the Rialto Bridge in Venice with the function of that city's Bridge of Sighs. Wright had been well schooled in the overlay of images by designers like Richardson, who regarded such riddles as the highest form of architectural wit. Were we to accuse Wright of contradicting himself with all these images, he could always find justification in Walt Whitman:

Do I contradict myself?
Very well then I contradict myself,
(I am large, I contain multitudes.)

I f Wright was so strongly drawn to amalgamating features of older buildings into Fallingwater, he was even more susceptible to drawing inspiration from buildings of his own era. Orthodox Wrightians regard the suggestion that Wright "borrowed" from his contemporaries as damnable heresy. The architect Eric Lloyd Wright would get livid—I observed this once myself—at any suggestion of a link between his grandfather's Fallingwater and other contemporary houses, particularly the Lovell house in Los Angeles, which is one of the links I propose here.

Scholars writing on Fallingwater for too long played the role of enablers to the fiction that Wright was influenced by no other buildings in his design of the house. The old literature on Fallingwater propagated that fiction even through its choice of illustrations. Five of the seven previous books on the house carried photographs of no building but Fallingwater itself. Robert McCarter's study carried pictures of six other buildings, but all were by Wright. Kaufmann Jr.'s coffee-table book on Fallingwater was similarly monopolistic, admitting only LeDoux's Loue River design and (in an introduction written by Mark Girouard) a smattering of country lodges. Depriving readers of comparisons with any other buildings greatly strengthens the fallacy that Fallingwater's design has nothing in common with the architecture that preceded it.

An assessment of artistic originality so perverse merits no rebuttal, but Wright rebutted it anyway, in a string of buildings that make crystal-clear how much he was influenced by contemporary architects. It was unremarkable that his Heurtley house of 1902 copied the side doorway of H. H. Richardson's Glessner house of 1886: for a novice architect that was a normal process of influence. But when in 1947 the world-famous Frank Lloyd Wright was *still* unable to forget Richardson's doorway when he designed the Morris store for San Francisco, then one must speculate that the man was exceptionally vulnerable to outside influences.

The peculiarity is that Wright often emulated architects who possessed less talent than he did. Borrowing from second-rate predecessors by itself constitutes no problem—Shakespeare got half his dramatic material that way—but the trick is not to lose your own artistic balance when you stoop to pick up someone else's work. For a quarter of a century after the Robie house had astonished Chicago, until Fallingwater, Wright would not speak with such artistic clarity again.

I earlier characterized Wright as the greatest assimilationist in the history of architecture, but as he got older, he learned how to borrow images without losing his own style. He was still too eager an assimilationist of the Bauhaus style in his 1931 "House on the Mesa" project, which with bitter humor he deliberately cast in the Germanic mode—flat roof, transparency, industrial precision—solely to get it admitted into MoMA's International Style show. Now, four years later, Bear Run would provide the perfect stage on which to exact final revenge on the European modernists.

In planning Fallingwater to exact artistic revenge, Wright was in lockstep with Kaufmann, who wanted it to exact social revenge against the snobbish bluebloods of Pittsburgh. Just as E. J. was a "social vaulter" rather than a social climber, so Wright sought not merely to catch up with the European modernists but to vault over them. Wright's daringly Europeanized design for Fallingwater said in effect: "I showed Europe how to do the new architecture in 1910; but they stripped it of life, made it a dry mechanical thing. Now, I'll remake the puny things they have done into something that will make them gasp all over again." Fallingwater would replay Wright's battle with Adler and Sullivan's draftsmen half a century earlier: Jews, British, Germans, Scandinavians—the whole of Europe to be whipped a second time.

If he was to beat Europe, especially Germany, at its own architectural game, Wright had taken on the right partner to achieve it. The 1932 MoMA exhibition showed how far Europe had moved ahead of the United States in contemporary architecture. Wright and Kaufmann knew how to beat German modernism better than most Americans because they knew the original so intimately: the former motivated by hatred, the latter by admiration for it. Fallingwater was not in use a month before critics pointed out how many features Wright had cribbed from the International Style. MoMA's January 1938 press release on Fallingwater acknowledged these borrowings, although it insisted that the borrowed features were American-born, and were simply being repatriated from Europe to the land of their birth. Wright, too, regarded these appropriations not as borrowings but as restitution.

For years Wright had been on record as belittling Gropius, Mies, Le Corbusier, and his other European modernist rivals. Now in 1931 he specifically anathematized them: "I believe Le Corbusier and the group around him are extremely useful, extremely valuable, especially, as an enemy." At first he mocked the European modernists as "Internationalists" to make them sound Communist, but later he called them the New Order to make them into Nazi-fascists. In 1934 he equated them outright with Hitler's storm troopers: "They ask for the formula and as much uniformity as they can get—so they can goose-step." To Wright, the most dangerous of the Europeans were Neutra and Schindler. Wright made clear he was out to beat them in 1931: "Richard [Neutra] has evidently gone head over heels—Le Corbusie [*sic*]. Rudolph [Schindler], too. It is a pity. But there is nothing to be done about it. I suppose I shall have to turn on them myself and show them up soon."

Wright's enmity toward the Europeans is comprehensible at one level, since he felt they had stolen modern architecture from him. At another level it bordered on the pathological: the more he copied from them, the more he needed to hate them. And copy from them he did. The architectural and urbanism critic Lewis Mumford displayed both insight and wit when he mischievously described Frank Lloyd Wright in 1928 as schooling himself through Le Corbusier—the opposite of what everyone else was saying at the time. Wright conceded his debt to Le Corbusier in his clever aphorism about the latter's usefulness as an enemy, but he never acknowledged the size of his debt.

It ought not surprise us that Wright began borrowing from Le Corbusier as early as 1923, because Le Corbusier, Mies, and Gropius were ideologically much closer to him than they had once seemed. Certainly the split between Wright and Le Corbusier was exaggerated: when Le Corbusier made outrageous statements such as "A house is a machine for living in," he was probably modeling himself on Wright. The two men were both much alarmed by urban sprawl; both had great reverence for building materials; both created prototypes for low-cost housing; and both used systematic proportioning scales (Wright in his Usonian houses, Le Corbusier in his customized "modulor"). Le Corbusier was hardly the fanatic of mechanized life that Wright made him out to be. A decade before Fallingwater, he combined rock-faced walls with high-tech industrial finishes and gave life to his buildings by lifting them up on concrete legs, or *pilotis*. Wright used both these innovations at Fallingwater. Le Corbusier's Pavillon de l'Esprit Nouveau of 1925 stepped aside to let a tree grow through: Fallingwater did the same thing. Wright evidently studied Le Corbusier's 1929 Villa Savoye with equal care. There, the stair tower marks the only curve in an otherwise rectilinear main floor; at Fallingwater the only significant deviation from the rectilinear is the far end of the "hatch" stairs leading down to the water. Originally, Wright made this feature straight-ended, then switched it to its current eye-catching curve.

Fallingwater works so differently from Wright's earlier homes that if not his revenge against the Europeans, it is surely his answer to them. The differences emerge the moment we compare Fallingwater with Kentuck Knob, the home Wright built not far south of Fallingwater in 1954 for the dairyman who sold milk from Kaufmann's cows. Kentuck Knob perfectly articulates what Wright meant by organic architecture or the "natural house." It is a modest one-story house, set low on the ground and respecting nature by standing well down from the brow of its hill. This differs markedly from the tall, complex, and industrial feel of Fallingwater, which assumes such a provocative stance against nature. Inside, Kentuck Knob has the warm and beguiling comforts of a typical Wright living room, with a sumptuous wood-paneled cathedral ceiling. Kentuck Knob is also marvelously decorated with a clerestory frieze intricately cut out with a jigsaw, letting light throw changing patterns on the walls and floor all day. Inside and out, the house echoes the intricate diagonalities articulated in the plan.

Visitors who see both houses on the same day are challenged by Fallingwater but charmed by Kentuck Knob. The unyielding rectilinearity of Fallingwater allows for neither decoration nor diagonals, making it exceptionally stark for a Wright house. This perhaps explains why Fallingwater, though twenty years older, looks more modern than Kentuck Knob. Fallingwater was obviously something new in the line of Wright's homes from the 1890s through the 1950s, but it formed a singular detour, not a new road. In design terms Fallingwater was a creation that Wright would never revisit.

So numerous are the departures from the usual Wright vocabulary at Fallingwater that we are compelled to see it as a virtual notebook of lessons that Wright took from the Europeans, starting with Le Corbusier, Mies, Gropius, Schindler, and Neutra. The most pervasive of these lessons was the avoidance of ornament. Wright learned the joy of ornament from Louis Henry Sullivan, and adorned all his works with art glass, paint, decorative bands of wood or concrete, and inscriptions. At Fallingwater, however, he used less ornament than in any previous building: just some shield-shaped light covers outside and one stylized cornice inside. Other major European-influenced elements are the use of concrete, the cantilevers, the widespread glazing, and the Cubist or minimalist plan. Wright claimed that the Europeans owed these features to him and not he to them, which may be technically true, since he had used cantilevered balconies and ribbon windows in embryonic form in his Gale and Robie houses decades before. But the fact remains that impartial observers regarded Fallingwater as the most Europeanized building of his career.

Wright's use of reinforced concrete is one example of transatlantic sharing in the design of Fallingwater, since he had never used the technique in a home before. Reinforced concrete (ferroconcrete) was a European technique that Ernest Ransome brought from England to the United States in the 1890s, but it proved slow to catch on. Wright's Unity Temple was a world landmark in expanding the nonindustrial use of the material, but the French and Germans took the lead in exploiting its artistic possibilities, particularly in Auguste Perret's factory and commercial projects around 1905, and in an elegant office building project by Mies twenty years later.

In the 1920s, as we saw, Wright incorporated reinforced-concrete cantilevers in the engineering of his Imperial Hotel, but the memorable exploitation of the cantilever for artistic effect in that decade belonged to Gropius's wall of glass at the Bauhaus. Wright had used a nearly all-glass corner window three decades previously, in the Gale house, but his first entirely glazed corner in which glass abuts against glass without any intervening support came only with his Ennis and Freeman houses in Los Angeles in 1923 and 1924. The mitered corner windows in the Freeman house look impressive as they rise in their horizontal frames up two continuous stories, but Gropius's Fagus factory had already captured this effect in 1911. The three-story glazed tower wall at Fallingwater was basically another restatement of that same effect, but made brilliant by the way Wright put two tiny casement windows together at the corners. When these windows swing open, the corner dematerializes altogether.

Among his various "enemies," Mies van der Rohe was the designer Wright most respected, so it is unsurprising that the plan of Fallingwater—among the most abstract and ethereal of his career—appears to show the influence of Miesian prototypes. For years Wright had sought to "break out of the box" of uninspired house design, but until Fallingwater he had generally retained conventional external walls. The discontinuous wall fragments at Fallingwater make you think that some drunk had begun to doodle with a T-square. Wright had never produced so powerful an architectural abstraction as the Fallingwater plan before, which makes it possible, even likely, that he was quoting from Mies and Theo van Doesburg, both of whom saw architecture as essentially a configuration of planes. Mies's widely published brick villa project of 1923 well conveys his high intellectualism and arbitrariness in a plan that does not merely break the box but explodes it. The plan of Fallingwater is less radical than the one proposed by Mies, but with the critical difference that Wright's plan was buildable, while Mies's was a theoretical demonstration. Fallingwater's plan also has parallels in Mies's 1930 Tugendhat house, which also has glazed front and side walls and a similar zigzag back wall. Mies's walls are disjointed but continuous, while Fallingwater's walls are both disjointed and discontinuous. In terms of plan, which architect was the more Miesian now?

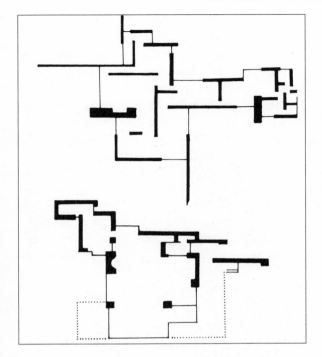

A comparison of
schematic plans
of Fallingwater (*bottom*)
and Mies van der Rohe's
1923 project for a brick
villa (*top*)

The three-story stone
tower and window wall

Fallingwater was by no means the first evidence of Wright's learning from the Europeans, but it was the first successful synthesis of what he had observed. For Wright the learning process from Gropius and Mies started in the 1920s in his four concrete-block houses for Los Angeles, which were more standardized and "industrialized" than the homes he had designed before. The highly mechanistic house he furnished his cousin Richard Lloyd Jones in Tulsa in 1929 shows him using concrete blocks in concert with two-story walls of glass. The Jones house was the most severe design of his career to that point, but it was so Europeanized that Wright appeared to have lost his own voice. By the time he came to design Fallingwater, Wright had subordinated the lessons of Mies to his own agenda. He was his own man again.

Gropius annoyed Wright more than Mies, probably because he formed a bigger ideological threat. In actuality, there was little Wright could have objected to in Gropius's curriculum at the Bauhaus, especially at the beginning. Like Wright, the Bauhaus showed great concern for integrity of materials and economy of design; it, too, sought the integration of all the arts, and its curriculum was based on an apprentice system in which the older students taught the younger. If Wright disdained the Bauhaus so much, why did he copy so much of its curriculum when he opened his rival school at Taliesin a decade later? Or did he just hate to share the spotlight?

Schindler and Neutra have a special place among the architects Wright studied, because Schindler worked for Wright in the years from 1920 to 1924 and Neutra in 1924–25. Wright knew their mature buildings firsthand, while he probably knew the work of Mies, Gropius, and Le Corbusier only from photographs. Schindler and Neutra had left Europe before the rise of the Bauhaus, but their California houses were among the earliest International Style designs anywhere.

Just as Richardson learned from his student Stanford White, and Sullivan from his assistant Wright, so Wright (who in person and in print emphasized his need to learn from younger people) was strongly influenced by Schindler. Schindler's impact came in several ways: it was he—even if not he alone—who alerted Wright to the vernacular adobe architecture of the Southwest; in the 1920s he was a main conduit of European design ideas to Wright; and Wright seems to have absorbed ideas from Schindler's later houses. Wright could not have escaped knowing Schindler's 1928 Wolfe house on California's Catalina Island, because it was shown in photographs and drawings at the same UCLA show that prompted Wright to call Schindler and Neutra thieves. The Wolfe house

R. M. Schindler's
1922–26 Lovell "Beach"
house at Newport
Beach, California

cascaded down a hillside, Fallingwater-like, with its four balconies pulled out like drawers. That is just what Wright would design for Bear Run seven years later, though his variant on Schindler produced something far more subtle.

Two other California residences appear to have been exemplars for Fallingwater, both of them commissioned by Philip and Leah Lovell. The earlier of these was the Lovell "Beach" house, still in use today by the Lovell family in the Los Angeles exurb of Newport Beach. Schindler produced a drawing for this house around 1922, although construction was delayed until 1925–26. Wright would have been fully informed about the beach house both through Schindler and from his direct contact with Leah Lovell (he worked for her sister Harriet Freeman and contacted Leah about the school she ran on the Barnsdall estate). There is the highest likelihood that he inspected the house personally.

Schindler's beach house is unforgettably striking even in its altered state today: when the Lovells took occupancy in 1926 there was not a more riveting modern house in the United States, and few enough anywhere in the world. Its *parti* of five reinforced-concrete bolsters lifting up a cantilevered balcony is almost incontrovertibly the origin for the structural system at Fallingwater (Wright installed bolsters around the same time at Taliesin, but these were puny both in form and function). The high all-glass end wall toward the ocean also looks stunningly similar to the glass wall in the tower at Fallingwater. These visual connections

Richard Neutra's Lovell "Health" house, Los Angeles, 1929

between the two houses were even closer when the beach house stood open below, as a bridge over the sand.

The only things missing in the equation of the Lovell beach house with Fallingwater are a dramatic site and a specific diagonal slope to the bolsters. These two features and much else were supplied by the Lovells' second famous house, by Richard Neutra. This was the so-called Lovell "Health" house in Los Angeles, completed in 1929 as a large steel-frame house that emerges in four levels from a hillside next to Griffith Park. Here we see prototypes, either exact or approximate, for Fallingwater's diagonal concrete bolsters, its prominent trellises, its ribbon windows, its cantilevers, its terraces, and even a goodly splash of water.

It is hard to see how the second Lovell house could *not* have exerted a huge influence on Fallingwater. Here was a site hardly less photogenic than Bear Run, a building hardly less dramatic, and clients hardly less charismatic than E. J. and Liliane. Inside were more prototypes for Fallingwater: indirect lighting in the living room, almost invisible mitering of the corner windows, and the same casement windows that Wright later used at Fallingwater. The Lovell house also had the customization that visitors appreciate at Fallingwater: every bedroom had its own sleeping porch, the windows admitted beneficial ultraviolet light so the Lovells could take a sunbath anywhere in the house, the bathrooms were painstakingly ventilated and fitted for sitz baths, and the kitchen presented the latest in labor-saving appliances.

There were other features of the Lovell house that Fallingwater was supposed to copy but which, for one reason or another, it never did. One was the top-down sequence of entry. Wright imbued Fallingwater with such a sequence implicitly with his elaborate penthouse steps; in 1947 he tried to impose the same sequence explicitly with a proposed expansion of the guesthouse that would have made it the principal point of entry to the whole complex, high up on the hillside. Another Lovell-like feature was Fallingwater's proposed sleeping porch, which the Kaufmanns and Wright gave up when the logistics of mosquito control got too complicated. A third was the Lovells' swimming pool in the balcony (actually an in-ground swimming pool with a balcony cradled around it). E. J. was so attracted to this feature—and it is hard to imagine where else he could have seen it—that he insisted Wright incorporate it in his private terrace at Fallingwater. The Lovell and Kaufmann houses have a distinctive cultural link, too: the first was top dog among the modern houses of America until displaced by the second.

I argued earlier that E. J. Kaufmann knew this thrilling house, and that he had requested Wright to incorporate it in his thinking on Bear Run. But Wright hardly needed Kaufmann to make him study the two Lovell houses with close attention. As we saw, Schindler was still under Wright's employ when he produced the beach house, and there still survives Wright's warm letter of congratulations to Neutra on designing the city house. Like Kaufmann, Wright literally could not miss seeing Neutra's house every time he stopped by his own Barnsdall house or Ennis house. Even when he began feuding with Neutra around 1930, Wright remained well informed about him either through the Lovell-Barnsdall friendship or through the Lovell-Freeman family connection.

It strikes me as a perverse misunderstanding of his grandfather's genius for Eric Lloyd Wright to deny that Wright borrowed from the Lovell house when he came to design Fallingwater. Wright could no more have abstained from tinkering with Neutra's design than Bach could have resisted toying with Vivaldi's concertos. Wright's genius did not consist in some impossible notion of originality, but in raising the quality of his sources to so high a level that today everyone knows Fallingwater, while specialists alone remember the two Lovell houses.

What makes the Wright-never-glanced-at-this-house pretense so counterproductive is that Neutra's design for the Lovell house left so much room for improvement. Its structure was both cheap and deceptive: the concrete was merely sprayed on, not integral to the house; the reinforced-concrete bolsters buttressed only the swimming pool, not the house itself; and the cantilevers were fakes, since the projections that looked cantilevered were actually suspended by steel cables from the framework above. One can imagine Wright looking at the Lovell house and saying: "What if I were to replicate this house on Bear Run not as the sham Neutra put up, but as an honest structure?"

It was the Lovell house, not Fallingwater, that made the most astonishing leap forward of any American home of the twentieth century, but both Wright and Kaufmann would have observed that this pioneering came at a high price. Wright would have critiqued the Lovell house's shabby structure. Kaufmann would have critiqued the house as too stridently modern, too futuristic, too "far-out" for mainstream America. E. J. knew that the fastest way for a retailer to lose his shirt was to get too far ahead of popular taste. Fallingwater became vastly more popular than the Lovell house not by being more modern but by being less so. Its futurism was tempered by its rough-hewn stone walls, by its comforting links to nature, and by its subliminal links to America's colonial and prehistoric past.

The weaknesses inherent in the Lovell house stemmed in large part, I believe, from Neutra's status as an immigrant. Immigrant architects are always likely to misread American taste, as I argued years ago in a study that made specific reference to Neutra. Wright had some egregious lapses of taste, too, particularly when he seemed almost self-alienated from the United States in the 1920s, but works like Fallingwater and the Guggenheim show him to have been generally expressive of mainstream America. In E. J. Kaufmann, Wright had a collaborator who was exquisitely attuned to popular taste. Fallingwater garnered popular acceptance where three important Los Angeles houses failed: David Selznick's fake-Colonial mansion because it was too backward, and Philip Lovell's hillside and beach houses because they were "ultramodern."

Mies, Gropius, Le Corbusier, Schindler, and Neutra—Wright profited from the lessons of these five celebrated designers while reviling them personally. But Wright had also a sixth teacher, and to this man he did show grudging deference: his son Lloyd. Lloyd Wright was one of the many architects who learned from Wright but surpassed him in the 1920s. His 1923 Derby house in Los Angeles is entered from the top, the better to emphasize the hillside from which it cascades. The artistic exploitation of reinforced concrete, the dramatic internal volumes, and the integration of house, hillside, and watercourses were all lessons that the son could have taught the father when he came to design Fallingwater. Here was one teacher Wright could respect.

Now it is September 22, 1935: Kaufmann is driving from Milwaukee, and Wright can no longer escape committing the Fallingwater design to paper. How will he do that?

In a moment of inspiration, the general conception of a symphonic work or a building may appear quickly, but both the composer and the architect require a much longer time to work out the thousands of details in an aural or spatial masterpiece. On his September date with destiny, Wright not only had to think Fallingwater, he had to render it on paper with enough specificity to guide its every essential detail later. That is why September 22 ranks so high in the annals of architectural history: not just for the rapidity with which Fallingwater was birthed, but the flawlessness of the birth in an art form more accustomed to botched deliveries. The whole history of architecture, beginning with the Egyptian surveyors who first scratched plans on papyrus five thousand years ago, provides no exact parallel.

The drawn-up-in-two-hours story is not above suspicion, however. We *want* to believe drawing up Fallingwater needed only two hours, just as we want to believe—despite massive contrary evidence—that Lincoln scribbled the Gettysburg Address on the back of an envelope. We don't want to hear that Lincoln struggled through five drafts on his historic oration, because that makes the speech less of a work of genius.

Wright seems to have designed his buildings in two completely different ways: some in a flash, others in painstaking deliberation. He tells us in the *Autobiography* that he devoted long hours to revisions on the Larkin Building, which cost his client $30,000 in last-minute changes. He similarly says that he redrew the plans for Unity Temple thirty-four times before he achieved the right solution. But in 1913, according to his son John, he was Mr. Speedy in designing Chicago's Midway Gardens. With only days remaining before the deadline, John exhorted his father to start designing the project. Wright answered that he was still thinking about it. At the last minute Wright walked into the drafting room, pulled out some blank tracing paper and said: "Here it is, John." "Where is it?" asked John. Wright answered: "Watch it come out of this clean white sheet." Within an hour, the project was drawn out in detail. Wright barked: "There it is. Now get into it. Get it out!"

. . .

The difference between the two design performances—so slow at Unity Temple, so fast at Midway Gardens—can be explained by a number of variables, but the most telling is the change in audience. Wright seems to have been slow and deliberate when working on paper by himself, but greased lightning by the time he allowed people to watch him. This suggests that he resolved the core problem of a building by himself—we know he would work nights at the drafting table in his bedroom-study at Taliesin while Olgivanna slept down the hall—then go before an audience for the rapid production of the secondary plans. The story that not a scrap of Fallingwater existed on paper before E. J. Kaufmann drove up to Taliesin on September 22 is, consequently, unlikely to be true: Wright almost certainly had made drawings for his own use before that date.

The not-a-scrap story was never adopted as Taliesin dogma, anyway: some of Wright's apprentices held to it, while others did not. Blaine Drake, for example, always asserted that Wright had drawn up some Fallingwater plans right after returning from Bear Run in early July. "He usually enjoyed an audience while he was working . . . ," Drake recalled. "But this day he said, 'Boys, I would like to work on this alone.'" Cornelia Brierly also maintained that the Fallingwater design began as Wright's solitary work in the early-morning hours. This corresponds closely to Wright's statement that he kept his design ideas "germinating, between three o'clock and four o'clock in the morning," and to the independent recollections of Wright's procedure by David and Annalise Dodge, who told me that Wright would typically think about a certain problem, sleep on it, wake up around four or five in the morning, draw the problem out on his bedroom drafting table, go back to sleep, and rise for breakfast hours later.

The Dodges' general recollection and Brierly's specific memory of September 22 both used breakfast as a common datum point, since Brierly further remembered Wright's initial Fallingwater drawings lying on the drafting table as the apprentices came in for breakfast around six-thirty. The recollections of Drake and Brierly mesh almost flawlessly with those of other apprentices who remembered Wright getting to work on the Fallingwater plans after breakfast. Wright doubtless did get to work after breakfast that famous September morning, but not from a tabula rasa: he had before him the plans that he had worked up beforehand. It was only the apprentices who were startled by Kaufmann's telephone call at breakfast; Wright himself had been expecting the call for a month.

The apprentices knew that at least one Fallingwater plan existed. That was the reworking by apprentices Edgar Tafel and Bob Mosher of the topographic survey of Bear Run that the Knowles firm had mailed to Taliesin the previous March. Wright had directed Tafel and Mosher to crop out everything but the immediate vicinity of the falls, and to redraw this portion in an enlarged scale. Today a draftsman would use a scanner and computer-aided-design software to do the job in half an hour, but in 1935 the task demanded the better part of several days. Tafel recalled that the reworked site plan sat on Wright's drafting table for weeks. Every day he would study it for a few minutes, but he never drew a line over it. Tafel's recollection does not, however, rule out the possibility that Wright was making midnight drawings for Fallingwater—the ones Drake and Brierly remembered—in the privacy of his bedroom. Again, the old man was sharing less with his apprentices than they imagined.

One of the odd things about the morning of September 22, 1935, is that each of the seven apprentices on record—Blaine Drake, Cornelia Brierly, Edgar Tafel, Bob Mosher, John Lautner, Jack Howe, and Cary Caraway—remembered it differently. Caraway put it this way:

> As I remember it, Mr. Kaufmann came to Milwaukee for some other function and said, "I'd like to know how you are doing, Mr. Wright," and Wright replied calmly, "Your house is finished," and we knew nothing had happened. Then we heard that Kaufmann was about to drive the hundred forty miles from Milwaukee to Spring Green. It could have been the morning of that day when word went out, "He's [Wright] in the studio." Then the next report was, "He's sitting down!" . . . [Wright] took three sheets of tracing paper in different colors, one for the basement, another for the first floor and a third for the second floor, and sketched it to a scale of one-eighth inch equals one foot. We were all standing around him. I'd say it took two hours.

Edgar Tafel recalled:

> [Wright] hung up the phone [with Kaufmann], briskly emerged from his office, some twelve steps from the drafting room, sat down at the table set with the plot plan [of the topography of Bear Run], and started to draw. First floor plan. Second floor. Section, elevation. Side sketches of details, talking *sotto voce* all the while. The design just poured out of him. "Liliane and E. J. will have tea on the balcony . . . they'll cross the bridge to walk into the woods. . . ." Pencils being used up as fast as we could sharpen them when broken. . . . Erasures, overdrawing, modifying. Flipping sheets back and forth. Then, the bold title across the bottom: "Fallingwater." A house has to have a name. . . .
>
> Just before noon Mr. Kaufmann arrived. As he walked up the outside stone steps, he was greeted graciously by the master. They came straight to the drafting table. "E. J.," said Mr. Wright, "we've been wait-

ing for you." The description of the house, its setting, philosophy, poured out. Poetry in form, line, color, textures, and materials, all for a greater glory: a reality to live in! Mr. Wright at his eloquent and romantic best—he had done it before and would often do it again. . . . Kaufmann nodded in affirmation.

They went up to the hill garden dining room for lunch, and while they were away, Bob Mosher and I drew up the other two elevations, naturally in Mr. Wright's style. When they came back, Mr. Wright continued describing the house, using the added elevations to reinforce his presentation. Second thoughts? The basic design never changed—pure all the way.

It does not greatly matter that Tafel's recollection of the extra elevations as lunchtime work conflicts with Mosher's recall that they were drawn overnight. It does matter, though, that the apprentices' recollections differ on the question of Kaufmann's expectations on the placement of his house. Mosher records Kaufmann saying: "I thought you would place the house near the waterfall, not over it," which suggests that E. J. already knew the basic location for the house within a few dozen yards. What numerous other sources depict E. J. as saying is entirely different: "I thought it would be on the opposite side from the waterfall." This portrays Kaufmann as having no clue where his house was going to rise, and clashes with Blaine Drake's memory that Kaufmann had known since July what site Wright had picked. Simple logic dictated in any case that there was neither sunlight nor space for a house on Bear Run's south bank.

As Wright began to draw out Fallingwater in detail, five plans would be critical to his task. The first was the Knowles topographic plan, the second its partial redrawing by Tafel and Mosher. After breakfast on September 22, Wright started the new plans by taping the Tafel-Mosher site plan to his drafting table and placing a clean sheet of tracing paper over it. The tracing became plan 166, which superimposed three floor levels in the future house as though one. Apprentice Carter Manny described exactly the same process in 1946. On that occasion Wright made preliminary drawings for three houses at four in the morning, then assigned each one after breakfast to a senior apprentice for drawing out into conventional plans. Wright's drawings were in colored pencil, with the elements superimposed one over the other—exactly like the base drawing for Fallingwater. In the middle of the night, Wright had created the conceptual designs of three different houses in as many hours!

The question "Did Wright draw Fallingwater out from preexisting plans or from nothing?" is important but incomplete, because it ignores a third possibility. My best guess is that Wright had indeed made preexisting plans in his bedroom, but when he stepped into his office, he had no further need of the original plans once he had committed them to memory. I liken this to Winston Churchill or any experienced orator, who works hard on a longhand draft of a speech but then hardly glances at his notes when he gives it. Wright could draw with great speed since he worked with a T-square and triangle, not freehand. Since he drew virtually to scale, he wasted little time in calibrating distances. The surviving drawings bear a scale of ⅛ inch to a foot, as Caraway recalled. If Wright wanted a certain wall to be 40 feet long, he would draw a line 5 inches in length at lightning speed. Such a drawing, hard-edged and kept to scale, might look hasty but never "rough": it would always look close to the final building. Wright then produced plans, sections, and an elevation. "There is no 'sketch,' and there never has been one," he wrote. "There seldom is in a thought-built building."

Plan 166 for Fallingwater came straight out of its site, specifically from three preexisting datum points: a wooden bridge that crossed the stream at its narrowest neck, some 45 feet upcurrent from the falls; the boulders over which Wright set the house; and the fall line of the upper falls. The bridge was Wright's only man-made determinant on the site. Though a human artifact, it was an important "gift" or given to Wright: it had a symbolic as well as practical rightness as the one thing that united the natural and the built environments at Bear Run.

Wright had to rebuild the bridge in concrete so the Kaufmanns' limousine could pass over it, but it had a far greater importance to him as a crucial element in Fallingwater's scenography. One of Hedrich's shots well captures the way the bridge acts as a literal and figurative parallel to the house itself (page 304). It sets up a dramatic perspective of Fallingwater in the eyes of anyone approaching it.

Now Wright turned to the three boulders that would frame the house itself. He seems to have begun with the fireplace as the functional and spiritual heart and hearth of Fallingwater. This he set at the cap of the eastern boulder, which rose to midlevel. He then set the west end of the house against the western boulder, on which he laid the three concrete buttresses that would anchor E. J.'s terrace. The middle boulder was the lowest, and mainly a nuisance: Wright had it blasted away to yield space for a basement.

Now the third and last determinant: the falls themselves. The lip of the falls provided the orientation of the house, which thereby came not from some compass abstraction but from nature itself.

Wright used the lip of the falls as the baseline from which to lay out the house with a 30/60/90-degree triangle, which produced Fallingwater's exceptionally tight fit between nature and architecture. It also accounts

Wright intimately linked Fallingwater to nature by making his walls correspond to the sides of triangles placed over the lip of the Bear Run waterfall on his site plan. As he developed the design, Wright removed the fourth diagonal "bolster" support at point A, changed the stairwell down to the stream from squared to rounded (B), extended Liliane's balcony from C to C1, and pushed the living-room end wall out from D to D1 and changed its doors to windows. To compensate for diminished light in the living room, Wright amalgamated five vertical glass strips into one large window by the hearth (E).

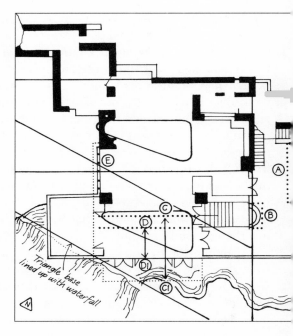

for Fallingwater's eccentric orientation of south-southeast to north-northwest, 36 degrees 41 minutes west of north, according to the most recent surveys.

Wright incorporated all these elements in plan 166, his base drawing for Fallingwater. Like many a plan, it carries the excitement of lines that seem to leap from the architect's pencil. Unlike most plans, however, this one did not dull as its lines translated over the next two years from graphite into masonry: the energy of these first lines was never lost. Plan

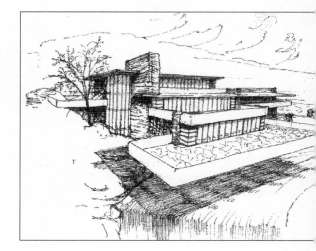

Reconstruction of Fallingwater halfway through Wright's design process. Wright has replaced the hip roof over the second floor with a flat-roofed penthouse, but Liliane's balcony still pulls back from the living room below it, rather than soaring into space.

166 is a tour de force of draftsmanship and spatial conception because it pulls together the stream and its banks (in blue), four concrete bolsters—not the three they later became—in light green, the main floor in black, and the second floor in orange. The plan gives no indication of a third floor.

Fallingwater is a strictly rectilinear building, but Wright used a multitude of triangles as hidden generators for this plan. I term these "hidden" because in the final building these design aids are invisible. As an analogy, we could think of George Bernard Shaw's play *Pygmalion*, which is based on a Greek myth but (apart from its last line) carries in its text no overt references to the Greek original. In the same way, Wright used many geometric forms in constructing Fallingwater that we cannot detect in the final product. To replicate the original plan requires the use of nothing more than a plastic 30/60/90-degree triangle of the kind that can be found in the desk of nearly any American home. Lacking that, the same triangle can be easily improvised from a folded piece of paper. Fallingwater gets both its cohesion and its tension from a plan that looks free but holds steadfast to a geometric tradition of great antiquity.

The orientation of the house was ideal for catching light all day: the sun shines from upstream in the morning (basically east), full-face before noon (basically south), and downstream toward evening (basically west). Wright set the back wall of Fallingwater against the hillside for protection against northerly winds and cold, which is no more than any Wisconsin farmer knows to do by instinct. All this and much more Wright incorporated into plan 166. After so many months of abstract thinking on the problem, he had his first concrete accomplishment at Fallingwater.

Wright's next task was to translate plan 166 into individual plans for each floor. To do this he either taped or tacked the drawing—it bears both kinds of marks today—to the bottom of his drafting table, and used overlay sheets to trace out the individual floors. The process was anything but seamless, however. The harsh light of morning brought out a half-dozen problems in plan 166. The house was at that moment quite different in profile from what Wright later worked out. The expansive orange X's and the broad overhangs on the plan seem to indicate that he intended Fallingwater to have a tiny basement and just two floors, the upper capped with pyramidal or hip roofs. It would have recalled Taliesin and the Prairie houses of pre–World War I days, an anachronism that was probably deliberate, since Wright called Hib Johnson's slightly later Wingspread a belated cousin to his Prairie house designs. But Fallingwater's hip roofs never got built: they might have been charming, but they were incompatible with the flat-roofed German idiom to which Wright needed to adhere to regain prestige within his profession.

As he translated his synoptic plan 166 into individual floor plans, Wright reworked his two-story home into a higher and more monumental building. He set a penthouse over the two lower floors, which gave greater privacy to Junior and allowed the senior Kaufmanns to have the separate bedrooms they preferred. We can see that Wright reduced the number of second-floor bathrooms from four to three, and he later took out a small bathroom at the entrance when Liliane asked for an extra closet. This was also the moment that Wright gave E. J. a balcony/terrace modeled on his own at Taliesin.

Up to this point Fallingwater resembled the first scheme for his Malcolm Willey house of 1932 (the Willeys had abandoned this for something cheaper). The key feature in the first Willey scheme was a living room that extended through a series of French doors onto a wraparound cantilevered terrace. But at the last minute Wright swerved from the Willey precedent and made the most important change of all. On plan 166, he had drawn an orange line to show Liliane's balcony ending 10 feet short of the lower balcony. This unbuilt Fallingwater would have been more conventional than the one that was built, though more practical functionally, easier to realize structurally, and more harmonious aesthetically. In short, it would have pleased Vitruvius in his three traditional categories of design. But it would not have yielded the most striking domestic profile of the twentieth century.

At some point that hectic morning Wright reconsidered the size of Liliane's balcony. He erased its original parapet line and set a new one 19 feet farther out, which made the upper balcony oversail the living room by 6 feet. Fallingwater now took on a totally new image, with the famous crisscross of its two main balconies. And only now did Fallingwater surpass Schindler's Wolfe house in drama, because it smashed the traditional idiom of sequentially receding balconies in favor of something that had rarely or never been attempted before. Wright's 1931 threat to punish Schindler and Neutra "and show them up soon" was proving chillingly accurate.

Fallingwater is unlikely to have become famous—certainly not *so* famous—had Liliane's balcony pulled back from the one below rather than oversailing it. Look how prominent Liliane's balcony is in Bill Hedrich's photograph of Fallingwater: the house just does not "fly" visually without it. But there was a price to pay for this photogeneity. Liliane's balcony was intended to work like a cantilever but never did, so almost its entire weight crushes down on the floor below. By putting photogeneity ahead of structural sobriety, Wright precipitated an engineering risk that

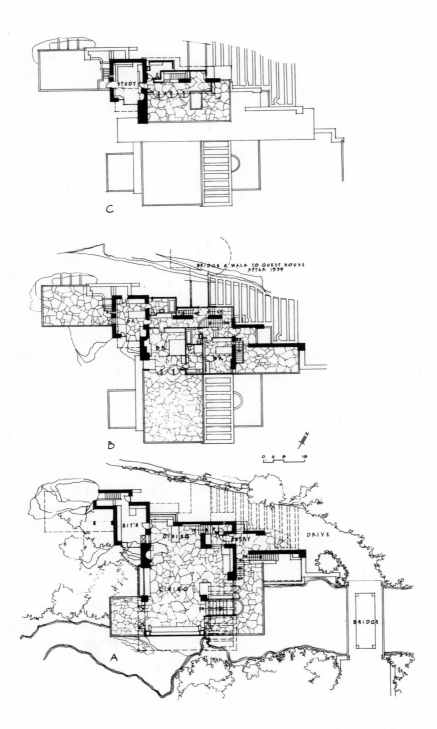

Fallingwater's floor plans: A is the main floor and site plan; B is the second floor, and C is the penthouse

came close to toppling Fallingwater in the 1990s. Fallingwater's eternity would have been short: sixty years or less.

Anyone who strolls on Liliane's balcony or studies it from above in a Fallingwater model, such as the one displayed at MoMA, must soon conclude that this oversized feature makes little functional sense, since it is located on a level that makes it useless for entertaining. But Wright knew what he was doing, because at Bear Run only the gods can view Liliane's balcony from above: we mortals can only view it from below, where it appears soaring rather than maladroit, active rather than passive, vigorous rather than bland, and drop-dead gorgeous. This is the "billboard architecture" with which Wright reproached his Beaux-Arts contemporaries. Now he too was engaging in billboard architecture, and the only difference was that he could do it better.

As he drew floor plans at each level, Wright had to calculate how he was going to engineer the building. It was as though he was playing against himself at chess. The erasures regarding the length of Liliane's balcony on plan 166 and second-floor plan 047 correspond perfectly, which means that Wright worked on them simultaneously. (Their dark paper is identical, too, whereas other drawings in the series carry a lighter tone.) Plan 166 shows clearly that the living room was supposed to end in balconies east, west, and south—not just east and west, as we have today. When Wright moved the south wall of the living room 10 feet out, he turned an uncovered balcony into a more usable living room that now ended not with doors (since there was no longer a south balcony to walk onto) but in a line of windows. The switch demanded numerous sacrifices, since the new living room was larger but darker. Plan 166 shows that Wright intended to give the living room two sets of "palisade" windows— a favorite device from his California houses—each comprising five vertical slits. One set of windows would have gone south of the fireplace, the other north of the dining area. To get more light into the living room, Wright turned the wall south of the fireplace into a huge window almost fifteen feet in length. He similarly opened two long clerestory windows in the dining alcove, just below his Italian-style cantilevered bathrooms.

Turning the south balcony into more living room put a snag in party circulation. To get from the east to the west balconies, today's guests have to troop through the living room. But someone sitting by the fireplace now has an unimpeded view of nature through the south windows, rather than being forced to peek through the gowns and tuxedos of guests on a balcony. Liliane got more entertainment space and unexpected seating on a 20-foot-long banquette—compensations any hostess would treasure.

· · ·

Ed Fisher's *New Yorker* cartoon of March 14, 1994, proposed marital discord as the reason why Fallingwater's upper balcony clamps down on the lower

"The story is that Wright was going through considerable domestic difficulties at the time he designed this one."

Do these last-minute switches detract from Wright's genius? Not in my view. Wright never claimed he was infallible. He made numerous changes while his buildings were under way; remember David Dodge crying out: "Mr. Wright, that wall has already been built in New York City!" If Wright did not hesitate to make changes when his buildings were going up, why should we be astonished if he changed a few lines on a plan?

We are almost but not quite done with Liliane's balcony. In anthropomorphic terms, nothing at Fallingwater expresses such anguish as that heavy balcony crushing down on the fragile strip of glass below it. With a little fantasy we could interpret this as Liliane clamping down on the liv-

Liliane firmly clamps down on E. J. at a family party around 1940

ing room in which E. J. was holding court. Was Wright using this gesture to give an architectural interpretation of the famously volatile Kaufmann marriage? He certainly knew all of E. J. and Liliane's secrets, even once acting as their sex counselor. The *New Yorker* cartoonist Ed Fisher specifically interpreted Liliane's balcony overbite in terms of marital discord, though he supposed it was the architect who had problems rather than the clients. Did Wright mean for Liliane's about-to-topple balcony to read metaphorically as the cry of the spurned wife? Or did he equate her threat to capsize the marriage with the structural peril to the house if her balcony ever came loose? The answer to both rhetorical questions is surely no, but we do have a hilarious family portrait that shows Liliane firmly clamping down on E. J., just the way her balcony clamps down on Fallingwater.

Wright probably guessed at the difficulties that would come his way when he extended Liliane's balcony so arbitrarily, but he also knew how much publicity it would reap. All artists occasionally put something outrageous in their works to get them noticed—signature pieces that guarantee their creators a *succès de scandale*. For Gertrude Stein it was deadening repetition, for Frank Gehry it has been undulating curves and titanium, for Picasso the distorted human forms in his *Demoiselles d'Avignon* and *Guernica*.

In Fallingwater, I see two such signature pieces: the illusion of water coursing through the house, and Liliane's oversailing balcony. Of the two, the second is the more photogenic and distinctive, because it defies all structural and functional logic. In 1999, I told Wright's apprentice Edgar Tafel that I had discovered that the oversailing balcony was a late change to the design, and I asked him if he remembered Wright making that change. After sixty-four years, Tafel could neither confirm nor contradict my finding, but a moment later he went into a sort of trance. His eyes grew set and disapproving, and he seemed to relive a long-ago battle when he intoned: "Architects will do things like that just to get publicity."

Now the apprentices were sharpening pencils in a fury, as additional drawings were traced out. We will never know precisely what Wright and his crew produced in those two hours, since no more than three or four of those drawings survive today. Sheet 166, with its superimposed plans, belongs to that historic group, although Wright probably kept it out of Kaufmann's sight because of its hasty quality.

On two more plans (047 and 046, respectively), Wright worked out the basic communication between the second floor and the penthouse. The penthouse has a small terrace to the south, over Liliane's bedroom,

Fallingwater from the east

Section through Fallingwater, as though viewed from the east

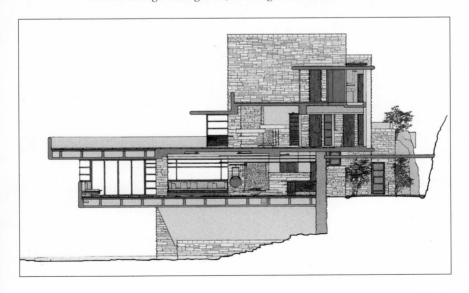

which required no cantilever support. On the west, outside Junior's bedroom, Wright placed the penthouse steps we looked at in detail earlier. E. J.'s terrace was one of the last elements in the house to be defined, since Wright was frustrated to find that the trees and the boulders at this spot had not been drawn accurately by the Knowles firm. He left E. J.'s terrace unresolved until he visited Bear Run again in October 1935. The perspective rendering of Fallingwater from that time still shows the mark where the terrace was crudely elongated a few feet at the last minute.

What holds Fallingwater's three floors together structurally and visually is the great vertical bulwark of the three-story stone tower. The tower imposes identical dimensions on the only three rooms in the house that are bounded by thick stone walls: the kitchen, E. J.'s bedroom, and Junior's intended bedroom in the penthouse. Part of the tower rises well above the roof to carry six flues from the furnace, the kitchen stove, the communal fireplace on the first floor, and the fireplaces from the three family bedrooms. What Wright seems to have done at this last stage was to "tease" the house from its block, like pulling taffy: he pulled E. J.'s terrace farther west, Liliane's balcony farther south, and the entrance and guestroom a little to the east. To the north went the stairways, the bathrooms, the heavy concrete trellis, and the thick stone walls that define the back of Fallingwater. These elements give the impression that the house is "anchored" into the hillside behind it, as though to balance the heavy balconies stretched out over the stream. (This balancing image serves only as a metaphor for the cantilever system, however, not as a true structural device.) Wright now had a design that captured the excitement of a stepped-down cascade from any angle.

Wright's two hours are now up, and E. J. Kaufmann is at the door. Nine months have passed since Fallingwater was conceived, and its birth has followed with impeccable timing. The two parents examine their offspring on the drafting table and see a house that is going to be very promising indeed.

Opposite: Fallingwater under construction, 1936

SIX

RAISING FALLINGWATER

I undertook this unbelievably difficult work under all but impossible circumstances.

—WRIGHT to Kaufmann

We can give Wright and the Taliesin apprentices a day off, even a week, to celebrate the extraordinary design that emerged on September 22, 1935. But they get no more than that, for all they achieved that bright fall day was a concept, not a building. A half-dozen people in the room and a hundred people outside it would suffer months of torment before Fallingwater gave corporeal shape to that concept.

E. J. Kaufmann, for his part, lost no time in getting his house built. The apprentices differed in their recollections of how long Kaufmann tarried after he saw his house on the drawing board: Mosher says he spent the night; Tafel, with higher probability, says he left after lunch. That meant Kaufmann was speeding home to Pittsburgh by the time the apprentices and a few Spring Green hangers-on filed into the Taliesin theater to watch *The Thirty-nine Steps,* the new Alfred Hitchcock thriller that Wright had obtained for a screening at three o'clock that afternoon.

Kaufmann probably reached Pittsburgh on Monday. He was at his desk on Tuesday the twenty-fourth and sent Wright his reactions to the events of Sunday. That letter does not survive, but three days later E. J. wrote again:

Dear Frank:
Following my letter of the 24th I hope you will continue to work on the house plan so that we can get our preliminary sketches, floor plans and elevations at the very earliest possible time—and when they are finished that you will come to Pittsburgh with them.

We learn something important about Kaufmann here, which is his familiarity with architectural graphics: dilettantes don't speak of "preliminary sketches, floor plans and elevations." Was that his year in engineering at Yale talking?

E. J. grasped Wright's intention for the house well enough (or thought he did) that he straightaway took Liliane and Junior to Bear Run, where he laid out the imaginary building in situ. This we know from Junior's letter to Wright on the twenty-seventh: "Father spent quite some time at Bear Run showing just where the various rooms would be and Edgar [Tafel] sent a rough drawing of the wall masses [one of several early drawings that later perished] so that we are all tremendously anxious to see just what the house will really look like. As far as I am concerned, it keeps floating around in a half-formed way almost continually asking for a little more information on which to complete itself."

. . .

A composer can play her own sonatina and a choreographer can perform his own dance, but architectural concepts take shape only when builders—not architects—construct them. The crucial intermediary between the architect's brain and the builders' brawn is the drawing. The concept drawings of September 22 constituted the first of eight different sets of architectural graphics that were needed to give Fallingwater the shape that Wright had in mind. The second set were the presentation drawings that he mailed to the Kaufmanns in mid-October 1935. Next, between October 1935 and January 1936, he had to oversee production of the measured or working drawings, which guaranteed that everything on the presentation drawings was logistically possible. The third set went through half a year of revisions until it emerged as a fourth set: the construction drawings of May 1936.

Most of Fallingwater was built from this fourth set of drawings, which also served as the legal basis for Wright's contract. Nonetheless, four additional sets of graphics followed. In July 1936, Wright's consultants produced structural drawings for the engineers in Pittsburgh, who revised them the next month in a new sequence of graphics to meet their own satisfaction: these constituted the fifth and sixth sets of drawings. In August 1936, Taliesin produced a seventh set of design-development drawings to guide the builders through particularly tricky details, and in early 1937 the eighth set emerged: these were the shop drawings for the furniture makers and the mechanical specialists who oversaw the windows, electricity, plumbing, heating, ventilation, lighting, and the sound system. These all came from Taliesin or from various suppliers to the house as needed, until everything was built and furnished by 1940. After 1940, changes to Fallingwater created new cycles of drawings.

The surviving presentation drawings consist of plans of the three floors, section views through the building looking east and west, and perspective views of the structure from front and back and from above and below. These were either black-and-white pen or pencil drawings or else quick color sketches. There was one spectacular exception: drawing 004, a colored perspective drawing of Fallingwater seen from below the falls. The signature block reads "FLLW/Arizona/36," but this is in error. Wright often signed his drawings years after the fact, and frequently misdated them: context makes clear that 004 was not drawn by Wright in Arizona in 1936 but in Wisconsin in October 1935. Its main author was probably not Wright at all, but his renderings specialist Jack Howe. Wright would not have assigned Howe so labor-intensive a drawing unless he felt the Kaufmanns needed a good deal of ardent wooing.

. . .

The unveiling of presentation drawings is normally the occasion for a love feast between architect and client. These seductive drawings can mask many dangers, however. Being free of budgetary and programmatic constraints, presentation drawings are notoriously impractical. They hide the demands of structure altogether, since concocting them requires no engineering skill. Presentation drawings need only make the building *look* structurally sound, not *be* structurally sound.

Historically, nothing is more important to an architect than a knowledge of structure, because that is what distinguishes architects from all other visual artists. The unskilled painter might displease his clients, but the unskilled architect will kill them. Designers can be notoriously callous on the question of structure, however; they recognize its importance but disagree with the engineers on its essence. In a perfect world, structure would determine architectural design; in an imperfect world, the reverse is usually true. In the real world, most architects regard structure as no more than a necessary evil that swallows up a quarter of a project's budget. That is why we pay homage to Fallingwater. Flawed it may be, but it is one of the rare buildings that honestly attempts to treat form and structure as one.

Wright's attempt to fuse form and structure explains, in part, why he was so minimalist in providing support to Fallingwater and his other structures. Most artists aim at economy as an aesthetic criterion, but for Wright (and, with different emphasis, Mies van der Rohe) economy of structure took on the force of a religious obligation. Wright's theory of architecture saw structure as the ultimate authority that dictated what the architect should build. One could say that he invested structure with a spiritual aura, because it alone conformed to a power higher than the architect's wishes and desires. This made structure a law of nature.

Such at least was the theory. In practice, Wright broke this law of nature whenever formalist concerns bid him do so. The roof overhang in his Robie house of 1909 stretched effortlessly beyond the walls of the building because Wright had hidden a steel beam inside. In theory, Wright's two moral guides, Ruskin and Viollet-le-Duc, should have restrained him from this structural dishonesty. At the least, he ought to have been deeply conflicted every time he used such concealed supports—but was he?

Wright was confident in his ability to create a structurally workable design for Fallingwater, but it is sobering to recall that when the concept drawings were unveiled at Taliesin in 1935, only two people in the room had even a dash of training in engineering—and one of those was E. J. Kaufmann. The other was Wright, with only a year of freshman engineering at the University of Wisconsin under his belt. The MIT-trained structural engineer William Wesley Peters should have collaborated on the design, but Peters had been banished from Taliesin for several months after he eloped with Wright's stepdaughter Svetlana, so that he had zero impact during Fallingwater's concept stage. Similarly, a year would pass before Wright called on Mendel Glickman to make structural diagrams for the house, so Glickman missed Fallingwater's concept stage as well.

That left Wright alone to figure out how Fallingwater would stand up. He had a good, or even brilliant, intuitive sense of structure, but he was not an engineer. Worse, his training with the engineer Dankmar Adler and the architect Louis Sullivan led him to acquiesce in that firm's fatal split between architecture and engineering. As partners, Adler and Sullivan worked hand in glove, but the former did no design work and the latter avoided all but the most elementary structural calculations. After they split in 1894, a notable flabbiness entered Sullivan's work, and Adler got no architectural commissions at all.

This means that Wright was initially trained to think of architectural design as something independent of—though never free of—structural restraints, which had both good and bad implications for his later work. Starting with his earliest houses, Wright opened up rooms by deleting walls and partitions, even though this deprived his buildings of conventional internal supports. This first structural deprivation was exacerbated by a second one: his extensive use of glass to bring his clients closer to nature. Wright had to experiment with new techniques to compensate for the absence of normal external walls. Beginning with the Tomek house of 1907, he employed hidden steel girders and cantilever technology to fling roofs past the edges of his homes. Some of these innovations were successful and some not: the Tomek house still bears the ugly pier that was later installed to support its sagging roof. Nor did Wright change much in later years: veteran Taliesin apprentices still tell story after story of how they bailed the old man out of a structural jam.

Starting with the cantilevered balconies of Fallingwater in 1935, the second half of Wright's career saw the erection of some of the more daringly engineered structures of the twentieth century: the pencil-thin lily-pad columns at Johnson's Wax (Wright called them "dendriform"—i.e., treelike), the folded canopy up to Bear Run's guesthouse, the inverted ziggurat of the Guggenheim, and the paper-thin roof at Beth Sholom Synagogue. Wright typically drew up these concepts by himself without outside advice, but the final structures were tailored for him by trained engineers, who were often hard-pressed to satisfy him because of his dangerous habit of inflating designs beyond their original concepts. He let the Guggenheim Museum and the Price Tower grow like weeds—the latter from three to nineteen stories.

All these designs tumbled out of a highly creative mind, but from a limited structural knowledge base. Wright had gained plenty of experience in structural design, but it is a dangerous thing to dream first and ask other people to produce reality later. Fallingwater's design is a consummate example of Wright's pure dreaming: between September 1935 and July 1936, when he finally assigned a structural engineer to review his plan, Wright had not asked any competent professional to back it up. We get some perspective on this from Wesley Peters, who fifty years later declared that it was not merely fortunate but essential that Fallingwater was built in the country rather than in a city, because "there is not a city in the United States, even today, where one could obtain a building permit to erect Fallingwater."

It would be months until Fallingwater's foundations were laid, so any miscalculation in the preliminary plans would have no immediate structural consequences, but Wright's push for a flashy profile at Fallingwater was risky to the building's long-term structural health. One example of this was his suppression of the fourth (easternmost) diagonal bolster, which one sees on preliminary drawing 166 but not in the building. Wright never said why he withheld this vital support from a building that was desperately in need of it, but his reasoning could only have been visual. The three diagonal bolsters as constructed are unobtrusive in the gloom under the main balcony, which is how Wright wanted them to be. The projected fourth bolster would have loomed much larger in the view from the bridge because it would have caught the light at the balcony's eastern edge. This would have deflated Fallingwater's magic lift into something merely prosaic. Carl Thumm, one of Kaufmann's site supervisors, remembered where this fourth bolster was supposed to go, and when he wrote Wright in 1936 about cracks that had developed on the east balcony, Thumm twitted him for having yanked out the bolster that would have prevented deformation at that spot.

After three weeks of hard work Wright sent his presentation drawings to Pittsburgh on October 15, 1935. He followed the precious bundle four days later, after a lecture at Yale University. His coming in person is another indication that Wright felt he needed all his persuasive powers to get the building started. The trip also gave him another look at Bear Run, so he could confirm certain peculiarities of the site for himself. We have no record of what took place during this site visit, since the letters exchanged immediately afterward are irrelevant to the main issue (Wright was cajoling Kaufmann into providing Pittsburgh coal to heat Taliesin for the winter). Nevertheless, the visit seems to have gone well, since there was discussion of future plans and talk of quarrying stone.

One document survives to record the first outsider reaction to Wright's design. Buried in the Fallingwater archives and until now ignored because it is in German, is a half-fictional east elevation of Fallingwater by Laszlo Gabor, the Austro-Hungarian refugee who had just become artistic director at Kaufmann's Department Store. The caricature shows E. J. Kaufmann hanging from a third-level cantilever in the form of a diving board. The text next to him says in German: "I always knew that on my fiftieth birthday I would easily see the waterfall!" while Liliane, descending on a parachute, looks at E. J. and says: "I see [the falls] even better [than E. J.]." Kaufmann's fiftieth birthday fell on November 1, 1935, which gives us the date for this parody. Evidently, Kaufmann had displayed the presentation drawings to his staff after Wright came to town. Gabor's humor turns on the classic analogy of cantilevers to diving boards, and what seems to have impressed him the most was the way Liliane's balcony extended in the air so far past the main floor.

Wright need not have worried how the Kaufmanns would take to the presentation drawings: they were enthralled, and E. J. gave Wright the go-ahead to proceed with construction drawings. This the Taliesin crew did by January 1936, with revision into yet more detailed working drawings at the end of May. The changes to the design between October 1935 and May 1936 are not easy to enumerate, since some key drawings are lost, but we can be certain of the most important of these, which was the switch in the balcony walls, the roof overhangs, and the penthouse steps from straight to rounded, a change that made the design substantially less mechanical and Germanic. We can suppose that Wright felt he had beaten the "Internationalists" at their own game as he had threatened to, and now it was time to return to his own sentiments. He had written Lewis Mumford several years before: "Nearly everything in Life is blended at the edges[.] No hard and fast lines in Nature you see."

Wright spent the last weeks of 1935 making other changes: he elongated E. J.'s terrace on the west, cut short the guest balcony and the corresponding overhang on the east, switched the east end of the hatch from rectilinear to rounded, and introduced horizontal rather than vertical windows alongside the doors to Liliane's balcony. Other modifications would pop up later in Fallingwater's construction. One of these was the swimming pool that E. J. wanted for his terrace. In the summer of 1936 the Knowles engineers created a plan showing how this could be done (this survives in Avery Library), and Carl Thumm corresponded with the engineers in July on "changing this terrace to a small diving pool." But it was not to happen.

T he holdup of four months between the completion of the first set of Fallingwater's working drawings in January 1936 and their revision in May was not, or not primarily, caused by Wright's habitual lateness: it came from Kaufmann's doubts about the design. On February 24, Wright mailed two sets of blueprints and three sets of specifications (notes on materials and procedures) to Kaufmann, who promptly sent one set to his longtime engineering consultants at Morris Knowles.

Kaufmann Jr. has characterized this incident as an act of treason by his father against Wright, though a more temperate view of Kaufmann's action would be to see it as simple prudence. Knowles reported back on April 3, 1935, with a three-page "Report on Review of Plans of E. [sic] L. Wright for House at Bear Run," now at Avery Library. In it, the firm advised Kaufmann of eight key points that made construction inadvisable:

- Knowles saw the Bear Run falls as continuing to recede, which would eventually take the proposed house with them. "We do not know the rate at which the falls are receding,—which may be very slow; and we do not know how hard the rock strata may be at the foot of the falls, where erosion and undercutting by the falling water take place." The firm told Kaufmann it would be prudent to find out the rate of erosion.*
- The process of erosion in the falls would be speeded up by the deflection of the water from the foundation walls of the house to the opposite (south) bank of the stream. This would ultimately change the appearance of the falls and have a possible impact on the house.
- The bolsters needed to be thickened to ward off the impact of driftwood in the stream at flood time.
- There could be a problem of stability from the incorporation of the main boulder into the living room. "We question seriously the advisability of utilizing it as a part of the building foundation."
- Wright's plans so far were not really structural: until Knowles saw detailed diagrams for the structural steel and the steel rein-

---

*This dour view of his scheme for the house on Bear Run nonetheless did Wright a favor: the Knowles report was the first to associate the phrase "falling water" with the house.

forcing in the concrete, they could not determine the potential stability of the house.
• The bridge looked wide enough for the projected water flow beneath, but Wright's plans did not specify the structural makeup of the bridge itself.
• The location of the boiler-room floor looked too low to survive damage in flood conditions.
• Knowles reminded Kaufmann of the state act of June 25, 1913, which stipulated that no one could restrict, alter, or obstruct a stream flow without permission of Pennsylvania's Water and Power Resources Board.

Kaufmann took the report seriously enough to ask Knowles to examine the site again and to make a specific pronouncement on whether he should proceed with construction. The Knowles engineers made an on-site survey on April 16, and two days later they sent Kaufmann a letter in which they warned him even more stridently to build nothing on the site:

> Briefly, we cannot recommend the site as suitable, from a structural standpoint, for a building of importance such as that contemplated. The rate of recession of the falls may be extremely slow, but cannot be predicted with any degree of safety. There is evidence of minor spalling off of the rock at the face of the falls and there is a possibility of further disturbance of the rock strata when channels are cut in the surface to provide necessary keyways for the foundation walls. If the entire structure were shifted to a safe distance from the crest of the falls, the building would encroach upon the bridge site and the space required for driveway. The question of utilizing the boulder as a base for the fireplace is perhaps a detail, but we do not consider the boulder suitable for incorporation into the foundation of the building.
>
> Of course, there is the possibility, or even a probability, that future deterioration of the rock ledge will not be sufficient to endanger the foundations; but in our opinion there could be no feeling of complete safety and consequently we recommend that the proposed site not be used for any important structure.

The engineers' warnings would not derail Kaufmann's determination to build Fallingwater, but they did haunt him for the rest of his life.

Who knew better, Wright or the Pittsburgh engineers? Knowles clearly had the better understanding of the physics of the site, since they had been observing it on Kaufmann's behalf for twenty years. The firm was

cautious, but Pittsburgh's engineers were in general among the more creative in the country. This was the city in which Benjamin Henry Latrobe
improved the design of steamships, John Roebling invented the first of his
suspension bridges, Alexander Holley laid out Carnegie's leading-edge
steel mill, and George Washington Ferris designed the first Ferris wheel.
The new Pittsburgh bridges of the 1920s and 1930s were—still are—
praised as among the most progressive in the world for that era. It was not
that the Pittsburgh engineers failed to appreciate the daring in Wright's
design: rather, they feared that at some point the house would self-
destruct or pull away from its anchors in the rock. Time has proved both
sides right: the fears expressed by the Knowles engineers were valid, but
Wright's concept proved viable nonetheless.

Legend has Wright turning furiously on E. J. for soliciting this second
opinion on Fallingwater's engineering. But here legend makes a bad mistake: Wright did grow furious with Kaufmann several times, but this first
involvement with Knowles was not one of them. The legend also holds
that a contrite E. J. buried the Knowles reports inside Fallingwater's foundations (Kaufmann Jr., among others, alleged this as fact). The existence
of full copies of both reports at Avery Library shoots holes in the "burial"
legend: Kaufmann may have buried something, but he kept one copy of
each report among his important papers until the day he died. Any blowup
between Wright and E. J. was soon smoothed over, since their next on-site
meeting on April 19, 1936, went without a hitch. Wright was downright
accommodating, agreeing to set thicker steel rods in the reinforced concrete (¾ inch rather than ½ inch in diameter), and promising to send Kaufmann new engineering plans that would convey this important change.

Construction drawings are supposed to precede construction
rather than follow it, but at Fallingwater—and at more building sites than the industry cares to talk about—this was sometimes true and sometimes not. Today the "fast-track" construction process
starts certain building operations before every last drawing has been
made, but this just legitimizes a situation faced by the building trades long
ago. We could compare it to a Hollywood filmscript undergoing revision
up to the last shoot. Much of Fallingwater was built from skimpy or missing drawings not because Wright was pioneering a new management
technique but because he kept sticking rewrites into the script.

Following his site visit in April, Wright had the working drawings for
Fallingwater revised again, then shipped to the work site on May 27,
1936. By then, however, construction on Fallingwater had already been

under way a full half-year under the highly questionable leadership of E. J. Kaufmann. Too excited to wait for final plans or the engagement of a professional builder, Kaufmann himself reopened the old Bear Run sandstone quarry late in 1935. (The overgrown quarry is still visible today several hundred feet uphill from the house, toward the Youghiogheny.) In November, E. J. asked Wright for specific dimensions on the stones needed for the walls. Wright's reply was guardedly generic, asking only that the stone be rendered in different lengths and heights. Kaufmann should set aside the smoothest ones, if not over 4 inches thick, to be used to pave the floors. The exterior walls would be a minimum of 18 inches thick, "so some bond-stones that width will be desirable." Kaufmann reported back that the stones coming out of the quarry measured about 12 to 14 inches in width and about 2 feet in length; he was stacking up about five cords a week. Great heaps of stone can be glimpsed in the home movies the Pittsburgh photographer Luke Swank periodically took of construction, starting in the spring of 1936.

The correspondence makes clear how experienced Wright was in using stone, which by the 1930s was an increasingly rare word in the design vocabulary in Europe and the U.S. His Victorian birth now turned into an asset: what he wrote about stone carries a wonderfully old-fashioned tone, almost as though the Industrial Revolution had never happened.

Wright and Kaufmann were in the meantime negotiating about fees, a ritual that both parties eased by sending gifts. Liliane dispatched some fine pottery to Taliesin and Wright reciprocated with three Japanese prints to Pittsburgh. They still hang in Fallingwater today.

Many Wright clients got sucked into building operations on their homes, as the memoirs of the Hanna and Jacobs families attest, but nobody in the group surpassed E. J.'s tenacity and skill as a gentleman builder. Even on holiday in Florida in 1937 he wrote the Fallingwater site supervisor: "[M]y thoughts have been daily, almost hourly, on the work at Bear Run, which has become part of me and a part of my life, and I hate to be separated until the work has been completed to everyone's satisfaction." Kaufmann "knows every inch of the plans," the site supervisor reported to Wright. Kaufmann may have appalled Wright with his new persona as construction foreman (in a typical take-charge reference, he tells Wright: "Meanwhile we will start putting up the forms"), but in the course of a running dialogue on a hundred questions large and small, he solved more than a few problems in construction and design. It was his idea, for example, to set the window glass directly into channels in the stone walls rather than in conventional steel frames.

Now Kaufmann poured much of the human and material resources of his store into Fallingwater. Two store managers in succession served as clerk of the works, numerous store staff did specialized jobs like wiring, and E. J. even threw his nephew I. D. Wolf Jr. into the work of dragging stone down the hill. A half-continent away, Sam Goldwyn was putting up his Beverly Hills palace in exactly the same way, on the back of peons from the construction crews on his movie sets.

Bizarrely, Fallingwater stumbled through much of 1936 without any professional builder at all. Norbert James Zeller was engaged in that capacity late in 1935, but he turned out to be a drunk and a family deserter. When he was hauled off to the local jail, Kaufmann refused to help free him, and he was fired in the late spring of 1936. Quarrying kept on nonetheless, with enough men employed to make Fallingwater look like E. J.'s private WPA. As many as eighteen masons were quarrying stone and hauling it on horse carts to the work site, most of the time without professional direction. The men were generally local farmers or unemployed laborers, and their Depression-era wages were 35 to 75 cents an hour. Later on, the masons working on the guesthouse got even less: just 25 cents an hour.

The construction techniques were primitive. Dimensioning of the stones in the quarry was done not by measurement but all'occhio (by the eye), the way Michelangelo had counseled his marble-workers to do at Carrara four centuries before. Closer to the house, a more skilled team of masons trimmed the stones—chipping rather than sawing them—to a variety of sizes before composing them into tapestrylike walls. A stump wall still stands next to the quarry to show the variety of effects you can get from Pottsville sandstone. It manifests some very subtle changes in coloration and demonstrates the flat levels that can be achieved from the stone merely by striking the rock the right way.

There was occasional blasting of some of the rock, but the account given me by Earl Friend, the last surviving mason, specifies that the individual stones were never sawed—they were simply pried out of the earth with crowbars and mallets. This gave the stones the shelflike feel we experience at Fallingwater today. An observer at Bear Run might have been reminded of the construction of King Solomon's Temple in Jerusalem, where "neither hammer nor axe nor any tool of iron was heard" (I Kings 6:7).

But heaps of stones do not make a house. The first practical step in giving form to Fallingwater came on April 16, 1936, when the Morris Knowles engineers staked out its foundations. They returned soon after to stake out the concrete bridge that was to replace the wooden bridge that Zeller had removed from the stream. Three days later, on April 19, Wright arrived for his fourth or fifth visit to Bear Run, and a formal arrangement was made that put his ex-apprentice Abe Dombar in charge of the work. Dombar was among the earliest Taliesin Fellows, but he had quit several months before, chafing at how little practical experience Wright was offering. (His lack of exposure to engineering at Taliesin prevented his ever registering as an architect in Ohio, Dombar told me.) What gave Dombar the inside track to command Fallingwater was his position as assistant to the art director at the Kaufmann store, a sinecure he owed to Kaufmann Jr.

On May 6, 1936—three weeks before Wright's definitive working drawings arrived—Zeller began building the stone piers and abutments for the concrete bridge. Informed of this, Wright sent up an emergency set of drawings for the bridge alone. By now, everyone recognized the absurdity of the builder's getting ahead of the architect. Zeller would soon be fired, but not without a spicy cultural note. He later declared that he had disapproved of the nude sunbathing at Bear Run ("Bare Run" to its neighbors), and his wife informed Kaufmann that her husband would not be a party to the creation of a nudist colony.

As a stopgap measure, Kaufmann deputized his store's assistant general manager, Carl Thumm, to oversee construction and expedite materials for the house. Wright bristled at having to report to an intermediary, and endlessly needled Kaufmann about the "Thumm in the soup."

On June 5, 1936, Wright showed up at Kaufmann's to sign his contract, for which the revised working drawings of late May served as the legal basis. The job eventually earned Wright about $10,000 of the $150,000 that the building cost Kaufmann. E. J. was either short on cash or chose not to disturb his regular investments, because most of Fallingwater went up on loan from Pittsburgh bankers.

Back at Taliesin the apprentices were grumbling at the unfairness of Wright's awarding the plum Fallingwater job to Dombar, who they (and Wright) regarded as a Taliesin renegade. Wright consequently fired Dombar just weeks after hiring him, and replaced him with Taliesin veteran Bob Mosher, who would carry construction through Fallingwater's second story.

If there is a hero to Fallingwater's construction, it is Mosher. As at so many building sites, the first months were the most productive, so it was Mosher who oversaw the most dramatic phase of the work, between June and August 1936. The basic "footprint" of the foundations had already been staked out in length and width by the Knowles engineers, but this gave Mosher no clue as to how to project the building's heights and depths. Taking Mosher out to Bear Run on June 6, Wright instructed him to jump on top of the main boulder by the falls—the fireplace hearth today—and use that as the datum point for everything else. That night, Mosher reviewed the working drawings with Kaufmann until one in the morning. For the next four weeks, Mosher was totally on his own, stranded in a virtual wilderness with a dozen stonemasons but no foreman.

The construction and furnishing of Fallingwater produced letters and memos by the thousands, but none render more tellingly the threadbare way in which this sophisticated house was built than Mosher's notes to his master and fellows at Taliesin. Mosher would work all day, take a swim in the old Camp Kaufmann pool or at the falls—until the night he nearly broke his neck—then write detailed memos to Wright through the night. He discovered the hard way that the Knowles engineers had made gross errors in staking out the wall alignments. Their topographic plans were equally erratic, so that trees and boulders cropped up where none were anticipated. (The Knowles firm denied this and, in truth, it would not have been the first time a Taliesin apprentice had read a plan wrong.)

Mosher found himself making ad hoc changes to Wright's design. His enduring monument is the plunge pool by the stream, which allowed the Kaufmanns to swim in deeper water than Bear Run itself provided in the

The bolsters, the "hatch" steps down from the living room, and the approach bridge beyond

Fallingwater's stone tapestry walls are among the most expressive in architecture; Wright planned the curved trellis beam to wrap around a tree

basin just above the falls. Not part of the original design, the plunge pool was a cosmetic answer to a four-foot discrepancy that Mosher discovered between the actual height of the streambed and the level at which the Knowles drawing said it was. By late June, Mosher had supervised construction of the stubby stone bases for the three concrete bolsters and the stone wall that rises from the stream west of the bolsters. His workmen then cobbled together the wooden formwork for the bolsters, and at the end of June 1936 Mosher guided the pouring of the concrete into them.

Then, crisis. To everyone's consternation, an entirely new concept for the bolsters arrived from Taliesin a few days after they had been poured. The old bolster design called for them to rise in three progressively wider tiers. Wright's new concept called for a sleeker V-shape: each bolster would widen from 15 inches at the bottom to 36 inches at the top, where it carried the first floor. Mosher tore down the just-completed bolsters and helped construct a new set in late July. Wright was determined to give Fallingwater a thrilling profile, whatever the cost.

The fiasco of the old and new bolsters showed that Wright and Mosher were out of synch not only on concepts but on factual questions of measurements. At one point Mosher sent Taliesin a plan of the bolsters on which he penciled the ominous reproach: "Showing heights of bolster piers, size of rocks used in relation to 8 in. coping. Your piers showed about 5 in. of stone. No! No! No!"

By now Mosher, though a born improviser, was clearly over his head in dealing with technical problems. Wright warned Kaufmann that he would send no further structural drawings until an experienced builder took over the helm. That builder was found in Walter J. Hall, who stepped in on July 13, 1936. Hall was an exact contemporary of Wright, with forty years' experience as a builder in the remote northern Pennsylvania town of Port Allegany, the deer-hunting mecca of the United States. Hall had glimpsed Wright in Buffalo thirty years before, while the architect directed construction either on the Darwin Martin house or the Larkin headquarters (Hall family lore sometimes cites the one building, sometimes the other). Ever since, he had made himself into something of a Wright clone: a dozen of his neo-Wrightian houses in Port Allegany still attest to this. Hall passed on his enthusiasm for Wright to his son Raymond Vinson Hall and to his grandson Ray Morton Hall. The son studied design through the International Correspondence School, then petitioned New York and Pennsylvania to allow him to register as an architect under the old apprenticeship rules. The grandson worked as a site supervisor, representing different architects at building sites, so that three generations of Halls made up a full century of building practice.

It could only have been Providence herself who brokered the partnership of Frank Lloyd Wright and Walter J. Hall, but rarely did she need so much mortal help. Against all odds, three different avenues of contact had opened up between remote Spring Green and remote Port Allegany. The first of these was Raymond Hall, who in 1934 wrote Wright to inquire how he could join the novitiate at Taliesin (in the end, he couldn't raise the money). In his letter Hall cited his father, Walter, as "a master builder in the real sense of the word."

It was probably young Hall's letter that led Wright to dispatch his son John in 1935 to Port Allegany. There John checked out Lynn Hall, the hotel that Walter Hall was building on the outskirts of town (long shuttered and abandoned, it stands there still). John was no doubt astonished to see how closely the walls of Lynn Hall recalled his father's Taliesin. Inside, John inspected the formidable 40-foot-long reinforced-concrete beam that spans the hotel's lounge. The beam is entirely self-supporting, with horizontal "rebar" rods inside the concrete that tie into a vertical parapet wall that acts like a beam. That integration of the horizontal slab with a vertical "stiffener" is one of the engineering effects Wright had in mind for Fallingwater. John evidently reported back to his father that Hall was a crackerjack builder quite equal to his reputation.

This second contact led to the third. Earl Friar was a Taliesin retainer who managed Wright's stables and barns. Friar was well informed on the technique of reinforced concrete, which, until the 1930s, was probably employed more in farm buildings than in any other building type in the United States. At Wright's bidding, Friar kept up a running correspondence with Hall on problems of reinforced concrete.

Port Allegany is hardly next door to Pittsburgh: it takes three and a half hours to drive there today, probably twice that long in the 1930s. But Wright was desperate for a builder to direct operations at Bear Run, and in May 1936 he advised Kaufmann to take Hall on. Hall decamped from Port Allegany in early July, made a quick survey of the work site, and signed on as builder in Kaufmann's downtown office the morning of July 13. He appeared for work at Bear Run the same day.

Walter Hall was a crucial figure in the creation of the stone-tapestry walls at Fallingwater, although it remains unclear exactly who invented their style. The walls take their basic inspiration from the natural layering of the Bear Run sandstone, but Wright had already captured a similar effect in the 1914 rebuilding of Taliesin, which was also built from local stone. Bob Mosher may have had some impact on the styling of Fallingwater's walls, but there was also a link, albeit a chronologically hazy one, with Walter Hall's buildings at Port Allegany. If not the inventor, Walter Hall was for certain the prime executor and maestro of Fallingwater's masonry style. It was he who teased the greatest possible richness out of the walls (his last, in the guesthouse, are universally regarded as the best of the lot). Hall also conjured up Fallingwater's rough-grained slab floors: you can still see the identical floors he had laid at Lynn Hall a few years before.

Hall made his mark at Bear Run from the get-go, taking charge of the perilous second casting of the concrete bolsters, with Mosher reduced to second fiddle. Hall's strong presence was crucial to success at Bear Run, because after July 1936, Wright was no more than an absentee architect at Fallingwater. His new and lucrative commission for the S. C. Johnson headquarters in Racine, Wisconsin, left him little time for the Kaufmann house. E. J. felt this inattention keenly. On September 7, 1937, before construction was over, he telegraphed Wright: "You seem to have forgotten your creation at Bear Run." Wright shot back: "Forgotten the creation at Bear Run? Never."

.   .   .

n August of 1936, Fallingwater took another precarious step: the pouring of concrete for the main floor. Wright had held up sending the detailed structural drawings for this floor until the last minute. The drawings had to address the placement and dimensions of the concrete slabs and beams in the floor, and particularly the amount of steel that was to reinforce the concrete so that the main floor could cantilever fourteen feet beyond the bolsters into midair. He knew better than to articulate the design of the cantilever himself: at the end of June 1936 he summoned Mendel Glickman to Taliesin to do it.

We have two ways of learning how highly Wright regarded Glickman: he trusted him to calculate the structures at both Fallingwater and Johnson's Wax, and he accorded Glickman and his wife the rare honor of burial in the ancestral Lloyd Jones cemetery at Spring Green. Glickman was an immigrant Jew who had trained in mechanical engineering in Russia before coming to America. When he introduced himself by letter to Wright in 1932, he had just served as chief engineer for the American contingent that was building the Stalingrad tractor plant in the USSR. His objective now, he wrote Wright, was to combine engineering with art. Glickman may have given Wright occasional engineering counsel, but he seems not to have been directly employed at Taliesin until the quandary over the Fallingwater cantilever. He was paired on the cantilever structural drawings with Wes Peters, Wright's errant son-in-law, who by mid-1936 had returned to Taliesin, where he presided as top apprentice and, later, director for several decades. Being younger and less experienced in real-world problems, Peters served as backup to Glickman. In late June and early July the two men worked together on the revised bolster design and on the steelwork diagrams for the first floor.

The task facing Glickman and Peters was as complex as the structure itself. Wright's design called for three terraces and four balconies: the nomenclature is fuzzy, but we may define the former as resting on something solid and the latter as pure projections in the air. Each family member had a terrace: Liliane's was partly over the living room and partly in the air; E. J.'s projected like a balcony but was anchored in a boulder; Junior's did not project at all. The four balconies carried the south end of the living room, its projections east and west, and the balcony off the guestroom. There were, besides, a half-dozen roof overhangs and the unsupported trellis beams over the east living-room balcony.

To understand how Fallingwater's balconies and overhangs work as cantilevers, in whole or in part, requires a short detour into the world of concrete, reinforced concrete, and beams. A cantilever is a particular kind of beam that, instead of being supported (engineers would say "fixed") underneath by supports in the middle or at both ends, is supported at one end only and floats free at the other. Nothing prevents cantilevers from being constructed of steel or even wood, but for aesthetic and practical reasons Wright envisioned the Fallingwater cantilevers in reinforced concrete.

Like so much of Fallingwater, concrete is at once new and old: the Greeks, Romans, and Mayans had exploited it for millennia to stunning effects. The basic component of concrete is cement, a sloppy mixture of sand, crushed stone, and water. Cement was adapted to industrial building uses in the nineteenth century, when British builders popularized a new type of cement made from stone quarried on the Isle of Portland. Portland cement combined lime, silica, alumina, and iron, which were burned together in a furnace and pulverized into powder. It was a stronger cement than any previously known, and did not weaken when it was exposed to water. When a stone aggregate like gravel was added to Portland cement, the resulting concrete was extraordinarily strong but still maneuverable during pouring.

Concrete was one of the materials with which Wright felt the greatest kinship, not aesthetically but for its versatility and economy. He claimed his Unity Temple of 1904 as the first concrete monolith in the world. Certainly it was one of the earliest designs to leave the concrete exterior exposed rather than covered with decoration or facing. By the time he designed Fallingwater, Wright had designated concrete for a score of built or unbuilt projects. He was also continuing to learn new properties of concrete from his advisors Glickman and Peters, from Earl Friar, the builder Walter Hall, and from two of his own children. Lloyd Wright had been working in poured-concrete houses in California since World War I, while David Wright represented the Portland Cement Association in Chicago.

Fallingwater's concrete is reinforced with steel, in a technique born in England around 1832, when concrete floors were first embedded with iron rods for added resiliency. Wright had used reinforced concrete for several buildings, but never on a house. Its use at Fallingwater was mandatory: an ordinary concrete structure would never be able to sustain those cantilevers. The reinforcing would be done with steel rods set in the bolsters, in the main floor and in the two floors above it, in the balconies and terraces, in the trellis beams, in the various overhangs, and even in the steps leading up to Junior's penthouse. Reinforcing rods stiffen at least some of Fallingwater's stone walls as well.

Fallingwater's concrete floors were poured in a manner that departed somewhat from standard operating procedure. Concrete floors typically consist of a slab on top and supporting beams and joists below, as in a wooden floor. Wright chose instead to flip the system upside down, so the beams and joists lie on top and the slab hangs below, not as a T but as a ⏌. This flipping of the joists brings to mind the way Filippo Brunelleschi set Gothic ribs outside the dome of Florence Cathedral, whereas French Gothic builders invariably placed them inside their vaults.

Wright never explained why he turned his floors upside-down, but evidently he saw this as the only way to give a smooth underbelly to the main floor, which otherwise would have had the haphazard look of the underdeck of a bridge. The flip was mandatory if Fallingwater was to achieve the serenity of the International Style. Wright seems also to have believed that the inversion stiffened the beams and joists, making them more resistant to the load that would be put on them. There was a possible functional payoff, too: the flipped system provided impregnably closed floors—highly important in a house that was sure to be drenched in moisture. It also answered the Kaufmanns' demands on Wright for acoustic control to keep down the roar of the waterfall in their living room. With the slab below and the joists on top, Wright obtained a sound-deadening airlock. Over the concrete joists he set redwood two-by-fours, and over them a subfloor of extra-thick sheets of plywood: nine-layered rather than the usual five. Over the plywood went asphalt roof sheeting, and over the sheeting a bed of sand to carry the flagstone paving slabs. It made for quite a sandwich.

Sunday, December 9, 2001. I am standing near Fallingwater's main fireplace, as I have a hundred times before, but today I hardly trust my eyes. All the built-in living room furniture, all the flagstones in the floor, all the

In 2002, post-tensioning cables of immense strength were inserted alongside Fallingwater's reinforced-concrete beams to halt further drooping of its cantilevers

roof sheeting and plywood flooring below that, all Wright's two-by-fours are gone, ripped away in the determination to give Fallingwater, belatedly, the strength that Wright promised but failed to give it sixty-five years earlier.

The texts and drawings of 1936 tell me what supposedly went into the making of this famous cantilever, but now I can see it for myself. I see, laid bare for only a few months, the four concrete beams 40 feet long, 2 feet wide, and 18 inches deep, on which the living room floor formerly sat. These beams run north-south over the stone wall and the three concrete bolsters coming up from the stream below. To give a distinctive shape to his hatch opening down to the stream, Wright designated the beam that marked the east end of the hatch as curved rather than straight. An enchanting idea, but a dangerous one, for here exactly is where the deflection in the cantilever has become most noticeable: a droop of a full 7 inches. Also visible are the narrower concrete joists that Wright and his engineers set east-west in order to crisscross the beams every 4 feet. Most of the joists have indentations, where until a month ago the redwood two-by-fours sat. Some joists have square cutouts to allow water pipes to reach the radiators. With the flooring and all the furniture gone, it feels as though someone has tossed the Shroud of Turin over a chair, or that the queen of England has entered Westminster Abbey without a stitch of clothing.

The cantilever deflections had been pronounced stable enough when evaluated by local engineers at the end of the 1980s and in the first site visits by the New York engineer Robert Silman in the early 1990s. Then, newly available computer modeling for structural systems indicated a higher possibility of collapse. To ward off such a danger, a steel cage was put up in 1997 to cradle the main floor and keep it safe from cantilever failure. Conceptually if not technically, though, the cantilevers *had* failed: it was only by luck—in Gothic times they would have said a miracle— that they had not crashed. Headlines in the *New York Times* spoke of "Fallingwater Falling Down," and called the house "America's Leaning Tower of Pisa."

Silman's solution: rip up the floor, lay bare the concrete beams, insert high-strength steel compound cables, or strands—from nine to thirteen per bundle—alongside the old beams and joists north-south and east-west, then tighten the cables (the technical term is post-tensioning) so the cantilevers would sag no more. The cables were in place when I visited Fallingwater again on February 12, 2002, and they were being prepared for their securing in huge concrete anchors. These anchor blocks were positioned immediately south of the fireplace and in a parallel line across the living room; other blocks were inserted in the balconies that extend east and west off the living room. The south ends of some of the cables poked through the window-wall of the living room so that they temporarily hung a few feet over the stream. In mid-March 2002 the cables were tightened by a hydraulic jack at the tremendous pressure of 350,000 to 360,000 pounds per square inch to restore to the floor the tautness it had before it went slack. The deflection in the cantilevers was reversed by little more than one-fifth of an inch—more would have been too dangerous—so that the ends of the balconies will always have a pronounced droop.

How in God's name did Wright bring us to this mess? He was well versed in the practice of cantilevers, but we can't tell how well he knew the theory on which they are based. Some of his cantilevers used very modest materials: the Laura Gale house of 1909 (the one Wright always claimed as the prototype for Fallingwater) has terraces and overhangs made of nothing more than wood covered with stucco. Fallingwater's balconies work on the same principle, but they are far more complex to analyze. For one thing, there are two systems at work: some of the joists are made of simple concrete, while the bolsters, beams, and other joists are made of reinforced concrete. In *The Natural House,* Wright observed that such complex structures defy the calculations of an engineer who analyzes everything as separate vertical and horizontal members, because he "has not yet enough scientific formulae to enable him to calculate for continuity."

Wright first called for a reinforced-concrete cantilever in his unexecuted 1912 project for the *San Francisco Call-Bulletin,* but, as we saw, his triumph of cantilever technology was the Imperial Hotel in Tokyo, which he made flexible enough to withstand seismic shocks but rigid enough to keep standing. When the hotel was hit by earthquakes in April 1922 and September 1923, it resisted, with only minor damage incurred. American newspapers declared that it was the only large building in Tokyo to survive the 1923 earthquake, though in fact dozens had. This gave an unmerited and lamentable boost to Wright's thinking of himself as an engineering genius.

How could the designer of the Imperial Hotel not spot the potential failure in Fallingwater's cantilevers? The basic answer is that Wright was overreaching and should never have pushed the cantilevers so far beyond their natural limits. One specialist has called Wright's cantilevering gesture "extravagant to the point of folly." Along with that intemperate decision, there were a number of design oversights: the steel rebars were probably too puny, and wrongly placed within the beams; the concrete mass was too heavy, and the upper cantilever (Liliane's terrace) was so poorly conceived—or so poorly constructed—that it transferred all its weight to the lower one.

Robert Silman published a lucid explanation of the cantilever collapse and his proposed antidote in the September 2000 *Scientific American*. He covered all the bases in an exemplary manner, but he allowed himself one bit of fiction: in his account, Mendel Glickman suddenly strikes his forehead and moans: "Oh my God, I forgot the negative reinforcement!"

There is no evidence—and no chance—that so experienced an engineer as Mendel Glickman forgot something as elementary as calculating the tension and compression in his concrete beams. But something else does appear to have been miscalculated or misconstrued in the summer of 1936. We know only that Glickman and Peters finished their calculations around mid-July and sent their drawings posthaste to Pittsburgh. As the wooden formwork for the main floor was being constructed, however, Kaufmann called in a second Pittsburgh engineering firm to check and ultimately replace Wright's structural drawings. This was the Metzger-Richardson Company, the engineers Kaufmann used a few years later to build a reinforced-concrete parking garage next to the store. Headed by the respected engineers F. L. Metzger, J. G. Richardson, and L. W. Cook, the firm specialized in the fabrication of reinforced concrete.

The Metzger-Richardson engineers went to work at once on the Glickman-Peters drawings, and on August 10 produced their own plans, which called for a much greater quantity of steel reinforcing for the main floor. The Metzger-Richardson drawings went to Kaufmann's site supervisor, Carl Thumm, rather than to Wright's supervisor, Bob Mosher. Thumm gave his approval for the addition of the steel and Mosher acquiesced: for several weeks Wright was kept in the dark about this momentous change. This time, at least, his knee-jerk fulminations about "treason" at the hands of his apprentices and clients were warranted.

The Metzger-Richardson plans called for 1-inch-square steel reinforcing rods, rather than the ¾-inch-diameter rods called for in Wright's drawings, and for many more of them. This meant a substantial upgrade in strength, but more weight, too. Silman is convinced that Metzger-Richardson's action saved Fallingwater. "Wright was clearly wrong about the cantilever beams: if Metzger-Richardson had not slipped in the extra steel bars, the beams surely would have failed."

But the beams very nearly reached failure anyway, so why was the additional steel inserted by Metzger-Richardson not enough? One factor Metzger-Richardson might have overlooked is that while the quantity of steel going in was significantly augmented, the weight of the concrete was never reduced. Structurally, Fallingwater might have proven its own worst enemy.

We might think that the most prudent engineer overseeing a reinforced-concrete cantilever is the one who calls for the most steel, but the science of engineering is a good deal more subtle than that. Steel acts in accord with its own internal needs in expanding in hot weather and contracting in cold: if these coefficients of expansion do not match those of the surrounding materials, then the addition of more steel can be calamitous to a structure like Fallingwater. There is also a ratio of helping to hurting: every time more steel was added to Fallingwater, the increased weight made it more prone to toppling over. The trick was not to blindly pile on more steel but to calculate what was the minimum appropriate amount of steel and where it should be placed within the concrete beam to strengthen the structure without increasing the risk of overturning it.

Suppose, however, that Fallingwater had been well designed but badly built? Sixty-five years later we can detect much negligence in the construction. The beams that Silman's technicians sliced open show the rebars fluctuating erratically in number and placement. Impulse analysis (a sort of sound-based X-ray) tells an even more frightening story on the upper floor: there is a gap of some 10 feet in Liliane's terrace where the joist rebars are completely missing. With the rebars wanting, Liliane's terrace no longer constituted the self-supporting structure Wright meant it to be. All these years it constituted a tremendous dead weight resting on the main cantilever below. Liliane's terrace projects about 19 feet south of the two stone piers that support it in the living room. Thirteen feet along, the upper terrace is supported by four T-shaped mullions that rise as part of the living room's window-wall (these mullions are disguised as oversized window frames, so they appear to be doing no structural work at all). The balcony then projects an additional unsupported six feet in the air. When Glickman calculated the stresses on the living-room cantilever, he had no reason to include the weight of Liliane's terrace, because each floor was conceived of as structurally independent. Walter Hall seems to have inadvertently turned the upper terrace from the self-supporting element Wright intended into a dead weight. Were it not for the overstressed mullions between the living-room windows, Liliane's terrace would have collapsed into the living room as soon as the temporary scaffolding was removed.

Wright gave a hint that he knew something was fundamentally flawed in Liliane's terrace. It was his intention to make an important structural support out of the low parapet walls that girdled the various terraces and balconies. Such parapets normally have only a minor structural role, but at Fallingwater Wright wanted the parapets to give added stability to the cantilevered slabs. He made them into "edge beams" to further stiffen the cantilevers, the way the bottom of a cardboard box gains stability from its sides. This was the procedure Walter Hall had already worked out in his quirky hotel at Port Allegany, but Wright could not finesse the same effect at Fallingwater. He was still mulling the question over a year later, and went out of his way in the *Architectural Forum* of January 1938 to express his regret that the parapets had not achieved the full structural role he had hoped to give them. "The cantilever slabs here carry parapets and the beams. They may be seen clutching big boulders. But next time, I believe, parapets will carry the floor—or better still we will know enough to make the two work together as one, as I originally intended." Whether his failure to do this at Bear Run was a flaw in the design or in the construction of Fallingwater, Wright never revealed.

The stress caused by the cantilever crisis of 1936 showed up not only in the beams and joists but in the anxieties felt by young Mosher, old Hall, Wright and his engineers, and Kaufmann and *his* engineers. The Taliesin apprentices had a wicked term for such conflicts, which was "Wes Is More." This conflated Mies's dictum "Less Is More" with the nickname for Wright's always-nervous engineer Wesley Peters. On numerous occasions Peters specified more steel for Wright's buildings than his father-in-law was willing to allow. Sometimes, Wright yielded to Peters and grudgingly confirmed the change orders to more steel. Twenty years after Fallingwater, for example, Wright had to admit that the nearby house at Kentuck Knob had so little steel in its roof that, unless it was strengthened, updrafts were liable to lift the roof into the air. But in at least a half-dozen cases Wright was unaware—or pretended to be—that massive quantities of steel were furtively inserted into his buildings by apprentices who felt the Master of Taliesin had dangerously underestimated the strengthening his buildings needed. Fallingwater was the most notable of these instances, and since the cantilever nearly failed, we have to assume that its deformation would have come earlier and been more serious had E. J. Kaufmann not countermanded Wright's wishes.

The extra steel recommended by the Metzger-Richardson engineers arrived on August 15. It was fixed in place within the wooden formwork for the living-room beams by August 19, and two days later Hall poured concrete into those forms. Mosher informed Wright of the pouring that same day, August 19, but he kept the master in the dark about the deviations in the Metzger-Richardson plans until August 25, by which time the extra steel had been securely laid in. Wright could do nothing about it.

Wright had probably never before suffered so harsh a rebellion at the hands of a client, at least as Mosher reported it. " 'I'm the one living in this house,' " Mosher quoted E. J. as saying, " 'not the architect, and I want it this way.' " The instant this letter arrived in Spring Green, Wright fired a telegram to Mosher: "Drop work and come back" until Kaufmann Sr. and Wright could "arrive at some basis of mutual respect." "Do not delay one hour," Wright emphasized, and when Mosher hesitated on receiving the first order, Wright sent him a second: "If you are unable or unwilling to carry out my instructions your connection with me ends." Wright then turned his fury on Kaufmann:

> Dear E. J.:
> If you are paying to have the concrete engineering done down there, there is no use whatever in our doing it here. I am willing you should take it over, but I am not willing to be insulted. . . . I don't know what kind of architect you are familiar with but it apparently isn't the kind I think I am. You seem not to know how to treat a decent one. I have put so much more into this house than you or any other client has a right to expect that if I haven't your confidence—to hell with the whole thing.

Kaufmann parried this thrust by mimicking Wright's telegram almost word for word:

> Dear Mr. Wright:
> If you have been paid to do the concrete engineering up there there is no use whatever of our doing it down here. I am not willing to take it over as you suggest nor am I willing to be insulted. . . .
> I don't know what kind of clients you are familiar with, but apparently they are not the kind I think I am. You seem not to know how to treat a decent one. I have put so much confidence and enthusiasm behind this whole project in my limited way, to help the fulfillment of your efforts that if I do not have your confidence in the matter—to hell with the whole thing. . . .
> Now don't you think that we should stop writing letters and that you owe it to the situation to come to Pittsburgh and clear it up by getting the facts? Certainly there are reasons which must have prompted you to write as you have.
> I am sorry that you are calling Bob [Mosher] back. He seems entirely wrapped up in his work and in its progress, but this is beyond my control and you must use your best judgment.
> It is difficult for me to conceive that a man of your magnitude and understanding could write such a letter. In deference to our past association, I must naturally put it aside as if it had never been written as it certainly does not conform to the facts.

That Wright would turn his venom on a client who dared question him was old hat, but it was uncharacteristic of him to reveal that he feared for a project. This he did regarding Fallingwater in the letter he wrote Walter Hall immediately after telegraphing Kaufmann:

> I have put too much into this house . . . to have it miscarry by mischievous interferences of any sort. The kind of buildings I build don't happen that way. (Several have been ruined that way, however.) And this one may be one of them.
>
> With a setup such as the present one turns out to be there can be only failure. I have not built one hundred and ninety of the world's important buildings without knowing the look of the thing when it turns up on the job.
>
> Failure, I mean, by way of treacherous interference.

At month's end Wright was still fulminating at Kaufmann that the extra steel surreptitiously slipped in would weaken the cantilever, but he gave E. J. a halfhearted statement that Kaufmann took as an apology, and the crisis was over. Kaufmann asked Wright for a second apprentice-supervisor to take over where Mosher had left off and Wright agreed, but Hall worked another several weeks on his own.

Wright now shifted his attention from the sorry proceedings at Bear Run to the triumph at Johnson's Wax. There he brilliantly resolved his design problem by placing the employees in a virtually windowless box, which he then illuminated with ceiling lights set among the lily-pad columns that Mendel Glickman had designed for him. Unlike the constant torment at Fallingwater, the design process at Johnson's Wax went smoothly. To prove the trustworthiness of Glickman's lily-pad columns, Wright devised a test in which a prototype column was piled up with about ten times its anticipated load, and easily withstood it. It remains the most famous structural test in the history of architecture.

Hall carried on as sole builder at Bear Run, grumbling all the while at the sketchiness of the plans that were being mailed to him from Taliesin. When he came to pour the living-room ceiling, he discovered that the plan calling for a recess 24 inches deep conflicted with the dimensions on Wright's steel diagrams, so Hall arbitrarily reduced the cove to the 16-inch depth it has today. He complained that he could not find the exact location Wright wanted for the two piers that were to rise in the living room: "To keep going I had to locate them by guess and by God rather than any figures I could find from the unit line. For the good of the party who made these plans I wish you would impress upon them how dumb Hall is and to give better measurements to builders of this kind."

It was obvious that a new Taliesin representative was badly needed at Bear Run, particularly to guide Hall with reference to the arcane modular system in Wright's design, which was producing weird fractional measurements. The pouring of the second floor was delayed two weeks because the plumbing, heating, and electrical details had not been worked out. This was the kind of task Mosher would have been working on while Hall urged on the masons. But there was the occasional good news from the work site, too. Hall poured the second floor on October 1, and six days later Edgar Tafel arrived as Wright's second on-site representative.

At the end of October the cantilevers struck back. As soon as Hall poured the second-floor roof overhang above the guest-balcony—a minor cantilever, but a cantilever nonetheless—it was obvious from its instantaneous droop that the overhang had been incorrectly reinforced. Work plodded into November, with the workmen now insisting on breaking for deer-hunting season. (Hall got each mason to return to work after bagging just one deer.) Tafel doggedly supervised the pouring of the joists and slabs for E. J.'s west-terrace floor and the raising of the third-floor walls, proving as ingenious as Mosher in solving on-site problems: he spaced the joists in E. J.'s terrace to allow three trees to grow through holes in the floor. Nature unfortunately refused to play ball, and the trees were dead within a year. The building season over, Wright ordered Tafel back to Taliesin, leaving Walter Hall as sole construction overseer a second time.

The cantilever problem now escalated into a crisis, and cracks were soon blooming all over Fallingwater. The cracks in the guest-balcony overhang were joined by two more in the parapet of Liliane's balcony. Tafel attributed these to Hall's inattention to the two T-shaped mullions in the bank of windows at the south end of the living room. The Taliesin drawings called for them to be welded at the top to form two independent structural rectangles. Hall, however, skipped that detail to save time, and merely placed horizontal steel bars over the mullions rather than welding everything together. It was no more reassuring for Wright to read Tafel's report of October 30 that the mullions had gone out of plumb soon after workers were seen pounding on them.

Wright sought to assure Kaufmann that cracks were normal in concrete shrinkage, and that they portended no weakness in the structural integrity of the house. He might have avoided the cracks by using expansion joints in the concrete, Wright explained on November 2, but he had chosen not to for aesthetic reasons. After the scare of the cracks in the second-floor roof overhang, Metzger-Richardson was commissioned to draw up a second set of steel diagrams, this time for the third floor. There was some structural soul-searching at Taliesin, too. Tafel, now back at Wright's side, informed Hall at the beginning of December: "We are trying to locate the exact cause of the cracks." By then the cracks were popping up ever more often: in early December a new one opened up in the guest-balcony parapet, and Hall morosely reported to Wright on December 7, 1936, that the parapet on the balcony extending west of the living room had now drooped a full inch below the level of the corresponding east balcony. The roof over the guest balcony continued to droop, obliging Hall to shore it up for a year with ugly steel bars. (Toward the end of 1937 he substituted the more aesthetic stone-wall crutch that remains today.) In mid-December, Kaufmann himself spotted a new crack in the living-room window-wall. "He has taken this very calmly considering the seriousness of it," Hall laconically reported to Wright.

As Glickman and Peters labored to find a definitive reason for the crack formations, Kaufmann ordered the Metzger-Richardson firm to conduct a full structural analysis. The engineers reported back that they had found cracks in five places where the cantilevers had been stressed beyond capacity. Their suggested cure, however, was far worse than the disease: each cantilever would have to be permanently braced from below. So equipped, Fallingwater would have been as pretty a sight as a ballerina maintaining her balance with a pair of ski poles.

At the moment this structural drama was unfolding at Bear Run, there was a parallel medical drama at Taliesin, where Wright spent most of December 1936 battling pneumonia. As Mosher hovered over him, Wright moaned in delirium that Fallingwater had become too heavy. There was a perfect irony here: in his *Autobiography* Wright admitted to experiencing the thrill of schadenfreude around 1890 every time his boss Dankmar Adler discovered a new crack in the Auditorium Building. Now construction cracks had come to haunt him, too.

Halfway recovered, Wright directed Hall to cut core samples from the concrete in the cracked areas for analysis. Kaufmann doubted the wisdom of these cuts, but Wright demanded an end to his interference: "I want an un-cracked structure. Know how to get it. Intend to have it." Undeterred, on December 11, Kaufmann telephoned Mendel Glickman and summoned him to Pittsburgh to "advise what must be done due to the checks." Kaufmann meant to write "cracks," of course—a Freudian slip that underlined his distress at the money he was wasting as the dream of Fallingwater began to slip away. Wright refused to let Glickman go to Pittsburgh, so Kaufmann had to content himself with a diagnosis over the telephone. Glickman would not lay eyes on Fallingwater until Kaufmann summoned him fifteen years later to resolve the very same problem.

The second year of construction opened to more acrimony in January 1937. On the second day of the new year, Wright admitted to Mendel Glickman: "We are on the spot at Pittsburgh and way behind with Racine, holding up the building." Two days later, Carl Thumm constructed an emergency wall under E. J.'s terrace, which the Metzger-Richardson consultants regarded as being in danger of imminent collapse (we will recall that Wright had significantly lengthened that terrace from its preliminary dimensions). Thumm and the Metzger-Richardson team then performed loading tests on the main cantilevers by stacking bags of sand, cement, and cast-iron pipes on E. J.'s new terrace and at the far ends of several balconies, which sounds as though they wished to replicate the heroic tests Wright had earlier conducted on the lily-pad columns at Racine. The weight tests caused no problem for Kaufmann's terrace, sustained by the new wall under it. The news was good at certain other points, too. "As I explained to Junior [Thumm wrote E. J. on January 21], the tests on the roof and the guest balcony under same were o.k." But when they put 2,700 pounds on the west balcony of the living room, it caused cracks to open in the parapet of Liliane's terrace above. It looked as though new walls would be needed to carry that terrace.

Not everything at Bear Run was bleak. Walter Hall's son Raymond made his first appearance there on January 6, 1937, and immediately wrote Wright that it was "positively the most beautiful structure I've ever seen."

It was all Kaufmann could do to keep up Wright's flagging spirits on Fallingwater—another role reversal between client and architect. "Cheer up, all difficulties must be overcome" and "With all the difficulties it still remains a noble structure" he telegraphed Wright on January 7. This was also the moment the Fallingwater publicity machine sputtered to life. On January 22 the Kaufmann house received its first-ever public mention in a piece by Bob Mosher in the "At Taliesin" column carried by the Wisconsin newspapers.

Taking advantage of the winter slowdown, Walter Hall went in late January to spend time with Wright at Taliesin. There they strategized over the deflection of the cantilevers and how best to finish the house internally. Wright sent Hall back to Bear Run together with Bob Mosher, who now began a second stint as supervisor.

At the end of January a second time bomb went off. It took half a month for Wright to learn about the loading tests that had been conducted on January 6. When he did, on January 24, he telegraphed Kaufmann that he would be held responsible if the tests caused damage to any of the balconies. Kaufmann merely mimicked and mirrored the threat back to Wright the same day, using the literary device he had used the previous summer. When Wright thunderously wired Kaufmann, "Are you prepared to take full responsibility for stability of concrete structure in view of tests you have conducted over my head?" Kaufmann wired back "You must take full responsibility for stability of concrete structure taking into consideration the results of our tests. Same were made for additional data during your illness after repeated attempts to have your engineer [Glickman] present."

The next day, January 25, Wright tried one of his sentimental appeals to Kaufmann. He berated E. J. for not having faith in his design:

> I have put my best inspiration and effort into creating something rare and beautiful for you, whom I respect and have conceived affection for, only to find that so far as you could add ruin to my work and reputation you did so behind my back when I was helpless, with no idea, apparently, that you were so doing. . . . I will get on the job now that I am around again. . . .
>
> I know the attitude of the shopper—the buyer and the seller where building matters are concerned. But if a man is his own lawyer he has a fool for a client. How much more than a fool is the man who tries to act between his architect and his building? Hall is not the experienced builder I needed but he has muddled through pretty well considering—though mixed up by your "Thumm" time and again.

Wright concluded by minimizing the "scare over the integrity of the structure"; the deflection in the cantilevers was "perfectly normal." Two days later Wright sent Kaufmann a long document that would have locked E. J. into deference to the architect in matters of construction. Wright demanded a signature but he never got it: the agreement sits today in multiple copies in multiple archives—all unsigned.

With the shell of the house complete by the beginning of 1937, it was time to turn to its interior finishes. Floors had to be laid, windows installed, steel-stud partitions set up for the interior walls. Plumbers and electricians, window-fitters and roofers—all had to be organized and supplied with mountains of shop drawings for their particular specialty.

At this point Fallingwater became a virtual branch of Kaufmann's Department Store, with plumbers, electricians, and half the store's maintenance staff (it seemed) working at Bear Run. Carl Thumm was prime coordinator at Fallingwater from 1935 on, just as he had been for a decade at the store. Now in 1937 he was joined by the store's architect, A. E. Vitaro, who began to build key parts of the house interior. Fallingwater would be a prime element of Vitaro's job at the store for the next twenty years, ending with his work on Liliane and E. J.'s tomb. It was also in 1937 that Kaufmann Jr. began to play a role in procuring interior furnishings for the house.

February 1937 was as fruitful a month as January had been barren. The electric piping and the radiator work were complete, with the redwood arriving for the subflooring. The first of the windows were installed by Pittsburgh Plate Glass. The Hope Window Company of Jamestown, New York, supplied the steel window sashes. Measuring the windows proved a trial in itself, and Bob Mosher had to reject wrong sizes fairly often. This was the moment at which E. J. came up with the idea of fitting the glass directly into the stone, where possible. The metal components of the frames as well as all railings and metal shelving in the house were painted Cherokee red in Duco paint supplied by DuPont (Wright sent the Kaufmanns an old Indian pot as a color guide). Stonemasons began to lay flagstone floors throughout the house, beginning in the living room. When it came time to shave down the tip of the boulder that protruded through the floor at the fireplace, Kaufmann persuaded Wright to leave it just as it was.

Attention now passed to the question of how to cover the concrete balconies. Early in 1937, Wright got the idea of sheathing them in gold leaf: "like the quiet gold of Japanese screens." A journalist reported in March of 1937 that this was about to happen, but it never did. Although it sounds fantastic, the concept had much to recommend it. Gold had become newly popular in the huge murals that were a staple of Art Deco buildings and ships in the twenties and thirties. Wright had used gold paint or gold-burnished plaster to striking effect at Taliesin, and he had set gold Japanese screens in the living room of the Barnsdall house. Gilding Fallingwater's balconies would have cost no more than a few thousand dollars, but E. J. obviously feared this would sound extravagant to his customers back in Pittsburgh, and no one knew how long the gold leaf would adhere in so damp an environment. Kaufmann shot down the idea and turned for an alternative solution to Lloyd Wright, who found him a waterproof cement paint from Super-Concrete Emulsions of Los Angeles. Kaufmann had the paint shipped from Los Angeles to Bear Run, and Fallingwater's concrete has been ocher-colored ever since. A small detail, but a significant one, because the International Style houses both in Europe and America were invariably painted white. Wright's tinted balconies have instead a sensuous quality that allies them with human experience.

A hundred other finishing details remained to be dealt with. By mid-

Construction on E. J.'s
terrace, December 1936, with
the stone tower that is a key
element in Fallingwater's
design

February half the windows had been glazed and the last of the stone
floors was complete. Not yet in place, according to a memo sent to Kaufmann at the beginning of April, were some details of the electrical wiring,
stonework, concrete, roofing, the bathrooms, plumbing, lighting, heating,
painting, and plastering; some special casement frames that were late in
arriving from Hope Windows; last-minute changes to the hatch stairs;
miscellaneous revisions to the ironwork, the kitchen, and the basement;
some special woodwork and metalwork, including the streamlined
shelves in the living room; and nearly all the built-in furniture.

Kaufmann's terrace remains
a spectacular display of
cantilever technology

Though Fallingwater was rushing to completion, the torment of the sagging cantilevers would not go away. In March, Bob Mosher calculated that both the east and west balconies opening off the living room had deflected more than two inches. Meanwhile, the old cracks in the parapets of Liliane's terrace had reopened. In May, Kaufmann sought a new evaluation on the cantilever deflection from the Metzger-Richardson firm, which reported back a week later. Metzger-Richardson minced no words: "The calculated stresses in the structure do not fall within the limits of those prescribed by accepted engineering practice. From this standpoint, therefore, the structure does not have a satisfactory factor of safety, or what might be termed reserve strength. We believe the recommendations we made from time to time, regarding the extension of supports at different points, should be carried out." Wright (who came on site both in September and October of 1937) continued to reassure Kaufmann that the cantilevers were adequate to their task, and Kaufmann allowed himself to be persuaded. He ordered Hall to tear away the wall that Thumm had stuck under the west terrace in January. In the end, Kaufmann defied the engineers who had urged him to place emergency struts under Fallingwater's balconies. He would let the balconies fly free.

Structural failure or no, the Kaufmanns were determined to move into their retreat, and in November 1937 they did. Just three years had passed since Wright and E. J. first discussed a waterfall cottage for Bear Run. Now the house was finished: an exceptionally fast track by any standard, and pretty miraculous for so complex a house.

The last word comes from the member of the Kaufmann family who was least involved in the building. Liliane wrote a lyrical letter of thanks to Wright on New Year's Day 1938, after the Kaufmanns' second holiday weekend at the house.

We have had the two happiest weekends of our lives in the House, the one over Christmas and this one. There are large balsam branches laid along the metal shelves around the living room and twined in the bars of the balustrade going up the staircase—you can't imagine how lovely it looks. We have had rather large house parties both weekends and it is a continual delight to see how beautifully the house adapts itself to large and rather scattered groups of people. . . . We . . . are more than grateful for the joy you have given us.

Opposite: Fallingwater's living room

SEVEN

FALLINGWATER
GETS AN INTERIOR

Mrs. Kaufmann, how will you get wallpaper to stick
on those walls?

—A VISITOR, to Liliane

What is it about the exterior of a photogenic building that makes some visitors so sure that disappointment awaits them inside? Such tourists—maybe one in ten—inevitably emerge from the Taj Mahal, St. Peter's, or the Dome of the Rock having been far less enchanted inside than they were outside. Roughly the same ratio holds true at Fallingwater. The only thing that would compel those one-in-ten visitors to love Fallingwater's interior would be to lock the house up and prohibit entry: make them press their noses to the living-room windows or study the house in color photographs such as the ones set among these pages.

Everybody who views the exterior of Fallingwater comes away enchanted, but the one-in-ten visitors carp endlessly about the interior. The futuristic appliances from the 1930s amuse them, the curiosities collected by the Kaufmanns intrigue them, and views of the falls from the balconies excite them, but they still find Fallingwater's interior too dark, or too cold, or too rough, its hallways too narrow, its ceilings too low, its walls too barren of ornament, the views outside too restricted. In the whole Wright industry, probably no tourist cliché is heard more often than their ". . . but I'd never want to live here." These are generally not crank comments, and they deserve a sympathetic hearing. But what Wright was trying to do inside Fallingwater deserves a sympathetic hearing, too. The tourists who are disenchanted, disappointed, or disoriented by the interior may simply not be ready for the most challenging part of Fallingwater's design.

Visitors bewildered by Fallingwater's interior—and some days they constitute more than one in ten—most often register their disappointment at three shortcomings: the confining proportions, the harshness of the materials, and the cavelike environment. The low ceilings evoke the most questions and complaints: visitors always want to know whether it was Wright or Kaufmann who was so short. Actually, both client and architect were of medium height, Wright claiming 5 feet 8½ inches. The house ceilings are typically 6 feet 4¾ inches tall, and rise to 7 feet at certain points. The guesthouse, added two years later, has a 7-foot-4-inch ceiling height, which does suggest that the Kaufmanns told Wright the ceilings in the main house were too low. Wright needed the low proportions to keep the external profile of Fallingwater low against its hillside, but they probably derive also from his mid-1930s thinking about a prototype Usonian house that could be produced inexpensively from standardized building components. The low ceiling height at Fallingwater is just one of many links between this luxury house and its proletarian cousins.

Once inside Fallingwater, visitors find themselves on three floors that appear smaller and more angular than what was promised by the exterior, since so much of the house is balcony. The rooms are few: a living room and two inconsequential servant spaces on the first floor; bedrooms for a guest, Liliane, and E. J. on the second floor; a study and bedroom for Kaufmann Jr. on the third. (Junior's double accommodation was not in the original plans: Wright had designated the second area as a portal for the bridge that would lead from the penthouse to a future guesthouse higher up the hillside, but he later connected the guesthouse bridge to the second floor instead.)

Packed into these few rooms are a significant number of innovations that later became commonplace in American housing. The linen and clothes closets with their openwork rattan shelves are always a visitor favorite, but the cork-lined bathrooms are also full of leading-edge equipment and finishes, and the living room pioneered foam-rubber cushions and indirect fluorescent lighting. (Fluorescent lights came on the market only in 1935, and only for industrial use.)

The rooms—Liliane's bathroom above all—are generally praised and sometimes even ecstatically received by visitors, but it is the connectors in the house that guests find perplexing. The narrow rock-faced halls and stairways threaten to (and occasionally do) scrape your limbs as you explore the building. Some visitors experience an almost claustrophobic reaction to those rock-faced walls. A cynic might say that the complexities of the program and of the site forced Wright to do what he despised in Beaux-Arts architecture: had he created a photogenic exterior at the expense of a livable interior?

Some of these negative visitor judgments are valid, others are not. A few visitors to Fallingwater expect the outside to be radical but the inside to be traditional, which would be rather like sticking Mount Vernon inside the Guggenheim. We can understand the wish for a traditional interior because visitors instinctively associate the Kaufmanns' home with their own; they want Fallingwater to be comfortable and comforting inside, and some get upset when the house refuses to be that.

Wright could easily have made Fallingwater more charming and seductive inside, but certain effects he could not provide and others he did not wish to. It is remarkable that even normally savvy visitors show little understanding of Wright's intentions for the interior of Fallingwater. They speculate that the house was somehow foisted on the Kaufmanns, though the record is clear that the family joyously embraced Fallingwater inside and out.

Americans are no better at space perception than anyone else, so it is understandable that visitors shuffling through Fallingwater expect to find spatial effects that Wright could not provide. If they are looking here for the type of sprawling single-level house they have seen him produce elsewhere (perhaps in the living room of the Little house, now in the Metropolitan Museum), then they have no comprehension of how tiny a footprint was demanded by Fallingwater's cramped site. If they anticipate the same cathedral ceiling in the living room that they loved in other Wright houses, then they don't realize that such a dramatic space inside would create an unsightly bump outside, and obliterate the upper floors besides. Nor, in spite of the guides' patient instruction, do they appreciate that cantilevered ceilings *have* to be flat, and that the floors had to be stacked low if the house were to achieve its waterfall-like stepped-down mass.

In the same mode, visitors who expect to find Fallingwater light and airy are not calculating that a house perched on a waterfall and nestled among trees and boulders must necessarily be dark, noisy, and damp inside. Observers who complain about the dark never seem to ask themselves whether Wright might have wanted Fallingwater to be dark: must the whole world be light and airy? In his highly penetrating spatial analysis and psychological reading of Wright's interiors, Grant Hildebrand makes exactly that argument. Hildebrand starts with the psychobiology theory Jay Appleton presented in *The Experience of Landscape*, which posits that the dangers lurking at places like Bear Run impel us to two linked responses: one is to protect ourselves, the other is to find a viewpoint from which we may safely observe the potential devastation going on outside. Appleton uses the term "prospect" to mean the excitement of looking out into danger; "refuge" is the comfort we feel in being protected.

Hildebrand interprets the thrill we experience inside Wright's houses as the action of prospect and refuge, which is certainly built into Fallingwater's living room: ceilings deliberately low, windows overlooking the falls to the south, a primitive hearth to the west, stone walls to the north and east. The rest of Fallingwater works in a similar manner: a dark, warm place of safety from which to see but not be seen. Kenneth Frampton memorably called it "a furnished cave."

Wright's prowess as an interior architect requires no affirmation here: Johnson's Wax, Unity Temple, and the Guggenheim join Emperor Justinian's Hagia Sofia as among the most beguiling interiors in the world. If some visitors are disenchanted inside Fallingwater, they may be misunderstanding Wright's objectives. Wright was an Emersonian transcendentalist: everything that was practical at Fallingwater had to have a spiritual side, too. He regarded the rough stone walls as the necessary validation of his metaphor of Fallingwater-as-waterfall. The narrow dark corridors put you metaphorically in the bear cave behind the falls; the narrow stone staircases reinforce the analogy of Fallingwater-as-pueblo.

Wright had to satisfy numerous practical considerations, too. Every design project involves trade-offs: more of this always means less of that, but this is especially true of Fallingwater. Wright had already calculated each of Fallingwater's overhangs and balconies to admit the low-angled winter light while cutting out the high glare of the summer sun, but extending Liliane's terrace was a different kind of decision. He knew it would put the living room in shadow, but he accepted this as a worthwhile trade-off, and today who among us would vote to curtail that outlandish balcony soaring in the air? The living room is in any case only dark on occasion: most days, light enters from windows or glass doors on all four sides, making it a transcendently radiant room.

Wright could easily have made the interior more seductive, but not without jettisoning his design philosophy. A light, cheery wood floor would have warmed up the living room, but what Wright sought was a highly polished flagstone floor that would mimic the wet rocks in the Bear Run streambed. Wooden beams on the ceiling might have had an equally rich effect, but they would have been dishonest in a house whose ceilings are poured concrete. Concrete beams are hard to love, but the way Wright uses them in his living room, they become integral to the structure and function of the house.

Wright felt obliged to link inside and outside through continuity of space and materials. This concern for continuity means that the visitor will look in vain for large expanses of wood inside Fallingwater: the stone, concrete, and glass that frame the house outside had to be the prime components inside. All interior floors except those in the kitchen and bathrooms are of Pottsville sandstone, and so are many of the walls; concrete makes up the ceilings and the remainder of the walls; and glass windows and doors fill the voids between the other materials. The rough walling recalls the exterior of both house and hillside; Donald Hoffman calls this "a rough and yet sophisticated abstraction of the native sedimentary beds."

We can now intuit why Fallingwater is Wright's least ornamental house. He called the two extremes in decoration "ornamentia," or obsessive love of decoration, and "ornaphobia," or the obsessive avoidance of it. At Fallingwater, he steered a middle path between these two extremes. As a master ornamentalist, he could have decked out Fallingwater in marvelously rich scrolls, brackets, and beams—had he wished to. But Wright had no such wish, because an external environment as lush as Fallingwater's demanded that the inside of the house lead you to look outside. Fallingwater does not lack ornament, but what it has is isolated and subtle: some stylized dentils inside the cove ceiling of the living room, some curved metal shelving, the hearth kettle, the shield-shaped trellis lights, and the natural richness (though artificially composed) of the stone walls.

What Wright engineered at Bear Run were two interdependent environments: the exterior mass of the building in cooperation with nature, and its internal environment in cooperation with the Kaufmanns. This second environment he created by laying out a sequence of rooms and spaces inside the house, animating them with furniture of his own design, and giving the residents and guests glimpses and mirror images of the natural world outside. The two environments are sometimes jarringly different, but both rest on the same assumption: Fallingwater is consistently analogous to nature.

Wright spelled out his philosophy of house design in 1954 in *The Natural House,* which (amid the usual tangle of Wrightian rhetoric) advances six principles of organic architecture:

- Integration of the house and its site
- Space as the reality of the building
- Emphasis on the articulative nature of materials used
- The logic of the plan
- Plasticity and continuity
- Grammar or congruity of all elements in forming the whole

The program sounds coherent, and Wright's houses generally follow it. But Wright was not averse to incorporating a little deliberate incoherence in his houses, too: nature is sometimes terrifyingly incoherent, after all. Wright's apprentice Donald Hoppen describes the spatial experience of Taliesin West this way:

> You are led down narrow galleries, up steps barely wide enough to pass; you are restricted, pulled, pressed, and taken through every kind of experience: light/dark, narrow/wide, low/high, beneath/above, mystery/revelation. Surprises everywhere!

The functions, settings, and layouts of Fallingwater and Taliesin West differ, but the two complexes have the kinship we would expect from designs that Wright executed just two years apart. We can see the deliberate twisting and turning in the circulation path at Taliesin West as a parallel to Wright's objective at Fallingwater.

But why should Wright have wanted to complicate our progress through Fallingwater and Taliesin West? Shouldn't all plans get us through a building with maximum speed and convenience? Yes and no. The architect of a hospital endeavors to give users a clear and straightforward plan—not the labyrinth those floors invariably become over time. But clarity of plan is not the objective of every architect at every job. The designers of King Zoser's mortuary temple at Saqqara, Hadrian's villa at Tivoli, or Mussolini's headquarters inside the Palazzo Venezia all wanted plans that were instead complex and hard to read. Call it creative disorientation, or calculated incoherence.

Some visitor disorientation at Bear Run comes from the contorted itinerary the guides follow to prevent the different tour groups from bumping into one another. But mostly it comes from the spatial complexity of the house itself. The disorientation begins with an entry sequence that is artfully hidden, then demands a turn left, a jump of three steps, and a right turn to arrive in the living room. The fluidity of these maneuvers makes you feel as fluid as water by the time you stand in the house.

Wright enjoyed the paradox of the house interior that he called "clear because so complicated." Touring Fallingwater *is* a labyrinthine experience. Wright saves Fallingwater visitors from becoming rats in a maze by placing a literal light at the end of every tunnel. At the end of the second floor is the window in E. J.'s bedroom; at the end of the third floor is the door in Junior's study. Visitors who head toward those lights—or to the sound of water—cannot lack for orientation.

Central to our complex spatial experience in Fallingwater is the complexity of its plan. We can trace the evolution of Wright's plans as they became more and more open, particularly after he was inspired by Japanese architecture and the use of movable screens. At Fallingwater, Wright sends us through a sequence of spaces sufficiently complex that we start to empathize with the trout caught in the eddies of Bear Run.

As the sole monumental space at Fallingwater, the living room encapsulates best how Wright worked as an interior architect at Bear Run. The shape and dimensions of the room necessarily relate to its structural role within the house, with bolsters below and two floors above. Its layout is also determined by the many functions of a weekend house. The south end is given over to conversation and viewing the forest and the stream; more energetic nature-lovers can walk out on the east or west living-room balconies, while the less energetic can sip Scotch on one of the built-in banquettes.

The living room's northwest corner is devoted to food, which is prepared in the kitchen and consumed in the dining alcove next door. A built-in dining table and credenza and a profusion of metal shelves gave the maids (Liliane did not cook) adequate storage and serving room. Dominating the west wall is the hearth that kept things merry at Fallingwater even on somber days. Alongside hangs the Cherokee-red swinging kettle in which the Kaufmanns hoped to serve mulled wine; the kettle copied one Wright used at Taliesin, but this one proved unworkable. Left of the hearth sits another banquette for intimate conversations, well illuminated by the biggest window in the house. Opposite the hearth, still another conversation banquette alongside a built-in radio and phonograph. In the southeast corner, two last functions: the admirably lit library, with skylight overhead, and the hatch steps leading down to the stream.

The living room measures roughly 40 by 50 feet, but it is anything but regular in shape: depending on how you count, it has about a dozen major corners and another dozen minor ones. Nonetheless, most visitors will remember the living room as square. This perceived squareness—and the solidity and tranquility that squareness implies—comes from two devices. One is the raised cove ceiling, which creates a room-within-a-room. Our eye is inevitably drawn to the cove because it is central and symmetrical, because it is higher than the rest of the living-room ceiling, and because it is flooded with light from hidden fluorescent tubes.

The other device involves the two freestanding stone piers in the room. The piers are there for structural purposes, but they have visual power, too. A ceiling supported by ordinary walls is visually inert: it neither floats nor rises but simply "is." A ceiling supported by piers or columns constitutes a far more dynamic structural system. You can feel it being lifted up. The piers may define better than anything else at Fallingwater the distance between Wright and the European modernists. The obvious comparison is with the minimalist steel supports in Mies's 1929 Barcelona Pavilion or in his Tugendhat house of 1930. We feel intellectual rightness in what Mies has done, but visceral rightness in what Wright gives us.

Compare the piers, the cove, and the concrete beams with parallel features in the Great Kiva at the Aztec Ruins National Monument in New Mexico, or with other rooms in which ceiling beams and piers work together to create a mesmerizing physiological magnetism. Visitors with a European background might read the cove and ceiling ridges as recalling the beams from some medieval great hall, or a Bronze Age megaron (throne room) from Knossos, Mycenae, or Tiryns. Hardly a photograph of the living room fails to include the ceiling that makes this space so much more meaningful than just a place for cocktails.

The hearth and dining area also follow historic precedents, in this

Fallingwater's hearth and dining area recall the Colonial New England houses that Wright observed in his childhood

case the timber-framed homes of seventeenth-century New England. Wright—we too often forget—spent a number of years of his childhood in New England. He lived at Weymouth, the venerable town south of Boston where Abigail Adams grew up. In the *Autobiography,* Wright described his home as "a modest, gray, wooden house near a tall white-brick church in drab old historic Weymouth." Wright generally avoided copying the Colonial style, but his George Blossom house of 1892 in Chicago is a spellbindingly perfect creation in that genre. We know of the English Gothic cathedral scenes his mother tacked up around the house, but even more popular right through the 1920s were the fake-Colonial interiors that photographer Wallace Nutting sold by mail order across the land. Americans were so in love with the Colonial Revival that views of both real- and fake-Colonial architecture dominated magazines for the first thirty years of Wright's architectural practice. It was impossible for him to open one of those magazines and not absorb both authentic and faux-Colonial detailing. During the Depression, the many publications of photographs and measured drawings issued by the WPA made Colonial interiors more popular than ever.

The flagstone floor, the low ceiling, the beamlike "trays" around the cove, the massive hearth, the swiveled kettle, the simple table, and the credenza with the best family china—all of these are American Colonial derivatives. Wright had a half-century of emphasizing fireplaces before Fallingwater, but nowhere did he build so many Colonial and early American allusions into a design as he did on Bear Run. Since his intent was metaphorical rather than archaeological, Wright required no specific model on which to base the design of this corner of the living room, but the result is nonetheless a powerful evocation of American colonial life. It is hard to think of any other modern movement designer except Aalto who would have done that.

The living room never lacked for light by day, but at night its large size and irregular perimeter posed a lighting problem. The original fixed lighting in the room was minimal: just a band of electric lights to ring the cove ceiling. Incandescent bulbs were used around the cove at first, but they tended to scorch the Japanese-style paper sheets that Wright had devised to shield them. The solution lay in the newfangled fluorescent tubes, with sheets of muslin as guards. This has worked fine ever since, and probably inspired Kaufmann Jr. to invent a second lighting accent in the fluorescent tubes that hide between the banquettes and the windows.

Fallingwater lacks the art glass that so pleases visitors to Wright's Prairie Style homes, but with good reason. Many of his buildings look so good because their settings are banal or outright hostile: decaying downtown Racine for Johnson's Wax, dusty Chicago for the Robie house, an arid Philadelphia suburb for Beth Sholom Synagogue, California freeways for the Marin County Civic Center. Wright was obliged to use art glass or other devices to shield these buildings from the outside world. Art glass was neither necessary nor appropriate at Fallingwater, where nature both guarantees privacy and supplies unsurpassed art for display. Why upstage the best ornament of all?

The distinguished architect James Speyer, who spent his summers at Bear Run, complained that Wright never opened up a full view of nature the way his own mentor, Mies van der Rohe, did: instead, Wright always put some architectural element in the way. I find this observation absolutely right, and absolutely wrong. Wright loved nature too much to allow himself to splurge on it. He deliberately kept the windows at Fallingwater from turning into International Style full walls of glass. (There was no technical limitation to the size of the glass, since Pittsburgh Plate Glass would have given E. J. any dimension he asked for.) Mies's huge windows allow us to view all of nature at once, while Wright's more stringent windows only permit us to glimpse nature, not to gorge ourselves on the view. Wright further crops our views by setting steel mullions between the panes. Through these devices he subtly underlines our distance from nature, while the low ceilings say that nature, rather than the society gathered inside the house, remains our ultimate focus.

Wright's self-imposed limitation on glass also testifies to his wider aesthetic philosophy. He regarded wall-sized plates of glass as dishonest for a material that by definition has no structural strength. Mies's glass walls lacked structural integrity, too, which obliged him to place his row of stainless steel columns through the living room of the Tugendhat house. Such columns can be exquisite, but they frustrate a true dialogue with nature. At Fallingwater one sees "walls of glass" only in two places: in the guesthouse, which was largely designed by Wright's students; and in the servants' sitting room beyond the kitchen, which was stuck on with minimal input from Wright. Like any philosopher, though, Wright harbored the occasional contradiction. Cedar Rock, his 1945 house for Lowell Walter in Quasqueton, Iowa, occupies a site as promising as Bear Run, but the house strikes me as much inferior to Fallingwater because of an overabundance of glass, which lets too much of the outside in. Bear Run is our perfect (artificial) cave and lair: as we peer outside our living room cave, the bears are us.

To guarantee consistency to the interior environment he had created for Fallingwater, Wright had to furnish the house himself, a task demanding no more than a few weeks from him but half a century for a parallel effort by the Kaufmanns. Fallingwater preserves 169 pieces of custom-designed furniture by Wright, a treasure far in excess of that found in any other of his homes. About half the pieces are built-ins ("client-proof," Wright slyly called them), the other half movable. This makes Fallingwater one of the most complete designed settings anywhere for the use of a twentieth-century family.

Whether movable or built-in, all the furniture that Wright designed for Fallingwater was fabricated in North Carolina black walnut by the Gillen Woodworking Corporation of Milwaukee. Gillen was a firm that seems to have incorporated in 1937 specifically to supply woodwork for Fallingwater. It was the successor to the defunct Matthews Brothers Company, an outfit that Wright had used for his Prairie houses. Auspiciously, two of the Gillen workmen were among the men who had faithfully translated his designs for the Martin house in Buffalo more than thirty years before. Immersed in the Johnson's Wax project, Wright could not draw every piece of Fallingwater's furnishings personally, but he checked and corrected the designs that were produced by the apprentices at Taliesin or by Bob Mosher at Bear Run. Edgar Tafel was constantly running over to Milwaukee when Gillen failed to grasp the effects Wright was aiming for.

Some of Mosher's letters as a furniture designer survive, snappy as usual. He wrote E. J. in February 1937: "In the meantime I am drowned in work. Wood-work, mostly. I have made diagrams for all ward-robes, position of all drawers, trays, hanging space, etc. I will send you prints, also doors and door frames, all of which has to work separately. Then next will come my drawings for all convector enclosures [radiator covers]. And cases, such as the dining alcove. If you have any especial desires concerning such I can work them in on this first attempt. Then furniture." To Wright the next month: "I am going ahead with what iron-work I can. With the exception of the three grates for the bedroom fireplaces as the Kaufmanns do not like them at all so will redesign them. I guess they were not very good, too much. Have to design ladle, fork and pokers for Living Room fireplace." Kaufmann also sent this memo to Mosher in May of 1937: "If you get around to detailing flower boxes we will get prices for you down here as well as some people in Scottdale and neighboring towns. Be sure to build these so they will not fall apart at the end of a year . . . the sooner we get these flower boxes the sooner we can get flowers planted and more joy will be added to finishing up the work."

By early June the design phase was over for a goodly part of the furniture, and Wright could send the Gillen firm his specifications for those pieces and for the millwork needed in the house. This represented a huge commission to Gillen, which rushed to respond with a bid just days later. It listed everything they were prepared to supply: doors and doorframes, the dining table and extensions, wardrobes in the bedrooms and bathrooms, desks, beds, headboards, nightstands, book shelves, occasional tables, and built-in and free seating. The text of their bids follows, but without the total price that must once have been attached to it:

10 Flush doors and jambs for same
1 pair flush doors and jambs at Utility closet, 3rd floor stair landing

LIVING ROOM
1 combination convector enclosure case #1 and Table #1
1 combination case, dining table, and 2 extension tables
1 seat #2
1 seat #3

MISCELLANEOUS LOCATIONS
1 Case at east end of Gallery
1 Set of wall book shelves at one side third floor stairway
1 convector enclosure at third floor stair well
1 wardrobe #1 second floor well

GUEST ROOM
1 Combination counter, convector, and wall shelf
1 wardrobe #2

MRS KAUFMANN'S ROOM
1 Combination bookcase convector enclosure
1 bookcase with open shelves above
1 back board at head of beds
1 wardrobe #3

MR KAUFMANN'S ROOM
1 desk and wall shelf
1 wardrobe #4
1 back board at head of bed

MR KAUFMANN JR'S ROOM
1 Combination desk and convector enclosure
1 wardrobe #5

MR KAUFMANN JR'S BATH ROOM
1 wardrobe #6

MR KAUFMANN'S BATH ROOM
1 Wardrobe #7
1 Seat

MRS KAUFMANN'S BATH ROOM
1 Wardrobe (this Wardrobe not on your list)
Bid #2 If we furnish three (3) night stands, add to Bid #1 the sum of
    Sixty-Eight dollars—$68.00
Bid #3 If we furnish six (6) single beds, add to Bid #1 the sum of Two
    Hundred Fifty-Seven Dollars—$257.00

Kaufmann speedily agreed to Gillen's terms, and by the fall of 1937 the furnishings were beginning to arrive from Milwaukee. The family—Junior particularly—was very stringent in judging what Gillen was shipping them, and they returned more than a few pieces for revision, enough so that Wright was afraid that the Kaufmann job would push Gillen into bankruptcy. In the end, it proved easier for E. J. to produce certain millwork in the workshops of his own store, beginning with the wood ceiling panels around the cove ceiling. Here again we see Kaufmann enjoying resources that were unavailable to Wright's other clients.

Much of the furniture was installed only in 1938, which explains why Bill Hedrich's views from mid-November 1937 show the interior so barren. But it was well worth the wait. Fallingwater's furniture is versatile, practical, elegant, and an affirmation of the design of the house itself: the tops of most of the pieces flare out in homage to the structural cantilevers at work on the floors above and below.

Wright took special care to incorporate the graining of the furniture as one of the secondary visual "systems" in the house. Just as he designated that the metal window frames be set vertically or horizontally depending on whether the glass was fixed or openable, so he directed that the wood grain run vertically on doors and cabinet doors but horizontally on drawers, shelves, and fixed elements. The result is a system in which each piece signals its special function.

He paid special attention to incorporating the grain of the wood veneers, called flitches. Flitches are not cut from trees in slices like salami, nor are they taken off lengthwise the way you peel a carrot. Instead, they are shaved from the trunks as the latter are turned, like meat on a spit, so they come off in rounded sheets that are thin enough to be pressed flat. Wright directed the Gillen woodworkers to use the entire tree, including sapwood—the outermost layer right below the bark—as well as the heartwood. The sapwood, being the most recently grown wood in the trunk, has light streaks that are normally regarded as blemishes, but Wright wanted those distinctive marks retained as integral to the growth of the tree and integral to his vertical/horizontal lexicon. To resist warping, the cabinetry was specified as shiplap, demanding the nine-ply thickness found on ships rather than the usual five-ply for home furnishings.

Every room at Fallingwater, even in the servant quarters, still preserves its Wright-designed furniture. The living room has the greatest profusion: the dining table and the extensions that allow a banquet for eighteen; the wood-encased floor cushions; the low tables in three different dimensions; the high table; the coffee tables; the high hassocks; the library table; and the low end tables. (The Fallingwater gift shop now sells costly replicas of several of these pieces.) Next door, Wright designed a Formica-topped table for the kitchen. Directly above the kitchen are the bedrooms for Kaufmann Sr. and Jr., each with a built-in desk featuring a cutout so the corner window can swing open unimpeded.

In the guest bedroom is one of the barrel chairs that Wright failed to convince the Kaufmanns to use with their dining table. It is semicircular, with a red wool cushion, and is an adaptation of his chair for the Martin house decades before. Each of the four bedrooms has a marvelous wardrobe, from out of which clothes and linens slide on the ingenious rattan openwork caning (a suggestion Kaufmann Jr. made to Wright), for maximum protection against mildew.

Wright also designed a score of desk lamps or task lamps for the house. These were typically of bronze with walnut shades, and normally rotate to change the direction of the light for the convenience of the user. Some of the lamps are for desk use, some for bedside use. The same basic types come in different dimensions, but all were designed specifically for Fallingwater.

The process of furnishing Fallingwater was not free of disputes between Wright and Gillen, Gillen and Kaufmann, Kaufmann and Wright. After two long construction campaigns everyone was exhausted, yet what comes through in the correspondence is still an extraordinarily high degree of civility and affection. Selling furniture was a big part of E. J.'s business, which made him all the more respectful and solicitous of Wright's higher powers of visual judgment. After Wright visited Falling-water in the summer of 1939 to iron out difficulties on the construction of the guesthouse, Kaufmann tried to get him to commit to visiting Falling-water twice a year "so that we may have the benefit of your judgment and advice to keep the interior arrangement in harmony with your architec-tural creation."

Wright also had some specific suggestions of color accents for Fallingwater, such as covering the throw pillows, hassocks, and ottomans predominantly in red and gold. This reflected his famous sensitivity to color. His apprentices still talk of the way he would change the planting of his fields at Taliesin to achieve the right color balance (he also tried to make the neighboring farmers conform, and once or twice bought their fields when they refused). Wright moved the livestock on his fields around to achieve bovine color harmony, too, and he did the same with his apprentices: any young man or woman who dressed in the wrong color for a Taliesin picnic was sent back to change.

Wright achieved another kind of accent in the placement of his fur-niture, which was also too important to leave to chance. The coffee tables and end tables in the living room currently have a kind of classical equipoise, but Wright's plan 078 makes clear that he intended these pieces to have a strongly asymmetrical placement. As others have pointed out, Wright may have regarded his Fallingwater furniture arrangements as analogous to the raked-sand gardens of Japan. Hassocks, ottomans, low tables, high tables, end tables—to Wright these pieces seem to have been players in some great cosmic scheme, just as the monks in Kyoto treated the rocks in their sand gardens as miniature mountains. (Bob Mosher regularly raked one of Taliesin's gravel courts as though it were a Japanese sand garden.) It was entirely consistent with Wright's organic philosophy for him to connect furniture arrangements and the cosmos. If

Fallingwater was truly to work as an analogy to nature, it should support a miniaturized version of nature inside.

Some scholars take the cosmic analogies further, and interpret certain features of Fallingwater as cryptic references to the four compass directions and the four prime elements (earth, air, fire, and water) of Pythagorean philosophy. For them the boulder outcrop in the living room represents earth; the trellis skylights, air; the fireplace, fire; and the steps down to the stream, water. This cosmological approach to Fallingwater would make it a kind of compass or sextant from which to read off the farthest removes of the universe. In this interpretation—a wonderful one, though unsupported by evidence—Fallingwater constitutes an *axis mundi,* or a link between heaven and earth. That makes the interior of Fallingwater quite a distinguished space indeed.

Opposite: Wright and Fallingwater on the cover of *Time* in 1938

EIGHT

FABRICATING FALLINGWATER I:
THE HYPE THAT SOLD IT

Time, Life and [Architectural] Forum; Fortune too, seem to
have been pretty good to me.

—WRIGHT to Henry R. Luce

Wright's need of publicity, of being newsworthy, cannot be
glossed over as a superficial part of his personality; rather, it
was a dominant feature.

—DONALD JOHNSON, Frank Lloyd Wright Versus America

On September 11, 2001, on a day that no American who was then over the age of ten will forget, a passenger jet that had been hijacked by Arab terrorists crashed into a meadow in southwestern Pennsylvania. The jet plunged to earth in the Somerset County township of Stony Creek, between the settlements of Shanksville (population 230) and the even smaller Lambertsville, seventy-eight miles southeast of Pittsburgh. Not to be bogged down with these obscure geographical details, the print and electronic media instantly defined the crash site as "near Pittsburgh."

Logical enough, but why do the same media define Fallingwater, thirty-three miles closer to Pittsburgh, as standing in Mill Run, a hamlet whose population—maybe 50 on a good day—makes Shanksville look like a metropolis? Or they assign Fallingwater to Bear Run, which has a large population of animals but not of the species *Homo sapiens,* which numbers zero. This warns us that the fame of Fallingwater defies logic. It rests instead on hype, which plays by its own rules.

Fallingwater emerged as a concept in 1935, as a finished building in 1937, and a third time in 1938 in a tidal wave of publicity so vast that the world celebrated it overnight as a masterpiece of modern architecture. The publicity campaign that nurtured this acclaim effected a stunning shift in public opinion. As recently as 1935, Americans had ratified their conservative taste in architecture by applauding the new but fake-Greek Supreme Court in Washington. What got them to turn 180 degrees to applaud the radically modern Fallingwater just three years later? By the time Ayn Rand made Fallingwater the centerpiece of a famous novel and movie in the 1940s, the house was an icon.

Any building that could become so famous so fast must have been launched with exceptionally cunning publicity. What is extraordinary is that of the four mass media that broadcast Fallingwater in 1938—the movies, radio, the photo magazines, and the newspapers—the first three were newcomers themselves. The movies had taken hold by the teens and twenties; by the thirties, movie theaters were pulling in 85 million Americans each week. Radio attained its following only in the late twenties, but its appeal soon became hypnotic. The mass-circulation magazines had just stepped out of infancy, too: the Wallaces' *Reader's Digest* began publication in 1922; Henry R. Luce launched *Time* in 1923, *Fortune* in 1930, *Life* in 1936. Before the movies, radio, and the photo magazines, there had been only the newspapers. *The Illustrated London News* startled the world with the pictorial layout of its engravings in 1851, but it took decades more to mesh newsprint and photography. In 1938, even the glossy rotogravure sections in the Sunday newspapers were regarded as new.

In the thirties, Americans increasingly measured their life spans by what they took from the mass media. Were a sampling of American adults asked in 1938 to name the most exciting events of their lifetime, two responses would have stood out: Lindbergh's flight to Paris in 1927 and the abdication of King Edward VIII in 1936. Why? Because both events were transmitted so widely on radio, in the newsreels, and through the glossy magazines. Half a generation earlier, epochal events like the sinking of the *Titanic* or the end of the Great War were made known by newspapers only. Of the Lindbergh and abdication stories, the latter was the more immediate, since listeners could hear the King's voice for themselves on a global hookup that had been technically impossible a decade before. The efficacy of the national or global hookup was demonstrated in October 1938, soon after Fallingwater's launch, in the hysteria that followed the radio production of Orson Welles's *War of the Worlds.*

Lindbergh and King Edward/the Duke of Windsor were not merely famous: they were world celebrities. The nineteenth century did not lack for celebrities, either, but Sarah Bernhardt, Oscar Wilde, and their like never had the worldwide recognition that the mass media of the 1930s could bestow. (Nonpersons could be celebrities, too: the racehorse Seabiscuit pulled in crowds of 20,000.) Celebrity power would grow exponentially with television, which was already in the wings: the BBC started to broadcast on television in 1935, and by the time the New York World's Fair was inaugurated in 1939, the host city had 20,000 sets that could follow the event.

Fallingwater was far from being the world's first celebrity structure. Four of the Seven Wonders of the World were buildings: any reader of Herodotus could reasonably discourse on the Pyramids, the Temple of Artemis at Ephesus, the Mausoleum of Halicarnassus, and the Lighthouse at Alexandria. A later age bestowed similar renown on the Dome of the Rock, St. Peter's, the Taj Mahal, and Beijing's Forbidden City. But those buildings, along with lesser landmarks like the Kremlin and Versailles, took centuries to get famous. By contrast, the architectural marvels of the nineteenth century attained fame in just a few years via the illustrated newspapers. Before the century was out, a moderately educated American could identify the Eiffel Tower from photographs as easily as she or he could recognize the Brooklyn Bridge or the Statue of Liberty.

The rapid acquisition of fame by those Victorian architectural stars nonetheless pales before the media blitz that made Fallingwater and some of its contemporaries famous. The structures hyped most shrilly in the 1930s were the Empire State Building, the Golden Gate Bridge, and Hoover Dam—plus, momentarily, the futuristic icons of the Chicago and New York world's fairs. It was natural for government bodies to promote such public or semipublic works in order to jack up morale in the midst of the Depression. Ordinary people knew them better than they would come to know Fallingwater: the astonishment is that Fallingwater garnered even a fraction of the attention lavished on the huge public projects. Being a mere house caused it to be overlooked by the public at first, but in later years that was a key element in its steadfast popularity. You could admire the Golden Gate but you could not love it, and the Empire State Building was even harder to dote on—as King Kong learned to his cost. As a house, Fallingwater was something people could identify with personally.

Who was behind the flood of publicity about Fallingwater? The old adage says, "Success has many fathers, but failure is an orphan." Since the promotion of Fallingwater turned into a success beyond anyone's expectation, its potential fathers and mothers are legion. There is an extra complication, too: no media mogul ever claimed responsibility for "puffing" Fallingwater, so the trail leading back to its promoters of more than half a century ago runs cold. We have to consider that a publicity campaign so big and diverse may have involved multiple producers. Alternately, there may have been no single Fallingwater publicity campaign, since the building was so adroit at promoting itself.

Still, there must have been at least a minimal publicity apparatus behind Fallingwater, and we should be able to estimate which player lay behind which part of it. The most efficient way to do this is to learn by analogy from the only comparable megahit in twentieth-century architecture: Frank Gehry's Guggenheim Museum at Bilbao. The Guggenheim Bilbao may have merited its popular success, but we can be certain that its PR was not left to chance. Its promoters commissioned a lavish book far enough ahead of time to allow publication the instant the museum opened in November 1997. The public relations payoff was huge: 1.4 million visitors appeared at the museum's door in its first year.

Like the Guggenheim Bilbao, Fallingwater was also publicized throughout the world even before it was fully furnished. Bilbao provides a rough analogue for Fallingwater in the rapidity of its acquisition of fame, but publicizing Fallingwater in 1938 was infinitely harder. Fallingwater got its message out without the benefit of television, cable, e-mail, the Internet, cell phones, CDs, chatrooms, music videos, faxes, or instant satellite transmission. Of the two public opinion triumphs, Bilbao and Bear Run, the production of Fallingwater's fame remains the more impressive.

Communications jargon distinguishes the molding of public opinion into two stages: hype and buzz. Hype manipulates the media to sell a product; buzz is a genuine public response that promotes buying it. Hype and buzz are complementaries, not opposites. At the 1936 Berlin Olympics, the German runners enjoyed all the hype the Nazi press machine could spit out, but it was Jesse Owens who got the buzz. Owens, in turn, got hyped on his return home.

Hype can be launched regardless of the merit of the product it is selling; buzz cannot. Every Hollywood movie gets hyped, but only the truly entertaining ones enjoy the buzz of word of mouth. Fallingwater enjoyed enormous buzz because the public saw it as one of the most interesting things the United States had produced in a decade buffeted by warfare and want. But Fallingwater had to be sold before it could be bought. Walter Gropius's 1939 house for Pittsburgh's Frank family is a fascinating work that should be a hundred times better known than it is, but the Franks had no wish to publicize it, and Gropius was too recently arrived in the United States to know how to hype it himself.

Guggenheim Bilbao shows us that when buildings get hyped, the beneficiaries fall into five categories:

- The architect: Bilbao vaulted Frank Gehry to number-one status in the design world.
- The patron: Bilbao was a godsend for the Guggenheim, a museum long dismissed as lackluster and indecisive, and for its highly ambitious director, Thomas Krens.
- The host city and region: for an instant, Guggenheim Bilbao transformed a decayed industrial city into one of Europe's major cultural centers.
- The culture industry and the media: no newspaper or cable service in the world dared ignore the new Guggenheim.
- Other linked products for sale: the Spanish airways, hotels, and restaurants profited handsomely from Guggenheim Bilbao, but the main product for sale was Basque nationalism, which is why the museum's $100 million cost was mostly borne by the Basque autonomous region of Spain. A museum built and run by Americans became a powerful thrust for Basque culture and autonomy.

The five corresponding persons or groups who profited from Fallingwater's success were the architect Wright, the patron Kaufmann, the United States (but *not* Pittsburgh or Mill Run) as the host region, Time-Life and MoMA as the leading representatives of the media and the culture industry, and—in the category of "other linked products for sale"—modern architecture itself.

S ince the biggest gainer from Fallingwater was Frank Lloyd Wright, does that unmask him as the mastermind behind the Fallingwater publicity campaign? Yes—and no. The great media manipulator of architectural history was perfectly capable of running such a campaign, but it now looks as though the old manipulator was asleep at the wheel: Wright seems never to have suspected how big the response to Fallingwater was going to be. Had he masterminded the Fallingwater publicity campaign, we would surely find a record of it in his meticulously preserved correspondence. But the correspondence points decisively *away* from Wright's crusading on behalf of Fallingwater. He would normally have thrown himself into every aspect of the promotion of the Kaufmann house, but in 1937 Wright's situation was anything but normal.

After years of professional famine, Wright was now caught up in a flood of building. For him the great project of the years 1936 to 1938 was not Fallingwater but Johnson's Wax in Racine, Wisconsin, followed by a luxury house for the wax king Herbert Johnson. Johnson's Wax was far more important to Wright than Fallingwater because it was the commercial building that Wright desperately wanted in order to discard the label of house designer with which he was tagged. The big news for Wright in 1937 was not that Fallingwater was nearing completion but that Johnson's Wax had fallen badly behind schedule. The best he could do on publicity for the Kaufmann house was to put out a few feelers.

Wright the media hound is a fascinating topic that has gone largely unstudied. Wright was always attentive to the way the media portrayed him, and how he could benefit from publicity. He was forever drumming up business by using publicity on his earlier work—one thinks of his sending a book on his work to E. J. Kaufmann early in their correspondence. He was also tireless in soliciting important figures for his social circle, for example his barrage of letters and telegrams to Albert Einstein.

By dint of his intuitive ability at public relations, Wright continued to be well known as a colorful old coot even during his dry spell of 1922 to 1935. He made sure, for example, that everyone knew of the triumph of his earthquake-proof Imperial Hotel in Tokyo. Nor did he exploit the sophisticated media only: the man who for decades had appeared in the pages of *Ladies' Home Journal* and *House Beautiful* kept up his exposure in the mainstream media in the early 1930s, including not one but two flattering articles in *Reader's Digest*. Publication of Wright's *Autobiography* in 1932 and his coauthored *Architecture and Modern Life* five years later were major literary events: scores of newspapers reviewed them.

We cannot document a specific PR campaign by Wright for Fallingwater, but there is at least some evidence of efforts he made in that direction. These efforts concentrated on the exploitation of his own persona, Fallingwater's structural and formal daring, the carefully calculated photogeneity of the house, and the name "Fallingwater" itself. The persona Wright had been so carefully shaping since the 1880s with his outlandish verbal statements guaranteed that when Fallingwater came to world attention in 1938 it would be treated not just as a building but as part of a great human drama: the return of America's greatest architect from the dead.

Wright knew the value of being outrageous not only in words but in images. We have already seen how he released a half-dozen drawings of his early projects around 1930 after they had been falsified to suggest that he was designing in Bauhaus style a generation before the Bauhaus. Not a few of Wright's stranger building proposals were floated purely for their media value. His much-touted "Mile High" skyscraper project of 1956, for example, was nothing more than a speculative notion, but it got him national publicity just when Mies van der Rohe was pulling ahead as the most acclaimed architect in the country.

The notion of architecture-as-publicity applies to real buildings as well as to theoretical projects. At Guggenheim Bilbao the unruly masses wrapped in titanium became their own architectural PR. Similarly, the dramatic cantilever in the Robie house and the International Style features in Fallingwater effectively guaranteed critical interest in these buildings. As we saw earlier, Fallingwater's two most photogenic devices are the illusion of water cascading through the building and the way the upper balcony oversails the lower. At least the latter feature, and maybe both, seem to have been devised to appropriate maximum publicity for the house.

Wright was a master at promoting his buildings. At nineteen he "placed" his first media mention—an exaggerated one—in a Unitarian bulletin in 1886, regarding his contribution to the building of his uncle's chapel at Spring Green. He got his first drawing published in 1887; the first published photograph of one of his buildings followed in 1892; his first printed promotional brochure came out in 1898; his first article byline in

1901. Wright first issued his own publication to promote a particular commission in 1906, for the Larkin Building, and, of course, it was the publication of his *Ausgeführte Bauten* in 1910 and 1911, far more than the construction of any single building, that fed his international reputation. In 1913, sensing in Wright a kindred spirit, the Press Club of Chicago made him a Life Member.

Early in his career, Wright had the insight and self-confidence to take control not only of what was written about his buildings, but who the writer would be. In 1903 he selected the preeminent critic Russell Sturgis to write up his work in *Architectural Record.* Dissatisfied with the results, Wright subsequently dropped Sturgis, and five years later he humiliated the old man when they quarreled in print over the Larkin Building.

While Wright had no time to oversee a major public relations campaign on Fallingwater, he could still orchestrate a few things with his left hand. That hand can be discerned behind the launching of the first mention of the Kaufmann house in print, in the construction narrative that Bob Mosher provided to the "At Taliesin" column that Wright periodically fed to the *Madison Capital Times* and to a half-dozen rural Wisconsin newspapers. The column ran in several papers in late January 1937, although completion of the house was still eleven months away.

But far from being a PR mastermind, Wright was mostly a lucky bystander in the publicizing of Fallingwater. One of his lucky breaks was the arrival in January 1937 of a telegram from the St. Louis newsman Max Putzel, requesting an interview on the Johnson's Wax Building and the Kaufmann house. Putzel left unsaid how he knew of the latter—the logical conduit was the Mosher article then on standby at the *Capital Times,* but he may have been set up by E. J. Kaufmann. Wright evidently divined some advantage in this request from a total unknown, and he invited Putzel to interview him at Spring Green the next month.

Putzel returned from Wisconsin in early March 1937 with a scoop on the Kaufmann house (Johnson's Wax was downgraded to a minor issue) and an even bigger prize in the waterfall perspective that Wright and Jack Howe had drawn up in October 1935. Later design changes had by then rendered the perspective obsolete, but Putzel was obviously mesmerized when he saw it, and he personally transported the drawing back to St. Louis to get the color plates made.

"A House That Straddles a Waterfall" appeared on March 21 in the Sunday rotogravure magazine of the *St. Louis Post-Dispatch,* with the full-color perspective splashed across the top of two pages and two accompanying construction photographs. It was the second published note on Fallingwater, but the world's first wake-up call to the astonishing news that Wright's career had roared back to life. Putzel's text was lyrical and prescient, capturing the organicity, the technical efficiency, and the spirituality of the Kaufmann house. The expected completion date for the Kaufmann house was given as June 1937, and Putzel announced that the balconies would be sheathed in gold leaf.

Putzel's article gave Wright his first inkling of the impact Fallingwater would have on the public, and he mailed fifty offprints of it to strategically placed operatives in the media. But then he hedged his bets, and ignored the house in a text that would have prepared the whole country for Fallingwater. That text was *Architecture and Modern Life*, the book he published in 1937 with Northwestern University professor Baker Brownell. Brownell had proposed the partnership in October 1936, and by February of 1937 the two men had drafted their respective texts (Wright's was basically recycled from his 1931 Kahn lectures at Princeton). With Wright's new office building and house for Herbert Johnson under way, the two authors pinned their hopes on selling quantities of books to Johnson's Wax as giveaways to their customers and employees. In Brownell's demurely cynical words: "It will be of great interest to the Johnson Company to have the two buildings in the book."

The galleys of *Architecture and Modern Life* would not be composed for several months, so Wright, after observing the electricity generated by Putzel's article in March, had ample time to insert Fallingwater in the book. But he chose not to. *Architecture and Modern Life* came out wordless on Fallingwater, and only by happenstance did the book carry a few views of it. The publishers, Harper & Brothers, informed Wright and Brownell in March that there would be eight illustrations in the book, and Brownell urged both Wright and the editor to place the highest priority on the two Johnson buildings. By the time photographs reached New York in May, several views of the Kaufmann house also showed up as candidates for inclusion, but Wright and Brownell agreed a second time that these would be the first to be thrown out if the publisher needed to economize.

When Harper & Brothers sent the first galley proofs of *Architecture and Modern Life* to its authors in June of 1937, Brownell again went on record that the three construction shots of Fallingwater were the least important illustrations in the book (these had by now jumped to a total of fifteen). To this Wright made no argument, so the book made its way to press with illustrations of Johnson's Wax, the Willey house in Minneapolis, and some Taliesin sculptures all ranked higher than images of Fallingwater. At the last moment, Harper & Brothers stuck in three construction views of Fallingwater as part of the ripple effect from the Putzel article. They appeared on a tipped-in sheet opposite page 86, with the caption "E. J. Kaufmann House During Construction, Pittsburgh, Pa."

The Fallingwater work shots obviously posed a conflict for Wright, since he made no effort to include them in the book. Architects were—are—generally opposed to the publication of construction photographs because of the confused image they give untutored viewers. Wright had allowed two such views to get into Putzel's Fallingwater piece the previous spring, but for him to have put three more views in a high-profile book was exceptional. In sanctioning their publication, he must have been persuaded by the publisher of a big payoff, and he got it. By October 1937 thousands of Americans knew that the old man was putting up an amazing house in Pittsburgh.

Fallingwater's PR momentum was clearly rolling, but Wright was still diffident about further attempts to promote it. He slammed a request from the journalist Beatrice Schapper, who wrote him on October 16, 1937, about her planned feature on the Kaufmann house for a national magazine. Schapper's appeal would normally have gratified Wright. She was an alumna of the University of Wisconsin (always a good sign), she came highly recommended by Kaufmann Jr., and she had excellent professional credentials. A former writer and promotion manager for the *Pittsburgh Post-Gazette,* Schapper now freelanced for *The Nation, Glamour, Reader's Digest, Good Housekeeping,* and *Redbook.* She was a far more important journalist than Putzel, and she represented the mainstream publications in which Wright loved to appear. Nonetheless, he peremptorily shot Schapper down, telling her only that the Kaufmanns' house would be featured in the January 1938 *Architectural Forum.* Although true, that was beside the point: Schapper's audience was not only completely different from *Forum*'s, it was potentially twenty times larger.

What made the notorious publicity hound now shy away from publicity? Such a posture is so atypical of Wright that it forces us to consider whether he actually feared risking exposure on Fallingwater. The last thing he needed was a Pittsburgh-based journalist asking about all those cracks. As 1937 progressed, Wright seems to have become increasingly anxious about whether Fallingwater would reach the light of day intact. A year earlier he had told Walter Hall that his designs lent themselves to being wrecked by builders, and that Fallingwater might prove to be one of them. This may have been whistling in the dark, but suppose he believed it? In 1943, Wright added dozens of lines in his revised *Autobiography* about Johnson's Wax, but next to nothing on Fallingwater. Was he even then fearful it might collapse?

Whatever the motive, Wright authorized publication of just the

Mosher and Putzel articles while Fallingwater was under construction, in addition to his mute illustration of it in his book. A third article, in the business section of the Hearst-controlled *Milwaukee Sentinel* for July 18, 1937, also covered Fallingwater, but Wright was on his way to lecture in Russia and probably had no advance knowledge of it. The article trumpeted the reestablishment of Milwaukee's "internationally known" Gillen Woodwork Corporation, which was providing wood cabinetry for a spectacular new house over a waterfall near Pittsburgh, the work of Frank Lloyd Wright of Spring Green.

Minor though it was, the *Sentinel* article was the first to illustrate Fallingwater substantially complete, since it ran a new photograph by Edgar Tafel (Wright took the earlier photographs with him to Russia). That meant that at least four photographers had recorded Fallingwater in two media when it was still half a year from opening. Beginning around June 1936, the Pittsburgh photographer Luke Swank had diligently covered its construction on both movie film and in prints. (Scores of these shots are preserved in the Kaufmann Archive in the Avery Library at Columbia University.) Swank, a native of nearby Johnstown, had a meteoric career among American photographers of the 1930s, and might today rank with Walker Evans or Margaret Bourke-White had he not died young, in 1944. He provided the Kaufmanns with scores of informal portraits over the years, in the late 1930s even accompanying E. J. and Liliane to their fishing lodge in Ontario. In 1936 he opened a photographic studio as a wholly owned subsidiary of Kaufmann's Department Store. This was evidently E. J.'s way of supporting Swank, who was as much a Kaufmann retainer as an employee.

Swank's films and stills were followed around May of 1937 by Bob Mosher's recordings in both media, then by Edgar Tafel's shots of the house in July. The New York architect Henry Churchill had also shot the house in October 1936. A longtime propagandist for Wright in professional design journals, Churchill probably intended to use the photographs for an article that never panned out. Did Wright kill that feature, too?

Midway through 1937, Wright got the biggest PR boost of his career, and the perfect vehicle to hype his comeback. This was the all-Wright January 1938 issue of *Architectural Forum*, which has no rival as the most famous issue of any architectural magazine in any language. The issue broke precedent in devoting all its editorial pages to a single architect, but it also ruptured Wright's decades-old publishing agreement with *Architectural Record*, which had put food on Taliesin's table right through the lean

1920s and early 1930s. This surprising jump to the rival *Forum* sounds like another instance of Wright's cynicism in the world of public relations, but he was lucky rather than prescient in the development of the *Forum* issue. Certainly he never suspected, right up to the last minute, that Fallingwater would be the star of the publication.

The genius behind the *Architectural Forum* special issue was William Connolly, the advertising manager for Johnson's Wax. Johnson's had revived its fortunes in the middle of the Depression with the newly developed Glo-Coat self-polishing floor wax. Connolly vigorously promoted Glo-Coat with his expertise in national consumer advertising (Johnson's claims to have been the first nationwide advertiser in the country). In the 1930s, Connolly kept Johnson's Wax alive by making it among the biggest advertisers on radio. Its sponsorship of the enormously popular "Fibber McGee and Molly" proved a gold mine.

As part of Hib Johnson's privy council, Connolly helped to select Wright for the company's new administrative headquarters in 1936. Within weeks of groundbreaking, he convoked an executive session to discuss how the company could exploit its new building with the public. Connolly felt Wright's standing—modern but not faddish—perfectly mirrored that of the firm. He was determined to translate Wright's radical design into millions of dollars in free publicity for S. C. Johnson & Sons.

In October 1936, Connolly presented Wright with a two-pronged publicity strategy, aimed at the popular press as well as the specialized architecture and engineering magazines. Connolly made clear who was in charge: "I believe our Advertising Department here at Racine should act as a clearing house for all releases. Our own publicity agent in Chicago can be used to take care of newspaper and lay publication releases." Wright responded the next day with the suggestion that his old friends at *Architectural Record* run the architectural story. It was the "best edited journal" in the field, Wright said, and the best place to sell architects on Johnson's Wax for building maintenance.

Connolly came to a different conclusion. Investigating the architecture magazines for himself, he picked *Architectural Forum* as having the image most in tune with Johnson's Wax. Being part of Henry Luce's Time-Life empire, *Forum* would also provide better linkage with the popular press than would the independent architecture magazines. Connolly got in touch with *Forum,* which jumped at the chance to gratify one of the nation's biggest advertisers with an article on its new building. Tom Maloney, so important to Wright in snaring E. J. Kaufmann in 1934, came to life again and got *Forum*'s editor Howard Myers to offer Wright $500 for a text and illustrations on Johnson's Wax.

But Wright wanted more than Johnson's Wax: he wanted *Forum* to cover his other recent buildings, too. Eight months of arduous horse-trading with Howard Myers yielded an unprecedented prize in August of 1937. *Forum* would turn over to Wright its entire January 1938 issue, in which he was free to publicize "four or five" new buildings besides Johnson's Wax. It was Myers, not Wright, who suggested that the Kaufmann house was something the *Forum* issue should cover.

It was either Wright's luck or persistence that got him George Nelson as the editor assigned by *Forum* for the special issue. Nelson, later one of America's leading industrial designers, was a longtime Wright supporter. On his visit to Taliesin in February 1937 he seems to have been smitten by Fallingwater, which to him represented the core issue of whether modern architecture in America would follow Wright or the International Style. That became his theme for the January *Forum* issue. As he wrote Wright's secretary Eugene Masselink in May 1937: "I spoke with Mr. Wright about the possibility of including the Kaufman[n] residence, the [Jacobs] house in Madison and others which were to be completed by the end of the summer. . . . Such a collection would, of course, be of the greatest interest and value as it would unmistakably call attention to the fact that while the so-called International Style has been taking advantage of every possible bit of publicity, the cause of organic architecture in America is still being vigorously carried on by its first and chief exponent." Editor-in-Chief Myers parroted the "American" line back to Wright in July: "We hear much these days that there is no leadership in American architecture; such an issue [of *Forum*] would definitely refute that view."

For six months Wright's apprentices worked on the *Forum* special issue, ending with a session of feverish all-nighters in the editorial offices in New York. As zero hour approached, the groundswell of interest in the forthcoming issue was so intense that even the rival *Architectural Record* swallowed its pride. Its editors pleaded to be allowed to publish the Johnson house or the lily-pad columns at Johnson's Wax, even though "we understand the building as a whole has been promised to the *Architectural Forum*." *Record* begged to carry at least the new Hanna house at Palo Alto, the new shop project for Oak Park, or any other bone Wright might toss them.

Architectural Forum's special issue came out on Monday, January 10, 1938, fat as a book. The cover revealed only the name "Frank Lloyd Wright": inside were some regular monthly features, but the 102 pages on Wright were set between special interior covers, so anyone could rip off the extraneous pages to get a self-standing spiral-bound book on Wright alone. Inside, readers were treated to an eye-catching layout and dazzling photographs wreathed with exhortations by Walt Whitman. The text recapitulated Wright's philosophy and early career, then presented the old man bursting with more creativity than any designer in America. Within hours readers flooded Taliesin and the *Forum* offices with congratulatory calls and telegrams; this went on for a month. In one shot, *Forum* vaulted Wright to the position from which he has never been dislodged: greatest architect in American or world history.

As Myers and Nelson had planned, the issue depicted Wright as an American whose lifelong commitment to modernism had been aped and usurped by the Johnny-come-lately Europeans. *Forum*'s readers got the Americanism message loud and clear: several letters to the editor in subsequent issues took up the magazine's thesis that the central issue of modern architecture was Wright versus the Europeans. Totally unplanned, however, was the adulation that fell on the building that became the lustrous star of the issue: not Johnson's Wax but Fallingwater. The Johnson headquarters had fallen so far behind schedule that it was represented in *Forum* only by some plans, some construction photographs, and an abstract elevation on the front cover of the interior "book." The Johnson mansion outside Racine fared as poorly. Fallingwater, by contrast, was gorgeously splashed over twelve pages of indelible images, and backed up by two pages on E. J.'s glamorous office in downtown Pittsburgh. The princess headquarters that was supposed to get world fame saw it bestowed instead on the Cinderella house that had only been admitted as window-dressing.

What dominated the *Forum* issue was photography, which guaranteed that no building on its pages would shine like Fallingwater. All architects know how photography can enhance or obstruct the public's perception of their buildings, but none grasped this better than Wright, who, as we saw, was himself a photographer as well as a collector of architectural photographs. In his fight with Russell Sturgis in 1908, Wright had raged against America's senior architectural critic for the sin of publishing unflattering photographs of the Larkin Building in *Architectural Record:* "murderous, wide-angle slanders," Wright called them. Now *Architectural Forum* gave him a blank check to show his buildings just as he wished.

Wright respected Luke Swank's views of Fallingwater, but George Nelson wanted consistent shots of Wright's works by a small number of freelance architectural photographers. Nelson made special arrangements for coverage of Wright's California houses, but he gave the rest of the work to the Chicago firm of Hedrich-Blessing. Ken Hedrich, the

Hedrich-Blessing manager, began taking the shots himself, but given the remoteness of Bear Run, he delegated the Kaufmann house to his kid brother Bill. Thus it was that a twenty-five-year-old rookie arrived to shoot Fallingwater at the last possible moment in the editorial process, in mid-November of 1937.

The account long floating around Taliesin West suggested that Hedrich was selected for the assignment because he was Wright's favorite photographer, and that Wright made him shoot Fallingwater looming over the water in explicit homage to the perspective rendering he had drawn up with Jack Howe two years before. There is no question that the breathtakingly close fit between the rendering and Hedrich's view of Fallingwater's balconies soaring over the diaphanous waterfall confirms Wright's phenomenal accuracy in creating a building in his mind. But the Taliesin story is wrong in every important detail: it was Ken Hedrich who was the Wright protégé in the firm, not Bill, and it must have been a let-down for Wright to learn that Ken had pawned off this low-priority assignment on his untested brother.

The parallels between the perspective and Hedrich's photograph were in part deliberate and in part happenstance. Bill Hedrich knew nothing of Fallingwater and had seen neither photographs nor drawings of it until he went to meet Wright before his assignment. During the visit, we know that Wright laid out his favorite views of the house, among which must surely have been the perspective from below the falls. The original rendering had probably gone to New York by then, since Valentino Sarra was incorporating it in *Time*'s cover for January 17. But Wright had many copies of Putzel's article lying around Taliesin, so Hedrich almost certainly had a color reproduction of the rendering in his kit when he got to Bear Run.

Hedrich drove to Pennsylvania, stopped over with the Kaufmanns, then spent a full day looking at Fallingwater. He saw that if he was to cap-ture the angle of Wright's perspective he needed to wade into the middle of icy-cold Bear Run. He straightaway bought hip-high fishing boots in Ohiopyle, and captured the shot that made Fallingwater famous. Apart from deep filtering of the sky, which heightened the drama of the view, Hedrich needed no special effects. Fallingwater was so photogenic that from any angle it virtually photographed itself.

Hedrich's celebrated interpretation of Fallingwater sparked a blaze of admiration for the house that has never subsided, but not everyone fell in photographic love at first sight. According to Hedrich himself, Wright at first scorned the exaggerated drama of the view, snorting: "Very acrobatic, very acrobatic. Did you think I designed this?"

A month later the photograph also displeased the curators of the

Museum of Modern Art's Fallingwater show, evidently because it was too romantic for their Germanic tastes. MoMA included the view in its exhibit, but they did not bother to include the historic image in the show's photo brochure. Instead, they used a different Hedrich shot for the cover of the brochure, one taken from below the second falls. In this more distant view, a mass of rhododendron blocks the view of Fallingwater's stone tower, and the uniformly strong light bleaches the balconies to a glistening white. As a result, Fallingwater emerges as Miesian rather than Wrightian, which is what MoMA evidently still preferred. *Architectural Forum,* trumpeting the house for its Americanism instead, loved Hedrich's more dramatic photo, which it enlarged into a two-page foldout. We could call it the first pinup in the history of architecture.

W e will recall that the first time Fallingwater was presented to the national public it was cited as the "E. J. Kaufmann House, Pittsburgh, Pa." Like a starlet needing a nose job or silicone breasts before a breakthrough movie, the Kaufmann house needed a makeover to make it more attractive. Rather than anatomical tweaking, the house required a less ethnic name and a less odoriferous geographical location. Of the two changes the geographical was the more radical and the more complete. One still on occasion finds the retreat listed as "E. J. Kaufmann House" as well as "Fallingwater," but never will you spot its location as "Pittsburgh."

I commented at the beginning of this chapter on the irrationality of denying the fact that Fallingwater stands "near Pittsburgh." Let us now see what reasoning lay behind the denial. Suppose that a travel writer was preparing an article on Cortona, Montepulciano, or one of the other enchanting but less famous hill towns of Tuscany: where would she locate these towns for her American readers? "Near Florence," of course. No matter that the town in question lies fifty to eighty miles outside Florence, or that its topographic coordinates put it more logically "near Prato" or "outside Arezzo": clear writing demands that an obscure site be illuminated by locating it with reference to the one Tuscan city most American readers know.

When the same journalist locates Fallingwater in "Mill Run, Pennsylvania" or "Bear Run, Pennsylvania," she is using locations that are not merely obscure but fictitious. Mill Run is a gaggle of houses in Springfield Township, which does not even encompass Fallingwater. It is a village, a status that may carry weight in England or New England, but in Pennsylvania a village means any segment of a township that *lacks* independent

Fallingwater from Bear Run

ABOVE: Plentiful water, verdant hills, a dramatic display of technology, and the Kaufmann family are among the prime threads that link Pittsburgh and Fallingwater
OPPOSITE: Airview of Fallingwater in the forest at Bear Run, bordered by the Youghiogheny River

Fortune magazine for November 1944 imagined Kaufmann's
Department Store as the soul of Pittsburgh

Kaufmann's Department Store, Pittsburgh, Pa.

ABOVE: Kaufmann's Department Store around 1905, shortly before E. J. Kaufmann planned its takeover

RIGHT: Interior of Kaufmann's Department Store after its remodeling in 1930

Hokusai's *View of Ono Falls* is one of several prefigurations of
Fallingwater that Wright encountered in his years in Japan

ABOVE: Wright and apprentice Jack Howe created this perspective
rendering for the Kaufmanns in October 1935
BELOW: Wright drew his base plan for Fallingwater on the
morning of September 22, 1935

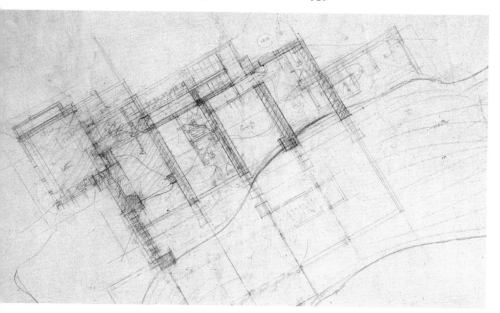

This evening view from the south captures the dual quality of
Fallingwater as both house and Cubist sculpture

The living room

ABOVE: The dining area, with steps to the second floor
BELOW: Kaufmann Junior's desk. More Wright-designed home
furnishings survive at Fallingwater than anywhere else.

ABOVE: The concrete canopy rises from Fallingwater to the
guesthouse with the grace of a Japanese origami
BELOW: The guesthouse exterior

ABOVE: Victor Hammer's *The Excursion* (at Fallingwater) shows E. J. Kaufmann as a hiker: Vienna 1929
BELOW: Hammer's *Vanitas* (Art Gallery, University of Kentucky), a portrait of Liliane Kaufmann: Florence, 1932

ABOVE: Peter Blume's *House at Falling Water,* 1938 and later
BELOW: Blume's 1948 painting *The Rock* is a "moral allegory"
about E. J. Kaufmann and Fallingwater

The richness of Richard Neutra's Kaufmann house at Palm Springs,
California, 1947, belies Wright's scorn for it as mechanistic and sterile

Edgar Kaufmann Jr.'s apartment in New York, with some of the
paintings that sold for nearly $100 million after his death in 1989

The Kaufmann tomb at Bear Run, with the bronze doors by Alberto Giacometti

status. Mill Run would not even have a name except for the presence of its post office. Legally speaking, it does not exist.

You can at least see Mill Run if you don't blink, and it has a welcome sign, whereas "Bear Run, Pennsylvania" is nothing but a stream. Recognizing this problem, some travel writers place Fallingwater in Ohiopyle, Connellsville, or Uniontown, but those stratagems won't work, either. Ohiopyle is a borough of 77 people; Connellsville a town of 8,000; Uniontown not much bigger. The citizens of Connellsville and Uniontown live miles away from Fallingwater; most have heard of the house, but few have gone to see it.

The legal address for Fallingwater is the one that appears on its deeds: "Stewart Township, Fayette County, Pennsylvania," but that won't help a prospective visitor from San Diego or Stuttgart. The only location that is logical and helpful for Fallingwater is "near Pittsburgh, Pennsylvania," which was how the earliest references cited it. Today the media repudiate a Pittsburgh address for Fallingwater as culturally incorrect. Already Max Putzel had created a second, more poetic, location for the house by the stream called Bear Run. MoMA turned the stream into the nonexistent "Bear Run, Pennsylvania," but by saying that the house stood "*on* Bear Run," MoMA at least distinguished that natural feature from a city. It was *Time* magazine that totally fictionalized the location as "*in* Bear Run, Pennsylvania," while *Architectural Forum* dropped all prepositions in favor of "Bear Run, Pennsylvania." After that, Fallingwater would almost never be found in or near Pittsburgh again.

Nonexistence was a useful quality for Fallingwater's site in the 1930s. Nobody had the money to go see it, so a practical address was little needed. The bucolic-sounding "Bear Run" portended a place as timeless and unreachable as an American Shangri-La (the *Lost Horizon* paradise also used as the original 1930s name for the presidential Camp David). Thus did this famously site-specific building get a site name better suited to no place: a literal utopia.

Now for the new name. For the makeover of the Kaufmann house into utopia to be complete, it needed a name so magic and universal that it sounded like an incantation and not a reminder of the merchant who had financed it. "Fallingwater" imparts utopianism and universality to the house, as though it no longer belonged to the Kaufmanns but to all humankind. The new name also removed the house from geographic and even temporal specificity, making it sound timeless, around forever. But the name Fallingwater came late, and obscurely. Edgar Tafel's claim that

Wright put the name on one of the earliest plans finds no second witness, and no such drawing exists today. One early drawing does bear the annotation FALLINGWATER, but in a hand so tiny and faint that it clearly belongs to a later archivist. The house went through 1935, 1936, and 1937 with nothing more than its client's name.

Bill Hedrich alleged that he godfathered the name through his famous photo, which he claimed made people first think of the house as "Fallingwater." This is possible, given that Wright first wrote out the name (in a draft text for the *Architectural Forum* issue) in November 1937, right at the time Hedrich took the photo. *Forum* is where the name appeared first, and inescapably, since its text on the Kaufmann house begins with a sentence exactly one word long: "Fallingwater."

Where did Wright get the name? The inverted "waterfall" represents exactly his kind of wordplay, akin to the name Wingspread that he gave Herbert Johnson's house. The name perhaps came to Wright subliminally from the common highway signs of western Pennsylvania that still warn of FALLING ROCK or from a map notation of Falling Waters, a West Virginia hamlet southeast of Bear Run. Alternately, Wright remembered the name because he was too tormented to forget it. The earliest documented use of the term in conjunction with the house came, as we saw, in the 1935 memo of the Morris Knowles firm that prophesied the building would self-destruct through the action of "falling water." Did that terrifying thought lock itself in Wright's subconscious, only to be released when the house was ready for its triumphant unveiling?

To this Freudian explanation we can append a Jungian one. The name Fallingwater may have served an even deeper psychic function for Wright. He was strangely taciturn on the subject of his most famous creation, but he obviously had a profound identification with the building that had saved his professional life. I believe it reflected not only his self-image but his very name. *Fa-Lling-Water* was the perfect cipher for the man himself: *Frank Lloyd Wright.*[*]

Since the "Fallingwater" nickname diminished their own glory, the Kaufmanns themselves never used it. That was ironic, because the social-climbing Liliane and E. J. would normally have loved such a gentrified name for their estate. America's historic houses have always borne fancy names: Mount Vernon, Monticello, San Simeon, Biltmore, Lyndhurst, Pickfair—even Elvis Presley's Graceland. In the United Kingdom, *Burke's Peerage* still receives no more frequent request than the plea to drop a

---

[*] I have no evidence for this theory of name association, but one suggestion that I am on the right track is that my idea was appropriated by *New Yorker* writer Brendan Gill, who used it in his *New York Life* after he heard me say it—and got hold of my text—at the 1986 Columbia University symposium on Fallingwater.

street address in favor of an estate name. According to a student of such names, the combination of gerund and noun in "Falling Water" (and the Mellons' nearby "Rolling Rock") is the height of pretentiousness. One nouveau riche tenant is supposed to have liked the formula so well that he christened his rented estate "Breaking Wind."

nadvertent criticality" is the way nuclear engineers define a chain reaction that feeds upon itself long after any external triggering has ended. That phenomenon now befell Fallingwater. In November 1937, as Wright's apprentices worked on the text and graphics of the special *Architectural Forum* issue, the house got the promise of another huge publicity boost in an unprecedented exhibit at the Museum of Modern Art.

Like the whole sequence of Fallingwater's PR history, details about this show are murky. At one level, MoMA's Fallingwater show made perfect sense, since it merely filled in for an Alvar Aalto exhibit after Aalto had begged for a delay. At another level, a Fallingwater show at MoMA was as likely as a Baby Face Nelson show at the FBI. Here was the institution that five years before had declared Wright outside the pale of modern architecture. Now it was bringing him back in triumph for its first major exhibit on a single work of art.

The path that led to the Fallingwater show at MoMA was tortured and complex. John McAndrew, MoMA's new curator of architecture and industrial design, heard that a Wright house was going up in Pittsburgh, wrote the Kaufmanns, and was invited to see their house in early November of 1937. McAndrew's source of information might have been Wright's new book, *Architecture and Modern Life*, but McAndrew specified that he learned about Fallingwater from the New York set designer Charles Alan.

Alan (actually Charles Allen Bernstein) was part of the Kaufmann clan, and it appears he was set up to call McAndrew by his sister Aline. Aline Bernstein Louchheim Saarinen (not to be confused with the older Aline Bernstein, who was the mistress of the novelist Thomas Wolfe) was much closer both to the Kaufmanns and to McAndrew than was her brother. After E. J., she was the most media-savvy member of the clan, a talent she later parlayed into a widespread following as a writer on art and architecture. Aline was a frequent visitor to Pittsburgh in the 1930s, and later lived there with her first husband, Joseph Louchheim Jr. She was a special favorite of her "aunt" Liliane Kaufmann, who bequeathed to her an enthralling mink cape that half a century later still made one Pittsburgh doyenne ache with envy. Aline was intimate enough with her cousin Kaufmann Jr. that the two were engaged to marry in 1953, but she wed the architect Eero Saarinen instead. Aline closely watched Falling-water go up, and knew better than anyone else in the clan the importance of what she was seeing, because she had been trained to discuss architecture by McAndrew himself—her old professor at Vassar College. Though McAndrew recalled "learning" about Fallingwater, it would be more accurate to say that he was ensnared into it.

Legend holds that McAndrew determined on the spot to mount a special exhibition on Fallingwater, but that ignores the reality of MoMA's byzantine exhibition politics. McAndrew could act only with a go-ahead from MoMA's Committee on Architecture and Industrial Art, which would not meet until November 19. On that day the ex-officio staff present were McAndrew, MoMA director Alfred Barr Jr., and Philip Goodwin, ex-curator of architecture at MoMA and now superintending the museum's new quarters. The outside voting members were academics: the art historians Winslow Ames, John Coolidge, and Henry-Russell Hitchcock, and Joseph Hudnut, dean of the Graduate School of Design at Harvard. The committee first voted to shift the delayed Aalto exhibit from January to March 1938, then deliberated on what to mount as its replacement in the small gallery devoted to architecture:

> Mr. McAndrew suggested the possibility of showing the house which Wright has just built for Mr. and Mrs. Edgar Kaufmann outside of Pittsburgh, during January, the same month that it is to be published extensively in the *Architectural Forum*. Mr. Barr pointed out that in two years the Department will probably want to hold a retrospective exhibition of Wright's work in honor of his 70th birthday. The Committee discussed the advisability of showing the Kaufmann house under those circumstances. It was decided that the exhibition of one house would not interfere with the probable exhibition in two years, and that this would be a good subject for the small exhibition for January.

The vote on November 19 was pro forma, since McAndrew knew the committee was willing to exhibit Wright before he proposed it. Actually, after humiliating Wright in its embrace of the Bauhaus in the epochal 1932 exhibition, MoMA had exhibited a glacial but perceptual warming up to him. Its curators could hardly ignore Wright's triumphant showing of the Broadacre City model in 1935 in Rockefeller Center, and in November 1935, MoMA's architecture committee had even considered asking Wright for a one-man show, though nothing came of it. Still, neither Wright nor Fallingwater would have crossed MoMA's threshold had Philip Johnson still been curator of architecture there in 1937. Not only did Johnson continue to champion German modernism throughout the

1930s, he now began to attack culturally progressive American Jews—people just like the Kaufmanns. The climate at MoMA ameliorated a bit in 1936 when Johnson quit as MoMA curator to organize a fascist movement in Ohio, and he then spent time with the real Nazis in Berlin. He accompanied the troops invading Poland in 1939, where, he wrote a friend, "The German green uniforms made the place look gay and happy."

Johnson remained on the Committee on Architecture and Industrial Art for a year after he resigned as a MoMA curator, but in September 1937 he finally quit that committee, too. When Fallingwater came up for a vote two months later, the remaining committee members were all well disposed to Wright. Dean Hudnut was an architectural moderate, but just that year he had appointed Gropius to head the architecture department at Harvard; he was known to respect Wright. Hitchcock was a Bauhaus enthusiast, but he had written a constructive book on Wright a decade earlier. The brilliant and patrician Coolidge, a gentleman architect like his ancestor and look-alike Thomas Jefferson, had sought to join Taliesin just the year before. The newest member of the committee, though absent from the November meeting, was George Nelson—the same George Nelson who was preparing the Wright issue of *Architectural Forum*. Nelson's presence guaranteed the viability of the Fallingwater show proposal—as the citation of *Forum* in the committee minutes reveals.

Something else that was propelling Fallingwater toward MoMA was geopolitics. The charge of bias against American artists had long bedeviled MoMA's exhibition program. In 1936, Hitchcock, who was both a Smith professor and MoMA's honorary curator of architecture, responded to this criticism by mounting an exhibition of the Victorian American architect H. H. Richardson. It was this aberrant exhibition of a Victorian at MoMA that first grouped Richardson, Sullivan, and Wright as the Holy Trinity of American architecture. Exaggerated that concept surely is, but not completely wrong: these three still strike us as the designers who struggled hardest to express American values in architecture.

But the Americanism issue would not go away, and at times it threatened to swamp MoMA. MoMA had been born in 1929 in Abby Aldrich Rockefeller's front parlor in the 53rd Street mansion that once stood where the shrine of modernism rises today. Abby's son Nelson became a MoMA trustee in 1932, was invested as treasurer in 1935, and was being groomed for a tenure as president to begin in 1939. Rockefeller had once dreamed of becoming an architect himself, and remained highly enthusiastic about the art of building. It was he who directed construction at Rockefeller Center during most of the 1930s, until it emerged as the most prominent modern complex in the world. He was schooled in architecture by a host of mentors, some of them quasi-moderns like Raymond Hood, others *echt* modern architects such as his favorites Wallace Harrison and Edward Durell Stone. Rockefeller had also learned that art can bite, in the infamous 1932 episode in which he invited Diego Rivera to paint a mural in Rockefeller Center, then ordered it destroyed.

As a businessman, Rockefeller was an active member of the Arts and Industry consortium, whose members saw modernism as good business. (This was the group on whose jury Rockefeller and E. J. Kaufmann were supposed to sit.) Rockefeller was also moving to modernism in his personal life. Around 1940 he had Wallace Harrison build him a modern summer home at Seal Harbor, Maine. Even his ancient father, John D. Jr., warmed up to the style, writing his son that he at first thought modern architecture a dreadful idea, but that he had come to like the house.

Ever since becoming a trustee, Rockefeller had been embroiled in the search for an architect to design MoMA's new building. The general sentiment was that the architect had to be European, and if possible German. In 1935, Alfred Barr got the trustees to designate Mies, Gropius, or the Dutch J. J. P. Oud as their three preferred architects. But the Nazi Party rallies in Germany did not play well in Manhattan: the MoMA board reversed itself the next year, and the architecture advisory committee unanimously expressed itself in favor of giving the commission to an American. The question of housing MoMA was also of substantial economic pertinence to Rockefeller because he still hoped to cut through a two-block street to join MoMA with Rockefeller Center as two halves of one complex. In 1936, Rockefeller ended years of bickering by picking MoMA's own Philip Goodwin plus Edward Durell Stone as architects for the new building, which finally began to rise between 1937 and 1939.

Philip Johnson's enthusiasm for the Nazis was evidently embarrassing to MoMA during 1936 and 1937. In the summer of 1937, Rockefeller wrote Hitchcock that MoMA's leadership was tiring of German modernism, and he asked Hitchcock to support more home-grown American architects. This meant that in the fall of 1937, Hitchcock and the MoMA curators were scrambling to mount a show by an American architect. How convenient that word was now circulating that the grand old man of American modernism was putting up a stone house in Pennsylvania.

MoMA mounted its Fallingwater show at a furious pace. McAndrew created the title, "A New House by Frank Lloyd Wright on Bear Run, Pennsylvania," and he scheduled the show to open only eight weeks later, on

January 25. On December 1 he telegraphed George Nelson, who was working with Wright at Taliesin, to ask Wright for plans and sections of Fallingwater. This request either went astray or was rebuffed—was Wright still licking his wounds from 1932?—so McAndrew repeated it with Kaufmann Jr. as intermediary. Junior in turn telegraphed Wright for his immediate assent: "Time is short. . . . Setup is elegant, McAndrew wants future exhibits and seems sincere, much unlike his predecessors [i.e., Hitchcock and Johnson], which can help us lots."

On the last day of 1937, McAndrew telegraphed Wright:

> Assembling photographs of Kaufmann House for exhibition in Museum of Modern Art. May we have your permission to show plans and text from Forum? Also we would like to issue 2500 copies of a sixteen page picture book of house, and would like to use your text again, as well as plans and some of Forum pictures. Yours would be the only text, all the rest pictures. Show to open about January twentieth, booklet appearing at same time. Photographs are really handsome and give quite a good idea of the house; it looks like a good show. I hope you will approve. Please wire answer collect. Hope you will have a fine New Year.

Wright responded on January 5:

> All right John let's see what you can do Coffman Junior has best photographs I have seen of house. Esther Born getting complete series of Hanna house Paloalto.

In his usual fashion, Wright was trying to force MoMA to include his other new houses in their show, too.

Wright's text in the MoMA show was identical to the one he had written for *Forum*; almost identical, too, were the plans that Wright's draftsmen had prepared for the magazine. The original intention was to show photographs by Luke Swank only, but at the last minute McAndrew secured some of the new Bill Hedrich views, and to these he added a few photographs he had taken at Bear Run himself. Twenty-two enlarged photographs were mounted on walnut boards with plans and explanatory text. MoMA called Fallingwater "Wright's most important house of the last 25 years, built at Bear Run, Pa., for Mr. and Mrs. Edgar Kaufmann." McAndrew produced an elegant fifty-cent brochure: *A New House by Frank Lloyd Wright at Bear Run, Pennsylvania*, which reproduced half the plans and views in the show, though it excluded what later became the most famous one, as we have seen. He also hoped to screen the Fallingwater construction movies that Swank had been taking for Kaufmann—

this in emulation of the much-publicized construction films on the Empire State Building and the Golden Gate Bridge—but technical difficulties ruled that out.

The media muse behind Fallingwater could not rest. Her efforts were sure to propel the house into orbit as an icon on the East Coast, but she would need to give it another promotional boost to achieve the same rank worldwide. That boost soon came from Henry R. Luce, king of Time-Life publications. Intimately involved in the weekly or monthly production of *Time, Life, Architectural Forum,* and *Fortune,* Luce was the one man who could send Fallingwater into permanent orbit in the ninth circle of fame. (He demonstrated this power a decade later when he sent the famous "Puff Graham" telegram to his office, and overnight turned Billy Graham into the world's most famous preacher.)

Until Time-Life unseals its archives we will never know exactly how much Luce personally involved himself in publicizing Fallingwater, but we can suspect that it was a great deal. Only Luce could have authorized Howard Myers to offer Wright the unprecedented and risky takeover of a whole issue of *Forum,* and only the man at the top of the Time-Life pyramid had the power to order the complex publicity linkage by which three of his magazines promoted Fallingwater on the same day.

The nexus of Luce, MoMA, Wright, and Fallingwater was so tight it was borderline incestuous. Luce, his celebrity wife, Clare Boothe Luce, and his son Henry III were personal acquaintances and later good friends of the Wrights. We don't know when the friendship started—a visit by Luce to the Manhattan showing of Broadacre City in 1935 is a good possibility—but their families were in close touch until Wright died in 1959. Wright and Luce genuinely liked each other, but they willingly used each other, too. Luce allotted copious publicity over the years to the man he affectionately addressed as "Maestro": *Time* ran seventeen favorable stories on Wright between 1945 and 1957; *Life* not many fewer.

Like Rockefeller, Luce was a longtime supporter of MoMA: in 1938 he was a year away from election to the museum board, and he, too, was an architect manqué. "To influence architecture is to influence life," he wrote in a 1935 mission statement for *Architectural Forum.* How much Luce loved the art of building it is easy to judge from his 1932 purchase of *Forum* as his third magazine. It followed *Time* and *Fortune* but preceded *Life* and (after Luce retired) *Sports Illustrated, People,* and others. *Forum* had three special distinctions within the Luce publishing empire. It was the only special-audience publication Time-Life ever put out: all its other magazines were written for a general public. It was the only publication in which Luce engaged in nepotism, installing his brother Sheldon as manager. And it was the only part of the business that lost money year after year. Luce's unsentimental successors at Time-Life rectified these three anomalies when they killed the magazine in 1964, just months after Luce retired.

Luce kept *Forum* alive because he was passionate about architecture and modernism. His political conservatism obscured this early passion, but it comes through with great sincerity in Luce's 1935 vision for *Architectural Forum*, in which he insisted that every new building be not merely new but modern. Like Rockefeller, he was a patron of Edward Durell Stone, and in 1937 he commissioned Stone to build a set of severely modern guest bungalows alongside his old plantation house outside Charleston, South Carolina. (The estate houses a Trappist monastery today.) These bungalows were both earlier and stylistically more radical than Fallingwater. Rockefeller may have waffled in his support of modernism in the arts, but in the 1930s Henry R. Luce was one of its most consistent promoters.

Even before Luce joined the MoMA board, his identification with MoMA was unmistakable. The old Time-Life Building at 14 West 49th Street—not the 1959 tower of the same name on Sixth Avenue—was one of the earliest parts of Rockefeller Center to be occupied. Luce worked in the penthouse; below him worked the staffs of *Time, Life, Fortune,* and *Architectural Forum.* Below them were the temporary quarters of the Museum of Modern Art, in a handsome basement concourse still preserved in amber today. In effect, MoMA mounted its Fallingwater exhibit right under Luce's feet.

The Fallingwater show could not fail to be hot, because three of Luce's four publications had been puffing Fallingwater for a fortnight. By dint of tight coordination, *Life, Time,* and *Architectural Forum* all carried features on Fallingwater when they hit the newsstands on January 10 (the first two with the cover date of January 17). Fallingwater also made its way into *Fortune* not long after, when it carried an effusive article on E. J. Kaufmann.

Time had never before conferred a cover on an architect or a building. Now here was Wright on the cover with a huge blow-up of Howe's Fallingwater perspective rendering. The new house for Edgar Kaufmann, *Time* pontificated inside, showed Wright to be "the greatest architect of the 20th Century." Nor was *Time* shy in reminding its readers to buy the ancillary *Forum* issue, which it claimed "broke all precedents for that magazine." Nonetheless, *Time* hedged its bets on which of Wright's works the public would like best. The cover caption referred not to Fallingwater but to Broadacre City. Inside, the article called Fallingwater Wright's "most beautiful work," but it devoted just four lines to the house, and neglected to plug the Fallingwater exhibition at MoMA (it corrected this oversight in its second mention of the house, the next month). By contrast *Time* gave forty-seven lines of text to Johnson's Wax. Were the editors uncertain how big a sensation Fallingwater was going to be, or were they just pandering to a corporation that advertised a great deal of wax?

The issue of *Life* that went on sale the same day carried a striking reproduction of Bill Hedrich's Fallingwater view in an advertisement for the *Architectural Forum* issue. Whether *Life*'s readers bought the *Forum* issue or not, the advertisement exposed a million or more Americans to the house. What was particularly arresting was its location on the inside front cover—normally a magazine's second- or third-most-lucrative advertising spot. *Life* had rarely squandered that page on a "house ad" before, but now it did. The ad portentously declaimed: "The editors believe that this issue is the most important architectural document ever published in America"—which is just what it became.

MoMA's Fallingwater exhibit opened the night of Monday, January 24. Within a week, as Wright was moving into his new quarters in Arizona's Taliesin West, excitement over the Fallingwater show and articles had risen to a frenzy. Wright had to write Johnson Wax's Bill Connolly in commiseration for the way *Forum* had downplayed Johnson's Wax in its pages. The Time-Life hierarchy—surely we see the hand of Luce again—was no less sensitive to the irony that Fallingwater had bested Johnson's Wax, and prepared itself for the loss of advertising dollars that might have come from a grateful Herbert Johnson. To recoup, *Life* devoted three full pages to Johnson's headquarters in its issue of May 8, 1939, when the tardy building was complete. *Life* called the Racine complex a truer view of the architecture of the future than the "gigantic mass of freak and futuristic buildings" then on view at the New York World's Fair. *Life*'s photographs of Johnson's Wax opened with a striking image of two figures on an interior balcony. These were Herbert Johnson and William Connolly—the two executives who knew from the first what a bonanza Wright's design would yield in free advertising.

Even though Wright defaulted on his promised deadline, Connolly's architecture-as-publicity strategy paid off. Johnson's Wax also appeared in *Scientific American* for May 1937; *Science* magazine for October 1937; *Business Week* for May 1939; and the *Saturday Evening Post* ran a profile of Herbert Johnson in April 1937. Wright keenly understood the financial implications of this publicity. In the 1943 update of his *Autobiography* he made a shrewd appraisal of the dollar value of his design to his client:

Bill Connolly, competent "man on the job" for the advertising of the S. C. Johnson Co., calculated that (with no help from him at all) two or more millions of dollars could not have bought the front pages in newspapers and top-notch magazines the building had attracted to itself—gratis.

The movie "shorts" took it up and carried on.

Radio came running. Meanwhile streams of visitors from all over the world went on and continue to go on to this hour.

The millions of dollars that Wright estimated his stunning administration building had brought Johnson's Wax in four years has by now amounted to hundreds of millions of dollars in free publicity. Johnson's Wax had still one further drop of free advertising to squeeze out of its connection with Frank Lloyd Wright. From 1937 until it went out of production in the late 1990s, nothing but Johnson's Glo-Coat was allowed to touch the stone floors at Fallingwater.

Word of Fallingwater spread fast through magazines not controlled by Luce, too. With just two exceptions, every magazine in the country—or on the face of the planet, so far as we know—that reported on Fallingwater did so with fulsome praise. The first specialized review of the house in the art and architecture magazines appeared in the February 1 *Art Digest*, followed by Lewis Mumford, America's foremost architectural critic, in the February 12 *New Yorker*. Mumford echoed *Time* in calling Wright the world's greatest living architect. Praise for Fallingwater now fell from the lips of critics and media barons far removed from the circles of modernism, and from some even hostile to it. The scholar and traditionalist Talbot Hamlin broke off his studies of Colonial houses and Greek Revival architecture long enough to review Fallingwater with zeal in the March issue of *Pencil Points*. Like the others, Hamlin saw Fallingwater as proof that Wright was the most creative architect in America.

Fallingwater now entered the orbit of the mass-circulation magazines. *Time*'s second mention of the house, on February 21, 1938, used a tone that assumed its readers were fully conversant with it. The house was then lauded by the leftist *New Masses* and by William Randolph Hearst's snooty *Town & Country*. Praising Fallingwater was probably the only point on which those two archantagonist publications agreed in the whole of their print history.

Of the two unforeseen conquests on the political left and right, the capitulation of Hearst was the more surprising. Hearst is mostly recalled today as the eccentric parodied in the 1941 movie *Citizen Kane* or as the prodigious stockpiler of relics from Europe's past at San Simeon ("Nazi nostalgia," the Italian novelist Umberto Eco witheringly called it). But socially and politically he was a far more dangerous force. He admired Mussolini and Hitler—and hired them both as free-lance columnists—and called Franklin D. Roosevelt the personal choice of Joseph Stalin for president of the United States. Already in 1935, Raymond Gram Swing's *Forerunners of American Fascism* classed Hearst with Huey Long and the rabidly anti-Jewish Father Coughlin as the three leading promoters of fascism in the United States.

Hearst ran a parallel though less consistent campaign against modernism, both through the example of his California castle and through his magazines. *Harper's Bazaar,* which Hearst took over in 1913, was the exception: it encouraged women toward modernism in their lives, and his other magazines would sometimes bestow faint praise on modernism when that tendency appeared "smart." *Town & Country,* for example, occasionally reviewed a titillating art show in New York, and *House Beautiful*'s exhibit on the modern house was written up extensively in its July 1934 issue. (This was, after all, the periodical that had praised Wright's work as early as 1897.) In 1936 *American Architect* carried an article on America's cities by Le Corbusier, and *Town & Country* ran an old drawing by Wright on its July 1937 cover. Overall, though, Hearst's magazines held to their conservative taste in architecture: a reader of *Town & Country, Country Life, Connoisseur,* or *American Architect* would barely perceive that modernism was storming the gates. In their magazines, as in their homes, Hearst and Luce were wrangling *mano a mano* on the issue of modern architecture.

It was Fallingwater that signaled the ebbing of Hearst's resistance. In 1936 *American Architect* merged with *Architecture* to get new readers, and inherited *Architecture*'s progressive editor, Henry H. Saylor. Saylor informed Wright on September 2, 1937, how impressed he had been by the *Milwaukee Sentinel*'s feature of "a home over a waterfall for some gentleman living near Pittsburgh." He hoped to publish Fallingwater in full when it was complete, he told Wright, but his magazine dissolved before its conversion to modernism could happen. In the end, it was *Town & Country* that signaled the end of Hearst's stonewalling of modernism. Not one modern construction had ever appeared among the scores of homes the magazine had discussed over the years, but now it devoted three pages in its February 1938 issue to Fallingwater and two lesser modern homes. The article was written by Augusta Owen Patterson, the same journalist who totally ignored modernism when she wrote her book on American houses a decade earlier.

. . .

The exposure of Fallingwater in the magazines was important and unprecedented, but an even greater tsunami of publicity came in the newspapers. The *New York Times* could not even wait for MoMA's official opening for it to run a positive review by its normally antimodern critic, Edward Alden Jewell. Even more surprising was the first lavishly illustrated story on the house, in the magazine section of the *New York Herald Tribune* of February 6. This must have come over the furious objections of the *Trib's* art critic Royal Cortissoz, the cranky old stegosaurus who, privately, was an "irate critic" of the house.

We have no idea how many hundreds—thousands?—of newspapers carried the boilerplate articles on Fallingwater that were offered up by the various news services, but a sampling of three dozen newspaper and magazine articles on the MoMA exhibition is preserved in that museum's archive. Feature stories appeared in publications as diverse as the *Christian Science Monitor;* the *Springfield* (Massachusetts) *Morning Union;* the *Des Moines Register and Tribune* (with an elaborate rotogravure feature); the *Albuquerque News;* and the *Dallas Times-Herald.* A long article appeared in *We the People: Pennsylvania in Review* for February 1, 1938. Other papers, from Los Angeles to Alaska and Colonial Williamsburg, ran the MoMA press release on the New York exhibition or reported on local showings of the Fallingwater traveling exhibit in the years following. Bill Hedrich's famous photo was plastered over newspapers by the hundreds. Was ever a private home so widely publicized?

What did the correspondents write about Fallingwater? Pretty much what their successors are still writing today. First came the fascination with the daring structure; second, admiration for Wright's achievement in harmonizing the house with its natural setting; third, the interior glamour and the labor-saving devices inside the house—devices that are naturally less remarkable today. A few newspapers and magazines alluded to Wright's resurgence as a creative designer, but only Max Putzel in the *St. Louis Post-Dispatch* bothered to say, in effect, "Welcome back, Frank Lloyd Wright." Neither *Architectural Forum* nor *Time* mentioned Wright's years-long famine before Fallingwater, perhaps because they themselves had once joined the orgy of praise for the European modernists.

It is peculiar, too, that none of the writers remarked how different Fallingwater was from Wright's ornamented and historicist work of the 1920s. Nor did they split hairs over his various disagreements with the Europeans. The few articles that tangled with the "European question" echoed MoMA's publicity release and talked about modernism returning to the United States "in the guise of a European influence." This theme is rarely found in popular articles on Fallingwater today, since the topic became a nonissue long ago.

Appropriately for a design that was itself so international, Fallingwater's publicity went international at warp speed. Beginning in February, Fallingwater was splashed in architectural magazines in English, French, Spanish, Italian, Dutch, Japanese, and Finnish. While their source was usually the *Architectural Forum* issue, the foreign architectural press generally dropped Johnson's Wax and Wright's other new buildings, and glorified Fallingwater alone.

A second wave of European publicity was set off when photographs of Fallingwater arrived in Europe for "Three Hundred Years of American Art," a show mounted by MoMA at the Musée du Jeu de Paume in Paris from May through July 1938. The French loved Fallingwater and made it the star of the show, along with American movies and photographs of early American architecture. (The American paintings bombed: "Better one meter of American film to fifty meters of American paintings," wrote one critic.) The June 1938 *Architecture d'Aujourd'hui* was typical in illustrating only Fallingwater from among the many buildings in the Paris show. Similarly, Eric Newton's review of the show in London's *Sunday Times* highlighted "the extraordinary beauty" of Fallingwater. Two English magazines, the June *Illustrated Carpenter and Builder* and the July 7 *Architects' Journal*, also discussed and illustrated the Paris show exclusively in terms of Fallingwater.

The only European architecture magazines of any significance that resisted falling in love with Fallingwater were the state-controlled journals in Germany, such as *Bauwelt*, which allowed nothing on its pages except the monumental fascist style or old-fashioned folk architecture. Outstanding was the highly enthusiastic article on the Villa Kaufmann in the Italian *Rassegna d'Architettura*, despite its status as the official organ of the Fascist League of Architects. The independent periodical *Casabella* waxed equally enthusiastic about Wright and Fallingwater, but there was a price to pay. The architectural journalist Bruno Zevi was convinced that Giuseppe Pagano, editor of *Casabella*, paid for his support of modern architecture with his life. The Germans deported him and executed him in the concentration camp at Mauthausen.

Fallingwater was even more rapturously appreciated by Italy's architectural underground, and it resurfaced triumphantly in May of 1945 on the cover of the very first book on architecture published in postwar Europe: Zevi's call for an organic architecture. Learning that a single picture on the cover was all that the paper- and ink-starved printer could afford for the whole book, Zevi breezily instructed the man to run nothing but a photograph of Fallingwater. "That one photograph," Zevi later recalled, "all by itself, was inspiration enough for an entire generation of Italian architects who had lived through Fascism and the war, to learn that modernism was not dead." To a Europe deprived of culture and freedom, Fallingwater promised a return to both.

Fallingwater got a second wave of public exposure in the United States in 1939, when MoMA revived the architecture segment that had proved so popular in its 1938 Paris show (but not the unpopular segment on American painting). It hung "Three Centuries of American Architecture" in its temporary Manhattan quarters in February and March 1939, then sent parts of it on the road as a traveling exhibit. All three formats— the Paris show, the New York reprise, and the traveling show—did much to solidify the image of Fallingwater. A year and a half after the first media blitz, Bill Hedrich's view of Fallingwater was still exciting enough to merit a huge reproduction in the *Cleveland Press*. MoMA also created three different exhibition formats that presented Fallingwater alone. Kaufmann Jr., by now on the MoMA staff, kept the shows touring in a hundred U.S. and Canadian cities for years. As late as 1949, the arrival of a traveling show on Fallingwater was treated as big news in the smaller American newspapers.

What drove this mass of stories? The bylines and the photo credits in the magazines and newspapers show that the articles were being fed to the media by two separate publicity machines: those of Time-Life and of the Museum of Modern Art. We know only a little about the former, but we can be certain of the potency of MoMA's PR, because there exists an unpublished account that documents how discerningly it was managed. MoMA's publicity in the 1930s and 1940s was run by Sara Newmeyer, who was famous in the trade for the rigor with which she pursued traditional PR and for her creativity at special publicity stunts. It was Newmeyer, for example, who cajoled the aristocratic Sara Delano Roosevelt into unveiling Whistler's *Portrait of the Artist's Mother* when it was mounted at a MoMA show. "All the leading newsreels showed Franklin D. Roosevelt's mother unveiling Whistler's," says MoMA's PR history. In the single year 1936–37, Newmeyer claimed to have spewed out 83,000 sheets of press releases or other publicity texts to a thousand publications around the world. In 1937, MoMA's self-congratulation garnered it 4,107 stories in newspapers or periodicals in the forty-eight states and abroad. "During this first year of *Life* magazine . . . the Museum made nine appearances in the new periodical, with from three to five full pages each. No other museum or art institution in the country appeared more than twice in *Life* in the same period." If we wish to decorate the soldier who, more than anyone else, slogged through the publicity battlefield to show the flag of Fallingwater, that warrior was Sarah Newmeyer.

B	ut Newmeyer was only the infantryman in one particular theater of the war: who was the generalissimo? It's too late to determine for sure, but all the circumstantial evidence points in the direction of the old master merchandiser E. J. Kaufmann. We cannot fully evaluate his efforts to publicize Fallingwater because not a scrap of paper survives to document them, but everything we know about E. J. tells us he would not leave the publicizing of his greatest cultural triumph to luck. He may have wished to cover up his tracks, however, so we should think of him as the prompter who resolutely stays hidden from view.

Kaufmann certainly had the connections and the ambition to have "placed" Fallingwater with MoMA, Time-Life, and the Hearst magazines and newspapers, had he chosen to. We will recall that Philip Johnson had sought to enlist Kaufmann as a MoMA supporter as early as 1932. Kaufmann also had a loyal protégé on the MoMA staff in the person of Catherine Bauer, whose career as an architectural critic he had launched by sponsoring her housing essay in *Fortune* in 1931. It was Bauer who got Johnson to contact E. J. in 1932, and she could easily have acted as E. J.'s private go-between with MoMA five years later. Two of Kaufmann's staff members also had professional links to MoMA: his designer Laszlo Gabor and Luke Swank, who had exhibited his photographs beginning with MoMA's second show in 1930. E. J. had made sure of the quality and quantity of Swank's portfolio on Fallingwater since 1936, which now paid off as a major inducement for McAndrew to exhibit the house despite his short lead time.

Kaufmann had a prodigious flair for publicity, as we have seen. His long-distance call echoing Lindbergh's flight to Paris, the store's use of early radio broadcasts, the airplane assembled on the ground floor—these were not merely stunts but demonstrations of how to get publicity from the application of new technology. E. J.'s professional film on combatting unemployment, in which he himself starred, makes clear how well he could exploit the new media.

Such a visionary would hardly have been less facile at manipulating the print media. Kaufmann was a publisher of sorts himself, putting out the monthly *Storagram* for his 3,000 employees, which was praised as the best retail employee publication in the United States. We still have the letters from dozens of rival stores who wanted to be placed on its mailing list. As the top advertiser in the Pittsburgh newspapers from the 1920s through the 1950s, E. J. was unafraid to throw his weight around in ways that we now regard as politically incorrect. The 1933 exposé on E. J. in the *Pittsburgh Bulletin Index* (impervious to Kaufmann's wrath, since it carried minimal advertising) alleged that in 1931 Kaufmann got the *Pittsburgh Press* to fire reporter Karl Krug for divulging that Liliane intended to file for divorce.

Nor was E. J. a greenhorn around the national media. He was friendly with Bill Paley and the top executives at the Columbia Broadcasting System, and he had at least superficial connections in Hollywood from years of wintering in southern California. Kaufmann had an even closer involvement with the national magazines. We already noted that his sponsorship of the essay contest in *Fortune* was worth a mint in free publicity for his store. The contest made Kaufmann and Luce working partners of sorts by 1930, even if they had not been previously acquainted. After E. J.'s success at Fallingwater, the two men worked together again in September 1938 in a joint venture to market house plans to Luce's readers.

Though Kaufmann left almost no tracks as a publicist for Fallingwater, we can reconstruct his probable modus operandi from the way he publicized his two other great houses, in Pittsburgh and in Palm Springs. The success of Kaufmann's publicizing of La Tourelle in the late 1920s can be measured in column inches, which exceeded what the architecture magazines carried on Fallingwater a decade later, though by then there were fewer of them. After it was completed in 1928, La Tourelle appeared first in Hearst's high-society *Country Life,* followed by a nineteen-page feature in the Forbes-controlled periodical *The Architect. Pencil Points* covered La Tourelle in 1929; *Architectural Record,* Hearst's *American Architect,* and the *Western Architect* weighed in with stories in 1930. *Architectural Forum,* the magazine Luce bought a few years later, was the one significant national architecture magazine *not* to carry La Tourelle: did its editors regard the house as too hopelessly antimodern?

La Tourelle had undeniable visual appeal, but its publicity was artificially induced. Each of the half-dozen articles on the house carried the identical photographs from the identical Pittsburgh studio. The aerial view that was so distinctive a feature of these articles was even more of a ploy: the Kaufmanns were part-owners of the company that took it.

The publicity Kaufmann snared for La Tourelle is instructive both in terms of how much he wanted it and how easily he got it. It was exceptional for a home outside the Vanderbilt or Rockefeller circles to get this much publicity, the more so since the house stood in provincial Pittsburgh. There had not been this much fuss over a Pittsburgh building since H. H. Richardson's courthouse opened in 1888. La Tourelle's appearance in the two Hearst magazines is unsurprising in artistic terms, since it was the kind of conservative design that Hearst's magazines favored. But its real triumph was in social terms. Hearst's publications all used architecture to propagate a distinctly white-bread view of American life. It was rare for Hearst periodicals to cover a "Jewish" house, and in the years from 1923 to 1931 the one exception among some three hundred dwellings that I counted as blessed on those pages was Kaufmann's. How Kaufmann made his way into *Country Life* and *American Architect* we do not know, but the likelihood is strong that he milked his professional and personal links with Hearst. The links that were sufficient to get La Tourelle into the pages of the Hearst magazines in the 1920s got Fallingwater and modern architecture into the same pages a decade later.

Now fast-forward to the 1940s. The strongest evidence for Kaufmann's manipulation of the architectural and general press in 1938 comes from an examination of the publicity he generated for his Palm Springs house a decade after Fallingwater. I will leave the details to their proper chronological place, except for two that are crucial for a reconstruction of how E. J. publicized Fallingwater. The first is the synchronization of the Time-Life publications on the Palm Springs house in the years from 1947 to 1949, which seems like a straight replay of their promotion of Fallingwater in 1938. There was a key difference between the two publicity campaigns, however: the publicity barrage of 1938 helped Wright as a Luce personal favorite, while that of 1947 to 1949 benefited Richard Neutra, the most hated of Wright's enemies. This points to Kaufmann as the force that squeezed the free publicity out of Time-Life both in 1938 and 1949. As near as we can determine, it was he who was the hidden generalissimo in the publicity war for Fallingwater.

Kaufmann's promotion of his Palm Springs house clears up a second curiosity about the publicity on Fallingwater, which is why it did not start at home. The explanation seems to be that Kaufmann knew, or at least feared, that the local architects and the artistically backward Pittsburgh aristocracy would attack him for bolting to modernism. (Remember that the 1933 *Bulletin Index* charged E. J. with being an artistic poseur.) E. J. also needed to sidestep his employees, who would not soon forget that his new estate on Bear Run had robbed them of their old summer camp. And the obvious fear: it was not good business in the Depression years for a retailer to play the millionaire. Wisconsin's Hib Johnson lacked Kaufmann's circumspection, and paid the price of looking too rich after *Architectural Forum* stressed the high cost of Wingspread.

For those and other reasons, Kaufmann wanted Pittsburgh to be the last place to hear about Fallingwater—and effectively it was. The *Pittsburgh Bulletin Index* in January 1938 noted that up to the last minute the curators of the Carnegie Museum of Art were oblivious to the fact that so experimental a house was going up in their backyard. When the *Pittsburgh Press* finally reported on Fallingwater—a month after its unveiling—its account was longer than those of most American newspapers but no more insightful: its information came not from the Kaufmanns but from the standard press releases that were cranked out of New York. With hindsight, we discover that in 1947 Kaufmann hired a Pittsburgh publicist for the specific assignment of preventing the *Press* from covering his new California house until E. J. could get national coverage for it. He clearly knew how to control publicity if he was willing to pay *not* to get it.

It finally makes sense why it was the *St. Louis Post-Dispatch* that rang up the curtain on Fallingwater. Kaufmann and Wright needed such a publication if they were to tease other magazines into publicizing the house, but they did not trust the job to Pittsburgh. Nothing in his prior life suggests that reporter Max Putzel dreamed up the Fallingwater story

The conservative architects of Pittsburgh reacted negatively to Fallingwater: a local publication of March 1938

on his own, nor did he ever claim to, but it would have been easy for E. J. to plant it with the Pulitzers, the progressive owners of the *Post-Dispatch*. In the late 1930s, the St. Louis summer opera became Kaufmann's specific model for bringing summer opera to Pittsburgh: it is reasonable to suppose that he made one or more trips there. Kaufmann's business ties to St. Louis could not have been closer, either: Morton May, CEO of the Famous-Barr retail chain, which was based there, was I. D. Wolf's first cousin, and within a few years E. J. would sell him the Kaufmann store. The Mays were the biggest advertisers at the *Post-Dispatch* and the main art collectors in town after the Pulitzers themselves. Business and culture combined to make St. Louis a perfect launchpad for Fallingwater.

Kaufmann was correct in fearing that conservative circles in Pittsburgh would attack him for building Fallingwater. The first—of exactly two—magazines that chose to ridicule Fallingwater was *Charette,* the house organ of the local architects of Pittsburgh. Its March 1938 issue mocked it in a drawing and text that likened the house to a gussied-up Tennessee Valley Authority dam. The drawing depicted the coffin in which Kaufmann supposedly buried the negative opinions of the Pittsburgh engineers who warned him not to proceed with Fallingwater. The attack was a severe case of sour grapes by the architects of Pittsburgh, whose favorite patron had abandoned them for modernism and Frank Lloyd Wright. Kaufmann was not insensitive to the attack, as we can tell from the fact that he kept a copy of the drawing among his personal papers until his death. But there was only a single publication to reprint the attack: the *Federal Architect,* another dinosaur of conservatism.

And that was it. The final tally in the entire world was two articles that disliked Fallingwater, and uncounted thousands that loved it. The hype on Fallingwater was solidly in place.

Opposite: Robert Day's cartoon of serial Fallingwaters: *The New Yorker,* May 3, 1952

NINE

FABRICATING FALLINGWATER II: THE BUZZ THAT MADE AMERICA BUY IT

What is this you bring to America? . . . What does it mean to me? . . . What are you, indeed, who would talk or sing to America? Have you studied out the land, its idioms, and men? Have you learned the physiology, phrenology, politics, geography, pride, freedom, friendship of the land? Its substratums and objects?

—WALT WHITMAN, *Leaves of Grass,* quoted by
Wright in *Architectural Forum,* 1938

I n the end, none of its promoters—not Wright, not Kaufmann, not Luce, not Hearst—sold Fallingwater to the American people as cunningly as the house sold itself. The hype on Fallingwater was soon overtaken by its buzz, and soon hundreds of thousands of Americans knew of it and cherished it.

What was it that made Fallingwater so attractive? It would be cynical to say that Americans cannot resist the combined assault of a talented architect and an ambitious client—and it would be mistaken as well. The collaboration of Mies van der Rohe and liquor tycoon Sam Bronfman in 1954 created a similar worldwide success for New York's Seagram Building, and the Gehry-Krens collaboration achieved the same result in 1997 for the Guggenheim in Bilbao. But no publicity assault can sell a bad building, in America or anywhere else. When the talented architect Edward Durell Stone and the immensely wealthy Huntington Hartford teamed up to build New York's Gallery of Modern Art in the early 1960s, critics greeted their Venetian rehash with nothing but derision.

No: money, ambition, and hype are *not* all you need to produce a classic building. A classic building demands resonance. Every CEO in America wanted a Seagram Building once they saw it, and the man or woman in the street knew even without full comprehension that something not merely novel but valuable had just been created. Ordinary people also tried to imitate Fallingwater after they learned of it, though for obvious reasons they would not get far. In the 1960s, for example, Craig Harper used Fallingwater as the model for the Mobil (now Shell) gas station that still stands at the I-95 off-ramp near Stafford, Virginia. No one seduced or bribed Harper to build this homage to Fallingwater: he did it from genuine love of the original.

T he paradox of Fallingwater is temporal: the building that is routinely called timeless went up with perfect timing. Of the many things never investigated about the house, one of the most significant is that Fallingwater was a child of the Depression. The two prime conditions that made Americans love Fallingwater were the same two that dominated the 1930s as a whole: the Depression and the drift into global warfare. Certainly any appraisal of the "meaning" of Fallingwater will fail unless it encompasses the harshness of the decade that caused Americans to fundamentally reevaluate the economic and cultural bases of their society.

The Depression was propagated by the mass media just as much as Fallingwater was. Had the media not made it "Great," the Depression might have struck most Americans as a series of disconnected local events. Had New Englanders not listened to the radio, watched the newsreels, or seen the photographs in *Life,* how much would they have known or cared about the drought in the Dust Bowl? The mass media made them care, just as it made them care about the larger-than-life figures of Roosevelt and Hitler.

Nothing gets famous without timing, and Fallingwater's timing was the best. It appeared before the public at the exact bottom of the Depression. The worst moment of the Depression was not the Stock Market Crash of October 1929, which was only a prelude; in terms of employment and industrial production the Depression reached its low point in 1932, after which these indices started climbing back. By 1936 industrial production was higher than it had been before the Crash. *Then* came the true depths of the Depression, in November and December of 1937, when production and employment disastrously slipped a second time, and any tentative optimism vanished. Word of a new luxury house called Fallingwater reached the world just one month later.

Here are some of the ways in which, I feel, Fallingwater was bound up with the Great Depression:

• It fed Americans' need for escapism in one of the country's terrible moments.
• It coddled Americans' need for reassurance on the core values of their beleaguered society.
• Like a thirties movie, it allowed the poor a vicarious association with the rich.
• It fed Americans' fascination with convenience and home appliances.
• Even though it was a luxury palace, Fallingwater was closely linked to the national aspiration for inexpensive housing.
• Fallingwater corresponded to Americans' disenchantment with the cities and their growing appreciation of nature.
• Fallingwater nicely balanced Americans' fascination with modernism and their fears of it. Specifically, it helped change their view of modernism in architecture from something foreign and suspect to something homegrown and patriotic.

We cannot state in five words or less what Fallingwater meant to Americans at the most wretched moment of the Depression, because its meanings were undoubtedly multiple and possibly contradictory. Like any group facing a crisis, the United States reacted to the Depression with a mixture of denial and realism, frivolity and seriousness. The denial emerged in a decade-long flirtation with escapism. The Okies migrating by the thousands to California were literally escaping their grinding poverty, and Edward VIII abdicating the cares of his crown made a literal escape, too. How many Americans wished they could leave their troubles behind, as Dorothy did in *The Wizard of Oz*? But thirties escapism was, naturally, far more often figurative than literal. Heroes served their purpose, as always: the Dionne quintuplets, Amelia Earhart as Lindbergh *redux*, Jesse Owens at the Berlin Olympics, even the racehorses Man o' War and Seabiscuit. Celluloid heroes suited the national mood best of all, most memorably in the Frank Capra classics *Mr. Deeds Goes to Town* and *Mr. Smith Goes to Washington* (Capra's *It's a Wonderful Life* was postwar). The most influential cultural institution of the thirties, Hollywood, was escapist to the core. Hitler, Mussolini, and Hirohito might have strutted through the thirties, but the dictator of the decade was Mickey Mouse. Walt Disney's first full-length cartoon film, *Snow White and the Seven Dwarfs*, came out in 1938, the same week Fallingwater was featured in *Time*. Another escapist Hollywood genre was the science fiction/horror film, represented in the thirties by *King Kong, Dracula*, and *Frankenstein*. A third was the moralizing crime-and-punishment film: *Scarface* and *The Public Enemy*. A fourth was the musical: *42nd Street, Top Hat, Gold Diggers of 1933*. Other escapist genres of the decade were the Westerns and the comedies of Charlie Chaplin and the Marx Brothers.

The typical 1930s movie setting was exotic, its stars wealthy and beautiful. This golden era culminated with *The Wizard of Oz, Gone With the Wind* (the book in 1936, the film three years later), and James Hilton's *Lost Horizon*. All three films appeared within a year or two of Fallingwater.

Escapism was not limited to books and movie screens: in the hard times of the Depression there was a constant public fascination with the wealthy and whatever was elegant, stylish, and modern. Henry Luce responded to this fascination by putting "*Life* Goes to a Party" in every issue of *Life*, right through the Depression and World War II. Thirties films were famous for their presentation of rich peoples' houses, and Fallingwater emerged as a rich peoples' house par excellence.

The fact that Bear Run was an unknown location added to its escapist allure. It was the Shangri-La that could have been in anyone's backyard. The unending passage of water below it added a soporific, even a hallucinogen, to the vision. It was Fallingwater, not one of the utopian escapes so carefully planned by Mies and Le Corbusier, that was a building without a care in the world.

Strangely, Fallingwater appealed both to the escapist and the realist aspirations of American society. The luxury house functioned as a prototype for the low-cost mass-produced housing that progressives were everywhere clamoring for. No one could look at Fallingwater even in a photograph and fail to see that it was an expensive house. It cost $166,000 (with the guesthouse) in an era in which some of its laborers were paid 25 cents an hour. (The cost of the house translates into about $4 million today, but it would cost far more to replicate it.)

The *Architectural Forum* issue that set Fallingwater before the public also included Wright's modest Willey house in Minneapolis, whose $10,000 cost was given in bold type, and the Usonian-style Jacobs house in Madison, whose $5,500 cost was likewise emblazoned on the page. Readers could figure out that Fallingwater—also a home for a family of three—cost some thirty times as much as the Jacobs house. There was nonetheless a formal kinship among the three houses that linked them beyond their shared appearance in the pages of *Forum*.

This perception was far from misplaced. Fallingwater was a luxury house brimming with futuristic appliances, but its overall effect was modest. It had to be: with Father Coughlin attacking rich Jews on the radio every week, and the German-American Bund fomenting boycotts of Jewish stores, Kaufmann dared not acquiesce to the rich appointments of Herbert Johnson's mansion outside Racine. Fallingwater appeared before the public basic and simple, a house that was rich but did not play rich. Hearst's castle at San Simeon was trademarked as Hearst's alone, but the untreated stone walls at Fallingwater matched the lodges then going up all over the country at the hands of the CCC boys. We could see Fallingwater as a kind of architectural FDR: a patrician dwelling that passed for the abode of one of the people.

No wonder Fallingwater ended up as the mythic ideal of American houses. We can judge that from Robert Day's cartoon in the May 3, 1952, *New Yorker,* which shows a whole suburb of Fallingwaters, each with its identical waterfall. We laugh because the Kaufmann house is the least banal dwelling imaginable, one that mocks the whole commodified and mass-produced basis of American life. Day's cartoon equally demonstrates that in just fourteen years—six of them in wartime—Fallingwater had become famous enough to be instantly recognizable to the nation's reading class.

Despite its glitz, Fallingwater appealed to the serious side of a country slogging through the Depression, because it addressed itself to America's need for reassurance of its core values. Just as Frank Lloyd Wright gained strength from the various fallows in his career, so the United States gained strength from the Depression, one of the great fallows in its history. While searing, the two fallows of the 1930s that concern us here—Frank Lloyd Wright's personal crisis and the national economic crisis—ultimately left both the man and the country better off.

We could see the brawling 1770s, the bloody 1860s, and the agonizing 1930s as the three decades that fundamentally altered the character of the American people. The terrible poverty of the 1930s goaded Americans toward a more serious and equitable society. Robert McElvaine notes in *The Great Depression:* "The Depression era may well be . . . the only time in the twentieth century during which there was a major break in the modern trends towards social disintegration and egoism." Social Security, the expanded national parks, the TVA, "God Bless America," Marion Anderson's voice lilting over the Lincoln Memorial, and Thornton Wilder's *Our Town* expressed the social cohesion of a generation that had been chastened by adversity, and emerged the stronger for it.

A number of excesses of the freewheeling 1920s were reversed by the Depression. The divorce rate went down, and Americans spent more time with their families. While the twenties ridiculed rural and small-town life, the thirties showed "a reverence for this way of life and the values it supported." Compare Sinclair Lewis's mocking *Main Street* (1920) and *Babbitt* (1922) with Wilder's loving commemoration of small-town America in *Our Town* (1938). There was new respect for working-class culture in general. Richard Llewellyn's 1940 novel *How Green Was My Valley* was set in Wales, but it was the American director John Ford who made it into the highly successful 1941 movie.

The return to domestic and folksy values seems also to have inflated the cult of Fallingwater. The house distanced itself from the snobby historicism of the eastern mansions of the 1920s, like La Tourelle, and also from the sybaritic glitz of the West Coast party houses of people like the Lovells. To people who did not know E. J. and Liliane personally, Fallingwater must have emanated sobriety and decency. It is a stretch to think that a house created by the libidinous Wright for the libidinous Kaufmanns could reflect the strengthened American family of the 1930s, but icons need not be true: they have only to *look* true.

The thirties' rejection of—or its inability to keep up with—the high-living twenties included a significant repudiation of the twenties' embrace of technology. The Depression seems to have made Americans skeptical of the promise of the machine. Charlie Chaplin enmeshed in the gears of an infernal contraption in *Modern Times* (1936) and the self-destruction of the *Hindenburg* in 1937 were in different ways emblematic of a generation that came to mistrust industry and technology. Robert McElvaine points out: "The twenties' embrace of things 'new' and its modern cutting off from the past was replaced in the Depression decade by a renewed affection for traditional ways. . . . The attraction of the land and the values of the small town and traditional communities for people in the Depression era are evident." These important shifts in social attitudes affected the way Americans saw modern architecture, too. The twenties modern of Neutra's Lovell house mirrored a carefree, dislocated, egoistic decade, standing free from the land and nature. The modernism of the thirties was equated instead with technology for social betterment.

The new attitude to technology would have affected how a Depression audience regarded Fallingwater's use of concrete. Wright had specific formal and structural reasons for making his balconies of concrete, but in the wider sphere concrete was the miracle substance of the 1930s (for the '40s it was nylon; for the '50s, plastic). Concrete was literally and figuratively shoring up New Deal America, from its new highways to its Hoover and TVA dams. Though the conservative architects of Pittsburgh drew a negative association between Fallingwater and the TVA dams, mainstream America would have made the same association—at least subliminally—in a positive way. The 1930s saw concrete as heroic both in formal and in social terms, as exemplified by Margaret Bourke-White's view of Montana's Fort Peck Dam on the cover of the very first *Life*, in 1936. Like the dam, Fallingwater married the formal beauty of concrete with its power for social betterment through public works.

Fallingwater's modernism mirrored the Depression's new purposefulness, social rootedness, and closeness to nature. With its historical quotations and old-fashioned stonework, it appealed to the public not as some avant-garde abstraction but as a kind of realism, akin to John Steinbeck's *Of Mice and Men* or the realist, folklore-based music of Aaron Copland. Fallingwater's glass, steel, and concrete were always acknowledged, but the house seems to have been perceived overall as rural, collective, historicist, and even (thanks to its hand-hewn stonework, again) antimachine.

The cultural shift from the twenties to the thirties was so marked that Fallingwater would probably have flopped had it appeared on the scene ten years earlier; it was too earthbound for the twenties. Perhaps this explains why Wright himself experienced such a decline in popularity during the hedonistic, machine-based 1920s, but rose in popularity and inner strength in the collectivist and machine-skeptical 1930s.

It is possible that Fallingwater was the swing building in the acceptance of modern architecture in the United States, but we lack the data to support such a claim. What we can say is that a sea change in Americans' attitude to modern architecture came just when Fallingwater was built, in the half-decade from 1932 to 1937. Only the foolhardy would try to assess whether that shift in taste popularized the house or whether the house popularized the shift in public taste. We will take refuge in saying that A affected B about as much as B affected A.

This much we can say with certainty: modern architecture as presented at MoMA in 1932 was something mannered and outlandish, the product of eccentric foreigners with four- and five-part names like Ludwig Mies van der Rohe and Charles-Édouard Jeanneret Le Corbusier. But what was eccentric and foreign in 1932 was perceived as nativist and homegrown just five years later. Modernism assumed an American face in the "streamline modern" of toasters and such practical-modern structures as the Chrysler and Empire State buildings, Rockefeller Center, the Philadelphia Savings Fund Society building, and Fallingwater. Rockefeller Center, with not one foreigner among its half-dozen main designers, was so much admired by the time it was finished in 1938 that the man in the street could think that Americans had invented modern architecture all by themselves. This attitude got reinforced in 1939 when the new MoMA was unveiled two blocks away, also designed by mainstream Americans. These buildings countered Americans' earlier antimodern prejudices and reformulated modernism as a native product.

As a social phenomenon, the triumph of modern architecture was nearly complete by 1938. Up to 1930, only Jews, Californians, and other marginal groups would associate with the style, but by 1936 bluebloods like the Vanderbilts, Fields, Browns, Goodyears, Rockefellers, and Luces were all happily living with it. Fallingwater contributed to this change in public taste because it Americanized modernism more than any other work. It helped that mainstream channels like *Reader's Digest* had already packaged Wright as a familiar, avuncular figure, but even without that PR boost, Fallingwater was perceived from the first as native and centrist. Staunch traditionalists like Talbot Hamlin rushed to praise its integration with the site, its functionalism, and its structural daring. Fallingwater's use of glass, concrete, and steel made it progressive, hence unlike the un-American excesses of San Simeon, but the house stopped short of being overly progressive. When it exploited the walls of glass, the cantilevers, and the corner windows that Americans typically reviled in modern work, these features came in not for criticism but for praise.

The key was the way Wright presented European themes in a muscular, down-to-earth, American manner. The International Style showcased industrial materials, but Fallingwater accentuated its natural components. The International Style shrouded itself in the bland anonymity of smooth transparent surfaces; Fallingwater presented itself instead with robust walls that were strongly colored and textured. In *The New Yorker*, Lewis Mumford said that Fallingwater "created a dynamic multidimensional composition that made Le Corbusier's buildings seem flat card-board compositions."

Then there was the question of nature. We saw earlier that Fallingwater showed up just when Americans were changing their attitudes to city and country. Robert McElvaine points out that four of the five most popular American books of the thirties dealt with a society trying to find its place in history or on the land: *The Good Earth* (1931), *God's Little Acre* (1933), *Gone With the Wind* (1936), and *The Grapes of Wrath* (1939). (The fifth book was Dale Carnegie's 1937 *How to Win Friends and Influence People*.) It was the cities, with their commerce and industry, that had failed the common people: Americans turned to nature as a force that could be counted on to sustain them. This became literally true under the Civilian Conservation Corps. Hardly a working-class family was to be found that did not have a husband, son, or brother in one of the CCC camps. The CCC was a tremendous impetus in the revived popularity and use of the state and national parks. Conservation sentiment blossomed as never before, both in government and through private initiative. The wide-spread flooding in the South and the disaster of the Dust Bowl were attributed less to the capriciousness of nature and more to its rapacious mistreatment by humankind. Industrial Pittsburgh was one of the cities that took the lead in protecting nature, with the founding in 1932 of the Western Pennsylvania Conservancy as the second nature conservancy in the country.

The Depression forced Americans to confront nature in intellectual terms as well. Certainly this was true of the photographers attached to the Historical Section of the Farm Security Administration or the WPA Federal Writers' Project. Walker Evans's bleak photographs of the depressed mill towns of Easton and Bethlehem, Pennsylvania, gave voice to many Americans' disenchantment with industry and the city, while Ansel Adams's intoxicating views of Yosemite and other natural sites typified their new respect for nature. Nature photography in the West grabbed most of the attention, but the East also discerned a new attractiveness to the land through the photographer's lens. Among the top-ranked nature photographers in the East was someone we have met before: E. J. Kaufmann's protégé Luke Swank.

Although we can never know exactly what the public saw in Falling-water in 1938, we can tell from its frequency of reproduction that Bill Hedrich's photograph defined the house best, the way a few years later the public embraced Joe Rosenthal's photo of the flag-raising on Iwo Jima as the definitive image of World War II. Hedrich's photograph conveyed the unmistakable message of man living in harmony with nature—just what the CCC was preaching. At a micro level, one of the most obvious associations of Hedrich's photograph was the almost palpable rush of pure Pennsylvania water. Healing the damage from America's profligacy with water was a central theme of the Roosevelt years. The ecological disasters of the 1930s woke America up to the need for wise water management; flood control, irrigation canals, and the TVA were Rooseveltian lessons in how to do it. Water, concrete, and conservation were all part of the image conveyed by Fallingwater. The house seemed to pick up Jefferson's credo of more than a century earlier: treat nature wisely and she will feed you, educate you, and lift you to a higher state of morality. Perhaps E. J. and Liliane sunbathing naked at "Bare Run" were not being so much racy as Jeffersonian.

One facet of Fallingwater that had a particular appeal in the 1930s was its Americanism. Psychologists and counselors advise clients who are in crisis to reexamine their roots. That is just what the Depression-buffeted United States did, resulting in the thirties being a prodigiously rich time for the exploration of early American folklore, folk song (as in the tenacious song-gathering of John and Alan Lomax), and folk art. This was no less true of architecture. In the 1930s architects and scholars delved into the roots of American architecture as they did in no decade before or after. A preponderant number of sourcebooks on American architecture date from the 1930s—those big, indispensable folios on southern antebellum mansions, New England timber-frame houses, Dutch Colonial farmhouses, Spanish Colonial missions, and pueblos. This impulse to rediscover America's architectural roots is the likely explanation (along with internal museum politics) for Henry-Russell Hitchcock's incongruous MoMA show and book on the architecture of H. H. Richardson in 1936. Hitchcock did not fall into the trap of distorting Richardson into a protomodernist, but he did define him as one of the earliest and best molders of forms to house specifically American rituals, whether in public libraries or commuter railroad stations.

On another level, we can see Fallingwater and the other artistic masterpieces of the 1930s as offering America relief from the stifling conventionality of the building world in the twenties. The twenties may have roared in social mores, but they were pretty banal in cultural terms. The United States passed up exhibiting at the 1925 Art Deco fair in Paris because the federal government could think of nothing in the country that Europeans would find of interest. The Depression chased away the frivolity of the twenties and the "business as usual" mantra of Mellon,

Harding, Coolidge, and Hoover. A broad spectrum of Americans, not just readers of *The New Masses,* was fed up with America's unrepresentative and unresponsive culture, which they saw as a reflection of a bloated and backward managerial class. Edmund Wilson observed: "To the writers and artists of my generation . . . these years [after the Crash] were not depressing but stimulating. One couldn't help being exhilarated at the sudden, unexpected collapse of that stupid gigantic fraud. It gave us a new sense of power to find ourselves still carrying on, while the bankers, for a change, were taking a beating."

Frank Capra's *Mr. Smith Goes to Washington,* which came out the year after Fallingwater, well articulated the political backlash to Hooverism, while Fallingwater's popularity articulated a parallel backlash in architecture. Symbolic of the bankruptcy of the old architectural order was the new Supreme Court building, whose icy classicism gave no hint of what America was actually like in the thirties. In reaction, architects began to employ early American buildings as quotes that they could incorporate into their academic designs. Such a process went back to the 1876 Centennial Exposition in Philadelphia, but it climaxed with Colonial Williamsburg, paid for by the Rockefellers and opened by President Roosevelt in 1934.

Wright saw the bewigged-Negro travesty of Williamsburg as a simplistic way of getting back to American roots, but he had no quarrel with the search for roots itself. That search was now more vital than ever: the abstract and context-free progressive architecture of the 1930s presented America with a future but no past, while traditionalist buildings gave the country a past but no future. Fallingwater by contrast tried to give Americans a future *and* a past. The future was conveyed by its materials and technology; the past was introduced through its vernacular building traditions and the imitation of nature, which is the most remote past of all.

Incorporating history gave Fallingwater one of its chief appeals, but it distanced the house from modernism on both sides of the Atlantic. The buildings of the modernist French and Germans were nonhistorical, even antihistorical in character: buildings like the Villa Savoye were made to look like nothing that had ever stood on earth before. Not so Fallingwater, which as we have seen is packed with historical precedents. These historical references give the house a humanity that keeps it from being merely modern. One could argue that the house Richard Neutra later built for the Kaufmanns in Palm Springs was superior to Fallingwater in formal, intellectual, and even functional terms. But as a human dwelling it is much the poorer, because it lacks the additional historical layering we decipher at Fallingwater.

The way Wright "Americanized" Fallingwater is one of the best things about the house. For about twenty years he had been putting awkward allusions to early American architecture in his buildings, as in his 1920s neo-tepee and neo-Mayan designs. Luckily, Fallingwater started life as an International Style abstraction, not some tepee or temple. That means that it was born without a specific meaning. To this core abstraction, however, Wright gave an unmistakably American overlay derived—it appears— from the Mesa Verde or other Anasazi ruins, the tapestried stone walls of Chaco Canyon, and the adobe steps from the kiva at San Ildefonso. The mill-like aspect of Fallingwater, with water rushing out from underneath, alludes to either European work or the immense nineteenth-century water-powered textile mills Wright knew from his years in New England. And the living room, as we have seen, is bristling with historical allusions, from colonial New England back to Bronze Age Greece.

What distinguishes Wright's living room from Colonial Revival interiors is the crucial difference between allusion and quotation. Wright abstracted from folk architecture the way Aaron Copland found inspiration in the common rhythms of American folk song, as in his 1930s compositions *Billy the Kid* and *Rodeo*. A few years later Copland hauntingly wove the Shaker melody "'Tis the Gift to Be Simple" into *Appalachian Spring,* to accompany the new ballet by Martha Graham. *Appalachian Spring* continues to be among America's most popular musical compositions today, but a Depression audience would have found added significance in the American allusions in Copland's work. Americanism in architecture, like Americanism in music, is a dead issue today, but we can still appreciate why it was important to Wright, and how superior his approach was to the commercial Colonialism of Williamsburg or the fake-Colonial A & P's that swept the country in the 1920s and 1930s. At the same time, Fallingwater appeals to us more than do the cool abstractions of the 1930s, such as the slick architecture of the Chicago and New York fairs, because those other buildings seemed not to recognize the trauma of the Depression at all.

The other factor that made Fallingwater stand out in sharp relief in 1938 was the shadow of Hitler. The house had neither a political use nor a political message, but nothing that made its debut in 1938 could be free of a political context, and Americans increasingly viewed their architecture in political terms. As we saw, *Architectural Forum's* editor Howard Myers intended from the first to emphasize Wright's work as an American style. That same appeal was echoed in the ad on the inside cover of *Life* for January 17, 1938, which reproduced Hedrich's photo of Fallingwater and ballyhooed the new *Forum* issue as displaying "architecture as thoroughly indigenous to America as the earth and rocks from which it springs." The next year, *Life* wrapped its praise for the Johnson's Wax Building in the Stars and Stripes even more blatantly when it assured its readers on May 8, 1939, that Johnson's Wax was "genuine American architecture, owing nothing to foreign inspiration, different from anything ever built in the world before." Such a jingoistic claim made sense only in nakedly political terms: formally speaking, it was baloney.

The same *Architectural Forum* issue that launched Fallingwater carried a photograph and a long caption mocking Nazi architecture. Three months earlier, the October 1937 issue of *Forum* reported that the last of the Bauhaus faculty had fled Germany, and that a new Bauhaus was about to open in Chicago. Born just when modern architecture was dying in Germany, Fallingwater *had* to be seen as a standard-bearer both for Americanism and modernism.

Fallingwater gave the country an appreciation of what it meant to be American in two ways. First, through the soul-searching occasioned by a collapse of the old status quo in the Depression, and second, through the rising German threat against all humanistic values, which now included modernism. The invasion of New York by European architects had been figurative in 1932, during MoMA's International Style exhibit, but a year later scores of modernists had become refugees from Nazism: Kandinsky and Klee fled Germany within months of Hitler's takeover. When Germany slandered all modern art as degenerate in 1936, the movement as a whole became a refugee. Americans traditionally mistrust foreigners but welcome refugees, which is what now happened to the Bauhaus. A movement that the country saw as eccentric, foreign, and stuck-up in 1932 had by 1938 turned into an occasionally funny but likable thing, like the funny but likable Professor Einstein.

Fallingwater's birth year—1938—was almost as tumultuous as the war years that followed. The year that began with Wright on the cover of *Time* ended with Hitler on the cover as *Time*'s Man of the Year. Guernica and Nanking had already become headline names in 1937 (the Buchenwald concentration camp started operations that same year, but Americans would learn about it only later). Now, in 1938, Germany and its allies took control of Ethiopia, Spain, Austria, Czechoslovakia, and much of China. January and February of 1938 were particularly hysterical. Those were the months Britain issued gas masks to its citizens, and Hitler picked January 10 for the Reichstag speech in which he swore to avenge the 10 million Germans living outside their homeland. Henry Luce picked the same day for *Life, Time,* and *Architectural Forum* to tell the world about Fallingwater.

While we know that modernism was a political topic in 1938, it is less clear what—if any—political reading Americans gave Fallingwater. Certainly the Kaufmanns took Hitler with dead seriousness right from 1933. Sometime later Liliane spirited one of her uncles out of Nazi Germany, and both she and E. J. were recognized on two continents as outstanding lifelines for refugee artists. Scores of German and Austrian designers and architects, Jews or not, owed their fortunes and possibly their lives to them. When Albert Einstein and other luminaries came to Fallingwater for a 1939 conference on how to save the Jews of Germany (details in the following chapter), the choice of site was symbolic, since modernism itself had suffered from Nazi brutality.

Wright, on the other hand, was a top-cadre isolationist. Jack Howe and several Wright apprentices went to jail rather than register for the draft, even after Pearl Harbor. Nor was Wright a silent pacifist: he supported America First and, as we saw earlier, kept open a pipeline to American fascists. Wright heaped praise on Charles Lindbergh even after he came home with an Iron Cross from Hitler. "We all knew you could fly straight," Wright cabled Lindbergh (with copy to Franklin Roosevelt) after he had delivered one of his fascist slanders in May 1940. "Now we know you can think straight and when talk is quite generally cheap and unreliable—you are brave enough to talk straight. I respect your integrity." Lindbergh's attack on Jews in July of 1941 left his standing with Wright untouched: he got fulsome praise in Wright's revised *Autobiography* two years later, and a warm welcome at Taliesin West after that. Kaufmann drastically reduced his contact with Wright in the early 1940s and left unanswered Wright's few letters during the last three years of the war. When the two at last got in touch, Wright was still the unrepentent isolationist. On July 16, 1946, he badgered E. J.: "I begged you during the imminence of the late war to be one Jew, at all costs, who stood out above and against the Jewish clamor for war."

Halfway through the war, Fallingwater was embraced by a third ideology, objectivism. The house caught the eye of the Russian immigrant Alyssa Rosenbaum, who had rebaptized herself in the name of her typewriter and emerged as the fanatical anti-Communist Ayn Rand. In 1934, Rand began research on a saga about the triumph and tragedy of a modern architect. The next year she moved from California to New York, and for three more years she read voraciously on modern architecture. In March 1936, Rand even began an apprenticeship with the designer Ely Jacques Kahn (Guy Francon in the eventual book) to observe firsthand how architects worked.

Then, nothing. After four years of work, Rand had amassed a research journal bulging with quotes and data, but she had not produced even page one of a book that had stalled in a near-terminal case of writer's block. But how could it have been otherwise? It was hard to describe the triumph of modern architecture in the United States when, up to 1938, no such triumph had taken place.

All that changed (if my hypothesis is correct) when Rand visited the 1938 Fallingwater exhibit at the Museum of Modern Art. Without having her ticket stub to hand (MoMA's early shows were free, actually), nor her appointments calendar for the 1930s, we cannot state as fact that she was among the thousands who studied Fallingwater in the concourse of Rockefeller Center between January 25 and March 6, 1938. But it beggars the imagination to think that an author who was writing on modern architecture in an apartment that stood just five minutes from MoMA by taxi, could have stayed away from the show. Besides, one document makes certain that Rand had scrutinized Fallingwater from the start: all her life she kept the January 17, 1938, issue of *Time* with Wright and Fallingwater on the cover. Here at last was a triumph of modern architecture she could write about.

Rand's liberation from writer's block corresponds in lockstep chronology with the Fallingwater show at MoMA. The month the show closed, March 1938, was the exact moment her creative energy recharged enough for her to sketch out the novel's plot. She began writing the text in June 1938, finished it in 1942, and had *The Fountainhead* published in 1943.

Everyone knows that Rand's architect-hero Howard Roark is a stand-in for Frank Lloyd Wright (she would end her letters to Wright with the tag line "Gratefully and reverently yours"), but unsuspected has been the way *The Fountainhead* specifically commemorates Fallingwater and the Kaufmanns. The several points of contact begin with Rand's title. She started the book as *Second-Hand Lives,* a phrase that remains embedded at several spots in the published text. It was after the MoMA exhibition that she changed the title to *Fountainhead,* which echoes *Fallingwater* in the identical twelve-letter length, the initial F, and a parallel aqueous image.

The Fountainhead particularly depends on Fallingwater in the passages describing the country houses that Howard Roark designed for Austin Heller, Whitford Sanborn, and Gail Wynand. The houses were supposedly all different, yet Rand based each on Fallingwater. The similarity of the three homes begins with their sites: each was a hillside or clifftop house cantilevered over water. Austin Heller built on a cliff above Long Island Sound in Connecticut, not on a woodland stream in Pennsylvania. Nevertheless, the subliminal connection with Bear Run is hard

Gary Cooper as the radical Wright-like architect Howard Roark in the 1949 movie version of Ayn Rand's 1943 novel *The Fountainhead*

to miss. E. J. Kaufmann (supposedly) wanted his house to view his favorite rock, contrary to the wishes of his architect, Wright, who wanted to build directly on the rock. Heller wanted just the opposite: a house that would sit over his favorite rock, while his academicist architect John Erik Snyte wanted the building to view the rock instead. Howard Roark, working for Snyte, designed a house whose rock ledges mimicked the rock ledges of the cliff. Rand underlines the fact that Roark proposed to build his house out of the same stone as the cliff itself.

It is hard, if not impossible, to imagine a house anywhere in the world closer to the Heller design than Fallingwater. The resemblance is made still tighter by Rand's giving her readers the story of Wright's lightning-fast conception of Fallingwater. In creating the Heller house design, Roark redrew its plan in a furious burst of creativity, incising lines on paper as though slashing a knife through canvas, in a dramatic performance that took just minutes.

The 1949 movie version of *The Fountainhead* backed this up. Warner Brothers' art director Edward Carrere rendered all but one of Roark's designs in the film as fake-Miesian rather than Wrightian (was this to punish Wright, who demanded an exorbitant $250,000 to design the sets?). Carrere's one exception was the Heller house, whose drawing bore a distinct resemblance to Fallingwater.

Whitford Sanborn discussed the project for his Hudson River weekend home with Roark in his Victorian living room, just as Wright talked at length with Kaufmann in his fake-Norman home outside Pittsburgh. The distinguishing characteristics that Rand gave the Sanborn home were just like the attributes she gave Heller's house: walls of common fieldstone, an abundance of glass, and prominent terraces. Again Rand's prose adequately if clumsily captured the synergy between the house and its site. The visual makeup of the second house, like the first, could only have been based on Fallingwater.

But the Sanborn–Fallingwater connections go beyond the visual. Like the real Fallingwater, the fictive Heller and Sanborn houses are presented in *The Fountainhead* as enormously difficult structural problems. "No reputable contractor would undertake the erection of the house," writes Rand of the Sanborn house. Contractors refused to bid, one saying of the Sanborn house: "It won't stand." The builder of the Heller house almost wrecked it, as did Walter Hall at Fallingwater.

The last of the three Fallingwater-clone homes in *The Fountainhead* was the Wynand house, which was also cantilevered out over water—this time a lake. Again Rand characterizes the home as organic, married to its hill. She also attributed to it Fallingwater's pueblo-like syncopation between floor and floor.

Rand additionally provided secure chronological links between the fictive Wynand house and the Fallingwater timeline, making the dates of the first correspond exactly with those of the second. In Rand's earliest plot sketch (partly altered in the final book), the Wynand house began in 1934, which was the year Wright embarked on the Kaufmann house. In the novel as published, Roark completed the Wynand house in 1937, the year Wright finished Fallingwater.

Not only their homes but the clients in *The Fountainhead* carried a marked resemblance to the Kaufmanns. Rand based numerous *Fountainhead* characters on real people, sometimes with concealed names, to titillate readers on the inside track. So, for example, Roark's ferocious antagonist at the fictive Stanton Institute of Technology bore the name of the New York traditionalist architect John B. Peterkin. Though the toponym "Pittsburgh" appears nowhere in the novel, Rand evidently wanted her readers to be subliminally aware of the Kaufmanns' city. She named New York's two most palatial bank buildings the "Frink" and the "Melton" in obvious allusion to the Frick and Mellon headquarters next to Kaufmann's Department Store.

To the best of my surmise, Rand inserted three or four hints about the Kaufmanns in *The Fountainhead,* but not in the obvious manner of calling them the Hoffmanns or Kaupmanns. Instead, she gave the name Austin or Austen Heller (the poorly edited novel carries both spellings) to Roark's first important client. "Austin Heller" conflated the name of Mr. Austin, an early benefactor in Wright's *Autobiography,* with that of Isodore Heller, his first Jewish client.

The Fountainhead also immortalized Edgar Kaufmann, Jr., in the role of Richard Sanborn, the son of Roark's highly quarrelsome client. Rand specifies that Richard Sanborn was twenty-four when Roark began his father's house: that was Junior's age when E. J. commissioned Wright to build on Bear Run. She furthermore characterized Richard as brilliant but lethargic, just like the brilliant but notably undirected Kaufmann Jr. The house being created for his father startled young Sanborn out of his lethargy, just as it catapulted Junior into a career in aesthetics. Rand even more presciently captured Junior's feeling that he was Fallingwater's true instigator. In *The Fountainhead,* the Sanborn parents prove too witless to appreciate their treasure: they abandon the house for something fake-Spanish, and the son takes over the house for himself.

Rand's inside-track knowledge about Fallingwater and the dynamics of its creation was so accurate that she must have relied on an inside source. Aline Saarinen or John McAndrew could have provided these details, but had Rand picked her gossip from Junior himself? We will see that Junior escorted the press around the 1938 MoMA show, and he made particular complaint about the women writers whose questions he had endured. Was Rand one of his questioners?

A truly indefatigable voyeur, Rand made another allusion to the Kaufmanns in her screenplay for the 1949 *Fountainhead* movie, in which Gary Cooper played Roark. She again showed herself well informed on the Kaufmanns, particularly E. J.'s decision in 1948 to deny Wright the chance to design a home for Pittsburgh's Civic Light Opera. She concocted a special scene for the film that has no counterpart in the novel. In this scene, Roark/Wright meets rejection as the architect for the "Civic Opera Company of New York," a name prominently revealed on the door as Roark limps out of the president's office. This was clearly a stand-in for the Civic Light Opera Company of Pittsburgh, of which the president at the time was E. J. Kaufmann.

The Fountainhead also seems to mirror the personal relationship between Kaufmann and Wright. Considering that her contact with Wright before publication of *The Fountainhead* was limited to a single handshake at a banquet, Rand was uncannily well informed about his friendship with Kaufmann. The mawkish passages in which Gail Wynand (a synthesis of Hearst and Kaufmann) declares how much he loves his architect are virtual repeats of Wright's expressions of tenderness for Kaufmann.

To make her story more dramatic, Rand raised the pitch of the relationship between the architect and his client to a near-homoerotic bonding. She situated a number of these exchanges on Wynand's yacht, which was both a clever and credible device. Kaufmann owned no yacht, but William Randolph Hearst did, and we know for a fact that he loved to take his favorite architect, Joseph Urban, out on it. *The Fountainhead* carries numerous passages on the same theme:

- *Roark:* "Gail . . . I'd give my life to save you." [In real life, Wright wrote Kaufmann: "I would deny you nothing I had to give, short of suicide."]
- Wynand and Roark, without another soul on board, sailed together on Wynand's yacht from December 1937 through April 1938 [these include the months of Fallingwater's show at MoMA, and in real life the beginning of Rand's progress on her novel]. "Nothing would enable [Wynand] to abandon this man. He, Gail Wynand, was the helpless one in this moment."
- *Wynand:* "Howard, this is what I wanted, to have you here with me."
- "Within a week, Heller knew that [in his architect Roark] he had found the best friend he would ever have."
- "Have you heard that Roark and Wynand are the best of friends?"
- "Howard . . . this preposterous business of Mr. Gail Wynand. You and he as inseparable friends upsets every rational concept I've ever held."
- *Wynand to his wife:* "Being with Howard [Roark] is like being alone with myself, only more at peace. . . . Dominique, I believe you're jealous. It's wonderful, I'm more grateful to him than ever—if it could make you jealous of me."

Rand obviously enjoyed peppering these various clues through her text, but the importance of her appropriation of Fallingwater for *The Fountainhead* is that she popularized not only fictive modern architecture but the real thing as well—and no building reaped more benefit from the novel than Fallingwater itself. No matter that these specific allusions to the Kaufmanns and Fallingwater have gone undetected; any reader of reasonable cultural background knew that Roark was Wright, and by subliminal association the Heller/Sanborn/Wynand cliffside house had to be Fallingwater. That makes *The Fountainhead* an important publication on Fallingwater: it was the most detailed textual exploration the building had received to that point.

The Fountainhead rendered a no less important service to architectural history by providing an understanding of Fallingwater as a human drama—something all the other accounts of its birth had missed. Years ahead of any scholarly publication, *The Fountainhead* established how crucial it was to understand Wright's personality as the basis for his architectural practice. Only *The Fountainhead* put sufficient weight on the drama of Wright's bouncing back from the humiliations of the 1920s and early 1930s (as noted before, the Time-Life publications kept silent on this important point). Only *The Fountainhead* records the constant fighting and making up between Wright and Kaufmann, the speed at which the house was designed, how much the house excited Junior, the construction difficulties, and the manipulated publicity that made Fallingwater famous. None of these important issues got any airing in the pages of *Forum*, but they did in *The Fountainhead*.

Rand was also insightful in discerning so early that Roark/Wright's most dangerous enemies stood not to his right but to his left. Rand's novel treated Wright's conservative adversaries fairly lightly, as he himself did. She was far tougher on the modernists who saw themselves as more radical than Roark/Wright, singling out the German modernists, whose formulaic and machine-based International Style (Rand specified its German origins) Roark mocked—as did Wright—for "putting up four walls and a flat top over them." She understood that even after Fallingwater a small circle of critics would always see Wright not as too modern but—compared to Mies and Le Corbusier—not modern enough.

Rand did Fallingwater a great service in forcing her vast audience to look carefully at the building, but she did it a disservice, too. Her self-identification with Roark and her facility with purple prose put too much stress on the romantic mythology of Fallingwater—a mythology that is still alive today. She thought it was romantic to have Roark/Wright draw up the whole design from scratch in a few minutes, whereas a duller but more balanced explanation would have done justice to Wright's design philosophy. She also understood before anyone else outside the profession how publicity could make or break an architect. Her pen was never sharper than in its characterization of the publicity battle between the architectural critic Ellsworth Toohey (a composite of the critics Lewis Mumford and Royal Cortissoz and the intellectual Harold Laski, perhaps) and the media baron Gail Wynand, who equivocated between modern and academic. In *The Fountainhead*, Roark's house for Austin Heller differed from Wright's house for E. J. Kaufmann in one telling respect: the critics neither reviewed nor published the Heller house, which made it useless in advancing Roark's career. A few years later, Roark found an uncertain champion in the publisher Wynand, who says: " 'I'll give him the fame he deserves. Public opinion? Public opinion is what I make it. . . . As an architect, he's public property.' . . . [Wynand's] twenty-two newspapers, his magazines, his newsreels were given the order: Defend Roark. Sell Roark to the public." That differed only in degree from what Henry R. Luce evidently told his editors late in 1937: "Puff Wright and the Kaufmann house."

Rand's timing in writing *The Fountainhead* was perfect, because Fallingwater exploded on the scene exactly halfway through her eight years of work on the novel. Had she begun work earlier, around 1930, her tale would have conveyed only Wright's woes in those years. Had she begun writing a bit later, around 1940, the book would have exclusively chronicled Wright's post-Fallingwater triumph. Instead, she observed Wright from just the right angle: half in shadow and half in sunlight. The book and film had tremendous impact in making both Wright and Fallingwater stars of American civilization. Wright even took on at least one aspect of the Howard Roark legend himself: the memoir he wrote about Louis Sullivan, *Genius and the Mobocracy* (1949), seems to be an explicit echo of Rand's *Fountainhead* thesis of the man of genius set against the mob.

The Fountainhead was one of the great popular successes in twentieth-century culture. Its sales of 5 million copies gave a tremendous boost not just to Wright but to all of modern architecture. Rand used Fallingwater as the vehicle for her tale because the public had already shouted its love of the Kaufmann house as something bold, radical, and modern. Publication of *The Fountainhead* led in turn to still more popularity for Fallingwater. Magnified by a movie that reached many times more people than the book, *The Fountainhead* constituted the single most powerful force for the acceptance of modern architecture in this country. If it was not already a leading icon of modernity before *The Fountainhead*, Fallingwater certainly became one after it. America's infatuation with modernism would prove short-lived, but it lasted long enough to make Fallingwater into the most famous private house in the world.

Opposite: E. J. and Liliane Kaufmann at Fallingwater around 1940

TEN

THE KAUFMANNS SHOWCASE FALLINGWATER, AND VICE VERSA

Kit tried to explain that [lavish spending] wasn't really a loss because a guy called Veblen said we make our reputations by how much money we can publicly throw away.

—BUDD SCHULBERG, *What Makes Sammy Run?*

An estate is a little kingdom: nothing could equal the egotism of a landed proprietor on a Sunday afternoon.

—BENJAMIN DISRAELI

E very tour of Fallingwater stops to admire the eighteenth-century *Virgen de Guadalupe* altarpiece at the top of the first flight of stairs. The guide will point out the charm of this bright Mexican folk painting, but he or she fails to add that the Kaufmanns originally treated the Madonna as a piece of merchandise. Photographs of the 1940 "Below the Rio Grande" promotion of old and new Mexican furnishings show the same altarpiece hanging on the wall at Kaufmann's Department Store. Nor was the Virgin the only leftover from that sale that E. J. and Liliane transported to Fallingwater. The same photographs document that Liliane took away the two Mexican milk glass bottles that tourists still glimpse in her bathroom, as well as the Mexican shadow box, Pueblo-ware majolica urn, and painted pumpkin or gourd bowl that today brighten up Fallingwater's guesthouse. And why not? E. J. and Liliane never stopped being merchandisers: it was natural for them to treat their weekend home as a branch of the store. Those half-dozen errant objects, and much else, remind us how much the Kaufmanns treated their week-end home as a showcase.

In making a commercial showcase out of Fallingwater, E. J. and Liliane demonstrated nothing more than simple adherence to the merchant's creed. Leon Harris, who grew up in his family's Dallas store, observed: "If the storekeeper . . . was authoritatively to set the style for what people should wear, the storekeeper's family had to set the style as to how families should live—how they should build, furnish, and decorate their houses, train and costume their servants, and how they should entertain."

Herbert Johnson could estimate how many millions of dollars he had made from his commission to Wright, but the Kaufmanns could make no similar calculation. Fallingwater had positive commercial implications for the store and the clan, but with just one location there was no alchemy by which the store could turn all the goodwill that flowed its way into gold. Not that the Kaufmanns did not try. The November 1944 *Fortune* article was correct in designating Fallingwater as one of E. J. Kaufmann's leading business assets because it ended up being the "model house" that Kaufmann's Department Store had several times tried to get Wright to build in the years 1935 to 1939, either at the store or in the Pittsburgh suburbs. Though they came to nothing, these efforts by the store to market a progressive "model house" are significant indications of the mercantile possibilities it attached to Fallingwater. There was no thought of shuttling potential shoppers to Bear Run, obviously, but Kaufmann's made certain that all of western Pennsylvania knew of the store's connection to the house. Even today you cannot enter the executive suite at the downtown Pittsburgh store without paying homage to Fallingwater through three striking color blowups.

No matter how luxurious Fallingwater may have seemed to a Depression audience, the house was always promoted as something futuristic but attainable, as though E. J. and Liliane were merely getting in advance a prize that the whole country would eventually enjoy. When Diego Rivera called Fallingwater "three hundred years ahead of its time" his timing was badly off. Unlike the never-attainable mansions of the rich, all Americans could expect to live in a labor-saving "home of tomorrow" like Fallingwater fairly soon, and by the 1950s, many did. Today Fallingwater's creature comforts strike us as advanced but practical: the only oddities are the lack of air-conditioning, which the Kaufmanns specifically rejected as unnatural in a forest retreat, and the low-slung toilets, which probably reflect the Kaufmanns' adhesion to the health cults of the 1920s.

For invention or application of the latest gadgetry and decorative touches, Fallingwater was hard to beat. This was especially true in the kitchen, with its St. Charles metal cabinets, a dishwasher (anticipated early but installed later on), a Frigidaire, double sinks, double warming trays, and a Formica-topped table and counters. The Formica underlines how new everything at Fallingwater was. The product was only patented in 1935, but Kaufmann probably learned of it immediately because it was invented locally by two engineers at Westinghouse.

The kitchen may look small to visitors who can only glimpse it from the doorway, but an efficient *small* kitchen was the ideal for housework reformers of the nineteenth century: anything bigger meant either inefficiency or the employment of servants. An American housewife of the 1930s would have been thrilled with such a perfectly equipped work-

Fallingwater's kitchen

Many suppliers exploited their links to Fallingwater. Thrush Heating Systems called the house "the world's most widely publicized residence" when it was only a year or two old.

space. But the stove brings us back to the reality of the 1930s. Provision of electricity was so shaky in rural America in that era that the original kitchen stove had to be a wood-burner. The current AGA stove is also wood-burning and coal-burning, but it is a technological marvel from Sweden, the invention of the Nobel Prize–winning physicist Gustaf Dalén. According to the original sales booklet, still on file in the Fallingwater archives, it guarantees "one cooker capable of every culinary technique . . . that could cook a variety of dishes simultaneously and one that delivered perfect results consistently."

Not a room at Fallingwater was built or furnished without Kaufmann's Department Store being in some way behind it. The glass was rushed in by PPG and the cork flooring and walling by Armstrong—both firms that were headquartered in Pittsburgh. DuPont supplied the paint, Dunlop the foam rubber, Thrush the heating, Hope the window frames, Capehart the record player. The alacrity with which these suppliers sprang to satisfy E. J. Kaufmann's every wish came not merely from their desire to get new business but to furnish what they understood to be a demonstration house of national importance. Any firm that wanted to expand its consumer base would have bent over backward to make sure the Kaufmanns were happy with its contribution to the new house. A dozen suppliers went on to publish Fallingwater-specific advertisements in national magazines. In its promotional brochure of 1939 or 1940 Thrush was already calling Fallingwater "the world's most widely publicized residence."

The Formica, the fluorescent-based indirect lighting, the foam-rubber cushions, and the cork-paneled bathrooms were among the dozen "firsts" claimed for the house. Fallingwater was also meant to have a whole-house sound system for radio and records, and it came close to being one of the rare country houses to have a teletype machine clattering in its living room all day. The most exotic item in the house was Liliane's bidet. Bob Mosher appears never to have seen one—in 1936 how many Americans had?—and referred to it guardedly as "a B-Dey (however it is spelled)."

The construction of Fallingwater was no mere building project for the Kaufmanns: it was the central fact of their lives. Literature presents us with numerous fictional American families whose lives were defined by their homes—*The House of the Seven Gables*, *The Rise of Silas Lapham*, *Gone With the Wind*, even *Mr. Blandings Builds His Dream House*—but not many people in the real world defined their lives through the act of building a house, as E. J. and Liliane did with their homes at Bear Run, Fox Chapel, and Palm Springs. Not just the three Kaufmanns of our story but the entire clan was marked by the building of the house. E. J.'s brother Oliver used his new status to make his own run in Pittsburgh society, and a dozen Kaufmann nephews, nieces, and cousins still remember the construction of Fallingwater as the highpoint of their lives.

We can presume that the main dividend the Kaufmanns sought from Fallingwater was respect. Not that they afterward became fixtures at the Duquesne Club or Rolling Rock: it was too late for that, and both sides knew it. Legend holds that when the Duquesne Club finally asked E. J. to join, he refused. Surely, though, E. J. must have taken some satisfaction at the flattery that came lightning-fast from the *Pittsburgh Bulletin Index*, which just five years earlier had mocked him as an uppity Jew. "Pittsburgh's Edgar J. Kaufmann . . . [has built on] Bear Run's wildest stretch . . . the latest, most beautiful and dynamic creation of America's most fertile and uncompromisingly modern architect." More *Bulletin Index* articles poured forth, as though in contrition: two servile stories on E. J. in 1938, another in 1941, still another—all superlatives—on Kaufmann Jr. With these articles and his glowing coverage in *Town & Country*,

Time, and *Fortune,* E. J. finally had a nationwide constituency that could free him from Pittsburgh's hobbling social mores.

Kaufmann had not long to wait before he could calibrate Fallingwater's payback in social prestige. On June 13, 1939, he convened at Fallingwater a national conference of high importance: a debate on how to nudge the Roosevelt administration to protect the Jews trapped in Nazi Germany. Attending in person or directly represented were men like the financier Edward Warburg, the legendary Impressionist-art collector Maurice Wertheim, the philanthropist and graphic arts king Lessing Rosenwald, and the philosopher Morris Raphael Cohen. Albert Einstein presided, as the most famous Jew in the world. As the Bible puts it, Kaufmann had formerly looked like a grasshopper in the sight of most of these men, but Fallingwater had nicely redressed the balance.

A showcase has no value unless it attracts customers, as Liliane and E. J. knew, so they employed two parallel strategies for broadcasting how well they were flourishing in their marvelously modern house. One was to propagate images in the media, in which, as we saw, they had a huge success. The other was to get important guests to visit Bear Run. Guests are in any case essential in giving life to a country house: a retreat into nature has little social value unless it gives you bragging rights.

The Kaufmann home movies show that the family had always been gregarious hosts to relatives and cronies at the old Hangover bungalow at Bear Run, but when Fallingwater went up, E. J. banished this crowd and kept Bear Run for himself. His sister Martha Wolf took a cabin on a hill toward Ohiopyle and his cousins the Bachmans and his friends the Speyers got their own places in Mill Run. Brother Oliver moved to an estate north of Pittsburgh that was big enough for it to serve today as the main campus of Robert Morris University.

Before 1937 the Kaufmanns did their serious entertaining in Pittsburgh, either in lavish banquets at the store or at La Tourelle; now the focus shifted to Bear Run. The problem was Fallingwater's distance from Pittsburgh. The old "Kaufmann" railroad depot ceased being a regular stop once the employees' summer camp shut down, and now the Baltimore & Ohio line was loath to halt its locomotives in order to help out a few guests. Motor travel improved greatly when the Pennsylvania Turnpike opened in 1940, but not all the Kaufmanns' callers wished to drive back to Pittsburgh in the middle of the night. The first of Fallingwater's guests had to make do with the scattered old cabins and the decaying Masonic Clubhouse, with an occasional spillover to the various hotels then still operating at Ohiopyle. The family always knew it would need a proper guesthouse at Bear Run. In early January of 1938, with the publicity on Fallingwater going full blast, Edgar Tafel visited E. J. to discuss some still-incomplete interior details of the main house and to start preliminary planning for a guesthouse. Soon after, E. J. sent Wright his specifications for a building that would include four servant rooms, lodging for four guests, and a four-car covered parking area. In a replay of 1935, a new topographic survey was conducted and a plan of the site was sent to Spring Green.

True to character, Wright waited nearly a month to respond. He came to Fallingwater in March 1938 to supervise placement of the furniture and to think through the linkage of the guesthouse to the main building. After the usual dawdling, he prepared plans for a combined guesthouse, garage, and servant quarters in May, but it evidently struck him as insufficient, and he did not send it on to Kaufmann. Two weeks later he produced a superior design that called for a spacious four-vehicle carport, canted at an angle, like sawteeth. This angle was repeated in the striking gravel forecourt in the shape of the 30/60/90-degree triangle that had given birth to the Fallingwater plan in the first place. The famous canopy between Fallingwater and the proposed guesthouse made its first appearance as a deep semicircle working around a high oak tree.

E. J. got these plans around May 28, looked them over for three days, and bluntly told Wright he had failed to capture what was wanted. The proposed guesthouse was too large and not right for the site, or, as Liliane put it, it was "too great a burden to put such a large addition on the present house." The site plan still has the word "VOID" prominently scratched in one corner.

At Kaufmann's request, Wright paid his thirteenth visit to Pittsburgh and Bear Run in late June, but the guesthouse project remained on hold for the rest of the year while numerous internal adjustments were made to the main house. On New Year's Day of 1939, E. J. broke the logjam on the guesthouse project in his usual decisive manner. He summoned the builder Walter Hall back to Pittsburgh and ordered him to get to work on the auxiliary complex. Hall complied, even though all he had to go by were the plans that Kaufmann had rejected the previous May.

"We are all thrilled that we are building again," Kaufmann wrote Wright. "It will help to fill up the first six months of 1939—so details are important. Please don't let us down—get to work!" Kaufmann wanted the guesthouse complete by June 22, 1939, the thirtieth anniversary of his marriage to Liliane. For his part, Hall appealed to Wright for a revised set of dimensioned drawings, but he began to excavate the hillside even before they arrived.

Kaufmann's power play triggered an instant rerun of the chaos of 1936: stone was being quarried, a foundation staked out, and grading of the hillside was under way—all on the basis of no more than a couple of sketchy plans. Nothing could have stirred the bear of Spring Green out of hibernation faster than this audacious jump-start by Kaufmann and Hall. Wright's creative process slipped into high gear, and by the end of January 1939, Kaufmann got a third and final plan. ("EJ. Here it is at last. Is it OK? If so put yours here," Wright scribbled on the plan where he hoped—in vain—to get Kaufmann's signature of assent.) The walkway to the guesthouse was reduced to half its projected length by Wright's inspired idea of folding the semicircular canopy into seven steps. Beautifully sashaying forth in imitation of the hillside and the waterfall, the canopy looks to be made of origami rather than reinforced concrete.

Hall was delighted with the concept of Fallingwater's guesthouse, less so with the reality of Wright's slapdash attention to detail: the servant wing was projected to rise five feet beyond his excavation line. Hall conferred with E. J. and Kaufmann Jr., and the three decided to change Wright's drawing rather than to rectify the error on the ground. Despite these occasional irritations, Hall increasingly saw himself as Wright's man on the site—no apprentice had yet come out from Taliesin—rather than Kaufmann's. "Can't be yes-man other than to your plans," he wrote Wright. "Leaving job. Too many bosses. E. J. OK, but led by Jr. and Thumm." Kaufmann Jr. was no less intransigent, wiring Wright: "I expect to see us get a Wright house, not a Hall house." To pacify the warring parties, Wright diverted his apprentice Harold Turner from a job in eastern Pennsylvania to serve as an interim site manager.

It was in character for Wright to be constantly modifying drawings as his buildings went up, but for so straightforward a construction as the guesthouse (the canopy was trickier) he displayed an inconsistency that made it seem as though in this project it was the architect who was meddling, not the client. The sideshow to Fallingwater was sapping more energy on all sides than had the main building.

Eventually the goddess of construction waved her wand over the building site, and by mid-March 1939 building was proceeding smoothly. By late April the exterior shell of the guest wing was nearly finished, and by summer it was in place. The guesthouse was an instant hit with the Kaufmanns' familiars, and within a year E. J. and Liliane shifted their main entertaining from Pittsburgh to Bear Run. In 1940 they turned over La Tourelle to the University of Pittsburgh as a chancellor's residence, and made do with an apartment at the William Penn Hotel.

The guesthouse is highly picturesque outside, an effect enhanced by the wisteria that intertwines in the trellis next to the swimming pool—a transplant from Taliesin East. The interior is less successful. Wright seems not to have concerned himself with it much, and its motel-like blandness bespeaks apprentice work. It has better ventilation than the main house because its ceilings are higher, which allows for a long clerestory window that gets opened from the outside. The guesthouse gives the impression that here the client—particularly Liliane—got the better of the architect, which rarely makes for good architecture. Liliane was nevertheless delighted with what became her favorite part of Fallingwater. She frequently took over the guesthouse herself, and made her guests sleep in the main house. E. J. was attached to the guesthouse, too. When his daughter, Betty Jo Harris, was about ten years old, he took her to see it while it was going up. All her life Betty Jo would remember her daddy's fib that he was building the little house just for her.

A trail of world celebrities made their way to Fallingwater even before they had a guesthouse to stay in. No guestbook survives to help us date these visits, but we can see that Alvar Aalto came in 1939, because his photograph of the main house shows the guesthouse under construction. Walter Gropius and Marcel Breuer came even earlier, when Fallingwater was only a few months old, at which time they invited Kaufmann Jr. to see the new Gropius home in Lincoln, Massachusetts.

By showing off Fallingwater to the top brass of MoMA and other cultural luminaries like Gropius, the Kaufmanns and especially Junior gave themselves instant prominence in the art world. One journalist who asked Kaufmann Jr. about these guests did not get far. " 'Who came to stay with you at the guesthouse at Fallingwater?' In the graceful way of aristocrats who prefer to keep their private lives private, he smiled and replied, 'Oh, just people who wandered out of the forest.' "

The classic appeal of villa life is its informality, as famously expressed by the Roman writer Pliny: "For besides the attractions which I have mentioned the greatest is the relaxation and carefree luxury of the place—there is no need for a toga, the neighbors do not come to call, it is always quiet and peaceful." Though life at Fallingwater was informal, it still had its protocols. Sunbathing was tops among them. Guests in the 1940s and 1950s were still regularly invited to disrobe on the various terraces, though not all complied.

As in any lordly house, there were certain unchanging rituals, such as the throwing of champagne glasses into Bear Run on New Year's Eve. At Easter the stairs going down from the living room to the stream were covered with lilies that had been grown in the Kaufmanns' greenhouse, giving the living room a heavenly scent.

Other reminiscences of Fallingwater come from its last cook, Elsie Henderson. Henderson worked for the Kaufmanns from 1946 until the Western Pennsylvania Conservancy took over the house in 1963. Later, she worked for the Mellons and for the Kennedys, two clans that she ranks poorly next to the Kaufmanns. Henderson recalls that a Fallingwater weekend would begin with guests gathering for cocktails and supper Friday evening, proceed to some sort of athletic exertions on Saturday (with or without the sunbathing), and break up at midday Sunday. What she remembers most vividly is that the Kaufmanns insisted she never create the same menu twice.

The most memorable account of a visit to Fallingwater is Frida Kahlo's Chaucerian recollection of her stay there in November 1938. Kahlo, who was separated from Rivera at the time, came to New York for the opening of her exhibit at the Julien Levy Gallery. E. J. came to the show, bought *Remembrance of an Open Wound,* and invited Kahlo and Levy to visit him at Fallingwater. As Kahlo's biographer Hayden Herrera recounts it:

> Once Levy took Frida to Pennsylvania to visit his client and friend Edgar Kaufmann, Sr., who, Levy said, wanted to be Frida's patron. The train ride was everything train rides are supposed to be—a slow but inexorable buildup of erotic anticipation. When they arrived, however, Frida flirted not just with Levy, but with their elderly host and his son as well. She was "very cavalier with her men," Levy recalled. She liked to play one off against the other, and she would pretend to one suitor that she thought the other was a nuisance or "a bore." At bedtime, Levy and the senior Kaufmann tried to wait each other out so as to spend the last moments of the evening in romantic solitude with Frida. When she retired, Fallingwater's complicated double stairway [the exterior steps up to the guestroom] served as the stage for the evening's drama. After biding his time until he thought everyone was peacefully asleep, Levy emerged from his room and started up one side of the staircase. Much to his astonishment, he found his host climbing the stairs on the other side. Both retreated. The same confrontation took place several times. In the end, Levy gave up. But when he returned to his bedroom, there was Frida—waiting for him!

For their own delight and that of their guests, the Kaufmanns brought into Fallingwater great quantities of what we can only call "stuff." Studies on architecture rarely attempt to draw out the

character of a building through "stuff," because the miscellaneous furnishings lying in full view in our living rooms are rarely accorded the status of Material Culture: they are merely stuff. Additionally, they have
nothing to do with the architecture; often what the client piles into a new
house can reduce the architect to tears.

Nonetheless, the objects the Kaufmanns stuffed into Fallingwater by
the thousands tell us much about them and how they used the house.
The Kaufmanns' stuff would fascinate us anyway for its excellent taste, its
wide range of eras, and its still wider range of national and ethnic origins.
In the living room alone we find the products of thirty different countries
or cultures. Asia is represented alphabetically by fourteen cultures from
Afghanistan to Uzbekistan; Europe by another thirteen cultures from
Austria to Switzerland; Africa by the Congo; and the New World by at
least five different cultures, from the potters and trappers of western
Pennsylvania to the potters and weavers of the American Southwest. If
we survey the national origins of the artisans and artists represented in
the whole house, from the founders of the Welsh brass plates in the
kitchen to the weavers of the Tutsi straw basket in the guest bedroom,
then the cultures represented at Fallingwater are as numerous as the flags
flying outside the United Nations.

What did Frank Lloyd Wright think about all this stuff? He was on
record as telling clients to liberate themselves from their possessions, and
we would expect that someone who dictated the appropriate color for his
fields, his cattle, and his apprentices would force his hand on his clients'
collectibles, too. Surprisingly, though, Wright was on record as saying
that any American had the right to decorate as he saw fit. As he wrote in
1910 in *Ausgeführte Bauten und Entwürfe von Frank Lloyd Wright:*

> In America each man has a peculiar, inalienable right to live in his own
> house in his own way. He is a pioneer in every right sense of the word.
> His home environment may face forward, may portray his character,
> tastes, and ideas, if he has any, and every man here has some some-
> where about him.

What the Kaufmanns displayed at Fallingwater certainly bears
Wright out. More than a few tourists remember the house better from the
profusion of the Kaufmanns' belongings than they do from Wright's
design. The Western Pennsylvania Conservancy Web site on Fallingwater
takes cognizance of this display of possessions when it refers to the house
as the "Fallingwater Museum." There are about 950 works of fine and
decorative arts on display at Fallingwater, some bearing major names like
Rembrandt, Audubon, Picasso, Feininger, Rivera, Arp, Aalto, Lipchitz,

Giacometti, Tiffany, and Lalique. That makes a notable collection in itself, particularly in the excellent examples of twentieth-century high-style furniture.

It would be pure masochism for us to examine all these artifacts in detail, and unnecessary besides, since our purpose is to understand the how and why of the Kaufmanns' decoration of their house, not to poke at their every Buddha and Bodhisattva. Still, it is worth pondering the meaning behind all this stuff. Many a house is heaped with objects; the Kaufmanns merely had more objects, and took better care of them, than the rest of us. For a building of only six rooms, plus the five rooms in the guesthouse and servant quarter, it had more stuff than any three mortals could possibly have needed.

The photographic record shows that there were scores or hundreds more items in the house before it went public: the interior as was photographed by Paul Mayén in 1962 and Ezra Stoller in 1963 was far breezier than the austere house museum pictured in Donald Hoffmann's book of 1978 and Kaufmann Jr.'s memoir of 1986. Junior had many of the family's personal belongings removed from Fallingwater in 1956 after E. J. died, and again in October 1963 when the WPC repackaged the house for public presentation. What was carted out the first time is not recorded, but on the second occasion the Pittsburgh storage firm of Haugh & Keenan removed enough suitcases, bronze statues, chairs, paintings, rugs, clothes, dishes, and books (nineteen cartons) to fill 152 separate containers, to wit:

28 barrels
75 cartons of 1.5 cubic feet
25 cartons of 3 cubic feet
8 cartons of 4.5 cubic feet
5 cartons of 5 cubic feet
2 wardrobe cartons
9 miscellaneous crates and containers

Mercifully, to understand the relationship between the family and its collectibles we need not examine the whole house. The living room will serve our purpose nicely, and not even everything in it, since Fallingwater's current inventory lists well over one hundred objects in that one room alone. Like most house museums, Fallingwater has rearranged certain items from the way the Kaufmanns displayed them and has brought in a few score items that Liliane and Edgar Kaufmann never saw at all. Most but not all of these new objects replace those that were once there or serve as general representations of the Kaufmanns' taste.

Among the furniture that has been subtracted from the living room are the several chestnut tree stumps that the Kaufmanns used, inverted and varnished on top, as occasional tables. Just one stump survives in the living room today, holding up liquor bottles by the fireplace. Another is currently on view in the guesthouse, with several more banished to storage. Gone from view now are the early-modern German lounge chairs the Kaufmanns bought in Berlin in 1921, which served as their standard easy chairs in the living room. They were visible in Ezra Stoller's photographs as late as 1963, then disappeared.

The one easy chair in the living room today is a latecomer, probably installed by Kaufmann Jr. after 1963 as part of his makeover of Fallingwater's furniture for public view. It was designed by T. H. Robsjohn-Gibbings, one of the dominant Anglo-American furniture designers and design critics of the 1940s and '50s, in whose career Kaufmann took a professional interest. (Robsjohn-Gibbings is remembered today for his critique *Goodbye Mr. Chippendale*.) Nearly everything else in the living room was custom-designed by Wright, except for the five Italian three-legged peasant chairs at the dining table. Liliane discovered these nineteenth-century chairs in Florence in the 1930s, and insisted on using them in place of the stiffly formal barrel chairs that Wright had intended for the eating alcove. She contended that they were more in character and more stable on the uneven flagstone floor.

The decor of the living room generally reflects the Kaufmanns' taste more than Wright's. The architect's preferences are represented by the Cherokee-red wine kettle in the fireplace, the metal shelves on the walls, and the tables, banquettes, and hassocks; but a hundred other items reflect the clients' taste. The prime color accents in the room come from a score of strikingly pigmented cushions, pillows, and coverlets that E. J.

Fallingwater's early decor was casual: here E. J.'s mother, Betty, uses a chair the Kaufmanns bought in Berlin; Kaufmann sits on a throw made of local skunk

and Liliane collected in a half-century of travels. One of the hand-woven coverlets, for example, is a Scottish wool tartan travel rug that Kaufmann bought at Eaton's Department Store in Montréal on his way to his fishing lodge at McGregor Bay. Complementing these are pillows and tapestries from Afghanistan, Indonesia, Turkey, Bhutan, Uzbekistan, Greece, Mexico, and Malaysia. The large couch cover was made of raccoon fur for the Kaufmanns by Ed Danko, a local trapper, using pelts from animals snared right on the property. Early photographs show E. J. on the same couch when it was covered in white skunk.

These objects provide a fair sample of the multiculturism evident throughout the house. Kaufmann Jr. bought the brass oil lamp in Greece, where he owned a house for many years. The turned wooden bowls come from Oregon, the hanging copper and brass planter from Belgium, the modern light-green ceramic bowl and the traditional tea-ceremony iron kettle from Japan, the large copper rooster over the buffet from France, the ceramic woodstove model from eighteenth-century Germany, the cylindrical boxes and the wedding chest under the portrait of E. J. come from Burma, the brass bells from Switzerland, the ancient unglazed clay bowl from Sicily. The polychromed earthenware pot that stands on the shelves over the second buffet is contemporary Zuni, while the two terra-cotta bulls on the shelf below it are Portuguese folk art from the 1920s. The Kaufmanns bought the terra-cotta male figure hanging in the music alcove in Berlin in 1921 (it is either Chinese, Korean, or a fake). On the desk in the reading alcove is an African wood statue of a chief and his heir, probably from the Congo; on the floor nearby is a geometric-design Pima Indian basket from the 1930s.

Other pieces—we still have not left the living room—are a seventeenth-century Chinese porcelain, a Japanese bronze vase and red lacquered bowl, a set of Imari china plates, an Indian handblown glass flycatcher and wooden cigarette box, an Islamic-origin green clay jug, a Syrian hanging copper container, and a Ming lacquer box. Flanking the closed-up pass-through that once opened into the kitchen are two bas-reliefs of stylized lions that originally stood as tomb guards in a Sung-dynasty grave. Among the miscellaneous knickknacks are bowls, mugs, and ashtrays of Venetian, Bohemian, and Mexican glass.

In addition to the furs, some other curiosities in the living room are local. The twenty-gallon stoneware crock was made in the Monongahela River town of Greensboro for shipping pickles, sauerkraut, or grains to Pittsburgh. (Western Pennsylvania pottery—a favorite Kaufmann collectible—was first sponsored by the inventive Albert Gallatin when he settled nearby.) The chunk of iron slag was found in a lime pit by the

Kaufmanns while they were hiking near Mill Run; the glass telescope lens was made in a factory in nearby Jeannette that was owned by the Kaufmanns' neighbor A. C. Speyer.

Set among these traditional or anonymous industrial artifacts—we *still* have not left the living room—are scores of works by high-style designers, many of them signed or otherwise securely attributed, such as the Robsjohn-Gibbings easy chair. From the Tiffany Studios came the Favrile turtleback glass panel leaning against the window next to the hearth, the Favrile Glass bowl with center stem (signed by Louis Comfort Tiffany himself), a bronze and Favrile Glass mosaic planter, a candlestick with blown-glass top, and a bronze gilt dish. These are all remnants from the Kaufmanns' important collection of Tiffany glass, other pieces of which the family donated to MoMA. The fireplace fork is signed by the master ironworker Samuel Yellin, who made it around 1930 for La Tourelle. The red stoneware vase is by the Dane Axel Salto, the green-glazed clay bowl by the Austrian-American industrial designers Gertrud and Otto Natzler. The oblong metal relief over the music-area couch was a commissioned piece executed for Kaufmann Jr. by Luisa Rota. The pewter cake plate was cast by Pietro Mezadona, and a Notsjo glass bowl and a sapphire glass bowl are both signed by Kaj Franck. The Cherokee-red enamel ice bucket with brass lid is by Russell Wright, the wooden and stainless steel serving spoons are by Dansk, and the Spanish glasses were purchased by Kaufmann Jr. at Lord & Taylor in 1985.

Edgar Jr. had a personal link to most of the contemporary high-style objects at Fallingwater. The glass vase is one that Alvar Aalto originally made for the Savoy restaurant in Helsinki in 1936: Kaufmann featured it in his 1950 MoMA booklet, *What Is Modern Design?* Kaufmann's friend Paul Mayén created *Red Cubic Sculpture* for the coffee table in front of the south wall banquette in the 1950s or '60s.

A few items survive at Fallingwater that depict the Kaufmanns or otherwise invoke their memory. In the coatroom hangs Kaufmann Jr.'s German-made poncho, his cane, leather bag, and Italian porkpie hat. At the entrance is a print of a raven by John James Audubon from his *Birds of America* volumes—one of four giant prints that the Kaufmanns brought from their old Hangover cottage. There is, finally, the tempera-and-oil portrait of E. J. as a hiker by Victor Hammer. After Hammer painted it in Vienna in 1929, it won the Best in Show prize at the Carnegie International exhibition in Pittsburgh the next year. Kaufmann Jr. gave the painting to the Western Pennsylvania Conservancy, but after a few years it was transferred to their corporate offices in Pittsburgh. When the painting began to warp in the dryness of the WPC offices, Fallingwater's then-curator and later director Lynda Waggoner suggested that Bear Run's humidity might help the picture, and E. J. was finally made visible in his old living room around 1990.

It is peculiar that no one at the Western Pennsylvania Conservancy thought Fallingwater was in need of a picture of E. J., and funny to think that only a technical problem with the portrait finally got him in. But E. J. has always been the missing man at Fallingwater. We have no idea what he thought of the place, for example, since neither he nor Liliane ever spoke about Fallingwater in public. All three Kaufmanns were supposed to contribute essays to the catalogue for MoMA's 1940 Frank Lloyd Wright exhibition, but nothing ever reached publication. Kaufmann Jr. wrote and lectured about the house for decades, but always with a certain ellipticality. That results in a dearth of insight on the house by the people most closely connected with it, including Wright.

This silence above the falls is broken—elliptically, again—by two paintings that the Kaufmanns commissioned for the house. Neither hangs at Fallingwater today, which is probably just as well, because tourists would find them more baffling than enlightening. The first is Peter Blume's *House at Falling Water,* which was hidden by its artist for so long that the definitive catalogue of Blume's works listed its location as "whereabouts unknown." The small oil on wood came to light in 1999, when a Boston dealer sold it to a gallery in New York. The painting immediately went on public view at Loretto, opposite Charles Schwab's estate, in the unrequited hope that the Western Pennsylvania Conservancy would buy it. Blume assigned the date "1938–1968" to the painting, which suggests that he never turned the work over to the Kaufmanns. *House at Falling Water* shows the family members in the house together but isolated: Junior and friends on the top terrace, E. J. and his aged mother, Betty, on the main terrace, and Liliane fishing in the stream below.

Around 1939 the Kaufmanns commissioned Blume to paint *The Rock.* A much larger painting, *The Rock* is a superb example of magic realism, Blume's signature style. (His 1937 *Eternal City* parody of Mussolini continues to be a great draw at MoMA.) Blume worked on *The Rock* intermittently from 1939 to 1945, then obsessively for three more years until 1948. It was voted Best in Show when the Kaufmanns entered it in the Carnegie International of 1950. E. J. then kept *The Rock* close to him either in Pittsburgh or in Palm Springs. In October 1955, Kaufmann Jr. shipped the painting to the Art Institute of Chicago, where it has been one of the museum's top crowd-pleasers ever since.

The Rock presents comically sweating laborers—one of them probably E. J. himself—intent on constructing a Fallingwater-like building on the left side, while tearing down a corresponding old building on the right side. There is a dead-ringer portrait of Betty Kaufmann hanging on the old building, but since she had died in 1942, Blume inserts her not as a living person but in an oval photograph. (The photograph Blume used is now among the Kaufmann papers at the Heinz Regional History Center in Pittsburgh.) Blume refused to tell either his biographer or the Art Institute of Chicago the meaning behind *The Rock,* so the work has never been "figured out," but we know that E. J. loved the painting and would often contemplate it with wonder.

The furnishings in the rest of the house and in the guesthouse extend the theme of the living room, with Wright's built-in furniture vying for attention with the traditional craftworks, artworks, and high-style design pieces collected by the Kaufmanns. The most important artworks are Diego Rivera's Conté crayon *Profile of a Man Wearing a Hat* in the second-floor guest-bedroom and his *Torrid Siesta (El Sueño)* watercolor in the bridge to the guesthouse; a Tiffany bronze lamp with lotus-leaf leaded glass shade, in the master bedroom; a fifteenth-century boxwood *Madonna and Child,* either Burgundian or Austro-Bohemian, in the same room; and Jean Arp's *Mediterranean II* abstract marble and Lyonel Feininger's *Church on the Cliffs VII,* both in Junior's study. There are six Japanese woodblock prints that Wright gave the Kaufmanns over the years, either by Hiroshige or Hokusai. Some of the other significant high-design pieces are a 1936 signed and dated bentwood maple easy chair by Bruno Mathsson, in the guest-bedroom; a leather-seated wooden armchair by the Austrian-American designer Josef Frank, in E. J.'s bedroom; and in the same room, an original metal and leather butterfly chair made by the Argentinian architects and designers Jorge Ferrari-Hardoy, Antonio Bonet, and Juan Kurchan; and a curvilinear wooden armchair with floating seat by the pioneer Danish modern designer Finn Juhl, which was executed by the Copenhagen cabinetmaker Niels Vodder in 1937. Kaufmann Jr. included both the Mathsson and the Argentinian chairs in his pioneering MoMA exhibit called "The Modern Chair," as well as in his 1950 catalogue on modern design.

The Kaufmanns did not stint in packing just as many objects into their guesthouse. Here again multiculturalism prevails, with pride of place going to Latin America. Among the 125 significant pieces in the guesthouse are folk objects from Norway, Greece, Japan, China, Peru, the Netherlands, England, India, and the Pennsylvania Dutch country, along with a Tiffany stained-glass panel. The guesthouse also features nearly a dozen small Mayan pre-Colombian heads. The Latin American theme is carried through with a large oil painting by José Maria Velasco from 1877, entitled *Landscape: Jalapa, Mexico,* which the Kaufmanns acquired around 1937. After hanging for years in Kaufmann Sr.'s apartment in downtown Pittsburgh, it came to the guesthouse around 1960. The government of Mexico regards the work as important enough that it has made entreaties to Fallingwater to get it back (Velasco was Rivera's teacher at one point). A William Morris chair, a Picasso aquatint and etching from 1963, and a cantilevered chair by Mies van der Rohe are some of the more important pieces here.

The collecting saga at Bear Run is far from over, because a modern storage building contains hundreds more objects: paintings, drawings, prints, photographs, and books, plus throws, tapestries, rugs, woven rugs, strips, shawls, beds, bedspreads, pillows, and old lawn chairs—all of them formerly in Fallingwater. This suggests that what some visitors perceive as a coldness in the house was once alleviated by a sea of textiles. It still makes it no less mysterious how three persons and their guests could possibly have put so many items to use.

Some of Fallingwater's most notable artworks stand outside the house, beginning with the bronze doors to the Kaufmann mausoleum along Bear Run, which were commissioned in 1954 from Alberto Giacometti. The most striking sculpture for visitors is the Sung Dynasty (10th–13th centuries) cast-iron head of Buddha that sits impassively on the west balcony off the living room. The Kaufmanns bought it in 1951, and Wright supposedly chose its final resting spot himself. At various points on the grounds stand stone folk sculptures by Mardonio Magana, whom the Kaufmanns appear to have known personally in Mexico in the 1930s.

The most notable museum-quality work inside or outside the house today is Jacques Lipchitz's bronze *Mother and Babe (Mother and Child).* Conceived by Lipchitz in Paris in 1939, the bronze was cast in New York in 1941. The Kaufmanns bought it the next year and installed it on the rim of the plunge pool in the streambed alongside the house. The once-a-century floodwaters of August 5, 1956, carried it off, but it was recovered and Lipchitz was able to repair it; at Wright's suggestion, the sculpture was then pivoted to face away from rather than toward the house. The bronze *Man on a Horse* by Marino Marini that had stood at the entrance to the bridge since 1950 was not so lucky: only three small fragments were ever found after it was swept away in the same deluge.

Fallingwater's works of art have been subject to a high degree of injury and loss. Not only the Marini but an important Rodin sculpture was damaged by the environment. This was Rodin's *Iris* (also listed in the inventories as *Messagère des Dieux* or *Bathing Woman*). Kaufmann Sr. installed it on a wall by the guesthouse swimming pool, but it suffered severe damage from frost and a fall into the pool in 1960. Kaufmann Jr. sent it to Jacques Lipchitz for conservation, but he later kept the restored piece in his New York apartment, where it stayed until it sold at Sotheby's in his estate auction.

More obscure is what happened to the Frida Kahlo painting(s) once at Fallingwater. *My Birth* was hanging at Fallingwater until 1957 or later, after which it went to Junior's New York apartment and was sold. The records do not specify where the Kaufmanns hung their second Kahlo, *Remembrance of an Open Wound,* bought in the late 1930s along with Rivera's *Torrid Siesta.* In 1954 it was hanging in Junior's New York apartment, after which it vanished.

The Kahlo or Kahlos remind us that at one time Fallingwater was a significant private museum of modern furnishings and art. A 1957 inventory additionally listed etchings by Picasso and Klee, Theodore Stamos's *Greek Orison,* a Modigliani sketch, and Piet Mondrian's *Diagonal,* all of which left Fallingwater a few years later. A schedule attached to Kaufmann Jr.'s insurance policy of July 11, 1960, documents still more treasures that were hanging in the house at the time. Gone a few years later were Lauren McIver's *The Streets Turn Young with Rain,* an untitled oil by Joseph Albers, Joan Miró's *The Cat,* Piet Mondrian's *Composition in Square,* four preparatory sketches for Peter Blume's *The Rock,* and two priceless canvases by Paul Klee: *With Thorns* and *Officially Flora.*

No one takes pleasure when works of art get lost or are destroyed, as were the two Klee paintings when Junior's country house in the Hudson River valley at Garrison, New York, burned down, but it may be for the best that Fallingwater today presents us with works of only secondary importance. Were really fine paintings hanging on its walls today, we would approach it as a museum and not as a home. The objects and the architecture might even come into conflict—an accusation that is still hurled at Wright's Guggenheim Museum.

Tracking down all the fine and decorative arts that are now, or were formerly, at Fallingwater is a bit exhausting, but thinking about these artefacts as a group tells us much about the house and its residents. As the writer Paul Eldridge perceptively remarked: "Possessions possess." These multithousands of items were not merely collected by the Kaufmanns: in the end they defined them as well. What emerges is a house that became a kind of battlefield of material culture. We have Wright defining an ideal interior landscape with his drawings for the Kaufmanns' built-ins in 1937, then the older Kaufmanns filling the house with their possessions from 1937 until Liliane died in 1952, an interregnum when E. J. lived there alone or with his second wife from 1952 to 1955, then Kaufmann Jr.'s taking possession from 1955 to 1963, the conversion of Fallingwater into a house-museum in 1963, and finally what the Western Pennsylvania Conservancy did with the house after Junior's death in 1989.

We can interpret the furnishings of Fallingwater along the lines of Ryunosuke Akutagawa's (and Akira Kurosawa's) *Rashomon*: an interior environment that was single in fact but multiple in its possible interpretations. Wright saw the house as a showcase for his own furnishings. Liliane and E. J. started off by seeking a rustic decor that would function as a foil to their city life, but they evidently wanted their house to be exotic, too. The exotic aura began at Fallingwater with the Chinese, Korean, and Indian artifacts the family began to assemble in the 1920s. The six Japanese prints from Wright intensified the non-Western imprint on the house. Then came all the Spanish, Portuguese, and Mexican pieces. What is especially intriguing is the way Fallingwater presents the Kaufmanns as peasants living in the bosom of High Modernism, akin to the decorative scheme in the two studios that their friend Juan O'Gorman designed in 1935 for Diego Rivera and Frida Kahlo. Given their close ties with Rivera and Kahlo, it is likely that the Kaufmanns saw those houses on their 1937 Mexico trip, or later. Peasants-living-in-modernism became the central theme that Liliane and E. J. enshrined at Fallingwater.

Kaufmann Jr. was ideologically modernist in taste, in contrast to his parents' nonideological nibbles at modernism—their modern furniture being mainly pieces made by their friends Laszlo Gabor and Josef Frank. The pieces now on display go hand in glove with the design philosophy of standardized utilitarian objects that Junior espoused at MoMA from the 1930s through the 1950s. Thanks to Kaufmann Jr., Fallingwater today is a good place to study mid-century furniture makers such as Mathsson, Juhl, and Robsjohn-Gibbings, and important houseware designers like Aalto, Salto, the Natzlers, Luisa Rota, Pietro Mezadona, Kaj Franck, Raymond Loewy, Paul Mayén, and Russell Wright. The house sometimes reads like an illustrated roll call for an article on the most important twentieth-century designers that Kaufmann Jr. wrote for the 1964 edition of the *Encyclopaedia Brittanica*. These mid-century pieces blend easily with the architecture and with Wright's built-ins, and keep up the informal tone that E. J. and Liliane set for the house.

After Junior's death in 1989, the Western Pennsylvania Conservancy unconsciously turned Fallingwater into a spatial portrait of the Kaufmanns. In the living room we find the oil portrait of E. J. hiking and in Liliane's room comes the photograph of him fishing; a sculpted bust of Kaufmann Jr. sits in his father's bedroom; a photograph of Liliane emerges in the third-floor hallway; and a photograph of the three Kaufmanns together brightens up Junior's study. The syncopation is perfect: E. J. in Liliane's room, Liliane in Junior's, Junior in E. J.'s. The problem is that of these five images, only the photograph of Liliane (formerly in E. J.'s bedroom) reflects how the Kaufmanns lived here. The other four images were brought in by the WPC either in the years 1963 to 1989 with Kaufmann Jr.'s help, or after he died. As we saw earlier, E. J. has gazed benignly at visitors to his living room only since the early 1990s. He began to busy himself fishing on Liliane's writing desk around the same time (Junior's 1986 book shows Liliane's desk spouse-free). Junior's bust appeared on his father's desk no earlier than the 1970s, and the portrait of the three Kaufmanns in Junior's study popped up there a decade after that.

It was Junior who started this manipulation of his family's material culture. He remade his parents into world-class collectors of exotica, though old photographs show that E. J. and Liliane ran the house with just a fraction of the pieces one encounters there today (they were not really world travelers, either: their Asian pieces mainly came from Kaufmann's buying offices in China or Europe). Junior made his parents look as decorous as he was: gone at once were their comfortable old lounge chairs and the funky chestnut-tree stumps on which they had balanced their drinks. A third fiction invoked propriety, if not outright prudery: even before Junior took Fallingwater public he had sequestered the blatantly sexual Kahlo paintings that his parents had nonchalantly kept on view there. *My Birth* went into a closet in his New York apartment; *Remembrance of an Open Wound* disappeared. In a more comic vein, someone ripped Liliane's hard-won bidet out of her bathroom around 1963, leaving the disused valves behind. Was Junior afraid that visitors would be shocked by it, too?

Prudery, or simple discomfort, led Kaufmann Jr. to make a fiction out of his parents' odd marriage. Wright's plans made clear from the first that Liliane and E. J. were to occupy separate bedrooms at Fallingwater, but

Junior's book persisted in calling his mother's room the main, or master, bedroom and his father's bedroom "the dressing room used by my father"—though readers could hardly miss E. J.'s manifestly single bed in the photograph. WPC, too, refused to accept that E. J. and Liliane did not sleep together. As late as 2001 their newsletter prissily referred to "Edgar Kaufmann Sr.'s dressing room/study," rather than just calling it his bedroom.

Kaufmann Jr.'s reworking of Fallingwater's furnishings also sanitized the image of his family in other ways. He de-Judaized the house by boosting the number and prominence of its Catholic images while doing away with the oil portraits of his Orthodox Jewish great-grandparents, Abraham and Sara Kaufmann. E. J. had commissioned those portraits himself, and they hung at Fallingwater until his death. Today's visitors see nothing in the house to suggest that the Kaufmanns were Jews, and the WPC guides see no reason to bring it up.

It was natural for Kaufmann Jr. to want to remake Fallingwater in his own image—he had lived so long in the shadow of his flamboyant parents, and he may have resented the overbearing way Wright had treated him not only at Taliesin but at Bear Run. The floor designated for him is not one of the significant elements in Fallingwater, and it is peculiar that Wright lodged him at the top of the stone tower in a bedroom that was a carbon copy of his father's below. These architectural slights, real or perceived, moved Junior to action: he bolted from the tower and moved his bed down the hall as far away from E. J. as he could go. Then he struck back at Wright, hammering bookshelves against two walls of his original bedroom, in the process covering up and immobilizing a window that Wright had inserted as a key provider of light and air. On the third floor, at least, Junior would have a showcase of his own.

Opposite: Richard Neutra: Kaufmann house, Palm Springs, California, 1947, in the Julius Shulman photograph that E. J. helped reproduce worldwide

ELEVEN

THE RENAISSANCE PRINCE IN WINTER

The picture [of Kaufmann's Palm Springs house at twilight] would become, in particular, one of modern architecture's most brilliant and famous photographs. . . . The house was internationally acclaimed.

—THOMAS HINES, *Richard Neutra and the Search for Modern Architecture*

We felt an obligation to you and your family for what you have done and made possible in the field of art and architecture.

—CHARLES EAMES to Liliane Kaufmann

When the Kaufmanns reopened Fallingwater after the war, Wright's ex-apprentice Edgar Tafel joined them on the last day of 1945. Family and friends cheered in the new year with toasts, then as usual threw their glasses off the living-room balconies into Bear Run. But the first day of 1946 gave E. J. less to cheer about. Tafel declined Kaufmann's offer to set him up as a residential architect in Pittsburgh. Worse, Junior scuttled his father's plan to groom him for the presidency of the store.

E. J. took the disconcerting news in stride. If Winston Churchill could not contemplate the liquidation of his postwar empire, E. J. could. Soon after learning of Junior's abdication as crown prince of the store, Kaufmann negotiated the sale of the business to his distant kin, the Mays of St. Louis and Los Angeles. It was an astute move: the Mays got E. J. to remain as nominal president for his public relations value; they relied on their cousin I. D. Wolf to keep the store profitable; and they even convinced Liliane to stay on as the public face of her Vendôme boutique. For their part, E. J. and Liliane finally became as rich as they had pretended to be all along.

Kaufmann was now hailed as a major art patron, but he carried his new status lightly. He never again sat on an art jury or wrote a quotable line about any building, including his own. He did what many a semi-retiree does, and spent his last decade in make-work projects. First he completed the transformation of the landscape at Bear Run, with a mixture of good and bizarre results. He resumed contact with Wright and gave him a string of commissions—all unbuilt—for buildings at Bear Run. He put up a world-famous house in California in collaboration with Wright's renegade protégé Richard Neutra, then irritated Wright still more with a set of to-die-for commissions for downtown Pittsburgh— none of which got built, either.

E. J. evidently regarded his unbuilt architectural projects as being almost as good as buildings, since he kept "building" to the end—and it was the end, since the last project was his own tomb. The first of his postwar projects was landscaping Bear Run. While Fallingwater's visitors are unstinting in their praise for everything the Kaufmanns achieved there, they fail to credit them with the natural beauty of the woods around the house. This is not for lack of appreciation—many call it the supreme joy of the place—but because today it is virtually impossible to realize how much of that beauty was conjured up not by nature but by the Kaufmanns. Wright had no motive for touching the physical environment around Fallingwater, but the Kaufmanns did. They imported so many species and moved plants and flowers around so energetically that the saying among their friends was "Best landscape God never created."

The flourishing environment of Bear Run today is not remotely the forest primeval: like the great English estates in the eighteenth-century Romantic tradition, these grounds show off "nature improved." We can measure the degree of improvement by comparing this postindustrial paradise with the the 1890s photograph of the treeless slopes behind the Bear Run depot on the B & O tracks. Kaufmann started this transformation as soon as his store began using the property in 1916. He made some forest and water improvements in the 1920s, and his 1933 application to turn Bear Run over to the CCC gave some hint of how he hoped to further improve its flora and fauna. When the application failed, Kaufmann continued to improve the water quality, reforest the most heavily logged parts of his grounds, and upgrade the animal and fish stock along Bear Run.

Until Fallingwater went up, Bear Run lacked any particular horticultural focus. When it was complete in 1938, Liliane became the estate's enthusiastic amateur gardener, with a special mission to intensify plant life around the house. She had local workmen uproot plants from the outlying parts of the property and mass them to highest effect for visitors entering or gazing out of the house. The lush banks of rhododendron that now flourish around the house and on both sides of the stream still testify to her intervention. Liliane's next step—a good deal more controversial in terms of husbandry—was to introduce nonnative plants into Fallingwater's environment. These include the Japanese iris, vinca, English ivy, ajuga, autumn crocus, Kaufmanniana tulips, narcissus, climbing euonymus, forget-me-nots, day lilies, hosta, lily of the valley, and Wright's wisteria from Taliesin East.

Modestly before World War II and extravagantly in the postwar years, E. J. determined to create forests at Bear Run where none had grown within living memory. This was the least successful of his ventures, since it involved the mechanical planting of trees. Between E. J. in the late 1940s and Junior in the late 1950s, the Kaufmanns planted a minimum of 50,000 trees on their land, and maybe twice that. This was largely in response to an economic incentive by the Commonwealth of Pennsylvania, which feared the loss of its once-vigorous logging industry. Some of this reforestation was reasonable and some not. The woods near Fallingwater were replanted with a new growth around 1950, with an eye to both aesthetics and profit. The odder results of E. J.'s arboreal enthusiasm appear not in the immediate vicinity of Fallingwater but across Highway 381, in the forests near the WPC Nature Center Barn. Anyone who treks for five minutes along the Arbutus and Wagon trails just beyond the parking lot finds that the natural helter-skelter distribution of the trees soon gives way to the precise mechanistic rows of a veritable pine plantation.

Even without the documentation that survives in the Fallingwater and WPC archives, it is obvious that these thousands of scrawny trees stand in what was a former cornfield turned forest overnight. In winter you can still make out the old corn furrows when they are crisply articulated by snow. The furrows were used by workers with planting machines to stick in saplings (here white pine, elsewhere spruce and red pine) at a furious clip. Numerous trees are dead now; others sustain live foliage only at the treetops. This moribund forest constitutes a fire hazard that could one day endanger Fallingwater.

A half-century of hindsight has turned the Kaufmanns' artificial forest into a textbook example of how not to achieve conservation. It also conflicts with the current philosophy at the Western Pennsylvania Conservancy and other land trusts, which now regard it as mindless to turn open farmland back into forest. WPC instead acknowledges that the early pioneers were engaged in a constant struggle to clear out the forests, which makes it a sign of disrespect to the pioneers to turn these fields into woods all over again.

We could say E. J. promoted forest conservation for both love and money, since he was an avid if idiosyncratic promoter of logging on his land. His last major logging operation took place between 1947 and 1954. When that campaign began to wind down in 1953, Kaufmann had the site newly surveyed for its remaining lumber value. In 1954, Kaufmann's consulting forester recommended logging the remaining scarlet oak, chestnut, white oak, red oak, yellow poplar, and black cherry throughout the estate, except for those stands of woods where "aesthetic values [are] paramount."

Charmingly, Kaufmann the tree merchant *had* aesthetic values, but the woodsmen of Bear Run knew how to outsmart him. E. J. loved to accompany the loggers at work, but on aesthetic or sentimental grounds he would always stop them from felling the more luxuriant trees. The lumbermen retaliated by switching their activity to the highest hilltops, where E. J. could not hike because of his arthritis. There, high up the slope, the loggers took down every tree in sight.

E. J. kept extending his property through the 1930s and 1940s. He purchased the Tissue family house and barn along Route 381 and turned them over to tenants who farmed the land and ran his start-up dairy for a decade. (Dairies seem to hold special appeal to patrons of architecture: Wright, Kaufmann, Marie Antoinette at Versailles, and Lorenzo de' Medici at Poggio a Caiano spring immediately to mind.) E. J. corresponded with Wright about cows, marketed his milk through a local cooperative, and got Wright to design (but not to build) new housing for his dairy workers. Then with equal suddenness E. J. switched back from farming to forestry. No new crops were planted after the early 1950s, and the dairy herd was auctioned off in the summer of 1951. Farmer Kaufmann had finally hung up his hat.

E. J. achieved two notable successes among the sometimes spotty results of his forays into natural resource management. One was the beauty of the trees, plants, and streams that complement the intellectual appeal of Fallingwater. The other was a major advance in the concept of conserving land as a public trust. In 1951 the Western Pennsylvania Conservancy appealed to Kaufmann to help it acquire Ferncliff Peninsula, opposite Ohiopyle, which at the time still housed several hotels and was about to be turned into an amusement park. Without hesitation E. J. put up the money to buy Ferncliff. His timely donation had multiple points of impact. It created the nucleus of what is today the most heavily utilized state park in Pennsylvania, which in turn began the physical and economic makeover of Ohiopyle; it launched WPC into the advocacy posture it still assumes today; and it forged a bond between the Kaufmanns and WPC that resulted in the donation of Fallingwater twelve years later.

A house, even a mansion, is just one building, but an estate carries outbuildings, and E. J. seemed always to have one more outbuilding for Wright to put up at Bear Run. The first was the guesthouse, but barely had this gone up in 1939 and 1940 when E. J. asked Wright for a farmhouse to crown his new purchase of the dairy farm he had just bought from the Tissue clan. Wright complied, drawing up five plans for a redwood cottage to go near the present WPC Nature Center Barn, but nothing got built. Or rather, a strikingly modern redwood cottage with a radiant-heat floor and other Wrightian features did get built for the site, but Wright got no credit for it. Its architect was Kaufmann Jr., who simply appropriated Wright's design. The next year, 1942, E. J. asked Wright for a gate lodge and caretaker's house that would have stood close by Highway 381 and the Bear Run stream. Six drawings survive for this building, but it was not executed, either.

Had either the farmhouse or the gatehouse gone up in the early 1940s, they would have had minimal impact on Fallingwater. Not so the projects that Kaufmann and Wright cooked up in the immediate postwar years, which could have had a stunningly adverse effect. These projects began with a letter from E. J. to Wright in late 1945—evidently his first communication in three years—requesting a proposal to alleviate crowding in the main house at mealtimes, both for the Kaufmanns' guests in the dining alcove and for the servant staff in the kitchen. Kaufmann included a sketch with the letter, showing how an overflow room to the kitchen—basically a servants' sitting room—could be tucked into the empty space under his own west terrace.

The sketch has not survived, but its existence means that Kaufmann had gone to some outside source—most likely the store architect, A. E. Vitaro—to force Wright's hand. Wright replied immediately with a counterproposal, but Kaufmann went ahead with his original scheme in 1946. The sitting room as we see it today is a *pastiche* (most Americans would call it a mishmash) of Wrightian features, its main focus a large mullion-free window wrapped around the corner of the room. While undeniably Wrightian down to the detail of radiant heat, the room lacks the character and organic spirit of the rest of the house. The participation of the Pittsburgh engineering firm of Hunting, Davis & Dunnell in the project might suggest that E. J. had an ulterior motive in insisting that the room be constructed his way. Since the sitting room stands immediately under E. J.'s terrace, it acts as a massive bolster to it, and would finally have relieved E. J.'s old worries about at least one of Wright's inadequate cantilevers.

Though he lost the battle for the servant room, Wright moved ahead on the problem of crowding in the dining area. At the end of 1945 he drew up plans for a dining-room extension, but Kaufmann was preoccupied with building operations in California, and the men did not meet at Fallingwater until May 1946. A year would pass before Wright was ready with plans for the requested alterations. What he proposed in 1947 was to tear out the back wall of the living room and insert a double-height dining room that would have radically changed the spatial experience of Fallingwater. The resulting misshapen bulk would have been high and wide enough to block the Shady Lane driveway that leads from the stream up to the guesthouse. Blocking the driveway meant that Wright also had to rethink the guesthouse, which he did in 1948 in a set of drawings that proposed doubling the capacity of the carport. The new solution had an unhappy resemblance to the Pennsylvania Turnpike tollbooths at Donegal.

Still, the guesthouse scheme of 1948 is instructive, and not only because it shows how bad Wright could be when he was not resisted by a tough client. The scheme documents that Wright conceived of Fallingwater as one of those radical houses like Neutra's Lovell house, Mies's Tugendhat house, or Lloyd Wright's Derby house in Los Angeles that are entered from the top. With Shady Lane blocked and the guesthouse reconfigured, Fallingwater's guests would have approached the guesthouse by a secondary road along the crown of the hillside, freshened up in their rooms, then walked down the hill and over the expanded dining

THE RENAISSANCE PRINCE IN WINTER • 329

room into Fallingwater. But either wiser heads or benign inertia prevailed, and Fallingwater escaped these disfigurements.

What are the chances that the same person would build two of the most important houses of the twentieth century? This is what came to pass a decade after Fallingwater, when E. J. got Richard Neutra to build the Kaufmann house (publicized as the "Desert House" to appease a furious Wright) in Palm Springs, California.

Kaufmann Jr. derided this house as both second-rate and traitorous to Wright, but a neutral observer would probably say that E. J.'s achievement as patron was actually more demanding at Palm Springs than at Bear Run. To get Fallingwater, E. J. had only to remind a brilliant architect where his anchor lay. To get the Palm Springs house, Kaufmann had to urge something brilliant from an architect who until then had produced only one outstanding work—the Lovell house of twenty years before.

Kaufmann Jr. upbraided his father for bolting from Wright to Neutra as another instance of E. J.'s inconstancy of taste. Had E. J. understood the profundity of Wright's philosophy of organic architecture, Junior's argument goes, he could never have deserted him for the slick Neutra. That argument works well so long as you know Desert House only from photographs. When you go through it in person, you see at once that it is a supreme achievement of technology raised to high art. Desert House is a dwelling of such clarity and even spirituality that one of the few other designers in America who might have matched it was Wright himself.

There are numerous features in the Kaufmann house in Palm Springs that seem to replay Fallingwater. The roll-back open corners (the walls are on rollers) of the living room and master bedroom amplify the flip-back open-corner windows in E. J.'s bedroom at Fallingwater. The pinwheel-shaped plan in Palm Springs further abstracts the implied pinwheel of Fallingwater. And when Neutra broached his antiorganic credo for the house, how could he have formulated it except in respectful opposition to the organic credo of Frank Lloyd Wright? "The house cannot of course be rooted in a soil," declares Neutra. "It is, frankly, an artifact, a construction . . . not grown there or rooted there, the building nevertheless fuses with its setting, partakes in its events, emphasizes its character."

More eerie still is the voice of E. J. Kaufmann egging on his architect, as it comes across in his scores of letters kept among the Neutra papers at UCLA. The voice is more brusque than any E. J. dared use with Wright a decade earlier, but Kaufmann must have felt he needed to use such a voice if Neutra were to achieve the Zen-like perfection of the house. Kaufmann's observations to Neutra generally made sense. True, he comes across as more meddlesome than he was at Fallingwater, but he was on vacation now, and would never again have serious business concerns to address. Architecture had become his full-time avocation.

Nonetheless, it would be inaccurate to think that Kaufmann involved himself in Neutra's design just as a diversion. The hundreds of tiny details in which E. J. interested himself manifestly raised the quality of the house. His obsession with shipping toilets, countertops, doors, and even nails from Pittsburgh (did he think California lacked such things?) can be understood as a tactic for wresting control of the building away from the architect. No more power-sharing for E. J. Kaufmann. Had he botched it, E. J. would have looked like the busybody William Randolph Hearst up the coast at San Simeon. But he did not botch it. Kaufmann in Palm Springs showed himself to be an alert pupil of Frank Lloyd Wright's.

Both Wright and Junior felt that Kaufmann chose Neutra specifically to wound Wright, but this is unlikely, since meanness was not part of E. J.'s character. Nor would he have picked Neutra unless he saw high potential in him: E. J. never hired suppliers of second-rate goods. But it did not hurt that Neutra's architecture was associated with the glamour of Hollywood. Neutra's clients were in general more glittering than Wright's, whether it was John Nicholas Brown or the famed director Josef von Sternberg. E. J. hired Neutra for the house in 1944 (after a meeting in Washington, D.C., perhaps). The house was designed in 1945, built in 1946, and publicized from 1947 to 1949.

It is relevant that the International Style first appeared in Palm Springs in Neutra's 1937 "desert house" for the St. Louis retail heiress Grace Miller. The Miller house was much publicized, including an appearance in one of *Fortune* magazine's early ventures into architecture. It still stands on Indian Canyon Drive, not far north of the site E. J. chose for his house. Palm Springs was so tiny in those days that Kaufmann of a certainty knew the Miller house firsthand (it was close to the Mirador, where he lodged), and he may have known Miller herself as part of the retailing aristocracy. E. J., meanwhile, was getting a taste of International Style himself: for some years he rented one of Albert Frey's Villa Hermosa apartments in downtown Palm Springs.

Kaufmann's Desert House cost him nearly half a million 1940s dollars, three times what he paid for Fallingwater, because it was intended from the first to be leading-edge. Neutra and not Wright was the man to build it, because Germans were no longer the enemy, and Kaufmann calculated that the Bauhaus style had a great future in postwar America. In this he was correct: Wright produced fine work in the 1950s in the Beth Sholom, Guggenheim, and Marin County complexes, and he had continuing impact on residential design, but in terms of influence, Mies was to become the dominant architect of the United States.

Losing the commission for Palm Springs to Neutra was hugely painful for Wright, who was not shy about reminding E. J. about it. He taunted Kaufmann by letter on January 23, 1950: "I went to work with you in high hope of making (with your help *as it used to exist before Palm Springs*) [italics mine] something really great for the Pittsburgh people. . . ." Most galling to Wright was the way Kaufmann publicized his showpiece home. Palm Springs would have immortalized E. J. as a patron of architecture had he built nothing else.

Now let us set architectural politics aside and look at the house, which by any standard is remarkable. It begins with the setting at 470 West Vista Chino, where at that time the street dead-ended. Even with the street cut through today, this is clearly the fringe of town, at the edge both of the desert and of the San Jacinto Mountains. The physical envelope of the house is surreal, both mimicking its environment and standing clear of it. The Kaufmann house is as flat as the desert around it, but its second-story "gloriette," or loggia, rises serenely over the living room in clear emulation of its mountain backdrop. The raised gloriette is perfect for catching evening breezes, and also restates a specific local precedent, since more than a few of the early Palm Springs homes had one.

Then there is the question of the relationship of architecture to nature, a theme done to death by the Taliesin acolytes. Actually, it is the Kaufmann house in Palm Springs, more than Fallingwater, that captures the sensation of living in an indoor-outdoor experience. The exquisitely proportioned gloriette and the "outdoor dining room" on the patio have walls made of aluminum louvers that alternately admit the sun and breezes or keep them at bay. The gloriette has only two walls, which mimic the "wall" of San Jacinto behind it: there is no wall whatever to spoil or mask the view east over Palm Springs and the desert. Most ingenious of all, the gloriette is equipped with a full roof, chaises longues with snugly blankets, and every technical convenience: a full fireplace, a sink, a dumbwaiter for food and drink, and a button to summon the servants. It suggests nothing so much as a sumptuous British picnic in colonial India, or the elegant picnicking in which Wright himself indulged at his own desert outpost.

The Kaufmann house may appear cold and mechanical in black-and-white views but is in reality colorful, warm, highly textured, and even intimate. Its floors, paneling, and structural accents are in rich wood, and the fireplaces and entrance walls of Utah limestone are as finely crafted as those at Fallingwater. The rooms of the Desert House extend on one level only, apart from the gloriette, so the circulation path is elemental in its simplicity. The apportionment of the house into public rooms, the two guestrooms, and the master bedroom suite (Liliane and E. J. sharing the same bed for once) is achieved with the serenity of a Japanese garden. Fallingwater is Japanese by implication, but Neutra's house is Japanese by emulation, down to its sliding walls, the gravel walkways, and its flawless proportions.

One gets the sense that E. J. kept goading Neutra until he reached a quality he had never achieved before and was never to capture again. You certainly feel Kaufmann's presence in the inspired gadgetry in the house, such as the peephole that shows the servants in the kitchen who is at the front gate. You sense it in the futuristic building technology, too: the banks of aluminum louvers, the radiant heating in the ceilings, and the sliding walls in the living room, dining room, and master bedroom. And you are certain you are in Kaufmann territory when you swing open the all-glass front door, which properly belongs not to a house but to a 1940s shoe store.

E. J. was only Wright's junior collaborator at Fallingwater, but he was much more than that with Neutra. Compare the hedonistic image of the heated pool here (E. J.) to the freezing guesthouse pool at Bear Run (Wright). We can imagine Kaufmann patiently instructing Neutra in such Fallingwater-like touches as the latex rubber cushions, the built-in phonograph, and sheets of glass that here, as at Bear Run, channel directly into the stone walls. Kaufmann's presence emerges ever more strongly in the bulging files on the house at the Neutra archive at UCLA. There, Kaufmann's memos to the architect, to the builders, and to various suppliers run to scores of pages, as he demands specific dimensions, finishes, and colors in the house and its garden. The UCLA papers also replay Fallingwater, with scores of documents showing Kaufmann's loyal retainers Ethel Clinton, Carl Thumm, and Roy Oliver playing the same roles for Palm Springs that they had assumed a decade before at Fallingwater. Even Wright made a grudging contribution. E. J. wheedled a promise of scores of cholla cacti out of Wright, then sent a truck to uproot them from Taliesin West and plant them around his new house, where they flourish still.

. . .

Like Wright, Neutra had not sought E. J. as a collaborator, only as a client. Unlike Wright, he was a man of patience. This we learn from his memo entitled "Edgar Kaufmann: Record of conversations, . . . Augmentations, corrections, modification on main drawings since April 23 1946." The memo goes on for four pages, detailing some eighty changes demanded by Kaufmann. Neutra's thirty-three-page "Index of correspondence" documents a total of six hundred separate changes involving Kaufmann, Neutra, and various contractors and suppliers on the house.

Finally, Neutra snapped. In the following undated memo he left to posterity—but not to E. J., since it was never mailed—is as baneful a howl of protest as any architect has ever expressed:

> I am considered a ranking artist in my profession, but I have not acted with artistic irresponsibility against you, as some of the men whose services you engaged. I have promptly, methodically worked and had my office work under all difficulties and communicated regularly. When I recommended Goggia, I had seen him faithfully make samples for ten days, and I was convinced that he is not a drunkard, nor that my judgment was poor, or my recommendations less sincere or more harm to you than Mr. Rivers recommendation.
>
> My nerves have been exhausted by overwork on your job, which we tried to cover and clearly document by a unique and amazing amount in detailing way over our own red mark. I have found it easy to agree with your good taste and very sensible and to the point wishes, I have found it hard to tolerate sentences and actions as the above cited.

In a second memo, Neutra seeks absolution from Kaufmann "whenever I or my staff have given you a little dissatisfaction or irritation on those five thousand occasions which occurred during a year and more on a wildly confused building market."

E. J. promoted the Palm Springs house with both creativity and an iron fist, until it became the third or fourth most widely publicized modern house in America, after Fallingwater, Mies's Farnsworth house, and Philip Johnson's Glass House. This documentation gives us a reliable indication of what E. J. had done to publicize Fallingwater a decade earlier. We find, for example, that Kaufmann was scheming to publicize his new house well before its completion. He financed the taking of construction photos, as he had at Bear Run, and an aerial flyover, just as he had for La Tourelle. On February 23, 1947, *Time* ran a short teaser about "[Richard Neutra's] desert hideaway for Pittsburgh Millionaire Edgar J. Kaufmann, whose famed house in Bear Run, Pa.—designed by Wright—

overhangs a waterfall." That same month Neutra telegraphed the editor of *Architectural Forum,* asking for details of what *Forum* needed in order to properly publish the Palm Springs house.

Kaufmann, displeased at Neutra's modest initiative, set the leash around his neck still tighter. Within a week he telegraphed from Pittsburgh:

> Following telephone conversation so that there can be no misunderstanding it is definitely understood between us that the pictures you had taken during the past week are for your own personal files and not to be released for publication through any media. The young lady who represents House and Garden should be advised by you as she came to the house through your introduction and no article is to be released excepting with my consent. I have notified Albert Kornfeld to this effect. Will you kindly acknowledge this telegram as a matter of record. E J Kaufmann.

Neutra got the point, and abjectly responded the same day:

> Wire received. Your intentions concerning publicity I believe fully understood and followed. All applying periodicals referred to you. Can you approve desk cabinet blueprints. Regards.

This telegram Neutra sent also to photographer Julius Shulman, with a complete set of instructions on how to shoot the house at dusk, with suggestions for the complex lighting that Shulman achieved in his famous photograph about a week later.

By now the architecture world was abuzz about the newest Kaufmann house. Neutra reported back to Kaufmann in early March 1947:

> Now, you realize that I have been accosted, it seems by everyone—all magazines etc. who want to talk about your "desert hideout," which becomes less of it, the more people come to see it. I have told all and everyone of these people, editors, reporters, photographers, clients of mine etc. that you and Mrs. Kaufmann are pacifists: that is, out for peace, and publicity is not interesting to you. Whenever I could collect myself, I have tried to do the talking to them in a courteous and friendly way, sometimes I have briefly to admit that I am too tired, at the moment, to be best mannered.

Shulman had already shot the Kaufmann house several times, without satisfying either Neutra or Kaufmann. Now he prepared to photograph the building again. Dione Neutra thought the news of sufficient import that she telegraphed Kaufmann, who immediately flew to Palm

Springs to be there. Shulman and Neutra trudged around the house for three whole days, Neutra terrified to impose any more on the Kaufmanns' privacy, Shulman certain the Pittsburghers would cooperate a little longer for the sake of the perfect shot.

The crowning glory came at dusk of the third day. Shulman took three separate time exposures during a frantic forty-five minutes, while he, E. J., and Neutra ran about the house, turning lights on and off so that both the house and its natural setting glow with surrealist energy. Shulman explained to me that Liliane lay statuelike by the pool to shade his lens from the glint of the harsh pool lights. The only thing not in Shulman's control was one of Liliane's dachshunds, who left puddles of water after he or she emerged from a jump in the pool. Shulman's photograph became hardly less famous an icon of modern architecture than Bill Hedrich's indelibly etched image of Fallingwater. The two photographs are often spoken of together as the most famous views of residential architecture of the twentieth century.

Then came the cold-blooded part of E. J.'s publicity strategy: he sat on Shulman's 125 photographs for two solid years, refusing, with only certain tactical exceptions, to release them to the media until he was satisfied with the expected outcome. An executive memo of March 1947 at Libbey-Owens-Ford, glass supplier to the house, noted that the building looked marvelous in the portfolio already in the hands of *Life*—but Kaufmann refused to allow *Life* to print those views until two more years had passed. The same memorandum makes clear that much of the fame of Neutra's new house stemmed from its link to Fallingwater. "I further understand that Edgar G. [*sic*] Kaufmann is the same party who has the famous home built over a waterfall near Pittsburgh, designed by Frank Lloyd Wright."

Meanwhile, Kaufmann was hedging his bets, acquiring Shulman photographs through Neutra while also paying the Bernard of Hollywood studio to take separate color views. Bruno Bernard specialized in subliminal sex, not in architecture: his New York stringer, for example, was one of the paparazzi who shot the famous photographs of Marilyn Monroe with her skirt flying up over a subway grate, from *The Seven Year Itch*. As with the Monroe photograph, we get a teaser about a personality cult of E. J. Kaufmann that was apparently in the offing. Neutra wrote Bernard of Hollywood on May 29, 1947: "Mr. Kaufmann who approved these pictures has acted as the sponsor for a significant experimentation and a close-up of him at his writing desk would probably enrich the story for readers who will like to know this great and fertile personality." But Kaufmann's strategy for the moment was restricting publicity, not encouraging it. He blocked *Arts and Architecture* from publishing the house, and made *Architectural Forum* wait for its coverage until 1949.

Kaufmann's bluff paid off magnificently. He allowed trial runs of publicity for the house in selected publications, among them a cover article for the *Los Angeles Times Home Magazine* in 1947 (illustrated by their in-house photographer). The first authorized printing of Shulman's twilight photograph took place toward the end of 1947 in *Marg,* a new arts magazine published half a globe away in Bombay. If Kaufmann hoped to escape the wrath of Frank Lloyd Wright by publishing Neutra's house in India, he was out of luck. Wright speedily picked up the *Marg* article, mailed the page with the "Palm Springs extravagance" to Kaufmann Jr., and hectored E. J. about it at once.

When he finally released American publication rights to his Palm Springs house, Kaufmann got heaps of publicity in *Newsweek* and other magazines, but most notable was the coordination among the Time-Life publications. A two-page spread of Julius Shulman's twilight view of the Kaufmann house dominated *Life* for April 11, 1949, in a conscious or

August 1949: Richard Neutra, the second architect on a *Time*
cover, with a second Kaufmann house as background

unconscious replay of Bill Hedrich's two-page spread of Fallingwater in *Architectural Forum*. The Palm Springs house got lavish coverage for a professional audience in the June 1949 *Forum,* and Kaufmann negotiated with *Fortune* for the kind of mention Fallingwater had received five years before. Then *Time* wrapped up the summer with an August 15, 1949, cover story on Richard Neutra. The backdrop to Neutra's cover portrait was his early plan for Kaufmann's house, in explicit replay of Valentino Sarra's use of Fallingwater for *Time*'s cover on Wright eleven years earlier.

With Kaufmann's fourth brilliant commission, after La Tourelle, Fallingwater, and the downtown office, his fame as a patron of the arts waxed exponentially. There are numerous testimonies to this, but two will suffice. Liliane Kaufmann had ordered special dining-room chairs for the Palm Springs house from the famous furniture designers Charles and Ray Eames. The chairs were late in arriving, and Charles Eames wrote Liliane that he had only accepted the commission as thanks for the family's patronage of good architecture and design. Bruce Goff, Frank Lloyd Wright's most talented disciple, wrote Neutra from the School of Architecture at the University of Oklahoma, asking him to plead with E. J. Kaufmann to allow "publication of the house in the desert," since "full documentation of his latest building would greatly benefit all those interested and devoted to the truly progressive phases of design."

Pittsburghers must have been alarmed at the news that E. J. and Liliane were building a home in California. Would they abandon the town where they had made their millions, as Carnegie, Frick, and the younger Mellons had? They need not have worried. Almost from the moment the Palm Springs house was launched, Kaufmann began planning his most spectacular contribution to Pittsburgh, and he was about to drag Frank Lloyd "cheaper to abandon it" Wright back as the man to get the job done.

The only Wright design that Kaufmann had achieved in Pittsburgh was his private office at the store. This wondrous little room was exquisitely paneled in an abstract design by Wright and beautifully furnished with Wright built-ins made at the same time and by the same Milwaukee concern that made all the cabinetry and tables for Fallingwater. Here was a perfect modern response to the kind of study a Renaissance prince would have enjoyed, such as the *studiolo* that survives in the Metropolitan Museum. This marvelous work was dismantled right after E. J. died in 1955. For a few years the office was resurrected in a Pittsburgh bank as the seat of the Edgar J. Kaufmann Charitable Foundation, then in 1973 Kaufmann Jr. gave it to the Victoria and Albert Museum in London.

Wright's 1937 office
for Edgar Kaufmann,
now at the Victoria
and Albert Museum
in London

From that office in the spring of 1946, Kaufmann invited Wright to work with him on several projects that constituted nothing less than a massive rebuilding of downtown Pittsburgh—essentially a replay of what the two men had discussed twelve years before. From 1946 to 1953, E. J. and Wright focused on four projects: the Point Park Civic Center, the Civic Light Opera Arena, a public parking garage for Kaufmann's, and an apartment complex for Pittsburgh's Mt. Washington.

Kaufmann seems to have conceived the Point Park Civic Center in March 1946, and he outlined the work to Wright during a meeting at Bear Run in May. Wright was still in the dark on the lavish architectural commission E. J. had just handed Neutra. He reacted with fury when he learned of it two months later:

> You have offered me a generous job working with you on the rehabilita-
> tion of a portion of Pittsburgh. And it looks like a real work in more than
> one sense. But, E. J., I cannot take you up. Henceforth you will never,
> as a Patron of the Arts, be in a position to help me with one hand and
> hurt me with the other, because I shall never trust my work to you again.

Kaufmann turned Wright's belligerence around in record time, and by the end of 1946 or the beginning of 1947 he had Wright drawing plans for a colossal building at the meeting of Pittsburgh's three rivers—the same Forks of the Ohio that the British and French had struggled to possess two centuries before. The scheme then already emerging from a New York architectural firm was for a set of office towers that would cohabit with a reconstruction of the old British Fort Pitt. Wright ignored these agreed-upon elements and created a counterproposal for a vast concrete megastructure one-fifth of a mile in diameter and a dozen stories high, capacious enough to accommodate a third of the city's citizens either at work or at play.

Wright estimated that his Point project could be built for a quarter of a billion dollars and that it would provide working space for 123,000 employees in government, business, and the arts. On the top deck of the circular ziggurat, and partly buried inside it, would have been a series of gigantic bubble-domed auditoria for sports events, exhibitions, conventions, cinemas, theaters, a zoo, a planetarium, an aviary, and a combined concert hall and opera house. Wright planned parking for thousands of cars at the base of the structure, and a water geyser to shoot out at its top. (The linkage with Wright's ramped Guggenheim Museum was not only conceptual but chronological: the two projects were on the Taliesin drawing boards together.) A car using the helical ramp encircling the building to get to the top and back would have traveled about four miles. An enthralled but horrified executive committee (royally entertained by both Wright and Kaufmann in their respective desert homes) rejected the scheme. The Taliesin archivist Bruce Brooks Pfeiffer later wrote that the Point Park Civic Center died because of anti-Jewish sentiment directed at Kaufmann. This might be true, but had Pfeiffer considered the length of the ramp?

In 1948, Wright roared back with a second scheme, which replaced the megastructure with a high "bastion" tower soaring a thousand feet in

Wright's Kaufmann-funded proposal for a new Pittsburgh civic center, 1947

the air. From this sprang a dreamlike cable-stayed bridge that, bifurcated, leaped over both the Allegheny and Monongahela rivers. This scheme elicited not much less befuddlement than had the first, and died just as quickly. Later Kaufmann egged Wright on to a third scheme on the site, for an open-air amphitheater for Pittsburgh's Civic Light Opera company at the point of the Point. Wright took the bait, but E. J. himself soon tired of the effort, and by mid-1948 the Point Park Civic Center was definitively abandoned.* A pity, because this thrilling structure of concrete, water, and bridges—was it not a kind of Fallingwater replayed on a vaster scale?

The projected Civic Light Opera Arena took a different turn, because the building did get built, but not by Wright. As president of the Civic Light Opera, Kaufmann or his store underwrote its annual deficits of $50,000 and more. The musicals were presented open-air in the University of Pittsburgh's football stadium, but to cope with the annoyance of rain Kaufmann directed Dahlen Ritchey to devise a system that could pull a roof over the audience should it begin to pour. Ritchey invented a fabric-suspension system to meet this challenge, but this visionary scheme was

*Not that Wright stopped nagging Kaufmann about it. As late as April 5, 1951, he wrote E. J.: "Remember what Eiffel Tower did for Paris. Our automobile objective [Wright's shorthand for the Point project] would do ten times as much for Pittsburgh for no more money."

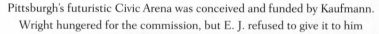

Pittsburgh's futuristic Civic Arena was conceived and funded by Kaufmann. Wright hungered for the commission, but E. J. refused to give it to him

overtaken by Wright's even more visionary Point Park Civic Center, the first and third versions of which contained accommodations specifically for Kaufmann's pet project. In mid-1948, Kaufmann definitively killed Wright's schemes, but he continued to finance Mitchell & Ritchey's plan for the world's first retractable dome, which would open for good weather but close against rain. This was the kind of showy architectural statement E. J. loved. He involved himself in every aspect of its planning, and left $1.5 million in his will for its completion.

Because he had already incorporated an embryonic solution for the Civic Light Opera in several schemes for the Point, Wright contended that Kaufmann had engaged and then dropped him as the Civic Arena architect. Infuriated, he wrote the sharpest of all his letters to E. J., on February 25, 1950:

Dear E. J.:

Now that (against my will and wish and understanding) I am being "paid off" I want to say some things that crowd on my mind.

I realize that we will never build any thing more together which is a genuine sorrow to me for I conceived a love of you quite beyond the ordinary relationship of client and Architect. That love gave you Fallingwater. You will never have anything more in your life like it because you seem to have changed greatly inside since then. There was a fire and courage in you that was trustworthy and could do great things, I felt.

Then you proceeded to waste it like a fool. The reasons for this were many and are not my story. You wouldn't believe me anyway. If you did believe me how would you escape being the child of your circumstances or I of mine. I gave you something I couldn't get back, that's all. I still look upon the efforts I made to give you the best of myself always with pleasure. But you weren't there after that and you aren't there now. What I see isn't good to see—another effect of the kind of culture we try to substitute for real feeling and honest thought—that's all.

Incidentally tell me . . . why, when you offered me ten thousand dollars less one-half my fee for an idea for a garage and I definitely told you I would do it for half or $30,000.00 but not for your figure and you let me go ahead and now send me the ten thousand dollars less than half (as paid by others)—do you feel square with yourself in the circumstances? If you do feel that way, alright.

I doubled on the work I did on the Point Park project at your own request because you were you, Edgar. Both schemes were practicable—buildable stuff—as will be seen someday—away from your advisers. Yes, our effort was wasted for now. But if you want a copy of the night-scene of Scheme II, I'll make for you an exact copy and send it to you to keep—but kindly send back the originals. I doubt if a cent came to me for my work on that project though.

Concerning the garage, I should have known better than to let you go to other architects and experts with the preliminary "bargain sketches." But I finally sent them to you and now will you kindly return these also?

This last scheme was not only buildable but a miracle of design-efficiency but you couldn't see the wood for the trees and you cheated yourself out of that too as you cheated yourself out of sponsoring a great playground for the people at Point Park. Too many adverse advisers either ignorant or insincere—and not sure of yourself.

So here we part with a prayer for your good health. What is life without it? Even money—then—can't make more of it than a bad mess. Money! See Dick Mellon now on the record for what. A philanthropist? Please laugh. And, E. J. I hope I can at least save you from the funny wilted prick [Wright here refers to a curved "mast" shown in certain proposals for the retractable dome at the Civic Arena] you would erect to carry a fluttering umbrella in the gale if ever the umbrella was used—a form of phallic-worship distressing in the extreme with the vulva lying so helpless beneath the poor emblem. I would save you from that caricature as a last service. But probably you have seen it for yourself, by now, anyway.

You are a fool for only short intervals, Edgar—but they will serve in the end.

When you are yourself you are the dearest and sweetest man alive as Lillian and Junior and I well know.

Affection,
Frank Lloyd Wright

Wright's letter ended his participation in the Civic Arena project, naturally enough, except for its afterlife on celluloid in the movie version of *The Fountainhead*. The Civic Arena opened after innumerable delays in 1962, a technical marvel as the pioneer of the retractable-roof dome that has been copied in skydomes a dozen times worldwide. But it was impractical for musical theater, and quickly settled down to hosting hockey games. It also became the object of resentment by the African-American community, thousands of whose members got displaced in its construction by the same Urban Redevelopment Authority that had once counted E. J. Kaufmann as its most prominent member.

Of the many unbuilt projects in the collaboration between Kaufmann and Wright, the parking garage adjacent to Kaufmann's Department Store had the least reason to remain on paper. The money was there, the need was there, and what seems to have been a fully realizable design was there, too. Wright generated $50,000 worth of drawings on the garage

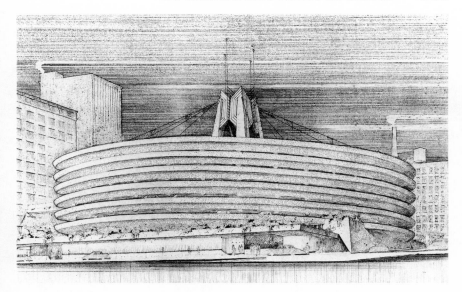

Wright's 1949 garage proposal for Kaufmann's Department Store (*at left*)

project around September 1949. His two slightly varying schemes called for twin interdependent stacks of reinforced-concrete helical ramps; support for the hollow-core structure came from steel cables that hooked to a central pylon. It was a fascinating design, linked both to the Point Park second scheme of 1948 and to Wright's ongoing schemes for the Guggenheim Museum. Then E. J. gave Wright his usual passive-aggressive body check, sending Wright's drawings for a critique by Mitchell & Ritchey— the same upstart firm that had wrested the Civic Arena commission from the old man. Wright shot back:

> Dear E. J.:
>   You are cheating, cheating me yes—but most of all cheating yourself. Cheating yourself out of a great lead along "the appropriate way."

This witty allusion to Kaufmann's adulterous past is followed by a classic six-page Wrightian screed that refuted the various objections to the proposed ramp, then closed with a set of aphorisms, among them the one defining a client as a timid sheep looking for a shepherd. Left unsaid was the fact that E. J. was an equal-opportunity cheater at least, since he simultaneously sent Wright's garage designs for a secret critique by Mitchell & Ritchey and showed Wright Mitchell & Ritchey's preliminary designs for the Civic Arena.

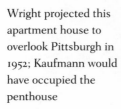

Wright projected this apartment house to overlook Pittsburgh in 1952; Kaufmann would have occupied the penthouse

The garage project limped through 1950 and 1951 but refused to die. By then Kaufmann had full knowledge of Wright's spiral-ramp design that was emerging for the Guggenheim Museum. Its obvious kinship to his garage apparently made E. J. now think of the garage as a museum prototype, and he tried to sell it to the Carnegie Museum of Art in Pittsburgh. In 1954 Kaufmann authorized construction of the conventional garage that still stands next to his store today. This banal structure shares with Wright's vision an identical function and approximately the same footprint—nothing more.

Kaufmann and Wright were not done with each other yet. Their last appointment with architectural destiny was the Point View Residences on Pittsburgh's Mt. Washington, a "mountain" about the height of Nob Hill in San Francisco. Kaufmann started the project in 1951 by paying for an option to build a luxury apartment block at 1000 Grandview Avenue. For Wright, however, the Mt. Washington project started in 1927, not in

Pittsburgh but in Los Angeles, in the stillborn commission for an apartment complex for Elizabeth Noble. He made this connection clear when he dated an early Mt. Washington plan as "1927–1952."

Wright, Kaufmann, and Kaufmann Jr. worked together for two full years on this project until abandoning it. Half a century after it died, the Point View Residences came to life for ten days in a full-scale reconstruction of one apartment unit that went on view at the Pittsburgh Home and Garden Show in March 1999. Three hundred and fifty thousand Pittsburghers—an enormous increase from the usual attendance—flocked to see this might-have-been marvel, which was executed from Wright's original working drawings by Gerald Lee Morosco, a Taliesin apprentice from the mid-1980s. The resurrected apartment showed Wright at his best: rich and crisp, it was so visually thrilling that guards got accustomed to seeing visitors shuffling by in tears.

Now Liliane Kaufmann sought the role of patron. Frank Lloyd Wright was little interested in women clients, and even less in clients' wives, exception made for Mrs. Cheney. He appreciated Liliane's good looks and good taste, but saw her as inconsequential. For her part, Liliane had little interest in architecture or in the male chauvinist architect who had invaded her life. She is supposed to have hated the Cherokee red that Wright demanded for the detailing at Fallingwater, but accepted it as part of the architecture. Her domain was furnishings, and when she clashed with Wright—as we know they did over the dining-room chairs—it was not she but he who retreated.

By the early 1950s, Liliane was declining in health and spirit, particularly when E. J. installed his mistress Grace Stoops at Fallingwater and in Palm Springs. This was the point at which Junior asked Wright for some marital counseling for his parents—a bit farcical, given Wright's poor credentials. Wright had met Stoops, and heard all about the parental imbroglio from Junior, who said of E. J.: "His jellification is due to his loins. He and mother are now separated and the girl (the one who visited you) is going to re-orient his interests, naturally enough." Wright later warned E. J. about the beguilements of sex: "So soon as sex is gratified, again ashes and vain regrets."

Wright tried to make hay from this turmoil by badgering the Kaufmanns to let him build a house in a boulder-strewn lot immediately adjacent to their Neutra-designed home in Palm Springs. You can see the intended site in Palm Springs today, still open and still filled with boulders. E. J. was client of record for Wright's projected "Boulder House" for this lot, but events would prove that it was Liliane who wanted it.

Wright could palaver about marital harmony all he wished, but his prime interest in the house was the chance to get revenge on his ideological enemies. He would turn the boulder field into a minefield, with an organic house that would shame the four International Style houses standing at each corner: the Kaufmann house to the south, the Thomas May/Jack Benny home to the southeast, and two celebrated neo-Bauhaus homes by Albert Frey that stood to the north and west: one for Frey himself, the other for the renowned designer Raymond Loewy. Wright apparently hoped his new house for Liliane would turn Palm Springs into a Waterloo for the International Style.

Wright started designing his Boulder House late in 1950, and soon he sent the Kaufmanns a beautifully rendered elevation and perspective of a globular house that incorporated boulders in its poured-concrete walls, and somewhat resembled a boulder, too. The perspective rendering showed the Neutra house just poking out in the distance. The boulder house had its own swimming pool, which linked directly to Liliane's bedroom by a water gate. Had the design been realized, E. J. and Liliane would have had separate His and Her houses: an indulgence better than anything Stanley Marcus could dangle before postwar America in his Neiman-Marcus catalogues.

"The house for the queen is designed," Wright wrote Liliane on January 15, 1951, when he sent over the drawings. "Boulder house it is. Feminine in essence, broad as the hills in feeling. I will get you out of the nasty nice cliché [the Neutra house next door] with a fine sweep." When the clients failed to bite, Wright ground out three closely identical letters to each of the Kaufmanns in little more than a week. To Edgar Sr. he wrote: "Have the cure here for all your troubles"; to Edgar Jr.: "Have the cure here for all family ills"; to Liliane: "It is no ordinary opus I have worked out but a prescription for genuine Kaufmann unity and happiness—real relief."

At that point the Kaufmanns were at two ends of the continent: Liliane in Pittsburgh, Junior about to sail to Europe from New York, E. J. recuperating from illness at the Biltmore Hotel in Los Angeles. Liliane told Wright she would see him at Taliesin West in March, "and I am sure the plans you have made will be well worth the journey and that I will love them." But when the plans arrived in Pittsburgh, Liliane did not love them, and on April 11 she killed the project with a minimalist telegram:

> Dear Frank I have always considered you infallible.
> This time I think you are wrong nevertheless many thanks for your letter your interest and your affections.

Though the tone of her April 11 put-down would not suggest it, Liliane had asked Wright to provide his architectural services on a different problem just a few weeks before. In a four-page handwritten letter to him from mid-March, she depicted herself as alienated from her homes in Pittsburgh, Bear Run, and Palm Springs. She had arranged to move into a new apartment block in downtown Pittsburgh, she told Wright (probably the now-demolished Plaza, where her brother-in-law Oliver later lived), but she needed him to create a home in the Laurel Highlands that she could call her own.

> I feel sure that by now you will have seen Edgar and will have gathered that the house in Palm Springs will in no sense have anything to do with me and Edgar and I will never share a house. That also means that when he returns I must leave Fallingwater which is a great sorrow to me. Therefore I have spent the last few week-ends motoring about the countryside and I believe I have found a lovely spot in which to build a small house for myself.

Liliane described her chosen location as Beaver Creek. She loved it, she said, because it provided superb trout fishing (one of her passions), and at that particular spot the creek sounded almost like a waterfall. She wanted Wright to visit the site.

Western Pennsylvania has many a Beaver Creek, but I have located the site at which Liliane meant to build, and can confirm that she was in no way exaggerating its attractiveness. The land lies about ten miles southeast of Fallingwater, on the fringe of the Nemacolin Woodlands Resort and Spa, the old Rockwell estate. In the 1970s the Rockwells parceled some of their holdings out to friends for weekend houses, including the lot once selected by Liliane. The lot lacks the bosky atmosphere and the dramatic waterfall on Bear Run, but it is exceptionally lovely. Liliane was quite right about the sound: bedrock protruding from the rushing brook replicates the sounds she was used to hearing from her Fallingwater balcony, only sweeter.

Liliane miscalculated badly in taking her anguish to Wright—not the architect but the human being. With the million-dollar Mt. Washington apartments, the Boulder House for Palm Springs, and the store's parking garage still on the drawing boards as projects Kaufmann promised to fund, Wright would never give offense to E. J. by siding with his wife. Wright ignored Liliane's cry for help, never bothering to answer her. Liliane must have grasped how unimportant she was in his scheme of things when she retaliated by quashing Wright's house of boulders. Beaver Creek was never mentioned again.

.   .   .

Wright would have to contend with Liliane a third time. In the late summer of 1951, Liliane and E. J. reconciled, and among the first to learn of it was the Sage of Taliesin.

> Dear Mr. Wright [wrote Kaufmann Jr. on September 2, 1951]: will you build a place of prayer at Bear Run? All three of us would like a focus of attention for the spiritual reality which we know underlies life and work and the joys we share here.
>
> Nature is the great restorer, concentrated here to balance our city living. The dignity and beauty of your architecture gives us a way of life in and with nature, beyond our best dreams. Mother brings a choice of flowers and foods and comforts, Father brings broad scope of action and activities, and I some ideas and music; all this combines into a rich life for which we are grateful and humbly so.
>
> Yet black storm clouds clash around us, often within us, born of wrongs, blindness and sin that bind the world and with which we bind ourselves. We know that only by special efforts of will can we be restored from these stormy depths to peace and well-being, even here among many blessings. For this we would like a spot set aside . . . [for] an oratory private in scale and carried out with perfection.

This letter brought forth eight drawings by Wright and his staff for two separate versions of a "Rhododendron Chapel" over the next year. The site was the same hillside on which Fallingwater stands, but a few hundred yards upstream. In both form and chronology the chapel falls halfway between the much-lauded Unitarian Church that Wright had just finished in Madison and the Beth Sholom Synagogue he would construct on the outskirts of Philadelphia in 1954. The half-glazed and tented

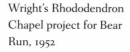

Wright's Rhododendron Chapel project for Bear Run, 1952

shape of the proposed chapel-oratory also recalled the aborted 1926 Steel Cathedral for New York.

For a small building, the Rhododendron Chapel has generated a disproportionately large amount of nonsense, beginning with speculation that the project was somehow meant to punish E. J. On the contrary, Junior specified to Wright that his father was supportive of the project, and an autograph note by Wright on one drawing entirely ignores the wife and son and offers the building to E. J. alone: "Rhododendron Chapel / 'Private to the Beauty of Thought' / (Temple of poetry / for EJ Kaufmann)," it says. As always, it was Kaufmann and no one else who played "Mr. Moneybags" opposite Wright in the chapel drama. Still, in light of the Boulder House and the Beaver Creek home that Liliane had sought for herself, it is reasonable to think that she was the driving force behind the chapel. Certainly, Junior's allusions to "black storm clouds . . . wrongs . . . blindness . . . sin . . . stormy depths . . . peace . . . well-being . . . [and] blessings" were words not much employed by E. J.

Speculation still envelops the chapel project today because it immediately preceded Liliane's death (which is true but irrelevant) and because of gossip that she needed a chapel after she converted to Roman Catholicism, which is simply untrue. This speculative fever in any case ignores a key passage in Junior's letter, which makes it clear that the family wanted the chapel not for themselves but for future generations of visitors to Fallingwater, who would discover "that the artists and people of our times wanted the special music of spiritual renewal as well as all the other joys provided here."

Visibly depressed after forty years in a stressful marriage, Liliane sought psychiatric help in New York. She fell unconscious at Fallingwater on Sunday, September 7, 1952; E. J. drove her to Mercy Hospital in Pittsburgh, where she died. Her burial was in Rodef Shalom Temple's cemetery near Pittsburgh, with a preceding memorial service in the couple's apartment in the William Penn Hotel. Liliane was propped up on a chaise longue, as though she were bidding guests a final adieu. E. J.'s mistress, Grace Stoops, served as hostess.

Liliane's death was front-page news in every Pittsburgh daily. The Allegheny County coroner's report was specific on both the cause of death (the sleeping pill Seconal) and the place of death, but gossip persists on both counts. Rumor holds that Liliane died by suicide, though the certifying physician, Lawrence Wechsler—for years the doctor at the Kaufmann store—told his family and associates nothing that would lend credibility to such hearsay. Seconal was a widely prescribed sleeping pill in the 1950s, but it is rarely recommended today because it lasts so long in the body and turns highly dangerous if mixed with alcohol. The likelihood is that Liliane took a drink while traces of Seconal were still in her bloodstream. E. J. was by all accounts grief-stricken at Liliane's death, and he commemorated her by building the Liliane S. Kaufmann Wing at Montefiore Hospital. At Kaufmann's Department Store, Liliane's Vendôme boutique survived her death by almost half a century, but is gone now.

In general, little remains of the Kaufmanns at Kaufmann's today. Except for the old downtown block, the sixty Kaufmann stores all stand in suburban malls. In 2002, Kaufmann's lost its independent status within the May Company: now it is a general manager and not a chain president who lords it over downtown Pittsburgh from the corner where E. J. used to preside. Benno Janssen's glittering Art Deco ground floor survived E. J. by less than half a year: the murals were ripped out, the ceiling lowered, the black carrara glass piers turned into ordinary mirrors.

E. J. waited two years to marry Grace Stoops, despite that young woman's aspirations to begin gold-digging at once. Kaufmann was dead (apparently of bone cancer) seven months after the marriage, a chronology the family always found too convenient to have been coincidental. After Stoops engaged in protracted legal battles with Kaufmann Jr. and the Kaufmann Charitable Trust, a contemptuous judge allowed her to snatch no more than the Palm Springs house and several hundred thousand dollars from the estate. She incinerated herself smoking in bed a few years later.

E. J. Kaufmann at Fallingwater in 1953 with his mistress, Grace Stoops, later his second wife

Wright did some gold-digging on his own after Liliane died. She was not buried a week when he preyed on Junior's grief with a push to build the failed Rhododendron Chapel as her memorial. "Your mother needs no sympathy. She shines the brighter now that she no longer suffers." Wright made the same pitch on the same day in a letter to E. J. Four days later Wright rescinded the chapel proposal in a curt note to Junior. He did the same thing the next month with Senior, both times without apology.

Today it is a tomb rather than a chapel that stands on the hillside upstream from Fallingwater. We would normally be affronted by the presence of death in a place once so alive with boisterousness, and yet it seems natural here, perhaps because Fallingwater itself seems hardly to age at all.

The tomb is one of death's more lovely shrines. A stone and earth-colored stucco mausoleum, it is reached by its own bridge over Bear Run. The design was the work of A. E. Vitaro, the Kaufmann store architect, but it followed an earlier concept fixed on paper by Edgar Kaufmann Jr. The tomb was Junior's one memorable architectural design, but it was more than that: it was an act of filial piety toward his mother and of reconciliation with his father.

The Kaufmanns put high emphasis on their tombs: the will that Liliane and E. J.'s uncle Henry Kaufmann drew up in 1941 left a perpetual endowment for fresh flowers on the family graves, and E. J. was no less attentive in caring for his parents' graves in Rodef Shalom Cemetery. It may have been just coincidence that E. J. started building Liliane's tomb in the summer of 1953, right before the first anniversary of her death, but I do not think so. For Jews the yearly commemoration of a death (*Yahrzeit,* in Yiddish) carries such weight that not even the freethinking E. J. could have escaped its gravitational pull. The first Yahrzeit imposes a specific architectural responsibility on the survivors: this is the moment—not right after the burial—when they are obliged to put up a tombstone.

E. J. threw himself into all the details of the tomb, including its hookups for steam heat and electricity. He had done this so many times for other projects, but it must have felt odd readying a building that he himself would soon enter. Liliane was reburied when the tomb was ready, in 1954, but the memorial lacked one key element—the bronze doors by Alberto Giacometti. When these arrived in 1957, they proved so heavy that a team of men needed a week to inch them into place.

Today we can see that the efforts of Edgar Sr. and Jr. are crowned with success; the tomb ranks with the best of the Kaufmann buildings. Giacometti's doors are greatly moving: two figures of indeterminate gender, but one a little more perceptibly male and the other a little more perceptibly female, gaze at each other in profound silence, at peace in a private Eden.

That the tomb resembles a little house cannot be an accident, since ancient peoples like the Etruscans also built their tombs and cinerary urns in the shape of houses. In this case the reference is specific to Fallingwater: the tomb's stucco walls are colored to match Fallingwater's balconies, and its oversailing roof imitates the house, too. Particularly moving is the entrance passage before the tomb, banked left and right with masonry retaining walls that long ago got encrusted in moss, and flagstone flooring and steps that recall the floors and steps at Fallingwater. Here Liliane would sleep forever in an eternal Kaufmann house.

It would not be long before E. J. entered that tomb. By the early 1950s he was in steep physical and mental decline. Dahlen Ritchey was shocked to see Kaufmann handling an elevation drawing for the Civic Arena and mistaking it for a plan. Locally, Kaufmann turned his civic responsibilities over to his brother Oliver and to I. D. Wolf. On the national and international scene, the Kaufmann most closely identified with Frank Lloyd Wright was no longer he but Edgar Jr. Then in 1951 Arthur C. Kaufmann, a first cousin of Liliane's and a second cousin once removed to E. J., came from nowhere to mount a lavish exhibit on Wright. Arthur, also Pittsburgh-born, had taken over Gimbel Brothers in Philadelphia, and now had the resources to launch "Frank Lloyd Wright: Sixty Years of Living Architecture," a scintillating exhibit of Wright's work that toured American, European, and Asian cities for years. The European opening was in the Strozzi Palace in Florence and marked the precise moment when Italian intellectuals began to admit that there might be something more to American culture than hot dogs. "Sixty Years" was probably second only to Fallingwater itself in exalting Wright's standing worldwide.

Wright, no slouch at transferring loyalties, loved having this new patron. He could not flatter and fawn enough over Arthur, and the two men worked on offering the public a "coordinated line of [Taliesin-brand] furniture, drapery fabrics and wallpaper," which would be publicized through the Gimbel Brothers stores and in *House Beautiful*—exactly the kind of tie-in that E. J. and Junior had discussed with Wright decades before. Naturally, Wright fawned as well over Arthur's wise and witty wife Dorothy. Already in July 1951 the mail from Taliesin brought Mrs. Kaufmann that supreme seduction gift—her very own Wright-inscribed Japanese woodblock print.

. . .

As he moved toward death, E. J. Kaufmann hadn't much free time to prop up Wright the showman: his preoccupation was double-checking Wright the engineer, for Fallingwater was in serious trouble again. Careful annual measurement of the deflection in the cantilevers showed Kaufmann that they were now sinking alarmingly. He sent engineers to measure the elevations at thirty-two different points, then informed Wright of their findings. The sinking was "very noticeable when one looks at the house." The two-inch deflection in the trellis was obvious even to the untutored eye, and some doors in the living room had buckled so badly that workers had to grind them down to get them open. E. J. also demanded a permanent cure from Wright for the chronic droop in the overhang above the guest-balcony, which began falling down in earnest during the summer of 1954. Kaufmann's characteristic solution was to make a direct appeal to Mendel Glickman, the man who had laid out Fallingwater's structural system two decades before. Still smarting from the imbroglio over the cantilevers, Glickman had never set eyes on Fallingwater. Now he did, and he promptly advised both Kaufmann and Wright how to rebuild the overhanging concrete roof slab that had failed.

In the fall of 1954 a flood rushed through the Bear Run valley, carrying debris down the stream at astounding speed. The suspended stairs that came down from the living-room hatch acted as a scoop that reached down into the swelling waters. Kaufmann wrote Wright for advice in mending the stairs, which he thereupon anchored into the streambed.

This was Kaufmann's last engagement in architecture. He died in his sleep in the Palm Springs house in the early morning of April 15, 1955. His timing was excellent, as usual, since just days later the world was distracted by the death of Albert Einstein; had Einstein died a bit earlier, there might have been no space in the national media for E. J. Kaufmann. Pittsburgh, on the other hand, took the two nearly simultaneous deaths as a token that both Einstein and E. J. had been men of genius. True or not, a story immediately got around that Wright was the last person to visit Kaufmann at his deathbed—another attempt to link men of genius.

The Pittsburgh newspapers could not fill their pages with enough tributes to E. J., and the service at Rodef Shalom Temple a few days later had all the trappings of a state funeral. The photographer W. Eugene Smith included a shot of the pallbearers among the 17,000 negatives he took of Pittsburgh that year. Immortalizing the rites was appropriate but bittersweet for Smith: he had been hired by the photojournalist Stefan Lorant, who in turn had been summoned to Pittsburgh by E. J. to create a huge book on the city. Smith and Kaufmann never met: his view of

E. J. Kaufmann's
funeral at Rodef
Shalom Temple,
April 1955: a farewell
by photographer
W. Eugene Smith

mourners pouring out of Rodef Shalom was the closest he ever got to E. J. The night before the service, Earl Friend gathered some of the farmhands from Bear Run, and together they drove to Pittsburgh to pay respects to the boss. Tears well up in his eyes and his voice breaks as he tells me this, forty-four years later.

Art has its price. So long as ordinary wooden doors covered the entrance to the tomb, E. J.'s secretary Ethel Clinton visited inside with him once or twice a month, reading psalms, singing hymns, or just talking to him. When the Giacometti doors were installed, Clinty had not the strength to open them, and her sojourns stopped. By now tourists were coming to Fallingwater in some numbers, and they wanted to see the tomb, too. In response, Junior directed the grounds crew to stop tending the trees and bushes around it, and the tomb retreated into nature. No matter: it is the legacy of Liliane and E. J. that we treasure, not their tomb.

Opposite: Edgar Kaufmann Jr. in his New York apartment, 1980s

TWELVE

EDGAR KAUFMANN JR., TRUE LORD OF FALLINGWATER

More than anyone else except, of course, Frank Lloyd Wright,
Edgar Kaufmann Jr. was responsible for Fallingwater.

—NEW YORK TIMES, 1989

A book on Fallingwater has to end with Professor Edgar Kaufmann Jr. as surely as it must start with Frank Lloyd Wright. Edgar Kaufmann (except as an author, he dropped "Jr." the day his father died, and from here on so will I) not only inherited Fallingwater: for a quarter of a century he shaped its image by educating the public about Wright and his parents' house through his books and through the creation of an educational environment at Bear Run. At considerable cost to purse and person he protected Fallingwater during a series of mishaps, including the flood of 1956 that swept tons of debris from Bear Run into the house. His choice of the Western Pennsylvania Conservancy to maintain the house and its nearly 2,000 acres of woods has proved successful beyond all expectations. In the long run, no one—not his father, not his mother, not even Wright—bound his life more tightly to the house than he.

Preserving Fallingwater was no simple matter: consider that one-fifth of Wright's buildings have already been destroyed. The most technically complex and geographically remote of all of Wright's major creations could easily have gone that route, too. Look at the fate of the three acclaimed California houses that preceded Fallingwater: Rudolf Schindler's Wolfe house on Catalina Island was pulled down in the summer of 2001 by a new owner who wanted something different. The two houses that Neutra and Schindler built for the Lovells in and near Los Angeles survive in adequate condition today, but hardly anyone gets in to see them. On the East Coast, John Nicholas Brown got weary of maintaining Neutra's Windshield and gave the house away. Untended, it burned to the ground in 1973.

It was clever of Ralph Waldo Emerson to say "No great man ever had a great son," but for the Kaufmanns the aphorism is not a perfect fit. We should say of them rather, "No great man ever had a son who was great in the same way." The two Edgar Kaufmanns were impressive in different ways. E. J. put a monetary value on everything, fitting Wright's nickname of "Mr. Moneybags." At times crude but always decisive and brilliant, he was contemptuous of what the world thought of him. The scholarly and arcane Edgar made his mark as an important American aesthete of the twentieth century. As intelligent as his father but contemplative where E. J. was not, he was much concerned with what people thought of him. History provides any number of businessmen who fathered aesthetes: one of the owners of Filene's Department Store in Boston, for example, fathered the dance patron Lincoln Kirstein. Journalists have drawn a parallel between the Kaufmanns and the industrialist Sam Bronfman and his architect daughter Phyllis Lambert, but this parallel is both flawed and mischievous, as we will see. More relevant is the first Benjamin D'Israeli, the hustling Italian-Jewish immigrant who made a fortune in commerce when he got to England, then watched in dismay as his son Isaac (father to the future prime minister) dedicated his whole life to English literary criticism. Since there is no obligation to choose between them, we ought to have the subtlety to discern the glory of both Kaufmann father and son.

We might be inclined to apply the term "singular" to a man who both inherited Fallingwater and rejected ownership of one of the most profitable stores in America; in botanical terms, *sui generis*. But it does not help our understanding of Edgar Kaufmann to imagine him as somehow unique. Moreover, it would not be true, for Edgar bore a striking resemblance to certain other Pittsburghers of his generation.

In the years 1955 to 1963, when Edgar was sole owner of Fallingwater, another expatriate Pittsburgher also lived in New York while keeping up a famous family home in western Pennsylvania. We may think it fantastic of Edgar to have ordered his servants to keep Fallingwater perpetually ready in case of a surprise visit, with lights on, heat turned up full blast, and packed with flowers from his private greenhouse. But Edgar was only following the model of the other expatriate, Helen Clay Frick, who for sixty-four years kept her father's Clayton in the same state of readiness, silver polished every day and table set every night. Helen designated Clayton as her legal residence; Edgar designated Fallingwater as his. Every year she returned from New York to vote in Allegheny County; he voted every year in Fayette County. Frick made her way back to Pittsburgh to die in her mansion, while Kaufmann gave his away; but the lordly manner in which they maintained their homes and transformed them into house-museums was otherwise identical. Even their mode of travel was the same: embark by train at Manhattan's old Pennsylvania Station (though Frick sometimes had her chauffeur drive her straight across Pennsylvania) and debark into a limousine at the other end: Kaufmann at Greensburg, Frick a half-hour later in Pittsburgh.*

Let's hope they rarely met, because apart from the servant problem, junior Frick and junior Kaufmann had little to say to each other. But Edgar

---

*Everyone in New York society knew about Helen Frick's spaniel and his "Pittsburgh" trick. Frick would tell the dog that they were staying in New York (she had an apartment on top of the Frick Art Reference Library as well as an estate in Westchester County), and it would play dead. Then she'd say they were off to Pittsburgh, and the spaniel would yelp with delight. To the best of my knowledge, Edgar owned no dog.

did fit comfortably into a clique of eight other Pittsburghers, all born in the late nineteenth or early twentieth century and all fleeing the family business for national or international distinction in cultural life and public service. The older men in the group were Walter Arensberg (1878–1954), America's first important collector of radical modern art; Duncan Phillips (1886–1966), who assembled a museum of stunning post-Impressionist canvases; the paleontologist and naturalist Childs Frick (Henry's son: 1883–1965); and the poet Robinson Jeffers (1887–1962). Somewhat younger were the art collector Paul Mellon (A. W.'s son: 1907–99) and John Walker III (1906–95), the man who shaped A. W.'s gifts into the National Gallery of Art in Washington. The most artistic of the group was James Laughlin IV (1914–97), who in 1936 founded *New Directions,* a key magazine and publishing house for literary modernism. The most unusual was a living saint: Edgar's old neighbor and exact contemporary, William Larimer Mellon II (1910–89), son of the founder of Gulf Oil. After raising hell at Princeton, Larry Mellon went to medical school and spent half his life and the whole of his inheritance tending the sick in Haiti. Pittsburgh would never come any closer to producing a Mother Teresa.

It would be hard to discern a group of rejectionists more productive than these nine young men. Phillips and Laughlin were cousins, and so were the two Mellons, but the others all knew one another socially, too. They had many traits in common: Each threw off the yoke of his family and abandoned smoky old Pittsburgh. Each—except for Laughlin—took years to find his niche in life, and each without exception used his family wealth to further his intellectual interests. Each seems to have found relative or absolute happiness—except for Edgar. Outstanding as a teacher, collector, curator, editor, and writer on architecture and design, Edgar was every bit as accomplished as the eight other rich boys, and he may have been the smartest of the lot. He deserved to be happy, but the man I interviewed for many hours and observed close-up on a dozen occasions seemed a tormented soul.

Were I to guess at Edgar's torments I would name them as his father E. J., his mentor Frank Lloyd Wright, his homosexuality, and his being Jewish. Edgar came to terms with his father and Wright, after their deaths if not before, and his quiet thirty-six-year companionship with the noted industrial designer Paul Mayén resolved the easier of his two outsiderships. What Edgar never seems to have resolved was the question of his Jewishness. There is something people enjoy in watching a clash between a stereotypical rich man—even better if a Jew—and his cultured offspring. Shakespeare wrung it for all it was worth when he invented Shylock and Jessica. Sometimes the stereotype holds true: Nathan de Rothschild supposedly once prefaced his daughter's harp concert by jin-

The two Edgar Kaufmanns around 1917

gling coins in his pocket and declaring that he, too, knew how to make beautiful music. Generally, our hilarity comes at the expense of the ignorant father, but occasionally the figure of fun is the learned aesthete-child. It was said of T. S. Eliot that he hated to watch Goldberg corner the Chicago market in grain futures, but what mortified him utterly was to see Goldberg's son take the school board's gold medal in poetry.

That is just what Edgar Kaufmann was: E. J. Kaufmann's gold-medal-winning son, not in poetry but in aesthetics. What made it ironic was how disconnected Edgar was to Judaism: he made sure Fallingwater was free of anything Jewish because so was his life. Whenever he revisited Pittsburgh he always stayed at the Duquesne Club, and when he revisited Fallingwater, he unfailingly slept at Rolling Rock. Whether by these activities Edgar felt that he had trumped the father who had been barred from these clubs or whether he felt that he had vindicated him, was hard to tell.

Edgar Jonas Kaufmann Jr. was born in Pittsburgh on April 9, 1910, and grew up in the two houses the Kaufmanns rented in Squirrel Hill. As "Kauffie," "Juni," or "Junior," he attended the private Arnold School in Pittsburgh's East End, where a schoolmate recalled him eighty years later as "very sheltered, a complete mama's boy." When he was ten, Kaufmann spent the year 1920–21 traveling with his parents in Europe, with a long stayover in Berlin. In 1924 he transferred to Shady Side Academy—his father's old school—in Fox Chapel, the suburb in which the Kaufmanns were building the first of their three showplace houses.

Surviving letters from Edgar's teenage years show him conscientiously preparing for the life of an aesthete. At sixteen he used his own money to buy the Rembrandt etching now hanging in the servant quarters at Fallingwater. For reasons unclear—estate taxes, perhaps?—E. J. and Liliane registered their half-dozen Old Master paintings of 1926 in Edgar's name. When he turned twenty-five, he sold them back to his father for the fractional but still imposing sum of $45,000.

By the age of seventeen Edgar was an active art collector, for example inquiring of Victor Hammer, the Viennese painter befriended by the family in the 1920s, whether any of his prints or fine-printing books were for sale. Kaufmann also moved to modernism with the acquisition of *Autumn Leaves* by the pioneer American progressive Arthur B. Davies.

In 1927, Kaufmann graduated from Shady Side (technically, he left school one credit short of graduation, he told me). *The Academician*, Shady Side's yearbook, cited him as the "poet and artist" of the graduating class. Edgar was clearly the school aesthete: his peers recorded in some awe that he was the only student there who spoke fluent French and understood Oswald Spengler. But there was a troubled side to the entry also. The epigram from *Hamlet* that accompanied Kaufmann's yearbook photograph warned: "One may smile, and smile, and be a villain."

Kaufmann was uncertain what course to take after high school. The class yearbook declares that he was going to follow his father's footsteps to Yale, but that summer Edgar expressed to Victor Hammer his wish to study painting and master printing with him in Vienna. In the end, he went neither to Yale nor to Vienna but to New York, where he studied painting during the academic year 1927–28. He then enrolled for 1928–29 and perhaps longer at the Kunstgewerbeschule in Vienna. There he explored applied arts—what we call industrial design today—in one of its most innovative centers. The Kunstgewerbeschule and other industrial-design centers in Vienna sold their products in the United States through the Wiener Werkstätte consortium, of which the Kaufmanns were significant financial backers. That may have been what brought Edgar to Vienna in the first place.

In 1929, still living in the city of Freud, Kaufmann corresponded with his old tutor José Alemany, a professor of languages at Carnegie Institute of Technology back in Pittsburgh. Edgar told Alemany that he had fallen

Edgar Kaufmann Jr. preparing
to study applied art in Vienna
around 1928

under the spell of P. D. Ouspensky's 1920 book *Tertium Organum,* which
deals with the problem of the fourth dimension and also invokes
Immanuel Kant. His excitement over Ouspensky was the first sign of
Kaufmann's propensity toward theosophy, in which he retained an interest all his life. Theosophy—"divine wisdom"—is a synthetic cosmology
that draws from all the religions of the world. Edgar's mystic interpretation of earth, air, fire, and water at Bear Run in his 1986 Fallingwater
coffee-table book reflects a theosophist train of thought.

Kaufmann was not the first eighteen-year-old to speculate on cosmology, but his dip into theosophy and the still more obscure discipline of
autopsychography tells us a good deal about his seriousness, precocity,
and budding spirituality. It also prefigures his lifelong attachment to
Frank Lloyd Wright, who knew and was probably influenced by the
theosophist guru Giorgi Ivanovitch Gurdjieff. Gurdjieff had mentored
Olgivanna Lazovich, the third Mrs. Wright, and he was an occasional
presence at Taliesin.

Edgar's broad if unconventional education in Europe culminated in his years with Victor Hammer. This apprenticeship covered the years 1930 through 1933, and took place mainly in Florence, where Hammer had established a fine-printing press called the Stampería del Santuccio. Edgar lived in Hammer's Florentine villa and participated in every aspect of the production of his books and graphic arts. E. J. and Liliane came to visit (the Kaufmann store had a buying office in Palazzo Strozzi), and purchased the various Hammer paintings that are now on view in Lexington, Kentucky, and elsewhere. It was in his villa that Hammer painted his half-nude portrait of Liliane in 1932. Edgar sent a reproduction of Hammer's portrait of his naked mother from Florence back to the United States to share with his old tutor, W. Frank Purdy.

Kaufmann was acquiring language skills as well as art techniques in Europe. His tutors in Pittsburgh had done a thorough job: his command of Spanish was good enough that years later MoMA director Alfred Barr selected Edgar as his interpreter in a grueling trip to buy modern paintings in Cuba and Mexico. To these languages Kaufmann now added fluent German from living in Vienna, and he would use that in the service of MoMA, too, when he crisscrossed postwar Germany to learn the truth about Philip Johnson's Nazi activities. His years in Florence left Edgar proficient enough in Italian that he later translated publications by the writers Bruno Zevi and Giuseppe Samonà into English. Edgar got to polish his literary English in Europe as well. His first publication came out of Florence: the prospectus to Hammer's 1931 edition of John Milton's *Samson Agonistes*. Kaufmann concluded his European years in 1933 with six months in London, where Hammer lived until his return to Austria in 1935.

No matter how long certain people may live, particularly in the case of heroes and Olympic athletes, their biographies invariably focus on just two or three critical years in their lifespans. So it is with Edgar Kaufmann and the years preceding the birth of Fallingwater. As he recounted it a thousand times in his books, on video, in his Columbia University classroom, and in numerous museum talks, when he returned from Europe he followed a friend's recommendation that he read Wright's *Autobiography*. Recognizing the genius of Wright, Kaufmann joined the Taliesin Fellowship and urged his parents to consider Wright as architect for their weekend house. This resulted in the meeting of Wright with the senior Kaufmanns, and the rest was history.

Kaufmann held to this account for decades, even when challenged by the journalist Donald Hoffmann in an exchange of letters between the two men from 1973 to 1977. Edgar had hired Hoffmann, the architecture critic at the *Kansas City Star,* to produce the first scholarly monograph on Fallingwater. Early on, Kaufmann told him: "I read *An Autobiography* in mid 1933. Went to Taliesin that fall. Left when the Broadacres model was trucked to the Radio City Forum the next year." Hoffmann immediately challenged that too-early chronology, since Taliesin recorded Edgar's arrival in 1934, not 1933. Didn't you return to the United States and go to Taliesin in 1934? Hoffmann asked. Edgar accepted this new date a week later ("I regret having misled you"), but in the next line he said that Wright first visited Bear Run in the fall of 1935, which was again wrong by a full year—now a year too late rather than too early. With one critical event displaced to 1933 and another to 1935, Kaufmann seemed to be trying to obliterate the year 1934 altogether.

Hoffmann and Kaufmann corresponded for two more years while the journalist tried to hammer out a reliable chronology. Then, in 1976, Edgar moved back to square one with 1933 as the year he had gone to Taliesin. He wrote Hoffmann:

> 33 Returned to USA for financial reasons, tried to paint in Pgh, expected to continue in NYC. There my friend (a Miss ? Adler, secretary at an art gallery) told me about the Wright autobiography. No sooner read than with my parents blessing I went to see if Wright would accept me. 33–34 Taliesin and Arizona.

This thicket of contradictions ultimately convinced the courtly, studious Hoffmann that Edgar was being manipulative and capricious on the chronology of events leading to the birth of Fallingwater. Hoffmann later confided in me: "Junior was awfully cavalier with the facts and anybody trying to find them out." Frank Lloyd Wright—notorious for what his editor, Frederick Gutheim, called his "systematic falsification" of dates and facts—had taught Edgar well.

Hoffmann eventually assigned 1934 as Edgar's return date from Europe only because he had no way of challenging it, and it seemed to mesh with Kaufmann's insistence that he signed up with Wright immediately on his return from Europe. Kaufmann, who read Hoffmann's drafts with care and made numerous changes, stuck with the fictitious return date of 1934 that Hoffmann had fed him, and used it in everything he published thereafter. In a 1986 newspaper interview, for example, the new version of the "facts" remained constant: "He studied painting in New York, Vienna, Florence, and London, returning to Pittsburgh in mid-1934. He then read Wright's autobiography, recommended by a friend, and for Kaufmann it was something of a turning point." The 1994 video on

Fallingwater replayed the 1982 interview in which Edgar told the same story, as we saw in the Prologue.

It is not difficult to establish that Kaufmann returned from Europe in 1933, not 1934. E. J. and Liliane inserted the following entry in the pages of the *Pittsburgh Jewish Criterion* for Friday, July 28, 1933: "Mr. and Mrs. Edgar Kaufmann of Pasadena Drive, Aspinwall [the old designation for Fox Chapel], are expecting the return home next week of their son, Edgar Kaufmann, Jr., who for the past two years has been abroad, studying in Vienna, Austria, Florence, Italy, and other art centers of Europe."

But it was possible to pinpoint Edgar's return with still greater precision. In 1989 the nonagenarian New York merchant Caroline Wagner recalled for me that she and Edgar occupied adjoining staterooms on board the *SS Champlain* as it crossed the Atlantic from Plymouth, England, to New York in the last week of July 1933. The two dined and talked together nearly every day of the voyage: Wagner was thirty-eight, Junior twenty-three. (Upon my reminding her that Kaufmann's art collection had just sold at Sotheby's for nearly $100 million, Wagner chuckled: "I should have married that young man.") Wagner remembered Liliane's meeting Edgar at the pier.

What struck Wagner in particular was Kaufmann's anxiety at being a Jew in Europe in the year that Hitler took over Germany. Edgar Tafel remembered Kaufmann talking about Hitler also: an important fact, because it makes it unthinkable that Kaufmann would have gone back to Europe after 1933. Edgar made it plain to Wagner that he was back in North America to stay.

So it was Hitler in 1933, not "financial reasons" in 1934, that brought Edgar back to Pittsburgh. This also makes it certain that Edgar did *not* immediately go to study with Wright, but let a year pass first—August 1933 to September 1934. At a distance of forty years, a date or two may shift in one's memory, but Edgar spoke of his role in the origins of Fallingwater as often as other people speak of their summer vacation. It seemed odd of him to cleave to a sequence of dates that made no sense, especially when cross-examined by Hoffmann. At one time he believed (correctly) that he had returned to the U.S. in 1933; now he told everyone 1934. Why?

There are other tales of Kaufmann's *Wanderjahre* in Europe that do not submit so easily to verification. The prominent scarring around Kaufmann's nose and upper lip—one Fallingwater director called it the tragedy of Edgar's life—gave rise to the persistent rumor that he had undergone a botched plastic surgery in Vienna. On occasion, he passed on this tale to his students in New York, and he told Caroline Wagner something similar, but involving France rather than Austria. At other times Kaufmann told friends the prosaic truth: the scarring was a side effect of radiation therapy he had undergone for teenage acne in the 1920s. Left unconfirmed and now probably unconfirmable is the rumor that Kaufmann used his spare time in Vienna to get psychoanalyzed by Sigmund Freud.

Unconfirmable, too, is a story that Edgar applied to join Wright in Taliesin in the summer of 1933 but got no reply for one full year. In any case, where did Kaufmann spend those thirteen months after returning to the United States? One report has him studying painting in Mexico, perhaps in the circle of Diego Rivera; another account has him studying at the famous Black Mountain College, which opened its doors in 1933. (Years later Edgar lectured at Black Mountain, but there is no record of him as a student there.) What is most probable is that he spent the year painting in the studio above the garage in Fox Chapel, which is where Karl Jensen found him, "dappling with painting," in September 1934.

We can understand why Edgar wanted to forget the year 1933–34. Hitler and facial scars were bad enough, but worse was the sex scandal involving his father's cast-off mistress Josephine Bennett Waxman and the repossessed diamond and platinum bracelets, a story that went public right after Edgar returned to Pittsburgh. Half a century later, Kaufmann made a face when telling me how much he hated his father's playing the buffoon.

Kaufmann's ease in suppressing a year of his life can only raise our suspicions about "a Miss ? Adler, secretary at an art gallery" in New York, who changed his life by recommending that Edgar read Wright's *Autobiography*. I can find not a single confirming detail about such a person. Edgar never cited Miss Adler by name in any public utterance, but she was a key part of his litany, beginning with his first publication on Fallingwater. This he wrote for a special issue of the journal *L'Architettura* as a favor to Bruno Zevi, who for half a century was the foremost spokesman for Frank Lloyd Wright in Europe. Zevi meant the August 1962 issue to have international distribution as the first monograph on Fallingwater, which is why it appeared in five languages. It was reprinted with a new layout the next year as a five-language book, *La Casa sulla Cascata di F. Ll. Wright / F. Lloyd Wright's Fallingwater*. The monograph contained two articles: a ponderous theoretical effort by Zevi and a reminiscence on the origins of Fallingwater by Edgar. The color photographs (the first published on the house) were by Kaufmann's partner, Paul Mayén. The 1962 magazine and the 1963 book were both sellouts, and Zevi kept reprinting the latter until (Edgar said) the plates wore out.

In his article in *L'Architettura,* Kaufmann referred to the person who recommended the *Autobiography* to him as his "good friend." English allows one to refer to a woman as a gender-neutral "good friend," but the other European languages do not. When the accompanying Italian translation rendered Kaufmann's "good friend" as *un amico,* it dropped his modifier and switched the gender that he had in mind. The French, German, and Spanish translations followed suit. Had "Adler" been a woman, it is inconceivable that Kaufmann would have allowed such a howler to get into print. But can we be certain he checked the galleys of *L'Architettura* before it went to press? Yes. Lisa Ronchi, the editorial assistant in charge of that issue, specifically recalled to me that she gave Kaufmann the galleys of the entire issue when she met him in 1962. Ronchi even remembered where: near the Colosseum in Rome.

Given a task like checking galley proofs, Edgar was not merely exacting but fastidious. He would have checked the galleys of his article not only in English but also in each of the translations into Italian, French, German, and Spanish—remember, he was not merely fluent but a whiz in those four languages. In seconds he would have rectified *un amico* and the equally wrong *un ami, ein Freund,* and *un amigo* into their correct feminine equivalents—had "Adler" really been a woman.

Suppose Kaufmann sent back revised galleys to Zevi but only after the magazine had gone to press? (I suggest this because of certain typographical errors in his essay, which Edgar must have asked Zevi to correct.) In that case, Kaufmann had a second chance to rectify the *amico/ami/Freund/amigo* error in 1963, when the galleys were reset into book format. This meant that neither economics nor logic justified preserving the gender error, yet it popped up again. To have left "Adler" as a man in four languages a second time was more than strange—it was bizarre. Didn't the woman whose act of kindness changed Edgar's whole life deserve to get her gender recorded right?

More than that, didn't "Adler" deserve to have her first name recorded for posterity? When quizzed by Hoffmann, all that Edgar recalled about this pivotal person in his life was her last name and unmarried status; he was unable or unwilling to come up with her first name. In the 1982 film interview, "Adler" lost her name but kept her feminine gender; in Kaufmann's coffee-table book four years later she lost both.

There must have been many Miss Adlers in New York in 1933 and 1934, but Kaufmann's particular Miss Adler appears at this moment to be fiction. The Adler family that has been active in the New York art market since the 1930s has no record of any corresponding Miss Adler working for their Manhattan gallery, nor for any other. The Weyhe Gallery, which sold Kaufmann both his architecture books and many of his prints through a quarter of a century, assured me that it, too, had never employed nor heard of a Miss Adler. Kaufmann's Miss Adler was perhaps a stand-in for Cornelia Brierly, the Pittsburgh woman who arrived at Taliesin in 1934 just when Kaufmann did. For Brierly, reading the *Autobiography* really had been an epiphany. Or "Adler" was transposed from Edgar's SS *Champlain* tablemate Caroline Wagner, who knew all about Wright and had already stayed at his Imperial Hotel in Tokyo. "Adler" might alternately have been Edgar's cousin Aline Bernstein Saarinen, who mentored him in architecture during the thirties, or she could have been someone in the circle of his painter friends in New York. Possibly, Adler existed but was not a female: was the "good friend" a man? Or, when pressed for details by Hoffmann in 1976, had Edgar simply taken the name Adler out of thin air—or from the arts pages of the *New York Times*?

Besides the problem of the year and the mentor who directed Edgar to Taliesin, there was confusion about his motives. On September 20, 1934, Frank Lloyd Wright wrote his ex-apprentice Philip Holliday that the son of Pittsburgh's "Marshall Field" was coming to Taliesin as a fellow. This reference to E. J. Kaufmann's status makes clear the naked cynicism by which Wright enrolled Edgar at Taliesin as bait to hook his rich father, but note that Wright wrote Holliday five days *before* Edgar came for his inspection tour of Taliesin on September 25. What made Wright so sure the young man would agree to sign up?

The French take seriously *l'art de bien mourir*—the art of dying well—and Edgar Kaufmann showed impeccable timing by dying (of leukemia) in 1989. Not only was the art market nearing the end of a frenzied cycle that would bring extra scores of millions to his estate, but making up false scenarios about Frank Lloyd Wright had recently become much more difficult. In 1988 the Getty Center in Los Angeles sponsored distribution of a massive (4,300 pages in five volumes) guide to the 103,000 letters in the Frank Lloyd Wright archives at Taliesin West. For half a century access to the letters had been grudgingly allowed only to those few researchers with the money and the gumption to try their luck at Taliesin West (at $40 an hour, Robert Twombly sourly remarked in his Wright biography). Donald Hoffmann, for example, had been refused admittance to the Taliesin archives in the 1970s by the dictatorial Olgivanna Wright, despite the fact that he was researching Fallingwater at Edgar's bidding. (Hoffmann was also peeved at Edgar for refusing to intervene: what was Kaufmann's motive for that?) Now 10 cents will get you a copy of any letter to or from Wright that you desire: I acquired several thousand, and flew to the Getty in 2000 to check thousands more.

The cache of letters published by the Getty cleared up many a Fallingwater mystery. They revealed, for example, that the meeting of Kaufmann Sr. and Wright at Taliesin in November 1934 was anything but the casual drop-in that Edgar had always made it seem. They also showed that E. J. was in contact with Wright well ahead of Edgar Jr., and the correspondence between Wright and E. J. revealed that their close emotional bond had nothing whatever to do with Junior. Edgar was mentioned (as "the boy") just once, we will recall, and Wright's secretary Jensen specifically warned Wright against enrolling Edgar at Taliesin until E. J. had been securely roped in as a client.

Jensen's memos constituted by themselves a denial of Edgar's claim that he had led his father to Wright. More remarkably, there is substantial indication that the opposite was true. In the memo to Wright about the business meeting he had just had with the elder Kaufmann in New York, Jensen wrote: "Kaufmann's son was at Taliesin Tuesday. His father wants him to go there ["there" because Jensen was writing from New York]." The reference is ambiguous, but a semiotician would—and the one I consulted did—observe that the phrase conveys not merely approval but preknowledge and volition on the part of the father. Nothing unusual about that: a score of parents beseeched Wright to take on their rudderless sons in the 1930s and 1940s. But it has major implications for Fallingwater if E. J. Kaufmann did not merely watch his son go to Taliesin, but sent him there.

Jensen's confidential memo rings true. Late in life, Edgar portrayed himself as the family rebel, but the fact is that he acquiesced each time his father set him on a career path. One occasion was his apprenticeship with Victor Hammer in Europe, which would not have happened without E. J.'s (and Liliane's) intervention. Going to Taliesin in 1934 was a second such step; joining MoMA without a salary in 1938 was a probable third. Is that why Edgar was so evasive when Hoffmann asked him how he discovered Wright? Everything now suggests that Edgar went to Taliesin not to enlighten his father about modernism but to do his bidding. We can be certain that the son did not direct the father toward Frank Lloyd Wright, and it looks now as if the father directed the son. *Rashomon* indeed!

Such a scenario constitutes a 180-degree turn from what Edgar alleged for decades, but it offers the best explanation for Edgar's missing year, 1933–34. Kaufmann might have spent the year moping at home until an exasperated E. J. sent him to join his new acquaintance, Frank Lloyd Wright. Edgar perhaps created "Miss Adler" because it was too embarrassing to acknowledge that it was his supposedly boneheaded father who first interested him in Wright. We know that at one point Wright sent E. J. a copy of H. T. Wijdeveld's *Frank Lloyd Wright: The Life-Work of the American Architect;* did he send along the *Autobiography* too? This would explain the haziness of Edgar's replies to Hoffmann and his refusal to help get him into the Taliesin archives. If word got out that he had been no more than E. J.'s pawn at Taliesin, it would have wiped out the central achievement of Edgar's life. A pawn could hardly claim to have been responsible for Fallingwater.

Wright was away from Taliesin on Tuesday, September 25, 1934, so Edgar did not get his blessing until a few days later. He joined the Taliesin Fellowship on October 15, but the column that Taliesin published in various Wisconsin newspapers could not wait that long to crow about its catch. It reported on September 27, 1934: "Edgar Kaufmann, also of Pittsburgh [as was the new apprentice Cornelia Brierly], came to see if we lived up to all that he had read about the Fellowship and wound up by signing up for himself and for one of his friends. He has only recently returned from studying painting in Florence and Vienna, so now he is coming here to learn something about it." The person alluded to as "one of [Kaufmann's] friends" never showed up, so we cannot now determine who it was. Possibly it was Edgar's lifelong friend A. James Speyer, who in 1934 was groaning under the Neanderthal architectural instruction at the Carnegie Institute of Technology.

Kaufmann's time at Taliesin began sunny and clear but ended overcast and murky. He stayed about five months, not the usual two to four years (apart from those apprentices who never left). He was gone by March or April 1935. This anomaly would have held only modest interest had Edgar ever explained it, but it grew more strange when he did not. Half a century would pass before Kaufmann spelled out why he left Taliesin so early, and even then his explanation was in code. In his Fallingwater book of 1986, Edgar gave only this tortured and nonsyntactic rationale: "So strong and convincing were Wright's principles that after a while—since I was not attuned to the Fellowship routine—it was time for me to leave."

Many Masks, Brendan Gill's 1987 life of Frank Lloyd Wright, alluded to Kaufmann's abrupt leave-taking from Taliesin, but (Edgar being still alive) Gill offered no explanation for it. Early in 1990, half a year after Edgar died, Gill told me privately that he was certain the cause was Kaufmann's engaging in homosexuality at Taliesin. Gill went public with that view in the March 1990 *Architectural Digest,* and repeated it in a book the next year. Edgar's friends were furious at this breach of confidence. They shunned Gill at Manhattan's Century Club and tried to have him punished elsewhere. They took pleasure in seeing *The New Yorker,* where Gill was an institutional mainstay, drop him (for unrelated reasons, actually) as its architecture critic, and they attempted to persuade *Architectural Digest* never to publish a word of his again.

With Gill's dismaying example before me, I would happily avoid the question of Edgar's leaving Taliesin were it not pertinent to our story. On why Edgar left, we can draw three conclusions of differing probability. There is no question that Wright persecuted Edgar during his stay at Taliesin, and that he eventually hounded Edgar out of the Fellowship. The only element in doubt is whether the cause was homosexuality. On the first point, several apprentices testified how much Wright humiliated Edgar at Taliesin, and all recalled the mocking "Whippoorwill" by which Wright addressed him. On the second point, there is wide agreement that Wright threw Edgar out. "Mr. Wright told him to leave," Edgar Tafel confided in me, and Bob Mosher independently reported the same thing. Wesley Peters and Cornelia Brierly also retained the memory of Edgar's being sent away from Taliesin at Wright's displeasure.

Less clear is Wright's motive for hounding Kaufmann out of paradise. Brierly declined to specify the nature of Edgar's transgression, while Peters called it high jinks and lack of discipline. As Wright's closest disciple, Peters would normally be an impeccable source, but he was not an eyewitness to these events, being in exile from Taliesin while Edgar was there. Eyewitnesses Edgar Tafel and Abe Dombar both recalled speculation that Kaufmann engaged in homosexuality at Taliesin. Dombar regarded the stories as true; Tafel said he had no basis on which to confirm or deny them.

Nonetheless, there exists a near-definitive statement on why Wright threw Edgar out of Taliesin, and it comes from Wright himself. He wrote E. J. in April 1935 that he wanted a face-to-face meeting in which the two men could discuss Edgar Jr.'s departure from Taliesin, including "some matter pertaining to the Junior which I don't care to put on paper." Eight years later he added a passage to his revised *Autobiography* about a few early apprentices he had sent packing from Taliesin because they were lacking in "circumspection," which sounds like a euphemism for sexual discretion. No one disputes that homosexuality was a significant subtheme to life at Taliesin. Wright in 1912 had joined his mistress (who now went by the name Mamah Bouton Borthwick) in editing and publishing an English edition of Ellen Key's book on free love. He probably turned a blind eye to homosexuality early on, but later he became harshly intolerant of it. Edgar Tafel wrote of Wright's suppression of homosexual behavior, then followed it with a story about Wright's visit to a homosexual ex-apprentice who sounds a good deal like Edgar Kaufmann. Homosexuality seems also to have been a verbal cudgel with which Wright beat his apprentice Bruce Goff. Hounded for decades by charges about his personal life, Wright could ill afford a lack of "circumspection" among his apprentices.

This clarification of Edgar's time at Taliesin fills in several odd gaps in the Fallingwater story. It makes clear that Edgar had no role whatsoever in designing Fallingwater—a point on which he had sometimes encouraged speculation. In the 1987 Fallingwater video, for example, a questioner asks Edgar whether he and Wright had clashed over the design of Fallingwater. Rather than replying that he was not present when the Fallingwater design emerged, Kaufmann wittily evades the question in a way that encourages us to take his unspoken no as a yes. The disclosure that Wright either expelled Edgar or hastened his departure from Taliesin deflates young Kaufmann's Fallingwater role even further. Wright would not have dared expel Edgar unless he regarded him as insignificant to the Fallingwater equation. E. J., after all, was Wright's only client in 1935; Wright must have been sure of his bonding with the father when he humiliated the son. How resentful Edgar must have felt toward both E. J. and Wright for the misery he suffered at Taliesin!

Leaving Taliesin in March or April of 1935, Edgar helped with the Broadacre model in New York and in Pittsburgh for a few months, then in mid-1935 he joined the management of the family store. For two years he worked in the bookshop and in home furnishings, then was promoted to merchandise manager. But his focus increasingly shifted to Fallingwater, first in furnishing it, then in showing it at MoMA. From November 1937 on, Edgar busied himself with details of the MoMA exhibition, above all in fulfilling requests by magazines like *Town & Country* for Luke Swank photographs. Just before the show opened, Liliane sailed for Europe and E. J. flew west, which left Edgar as the sole family spokesman in New York. On January 24, 1938, Edgar greeted MoMA's top patrons at an advance showing of Fallingwater, as he reported to Wright:

I found myself explaining away the misconceptions of journalists and journalistes, the latter the worse. The elder mesdames Rockefeller and Guggenheim appeared, asked some shrewd housewifely questions, seemed to appreciate the charm of the house and left. A Mrs. Hay, chairman of the advisory board, was quite enthusiastic. She was young. The total effect is strong and pleasant; I think you'd find it decent, tho'

E. J., Edgar Jr., and Liliane Kaufmann at Fallingwater soon after its completion

not in your manner; and much of the public, warmed up by the publicity in periodicals, will give it some study.

The help Edgar rendered to John McAndrew and his palaver with Abby Aldrich Rockefeller and Olga Guggenheim resulted in his engagement at MoMA as one of McAndrew's unsalaried assistants. His first job was to shepherd the traveling version of MoMA's Fallingwater exhibition as it made its way around the country in 1938, 1939, and 1940.

Edgar at first defined his work at MoMA essentially as advancing Wright's career by playing the unpaid publicist. He tried hard to book the traveling Fallingwater show at the University of Wisconsin at Madison, for example, because Wright was fishing for a major commission there. Three years earlier, Edgar had already foretold such a role for himself when he told Wright: "I am not good material for your real needs; but I hope always to fulfill the less enviable role of sincere, and I trust a little useful, propagandist." Kaufmann would serve for fifty-four years as one of a score of people who played that role.

Edgar broadened the scope of his work when James Laughlin asked him for a roundup of developments in architecture and design for *New Directions*. This laid the groundwork for turning Kaufmann into a tastemaker for modern design, which finally liberated him from E. J.'s shadow. After the *New Directions* piece appeared, Edgar was the subject of a flattering article in the October 27, 1938, *Bulletin Index,* back in Pittsburgh. For the first time in his life people seemed interested in him for himself.

Kaufmann later composed two more articles for *New Directions,* which began the line of 229 articles, catalogues, and books on architecture and design that he would publish over the next half-century. At the suggestion of Alfred Barr, he organized a MoMA exhibit called "Useful Objects," but the museum refused to give him a clear line of authority to promote industrial design, and Edgar returned to Pittsburgh in 1939 as the new secretary of Kaufmann's Department Store.

Buried in the Museum of Modern Art's 1940 *Guide to Modern Architecture in the Northeast* is a glimpse of Edgar's short-lived attempt at becoming a store executive like his father. The entry on modern architecture in Pittsburgh, which Edgar wrote as part of the sponsoring committee for the guide, listed four designs in the city as worth seeing. These were a house by Edgar's fellow apprentice Cornelia Brierly, the new Metzger-Richardson garage for Kaufmann's Department Store, Wright's office for his father in the store, and Edgar's own office there. The two offices are described in the guide as though twins: "Private office for Edgar Kaufmann, Sr., . . . Frank Lloyd Wright, architect, 1936" and "Private office for Edgar Kaufmann, Jr., . . . designed by Edgar Kaufmann, Jr., 1940."

Kaufmann spent from September 1942 through November 1945 as a lieutenant and captain with Fifth Army Air Force intelligence in Australia, New Guinea, and the Philippines. Half a world away from Pennsylvania, Australia knew all about Fallingwater and welcomed Edgar as a minor celebrity. The war over, Edgar renounced a career at the store and moved to Manhattan. He lived well, particularly after Liliane's death brought him a pass-through inheritance of a million dollars from the estate of his grandfather Isaac.

Edgar's second tenure at MoMA lasted from 1947 until 1955—a productive but unhappy time. The atmosphere at MoMA grew thick with suspicion and enmity when Philip Johnson returned to power despite Edgar's attempt to sidetrack him for his Nazi involvement. As brilliant and mercurial rich boys, Johnson and Kaufmann were much alike. Both were high achievers, but Johnson was about to catapult to world fame with his Glass House in Connecticut. Johnson got the department split into two: he took Architecture and Kaufmann got Industrial Design. Johnson's biographer Franz Schulze characterized Kaufmann as Johnson's great enemy at MoMA:

> Philip did encounter a genuinely pugnacious adversary during the early postwar years. He was Edgar Kaufmann, Jr., [Eliot] Noyes's successor in Industrial Design and a man capable of matching Philip insult for insult with a few left over for anyone else in the museum he didn't care for. . . . There was ample room for bile to build up between the two of them. Kaufmann was the one person at the museum, at least in Philip's recall, who not only knew of his political past [as a Nazi sympathizer] but saw no reason to forgive him for it.

In 1950, Kaufmann inaugurated a series of exhibits called "Good Design" that would show for the next five years both at MoMA and in the gargantuan Merchandise Mart in Chicago, which Joseph P. Kennedy had just taken over. Some of the designers were unknowns; others were famous names like Knoll and Herman Miller. After exhibition the items went on sale by special arrangement at the Bloomingdale, Abraham & Straus, and Lord & Taylor stores. They even bore a "Good Design" insignia in imitation of the "Good Housekeeping" stickers that every American in those days could recognize. Kaufmann followed through on the concept by issuing his small book *What Is Modern Design?*

The design shows found an enthusiastic following in a postwar America awash with money but short on confidence in its own taste. But there was grumbling at MoMA that Kaufmann was commercializing the institution. He became vulnerable after the avuncular Alfred Barr was forced out as MoMA director; he never had a close relationship with Barr's successor, René d'Harnoncourt, and at some point his status dropped from salaried to unsalaried (his IRS forms from the early 1950s list no income from MoMA at all). In 1954, Edgar took an extended trip to India to organize a show of textiles and ornamental arts; distressed on his return by another dilution of his authority, he submitted his resignation to d'Harnoncourt. This standard operating procedure had gotten him his way a dozen times before, but now it was accepted, and Edgar's MoMA days were over.

Kaufmann left a significant but unheralded legacy at MoMA. The architecture and design galleries carry no mention of the Kaufmann name today, except indirectly in the costly model of Fallingwater that remains one of the museum's popular artifacts. The galleries constitute the one place at MoMA where you can measure the artistry of ordinary objects, as for example the molded polyester side chair made by the millions from Charles Eames's design of 1950. We could call this true art for the masses, and it represents what E. J., Liliane, and Edgar were trying to achieve in Pittsburgh and Vienna as early as the 1920s.

In the end, the Pittsburgh and New York halves of Kaufmann's life reinforced each other. What Edgar learned from his parents and the store culture in Pittsburgh translated into a keen understanding of how good design could be made available worldwide. Through MoMA and his publications, Edgar sold more merchandise than any other Kaufmann. The only difference is that the clan made millions from selling it, and he did it for free. Literally and figuratively, Edgar gave away the store.

L eaving MoMA, Kaufmann signed up as an art editor for the *Encyclopaedia Britannica*, but the most important job of his life began with E. J.'s death in April 1955, which made Edgar the second lord of Fallingwater. His main task over the next half-dozen years was winding up E. J.'s $10 million estate, which was challenged until 1963 by Grace Stoops. Edgar was forty-five when he inherited Fallingwater. For the remaining thirty-four years of his life, he worked with the house in four separate ways. He administered Bear Run, as his father had before him, including new commissions to Wright; he wrote the first history of Fallingwater; he drew up the protocols for its preservation; and he set its tone as a house-museum.

On paper, Edgar should have been Wright's dream client, having the time, the money, and the erudition to have held up his end of a marvelous collaboration. But the two men produced nothing together beyond some drawings, and their contact betrayed a sourness that was never present when Wright worked with Kaufmann Sr. E. J. had been dead just a month when Edgar stepped into his shoes as a Wright patron. In May of 1955 he tried to get Wright to come to Bear Run for the Memorial Day weekend to explore several new projects. Later that summer Edgar sent Wright a contour map of the entry area at Bear Run: "as you know, I am eager to build a gatehouse there to replace many scattered old buildings that should be torn down, and principally to control access to the main house." The program called for a complex of twelve servant bedrooms, a garage for six cars or trucks, and (eventually) a swimming pool. Kaufmann also asked Wright to strengthen the hatch steps descending into Bear Run. E. J. had anchored the steps into the streambed below; now Edgar and Wright worked to further stabilize the steps with steel columns inserted into the balcony above.

Then Edgar administered to Wright an astonishing insult: he told

Wright to get started on making plans at the standard professional fee of $12 per square foot. Wright had probably not been treated in so cavalier a fashion since moonlighting in house plans in Oak Park seventy years earlier. He kept calm, however, until Edgar weighed in again with these still more galling lines: "If that is satisfactory to you, no one will worry about your ability. If it is not, the project cannot be undertaken between us. Let me know. Fondly and faithfully, Edgar K." No one, certainly not E. J., had ever dared subject Wright to such lèse-majesté. Wright's rebuke arrived the next week:

> Edgar!
> All my life I have been more interested in the birth of the beautiful than in money. And now I do not know how (even owing you for so much) to give you $4,111.57 worth of it. [Wright is sarcastically calculating the job at the stipulated $12 a square foot.] It is too late in my day for me to try now. There are so many young aspirants to fame and fortune who will perform for you and I think you would enjoy working with them as "employer" more than you would with me.
> So (all things considered) why should either of us make the sacrifice? I am not sure you intended to insult me. But so it is.
> A severe pain in the region of the heart goes with this—but affection as ever. It is "built in."
>
> Frank Lloyd Wright

The next year Edgar was successful in dragging a half-dozen drawings out of Wright. These were more curious than lovely, a throwback to Wright's concrete-block houses that E. J. had explored in Los Angeles in the 1930s. Early in 1957, Kaufmann visited with the Wrights at Taliesin West, and he subsequently reconfigured the gatehouse project into a complex involving a caretaker's house, a guesthouse, a parking shed for ten or twelve cars, a workshop, and a drying yard. Wright tried gamely to fulfill this new request with preliminary plans in April and full working drawings in September, but Edgar never executed them. In the end, he put up a utilitarian garage and designed the caretaker's house himself. This commonplace dwelling stands close to Fallingwater today.

Disappointing he may have been as an architectural patron, but Edgar was a first-class manager of the Bear Run estate. His indispensable helper was Ethel Clinton Appel. Clinty had entered the Kaufmann store during World War I, probably as a teenage salesclerk, then served as E. J.'s faithful secretary for thirty years. Now she became overseer of

Bear Run, driving out from Pittsburgh for fortnightly visits and reporting in detail to her new boss in New York. Apart from the few references to mechanized farm equipment, her detailed and lively reports could have been prepared by a majordomo working for George Washington or for Lorenzo de' Medici.

Edgar reorganized the estate in 1955 with a staff of six, plus Clinton in Pittsburgh. By 1961 a staff of three cared for Fallingwater, three more attended to the grounds, three clerical workers managed finances in the office in Pittsburgh, and a dozen part-time laborers farmed in the warm months and logged in the cold months. Even paying part-time salaries of $1 an hour and full-time salaries of about $130 a month, it probably cost Edgar $100,000 a year to run the farm.

History will regard the names of Edgar's employees as unimportant, but I include some here because they provide us with personal details on the way Kaufmann re-created a medieval manor in the middle of the twentieth century. Jesse Hall managed the farm and sawmill, for which Kaufmann gave him a salary, free use of the Merle Taylor house (a dozen cottages from the old Masonic camp survived), and three acres to farm for himself. Hall then split his crops with Kaufmann in the *mezzadria* system known to every medieval serf. George Green supervised landscaping and managed the grounds around the house. The store architect, A. E. Vitaro, had designed a fine house for Green on the banks of Bear Run, where Fallingwater's financial staff works today. Ralph Miner ran the management of the Fallingwater house, the old swimming pool, the greenhouse, and the Kaufmann tomb. Eventually, he was put in charge of house tours, too.

Living in Wright's servant quarters were Harold Jones, E. J.'s old butler-houseman-chauffeur; the cook and weekend chambermaid, Elsie Lee [Henderson]; and Elsie Harbaugh, in charge of housecleaning and laundry. Working in the Oliver Building in Pittsburgh were Ethel Clinton Appel as the estate supervisor, and her assistants, Joseph Johnson and Julia Tompkins. Those three, plus E. J.'s old accountants Philip Smith and A. E. Rowland, also ran the Kaufmann Foundation out of the same office. Smith and Rowland were forever engaged in paying Edgar's bills both in Pittsburgh and New York, as well as balancing his checkbook.

The reconstituted Bear Run Farm had an organizing meeting on August 29, 1955, Edgar presiding. The first of Clinton's scores of reports to Edgar in New York followed on September 12. The reports were basically letters to Edgar; when he was on vacation they were sent in more businesslike form to Smith and Rowland in Pittsburgh. They usually ran to four pages, and their degree of specificity could be extraordinary. One paragraph in the September 12 report concerns nothing but manure:

"There isn't any manure at Bear Run. Green has written Isler and Butler asking the cost of three loads of spent mushroom manure—spent mushroom manure is horse manure from which a crop of mushrooms has been taken. All the trees he plans to move will take extra manure for a mulch around them. Local manure, he states, is full of sawdust. Within another year he hopes to solve the manure problem."

Most of the details were professional in nature: the less usable of the Masonic camp cabins were being torn down one by one; one young beef will be slaughtered this week; all cattle are now registered in Edgar's name; five lambs are being slaughtered and put in deep freeze. More paragraphs followed on farming, logging, farm equipment, planting of corn and eight acres of wheat, and new trees. The electricity to the family tomb and the greenhouse is now to be separate from that supplying Mr. Green's house. A few questions were personal: did Edgar like the bedspread Mrs. Harbaugh had put on his bed?

Clinton later reported that the "Frick sawmill" on the grounds was turning out commercial lumber: 25,000 feet were ready for sale.* Seven tons of fertilizer will be needed next year; new laurel plants are being planted near the stream; five more lambs are going to slaughter. The references to food in Clinton's reports make Bear Run sound all the more like a feudal fief. Elsie Henderson was serving the beef raised at Fallingwater, Clinton says. In another report, the calves have been weaned and Jesse Hall was starting to sell them. In October 1955, Clinton observes that apples are being harvested and will be sent to Edgar's apartment in New York; sides of lamb and beef, ducks and chickens will shortly follow. Clinty does not say by what mechanics all this food is to show up in Manhattan, but the Fallingwater estate had capacious freezers, and train service would have taken the frozen food quickly from the Greensburg station to New York. Many people eat away at their inheritances; Edgar Kaufmann was eating his up.

Early in 1956 comes the first of scores of mentions of eggs. "Oakey Harbaugh was cleaning in the barn and had fifty dozens of eggs ready for us to bring to the office. People clamor to buy them . . . many of the steady customers we had at the store come to our offices and pick them up and we have a few new customers in our office building. In a couple of hours the 50 dozens will be gone." This unambiguous reference tells us that Bear Run's eggs had earlier been sold in the Kaufmann store, and

---

*Clinton's "Frick" modifier—necessary because there were other sawmills at Bear Run—most likely derived from the name of its builder, one of the country Fricks who got left behind when the clan got rich in Pittsburgh. A man named Frick was the main builder of the Kaufmanns' tomb.

were now being distributed from the offices of the Kaufmann Foundation in the Oliver Building. This near-feudal disposition of the riches of the estate, above all its meat and eggs, will be familiar to anyone who knows the medieval and Renaissance palaces of Rome and Florence. From the main street, those palaces are the most elegant buildings on earth, but from the side alley you can still see the counters where servants once sold the wine, eggs, butter, and olives that the Medici and Rucellai produced on their estates.

Knowingly or not, Edgar was practicing refeudalization, the process by which rich merchants attained the ultimate power of owning land. The economist Walt Whitman Rostow called this the "pattern of *Buddenbrooks* dynamics," as in Thomas Mann's novel. E. J. Kaufmann acted as though he were wedded to the country, but only Edgar, the aesthete totally removed from making money, qualified as an authentic country lord.

Along with land, animals, and the consumption of so much food, the other distinctive medieval feature on Edgar's fief was accommodation for his retainers. The English crown has nearly 1,000 rooms at Hampton Court and other palaces to dispense as grace and favor apartments to retainers who have served it faithfully. E. J., as we saw, cleared out most of the retainers at Bear Run, but Edgar brought several back. He designated one cabin for Clinton herself, and about half a dozen others to people who had served the Kaufmanns at the farm or the store: David Wolfe, Oakey and Gertrude Harbaugh, Jesse and Mary Hall, Earl Friend, George Green, Ralph Miner, Joseph and Ruth Hamborsky. Edgar also allowed his cousin Joan Kaufmann Mendelsohn to park her camper on his grounds. He tried to evict Hilda Schlosser, who seems to have been an old store employee, but when she protested, Edgar relented and even built a pool next to her cottage. The downside? Schlosser was henceforth forbidden to set foot anywhere else on the grounds.

A country lord dispenses drink as well as food, and (though it was not distilled at Bear Run) Edgar sent rivers of liquor to friends at Christmas. His employees in the Oliver Building were kept busy all December sending out fine Scotch, bourbon, and brandy to old friends and favorites like the architects Max Abramovitz and Wallace K. Harrison, the sculptor Richmond Barthé in Jamaica, the writers and scholars Brendan Gill, Henry-Russell Hitchcock, Leo Steinberg, Sibyl Moholy-Nagy, James Laughlin, Ada Louise Huxtable, and George Nelson, the editor of the *Architectural Forum* special issue of 1938. Not forgotten was Edgar's old mentor Victor Hammer.

After the liquor came the largesse: checks to the nine turnpike tolltakers at Donegal, to his father's old retainers at the fishing lodge in

Ontario, and to his apartment building's staff in New York: thirteen elevator operators, both day and night; fourteen janitors, day and night; and fifteen miscellaneous maintenance workers—each listed by name, occupation, and specification of the cash or liquor they were to receive.

Finally came Christmas cards by the hundreds, newly designed each year. These went to his distant cousins Charles Alan and Aline Saarinen; to artists, architects, and designers like Josef Albers, Charles Eames, Marcel Breuer, Mies van der Rohe, Mark Rothko, Paul Rudolph, Saul Steinberg, Ezra Stoller; to his old MoMA boss John McAndrew; and to the Time-Life heir Henry Luce III. A fair number of Pittsburgh cousins and old friends were also greeted at Christmas, as were a dozen "people with whom we trade," including garagemen and oil suppliers in Ohiopyle, Connellsville, and Mill Run. Six couples were still remembered from Edgar's war years in Australia, and from an even earlier era, Edgar sent money to Hugo Leinwetter, the chief porter at the Hotel Bristol in Vienna—Liliane's favorite place from the 1920s. All these bottles, checks, and cards came out in Edgar's name from his staff in Pittsburgh: he never saw any of it himself.

Two final notes before all these protocols turn us numb. One is commercial: as a gentleman farmer, Edgar lost impressive amounts of money on Bear Run each year, but he nonetheless ran it as a commercial enterprise. The estate's sawmills produced about 3,000 board feet of lumber each day. Other wood was used on the spot: the scaffolding that went up whenever Fallingwater got painted came from poplar trees nearby. In February of 1956, Clinty reported that lumber sales had produced $1,300; oats yielded 500 bushels at 70 cents a bushel; shelled corn is selling at $1.35 per bushel; there are twenty-five baby ducks and a hundred new baby chicks. Another steer will be fattened and slaughtered in ninety days; hay is selling at $10 a ton, then for $20 and $30 a ton; twenty-seven dozen chickens are going for sale in town. Other entries record the planting of gooseberries and raspberries, the weaning of the calves and heifers, the sale of sheep, the birth of lambs, and the revenue from sheepswool: $144.59.

The other note sounded in these accounts was sentimental. Clinton's first report ended with a visit to E. J. inside his tomb, one of scores to follow. "The day was beautiful . . . the foliage magnificent . . . and my day always seems to go smoother when I pay my little visit to the crypt and offer a little prayer.—Clinty." (To this note Edgar added a marginal "Me too.") On February 20, 1956: "As usual I paid my visit to the Crypt with happy reminiscences but with a very heavy heart. We should not be sad— should we? I am sure he guides both you and me always." April 17: "Green and I together visited the crypt—I read the 23rd psalm and together we offered up a little prayer . . . it impressed me greatly when Mr. Green asked if he might go with me into the crypt."

July 17, 1956: "Ma Purdy and I visited the crypt—sat down and meditated for a few minutes, were comforted by reading a Psalm and offered up our thanks for the privileges allowed us and the blessings innumerable that had come our way.—Clinty." October 8: "We [she and Mr. Brennan] both read a Psalm from the little prayer book and had a wonderful little chat about Poppy. It made me feel so good." December 17: "I had an extra long visit to the crypt today . . . called it my Christmas visit . . . and offered up prayers of thanks for both of us."

Then there were the visitors, whose number exploded the moment Edgar took over Fallingwater. The first note of these visitors comes in Clinty's fortnightly account to Edgar of March 5, 1956. By October of 1957, she warned him that careless and aggressive visitors were taking pictures at all moments, tracking dirt into the house, and leaving cigarettes on the floor. Ralph Miner organized forty-five-minute tours, but banned photography when it dragged out the visits to three times that length. One architecture student from Carnegie Tech got badly injured when he put his knee through a glass door. In 1957 there were 312 visitors from January to October, with many more refused. "And too, we have had many requests for visitors to see the crypt . . . but I have been reluctant to grant this permission and up until now have not done so, awaiting your decision."

Kaufmann and Clinton worked out a visitors' policy in the spring of 1957. No tours Saturday and Sunday. Visits inside Fallingwater Monday, Tuesday, and Wednesday but not Thursday or Friday, when it was being cleaned for possible arrival by Edgar. Visitors were allowed on the grounds those two days, however, which immediately distinguished Fallingwater from other historic houses: an outside-only visit to the White House, San Simeon, Monticello, or Mount Vernon would find few takers, but Fallingwater was so famous for its exterior and its site that even an outside glimpse gratified many tourists. Fallingwater still divides its visitors into insiders and outsiders today.*

It was peculiar to visit a private house with the lord away, but the Duke of Devonshire allowed it on his estate, and so did Peggy Guggen-

---

*Fallingwater is open every day but Monday and certain holidays from March through November, and on weekends in the other months. Reservations are taken at (724) 329-8501; the Web site is <www.wpconline.org>; e-mails to wpc@paconserve.org

heim at her palace in Venice. Edgar, though, was far more careful about his visitors than Guggenheim was. At first every tourist needed either his personal approval from New York or Clinton's OK from Pittsburgh. As an experiment, visits were limited in 1958 to just four hours each Monday. The future Postmodernists Charles Moore and Donlyn Lyndon were among the two hundred people admitted that year. This schedule was soon liberalized to allow visits between ten and four on Mondays, Tuesdays, and Wednesdays. Groups were admitted only if Edgar permitted them, and interior photography was still proscribed.

Edgar enjoyed a certain voyeurism from inspecting visitors to Fallingwater at arm's length. When his lawyer Ralph Demmler wrote him on May 25, 1960, as intercessor for a visit by Dr. Josiah Eisaman, Demmler concluded his request by saying, "I am sure you would enjoy meeting him." Kaufmann sent the letter back to Julia Tompkins in the Pittsburgh office with the marginal addendum, "I can live without it."

E. J. had built Fallingwater, but Edgar was the one destined to enjoy it. Every week or two he and Paul Mayén would meet at Penn Station after work on Friday evening, take the overnight sleeper to Pittsburgh, emerge in the morning at Greensburg, and be chauffeured to Fallingwater. Sunday night the men did the reverse, and got back to Manhattan in time for work on Monday. The staff never knew when Edgar might also pay a surprise visit, so they kept Fallingwater in perpetual readiness. God help the servant who was derelict in any duty. Once Kaufmann arrived with only a last-minute call from Greensburg, and he found the pansies missing from the flower box over the hatch. He fumed for a whole hour until new ones were brought over from Uniontown, rapping his walking stick on the stone floor all the while.

On November 1, 1961, Kaufmann drew up a protocol of how each servant was to prepare for the weekend visits. The office staff in Pittsburgh was kept equally busy: he would tell them what guests were coming and have them dispatch plane or train tickets all over the United States.

Like any great country house, Fallingwater kept meticulous inventories not only of its paintings but of its china and silver, its linens, and all other furnishings. In 1957, Clinton observed that Fallingwater had 34 good handtowels and 24 worn ones; 18 bathtowels plus 5 worn; 20 good washcloths plus 8 worn; and numerous bathrobes. Still preserved is the Fallingwater liquor list from October 11, 1960, which details the fourteen different brands of liquor that were always to be in stock. Nearly all the same brands are kept for show and the occasional delectation of visitors today.

. . .

The other side to the coin was Kaufmann's life in New York. From 1947 until 1971 he lived in a ground-floor apartment at 450 East Fifty-second Street, in the same building as Greta Garbo; after that he took most of a floor in a gracious old building at 535 Park Avenue. By 1947, Kaufmann was collecting art in quantity, and both apartments would eventually be packed with painting and sculpture. By 1949, Alfred Barr classed Edgar's art collection along with those of Nelson Rockefeller and John Hay Whitney for its high interest, if lesser richness. Kaufmann's most notable purchases in paintings came after he inherited E. J.'s estate. In 1955 he spent $4,000 on Willem de Kooning's *Interchange*, which sold to a Japanese collector in 1989 for $20.7 million dollars—the highest price ever paid for contemporary art. Kaufmann's paintings fetched a total of $98.3 million after his death. Once again Edgar proved himself the smartest merchant in the clan.*

Kaufmann left the Park Avenue condominium, his property in the Hudson River valley at Garrison, New York, and his house on the Greek island of Hydra to Paul Mayén. His will directed that all the paintings were to be sold and the proceeds given to Fallingwater and some other charities, except for whatever canvases of sentimental value that Mayén might choose to retain. Mayén professed a sentimental interest in every one of the paintings, so the entire $98 million, less commission and taxes, went to him. When Mayén died a decade later, his bequest to Fallingwater was decent enough, but just a portion of this colossal harvest.

Starting in 1959, Edgar entered into a competition of sorts with MoMA, giving out the Kaufmann International Design Awards to a designer, educator, historian, philosopher, or design critic of his choice. The awards were funded at $40,000 a year by the Kaufmann Foundation and administered through the Institute of International Education in New York. The first Kaufmann Award went to Charles and Ray Eames in 1961, the second to Walter Gropius in 1962. The 1963 winner was Olivetti, with a special commendation to Volkswagen, after which the competition abruptly

---

*Edgar's 10,000 percent markup on Frida Kahlo's *My Birth* was less impressive than his 50,000 percent markup on the de Kooning, but its sale occasioned a more interesting story. In the mid-1980s a dealer brought the entertainer Madonna to Edgar's apartment to view the painting. Edgar and Madonna quickly settled on a price, but by then word of Madonna's presence on Park Avenue had gotten out, and there was a knot of fans trying to get into the lobby. All of this puzzled Edgar, who called the star "Miss Madonna," and had no idea who she was.

folded. When the same institute built a new headquarters at 809 United Nations Plaza, from 1961 to 1966, Edgar paid out some $200,000 of his father's money for the creation of the Edgar J. Kaufmann Conference Rooms, a suite of stunning wood-paneled rooms designed by Alvar Aalto. For twenty years he also supported the philosopher and aesthetician Suzanne Langer.

What got sidestepped in Edgar's years at the helm at Fallingwater was the problem of the cantilevers. Edgar stopped his father's practice of having their deflection checked each year. Back in 1952 he had written Wright: "We also discussed the deflected cantilevers at Bear Run, and think you are right in dismissing the structural problems." (Left undefined is who "we" were, since this was assuredly not E. J.'s view.) In his 1986 book, Kaufmann still comes across as an unreconstructed believer in Wright's engineering expertise. The cantilevers habitually "bounce up and down" with the seasons, he told readers. If anyone was to blame for their deflection it was E. J., with the testing of the balconies in 1937. It would have been a mark of disrespect to Frank Lloyd Wright to think that anything could go wrong, Kaufmann wrote.

WPC believed Edgar when he said the cantilevers were not in trouble. In consequence, the balconies went unchecked not only for the eight years of Edgar's ownership but for the first quarter-century during which WPC operated the house. Edgar's death in 1989 finally liberated WPC to authorize testing, and findings almost at once showed that Fallingwater had for years been committing structural suicide.

It was time for Edgar to let go of Fallingwater. Already in the early 1950s E. J. had told the Western Pennsylvania Conservancy that it would eventually get the house. Now, on July 31, 1959, Edgar met with three of E. J.'s old loyalists to see how this could be made to happen. These were his father's lead lawyer, Ralph Demmler; his chief banker, Frank Denton; and E. J.'s brother Oliver. Four years of negotiations with WPC followed, after which E. J.'s old lawyers at Reed, Smith, Shaw & McClay produced the Trust Agreement of October 14, 1963, by which Edgar gave Fallingwater to WPC. The Kaufmann Foundation gave half a million dollars as endowment for an outreach program to go along with the house. Attached to the agreement were 7,187 shares of May Department Stores common stock at $69.5625, worth a total of $499,945.69, plus $54.31 in cash. On October 29, 1963, with the governor of Pennsylvania in attendance, Kaufmann deeded Fallingwater to the Western Pennsylvania Conservancy, whose crown jewel it has been ever since.

In giving Fallingwater away, Edgar exhibited one more instance of a lifelong sense of timing that was just like his father's: perfect. He had joined MoMA in 1938 when it was swept up in a wave of Fallingwatermania, and reentered it in 1947 when his expertise in home furnishings dovetailed with the postwar boom in consumer spending. He quit MoMA in 1955 to get back to Fallingwater, then quit Fallingwater in 1963 to get into teaching. The Bear Run Farm had already depleted his capital by about a million dollars, but the last straw was the decision of the dying Pennsylvania Railroad to cut off overnight sleeper service from New York to Pittsburgh. What is the value of a fief if you can't reach it in comfort?

Giving Fallingwater to WPC was nonetheless a masterstroke worthy of his father. It stanched Edgar's hemorrhage of cash by moving his farmhands and overseers from his payroll to the coffers at WPC, but it allowed him to keep running the place as though he yet owned it. For the quarter-century until his death, Fallingwater still had to be perfect for his return at any moment: lights, heat, and fresh flowers just as before. The only change was that Edgar no longer slept at Fallingwater: now he lodged with the Mellons at Rolling Rock.

The move to Rolling Rock documented Edgar's rise in social status, as did the elegant new friends he made at WPC. The longtime director at Fallingwater was Thomas Mellon Schmidt and the WPC president in the same decades was a Mellon in-law; in the 1980s, that presidency fell on John Oliver, the descendant of a major partner of Andrew Carnegie's. By his gift Edgar also added to his titles: after 1963 he was not only lord but guru of Fallingwater. He remade the house in his own image not only by altering its furnishings but by training the guides who reverently invoked his name as they led their charges through Fallingwater. Forty years later their successors still do.

In 1964 Kaufmann joined the Columbia University faculty as adjunct professor of architectural history in the School of Architecture, where he taught until 1980. He enjoyed the prestige the title conferred on him, although he was only "adjunct," he told me with glee, because he had graduated from neither college nor high school. He was a generous benefactor to Columbia as well, beginning in 1963 with funding for publication subsidies and $100,000 to air-condition the Avery Architectural Library. Another $100,000 was forthcoming for Columbia to purchase some drawings that Louis Sullivan had given Wright, which the Wright Foundation had put up for sale.

One has the impression of Edgar's buying his way into Columbia the way he had at MoMA (and faculty gossip was not shy about saying so), but he nonetheless proved an effective teacher who is still fondly remembered by numerous students. The core of his teaching was the work of Wright, including Fallingwater, but he offered courses of broader scope as well. His "Architecture in the Modern Age (1750–1960) with special attention to concepts and forms influential today" featured some mindbogglingly obscure structures that only he could have known from his travels in Europe, but he discoursed on wider design issues in his lectures, too.

At the point of entering academic life as a gentleman architectural historian, Kaufmann evidently realized how odd it was that his own famous home had never gotten the history it warranted. Fallingwater was about to turn twenty-five without ever having been the subject of a book or any scholarly (as opposed to journalistic) articles. In 1962, Kaufmann was given the chance to rectify this by working on the Fallingwater special number of Bruno Zevi's magazine, *L'Architettura*.

The issue of *L'Architettura* and its book derivative the next year were fundamental to a whole generation's thinking about Fallingwater. *L'Architettura*'s key message was that it was Edgar and not E. J. Kaufmann who was responsible for Fallingwater. As the text declared:

> *Fallingwater fu costruita perchè Edgar Kaufmann Jr. la volle.*
> Fallingwater was built because Edgar Kaufmann Jr. wanted it.
> *Fallingwater fut construite parce que voulue par Edgar Kaufmann Jr.*

Shortly before his death Zevi told me that he alone was responsible for that claim, which he said was made without Edgar's assent or preknowledge. I accept that, but the question remains whether Edgar believed that this was an accurate assessment of his role at Fallingwater. Surely he was not too awed by Zevi to force a retraction of the claim: at fifty-two, Edgar was no timorous youth. Nor was it a case of one author writing part of the issue in New York and the other writing an ocean away: Kaufmann says right in his text that he wrote his memoir in Florence. And (as we saw earlier) Zevi's editorial assistant remembered handing Kaufmann the entire text of the issue in Rome for his review. Even if by chance Zevi had slipped the comment in without Kaufmann's approval in 1962, its reappearance in the 1963 edition guarantees that it had Kaufmann's imprimatur.

The 1963 book clearly had Kaufmann's stamp all over it anyway, from the reprinting of his own text to his authorization for the reprinting of

Paul Mayén's color photographs. Curiously, Zevi's key phrase appeared only in Italian, English, and French—not in German or Spanish. Those nine missing words constitute the sole important deviation of the German and Spanish texts from those in the three other languages.

It was probably an innocent mistake, though a remarkably careless one, for Zevi to have inflated Edgar's role at Fallingwater; he surely would not have made it had he known E. J. personally. Instead, Zevi encountered only Edgar Jr. as owner, preserver, historian, spokesman, and interpreter for Fallingwater, so it was natural for him to assume that he had served as its patron as well.

But it is a separate question why Edgar allowed this inflated claim to be published. In his essay he acknowledged that it was his father who had paid for the house, but by stating that Wright had come to Pittsburgh "at our request" and that "we received the first sketches" and the like, Edgar presented himself as a full partner with his father in its creation. He had never sought credit for Fallingwater while his father was alive, but his memoir in *L'Architettura* and the *Casa sulla Cascata* book ended this reserve. After 1962 he identified himself more aggressively as catalyst and midwife to Fallingwater. That is the way he presented himself in his 1982 film interview, in his 1986 book on Fallingwater, and in no end of interviews and articles.

After E. J., Liliane, and Wright died, and especially after Edgar began to play host to Fallingwater's tourists, the assumption grew ever more insistent that the real client at Fallingwater had been the son and not the father. Once in a while, Kaufmann downplayed the assumption, as in a letter to the editor of *Time* in 1964 and at least once in his lectures at Columbia; but generally he allowed his interlocutors to give him the benefit of the doubt. After years of carefully pigeonholing his father as "client of record" at Fallingwater (thereby implying that there was another client who was not of record), Edgar should not have been surprised when his fellow historians followed the lead of the influential Zevi and praised him as the intellectual and artistic patron of Wright's masterpiece.

There was also a mischievous analogy at work. In a clamorous architectural putsch in 1954, Phyllis Bronfman Lambert made her father Sam Bronfman drop the original architect for the Seagram Building in New York and engage Mies van der Rohe instead. Just a few years before, Joe Price had similarly pushed his father to use Wright for his Price Tower in Bartlesville, Oklahoma. It was natural—though mistaken—for journalists to assume that Edgar Kaufmann had played the same role of catalyst with his father in the 1930s that Lambert and Price played with their fathers twenty years later. By the 1960s and '70s, most scholars and journalists active in architectural history were too young to have known any of the major players from the 1930s except for Edgar. Tafel and Mosher were alive, too, but they were not architectural stars of Edgar's magnitude.

I shared the same assumptions about Fallingwater as everybody else until Edgar asked me to do specific research on the house. He had a copy of one of my books, *Pittsburgh: An Urban Portrait,* and he had thought enough of it to place it on the shelves at Fallingwater. (Updating Fallingwater's books was one way that Edgar made certain he remained a palpable presence there.) During the research phase for that book in the early 1980s, I got in touch with Edgar about the family store and the architectural patronage of his father before he got involved with Wright. In 1985, just before my book came out, Kaufmann told the architect Robert A. M. Stern, then director of Columbia University's center for the study of American architecture, to invite me to speak at the symposium Stern was organizing for the fiftieth anniversary of Fallingwater in 1986. Edgar funded me specifically to address the Pittsburgh and Kaufmann connections to Fallingwater. The keynote speaker was the dean of Wright scholars, Yale's Vincent Scully. Scully and all the other symposium speakers lectured on Frank Lloyd Wright; I talked about E. J. Kaufmann.

For background on E. J., I conducted two interviews with Edgar and received his permission (necessary in those days) to explore the Fallingwater materials he had deposited at Avery. The first document I encountered there was E. J.'s 1946 note to Edgar about the house he was building with Neutra at Palm Springs. E. J. seemed so entirely in control both of the building process and of Neutra's ego that it was no surprise to turn to the other letters and find that he had handled Frank Lloyd Wright in much the same way. It was a small but revealing point to see that E. J. addressed the considerably older Wright both as "Mr. Wright" and "Frank." Wright's associates and followers, even those who were born long after the Master died, call him only "Mr. Wright" to this day.

Among the secondary sources I used on Fallingwater (these were many fewer in the 1980s than today) was Edgar's memoir in *L'Architettura* and the *Casa sulla Cascata* book. I had always accepted the analogy of his being midwife to Fallingwater, and had no intention of questioning it in my Columbia talk, with Kaufmann sitting as guest of honor in the third row. I stuck to my theme of Kaufmann Sr. and his involvement with Pittsburgh architecture before and after Fallingwater. But as I researched the topic, I could not help wondering: who really had played the major role in the heroic events of the mid-thirties at Bear Run—the father or the son?

The way Edgar presented his role in the creation of Fallingwater started to give me a certain unease. Beginning with the article in *L'Arch-itettura*, he habitually displayed inexplicable lapses in memory. The key events at Fallingwater had taken place no more than twenty-five to twenty-eight years before publication of the 1962 article, yet there was a pervasive vagueness and unreliability to Kaufmann's account. Eight hundred miles away in Missouri, Donald Hoffmann had already discovered the same thing, but years would pass before he and I got together to share impressions.

Some elements were minor, perhaps. In his 1962 piece Edgar claimed that 30,000 visitors were already pouring through Fallingwater each year, which was one hundred times the true number. Kaufmann misrecollected that his parents first met Wright in Arizona, rather than Wisconsin, and his memory played tricks again when he stated that the rhododendron on Bear Run were in full bloom when Wright first saw the family property. Edgar recalled the interval between Wright's first site visit and the arrival of his sketch plans as a few weeks; actually it lasted nine months. He also left out the crucial design meeting between Wright and E. J. at Taliesin in September 1935 and anything else that would have shown his father in charge of the building. Where E. J. was mentioned, he came off as an ignorant strawman. Phrases such as "I was able to persuade my father" and "It was up to me to fight it out with him" made Edgar sound like Jesus jousting with the Scribes and the Pharisees.

As we saw in the Prologue, Edgar's crucial misrecollection was the claim he made in both his 1962 and 1986 texts that he had accompanied his father on Wright's first visit to Bear Run: this was pure falsehood. His explanation for quitting Taliesin—it was so wonderful that he had to leave—was so bizarre that it gave me less confidence than ever in his veracity.

My talk at Columbia in November 1986 marked the first time anyone had presented E. J. Kaufmann as a subject worthy of architectural study in his own right. I had by then immersed myself in so many unresolved Fallingwater issues that I kept working on the origins of the house out of pure curiosity. In February 1987, I mailed Edgar a letter with three pages of questions about his father, to which I got the following reply:

Dear Frank,
   your inquiries are quite sensible, but deal with social and personal problems which I left behind me in 1940 and have no more relish for now than then.

With all good wishes,
yours truly,
Edgar

Edgar was sandbagging my investigation in just thirty-seven words, all the more curious since my letter had been about his father, not about him. Why then the reference to "social and personal problems"? The letter made me ask myself for the first time whether Edgar was more than merely careless with facts. Was he an outright manipulator of the truth, as Hoffmann later alleged? Kaufmann had been the soul of amiability to me, subjecting himself to the long interviews in his Park Avenue apartment and treating me to two unforgettable lunches in a Viennese restaurant around the corner. (Never had I seen a waiter literally bow to a client until Edgar and I walked in.) But there is no question that Edgar was telling me only what he wanted me to know.

Brendan Gill's two published evaluations of Kaufmann dwelled on this habit of dissimulation. Gill saw Kaufmann as a "mischief-making lemur" and as a "difficult, prickly man":

> Over the years, that was the impression I gained of Edgar Kaufmann, Jr. . . . Although an architectural historian by profession, age had not encouraged him to tell all that he knew but only what he wanted to have known. His discretion leaves many questions unanswered, and one detects in it an element of the mischievous, like a child's singsong chanting of "I know a secret." Edgar did indeed possess a number of secrets and it was hoped that, as a historian, he would feel obliged to share them with us. Not he, not ever, and with his death they will remain tantalizingly undisclosed.

This was Gill's opinion, not a fact, but it was an opinion widely shared in Edgar's circle. Edgar Tafel, who had begun to publish his own books on Wright, also believed that Kaufmann had muddied the historical record on Fallingwater. Tafel wrote me in 1989: "I don't think you will ever solve that mystery [of the origins of Fallingwater], but you can ferret out about all there is to know—too bad 'Junie' tried to obliterate all before 1940— but it's interesting also." Since no inventory of E. J. Kaufmann's papers survives, it would be hearsay to speculate that Edgar dispersed them, but sending E. J.'s office to London and key family paintings to Chicago, Lexington, Kentucky, and elsewhere looks like a deliberate attempt by Edgar to blot out his father's memory—what the ancients called *damnatio memoriae.*

The other element of *damnatio memoriae,* it seemed to me, was the campaign of words that Edgar waged against his father, strong enough to count as verbal parricide. In the 1962–63 Italian book and the 1982 film interview, Edgar was generally respectful to his father, presenting him as a vibrant and creative person even though in need of his son to guide him through the subtleties of Fallingwater. Edgar also threw E. J. a few positive adjectives in his 1986 book, but by and large the father came off look-ing dim-witted. We meet E. J. in the second paragraph of Kaufmann's narration as the patron who had commissioned the family's fake-Norman house in Pittsburgh, and we immediately hear Wright's mockery of it. A few pages farther on, Edgar accuses his father of false economy at Fallingwater in his attempt to cut costs. On subsequent pages, Edgar calls E. J. "ignorant," "wrong," devious, and insubordinate to Wright, and full of unsuitable suggestions for the house. His final belittling adjective for his father was "captious" (i.e., cantankerous), a man in need of con-stant attention as he took on a quarrelsome second wife. In short, Edgar presented E. J. as unworthy of being a Wright client. This echoed what Wright told E. J. more than once: he hadn't really deserved Fallingwater.

All sons probably want to rival their fathers at some point, but few do it as energetically as Edgar. In one particularly farcical detail Edgar flew in the face of both eyewitnesses and scholars when he denied (at the 1986 Columbia symposium on Fallingwater, and elsewhere) that it was his father who had had the insight to leave uncut the top of the boulder that stuck out next to Fallingwater's hearth. In his *Autobiography*, Wright gave E. J. unstinting and unambiguous credit for this dazzling idea. How could Edgar possibly deny it?

Edgar Kaufmann Jr.
with Wright and E. J.
at Taliesin West, 1947
© Pedro E. Guerrero

Edgar's literary parricide jumps out as all the more surprising because in his last decades he had assumed a kinder, gentler persona. People who remembered him as brusque or brutal in the 1930s found him mellow half a century later. He seemed notably more relaxed after E. J. died in 1955 and Wright died in 1959.

It must have been strange for Edgar to have had two fathers: one can almost feel the strain in a late 1940s photograph showing him standing awkwardly to the side as Wright and E. J. lock into each other's gaze like lovers. His relationship with Wright was certainly complex. Wright showed him ample cruelty at Taliesin, but there was much genuine concern in his letters to the younger Kaufmann, and as late as 1950, Wright advised E. J. to be less demanding of his son. When E. J. died, Wright told Edgar to think of him as his second father.

After Wright himself died in 1959, Edgar constructed a posthumous relationship with him that was substantially more harmonious than the one they had had when Wright was alive. The first manifestation of the new relationship was monetary. Edgar wrote Olgivanna that he was giving the revenue from his Fallingwater visitors to the Wright Foundation, and such moneys did in fact go to Taliesin. After repeated entreaties Olgivanna accepted Edgar's invitation to Bear Run one last time, in 1971, though she refused to set foot inside Fallingwater, calling it Liliane's place of death.

With Wright dead, Edgar could take him over as he had already taken control of his other dead father. He began to dress like Wright, with the same neutral-tone clothes, the same cane, an identical porkpie hat, and an endless coat to simulate Wright's cape. He arranged his bedroom on Park Avenue in the manner of Wright, with a daybed rather than a conventional bed. Brendan Gill discerned a parallel takeover tendency in Edgar's articles about Wright, in which Edgar made a habit of correcting his old mentor. As Gill said: "Kaufmann over the years has succeeded in reversing their roles [i.e., his early role as apprentice to Wright]: he speaks of Wright as a kindly father might speak of an errant son, not to debunk him but to ensure that his beguiling exaggerations be kept in perspective."

It was no accident that Edgar's several commissions to Wright came to nothing. It is a poor idea to hire your father under the best of circumstances, but the loony way in which Edgar asked Wright to price his design by the square foot like a carpet salesman was grotesque. Edgar was unlikely in any case to be a decisive architectural patron after subjugating himself for twenty-one years to his father and Wright. The medieval painter Taddeo Gaddi apprenticed himself to the great Giotto for that long, and when he was finally free of his master, he had nothing left to say.

In the end, Edgar outlived and outlaughed nearly all his critics save Philip Johnson and Brendan Gill. He could enjoy himself after he gave Fallingwater away in 1963, and after his retirement from Columbia in 1980 he had no job at all except to be Lord of Fallingwater. He was lionized at a 1982 reunion of the Taliesin apprentices and at the fiftieth-anniversary galas held at Columbia and Fallingwater. He was fêted at the Carnegie Museum of Art in Pittsburgh, twice, and at my request he held court at Fallingwater again when the Society of Architectural Historians came there for a magical candlelight dinner in 1985. Everyone who met Edgar in those years found him approachable, courtly, knowledgeable, and still ardent in the furtherance of modern design.

Socially, Edgar never left Pittsburgh. He retained close ties to his Kaufmann and Mundheim cousins in New York and elsewhere, and at the end of his life he contributed to the restoration of Rodef Shalom, the temple his grandfather Morris had helped build eighty years earlier. In New York, Edgar lived in the same apartment building as his childhood friend Tom Frank; on the island of Hydra his villa was a few minutes' walk from that of his lifelong friends James and Darthea Speyer. Even the subtlety of his friendship with Paul Mayén bespoke Pittsburgh more than New York. It clearly gave Edgar great satisfaction to bring Mayén into the creative work at Fallingwater, first as the photographer for the 1962–63 Italian book, then as designer of the captivating Visitors Pavilion at Bear Run.

The minuscule size of Edgar's social world defies probability. The bride he chose in 1953 was his distant cousin (and his mother's favorite) Aline Bernstein Louchheim, who had been so central in publicizing Fallingwater decades before. When Aline chose instead to marry the architect Eero Saarinen, she already knew her mother-in-law, because it was Loja Saarinen who had woven the rugs for E. J.'s famous office.

Edgar preferred to hire African-Americans from Pittsburgh for his servant staff in Manhattan, for he could be finicky about caste but he was free of prejudice when it came to race. His Fallingwater cook, Elsie Henderson, loved him for his countless acts of generosity, but Edgar's commitment to African-Americans was not limited to people he knew. He took much pleasure in 1967 when he gave the family's old Irene Kaufmann Settlement on the Hill to the African-American community, in whose hands it flourishes still. Far more moving than the scores of obituaries on Kaufmann the connoisseur was the account by the African-American activist Nate Smith about his close relationship with Edgar, despite their having been born on very different sides of the Pittsburgh tracks.

No question, then, that Edgar Kaufmann Jr. could be a lovely man, but was he also a liar? If he was, why would a person of so many accomplishments and of such gentleness—most days—feel compelled to lie about his role at Fallingwater?

I do not see Edgar as a liar. When he claimed to have been the catalyst for Fallingwater, he was probably telling the truth as he knew it, although there was considerable stretching of the envelope. I propose three scenarios in which Edgar emerges as truthful, or relatively truthful, about his actual role. These I call the Kissinger, the Zuckerman, and the O. Henry scenarios. The first derives its name from an apocryphal story about the famously calculating secretary of state. A lady meets Kissinger at a reception and gushes, "Oh, Dr. Kissinger, thank you for saving the world," to which Kissinger replies, "You're welcome, madam." Journalists and historians were so obdurate in wanting Edgar to be the patron of Fallingwater that at some point it became churlish for him to refuse. Like Kissinger in the story, Edgar finally consented to play the role in which the public wished to see him. In part he had the role thrust upon him, and in part he assumed it himself. Like Kissinger, at some point he could no longer withdraw from the role even if he wanted to. In 1987, for example, the University of Pennsylvania made him a Doctor of Humane Letters, *honoris causa*, with the citation, in part:

> Both catalyst and witness to "Fallingwater," the country house designed fifty years ago by Wright in the woods of Pennsylvania, you secured this twentieth-century masterpiece of America and the world under the auspices of the Western Pennsylvania Conservancy, while preserving the record of its construction and habitation for all time in your lyrical prose.

The earlier part of the citation was accurate enough in calling Kaufmann a renowned "architectural historian, museum curator, teacher, philanthropist, patron of the arts, and a leading expert on modern design." When the university president got to the words "catalyst and witness to 'Fallingwater,' " what was Edgar to do—drown him out? Besides, he *was* a witness to the construction of Fallingwater, and its most eloquent champion. And when Donald Hoppen, a Wright apprentice who knew Edgar personally, wrote, "Edgar . . . was destined to be the genie who would make the miraculous possible," was Kaufmann obliged to sue Hoppen for a retraction? When the *New York Times* wrote that it was Edgar more than anyone else, except Frank Lloyd Wright, who was responsible for Fallingwater, this praise was patently misdirected, but Kaufmann could not dispute it, either, because by then he was dead.

The Zuckerman scenario is darker. My friend Zuckerman had a father who was so competitive that when the son started publishing in psychology the father entered the field just to rival his son with a magnum opus of his own. We will recall that Karl Jensen's long report on the Kaufmanns informed Wright in 1934 that "[Edgar Jr.] has been responsible to some extent in making his father acquainted with you." E. J. did not need his son to tell him about Wright: the media or the numerous friends they had in common (Urban, Benno Janssen, Bel Geddes, Frankl, and Frank) would already have done that. Nevertheless, he may have paid serious attention to Wright only when Edgar Jr. told him he wanted to study at Taliesin. (The confused 1933–34 chronology and the ambiguous "his father wants him to go there" remark will never permit us to know for sure.) In that case the son might indeed have provided the spark that led to Fallingwater—an aboriginal spark that E. J. soon obliterated with a great burning bush of his own.

The O. Henry scenario is more comic. In the short story "Mammon and the Archer," Richard Rockwall wins the hand of Miss Lantry through what he believes was his persistence and a grand stroke of luck. He is unaware of the hidden manipulation by which his father had shelled out a turn-of-the-century fortune of $6,300 to manipulate the "stroke of luck"—a monster carriage jam on Broadway—that precipitated the engagement. Clumsy as E. J. was as a father, prickly as Edgar was as a son, it is clear from the father's every letter how much he loved Edgar and how much he encouraged him in his enthusiasm for architecture. Had E. J. deliberately contrived events (we know he was a master contriver) to make Edgar Jr. mistakenly think that he, rather than his father, was the catalyst for the creation of Fallingwater?

So different from his father in life, Edgar was bound to depart from E. J. in death. Two ceremonies marked his passing. The more elaborate was an elegant gathering in Henry Clay Frick's Manhattan palace—a last affirmation of their common Pittsburgh roots. The more meaningful was a short commemoration held by the Western Pennsylvania Conservancy on the banks of Bear Run. There was room for Edgar in the family tomb, but his will stipulated that his body be donated to science. Edgar's loyal friend Paul Mayén attempted to get various New York medical schools to take the body, but none had need of it. Mayén then had Edgar cremated and brought the ashes to Fallingwater for the memorial ceremony. When Mayén entered the family mausoleum, he felt it was not the right place for Edgar's restless soul, and he scattered the ashes over the hillside instead. Edgar's self-identification with Fallingwater was now complete.

It was appropriate for Frank Lloyd Wright to call Fallingwater a great blessing, and millions of us have found it so. But ultimately blessings take shape as lives, not as buildings. E. J. and Liliane, Edgar and Wright: what a constellation of blessings those lives have proved to be.

Opposite: Fallingwater crowded with tourists. The house has become the national monument E. J. Kaufmann intended it to be.

FALLINGWATER FOR OURSELVES

Well the building stands. Your home. It is yours for what it has cost you. It is mine for what it has cost me. And it's for all mankind according to its costs in all its bearings.

—FRANK LLOYD WRIGHT to Aline Barnsdall

With Wright and the Kaufmanns dead, ownership of Fallingwater falls to us, the living, and we are obliged to ask not just what Fallingwater meant in the past, but what it means today. Like everything else, Fallingwater takes on new meanings each year. The hype that was set in place in 1938 was so compelling that it has not entirely worn off even now. The main spinners of that hype, particularly Henry Luce and E. J. Kaufmann (though not Wright and Ayn Rand) have dropped in status to little more than historical footnotes, but the house gains in celebrity every year. As its new owners, we need to ask why.

For modern architecture Oscar Wilde's aphorism that nothing is more dangerous than being modern has proved half right and half wrong. The trinity of modern structures that received such adulation at MoMA in 1932 has aged surprisingly well: Gropius's Bauhaus and Le Corbusier's Villa Savoye were restored after war damage and abandonment, and Mies's temporary pavilion for the Barcelona exhibition looked so intriguing in old photographs that the municipality rebuilt it fifty years after it was taken down. What has aged less well are the reputations of the three architects who were MoMA's stars in 1932. Gropius's reputation has fared the worst. He committed hara-kiri as a serious architect when he allowed his name to go on the travesty that was the Pan-Am Building, behind Grand Central Station in New York. Le Corbusier retained the purity and lyricism of his early work all his life, but his buildings fell prey to easy imitation. It is hard to thrill to his monastery of La Tourette after you have seen its string of knockoffs from Boston's City Hall to the FBI headquarters in Washington. For some years Mies suffered a similar fate. The brilliance of his Seagram Building shone the length of Park Avenue in 1958 because there was nothing like it in New York, but today Park Avenue carries so many cigar-box skyscrapers that it takes a knowledgeable tourist to spot Seagram's. But that should have been predictable even in 1958. The glory of Mies is that you can (superficially) reproduce him; the glory of Wright is that you cannot.

This does not automatically declare Wright the winner in his bitter rivalry with Gropius, Le Corbusier, and Mies. In terms of volume it was the Europeans—Mies above all—who were the winners: the world outside our doors looks far more like the Seagram Building than Fallingwater. Ideologically, though, the Europeans are in the weaker position. Theirs was a movement that was insistent on breaking with the past: now they are the past themselves.

By and large Wright's reputation has aged well, and Fallingwater's popularity certainly grows every year. It is a popularity that transcends both time and space. Time, because unlike other famous early modern buildings, it has not become a period piece. The houses of Gropius and Le Corbusier, especially, give us the pleasurable feeling of revisiting the thirties, but Fallingwater does not. We don't love Fallingwater because it is a monument to the 1930s—we love it for the excitement it brings us today. In geographic terms, Fallingwater's popularity was always international, and it remains so. It sometimes appears to be more popular abroad than it is at home: Japan, for example, accords Fallingwater the veneration it normally reserves for its own national treasures.

Fallingwater also stands up well compared to the thousands of excellent buildings that have been constructed since 1938. One of the few pleasures that came from the overblown celebration of entering the third millennium was the discovery that the twentieth century had been a great era for architecture. Its succession of fine buildings began with Wright and his European contemporaries; restarted after World War II with masters like Kahn, Saarinen, Barragán, and Tange; and ended with our cities bedecked in "spectacle" or "diva" architecture in a stylistic tendency variously called Postmodern or Second Modern. Fallingwater has little to fear from these competitors. Already the Guggenheim Bilbao is dropping in public esteem. Its hype was the one great success of the twentieth century that matched Fallingwater's, but few are the visitors who could say that seeing it changed their lives, as they still do of Fallingwater.

One of the things that gave new relevance to Fallingwater in recent years was the need to save it. When the building came perilously close to collapse in the 1990s, it reminded a new generation how audacious it had been at birth. "America's Leaning Tower of Pisa" was a good description for Fallingwater in its beleaguered state, because preventing its crash was a striking parallel to what Italian and British engineers accomplished in halting the self-destruction of another great monument of engineering at the other end of the millennium. The world marveled at the use of modern procedures to reverse the problems caused by primitive technology, and in the process we realized how much we loved these two (relatively) old buildings.

Stopping the cantilever deflection was the most urgent of a number of tasks facing the Western Pennsylvania Conservancy at Bear Run. The sash holding Fallingwater's hundreds of windows had decayed to the point of having to be rebuilt. Bear Run's water had become polluted, which required a costly reworking of the sewage system that crisscrosses the estate. (Fiber-optic cable was laid through the grounds in the same new conduits.) While they were wrestling with these high-tech questions, the WPC administrators also had to work out a preservation strategy for the natural riches of Bear Run, which were being compromised by the influx of tourists. As one study put it, "Fallingwater has suffered from being loved too much."

The past keeps changing because we keep viewing it differently, so Fallingwater must change as we view it through the filter of everything that has been built since. But Wright's design has a decided advantage over every other architectural masterpiece: there is still nothing else in the world that looks like it. Putting later buildings alongside Fallingwater, literally or metaphorically, would be like moving Picassos into the Velázquez room at the Prado. Velázquez's *Las Meninas* would look even better, not because the Picassos are bad, but because they would bring out the core strength of the earlier master.

It is impressive that the American architectural profession consistently votes Fallingwater as the best building of any period in the United States and the best building of the last hundred years anywhere in the world— but what does the general public say? Lacking any popular poll, we might start by counting what buildings get the most visitors, though such tallies mean little out of context. In the United States, the U.S. Capitol, the Statue of Liberty, the United Nations, and the White House each attract two million visitors annually, but people are drawn to those sites for their history and symbolism, not for their architecture. On a world scale, the most important building on the planet should be Mao Tse-tung's mausoleum in Beijing, but its eight million annual visitors are not there to study its architecture, either. The Ka'ba at Mecca, the Pyramids, Lenin's Tomb, and Buckingham Palace fall into the same category. Of the millions of visitors who gape at Buckingham Palace each year, how many could draw even a simple sketch of it from memory?

Raw visitorship figures are also skewed because some sites are easy to access and some difficult. Many thousands more people have viewed the Sistine Chapel and clambered up the Eiffel Tower than have seen Fallingwater, because those monuments are always in the public eye and easy to reach. Fallingwater must be one of the world's least-seen masterpieces of art. The 3.5 million people who have toured it represent about half a percent of living Americans. More people glimpse New York's Guggenheim Museum in a day, if only from a Fifth Avenue bus, than see Fallingwater in a year.

Since Fallingwater is a house-museum, we can learn something by comparing it with its thousands of similar competitors. Its 140,000 annual visitors put it in twentieth place among the top twenty-five attractions in this category—a strong performance in a business whose prime lure is not architecture but the ghosts of the rich and famous. George Washington's Mount Vernon leads this list with over a million visitors a year (as a public building, the White House is excluded). The Vanderbilts' Biltmore in Asheville, North Carolina, ranks second, with something under a million visitors; William Randolph Hearst's San Simeon ranks third; fourth is Elvis Presley's Graceland in Memphis, Tennessee, which pulls in about 600,000 middle-aged visitors a year (younger people are less interested); and Thomas Jefferson's Monticello takes fifth place, with half a million visitors. The remaining top house-museums are mainly presidential abodes (Andrew Jackson's, Lincoln's, and two of Franklin D. Roosevelt's); the estates of Thomas Edison, Henry Ford, and six other industrialists; then the houses of miscellaneous notables like Paul Revere, Betsy Ross, Robert E. Lee, and (number twenty-four on the list) Frank Lloyd Wright's Taliesin West at Scottsdale, Arizona.

Only four of the twenty-five homes—Monticello, Mount Vernon, Taliesin West, and Fallingwater—have significant architectural value, but even the first three of these four are primarily visited for the mystique of the great men or women whose presence dwells there, Wright's included. Most of the homes on the top twenty-five list are authentically historic, whereas nothing important ever happened at Bear Run: neither treaties nor surrenders were signed there, neither massacres nor witch trials took place there, and neither inventions nor great works of music or literature were inspired there. Apart from Wright and Einstein, no one of universal fame ever visited Fallingwater, either. The Kaufmanns' house is the only one on the top twenty-five list that is visited exclusively for its architectural excellence.

The question "What is the meaning of Fallingwater today?" demands the delimiter "To whom?," because the house has diverse and overlapping meanings for Pittsburgh, for southwestern Pennsylvania, for America, and for the world. For Pittsburgh, the most basic meaning of Fallingwater should be counterimage. Wright took the glass and steel that Pittsburgh produced better than any city in the world and set them on a water-drenched hillside that mirrors Pittsburgh itself. Ideally, Fallingwater should embrace Pittsburgh as its mother and Pittsburgh should love Fallingwater as its son, but Fallingwater wants to have nothing to do with its mother today, no matter how cleaned up she is. Pittsburgh would nevertheless be justified in bellowing to all the earth how it gave birth to Fallingwater—but that is not its style.

Southwestern Pennsylvania is more astute in exploiting Fallingwater. The various counties use the house to quarterback the ecotourism that drives their new economy, which is fairly ironic for a region that for two centuries lost no chance to wallop nature into submission. After half a century of decay, Ohiopyle has regained and even exceeded the numbers of visitors it attracted in the early twentieth century. This it owes to E. J. Kaufmann and the gift that saved Ferncliff Peninsula a half-century ago. In summer, the resident population of Ohiopyle swells as thousands arrive to hike, camp, bike, fish, kayak, and go white-water rafting. About two million visitors from all over the United States use the state park in some way every year, though only a fraction go on to explore the "white-water" house that sits five minutes up the road.

Ohiopyle has a fine breezy feel to it today. You can still shop in the general store that the Kaufmanns patronized when Wilson was president, and other Ohiopyle merchants are prospering as outfitters for the rafters on the Youghiogheny. In E. J.'s old retail base of Connellsville, the merchants outfit hikers and cyclists for the Great Allegheny Passage, a walking and bicycle path that you can soon take uninterrupted from Pittsburgh to Washington D.C. Half a million visits are made each year to different segments of the GAP, part of which is the old rail path on the opposite bank of the Youghiogheny from Fallingwater. The rails-to-trails movement is stronger in western Pennsylvania than anywhere else in the country, and the seventy miles of trail between Ohiopyle and Pittsburgh are particularly dense with users. Eventually, ecotourism may forge new topographical and cultural links between the Laurel Highlands and the Forks of the Ohio like those that existed when George Washington passed by 250 years ago.

For America as a whole, the fundamental meaning of Fallingwater still seems to be the one sketched out by Walt Whitman in "Song of the [Philadelphia] Exposition," when Wright was nine. What the Pyramids were for Egypt, Whitman says, our audacious new architecture will be for America, if we will but see it so:

> Mightier than Egypt's tombs,
> Fairer than Grecia's, Roma's temples,
> Prouder than Milan's statued, spired cathedral,
> More picturesque than Rhenish castle-keeps,
> We plan even now to raise, beyond them all,
> The great cathedral sacred industry, no tomb,
> A keep for life for practical invention. . . .
> (This, this and these, America, shall be your pyramids and obelisks,
> Your Alexandrian Pharos, gardens of Babylon,
> Your temple at Olympia.)

Like his adored Whitman, Wright addressed himself to a specifically American audience when he called Fallingwater the architecture of American democracy. For him, the horizontal planes of its balconies reflected the earth, hence "grounding" the building from any harm. Wright gave this horizontal emphasis a metaphorical meaning, too. "I see this extended horizontal line as the true earth-line of human life, indicative of freedom. Always."

The architecture critic Montgomery Schuyler said of another wonder of Wright's youth, the Brooklyn Bridge, that it was "one of the greatest and most characteristic" structures of its time. Great art generally goes hand-in-hand with great wealth, but not always. Not one of America's "greatest and most characteristic" buildings came out of the rich 1920s except for the counterculture Watts towers built by hand by Simon Rodia in Los Angeles. By contrast, the poor 1930s gave us the Empire State Building, Hoover Dam, the Golden Gate Bridge, and Fallingwater. The Kaufmann house, I speculated earlier, would probably not have emerged from the wealthy and profligate twenties: it needed the austere thirties to give it the drama and even the sadness that can be found in it.

I argued above that the Great Depression made Americans conscious of their vernacular heritage, a good deal of which is incorporated into Fallingwater. Aside from Aalto, European modern architects only rarely cited the vernacular in their buildings: theirs was the utopian dream-world of Le Corbusier's Villa Savoye or Mies's Barcelona Pavilion. Wright wanted instead to weave American vernacular folk rhythms throughout Fallingwater, the way Dvořák, Ives, Gershwin, and Copland had in their music. But Fallingwater did not just take from popular culture: it gave also. It helped shape the common postwar vernacular in the wave of ranch and split-level houses that began to cover the country as soon as wartime restrictions ended.

One reason Americans are so comfortable with Fallingwater is that many of them grew up in its ranch and split-level copies. The various Levittowns of the postwar years retailed Fallingwater far better than Wright himself did. Wright's Usonian houses never reached more than a few score clients, while the Levitts and other speculators selected certain elements of Fallingwater—the rock-faced stone, the uninterrupted horizontal lines, the window-walls and the flagstone-covered patios—and marketed them with an acute understanding of their potency as symbols of a richer life.

While some readings of Fallingwater are specific to the United States, its worldwide following makes clear that Fallingwater holds meaning for the rest of the world, too. This probably stems from its radical modernism. Today, not many Americans think of Fallingwater as a "home

A 1951 housing
development in
Mexico City lured
buyers with this
false representation
of Fallingwater

of tomorrow," but it still represents the future in many other countries. In 1951, for example, a draftsman working for the great designer Luis Barragán, or possibly Barragán himself, drew Fallingwater as a come-on for a housing development in Mexico City, not because the developers were actually putting up Fallingwaters, but because the house so perfectly represented the middle-class residential dream.

There is, however, a totally different and even contradictory reason for Fallingwater's global popularity, which is the deep spirituality that people intuit in the house. This I attribute to the numerous allusions Fallingwater makes to the architecture of the past. Some of these allusions are culture-specific, but most people can "decode" Fallingwater no matter what culture they come from, because its key allusions are to nature. The building cascades like the waterfall in front of it and the stone ledges behind, and its walls look as though nature itself had laid them up. Everyone understands these allusions, because nature is the one universal element on earth. Every visitor and viewer seems to find in Fallingwater some echo of his or her own culture.

The architect Paul Rudolph wisely called Fallingwater "a realized dream . . . [that] touches something deep within us about which, finally, none of us can speak." We can never fully articulate its hold over us. There are few parallels to the Fallingwater experience in architecture, but there is one in the Bible. An ancient commentary holds that the *manna* God fed the Israelites in the desert year after year was enticing because it took on the taste of any food the recipient wanted it to be. We could call Fallingwater architectural *manna*: we respond to it eagerly because it reminds us of those buildings or styles we love most. Depending on our own taste, it attracts us as rational or as romantic, abstract or representational, old-fashioned or high-tech. This makes Fallingwater one of the few buildings to be authentically beyond fashion. It will never grow unpopular so long as everyone projects his or her favorite image or ideology onto it.

In the Prologue I promised to substitute for the myths and miracles about Fallingwater a factual chronology of how the house came into being. I hope I have done that, but I admit that the birth of Fallingwater was affected by so many coincidences that it seems at times to have been conceived by the law of unintended consequences. If Joseph Urban hadn't

Tourists at Bear Run prepare to enter Fallingwater

died in 1933 and Benno Janssen hadn't become rich working for the Mellons, then either architect would have built Fallingwater as an elegant but unexceptional country house. If E. J. Kaufmann had not been ridiculed in the *Pittsburgh Bulletin Index* in 1933, he would not have needed to compensate by building himself an architectural marvel. If Frank Lloyd Wright had not been humiliated at MoMA in 1932, he might have lacked the fire to design a building so radical that he regained his standing in modern architecture. If Hitler had not taken over Germany in 1933, Kaufmann Jr. would have lingered on in Europe and his father would have pursued his architectural schooling there rather than in Los Angeles. Fallingwater's makeup also demanded a bucolic natural setting near a city of great industrial strength, and for its launch into instant fame it needed a circulation gimmick by Henry Luce, a once-in-a-lifetime image by a rookie photographer, and Ayn Rand working her way out of writer's block. Fallingwater's popularity depended as well on a new social sensitivity and the new cultural values spawned by the Depression, and a heightened American nationalism as the country moved to war.

In the end, though, and despite all these coincidences, the building owes its fame to nothing but itself. There was never a house like Fallingwater before, and there will never be a house like Fallingwater again.

I have acquired many debts in four decades as a scholar, but never so many as in the writing of this book. I have noted scores of individual contributions in my endnotes, including the many people who consented to interviews with me. But there are others whose help I want to acknowledge here in greater detail.

Foremost among these is Edgar Kaufmann Jr., who first encouraged me to study Fallingwater. I thanked him for that encouragement before he died and I repeat those thanks now, even though my findings would be unlikely to gratify him were he still alive. Any reader will see that my understanding of the origins of Fallingwater departs radically from Edgar's. I felt it imperative that I define clearly those differences in fact or interpretation: anything else would have made a mockery of historical method. But our differences were intellectual only, never personal. I was not only indebted to Edgar but much impressed by the man as a scholar, curator, and collector. Like everyone who loves Fallingwater, I acknowledge and respect the tenacious way in which he completed his father's dream of turning a private house into a national monument.

My second-largest debt is to the students who heard me out as I developed my ideas on Fallingwater. I thank particularly John Conti (also my patient traveling companion and fellow researcher in New York, Chicago, Wisconsin, and California), Alex Barron, Betsy McLean, Adam Young, Ken Kremer, Bill Boyle, Thad Pawlowski, and other members of the seminar on Fallingwater that I taught at the University of Pittsburgh in 1999.

The audiences at my various public lectures on Fallingwater reacted with many good ideas, too, and I particularly thank Robert A. M. Stern, for coordinating my participation in the fiftieth-anniversary symposium on Fallingwater at Columbia University in 1986; the Facoltà di Architettura, Università di Reggio Calabria, for inviting me to lecture on the "Casa sulla Cascata" in 1996—the first time in thirty years of lecturing in Italy that I was asked to discourse on an American subject; and ARLIS, the association of art librarians, for an especially helpful reaction when I lectured before them in 2000.

I extend special thanks to Bruce Brooks Pfeiffer, Margo Stipe, Indira Berndtson, and others on the staff of the Frank Lloyd Wright Foundation and to the staff of the Frank Lloyd Wright Building Conservancy.

At Fallingwater, I was given unfailingly generous assistance by the director, Lynda S. Waggoner, and by her predecessor, Thomas Mellon Schmidt, as well as by staff members Clinton Piper, Scott Daley, Denise Miner, Sarah Beyer, Michele Risdal-Barnes, Cara Armstrong, and Earl Friend. The staff of the Western Pennsylvania Conservancy was also helpful.

In Pittsburgh the following rendered me invaluable help: the staffs of both the Music and Art and the Pennsylvania departments of Carnegie Library of Pittsburgh, and the Carnegie reference librarians, particularly Marian Strieff; Martin Aurand at the Architecture Archives of Carnegie Mellon University; Susan Melnick at the Rauh Jewish Archives at the Senator John Heinz Pittsburgh Regional History Center, and many others at the Center; and Ray Anne Lockard and Marcia Rostek and the other highly supportive staff of the Frick Fine Arts Library at the University of Pittsburgh. My teaching colleagues in History of Art and Architecture at the university were also supportive, particularly David Wilkins, Fil Hearn, and Ken Neal, as were Lucy Fischer in Film Studies and Jerry Rosenberg and his successor deans in the university's Faculty of Arts and Sciences.

Other aid was rendered to me in Pittsburgh by Harold Corsini, Marlene Boyle, Louis Astorino, and Kai Gutschow; by Carole Mazzotta at Kaufmann's Department Store; by Al Tannler at the Pittsburgh History & Landmarks Foundation; and by Anne Swager at the Pittsburgh chapter of the American Institute of Architects. At the Carnegie Museum of Art, I was given support by Tracy Myers, Joseph Rosa, Charlene Shang Miller, and Lucy Stewart.

Other observers of the Pittsburgh scene to whom I am indebted are Donald Miller, Lu Donnelly, David Brumble, Jerry Morosco, Cyril Wecht, Ray Gindroz, David Lewis, Susan Schmidt, David Lambert, Alan I. W. Frank, Kenneth Love, C. Holmes Wolfe, and Dennis Kelleher, the current owner of La Tourelle. Always on the lookout for me were the late Fannia Weingartner, my wife Ellen, and our three children.

Many institutions around the country helped in my research. In New York, Janet Parks, Angela Giral, and Ted Goodman at Avery Fine Arts and Architectural Library; the archivists at Butler Library at Columbia University; and Sherman Clark, librarian at New York University. At the Museum of Modern Art I was much helped by Peter Reed, Terence Riley, Claire Dienes, and the library and archives staff. Other helpful New Yorkers were Carole Rifkind, Henry R. Luce III, Michael Schwarting, and Frances Campani.

In Boston, I profited from the use of the Boston Public Library, the Harvard College Library, Harvard's History of Art and Architecture Library, and its Frances Loeb Library of the Graduate School of Design.

In Chicago and Wisconsin, I was helped by Daniel Schulman and the curatorial and library staffs at the Art Institute of Chicago; by the owners of private Wright homes in Oak Park; by many associates at Wright's home and studio at Taliesin East; and by the archivists at Johnson's Wax in Racine.

In California, I was aided by Mark Henderson, Wim DeWitt, and others at the Getty Center for the History of Art and the Humanities. The archival staff at the Department of Special Collections at the UCLA Library was of outstanding help in making the Richard Neutra papers available to me. The owners or conservators of important California homes by Wright, Lloyd Wright, Neutra, and Schindler gave me extraordinarily kind cooperation: I thank particularly Brent and Beth Harris, Liz Topper, Barbara Jean Lovell, and Virginia Kazor; other supportive Californians were Julius Shulman, Steve Harby, Michael and Carole Dougherty, Kathryn Smith, and Thomas Hines.

Elsewhere around the country I was aided by James Rees at Mount Vernon; by the staff of the Pope-Leighy house; by Mark Dimunation and the Special Collections archivists at the Library of Congress; and by Cristiane Collins, Keith Eggener, and Grant Hildebrand. The Reverend Paul Evans Holbrook was extraordinarily helpful in tracking down connections between the Kaufmanns and the painter and master printer Victor Hammer.

In Italy, Lisa Ronchi and the late Bruno Zevi helped greatly with details on Zevi's pioneering book on Fallingwater, and in Israel, I was treated with exemplary courtesy by Barbara Wolff of the Albert Einstein Archives at the Hebrew University of Jerusalem.

Quotations from the letters of Frank Lloyd Wright are copyright © 2003 The Frank Lloyd Wright Foundation, Scottsdale, Arizona; used with permission. The quotation from *Fallingwater: A Conversation with Edgar Kaufmann, Jr.* is used by permission of Kenneth Love; quotations from the Richard Joseph Neutra Papers (Collection 1179) appear by permission of Dion Neutra, Architect, and of the Department of Special Collections, Charles E. Young Research Library, UCLA. Fallingwater is a trademark and a registered service mark ot the Western Pennsylvania Conservancy.

I am greatly indebted to the dedicated readers of all or parts of my early draft texts:

Ivan Chorney, Leslie Aizenman, Tom Hanchett, Lynda Waggoner, Kathryn Smith, and David DeLong. I am much beholden also to my editor, Robert Gottlieb, to Knopf's managing editor, Katherine Hourigan, to Lydia Buechler, Iris Weinstein, Romeo Enriquez, Eric Bliss, Paul Bogaards, Sheila O'Shea, Nicholas Latimer, Kathryn Zuckerman, Farah Miller, and to many others on the Knopf staff. It was a pleasure working with them and with my literary agent, William Clark.

Writing this book made me reflect several times on my late mother, who loved Fallingwater. Ethel was the kind of woman E. J. Kaufmann doted on: rich (at birth, anyway), aristocratic in breeding, elegant but high-spirited. There was a chronological fit between her life and that of the Kaufmanns, too. Her great-grandparents descended from an Austro-German merchant caste very much like E. J. and Liliane's, with the same proclivity for marriages between cousins. Ethel's lifespan of 1912–1992 closely matched that of Edgar Jr., and she and Father got engaged in the summer of 1934, when Kaufmann and Wright were courting, too. As was true of Wright and the Kaufmanns, my parents' lives were rich and full, and their memories are a blessing.

Pittsburgh–Isle au Haut–Pittsburg,
1985–2003

The bibliography on Wright and Fallingwater is vast: I list only the main archival materials, books, and articles below. Of particular note are the Sweeney bibliography, which carries nearly all the relevant literature up to 1978; the Storrer *Companion,* which gives reliable dates, names, and locations for Wright's standing buildings; and Anthony Alofsin's *Frank Lloyd Wright: An Index to the Taliesin Correspondence,* a guide to nearly all letters to or from Wright, indexed by author, recipient, and date. Unless otherwise indicated, the Wright letters that I quote here form part of the Frank Lloyd Wright Foundation Archives at Scottsdale, Arizona, which may also be ordered in reproductions from the Getty Center in Los Angeles. The MoMA Archives preserve important materials on the Fallingwater exhibit that was held there in 1938.

Learning about E. J. Kaufmann Sr. is a good deal more difficult. The only comprehensive biographical sketch on Kaufmann is provided in my "Edgar Jonas Kaufmann, Sr." in *American National Biography* 12 (1999): 400–01. Kaufmann listed the bare facts of his life in a paid entry in Frank Harper, *Pittsburgh of Today: Its Resources and People* 4 (1932): 551–53. On Kaufmann's business life, see "Seller's Market: In war Kaufmann's of Pittsburgh, like all U.S. department stores, has sold everything it could buy. It expects soon to buy more," *Fortune* 30/5 (November 1944): 122–31; on Kaufmann's flamboyant personal life, see Leon Harris's *Merchant Princes;* for his context in Pittsburgh and as a Wright client, see the studies by Cleary, Feldman, Toker, and Wilk, as noted below. In terms of firsthand materials, Kaufmann as a builder is well represented in the archives at Taliesin, at Fallingwater, at Avery Library at Columbia University, and in the Neutra Papers at UCLA. Nothing but scraps survive on Kaufmann's personal life except for his letters to and from Wright. Kaufmann's business papers were never saved, either: some store records that are now at the Senator John Heinz Pittsburgh Regional History Center preserve interesting fragments on the family business under his leadership, but they do not constitute a real archive on Kaufmann. The same center has some general Kaufmann family materials, and the Fallingwater archives has more, plus some of E. J.'s legal papers.

MoMA has a small file on Edgar Kaufmann Jr., and the Fallingwater Archives record how he managed the house and grounds from 1955 to 1963, with occasional later notes; otherwise Kaufmann Jr.'s papers have been dispersed, too.

Most of the American buildings cited in the text are found in G. E. Kidder Smith's *Source Book of American Architecture: 500 Notable Buildings from the 10th Century to the Present* (Princeton, 1996, and later eds.). For modern architecture around the world, two convenient sources are William Curtis's *Modern Architecture Since 1900* (1982, and later eds.) and Kenneth Frampton's *Modern Architecture: A Critical History* (London, 1980, and later eds.). For the progress of modernism in the United States in the 1930s, see Terry Smith's *Making the Modern: Industry, Art, and Design in America* (Chicago, 1993).

INTERVIEWS

For E. J. Kaufmann, I conducted interviews with his son, Prof. Edgar J. Kaufmann Jr. (November 18, 1985, and April 15, 1986); his grandson Ted Stanford (October 12, 2000); his nephews Irwin D. Wolf Jr. (March 10, 1987) and John Wolf (October 21, 1998); his nieces Joan Kaufmann Mendelsohn (February 22, 1995) and Betty Wolf Loeb (January 12, 2003);

his cousins Stanley Baer (a dozen conversations in the mid-1970s) and James and Ruth Bachman (April 22, 1999); the Kaufmann clan historian Karl Kaufmann Jr. (July 21, 2002); E. J.'s friend and literary protégé Stefan Lorant (June 4, 1988); his close friend Dorothy Hast Blumenthal (December 12, 1989); his lawyer Ralph Demmler (October 28, 1986); his business rival Stanley Marcus (March 6, 1987); his architectural protégé Dahlen Ritchey (August 6, 1998); Kaufmann's employee Irene Pasinski (April 24, 1999); Ermalee Desenberg, who met the Kaufmanns after her escape from Nazi Germany in the late 1930s (February 15, 2002); Stanley Rosin, president of E. J.'s Temple Isaiah in Palm Springs (February 16, 2001); family friend and Bear Run neighbor Darthea Speyer (December 4 and 5, 1997); and E. J.'s cactus gardener and friend Patricia Moorten (May 6, 2000) and her son, Kaufmann's teenage pal Clark Moorten (February 19, 2002).

Specific to Fallingwater, I interviewed Fallingwater's current director, Lynda Waggoner, and its former director, Tom Schmidt, numerous times since 1985; its reconstruction engineer Robert Silman and its concrete specialist Norman Weiss (April 10, 1999); its post-tensioning specialist Mario Suarez (February 12, 2002); Ray Hall, grandson of Fallingwater's builder Walter J. Hall (December 21, 1999); longtime Bear Run employee and Fallingwater mason Earl Friend (July 30, 1999); Fallingwater's former cook, Elsie Henderson (April 9, 1999); Fallingwater researcher Denise Miner (February 12, 2002, and numerous earlier conversations); Fallingwater guide Sue Rugg (December 9, 2001); and former Fallingwater guests William Block (September 19, 1998) and Richard Wechsler (March 21, 1999).

For Frank Lloyd Wright and his circle I interviewed his grandson, Eric Lloyd Wright (April 9, 1999); Wright's early apprentices Edgar Tafel (December 8, 1989, July 13, 1999, and numerous other times), Cornelia Brierly [Berndtson] (December 8, 1989, and June 24 and 26, 1999), Abe Dombar (June 25, 1999), and Wesley Peters (December 8, 1989); Wright's draftsman David Dodge (June 24, 1999); Frank Lloyd Wright School of Architecture graduates Harold Hanen (March 12, 1999) and Gerald Lee Morosco (June 24, 1999); Wright scholars Donald Hoffmann (December 29, 1989, December 6, 1997, and other times), Richard Cleary (April 15, 1988, April 10, 1999, and other times), Bruce Brooks Pfeiffer (April 15, 1988, and June 24, 1999), Kathryn Smith (May 8, 2000), Brendan Gill (March 20, 1990), Anthony Alofsin (April 17 and June 21, 1993), and Bruno Zevi (September 1, 1999); and Gus Brown, owner of Wright's Ennis-Brown house (May 8, 2000).

On miscellaneous questions I also interviewed James S. Ackerman (September 20, 2000); Rachel Adler and Ann Yaffe Phillips (January 8, 1993); the Arensberg clan historian Charles Arensberg II (October 12, 2000); Gilbert Boddy Jr. (November 1995); former Palm Springs mayor Frank Bogert (February 19, 2002); Mosette Broderick (April 24, 1991, and May 3, 1999); John Carter Brown (April 17, 1993); Newton Chapin Jr. (June 6, 1998); architects Gary Coates and Mark Schapiro (March 6, 1998); John Coolidge (January 19, 1990); independent scholar George Goodwin (May 27, 1998); the writers Harriet Gross (January, 1987) and Leon Harris (June 25, 1999); the architectural historian Thomas Hines (May 8, 2000); architect Tasso Katselas (April 9, 1999); Aline Saarinen's son Donald Louchheim (August 26 1998); the survivors of Philip and Leah Lovell: their daughter-in-law Barbara Jean, their son Hap, and their great-niece and clan historian Susan Bernstein (February 15–19, 2002); Paul Mayén (April 14, 1999); Palm Springs historian Tony Merchell (May 3, 2000); Dion Neutra (May 2, 2000); Harry Sampey (July 21, 2000); Frick family historian Martha Sanger (September 13, 2002); Richard Mellon Scaife (May 15, 2002); the architectural photographer Julius Shulman (May 2, 2000); Richard Tobias (February 13, 1999); Caroline Wagner (December 8, 1989); Paul Wiegman, senior naturalist for the Western Pennsylvania Conservancy (July 30, 1999); Glenn Willumson (December 1, 2002); and Edward Zuckerman (June 9, 2002).

ARCHIVAL SOURCES

Certain archives are indicated by the words and abbreviations listed below:

Avery: Kaufmann Papers, Avery Library, Columbia University, New York

Carnegie: Clippings in the Pennsylvania Division, Carnegie Library of Pittsburgh

FLWF: Frank Lloyd Wright Foundation Archives, Scottsdale, Arizona

Fallingwater Archives: Fallingwater Archives at Bear Run

Heinz: Senator John Heinz Pittsburgh Regional History Center, Pittsburgh; contains both Kaufmann Family Papers and the Media Relations Department files of Kaufmann's Department Store

Library of Congress: Victor Hammer Papers, Library of Congress

MoMA: Library and Archives, Museum of Modern Art, New York

UCLA: Richard Neutra Papers, Charles E. Young Reference Library Special Collections, University of California at Los Angeles

WPC: Kaufmann and Fallingwater Files, Western Pennsylvania Conservancy headquarters, Pittsburgh

SELECTED PUBLISHED SOURCES

The following works are cited throughout the Notes in abbreviated format (for example, Hoffmann, *Fallingwater*). Other more specialized works are cited in full in their first appearance, and subsequently with a short title only. New York is the place of publication unless indicated otherwise.

Alofsin, Anthony, ed. *Frank Lloyd Wright: An Index to the Taliesin Correspondence*. 1988; 5 vols.

Cleary, Richard. *Merchant Prince and Master Builder: Edgar J. Kaufmann and Frank Lloyd Wright*. Seattle, 1999.

Frank Lloyd Wright's Fallingwater. Photographs by Ezra Stoller, introduction by Neil Levine. 1999.

Futagawa, Yukio, and Paul Rudolph. *Frank Lloyd Wright: Kaufmann House, "Fallingwater," Bear Run, Pennsylvania, 1936*. Tokyo, 1970.

Futagawa, Yukio, and Bruce Brooks Pfeiffer. *Frank Lloyd Wright*. 12 vols. Tokyo, 1984–92. Contains an eight-volume monograph on the completed works, three volumes of preliminary studies, and one volume of color renderings, with Fallingwater documented in vols. 5, 11, and 12.

Gill, Brendan. *Many Masks: A Life of Frank Lloyd Wright*. 1987.

Harris, Leon. "The Kaufmanns of Pittsburgh," in *Merchant Princes*, pp. 91–111. 1979.

Hildebrand, Grant. *The Wright Space: Pattern and Meaning in Frank Lloyd Wright's Houses*. Seattle, 1991.

Hoffmann, Donald. *Frank Lloyd Wright's Fallingwater: The House and Its History*. 2nd ed., 1993.

Hoppen, Donald. *The Seven Ages of Frank Lloyd Wright: The Creative Process.* 1993. Contains a listing of over 1,000 buildings and projects by Wright, pp. 173–81.

Johnson, Donald. *Frank Lloyd Wright Versus America: The 1930s.* Cambridge, Mass., 1990.

Kaufmann, Edgar J., Jr. "Twenty-five Years of the House on the Waterfall," in *L'Architettura* (August 1962): 255–62. This was republished in Bruno Zevi and Edgar J. Kaufmann, *La Casa sulla Cascata di F.Ll. Wright / F. Lloyd Wright's Fallingwater,* pp. 20–25, Milan, 1963, and in *Writings on Wright: Selected Comment on Frank Lloyd Wright,* ed. H. Allen Brooks, pp. 69–72 (Cambridge, Mass., 1981).

———. *Fallingwater: A Frank Lloyd Wright Country House.* 1986.

———. *Nine Commentaries on Frank Lloyd Wright.* Cambridge, Mass., 1989. Contains Alfred Willis's bibliography of Kaufmann's writings, pp. 137–56.

Levine, Neil. *The Architecture of Frank Lloyd Wright.* Princeton, 1996, esp. "The Temporal Dimension of Fallingwater," pp. 217–53.

McCarter, Robert. *Fallingwater.* 1994.

———. *Frank Lloyd Wright.* London, 1997. Contains a complete listing of Wright's works by Bruce Brooks Pfeiffer, pp. 344–59.

Mumford, Lewis. "The Sky Line: At Home, Indoors and Out," *The New Yorker* (February 12, 1938): 31.

Rand, Ayn. *The Fountainhead.* 1943; repr. 1968, and later eds.

Secrest, Meryle. *Frank Lloyd Wright.* 1992.

Silman, Robert. "The Plan to Save Fallingwater," *Scientific American* 283/3 (September 2000): 88–95.

Storrer, William. *The Frank Lloyd Wright Companion.* Chicago, 1993. Also on CD-ROM, this augments Storrer's earlier *Architecture of Frank Lloyd Wright* (Cambridge, Mass., 1982, and later eds.). All three versions illustrate each building.

Sweeney, Robert. *Frank Lloyd Wright: An Annotated Bibliography.* Los Angeles, 1978.

Toker, Franklin. *Pittsburgh: An Urban Portrait.* University Park, Pa.; 2d ed. Pittsburgh, 1995.

Twombly, Robert. *Frank Lloyd Wright: His Life and His Architecture.* 1979.

"Usonian Architect," *Time* 31 (January 17, 1938): 29.

Waggoner, Lynda. *Fallingwater: Frank Lloyd Wright's Romance with Nature.* 1996.

Wright, Frank Lloyd. *An Autobiography.* 1932. Quotations come from the 2nd rev. ed., 1943 (repr. 1998) unless specified otherwise.

———. *Collected Writings.* Bruce Brooks Pfeiffer, ed. 1992–95; 5 vols.

NOTES TO THE TEXT

PROLOGUE: APPROACHING FALLINGWATER

Fallingwater's fame: The oft-repeated citation of Fallingwater as "unquestionably the most famous private residence ever built" first appeared in Futagawa and Pfeiffer, *Frank Lloyd Wright* 5 (Tokyo, 1985), 164.

Wright standing under the balconies: Kaufmann, "Twenty-five Years," 23; Donald Hoppen, *Seven Ages,* 101.

ONE: THE DEAD MAN OF MODERN ARCHITECTURE PLANS A COMEBACK

Wright the forgotten man: Hoppen's *Seven Ages* dissects the various fallows in Wright's career. John Cushman Fistere commented on Wright in his "Poets in Steel," *Vanity Fair* (December 1931): 58–59, 98; Ayn Rand's reaction to Fistere appears in the *Journals of Ayn*

Rand, ed. David Harriman (1997), 150. Harold Sterner's appraisal of Wright appeared in *Architectural Forum* (February 1936): 7—a citation I owe to Meryle Secrest's *Wright,* 396. Wright made his remark to Fiske Kimball in a letter of 1928 that was reprinted in "American Architecture: Correspondence of Walter Pach, Paul Cret, Frank Lloyd Wright and Erich Mendelsohn," *Architectural Record* 65 (May 1929): 434.

Wright as father of modern architecture: The question of what Wright gave to modern architecture and what he derived from other practitioners of the style is well summarized in Vincent Scully, "Frank Lloyd Wright vs. the International Style," *Art News* 53 (March 1954): 32–35, 64–66. See Henry-Russell Hitchcock, "American Influence Abroad," in *The Rise of an American Architecture,* ed. Edgar J. Kaufmann Jr. (1970), 3–48, at p. 37, with particular attention to Gropius's Administration Building for the 1914 Werkbund Exposition in Cologne.

America turning away from modernism: The *retour à l'ordre* is discussed in Levine, *Wright,* 151, 457 n. 11. For a detailed explanation of why the United States turned its back on modernism in the 1920s, see T. J. Jackson Lears, *No Place of Grace: Antimodernism and the Transformation of American Culture, 1880–1920* (1981), and *The Culture of Consumption: Critical Essays in American History, 1880–1980,* ed. Richard Wightman Fox and T. J. Jackson Lears (1983). The competition entries for the Chicago Tribune Tower are fully illustrated in *The International Competition for a New Administration Building for the Chicago Tribune MCMXXII* (Chicago, 1923). Russell Lynes, *The Tastemakers* (1954), 247, noted: "Some suburbs had zoning laws that prohibited the construction of Modern houses lest they spoil the character and atmosphere of the community." The various camps in American interwar architecture are delineated by Susanne Ralston Lichtenstein, "Editing Architecture: *Architectural Record* and the Growth of Modern Architecture, 1928–1938," Ph.D. thesis, Cornell University, 1990.

Modern versus modernistic: The attack on modernistic comes from the Museum of Modern Art's *Guide to Modern Architecture: Northeast States,* ed. John McAndrew (1940), 15 n. 2. "Art Deco" as a stylistic term had almost no prevalence in the United States until after World War II. That term and "Moderne" both derived from the title of the Exposition Internationale des Arts Décoratifs et Industriels Modernes held in Paris in 1925, but in the twenties and thirties the style was generally known as Zigzag or Jazz Modern. An excellent summary of the social meaning of Art Deco in the United States is Lucy Fischer's *Designing Women: Cinema, Art Deco, and the Female Form* (2003).

Curtiss and Polk: Curtiss's Boley Building is described and illustrated in Kidder Smith, *Sourcebook,* 331; Polk's Hallidie Building on p. 344. Albert Kahn's attack on European modernism is reported and analyzed in Smith, *Making the Modern,* 59, 81–82. The threat to remake the Bauhaus into a traditional German architectural idiom was reported in *Architectural Forum* (October 1937): 22. For the Nazi position on architectural modernism, see Barbara Miller Lane, *Architecture and Politics in Germany, 1918–1945* (Cambridge, Mass., 1968, 1985).

Wright's rivalry with the Europeans: Mies's discussion of his glass tower project of 1922 and his Eliat house project of 1925 appeared in the February 1927 *Kunstblatt,* 58, including the phrase *"Der Gesamtraum wird nach der Verwendungszwerk organisch gegliedert"* (The whole space will be organically partitioned, according to its function). Wright's view of the International Style is discussed in Levine, *Wright,* 151 and 457 n. 11. The fly-swatting monologue was confirmed for me by Wright's draftsman David Dodge.

Falsifying Wright's old drawings: Johnson, *Wright Versus America,* 100–01, cites the recollection of Henry Klumb that it was his idea to rework certain of Wright's old drawings, but Wright still bears responsibility for allowing the resulting drawings to be reproduced scores of times as though they had been executed thirty years ahead of their time. Wright's slicked-up perspective of Unity Temple appears in his *Autobiography* (1932 ed.), opposite p. 156.

Recognition in Europe, disdain in U.S.: The Wright monographs appearing in the 1920s were *The Life-Work of the American Architect Frank Lloyd Wright*, ed. H. Th. Wijdeveld (Santpoort, Netherlands, 1925); *Frank Lloyd Wright: Aus dem Lebenswerke eines Architekten*, ed. H. de Fries (Berlin, 1926); and Henry-Russell Hitchcock's short photo book, *Frank Lloyd Wright* (Paris, 1928), a reprint of his article on Wright in *Cahiers d'Art* 2 (1927): 322–28. On Wright's reputation in Europe: Bruno Taut, *Modern Architecture* (London, 1929), 68. Ralph Flint's comments appeared in *Art News*, February 13, 1932 (I owe this reference to Franz Schulze, *Philip Johnson: Life and Work* [1994], 80).

Schindler, Neutra, and Frey: Esther McCoy, *Five California Architects* (1960), reliably summarizes the development of California modernism, while Robert Sweeney, *Wright in Hollywood* (1994), 76–79, succinctly encapsulates Wright's relationships with Schindler and Neutra. Wright's "two thieves" remark is recorded in Hoffmann, *Fallingwater* (1978 ed. only), 89 n. 14, with the date of 1932. Wright complained of Neutra as a copyist of his work in a letter of January 19, 1932, to Lewis Mumford, reproduced in *Frank Lloyd Wright and Lewis Mumford: Thirty Years of Correspondence*, ed. Bruce Brooks Pfeiffer and Robert Wojtowicz (2001), 124. The relevant part of Hitchcock's letter to Wright is reproduced in Arthur Drexler and Thomas Hines, *The Architecture of Richard Neutra: From International Style to California Modern* (1982), 49. The standard monographs on Neutra are Willy Boesiger, *Richard Neutra: Buildings and Projects* (1966), and Thomas Hines, *Richard Neutra and the Search for Modern Architecture: A Biography and History* (Berkeley, 1994). The question of Wright's alienation from American culture of the thirties is well explored in Johnson, *Wright Versus America*. Deborah Pokinski, *The Development of the American Modern Style* (Ann Arbor, 1984), assesses American and European attitudes to the International Style. Frey and Kocher's Aluminaire House now stands on the Central Islip campus of the New York Institute of Technology on Long Island. On its chronology and links to Le Corbusier, see Michael Webb, *Modernism Reborn: Mid-Century American Houses* (2001), 58.

Attacking the International Style: The continuing struggle against the International Style by Wright and the Wrightians in the 1950s is summarized in Secrest, *Wright*, 551–53. Wright's attack on the International Style appeared in *Architectural Record* (June 1953): 12, 332.

The Taliesin Fellowship: Fellowship life is vividly recalled in two books by Edgar Tafel: *Apprentice to Genius: Years with Frank Lloyd Wright* (1979), and *About Wright: An Album of Recollections by Those Who Knew Frank Lloyd Wright* (1993; repr. 2001 as *Frank Lloyd Wright: Recollections by Those Who Knew Him*). Additional information is put forward by apprentice Cornelia Brierly in her *Tales of Taliesin: A Memoir of Fellowship* (Tempe, Ariz., 1999) and in Myron Marty and Shirley Marty, *Frank Lloyd Wright's Taliesin Fellowship* (Kirksville, Mo., 1999). Harold Zellman also has a Taliesin Fellowship history in progress. The 1930s tuition figures for Yale come from James S. Ackerman; those for Harvard come from the Harvard University Archives. The Frank Lloyd Wright School of Architecture continues apprentice traditions at both Taliesin East and West today. Apprentices still do communal labor, and the day still starts with an early breakfast.

Wright and MoMA: The epochal 1932 exhibition was meticulously researched by Terence Riley in his book *The International Style: Exhibition 15 and the Museum of Modern Art* (1992). In 1931, the co-curator of the planned 1932 show, Philip Johnson, wrote to the Dutch architect J. J. P. Oud: "Frank Lloyd Wright was included only from courtesy and in recognition of his past contributions" (Riley, *International Style*, 41, 206 n. 5). Hitchcock's dismissive comment on Wright appeared in Henry-Russell Hitchcock and Philip Johnson, *The International Style: Architecture Since 1922* (1932), 27. The 1995 revised edition of this book contains afterthoughts by the curators about their attempt to exclude or minimize Wright. Wright's comments on the MoMA show appeared in Thomas Craven's *Modern Art: The Men, the Movements, the Meaning* (1934), 289; his response to Hitchcock appears in *Frank Lloyd Wright on Architecture: Selected Writings, 1894–1940*, ed. Frederick Gutheim (1941), 136; his rebuttal to Johnson is reproduced in Schulze, *Johnson*, 427 n. 82. Wright's rebound was truly the stuff of legend. The humiliating exhibit on the International Style opened at MoMA on January 24, 1932; his triumphant Fallingwater show at MoMA had its patrons' opening six years later, to the very day.

TWO: E. J. KAUFMANN OF PITTSBURGH
SUFFERS HUMILIATION OF ANOTHER SORT

Sources on Kaufmann and his family: A brief summary of the archival and published sources on E. J. Kaufmann is provided in the introduction to these notes. A detailed and generally accurate Kaufmann family tree survives among the Kaufmann Family Papers at the Heinz Regional History Center in Pittsburgh. Details on a half-dozen individual Kaufmanns reside in the clippings files in the Pennsylvania Department of the Carnegie Library in Pittsburgh. Notes on the first generation of Kaufmanns are also scattered through Jacob Feldman, *The Jewish Experience in Western Pennsylvania* (Pittsburgh, 1986). J. A. Caldwell's *Atlas of Washington County* (Condit, Ohio, 1876; repr. Rimersburg, Pa., 1976) shows a peddler exactly contemporary with the Kaufmanns plying his wares in an adjoining county, as I learned from Terry Necciai. The Kaufmann family tombs survive in Rodef Shalom's cemetery at West View, north of Pittsburgh, and a half-dozen family portraits constitute a Kaufmann family shrine of sorts at the Jewish Community Center in Pittsburgh's Squirrel Hill.

The Kaufmann store: The ranking of Kaufmann's is featured in a newspaper clipping of February 27, 1925, in the Kaufmann's Department Store Files, Pennsylvania Department, Carnegie Library of Pittsburgh. Other information comes from *Kaufmann's: A Pittsburgh Tradition*, a video issued by the store in 1997.

The Kaufmanns as builders: The architectural character of Kaufmann's North Side neighborhood is described in Toker, *Pittsburgh*, 153–76, esp. 171–72; and in James Van Trump, *1300–1335 Liverpool Street, Manchester, Old Allegheny, Pittsburgh* (Pittsburgh, n.d. but ca. 1965), 17. Morris Kaufmann's first house in Squirrel Hill was cited in the *Inland Architect and News Record*, 24/5 (December 1894): 51; his second mansion appears in *Palmer's Pictorial Pittsburgh* (Pittsburgh, 1905), 34. The Kaufmann homes appear in the *Directory of Pittsburgh and Allegheny Cities* (Pittsburgh, 1881, and later eds.) and in *Diffenbacher's Directory of Pittsburgh, Allegheny, and Vicinity* (Pittsburgh, 1896). The Kaufmann donations in the medical field are listed in Carol Stein Bleier, Lu Donnelly, and Samuel Granowitz, *A History of Montefiore Hospital of Pittsburgh, Pennsylvania, 1898–1990* (Pittsburgh, 1997), 11, 15, 26.

Rodef Shalom as rebuilt in 1901 is illustrated and described in Feldman, *Jewish Experience*, 14, 186–87; the 1907 building is discussed in Toker, *Pittsburgh*, 114–15. The Irene Kaufmann Settlement is illustrated and minutely described in *Pittsburgh: How to See It*, ed. G. Fleming (Pittsburgh, 1916), 248–49; a standing remnant is described in Toker, *Pittsburgh*, 239. Additional photographs, including one of Edward Stotz's design for the 1928 wing, are in the Irene Kaufmann Settlement File, Archives of Industrial Society,

Hillman Library, University of Pittsburgh, and in the Kaufmann Family Papers at the Heinz Pittsburgh Regional History Center. The latter archive also contains notations on the donations advanced by Carnegie and Frick.

The Archives of Industrial Society also preserves the city building permit for the Kaufmann Settlement house, which lists the builder as New York's Thompson-Starrett Co. The main designers for the firm were Theodore and Goldwyn Starrett, who were prominent in the design of Bloomingdale's and other large department stores—which is probably how the Kaufmanns got to know them.

E. J. branching out, and taking over: Though he dropped out of Yale's Sheffield School after just a year, Kaufmann sent detailed reports of his activities to the *Sheffield Scientific School Alumni Reports* for 1906 and 1912: my thanks to the Yale University Archives for locating these records for me. Paul Mellon, *Reflections in a Silver Spoon* (1992), 114, recalled that the men in Yale College and Sheffield had almost no social connections. The case of "Kaufmann v. Kaufmann," Nos. 201–18, Supreme Court of Pennsylvania, was argued November 4, 1912, with the decision of January 6, 1913, being linked to an earlier court case in 1907. My main source on the fight among the Kaufmann was Stanley Baer, E. J. Kaufmann's distant cousin. E. J. listed his time in Europe in 1907–08 and in Connellsville in his entry in *Pittsburgh of Today*; further details are from his obituary in the *Pittsburgh Post-Gazette*, April 16, 1955. M. Graham Netting, who knew Kaufmann well, confirmed Kaufmann's time in Connellsville in his *Fifty Years of the Western Pennsylvania Conservancy* (Pittsburgh, 1982), 140. The name of Kaufmann's general store in Connellsville remains undetected because E. J. seems to have bought a store without changing its old name. The *Connellsville Sesquecentennial History* of 1906 lists a dozen prominent Jewish-owned stores: Kaufmann might have bought any one of these, or one of the dozens of other stores in town in 1908 or 1909.

An early Kaufmann's stock certificate survives in the store archives. The store's reincorporation date of January 13, 1913, comes from an article on operations at Kaufmann's in the *Pittsburgh Bulletin Index* of July 31, 1941. The article gave family ownership percentages for the store as: E. J. Kaufmann, 44.6%; Liliane, 3%; their son Edgar Jr., 2%; E. J.'s brother Oliver, 8%; Oliver's wife, 4%; E. J.'s sister Martha Wolf, 1%; Martha's husband I. D. Wolf, 5%; and E. J.'s sister Stella Mundheim, one tenth of one percent.

Kaufmann and Pittsburgh: I am indebted to the writer Harriet Gross for her recollection of her talk with Kaufmann in 1953, which elicited his "I love my city" quote (Gross went to ask E. J. for permission to form a chapter of Hadassah in Liliane's name). E. J. was recalled as "the most brilliant mind in Pittsburgh" in an unpublished quote by Park Martin, executive director of the Allegheny Conference on Community Development, in 1955 (Stefan Lorant Files, Pennsylvania Department, Carnegie Public Library). Plans for Kaufmann's funeral were detailed in the *Pittsburgh Sun-Telegraph* for April 15, 1955, and in the *Pittsburgh Post-Gazette* for April 16, 1955. Kaufmann made his lament that he was worth only one-tenth as much as A. C. Speyer to his cousin Sidney Bachman, as recalled by Sidney's son James.

Culture and the department store: The linkage between the popularization of modern art and the department stores was explored in William Leach, *Land of Desire: Merchants, Power, and the Rise of a New American Culture* (1993). The Pittsburgh venue of the Armory Show was documented in Aaron Sheon, "1913: Pittsburgh in the Cubist Avant-Garde," *Carnegie Magazine* 56 (July-August 1982): 12–17, 38–39; and Sheon, "1913: Forgotten Cubist Exhibitions in America," *Arts Magazine* 57 (March 1983): 93–107. The showing of MoMA's architecture show at Bullock's Wilshire is documented in Robert A. M. Stern et al., *New York 1930: Architecture and Urbanism Between the Two World Wars* (1987), 792 n. 106. Philip Johnson wrote a long letter to E. J. Kaufmann about MoMA's proposed exhibition on public housing on March 18, 1932, in which he noted that Catherine Bauer "has told me of your interest in housing." Johnson's April 22, 1932, telegram to Kaufmann reads in part: "I understand from Mr Hitchcock that you are seriously considering taking the architectural exhibition of the Museum of Modern Art in Jan 1933 stop the Museum is very anxious to have this date settled stop they would very much appreciate receiving word from you as to what decisions you have reached (signed) Philip Johnson, director of the exhibition." I. D. Wolf responded to Johnson on April 23, 1932. Johnson sent other letters to the Pittsburgh Housing Association, the Pittsburgh Architectural Club, and to Sidney Teller, executive director of the Irene Kaufmann Settlement (and part of E. J.'s brain trust), with the same objective of sending the show to Kaufmann's Department Store. Johnson informed Kaufmann that the show would later appear at Bullock's Wilshire in Los Angeles and at Sears, Roebuck in Chicago (MoMA: Records of the Department of Circulating Exhibitions).

Kaufmann's business innovations: The curvilinear counters are illustrated and discussed in "Seller's Market," 130. The counters were also illustrated in Emrich Nicholson's *Contemporary Shops in the United States* (1945), 152, which attributed their design to Kaufmann's art director, Laszlo Gabor (Cleary, *Merchant*, 33). Sonnenberg and Bernays's work with department stores appears in Harris, *Merchant Princes*, 27, 181ff. The minute surviving fraction of the store archive does not specify whether E. J. employed a national PR firm, but we know that Kaufmann worked closely in the 1930s with the Pittsburgh PR consultant Frank Harper, and in 1947 he used the Pittsburgh publicist Harry Kodinsky to help control publicity on his new house in Palm Springs. Kaufmann's contest on the subject of arts and industry was announced in *Fortune*'s May 1930 issue; Catherine Bauer's winning essay was published in *Fortune*, May 1931: 94ff. The request from the Catholic diocese for Kaufmann's spare angels is preserved among the miscellaneous clippings from Kaufmann's Media Relations Files that are now in the Heinz Center. Gerard Wolfe, *New York: A Guide to the Metropolis* (1975), 173ff., well describes the stores that once flourished on Sixth Avenue above 18th Street in Manhattan, from which the Kaufmanns learned many of their marketing techniques. These stores constitute an extraordinary relic of American commercial architecture.

Kaufmann's contacts with Germany: E. J.'s cousin James Bachman keeps several postcards, written in German, that document how frequently the Kaufmanns visited Germany until World War I. E. J.'s own German is not in doubt, either: the all-German card that Laszlo Gabor drew up for E. J.'s fiftieth birthday in 1935 would have made no sense were Kaufmann not able to read the jokes. Liliane's German letter to Victor Hammer of 1927 is among the Hammer Papers at the Library of Congress. Peter Hall, *Cities in Civilization: Culture, Innovation, and Urban Order* (London, 1998), 242–43, gives an excellent summary of the advanced German technology then on view in Berlin. Stanley Marcus's recollections about E. J. came from an interview and his communication of October 12, 1987. *The Pittsburgh Plan* newsreel survives in the Fallingwater Archives.

Kaufmann's identification with his store: The Elbert Hubbard quote comes from Leach, *Land of Desire*, 42. E. J. was described as an "art-lover" in the *Pittsburgh Bulletin Index* of September 28, 1933. Kaufmann described hosting Einstein in his letter to Wright of December 30, 1934.

The Kaufmanns as Jews: The ritual bath on the Kaufmann farm was recalled by James Bachman and confirmed by Karl Kaufmann Jr. The "Pittsburgh Platform" of 1885 was repudiated by a gathering of rabbis who met in Pittsburgh 111 years later. The Kaufmanns' collection of Old Masters survives today only in the inventories among the Kaufmann Papers in the Heinz Center. The circumstances of E. J.'s joining Temple Isaiah in Palm Springs were recalled for me by Stanley Rosin, the temple's founder, who enlisted his membership. Kaufmann was a founding member of Palm Springs's all-Jewish Tamarisk Golf Club, which was started in 1953 after the applications of twenty Jewish candidates for membership (including that of Kaufmann's neighbor Jack Benny) were thrown out of the Thunderbird Golf Club, according to former Palm Springs mayor Frank Bogert.

The criticism of Joseph Pulitzer as a renegade Jew is documented in J. Douglas Bates, *The Pulitzer Prize: The Inside Story of America's Most Prestigious Award* (1991), 70. On Otto Kahn: Kate Simon, *Fifth Avenue: A Very Social History* (1978), 254; on E. J.'s crucifix-crowned headboard at La Tourelle: Donald Miller, *The Architecture of Benno Janssen* (Pittsburgh, 1997), 91.

Kaufmann as social climber: E. J.'s listing of the Loyal Order of Moose comes from the 1918 compendium *Distinguished Jews of America. Pittsburgh of Today* listed his memberships in seven clubs. In a 1954 Social Register, Kaufmann stated his membership in the Harmonie Club in New York, the Tamarisk in Palm Springs, and the Pittsburgh Field Club. This latter claim is demonstrably false (communication from club historian James C. Hayes, March 6, 1991).

Harris's references—probably exaggerated—to the Kaufmanns as track lords in his *Merchant Princes,* 96, were fed to him by Oliver Kaufmann, but these can now be confirmed in detail by scores of newspaper and racing-form references to E. J.'s French-bred horses such as Libertin VIII and Sardaneza in the 1920s (archives of the Rolling Rock Club at Ligonier, Pennsylvania, communicated to me by Denise and Donna Miner on January 11, 2001).

We lack comparable hard data on Liliane's success as a breeder of long-haired dachshunds. Family lore says the dogs won prizes, but none have yet been confirmed by the various dog shows around the United States. The dogs evidently had good breeding, though: after Liliane bequeathed some to her cousin Sidney Bachman in 1952, he turned several into winners, according to his son James. In the 1930s, breeding dachshunds was the height of fashion: Henry Clay Frick's daughter-in-law Frances had herself depicted in an oil portrait in 1935 with her long-haired dachshund. See Martha Sanger, *The Henry Clay Frick Houses* (2001), 243. My thanks to Ray Anne Lockard for pointing this out.

Anti-Jewish prejudice: Rockefeller's letter appears in Joe A. Morris, *Nelson Rockefeller: A Biography* (1960), 77. The quota on medical students at the University of Pittsburgh is cited in Bleier and Donnelly, *Montefiore,* 50–51, 112. Ziegfeld's hiring practices are defined in Linda Mizejewski, *Ziegfeld Girl* (Durham, N.C., 1999), 6, 34, 116, 151. Wright informed Kaufmann of his exclusion from Chandler's San Marcos Hotel by letter of January 11, 1935 (the reason is not given, but is obvious from the context). The recollection of the Kaufmanns' staying at the abandoned La Hacienda Motel came in a lecture by Edgar Tafel at the Carnegie Museum of Art, July 13, 1999; Liliane and E. J. later occupied a bungalow at the San Marcos Hotel, according to apprentice Robert Bishop (Tafel, *About Wright,* 114, with a drawing of the Hacienda, p. 113). The detail of the Marcuses barely getting into the Arizona Biltmore is in Tafel, *About Wright,* 257. The famed German-born historian George Mosse cited the severity of anti-Jewish prejudice in the United States in his autobiography, *Confronting History* (Madison, Wis., 1999), 119, and gave more dismaying details in a lecture at the University of Pittsburgh in January 1997. The identical report came from Ermalee Desenberg, who met the Kaufmanns immediately after her escape from Nazi Germany in the 1930s.

Kaufmann was mocked as "Warren Kamen" in Al Hine, *An Unfound Door* (1951), 115. The Mellons' loan of $3,500,000 on October 18, 1929, is in the Kaufmann's Department Store ledgers, now at the Heinz Center. The perception of the Mellons as strongly anti-Jewish came in an interview with a fourth-generation scion of the Pittsburgh establishment and close Mellon- and Kaufmann-watcher, who prefers to remain anonymous.

Judge Josiah Cohen used to relate the day he appeared as a novice lawyer before Judge Mellon with a petition to incorporate a Jewish cemetery. "A place to bury Jews?" "Yes, sir." "With pleasure, with pleasure" (William Hoffman, *Paul Mellon: Portrait of an Oil Baron* [Chicago, 1974], 30–31). The reported exclusion of the Kaufmanns even from lunch at Rolling Rock is surprising but reliable, coming from so close a Kaufmann confidant as Ralph Demmler. The only contradiction might be a *Pittsburgh Post-Gazette* (October 2, 1947) report of the Kaufmanns at Ligonier, which, however, specified that E. J. and Liliane had brought their own lunch in a "beautifully decorated basket."

Denton, Beal, and Demmler are documented in *Story of Rolling Rock*, ed. J. B. van Urk (1950). Roy Oliver's stay at the Jonathan Club is documented in Kaufmann's handwritten note of December 7 of an unspecified year that by context was 1946 or 1947 (UCLA). On the wider phenomenon of Jews reacting to prejudice in the 1920s and '30s: Budd Schulberg, *What Makes Sammy Run?* (1941); Neal Gabler, *An Empire of Their Own: How the Jews Invented Hollywood* (1988); Heywood Broun and George Britt, *Christians Only* (1931); Albert Lee, *Henry Ford and the Jews* (1980). On E. J.'s being shunned by Jews: Corrine Krause, *Isaac W. Frank: Industrialist and Civic Leader* (Pittsburgh, 1984), 145–46 (Kaufmann is unnamed but obvious, and was later specified in conversation with the author).

Calvinist Pittsburgh: Both Paul Mellon, *Reflections in a Silver Spoon* (1992), 77, and R. L. Duffus, "Is Pittsburgh Civilized?" *Harper's Monthly Magazine* 161 (October 1930): 537–45, are good sources on some of Pittsburgh's more egregious social restrictions.

Kaufmann in private: E. J.'s plaint that Junior "refused to be a son" was recalled by his nephew I. D. Wolf Jr. Kaufmann's fondness for the Ziegfeld Follies is documented in Harris, *Merchant Princes*, 97. The Kaufmanns' near-divorce was cited in the *Pittsburgh Bulletin Index* of September 28, 1933. Intimations of Paul Mellon's illegitimate birth: Mellon, *Reflections*, 82.

Kaufmann in California: It has so far proved impossible to document how Pasadena Drive in Fox Chapel got its name, but as the developers of that street, the Kaufmanns would have had a major say in its determination. The *Pittsburgh Jewish Criterion*, January 22, 1915, recorded Kaufmann's uncle Henry going to California in 1915, and E. J.'s parents two years later (February 9, 1917). In 1928, Kaufmann composed a list of about seventy special contacts to whom he wanted a lavish 1928 issue of his employee *Storagram* sent. Half of these contacts were in Pittsburgh and on the East Coast, as we would expect, but a surprising thirty names on the list were Californians (the list from the Kaufmann store archives survives at the Heinz Center). Years later, Betty Kaufmann left Pittsburgh to reach California by boat (*Jewish Criterion*, January 4, 1935); E. J. and Liliane flew from Pittsburgh to Arizona to stay with Wright on February 15, 1935, then proceeded by air to California. Former mayor Frank Bogert vividly described the Palm Springs social life of the 1930s for me, and also published a sanitized account of those days in his *Palm Springs: The First Hundred Years* (Palm Springs, 1987), which also carries a photograph of Albert Einstein at the Mirador. I am indebted to Barbara Wolff of the Albert Einstein Archives at the Hebrew University of Jerusalem for confirming Einstein's brief stay at the El Mirador in 1933.

Hearst and Kaufmann: Hearst as a power in radio broadcasting in Pittsburgh is documented in Stewart Holbrook, *Age of the Moguls* (Garden City, N.Y., 1953), 312, 317, which also conveniently summarizes his national newspaper, magazine, film, and radio holdings. Kaufmann's sponsorship of radio broadcasts is documented in the store archives. Holbrook, *Age of the Moguls*, 312, links Hearst and Pathé as early as 1913; Pathé's production of Kaufmann's unemployment documentary is specified in the film's opening credits. The links among Block, Hearst, Kaufmann, and Urban are documented in part in Frank Brady, *The Publisher: Paul Block, a Life of Friendship, Power, and Politics* (Lanham, Md., 2000); in part in the Joseph Urban Papers at Columbia University; and in part from his son William, long-time publisher of the *Pittsburgh Post-Gazette*.

Liliane's private life: Kaufmann, *Fallingwater*, 34, documented his mother's separate apartment but did not specify a location. In 1927, Liliane wrote Victor Hammer from the Schenley Apartments in Oakland, which may have been the pied-à-terre of which Kaufmann speaks, or else she was simply living near her mother-in-law while the Kaufmanns' new home was being built in Fox Chapel (Hammer Papers, Library of Congress). Liliane's liaisons are, understandably, not documented, but the candidates of most frequent mention are Luke Swank and Laszlo Gabor, two artists with whom she had frequent contact. Swank ran the photographic studio in the store and spent much time with the Kaufmanns at Fallingwater and on vacations with them. As the store's artistic director, Gabor designed Liliane's Vendôme boutique. Liliane's expertise as an administrator is cited in Bleier and Donnelly, *Montefiore*, 74, 87, 88.

Liliane's portrait: Victor Hammer (Graz, 1936), plate 10 carries this portrait as a "half-nude" in the possession of E. J. Kaufmann, but the identification with Liliane was made unequivocal by her niece, Betty Wolf Loeb (communication, February 4, 2003). It closely follows Hammer's 1926 pencil sketch of her, now in storage at Fallingwater. The portrait appeared in family inventories through the 1950s, after which Kaufmann Jr. gave it to the University of Kentucky Art Museum at Lexington. My deep thanks to Rev. Fr. Paul Evans Holbrook, literary executor to Victor Hammer, for a full discussion of the portrait. Among the more notable paintings that Hammer sold the Kaufmanns are *Borgo degli Albizzi* (known also as *Two Men: One in Red Robe, the Other in Black*) and one version of his *Christ and the Adultress*. See John Rothenstein, *Victor Hammer* (London, 1948), and *Victor Hammer: An Artist's Testament,* ed. Carolyn R. Hammer (Lexington, Ky., 1988).

Kaufmann's buildings: The following list cites Kaufmann's main transactions in architecture. Dates generally indicate the year of completion; the location is Pittsburgh unless indicated otherwise:

- Secondary involvement with uncle Henry Kaufmann in Irene Kaufmann Settlement, 1910: Thompson-Starrett Company (original building demolished).
- Rented home at 5739 Baum Boulevard, 1910 (demolished).
- Kaufmann's Department Store, Fifth and Smithfield wing, 1913: Benno Janssen.
- Secondary involvement with father Morris Kaufmann in Concordia Club, 1913: probably by, or involving, either Henry Hornbostel or Benno Jannsen.
- Rented home at 5423 Darlington Road, 1913–20: Janssen.
- Cherry Way wing for store, 1914: Janssen.
- Prefabricated fishing lodge at McGregor Bay, Ontario, 1918.
- Reinforced-concrete warehouse on North Side, ca. 1920 (demolished 1999).
- Rented home (from Benno Janssen) at 5625 Darlington Road, 1920–25: Janssen.
- Fifth Avenue wing of store, 1922: Janssen.
- Prefabricated weekend house at Bear Run, ca. 1921; enlarged 1931 (demolished 1950s).
- Speculative office block, Smithfield Street at Sixth Avenue, 1924: Janssen.
- Conversion and installation of Hanseatic merchant's house (also called Austrian monastery) in store as executive conference room, mid-1920s (demolished).
- Apartment for Liliane Kaufmann, mid-1920s: Joseph Urban, architect; Paul Frankl, decorator.
- Kaufmann Development Co. builds one or more prototype homes in Johnstown, Pa., 1925: Theodore Eichholtz.

- La Tourelle residence, Fox Chapel, ca. 1925–28: Janssen.
- Oakland YMHA, 1926: Janssen.
- Projected ground-floor remodeling of Kaufmann's Department Store, 1928 (unbuilt): Joseph Urban.
- Expansion of Irene Kaufmann Settlement, 1929: auditorium by Edward and Charles Stotz (standing); poolhouse by Joseph Urban (demolished).
- Remodeled Kaufmann's Department Store ground floor, 1930: Benno Janssen, architect; Boardman Robinson, muralist.
- Miscellaneous public works projects (bridges, highways, riverfront), 1934–35 (unbuilt): Frank Lloyd Wright.
- Projected planetarium for Kaufmann's Department Store, 1934–36 (unbuilt): Wright.
- Broadacre City model (subsidy), 1935: Wright.
- Fallingwater, 1937: Wright.
- Private office in store, 1937: Wright (removed 1955, now reinstalled in Victoria and Albert Museum, London).
- Parking garage for store, 1937: Metzger-Richardson, engineers (demolished).
- Guesthouse for Fallingwater, 1939: Wright.
- Kaufmann Usonian house project, 1939 (unbuilt): Wright.
- Projected farmhouse for Bear Run, 1941 (unbuilt): Wright; substitute built by Edgar Kaufmann Jr.
- Projected gatehouse for Bear Run, 1942 (unbuilt): Wright.
- Desert House, Palm Springs, Calif., 1946: Richard Neutra.
- Kitchen addition for Fallingwater, 1947: A. E. Vitaro.
- Projected dining room extension for Fallingwater, 1947 (unbuilt): Wright.
- Projected expansion of guesthouse and servant quarters for Fallingwater, 1947–48 (unbuilt): Wright.
- Projected Pittsburgh Point Civic Center, including "tall shaft" at Point, Point Park bridges and other variants, 1947–48 (unbuilt): Wright.
- Civic Arena, planned from 1947 with Wright (unbuilt); commissioned from Mitchell & Ritchey in 1949, opened 1962.
- Architectural services for Tisherman house, Squirrel Hill, 1948: Mitchell & Ritchey.
- Purchase of Frick Annex Building (Daniel H. Burnham, 1906) and conversion as annex to the store, 1948.
- Projected garage for Kaufmann's Department Store, 1949 (unbuilt): Wright.
- Projected Point View Residences (apartments), 1951–54 (unbuilt): Wright.
- Projected Boulder House for Palm Springs, 1951 (unbuilt): Wright.
- Projected chapel for Bear Run, 1951–52 (unbuilt): Wright.
- Liliane S. Kaufmann Wing at Montefiore Hospital, 1953: James H. Ritchie.
- Purchase and demolition of Carnegie Building (Longfellow, Alden & Harlow, 1892), 1953, and replacement by ten-story annex for the store, 1954: Hoffman & Crumpton (successors to Janssen).
- Tomb for Bear Run, 1953, designed by Edgar Kaufmann Jr. and A. E. Vitaro.
- New parking garage for store on Smithfield Street, 1955.

Kaufmann and Benno Janssen: These works by Janssen are discussed and illustrated in Toker, *Pittsburgh;* in James Van Trump, "Yet Once More O Ye Laurels: Benno Janssen," *Charette* 45/2 (February 1965): 8–13; and in Miller, *Janssen.*

Kaufmann and Mellon buildings: It is hard to say whether the Kaufmanns or the Mellons got the last laugh in this game of architectural musical chairs. Pittsburgh's Civic Arena, which should have been named for E. J. Kaufmann as its founder and chief bene-factor, sold its naming rights to the bank in 2000 and emerged as Mellon Arena. But that same year the May Company, Kaufmann's corporate parent, gutted Mellon's banking hall—in the literal shadow of Kaufmann's—and turned it into a Lord & Taylor. The build-ing activities of Carnegie and Frick are documented in Toker, *Pittsburgh*, 70, 81, 94–100, 105–109 and 21, 40, 69–72, 223–24, 246, 254, respectively.

La Tourelle: My thanks to Dennis Kelleher for his hours-long hospitality at La Tourelle in 1998. Frances C. Hardie, *Fox Chapel* (Pittsburgh, 1989), 78, 96, 103, documents discrimi-nation against Jews in the local golf and riding clubs of the era. More than a few Jews were uncomfortable about medieval mannerisms in their lifestyles. Jacob Schiff was displeased that his son-in-law Felix Warburg put up a Gothic rather than a Renaissance palace on Fifth Avenue, feeling that a medieval style was non-Jewish. It ended up as the Jewish Museum anyway (Simon, *Fifth Avenue*, 307). La Tourelle voted best new house in Pittsburgh: "The First Annual Architectural Exhibition," *Western Architect* 39 (August 1930): 122.

Society and architectural style: Leach defines the "brokering class" in *Land of Desire*, 11. On Selznick's house, see Peter Holliday, abstract submitted to the 1993 annual meeting of the Society of Architectural Historians, Charleston, S.C. Augusta Owen Patterson, *Amer-ican Homes of To-day: Their Architectural Style, Their Environment, Their Characteristics* (1924), carries the word "modern" only as a trivial substyle called "modern picturesque."

No comprehensive study relates social stratification to architectural style in the 1930s the way Leonard K. Eaton did in his classic work on Wright's early clients thirty years ear-lier: *Two Chicago Architects and Their Clients: Frank Lloyd Wright and Howard Van Doren Shaw* (Cambridge, Mass., 1969). In Eaton's study we find that more Chicago Jews went to the conservative architect Shaw than to the radical Wright. Pertinent on the topic are William Jordy, *American Buildings and Their Architects, IV: The Impact of European Mod-ernism in the Mid-Twentieth Century* (Garden City, N.Y., 1972), esp. 123–64; Stern, *New York 1930*, esp. 329–56; and the proceedings of a 1964 symposium on modern architecture at Columbia University, in the *Journal of the Society of Architectural Historians* 24 (1965): 3–95. Lears, *No Place of Grace*, and S. Guilbaut, *How New York Stole the Idea of Modern Art* (Chicago, 1983), make some striking observations on the cultural and social climate in America before and after the 1930s.

Kaufmann and the Mexican muralists: A good background to understanding the lure of Mexico for the Kaufmanns is provided by Helen Delpar, *The Enormous Vogue of Things Mexican: Cultural Relations Between the United States and Mexico, 1920–1935* (Tusca-loosa, Ala., 1992). The walls of the YMHA that Kaufmann closely supervised in the mid-twenties have a conspicuous series of blank fields in the upper lobby, as though waiting for murals. E. J. brought the muralist Juan O'Gorman to Pittsburgh in the late 1930s to paint such a cycle, but the project aborted after a few months.

Kaufmann and Boardman Robinson: My evaluation of Robinson's murals is based on a communication from Henry Adams, February 16, 2001; see also Adams, *Boardman Robin-son: American Muralist and Illustrator, 1876–1952* (Colorado Springs, 1996), with color reproductions, and Adams's forthcoming Robinson biography; Oliver Larkin, *Art and Life in America* (1949), 419–21.

Kaufmann and Kahlo: *Frida Kahlo: Das Gesamtwerk*, ed. Helga Prignitz-Poda et al. (Frankfurt am Main, 1988), cites *Birth* as cat. no. 37 and *Remembrance of an Open Wound* as cat. no. 63. I owe the characterization of the Kaufmanns' "fairly bizarre taste" to the Kahlo specialist Laura Crary (communication, June 4, 1998).

The Kaufmanns and Austrian modernists: The best source on the neglected Austrian contribution to the acceptance of modernism in the United States is *Visionäre und Ver-triebene: österreichische Spuren in der modernen amerikanischen Architektur*, ed. Matthias Boeckl (Vienna, 1995), 201–15, with specific discussion of the Kaufmanns' involvement with the Austrians. Frankl decorated Liliane's hideaway apartment (Kaufmann, *Fallingwa-ter*, 34), and Urban seems to have supplied its architectural design, according to Richard Cleary. Gabor is documented in Cleary, *Merchant*, 27. On Paul Theodore Frankl in Pittsburgh: Kaufmann, *Fallingwater*, 34.

Wiener Werkstätte: Much correspondence with the Werkstätte survives in the Fallingwater archives, most of it appeals for financial support from the Kaufmanns. We have no specific timetable for the Kaufmanns' visits to Vienna, but the city where Hammer painted E. J.'s large portrait was clearly of highest importance to them. Liliane's will left a bequest to the doorman of the Hotel Bristol, though she had not stayed there in twenty or thirty years. A standard source on Joseph Urban is Randolph Carter and Robert Cole, *Joseph Urban, Architecture, Theatre, Opera, Film* (1992); further information is in Stern, *New York, 1930*, 235ff; Boeckl, *Visionäre*, 69, 345–46; and Mary Beth Betts, abstract of a lecture to the College Art Association Annual Meeting, 1993. Urban's pool at the Kaufmann Settlement is documented by photographs in the Archives of Industrial Society, University of Pittsburgh, with snapshots of Kaufmann laying its cornerstone in 1929. Kaufmann's uncle Henry paid the half-million dollars for the project, but E. J. was definitely the main client in the mind of the public.

The rebuilding of Kaufmann's ground floor: Albert Christ-Janer, *Boardman Robinson* (Chicago, 1946), 50–51, contains the report that Kaufmann had earlier contacted the designer Eugene Schoen about his remodeling needs. Cleary, *Merchant*, 24, follows earlier writers in saying unequivocally that Kaufmann "commissioned a scheme" from Urban, but July 28, 1928, strikes me as an impossibly late date at which to submit a serious proposal for a project that had already started in 1927 with Kaufmann's commission for Robinson. More likely, Urban, whose sumptuous drawings are preserved at Columbia University, was taking a chance on his own. On Bullock's Wilshire in Los Angeles, which is the best surviving Art Deco commercial work in the U.S. today, see Robert Winter's privately printed notes, *Society of Architectural Historians Tour of Los Angeles* (September 1989), 39–40, including a partial reprint of Pauline Schindler's 1930 article on the store.

Modernism and merchandising: The January 1929 *Vogue* advertisement that centered on modernism was for its sister publication, *Vanity Fair*. I owe this finding to Lucy Fischer, who kindly shared with me an advance text of her *Designing Women: Cinema, Art Deco, and the Female Form.*

Germany and modernism: In several conversations in the mid-1970s, E. J.'s cousin Stanley Baer told me about Kaufmann's regular visits to his German cousins right through the 1920s, including his recollection of E. J.'s flawless German. E. J.'s cousins James Bachman and Karl Kaufmann Jr. both noted that E. J.'s continuing involvement with Germany contrasted sharply with the pattern in the other branches of the family, which mainly ended their social visits by World War I. Bernt Engelmann's popular history *Germany Without Jews* (Berlin, 1979; American ed., 1984) documents the exceptional participation of Jews in the cultural, commercial, and even military life of pre-Nazi Germany. A more sober evaluation, but all the more impressive for being sober, is that of W. E. Mosse, *Jews in the German Economy* (Oxford, 1987), esp. chap. 8: "Weimar: Decline and Fall?" pp. 323–79. I owe my information on Karstadt's to Christiane Collins (communication with company brochures, April 1987).

German-American exchanges: For details of how the Fagus corporation was both capitalized and inspired by its American joint-venture associates, see Annemarie Jaeggi, *Fagus:*

Industrial Culture from Werkbund to Bauhaus (2000), 13–15. The transatlantic factor in modern architecture is well documented in Reyner Banham, *A Concrete Atlantis: United States Industrial Building and European Modern Architecture* (Cambridge, Mass., 1986); Julius Posener, *Berlin auf dem Wege zu einer neuen Architektur* (Munich, 1979 and 1995); and Jean-Louis Cohen, *Scenes of the World to Come: European Architecture and the American Challenge, 1893–1960* (Montreal, 1995). On the Mosse family's borrowing in the United States: Mosse, *Confronting History,* 213. American architecture was featured in Erich Mendelsohn's *Amerika: Bilderbuck eines Architekten* (Berlin, 1926); Richard Neutra's *Wie Baut Amerika?* (Stuttgart, 1927) and the same author's *Amerika: Die Stilbildung des Neuen Bauens in den Vereinigten Staaten* (Vienna, 1930); and in Bruno Taut's *Die Neue Baukunst in Europa und Amerika* (Stuttgart, 1929), with the English translation, *Modern Architecture,* published in London the same year.

"[T]he most beautiful department store": R. L. Duffus, "Is Pittsburgh Civilized?" *Harper's Monthly Magazine* 161 (October 1930): 537–45.

THREE: BEAR RUN: THE LAND AWAITING

Vicinity of Bear Run: The Pennsylvania Railroad bought the land for the Mill Run reservoir from August Stickel in 1892 and had it operational by 1905. It was abandoned with the switch to diesel engines. See the Mill Run Historical Society, *A History of Mill Run, Fayette County, Pennsylvania* (Mill Run, 1971), 17. The coordinates of Fallingwater are provided by the U.S. Geological Survey map entitled *Mill Run Quadrangle, Pennsylvania* (Washington, D.C., 1999).

Continental divide: The tale of the continental divide's splitting a house in Cresson comes from David McCullough, *The Johnstown Flood* (1979), 47. Tim Palmer, *Youghiogheny: Appalachian River* (Pittsburgh, 1984), 5, gives a more scientifically exact location for this "continental divide of the East."

Water system of Bear Run: I am indebted to Paul Wiegman for a field visit and wide-ranging discussion of the natural history of Bear Run. The terrors of the Youghiogheny are discussed in Tim Palmer, *Rivers of Pennsylvania* (University Park, Pa., 1980), 134; in Palmer's *Youghiogheny,* 162; and in the *Pittsburgh Post-Gazette,* June 28, 2000.

Landforms of North America: De Tocqueville, *Democracy,* 19–20. There are excellent discussions of the geological formation of Appalachia in Palmer, *Youghiogheny,* 122, 132; and John McPhee, "Appalachia and Plate Tectonics," in his *Annals of the Former World* (1988), esp. 115–26, 209–18, 235–51.

Flora and fauna of Bear Run: Netting, *Western Pennsylvania Conservancy,* 138; and discussion with Ralph Demmler, the major power in the Edgar J. Kaufmann Charitable Trust. John F. Lewis, *A Guide to Plants at Bear Run Nature Reserve* (Pittsburgh, 1968); Hoffmann, *Fallingwater,* 6; Robert P. Harrison, *Forests: The Shadow of Civilization* (Chicago, 1992), 232–37.

Settlement history of Bear Run: Franklin Ellis, *History of Fayette County, Pennsylvania with Biographical Sketches of Many of Its Pioneers and Prominent Men* (Philadelphia, 1882), 14, 16–17, 20; *History of Mill Run,* 11–12. This chapter draws considerably on research conducted by Adam Young for my Fallingwater seminar at the University of Pittsburgh in 1999.

Washington's land holdings: The exact acreage and location of some of Washington's parcels is unknown, the main difficulty being that Fayette County did not yet exist when those purchases were made. Edgar Kaufmann Jr. made the claim about George Washington in his "Twenty-five Years," p. 22.

Post-Revolutionary settlement: Ellis, *Fayette,* 21; and *History of Mill Run,* 11–12. Route 30 is fully documented in Brian Butko's *Pennsylvania Traveler's Guide: The Lincoln Highway* (Mechanicsburg, Pa., 1996).

Development of Mill Run and Bear Run: I follow here the indispensable *History of Mill Run* and other data collected by Adam Young. For other Bear Runs and similar-sounding Pennsylvania place names, see *Pennsylvania Atlas & Gazetteer* (Yarmouth, Maine, 1999). Numerous typescripts of deed abstracts for the Kaufmanns' land purchases survive among the Kaufmann Papers in Avery Library.

Early industrialization of the Youghiogheny Valley: *History of Mill Run,* 12–15, 22; Palmer, *Youghiogheny,* 150. My thanks to Terry Necciai (communication, October 13, 2000) for explaining the odd term "iron plantation." Richard Scaife kindly clarified for me that the train he hired actually stopped nearer to Mill Run than to the old "Kaufmann" depot, from which point buses brought the partygoers to Fallingwater.

Mineral resources in Fayette County: J. J. Stevenson, *Report of Progress in the Fayette and Westmoreland District of the Bituminous Coal-Fields of Western Pennsylvania* (Harrisburg, 1877); *Topographic and Geologic Survey of Pennsylvania* (Harrisburg, 1908); W. O. Hickok and F. T. Moyer, *Geology and Mineral Resources of Fayette County* (Harrisburg, 1940); and Walter J. Story, *Brief History of Coal and Coke in Fayette County* (n.p., 1982). The dispersion of the 1891 strike is documented in Milan Simonich, "118 Killed in 1891 Frick Massacre and Mine Explosion to Get Markers," *Pittsburgh Post-Gazette,* September 24, 2000. The WPC Archives preserve some of the oil and gas leases for land that now forms part of the Kaufmann Conservancy.

Fayette County today: "Fayette County Has Highest Illiteracy," *Uniontown Morning Herald,* April 7, 1972; Barbara White Stack, "Caught in the Web of Poverty," *Pittsburgh Post-Gazette,* November 1, 1998; S. M. Berg, *Some Facts and Figures About Fayette County, Pennsylvania, 1935* (np, nd), and Berg's *Some Facts and Figures About Fayette County, Pennsylvania, 1951* (np, nd); *The Population of Pennsylvania Municipalities: 1960 to 1998* (Harrisburg, 1999).

Architecture and painting in the Laurel Highlands: McCullough, *Johnstown Flood; Story of Rolling Rock.* On Henry Clay Frick's purchase of George Hetzel's *Woodland Stream,* see Gabriel Weisberg et al., *Collecting in the Gilded Age: Artistic Patronage in Pittsburgh, 1890–1910* (Pittsburgh, 1997), 56, 132.

Camp Kaufmann at Bear Run: Kaufmann's account of discovering Bear Run appears in Netting, *Western Pennsylvania Conservancy,* 140–41. Netting recorded the year as 1905, but Kaufmann did not take over the Connellsville store until 1908 at the earliest. The Kurtz store was listed in advertisements in the *Connellsville Daily Courier* for 1908 and 1909 — I thank Ken Kremer for this reference. A memo of March 5, 1920, from the Pittsburgh engineering firm of Morris Knowles Inc. identifies Kurtz as an officer of the Bear Run Country Club, which still owned the property at the time (Avery). Hoffmann, *Fallingwater,* 8, suggested certain plausible links between E. J. and the Masons, but there is another curious connection. On June 20, 1962, Spencer J. Holland, instructor at the Masonic lodge in Karns City, north of Pittsburgh, wrote Kaufmann Jr. with an appeal for funds based on Junior's being a fellow Mason (the letter in the Fallingwater Archives is addressed to Bro. Edgar Kaufmann Junior, and begins "Dear Bro. Kaufmann"). Nobody was less of a joiner than Kaufmann Jr.: it takes a considerable leap of faith to think of him as a Mason. Holland must have confused the son for the father, but his identification of E. J. as a Mason may well have been correct.

The 1909 deed of sale of Bear Run to the Syria Land Improvement Association survives in Avery Library. Little is known of the camp operations between 1916 and 1920, because the *Storagram* employee newsletter did not begin publication until the latter year. Camp Kaufmann was cited in numerous issues of the *Storagram*, particularly those of September-October 1920, June 1921, and June 1927. A 1937 "Memo re. Bear Run Property of Liliane S. Kaufmann" summarizes the property's full ownership history (Avery). Other Kaufmann titles to smaller parcels at Bear Run are preserved in the Fallingwater Archives. I owe the tale of the Kaufmanns' untended laundry to Denise Miner.

Kaufmann and nature: The recollection that Kaufmann preferred The Hangover to Fallingwater comes from his cousin and former neighbor James Bachman.

Kaufmann's options in 1933: The new road is cited in an undated clipping in the Fallingwater Archives. A good capsule history of the CCC appears in Robert McElvaine, *The Great Depression* (1984), 154–55; full details in Leslie Alexander Lacy, *The Soil Soldiers: The Civilian Conservation Corps in the Great Depression* (Radnor, Pa., 1976). An April 18, 1933, memorandum by E. F. Twomey of Morris Knowles Inc. describes Kaufmann's CCC application in detail (Avery). Kaufmann's close friend Dorothy Blumenthal remembered E. J.'s intent to build a more permanent weekend house at Bear Run as early as 1923, though nothing came of it then. The reports from forester Bearer are quoted in Hoffmann, *Fallingwater*, 10. The cabin names are given in a map and attachments to the Knowles memo to Kaufmann of March 5, 1920.

FOUR: FRANK LLOYD WRIGHT SEEKS A CLIENT, GETS A PATRON

Greatest architect: Wright's aphorism is reported in Twombly, *Wright*, 385.

Wright and his clients: Roxanne Williamson's *American Architects and the Mechanics of Fame* (Austin, 1991) gives a quantitative analysis of architectural fame, but does not specifically address how architects make themselves famous, nor how they come back after a fall from grace. Wright's comments on Albert Johnson were in his letter to Norman Guthrie of October 26, 1927.

Wright and Kaufmann: Liliane's "my one education" remark comes from her birthday greeting to Wright on June 8, 1951, which resides today in a restricted section of the Kaufmann Papers in Avery Library. My thanks to Janet Parks for sharing with me this letter, which is often selectively quoted but rarely seen. Kaufmann's promise to create a book of Wright's drawings evaporated in 1935 but revived around 1952 as a projected series of eight volumes. *Frank Lloyd Wright: Drawings for a Living Architecture* (1959) was edited by Kaufmann Jr. and funded by the Bear Run Foundation and the Edgar J. Kaufmann Charitable Foundation. Wright's comments on E. J., women, and architects comes from his letter to Kaufmann Jr. of January 25, 1950. He wrote his angry letter about never trusting E. J. again on July 16, 1946.

Hypnotizing clients: The quoted passage comes from Wright's *Autobiography* (1932 ed.), 342. Wright wrote William Kittredge on September 27, 1932. Wright called Kaufmann a "shopper" in his letter of January 25, 1937, and elsewhere.

Architectural patrons: Wright flattered Kaufmann as an "Idea Man" in his letter of March 10, 1948. The analysis of Sir Francis Willoughby's library comes from Alice T. Friedman, *House and Household in Elizabethan England: Wollaton Hall and the Willoughby Family* (Chicago, 1989). John Carter Brown kindly discussed the design sequence for his parents' house with me in 1993; his general recollections appear in *Richard Neutra's Windshield House*, ed. Dietrich Neumann (Cambridge, Mass., 2001), 108–20. The episode of Hearst and the garden wall comes from Lindsay Chaney and Michael Cieply, *The Hearsts: Family and Empire* (1981), 153–54.

Weekend and "tomorrow" houses: The architect Knud Lönberg-Holm wrote the definitive article on "The Week-End House" in *Architectural Record* (August 1930): 175–92, with

Wright's Ocatilla desert camp in Arizona as its somewhat curious centerpiece. A complete chronology of the Dymaxion House is provided in Webb, *Modernism Reborn*, 58. Stern, *New York 1930*, 352–54ff. catalogues in detail the efforts of the New York department stores to put up model houses. The Steelaire House at Kaufmann's is documented in clippings in the Kaufmann Store papers at the Heinz Center.

Kaufmann's nephews John and I. D. Wolf Jr. attended the Chicago fair, and recalled their uncle being there also. E. J. copied the fair's name for the "Paths of Progress" exhibits he later produced at Kaufmann's. Six of the fourteen model houses at the fair were later rebuilt in Indiana, five of which still stand today. Mies's model house for the 1931 "Dwellings of Our Time" show in Berlin is documented in Terence Reilly and Barry Bergdol, *Mies in Europe* (2001), 264–65.

Kaufmann as a commercial house builder: An unremarkable house at 420 Orchard Street in the Johnstown suburb of Westmont was built in 1925 by the Kaufmann Development Co., based at 413 Fourth Avenue in Pittsburgh. My thanks to Charles Strandquest Jr. for information on both the house and its architectural drawings. We can be certain that the otherwise unknown "Kaufmann Development Co." was part of the store because its address was that of the headquarters for the store's art and display departments (information from Irene Pasinski, who worked there). We also know that Kaufmann was closely connected to Theodore Eichholz, architect of the Johnstown house, since it was he who built the Irvin Lehman house on part of Kaufmann's Fox Chapel estate. Eichholz later built a parody of La Tourelle in Pittsburgh's Highland Park district (Toker, *Pittsburgh*, 215), which I regard as another testimony of his closeness to E. J.

Wright's model house project for Kaufmann's: Kaufmann's vice president I. D. Wolf several times asked Wright to produce a house prototype that the store could mass-produce. Wright alluded to the first such request in a letter to Karl Jensen on June 17, 1935. Wolf meant to attend the Fallingwater design meeting at Taliesin on September 22, 1935, specifically to "discuss with you the possibility of your designing a house for the store such as we talked about when you were here," but he returned to Pittsburgh instead (I. D. Wolf to Wright, August 20, 1935). Kaufmann Jr. also told Wright by letter of August 1, 1935, that "the project of building a or more house(s) designed by you . . . [will be] really worth while . . . for the store." In 1938, Wolf took up this initiative again, and asked Wright for a mass-production version of the low-budget home he had just constructed for Herbert Jacobs in Madison, Wisconsin: "Would it be possible for us to reproduce the Jacobs house on a piece of property here—if so what would the cost be to us for your plans?" Wright was willing, but wary: "I suppose doing a model house for you and Pittsburgh is tantamount to handing the whole thing over to all and sundry by and large to horse with as they like. If the thing were done it would be no replica but an improvement and would cost you the same 10 percent fee for which we always work plus the agreement to refrain from conniving at reproduction except under our own auspices" (Wolf to Wright, April 14, 1938; Wright's reply April 26). Right through 1939, Kaufmann's kept trying to get Wright to design a Usonian house it could sell; the Taliesin Archives lists Wright's project 3919 as "Kaufmann Usonian house, 1939."

Modernism grows in popularity: James Ford and Katherine Morrow Ford, *The Modern House in America* (1940); Tom Wolfe, *From Bauhaus to Our House* (1981), 86; Augusta Owen Patterson, "Three Modern Houses: No. 3: Owner, Edgar J. Kaufmann, Pittsburgh; Architect, Frank Lloyd Wright," *Town & Country* (February 1938): 64–65, 104.

Modernism comes to Pittsburgh: The MoMA International Style show was on view in Pittsburgh from June 3 to June 25, 1932—a showing evidently improvised at the last minute. Robert Schmertz's critique of the exhibition: "International Architecture: A Review of the Current Exhibition of Modern Architecture," *Carnegie Magazine* 6 (June

1932): 69–71, highlighted the work of Wright, though the exhibition itself did the opposite. On Scheibler, see Martin Aurand, *The Progressive Architecture of Frederick G. Scheibler, Jr.* (Pittsburgh, 1994); on Kiehnel and Elliott, see Toker, *Pittsburgh,* 119n., 124. On Wright's drawings exhibited in Pittsburgh, see the catalogues of the Pittsburgh Architectural League exhibitions in Pittsburgh, 1902–17. Frank Ullom wrote Wright on February 3, 1913.

Despite its tentative moves to modernism, Pittsburgh had plenty of architectural conservatives. The July 1932 issue of *Charette,* the official journal of Pittsburgh's architects, contained an attack against the frank expression of steel and concrete that was remarkable only for its late date; hardly anyone the world over was still fighting that old battle.

For the reinforced-concrete factory in McKees Rocks, see Lu Donnelly, David Brumble, Franklin Toker, *Buildings of Pennsylvania: Pittsburgh and Western Pennsylvania* (forthcoming); for the International Style warehouse in the Strip, now destroyed, see Toker, *Pittsburgh,* 94. Kaufmann referred to his work on the building committee of Allegheny General Hospital in a letter to Wright of January 19, 1937. The Swan Acres houses were announced in 1934, and a number of them opened in 1936; see " 'Homes All to Be Modern' Is the Startling but Financially Sound Restriction in a Pittsburgh Subdivision," *Architectural Forum* (November 1937): 442–43, with illustrations; and Toker, *Pittsburgh,* 300.

Pioneer modernism in Los Angeles: My information on the Lovells comes largely from family members Barbara Jean and Hap Lovell, and Susan Bernstein. See also Philip Lovell, *Los Angeles Times Sunday Magazine,* December 15, 1929; and "Newest in Modern Architecture Is Here," *Hollywood Daily Citizen,* December 15, 1929. My thanks to Dion Neutra and the administrators at Special Collections in the UCLA Library for allowing me access to the archive on the Lovell house, and to Betty Lou Topper for graciously showing me through the house in 2000. For a full history of the Lovell house, see Hines, *Neutra,* 78–91, 223ff. Aline Barnsdall and her Pittsburgh connections are fully investigated in Norman and Dorothy Karasick, *The Oilman's Daughter: A Biography of Aline Barndall* (Encino, Ca., 1993), 11–32. My information on the Ennises comes from Gus Brown, owner of the Ennis-Brown house, and from Norma Gross, a former volunteer there. Details on the Arensbergs in Los Angeles were kindly provided by their cousin Charles Arensberg II. Neutra and Schindler, Bel Geddes, Harriet and Sam Freeman, Lloyd Wright, and Walter and Louise Arensberg are characterized as among the crucial figures in bringing modernism to Los Angeles in *LA's Early Moderns: Art, Architecture, Photography,* ed. Victoria Dailey, Natalie Shivers, and Michael Dawson (forthcoming).

The Lovell house appeared in the Spring 1930 building supplement to the *Literary Digest,* along with features on the new Bullock's Wilshire store. The same issue devoted its cover to the Robinson murals. Neutra ripped out and stapled together the cover and the Lovell house article, which both reside today with his papers at UCLA. (I thank Ray Ann Lockard and Sherman Clark for yeoman service in tracking down this issue, of which only a single intact exemplar could be found in the whole United States.) Neutra's son Dion had the impression (communication, May 2, 1999) that his father and Kaufmann had met during World War II, perhaps in Washington. This is certainly possible but does not rule out an encounter in earlier years that Dion would have been too young to remember. Wright made the "popular architects" reference in his letter to Jensen, November 9, 1934.

Popular literature on Wright: Alexander Woollcott's profile of Wright, "The Prodigal Father," *The New Yorker* 6 (July 19, 1930): 22–25, was reprinted in *Reader's Digest* 17 (September 1930): 388–90. Wright's *Autobiography* was reviewed in the *The New York Times,* April 3, 1932; the *San Francisco Chronicle,* April 10, 1932; *Saturday Review of Literature,*

April 23, 1932; and in many other publications. Wright was also the subject of a complete chapter in the most important introductory text on modern art in America in the thirties, Thomas Craven's *Modern Art: The Men, the Movements, the Meaning* (1934). Dorothy Blumenthal and Caroline Wagner's recollections of what they knew of Frank Lloyd Wright as early as the 1920s emerged in interviews.

Friends and contacts in common: Jensen's remark that Wright and Kaufmann knew many people in common came in his letter to Wright of September 28, 1934. Urban was sufficiently devoted to Wright that he agreed to advance $7,500 in 1927 to "own" about a tenth of him, in a harebrained but charitable scheme to save the Master from bankruptcy (details in Secrest, *Wright,* 333–35). Wright emphasized Kaufmann's wealth right from the beginning of their association: he called E. J. "Pittsburgh's Marshall Field" in a letter to Philip Holliday on September 20, 1934, and again in a letter to Alexander Chandler on December 26, 1934. On Bauer's connection with Wright, see Pfeiffer and Wojtowicz, *Wright & Mumford,* 115 and following.

Request for a photograph: Ethel Clinton to Wright, January 2, 1934. Virtually all writings on Fallingwater (Cleary, *Merchant,* 28; Hoffmann, *Fallingwater,* 13; and Levine, *Wright,* 226, among them) make the assumption that Kaufmann and Wright came into contact only in November 1934. E. J. wrote of an "interesting matter" to Wright on August 16, 1934; Wright to Kaufmann, September 18, 1934; Karl Jensen to Wright, undated letter from mid-September and a second letter on September 28, 1934.

Kaufmann's involvement with the CWA: On the CWA, see McElvaine, *Depression,* 153–54; Kaufmann to Wright, October 20, 1934; and *Pittsburgh Bulletin Index* 105 (October 4, 1934): 6–7. California used CWA funding to build the Golden Gate and Oakland bridges in San Francisco and numerous public works in Los Angeles; Pennsylvania built the first part of its turnpike out of the same fund. (The CWA was soon phased out, but regular Public Works Administration funding continued for designated projects.) In the end, Pittsburgh lost out on public funding in the 1930s, but Pennsylvania's governor David L. Lawrence specifically credited Kaufmann for creating the vision of the tunnels, roads, and parks that were eventually built in the late 1940s.

Karl Jensen as intermediary: Jensen's letter about Kaufmann and Pittsburgh is undated, but its context places it in early September 1934. Wright sent Kaufmann a brochure on the Taliesin Fellowship with his letter of September 18, 1934. Jensen described his second meeting with Kaufmann in New York in an undated telegram that is datable by context to September 28, 1934. Wright then scribbled a cryptic response to Tom Maloney that made reference to another letter about the Kaufmann planetarium project, but his full responses to both Jensen and Maloney are lost. Stern, *New York 1930,* 349, 352 gives specifics on the industrial arts expositions of 1934 and 1935.

Preparations for Broadacre City: Thomas J. Maloney was a freelance writer in New York who promoted Wright's career and the interests of the National Alliance of Art and Industry both for love and some profit. His obituary in the *New York Times* on January 28, 1988, cites him as the founder of *U.S. Camera* magazine in the 1930s. Maloney's links to Wright are confirmed in Johnson, *Wright Versus America,* 110, 115, 148. Jensen and Maloney were evidently close: Jensen got his mail at Maloney's home in New York and he used Maloney's typewriter for some of his correspondence. On the eventual Broadacre City exhibition in 1935, see Stern, *New York 1930,* 346–47, 352, 792 n. 136. The show was praised by Lewis Mumford, "The Sky Line: Mr. Wright's City—Downtown Dignity," *The New Yorker* 7 (April 27, 1935): 79–81. Jensen asked Wright for a bounty of 10 percent on new apprentices in his letter of November 11, 1934. Sixty years later Wright's apprentice Edgar Tafel remembered that Wright had used Jensen to reel in Kaufmann as a client.

Stanley Marcus as client: Marcus asked Wright to build him a house by letter of November 6, 1934. Wright's virtually identical letters to Marcus and Kaufmann went out on December 26, 1934.

Kaufmann as sponsor of Broadacre City: Wright described the Broadacre City concept in his book *The Disappearing City* (1932), in the *New York Times Sunday Magazine* of March 20, 1932, and in a special "Book Six" that he wrote for his revised *Autobiography* in 1943, but which was separately printed instead. In a letter to Wright (dated only as "Friday," but from context datable to November 23, 1934), Jensen insisted that he had been the first person to plant sponsorship of the Broadacre City model in Kaufmann's mind. Alistair Cooke commemorated Wright in the *Washington Post* of April 26, 1959 (Secrest, *Wright*, 443). E. J.'s visit to Taliesin is documented in *"At Taliesin": Newspaper Columns by Frank Lloyd Wright and the Taliesin Fellowship, 1934–1937,* ed. Randolph Henning (Carbondale, Ill., 1992), 87. Tafel recounted Kaufmann's sponsorship offer in *Apprentice*, 2, but it is clear that well before the Kaufmanns arrived in Spring Green, Wright and Kaufmann had agreed on a $1,000 subsidy for the Broadacre City model. On November 9, Tom Maloney had urged Wright to create "a striking model layout to cover an area of about ten feet square [ten feet a side], I think it could be the most interesting thing in the show." Maloney set the cost at about $1,000. That is just what Kaufmann granted Wright: $1,000 to craft a 12-by-12-foot model in painted wood, cardboard, and paper. Leaving nothing to chance, Maloney wrote Kaufmann about subsidizing the model both before and after E. J.'s trip to Taliesin. The moment Kaufmann returned from Wisconsin, Maloney paid him a visit from New York to make sure there were no slip-ups. (Jensen to Wright, undated telegram, by context November 21, 1934, and undated letter, presumably November 23, 1934; Maloney to Wright, November 26, 1934, and Maloney to Kaufmann, same day.) The projected national tour for the model never worked out: after New York, it showed only at Kaufmann's and in the Corcoran Gallery in Washington, D.C. The model still survives at Taliesin West.

Wright in Pittsburgh: Preparations for the visit appear in Kaufmann's letter to Wright, December 4, 1934, and Wright's note to Jensen, December 7. Wright's letter to Kaufmann, December 26, 1934, makes it unambiguous that Kaufmann Jr. had stayed at Taliesin while Wright was in Pittsburgh. "Oral History of Bill Hedrich," typescript at Chicago Art Institute, 1992, contains the detail about Kaufmann's strip joints. Wright's purchases in Pittsburgh are documented in a letter from Charles Caputo of C. G. Conn, Ltd., "world's largest manufacturers of band instruments," to Wright via Kaufmann, December 20, 1934, and by Clinton's two letters to Wright of December 21.

Einstein in Pittsburgh: *Pittsburgh Post-Gazette:* "Atom Energy Hope Is Spiked by Einstein" and "Mass Theory Proved Anew by Einstein," both December 29, 1934; Kaufmann to Wright, December 30.

Wright bonding with Kaufmann: Wright's longtime supporter George Nelson recalled that Wright was sincerely fond of Kaufmann (Hoffmann, *Fallingwater,* 73). No comparable closeness emerges in Wright's published correspondence with Aline Barnsdall, Solomon Guggenheim, or the Robie, Hanna, and Jacobs families. On Sullivan and Richardson and their clients: Robert Twombly, *Louis Sullivan: His Life and Work* (1986), 399–402; James O'Gorman, *H. H. Richardson: Architectural Forms for an American Society* (Chicago, 1987), 25. Wright to Kaufmann, September 27, 1948; Kaufmann to Wright, May 6, 1946.

Wright as a businessman: Tafel spoke about Wright's billing clients in an interview in 1999; see also Tafel, *Apprentice*, 80. Wright's 1922 letter to the Metropolitan's curator of Far Eastern art, C. Bosch Reitz, was quoted in Julia Meech, *Frank Lloyd Wright and the*

Art of Japan: The Architect's Other Passion (2001), 170. Kaufmann's self-identification with tradespeople comes in his letter to Wright of April 16, 1936: "I am having the foundations staked on the property this week and other points more for my own visualization as well as Liliane's. After all, we are only trades people and cannot see things quite as clearly as others."

Wright battling Jews: Wright recounted his verbal and physical battles with the Jews in Sullivan's office in his *Autobiography,* 95–102. Peter Blake, *Frank Lloyd Wright: Architecture and Space* (Baltimore, 1964), 20, deals interestingly with the question of what city life meant to a farm boy like Wright. We can identify two of Wright's Jewish adversaries with precision. One was the Chicago architect Harry A. Ottenheimer, who years later was Rudolph Schindler's first employer in America; another was the Beaux-Arts architect Simeon B. Eisendrath, who in 1902 produced a scheme for an elegant "Hebrew Hospital" on the Hill in Pittsburgh. Had the Kaufmanns built it, they would have had the distinction of financing both Wright and the first of his many make-believe enemies.

Wright's 1926 attack on Jewish lawyers is cited in Gill, *Many Masks,* 296; the original letter is preserved in the Wright Archives at the University at Buffalo. After a 1931 court battle in Milwaukee over a trust fund that he claimed was his, Wright lashed out at "the kike-attorney" and "the kike-lawyer" who had opposed him (Wright to Henry Churchill, January 16, 1931). A typically pejorative use of the word "Jewish" in Wright's lexicon appears in his December 3, 1932, letter to his lecture agent W. Colston Leigh, whom he accused of cheating: "My dear Leigh: your logic concerning the Madison deduction is too jewish for me, or anyone here, to grasp." Wright specified Schindler and Neutra as Jews in a venomous attack he sent to Lewis Mumford on January 19, 1932, cited above (Pfeiffer and Wojtowicz, *Wright & Mumford,* 123–26). Working with Wright on a proposed counterexhibit to the 1932 MoMA show, Henry Churchill referred by letter on February 29, 1932, to "Gropius and J. J. P. Oud (two J's, by the way)."

We cannot now determine exactly what Wright and Kaufmann argued about concerning Jews and Zionism because both parties destroyed their copies of what must have been a highly inflammatory letter from Wright to Kaufmann in the early summer of 1946. Wright also destroyed E. J.'s reply. When he next wrote, on July 16, 1946, he offered "some explanation of my reference to 'race' as a probable factor in the slippery character of your patronage," and concluded with the tired classic "My best friends are Jews and I shall always be their friend." But Wright was in fact a cordial correspondent with Rabbi Norman Gerstenfeld—a Kaufmann relative—in Washington; he invited Rabbi Max Kadushin of the University of Wisconsin to conduct a Jewish service and join in a picnic at Taliesin (a great success); and he insisted on calling Rabbi Mortimer J. Cohen his design partner at his Beth Sholom Synagogue. He also counted as a good friend the esteemed Jewish leader Cyrus Adler. George Goodwin has written an unpublished "Jews in the Circle of Frank Lloyd Wright," which looks at both Wright's Jewish clients and at his numerous Jewish apprentices. See his "Wright and the Jewish community: Meyer May," *Bulletin: The Quarterly Newsletter of the Frank Lloyd Wright Building Conservancy* (Summer 1997). Goodwin regards Wright as highly intolerant of homosexuals, African-Americans, Jews, and Latinos.

Wright flirting with fascists: The identification of *Scribner's Commentator* as a Nazi propaganda tool is made in J. C. Furnas, *Stormy Weather: Crosslights on the Nineteen Thirties: An Informal Social History of the United States, 1929–1941* (1977), 242. Edward Arps asked for "divine protection" for Hitler in his letter of July 23, 1941, to Jesse Howell, chairman of the Conservative Party in Los Angeles. Arps copied the letter out and mailed it with his personal greeting to Wright the same day.

FIVE: THE DESIGN OF FALLINGWATER STRUGGLES NINE MONTHS TO BE BORN

Two views on architectural design: The dialogue of Heller and Roark comes from Rand, *The Fountainhead*, 252; Wright recollected his design process for Fallingwater in a televised interview with Hugh Downs on NBC, May 17, 1953, later published in emended form in Wright, *The Future of Architecture* (1953), 13–14.

The Vitruvian formula: Vitruvius, *Ten Books on Architecture,* trans. Morris Morgan (Cambridge, Mass., 1914, repr. 1960), 17.

Wright's knowledge of the kiva: The Kiva at Taliesin West is illustrated in Curtis Besinger's valuable *Working with Mr. Wright: What It Was Like* (Cambridge, 1995), figs. 52 and 53.

Parallel creation of Porgy and Bess: George Gershwin marked the dates of his orchestration of the opera on the first page of the original musical score, today one of the treasures of the Library of Congress.

Wright's trips to Bear Run: Eugene Masselink's accounting to Ethel Clinton on July 2, 1936, listed five trips that Wright had by then taken to Pittsburgh: May 18, July 3, and October 19, 1935; April 19 and June 5–6, 1936. There were additional stopovers on December 18, 1934, and June 29, 1935, and Wright almost certainly also made a visit on June 13, 1935, on which date George Sherman telegraphed him in Pittsburgh, and got a reply from Wright there.

A year later, on October 25, 1937, Wright claimed in a letter to Kaufmann that he had visited Pittsburgh or Bear Run eleven times during construction of the main house. That would include the seven main visits listed above (excluding June 13, 1935), plus four later visits on August 30 and October 20, 1936, September 13, 1937, and around October 7, 1937. More visits relative to the guesthouse and the interior furnishings followed in March and June 1938 and in August 1939.

Recollections of July 3, 1935: Cornelia Brierly's recollection of Wright's "beat the Internationalists" remark was first published in "Exploring Wright Sites in the East," *Frank Lloyd Wright Quarterly* 7 (Spring 1996): 14. Ms. Brierly and I reviewed the statement in detail during several interviews in 1999, and, while anyone's memory can play tricks, her account strikes me as entirely trustworthy. Brierly's book, *Tales of Taliesin: A Memoir of Fellowship* (Tempe, Ariz., 1999), is replete with what appear to be verbatim dialogues with Wright. Blaine Drake's recollections are cited in Hoffmann, *Fallingwater,* 16; those by Kaufmann Jr. are in his "Twenty-five Years," 22.

Budget and design development: Three letters confirm that architect and client had discussed a global price for the house in early July 1935: Kaufmann to Wright, July 5 and November 24; and Wright to Kaufmann, November 18, 1935. A price of $35,000 was about five times what the average American house sold for in 1935. The September 1935 meeting was cited in Wright to Kaufmann, August 21, 1935; Masselink to I. D. Wolf, August 26; Wright to Kaufmann and I. D. Wolf, September 18. Kaufmann Jr.'s letter to Wright about Fallingwater's being "to some extent on paper" is undated but from context came in late August 1935.

Wright drawing at night: Wright's first quote comes from Hoppen, *Seven Ages,* 97; the second from his "In the Cause of Architecture: The Logic of the Plan," *Architectural Record* 63 (January 1928): 49.

The Beaux-Arts design method: Wright, *Autobiography,* 126; Franklin Toker, "Richardson 'en concours': The Pittsburgh Courthouse," *Carnegie Magazine* 51 (November 1977): 13–25; Richard Chafee, "The Teaching of Architecture at the École des Beaux-Arts," in *The Architecture of the École des Beaux-Arts,* ed. Arthur Drexler (1977), 61–110, esp. pp. 84–85.

Wright praised Richardson's Pittsburgh courthouse in a newspaper column published on August 9, 1935, reproduced in Henning, "At Taliesin," 149–50. The link between his Imperial Hotel in Tokyo and a Beaux-Arts Grand Prix design was explored in Levine, Wright, 115–17.

Wright at the drafting table: Wright's last-minute changes to the Guggenheim and the way he drew almost perfectly to scale were recounted to me by David Dodge. For a different perspective on Wright's design process, see Joseph Connors, "Wright on Nature and the Machine," in The Nature of Frank Lloyd Wright, ed. C. Bolon et al. (Chicago, 1988), 14–16.

Wright's design gifts: Insight on the way Wright worked with nature is provided in Hoppen, Seven Ages, 97; Donald Hoffmann, Frank Lloyd Wright: Architecture and Nature (1986). Wright's aphorism on Taliesin as "a house that hill might marry" is reported in Levine, Wright, 104.

Wright and his clients: Ayn Rand to Wright, October 10, 1946. Kaufmann, Fallingwater, 121, stresses how accommodating Wright was to the Kaufmanns' requests. At the last minute he made a cloakroom out of a bathroom, then created a banquette and music-listening nook where the original coat closet was supposed to have gone. He added unanticipated exterior steps up to the guest-balcony in response to Liliane's fear of wet bathing suits in the living room, and made numerous additional changes in the bathrooms and elsewhere. The "Imaginary Letter from Liliane Kaufmann, owner of Fallingwater, to me" forms part of Frances Balter, The River's Bend (Amherst, Mass., 1998), 9–10.

Analysis of Wright's house plans: Hildebrand, Wright Space, 93–105, offers a spatial analysis of Fallingwater in part based on the psychobiology theory of Jay Appleton in The Experience of Landscape (1975). See also the assessment of Fallingwater as the supreme achievement of organic design, in Norris Kelly Smith's Frank Lloyd Wright: A Study in Architectural Content (Englewood Cliffs, N.J., 1966), 127–36. For Jung's analysis of domestic space, see Marjorie Garber, Sex and Real Estate: Why We Love Houses (2000), 100–04.

How Wright designed Fallingwater: My discussion of Wright's design method benefited from the analysis presented by Bill Boyle to my Fallingwater seminar at the University of Pittsburgh in 1999, and from later discussions in front of Wright's Fallingwater plans. For Fallingwater's dimensions I follow the new plans in McCarter, Fallingwater, 59.

Fallingwater's bolsters: Wright spoke of his use of the cantilever at the Imperial Hotel in his Autobiography, 147, 215–16, in which he evoked the image of the cantilever akin to a tray held by a waiter with outstretched fingers. He may have enjoyed flaunting convention with the cantilever, too. Cantilevers were forbidden to students at the École des Beaux-Arts in Paris, the institution Wright loved to hate (Hoppen, Seven Ages, 102).

Design with nature: Jan Peterson, "Nature's Architect," New Masses 26 (February 8, 1938): 29–30. Alexander Purves, "This Goodly Frame, the Earth," Perspecta 25 (1989): 178–201, used Wright's Fallingwater and Aalto's contemporary Villa Mairea to explore the Modern Movement's relationship of architecture to nature. Wright's comment about seeing how nature built the Grand Canyon appears in Hoffmann, Fallingwater, 13 n. 8. The legend of Indians supposedly siting campfires on the main boulder undergirding Fallingwater comes from Hoppen, Seven Ages, 95.

Wright and waterfalls: Kathryn Smith, "A Beat of the Rhythmic Clock of Nature: Frank Lloyd Wright's Waterfall Buildings," in Wright Studies 2 (Carbondale, Ill., 2000): 1–31, carries illustrations of some of Wright's waterfall photographs from Japan and discusses all of Wright's designs with water. The observation about the two Fallingwater balconies reflecting the two different angles of the Bear Run falls comes from this paper. The waterfall at

Taliesin is documented in Anne Whiston Spirn, "Frank Lloyd Wright: Architect of Land-scape," *Frank Lloyd Wright Quarterly* 11 (Summer 2000): 23. The trout stream running through the bedroom was hypothesized in "Modern Home Built over a Mountain Brook," *We the People: Pennsylvania in Review* 3 (February 1, 1938): 12–13.

Fallingwater and other waterfall buildings: LeDoux's image is discussed in Levine, *Wright,* 473 n. 100. Jules Saulnier's widely publicized Menier Chocolate factory of 1870–71 stood atop a power dam on the Marne River: see Siegfried Giedion, *Space, Time, and Architecture* (Cambridge, Mass., 1941), 204–06. L'Enfant's concept of placing an artificial waterfall at the base of the U.S. Capitol is documented in Pamela Scott, "'This Vast Empire': The Iconography of the Mall, 1791–1848," in *The Mall in Washington, 1791–1991,* ed. Richard Longstreth (Washington, 1991), 37–58, at pp. 42 and 56 n. 34.

Fallingwater, industry, and Pittsburgh: Wright's editorial "Broadacres to Pittsburgh" appeared in the *Pittsburgh Sun-Telegraph,* June 24, 1935. His "abandon it" quote on Pitts-burgh appeared in the *Sun-Telegraph* on June 30. Wright recalled the Bessemers in his article "The Nature of Materials," *Architectural Record* (October 1928). Wright cited the power of Pittsburgh architecture in a column reproduced in Henning, *"At Taliesin,"* 149–50. Maloney wrote Tafel and Masselink about Wright's criticism of Pittsburgh on July 27, 1935. For Evergreen Hamlet, see Toker, *Pittsburgh,* 300–02.

Wright's appreciation for history: Wright was quoted on the importance of incorporating history in architectural design in "A New Debate in Old Venice," *New York Times Maga-zine,* March 21, 1954: 8 (Levine, *Wright,* 493 n. 47, and discussion of Wright's design for Venice, 374–83). Joseph Connors's review of Hoffmann's *Fallingwater* appeared in the *Journal of the Society of Architectural Historians* (December 1979): 397. Other sources on Wright's eclecticism in Levine, *Wright,* 468 n. 14. The story of Wright's hiding his sources was told many times: the version in the text comes from Robert Winter's first-person account in his brochure for the 1989 Los Angeles tour of the Society of Architectural His-torians, p. 9. The Horiu-ji "tree" system for the St.-Mark's-in-the-Bouwerie towers comes from M. F. Hearn Jr., "A Japanese Inspiration for Frank Lloyd Wright's Rigid-Core High-Rise Structures," *Journal of the Society of Architectural Historians* 50 (1991): 68–71.

The Gale house as prototype for Fallingwater: Frank Lloyd Wright, *A Testament* (1957), 75; Storrer, *Companion,* 94. The fake date on the Gale house drawing is cited in Hoff-mann, *Fallingwater,* 73, and Robert McCarter, *Fallingwater,* 8, and elsewhere. I thank Kort Gustafson for allowing me to inspect the Gale house in 1999. Robert van 't Hoff's Villa Henny at Huis ter Heide, near Utrecht, is illustrated in Curtis, *Modern Architecture* (1996 ed.), 154. Already in 1918 van Doesburg's *Rhythm of a Russian Dance,* today in MoMA, looked like a free two-dimensional adaptation of a Wrightian Prairie house plan; van Doesburg's 1923 project moved from a two-dimensional abstraction to three-dimensional. Full documentation on Rietveld's design is in *The Rietveld Schröder House,* ed. Paul Overy et al. (Cambridge, Mass., 1988).

Italian and Native American elements at Fallingwater: Wright recalled his time in Italy in his *Autobiography,* 164–65; his house in Florence is documented in photographs and text in Anthony Alofsin, *Frank Lloyd Wright: The Lost Years, 1910–1922* (Chicago, 1993), 48–53. The description of the Picuries Pueblo is reproduced in Eleanor B. Adams, *The Missions of New Mexico* (Albuquerque, 1956). Kathryn Smith, *Schindler House* (2001), 10, reproduces Schindler's view of the pueblo at Taos. Wright told Kaufmann of his impend-ing visit to the "cliffdwellers" by letter of March 8, 1935. Wright's citations of Southwest-ern architecture are discussed in Levine, *Wright,* 188 and 460 n. 76. Cornelia Brierly told me of Wright's travels in the Southwest in 1999, while Christopher Curtis Mead gener-ously reviewed different cliff-dweller sites with me (communication, July 28, 2000). Walt Whitman, "Song of Myself," 1855, in *Leaves of Grass* (New York, 1892), 72. Wright demonstrated his fondness for Whitman in the sequence of Whitman quotes he used as marginalia in the January 1938 issue of *Architectural Forum* devoted to his work.

The influence of other architects and buildings: Eric Lloyd Wright denigrated the idea of any influence of the Lovell house on Fallingwater at the symposium on Fallingwater's engineering, Carnegie Museum of Art, Pittsburgh, April 20, 1999. The prime exceptions to the narrow-focus discussions of Fallingwater in the earlier literature are Vincent Scully, *American Architecture and Urbanism* (1969), 156–60, and Levine's chapter on the house in his *Wright*, 217–54. The argument that Wright was particularly vulnerable to outside influences was presented by James O'Gorman in a lecture on Wright at the Carnegie Museum of Art, June 1999.

Wright attacking the European moderns: Twombly, *Wright*, 384–85; and a report on Wright's address to the Michigan Architectural Society, *Architectural Forum* 55 (October 1931): 409. Le Corbusier was fully aware of Wright's hostility toward him. In 1947 he asked the young Pittsburgh architect and would-be Wright apprentice Tasso Katselas: "Why does Wright hate me so?" Wright used the term "goose-step" in describing the followers of the European modernists in an unpublished letter to Kenneth Conant, October 31, 1934 (Frances Loeb Library, Harvard University). He also summed up his differences with the German modernists in a 1931 circular "To My Critics in the Land of the Danube and the Rhine" (Levine, *Wright*, 468 n. 14). Wright threatened to turn against Neutra and Schindler in a letter to Pauline Schindler that is datable by context to January 1931. In his review of Le Corbusier's *Towards a New Architecture* in *World Unity* (September 1928):393–95, Wright alleged that everything good in Le Corbusier's work had been invented twenty-five years earlier either by Sullivan or himself (Twombly, *Wright*, 163). Mumford's evaluation of Wright and Le Corbusier came in his "Frank Lloyd Wright and the New Pioneers," *Architectural Record* (April 1929): 414–16.

Overlapping with the Europeans: Scully, *American Architecture*, 158, points out the dependence of Wright's first *parti* for his Millard house in Pasadena on Le Corbusier's Citrohan house project, as had already been noted by critics at the time. Connors pointed out similar connections in his review of Hoffmann's *Fallingwater* in the *Journal of the Society of Architectural Historians*: 397. Henry-Russell Hitchcock, *In the Nature of Materials: The Buildings of Frank Lloyd Wright, 1887–1941* (1942), 91, also explained Fallingwater largely in terms of Wright's interaction with the Europeans. See also the excellent analysis of what Wright learned from the Europeans in Johnson, *Wright Versus America*, 93.

Kentuck Knob: Complete analysis of the house in Donald Hoffmann, *Kentuck Knob* (Pittsburgh, 2000); plans and views in Storrer, *Companion*, 405.

Wright's use of concrete: Frank Lloyd Wright, "In the Cause of Architecture—Concrete," *Architectural Record* 63 (August 1928): 98–104. For Ernest Ransome and pioneer work in reinforced concrete in the United States, see Reyner Banham, *A Concrete Atlantis: U.S. Industrial Building and European Modern Architecture, 1900–1925* (Cambridge, Mass., 1986), 32ff. The early history of reinforced concrete is sketched out in Marvin Trachtenberg and Isabelle Hyman, *Architecture: From Prehistory to Post-Modernism* (1986), 463, 520–22.

Impact of Gropius and Mies on Fallingwater: The mitered corner windows in the Ennis and Freeman houses are illustrated and discussed in Sweeney, *Wright in Hollywood*, 76–79. Mies's Tugendhat house is well documented in *Ludwig Mies van der Rohe: The Tugendhat House*, ed. Daniela Hammer-Tugendhat and Wolf Tegethoff (2002). The Bauhaus curriculum is discussed in *The Bauhaus, 1919–1928*, ed. Herbert Bayer (1938) and in the fascinating memoir of an American who studied there: Howard Dearstyne's *Inside the Bauhaus*, ed. David Spaeth (1986).

Wright, Schindler, and Neutra: Wright spoke of his need to gain energy from contact with younger architects and apprentices (*Autobiography,* 449–50, and in many other passages), as the apprentices in turn affirmed (Tafel, *About Wright,* 105–86). On Schindler's Wolfe house: *R. M. Schindler: Composition and Construction,* ed. Lionel March and Judith Sheine (London, 1993), 162–69. The 1931 architecture show at UCLA was curated by Schindler's ex-wife Pauline; details in McCoy, *Five California Architects,* 167. The direct contact between Wright and Leah Lovell was reported to me both by Leah Lovell's daughter-in-law Barbara Jean Lovell and by her great-niece Susan Bernstein, the Lovell family historian. I thank Dr. Lovell for graciously showing her house to me in 2002. The diagonal bolsters that Wright added to Taliesin around 1925 have a shape that is closer to Fallingwater's bolsters than are Schindler's, but Schindler's bolsters are incomparably more dramatic, and chronologically precede those that Wright added to Taliesin.

The second Lovell house and Fallingwater: See the illuminating discussion of Fallingwater's sources in Vincent Scully's *American Architecture,* 159–60. Wright's letter of congratulations to Neutra on the Lovell house is quoted in part in Hines, *Richard Neutra,* 84. On the architect as immigrant: Franklin Toker, "James O'Donnell: An Irish Georgian in America," *Journal of the Society of Architectural Historians* 29 (1970): 132–43.

Frank Lloyd Wright learning from his son Lloyd: *Lloyd Wright: The Architecture of Frank Lloyd Wright Jr.,* ed. Alan Weintraub et al. (1998), 90–97. I thank Michael and Carole Dougherty for showing me through the Derby house and its grounds in 2000.

Could Wright have designed Fallingwater in two hours?: Jack Quinan, *Frank Lloyd Wright's Larkin Building: Myth and Fact* (Cambridge, Mass., 1987), 26–33, questions the accuracy of Wright's account of his tortured revisions on the Larkin design, which may have been posturing for his readers. Wright recalled his design process at Unity Temple in the *Autobiography,* 158. John Lloyd Wright's recollection of the birth of the Midway Gardens design comes from his book *My Father Who Is on Earth* (1946; repr. Carbondale, Ill., 1994), 71–72. My thanks to Ken Kremer for reminding me of this incident.

Wright's drawing procedure: Blaine Drake to Donald Hoffmann, May 19, 1975, and Brierly's undated recollections (both in Hoffmann, *Fallingwater,* 17). Brierly presumably talked with Hoffmann while the latter was researching his book at Taliesin in the 1970s. The Dodges' recollections to me are confirmed almost word for word by apprentice Donald Hoppen, who quoted Wright as saying that his special hour of inspiration was between three and four in the morning (Hoppen, *Seven Ages,* 97). The original Knowles drawing C-9284 was in a scale of 1 inch = 20 feet, conventionally called a ¹⁄₂₀″ scale; the redrawing (FLWF no. 3602.129, henceforth 129) was in the much larger ⅛″ scale. Tafel recalled his role in making this site plan tracing when we spoke in 2002.

The apprentices recalled September 22, 1935: Caraway was recorded by Secrest, *Wright,* 419. Jack Howe recalled Kaufmann saying after the brief meeting, "Don't change a thing" (Secrest, *Wright,* 420). Tafel's account comes from his *Apprentice,* 1–7, and in variants in Hoffmann, *Fallingwater,* 15–17, and Gill, *Many Masks,* 345–47. Bob Mosher's version is quoted in Hoffmann, *Fallingwater,* 17. Cleary, *Merchant,* 39, states: "Kaufmann was surprised to see the house perched above the waterfall rather than on the opposite bank oriented with a view of the falls."

The Fallingwater conceptual drawings: Kaufmann, *Fallingwater,* 176–77, gives a half-size color reproduction of drawing 166. I cite the Fallingwater drawings wherever possible with their inventory numbers at the archives of the Frank Lloyd Wright Foundation (FLWF) at Taliesin West, in Scottsdale, Arizona. The majority of the drawings are reproduced on four CD-ROM diskettes in *Frank Lloyd Wright: Presentation and Conceptual Drawings* (Urbana, Calif., 1994). Futagawa and Pfeiffer, *Frank Lloyd Wright,* 11:28–40, illustrates a selection of preliminary studies for Fallingwater as figures 42–58. Carter

Manny Jr. recalled Wright's simultaneous creation of three different house plans in Tafel, *About Wright,* 145. Wright declared, "There is no 'sketch,'" in his *Autobiography,* 158, as pointed out in the excellent discussion of Wright's design method in Connors, *Robie House,* 40–41. Levine, *Wright,* 264–65, notes that Wright did nonetheless make occasional conceptual sketches, and illustrates two of Taliesin West that bear a scant relationship to the final design.

Wright's "hidden" triangle: Wright spelled out his triangle-based design method in detail on another job six years before Fallingwater: Levine, *Wright,* 465 n. 60, and Hoffmann, *Fallingwater,* 19.

Extending Liliane's terrace: My observation of Wright's last-minute extension of Liliane's terrace is new, but the general linkage of Fallingwater to the first Willey house scheme was already pointed out in Levine, *Wright,* 222, with the reproduction of the original perspective view and plan. Lewis Mumford cited the two houses together in his review of MoMA's Fallingwater exhibit in *The New Yorker,* February 12, 1938. Confirmation that Fallingwater's extended terrace was a true change of plan rather than a banal transcription error comes from the suppression of the two sets of palisade windows on plan 166 and erasures and extensions on second-floor plan 047 that exactly correspond with those on plan 166. Note, too, the addition of the word "deck" on Liliane's ample new balcony on plan 047, whereas Wright had earlier written "terrace" on the much smaller patio he had devised for her. I thank Charles Rosenblum (two communications, both October 9, 2002) for discussing these changes with me after I outlined them in a lecture to my University of Pittsburgh colleagues the preceding day.

Sequence of drawings: Tafel and I discussed plan 166 as we stood in front of it in 1999. None of the drawings made in 1935 bear dates, and their sequence gets complicated because numerous intermediary drawings disappeared long ago. The discussion in Cleary, *Merchant,* 174–83, only intermittently distinguishes between drawings created in 1935 and those executed in 1936; it additionally fails to isolate the drawings of September 1935 from those of October 1935. The Taliesin Archives also merge the September and October groups together. But the two series can be distinguished by certain telltale characteristics. Belonging to September 22 or immediately thereafter are the first-floor plan (Taliesin inventory number 048), the second-floor plan 047, the third-floor plan 046, and two aerial views of Fallingwater's front and back (Taliesin numbers 001 and 002, now at the Canadian Centre for Architecture in Montréal). The dozen plans that were mailed to Pittsburgh in October 1935 were all on distinctive paper 32″ tall by 41″ wide, and they rendered the house in a ¼″ scale that had not been used before.

Connors, *Robie House,* 40–41, shows in two plans for the Ullman house how Wright would "pull" a perspective view from a plan to check the massing of the building as it took shape. In his *Autobiography,* Wright derided the dexterity of his early boss Joseph Silsbee in making a perspective view and then forcing the plan of the building to respond. Wright worked the opposite way: if need be he would change the plans, then force the perspective to respond. Fallingwater plans 047 and 048 carry baselines from which perspective views seem to have been "pulled," but no corresponding perspective renderings survive today.

SIX: RAISING FALLINGWATER

The preliminary sketches: Kaufmann to Wright, September 27, 1935, and Kaufmann Jr. to Wright, same day.

The Fallingwater detail drawings: Cleary, *Merchant*, 175–83, lists several hundred master sheets for Fallingwater from the 1930s through the 1950s, nearly all of which reside today in the archives at Taliesin. Taliesin and Avery Library also contain hundreds more blueprints that were created in various mechanical-reproduction techniques from the hand-drawn originals: these have never been numbered. Here and throughout this chapter I have been assisted by Ken Kremer on both the philosophy and the technique of engineering at Fallingwater.

Early appraisals of Fallingwater: Wes Peters's insightful remark that Fallingwater was too radical to obtain a building permit either in the 1930s or in the 1990s appears in *Frank Lloyd Wright: The Masterworks,* ed. David Larkin and Bruce Brooks Pfeiffer (1993), 161. (Peters is not identified by name in the text, but Pfeiffer so informed me privately in 1999.) Carl Thumm to Wright, January 20, 1937. Wright and Kaufmann discussed coal in their letters of October 23, 25, and 28, 1935. The original wording of Gabor's parody reads: "Ich wußte ja, daß ich zu meinem 50. Geburtstag den Wasserfall ganz leicht sehen werde! Das allerbeste zum fünfzigsten wünsche. Ihr Gabor." Liliane says: "Ich sehe ihn noch viel besser." Wright's comment to Mumford that there were "no hard and fast lines in Nature" came in his letter of April 7, 1931 (*Wright & Mumford,* 105–07).

Kaufmann's "second opinion": The "second opinion" is chronicled in Kaufmann, *Fallingwater,* 46. References to the April 19 meeting are in Kaufmann to Wright, April 20, 1936, and Wright to Kaufmann, May 4, 1936. Discussion of stone: Wright to Kaufmann, November 11; Kaufmann to Wright, December 12, 1935. Negotiating about fees: Kaufmann to Wright, November 5 and December 12, 1935; Wright to Kaufmann, December 16. For a comparison with other Wright clients, see Paul and Jean Hanna, *Frank Lloyd Wright's Hanna House* (1982), and Herbert and Katherine Jacobs, *Building with Frank Lloyd Wright* (San Francisco, 1978). Kaufmann wrote Mosher from Florida on February 10, 1937; Mosher referred to E. J.'s knowing every inch of the plans in his letter to Wright of July 16, 1936. On putting up forms: Kaufmann to Wright, July 7, 1936. Other observations on E. J. in Hoffmann, *Fallingwater,* 33–56ff. I. D. Wolf Jr. recalled hauling stones in an interview in 1987. On Zeller: Mosher to Wright, June 16, 1936, and in an undated letter probably from May or June 1936. Depression wages: Hall to Wright, March 10, 1939. Paul Wiegman and Earl Friend provided much insight on the Fallingwater quarrying process in interviews.

Start of construction: Dombar to Wright, April 29, 1936, and Dombar interview in 1999. The original surveyor's notebook survived in the Knowles offices until 1998; at the point of the company's dissolution, the firm gave it to Fallingwater, where it now resides. Norbert Zeller lived until 1976, long enough for his complaints about nude sunbathing to be absorbed into the lore of Fallingwater's guides; I thank Ken Kremer for this particular story. Wright's contract of June 5, 1936, is preserved at Avery Library. The financing of Fallingwater emerged in an interview with Ralph Demmler in 1986.

Changing the bolsters—and the builder: Mosher to Wright, July 21 and August 19 and 21, 1936. Tafel's letter to Mosher of June 30, 1936, enclosed a detail drawing for the revised bolsters. On July 4, 1936, Mosher informed Wright that "the bolsters have been stripped and floated." Mosher acknowledged receipt of the revised bolster design by letter to Tafel on July 5, 1936. Wright chastised Kaufmann about the lack of a professional builder at Bear Run by letter of July 10, 1936. My thanks to Walter J. Hall's grandson Ray and his wife Ronda for their hospitality to me and my son Jeffrey at Lynn Hall in 1999. My information on Walter Hall comes from his extensive records and his correspondence with Wright and Kaufmann, all preserved among the Hall family papers at Lynn Hall. Raymond V. Hall's introductory letter to Wright of March 19, 1934, survives at Taliesin. I learned much about Earl Friar from Norman Weiss, the concrete specialist for the reconstruction of Fallingwater's balconies. Wright to Hall, May 13, 1936, and Hall to Wright, May 23. Hall's original five-page contract with Kaufmann survives in the Hall family archives. It gives Hall's estimated cost for the work as $29,000 and his salary as $50 a week. Kaufmann promised Hall a $25-a-week bonus if the work came in under $29,000 in cost.

First cantilever crisis: Kaufmann to Wright, July 7, 1936, expressing frustration that plans for the steelwork in the main floor had not yet arrived. Wright's summons to Mendel Glickman was reported in a letter of Tafel to Mosher, June 30, 1936. Glickman introduced himself by letter to Wright on September 6, 1932.

The popularization of reinforced concrete in the U.S. is documented in Amy Slaton, *Reinforced Concrete and the Mechanization of American Building, 1900–1930* (Baltimore, 2002). Kenneth Frampton's important essay, "Modernization and Mediation: Frank Lloyd Wright and the Impact of Technology," in the 1994 MoMA catalogue *Frank Lloyd Wright, Architect*, 58–79, esp. pp. 72–73, gives a good summary of the challenges facing Wright at Fallingwater. It was Frampton, in his *Modern Architecture* (1991 ed.), 189, who called Fallingwater's balconies "extravagant to the point of folly."

Cantilever failure and reconstruction: I thank Lynda Waggoner (communication, August 9, 2002) for her substantial contribution to my account of the rebuilding of Fallingwater. Ken Kremer has been my faithful guide in all technical aspects of Fallingwater's construction, especially in our site visit of February 12, 2002, during which we discussed the reconstruction with Mario Suarez, the project's post-tensioning specialist.

Calculating the cantilevers: Frank Lloyd Wright, *The Natural House* (1954), 47. Robert Silman, "The Plan to Save Fallingwater," *Scientific American* 283:3 (September 2000): 88–95. Metzger-Richardson drawing 3784-1 for "Residence for E. J. Kaufmann, Bear Run Pa.," and cover letter from L. W. Cook to Carl Thumm, August 10, 1936 (both preserved in Avery Library). Edgar Tafel reported to me the general feeling among the apprentices at Taliesin at the time that there were not enough rods in the concrete, and that the rods might have been placed too high within the beams.

E. J. adds extra steel: Wright's underestimation of the steel needed in the roof at Kentuck Knob is documented in Donald Hoffmann, *Kentuck Knob* (Pittsburgh, 2000), 43. Edgar Tafel recounts that Wright fired him in fury at the extra steel he had added to one house, but then rehired him when he realized that the house would probably have collapsed without that amount of steel (*About Wright*, 252). The main letters chronicling the cantilever crisis are: Mosher to Wright, August 25, 1936; Wright to Mosher, August 27, and an undated telegram, by context August 29; Wright to Kaufmann, August 27; Kaufmann to Wright, August 28; Wright to Hall, August 29; and Hall to Wright, September 12 and 16, 1936.

Cracks everywhere: Hall described his pouring of the second floor by letter to Wright of October 1, 1936. The troublesome second-floor roof overhang was designed to Mendel Glickman's specifications, not those of the Metzger-Richardson engineers. Glickman sent Wright a steel diagram for the reinforcement of the roof slab on October 15, 1936, noting that the slab was reinforced both in compression and tension "in order to keep the thickness down to 5 [inches]." Mosher's August 25, 1936, letter to Wright reported: "I am inclosing some calculations made in Pittsburgh by engineers hired by Kaufmann: their contention was that more steel [was] necessary in beams because they discovered that the weight of second floor transposed through T-iron window frames was not figured." Robert Stilman told me in 1999 that it did not matter whether Hall welded the mullions and the steel lintels together into one complete system or not: so long as Fallingwater was stable, the act of welding was immaterial.

Furnishing the interior: Thumm sent Hall a schedule for internal furnishings on January 19, 1937; it covered fifteen separate topics in the manner of a legal brief. The redwood subflooring was mentioned by Hall to Wright in a letter of February 4, 1937. Mosher wrote of his frustrations with the windows to Wright, August 3, 1936, and February 11, 1937; Carl Thumm to Kaufmann, January 21, 1937. Wright's sending the Kaufmanns an old Indian pot is documented by letter of Mosher to Wright, March 27, 1937; this phase of construction is well evoked by the memorandum of "Work to Be Done/Kaufmann House Bear Run April 1 1937" (Avery).

Sheathing the balconies in gold leaf: Max Putzel, "A House That Straddles a Waterfall," *St. Louis Post-Dispatch Sunday Magazine,* March 21, 1937, cited "[the] concrete shelves, which will probably be trimmed in dull gold leaf—the quiet gold of Japanese screens." Hoppen, *Seven Ages,* 102, reported Wright's allusion to Fallingwater's abortive gilding in connection with the temple in Kyoto, but a more specific precedent can be found in Wright's own work. His Winslow and Dana houses of 1893 and 1903, respectively, carry plasterwork bands just below the roofline that give those buildings substantial color accents. In 1907, Wright veneered large patches of the exterior of the Avery Coonley house in Riverside, Illinois, with tiles that emit so lustrous an aura they may as well be golden (see the photograph in Thomas Heinz, *The Vision of Frank Lloyd Wright* [Edison, N.J., 2001], 133). The waterproof cement paint was mentioned in a letter of Lloyd Wright to Kaufmann, March 19, 1937; Kaufmann wrote the Super-Concrete Emulsions Company of Los Angeles on May 13, 1937.

Last details on the house: The reappearing cracks in the parapets of Liliane's terrace were reported by Mosher to Wright on March 27, 1937; Kaufmann sought a new evaluation on the cantilever deflection by letter to Metzger-Richardson, May 21, 1937; Metzger-Richardson reported back to Kaufmann on June 1, 1937 (Avery).

SEVEN: FALLINGWATER GETS AN INTERIOR

Interior proportions and innovations: Storrer, *Companion,* 246, 258, discusses the typical plan and proportions in Wright's Usonian houses. On fluorescent lights, see Stephen von Dulken, *Inventing the 20th Century: 100 Inventions That Shaped the World* (London, 2000), 42.

Prospect and refuge: Hildebrand, *Wright Space,* 93–105, and the same author's *Origins of Architectural Pleasure* (Berkeley, Calif., 1999), 71–72, expand on the concept of Fallingwater as a refuge from the dangers that swirl around it. Robert Pogue Harrison, *Forest: The Shadow of Civilization* (Chicago, 1992), 232–38, also sees Fallingwater primarily as shelter. Frampton's appraisal of Fallingwater's interior as a "furnished cave" appears in his *Modern Architecture* (1991 ed.), 189.

The "natural house": Hoffmann characterized the walls as "a rough and yet sophisticated abstraction" in his *Fallingwater,* 33. Wright spoke of the two extremes of decoration in his *Autobiography,* 348; he listed his six points of house design in *The Natural House* (1954), esp. pp. 16–19; as trimmed down in Charles Rosenblum's talk, "Precedent and Principle: The Work of Cornelia Brierly and Peter Berndtson," Pittsburgh, June 21, 1999. Hoppen's analysis of Taliesin West appears in his *Seven Ages,* 67.

The living room: Wright spoke of his old home in Weymouth in his *Autobiography,* 32.

Wright's windows: "Oral history of A. James Speyer," typescript at the Art Institute of Chicago, ca. 1980.

Wright's furnishings: My discussion of Wright's furniture was materially aided by Fallingwater's curatorial files and by explanations of arcane points by the furniture designer Dan Droz. The standard references on the topic are David Hanks, *The Decorative Designs of Frank Lloyd Wright* (1979), and Thomas Heinz, *Frank Lloyd Wright: Interiors and Furni-*

ture (London, 1994). Mosher's memos on furniture design went to Kaufmann, February 4, 1937, and to Wright, March 27, 1937; Kaufmann's note to Mosher is dated May 17, 1937. Wright's "Specifications for Kaufmann House Mill Work" is undated, but its context suggests a date around June 1, 1937; the answering "Bid for Walnut Wood Fixtures" came from the Gillen Woodwork Corporation of Milwaukee to Wright on June 4, 1937. Edgar Tafel sent the bid and a cover letter to Kaufmann on June 5, 1937; the contract between E. J. Kaufmann and Gillen Woodwork was drawn up on June 16, 1937 (Avery). Other furniture-related memos were from Kaufmann to Wright, October 16 and 18, 1937; Edgar Tafel to Kaufmann Jr., March 14 and 17, 1938. The March 14 letter shows the first use (to my knowledge) of the term "Fallingwater" by either the clients or the designers—months after it had been independently popularized in the press. Kaufmann made his request for Wright's ongoing consultation concerning furnishings on August 24, 1939. The recollection of apprentices being sent back to change the color of their clothes comes from Cornelia Brierly.

Furniture arrangement and cosmology: Heinz, *Vision*, 419, created and photographed a rearrangement of the furniture according to what he believed was Wright's conception of "overlapping and cantilevered elements," rather than the Kaufmanns' more formal arrangement. The main courtyard at Taliesin West was raked in the manner of a Japanese sand garden, such as that of the Ryoanji Temple in Kyoto (Tafel, *About Wright*, 142–43). Cosmological/Pythagorean analyses of the house are offered in Kaufmann, *Fallingwater*, 178; Levine, *Wright*:46ff; and Arnold Klukas, "Fallingwater: Villa or Shrine," *Fallingwater Newsletter* 10 (1993): 1–5. I recognize that such readings are possible, but there is no evidence that Wright worked in so mystic a vein.

EIGHT: FABRICATING FALLINGWATER I: THE HYPE THAT SOLD IT

Fallingwater and the media: My thanks to John Conti for his report on the publicizing of Fallingwater for my Fallingwater seminar at the University of Pittsburgh in 1999, which influenced my discussion here.

Wright as media manipulator: The closest thing to a study on Wright the media hound is a paper by Martin Filler, "The Master and the Magazines: The Media of Mobocracy," delivered at the annual meeting of the Society of Architectural Historians, April 1983. Of value are the instructive passages on Wright in Andrew Saint, *The Image of the Architect* (New Haven, 1983), 1–14, and the biographies by Gill and Secrest, but much more needs to be researched. The 1886 mention of Wright in a Unitarian newsletter is carried in Sweeney, *Bibliography*, 1. Wright's quarrel with Sturgis is documented in Jack Quinan, "Frank Lloyd Wright's Reply to Russell Sturgis," *Journal of the Society of Architectural Historians* 41 (1982): 238–44.

Early publications on Fallingwater: Mosher's construction narrative is reprinted in Henning, "At Taliesin," 232–34. Baker Brownell to Wright, February 1 and March 1, 1937; Brownell to Eugene Saxton of Harper & Brothers, May 28, 1937; Saxton to Brownell, June 4, 1937; Brownell to Wright, June 29. Saxton to Eugene Masselink, August 9, 1937, describing the book as in final galleys. That the galleys were still open to change is clear from Saxton's separate letters to Brownell and Wright of August 12 on certain incendiary passages by Wright that had to be excised from the book. See also Johnson, *Wright Versus America*, 174. Beatrice Schapper's obituary appeared in the *New York Times*, January 28, 1974; see her *Writing the Magazine Article: From Idea to Printed Page* (Cincinnati, 1970). Masselink to Arch Ely, author of the *Sentinel* article, July 14, 1937; Ely to Masselink, July 17; Masselink to Kaufmann, July 19, 1937.

Fallingwater illustrated: Mosher's movies are cited in Tafel's letter to Kaufmann of June 5, 1937; Swank's movies are cited in the MoMA Archives relative to its exhibition on Fallingwater in January 1938. On Swank, see Clyde Hare, *Luke Swank,* exhibition at the Carnegie Museum of Art (Pittsburgh, 1980). The Churchill photographs now reside among the Kaufmann papers at Columbia University.

Origins of the January 1938 Architectural Forum issue: Connolly to Johnson's Wax general manager J. R. Ramsey, November 9, 1936; Connolly to Wright, October 8, 1936; Wright replied the next day. Howard Myers to Wright, November 27, 1936: "Tom Maloney has been kind enough to transmit your wire in response to our request for publishing rights on your new building for the Johnson Company, of Racine"; Wright to Connolly, November 28, 1936; Jonathan Lipman, *Frank Lloyd Wright and the Johnson Wax Buildings* (1986), 46–47. Wright to *Forum's* George Nelson, June 7, 1937; Myers to Wright, July 28 and August 6, 1937; Nelson to Masselink, May 11, 1937. A. Lawrence Kocher of *Architectural Record* to Wright, June 4, 1937, and Mabel Morgan's reply on Wright's behalf, June 8; James M. Fitch Jr. of *Architectural Record* to Wright, August 19 and 25, 1937; Kocher to Masselink, October 11, 1937.

Hedrich's photographs: Quinan, "Wright's Reply to Sturgis": 238–44. The folkloric account of Hedrich's relationship to Wright was reported in Jack Quinan, "Wright, Photography, and Architecture," in "Fallingwater: A Symposium to Honor Edgar Kaufmann, Jr., on the 50th Anniversary of the Completion of Frank Lloyd Wright's House at Bear Run, Pennsylvania," Temple Hoyne Buell Center for the Study of American Architecture, Columbia University, November 8, 1986 (unpublished). "Oral History of William C. Hedrich," 1994, unpublished manuscript at the Art Institute of Chicago; excerpts in Tony Hiss, *Building Images: Seventy Years of Photography at Hedrich Blessing* (San Francisco, 2000), 32–37. Wright's negative reaction to the photograph is also recorded in the same interview. *Architectural Forum* incorrectly credited the Fallingwater photographs to Ken Hedrich rather than to his brother Bill.

Fallingwater's geographical location: The designation of "village" for an unincorporated settlement comes from Pennsylvania Statutes 53 P.S., paragraph 0107 (Harrisburg, 2001); my thanks to Wendy Mann-Eliot, University of Pittsburgh government documents librarian, for locating this. *The Population of Pennsylvania Municipalities: 1960 to 1998* (Harrisburg, 1999).

Fallingwater's name: Tafel, *Apprentice,* 3; and "Oral History of William C. Hedrich." Brendan Gill, *A New York Life: Of Friends and Others* (1991), 111–12. An amusing discussion of estate naming appears in Garber's *Sex and Real Estate,* 198–204.

The Fallingwater exhibit at MoMA: MoMA Archives, Minutes of Committee Meetings, Box 7: Minutes of the Committee on Architecture and Industrial Art, Friday, November 19, 1937, at 5 P.M. in Mr. Goodwin's Office. I thank John Conti and the MoMA archivist Clare Diens for assisting in the retrieval of these materials. MoMA had previously mounted minor shows on homes by the architects Richard Wood and William Priestly (Levine, *Wright,* 467 n. 2). Hoffmann, *Fallingwater,* 91, carries McAndrew's earliest recollections about Fallingwater. Charles Alan [Bernstein] was a son of the sister of Henry Kaufmann's wife Theresa Lissberger Kaufmann, and a good friend of Kaufmann Jr.'s. The link sounds more tenuous than it was: Henry's will in the Fallingwater Archives includes Alan as a beneficiary. Aline Saarinen's role in publicizing Fallingwater was recalled by her son Donald Louchheim in 1998, including the memory that when the family lived in Pittsburgh, Kaufmann Jr. once dropped over with a Picasso that he lent the Louchheims to brighten up their walls. Edgar Tafel recollected Saarinen's involvement with Fallingwater for me in 1989. Tafel specifically recalled attending a Marian Anderson concert with Saarinen and the Kaufmanns in Morris Kaufmann Hall at the Pittsburgh YMHA. Anderson sang there on Saturday, April 10, 1937, which fits perfectly with both the construction sequence on Fallingwater and with McAndrew's visit half a year later (Kathryn Logan of the Carnegie Library of Pittsburgh kindly located the concert program).

Philip Johnson: One of Johnson's attacks on American Jews is quoted in Schulze, *Johnson,* 135; Johnson's letter documenting his participation in the Nazi invasion of Poland is quoted in Schulze, 139. Another insight into Johnson and the climate of the era is provided by Geoffrey Blodgett, "Philip Johnson's Great Depression," *Timeline* (June–July 1987): 2–17. Johnson was cited as a leading Nazi sympathizer in William Shirer, *Berlin Diary: The Journal of a Foreign Correspondent, 1934–1941* (1941), 213. There was no significant successor to Johnson until McAndrew entered MoMA in 1937.

MoMA's architecture committee: Joseph Hudnut is a major figure in Anthony Alofsin, *The Struggle for Modernism: Architecture, Landscape Architecture, and City Planning at Harvard* (2002). John Coolidge applied to join Taliesin by letter to Wright of April 19, 1936. I studied with Coolidge at Harvard University in the 1960s, and I laid out my progress on the "Fallingwater problem" to him in a three-hour chat in 1990. Coolidge never revealed to me his role in popularizing Fallingwater, which at that point I had not yet discovered. Had he forgotten that detail after half a century, or was he testing me to see whether I would find it on my own?

Nelson Rockefeller: Morris, *Nelson Rockefeller,* 75, 76, 106; Betty Chamberlain, "History of MoMA," undated and unpublished typescript in the MoMA Archives; Lynes, *Good Old Modern,* 76, 83. Secrest, *Wright,* 463, first reported the Rockefeller-Hitchcock exchange about MoMA's disenchantment with German modernism, though mistaking Nelson for his father John D. Rockefeller Jr. The exchange was reported by the Anglo-Russian architect Bernard Lubetkin, and confirmed for me by Lubetkin's biographer, Gavin Stamp (communication, June 2, 1999).

Mounting the MoMA exhibition: Kaufmann Jr. to Wright, undated but by context early December 1937; Hoffmann, *Fallingwater,* 91. McAndrew to Wright, undated telegram but by context December 31, 1937.

Henry Luce and Fallingwater: References by Luce to architecture and modernism are cited in *The Ideas of Henry Luce,* ed. John Jessup (1969), 262–80. I am grateful to Glenn Willumson, who has published on Luce's direct involvement in the art content of the Time-Life magazines, for consulting with me in 2001 on how extensive Luce's role in publicizing Fallingwater must have been. Willumson agreed that only Luce could have ordered the extraordinary "puffing" that Fallingwater got from the Time-Life empire. Communications about the Time-Life archives from Henry Luce III, April 26, 1999, and from the archivist, Bill Hooper, May 9, 1999; Myers to Wright, August 6, 1937. The interconnectedness of the four Time-Life magazines under Luce's watchful eye was detailed in *Time* (February 28, 1938): 40. As early as 1933, Luce lured potential advertisers with the promise that any message published in *Architectural Forum* could appear simultaneously in *Time* and *Fortune.* By 1936, this was true of *Life* as well.

The personal closeness of Wright and Luce comes through in their extensive correspondence from the 1930s through the 1950s. *Time's* favorable stories on Wright are cited in Luce's letter to Wright of March 20, 1956, and the statistical analysis provided by Twombly, *Wright,* 384. The architectural community seems to have sensed Luce's affinity for its profession, to judge from a letter from the architectural renderer Charles Morgan to Luce on April 2, 1931; there Morgan (citing a recent *Time* article on Wright) calls Luce a "brother architect."

Wright and Johnson's Wax: Wright to Bill Connolly, January 19, 1938; Brian Carter, *John-*

son *Wax Administration Building and Research Tower* (London, 1998), 4. Wright's comment on the free publicity that his building gave Johnson's Wax comes from *An Autobiography,* 2nd ed. (1943), 470, 496.

Secondary publications on Fallingwater: See the partial listing of articles from around the globe in Sweeney's *Bibliography,* 62–66. On architectural publications in the 1930s: Lichtenstein, "Modernism": 10. Talbot E. Hamlin, "F.L.W.—An Analysis," *Pencil Points* 16 (March 1938): 137–44 (the journal later renamed itself *Progressive Architecture*). Fallingwater's second appearance in *Time* came in "Fairs & Furbelows," *Time* (February 21, 1938):53. Jan Peterson, "Nature's Architect," *New Masses* 26 (February 8, 1938): 29–30; Augusta Owen Patterson, "Three Modern Houses": 64–65, 104.

Hearst and Fallingwater: Raymond Gram Swing, *Forerunners of American Fascism* (1937); Rodney Parker Carlisle, "The Political Ideas and Influence of William Randolph Hearst, 1928–1936" (Ph.D. dissertation, University of California, Berkeley, 1965). On Hearst's being out of date politically and artistically in the 1930s, see the stimulating ideas of Madeline Caviness in "Learning from Forest Lawn," *Speculum* 69 (1994): 963–92, at p. 983. Umberto Eco's remarks are in his *Travels in Hyper Reality: Essays* (San Diego and New York, 1986), 62. For Le Corbusier's article in *American Architect,* see Mardges Bacon, *Le Corbusier in America: Travels in the Land of the Timid* (Cambridge, Mass., 2001), 152, 242.

Fallingwater in the newspapers: Edward Alden Jewell, "Pictures Analyze 'Cantilever' House," *New York Times,* January 25, 1938, 24. Though no older than Wright, Royal Cortissoz (1869–1948) was the supreme antimodernist of his generation. G. E. Kidder Smith's remark (*Sourcebook of American Architecture,* 382) that Cortissoz was "an irate critic" of Fallingwater carries no source citation and was probably based on a private conversation. The *Des Moines Register and Tribune* clipping is undated, but appears to be from late January 1938; the *Pittsburgh Press* article appeared on February 6, 1938, that of the *Dallas Times-Herald* on February 27. The phrase that Fallingwater brought modernism back to the United States "in the guise of a European influence," which appeared in the *New York Times* review and in numerous other stories, came direct from the original publicity material distributed by MoMA.

Fallingwater around the world: Bruno Zevi, *Verso un'Architettura Organica: Saggio sullo Sviluppo del Pensiero Architettonico negli Ultimi Cinquant'Anni* (Turin, 1945). Zevi's comment on Wright's influence in Italy came in his talk to the Society of Architectural Historians' symposium on Wright at MoMA on April 27, 1994 (reprinted as "Wright and Italy: A Recollection," in Alofsin, *Wright: Europe and Beyond,* 66–75). Zevi added further details in a 1999 interview and in a communication of September 22, 1999. My thanks to Ted Goodman for his help locating foreign publications on Fallingwater.

MoMA's traveling show on Fallingwater: The MoMA Exhibition Archives, folder 86(4) lists: "A New House by Frank Lloyd Wright," which circulated between 1938 and 1946 at a fee of $15 at each venue. Just in its first three years the exhibit was booked for showings at twenty-one schools and museums. In 1940 a second traveling show was sent around the country, again with a focus on Fallingwater. This exhibit was being booked as late as 1946 at Swarthmore and Williams colleges and at the Universities of Kansas, Minnesota, and Oregon. A third exhibition of "Houses by Frank Lloyd Wright" was then sent in circulation to another score of cities from 1946 through 1949. This included some of Wright's earliest houses plus what the public relations release called "the romantically conceived Bear Run, Pa. home of Edgar Kaufmann which marked the beginning of a new creative development in Wright's work."

MoMA and the media: Betty Chamberlain, MoMA's publicity director in the postwar years, wrote an unpublished account on MoMA's PR operations that survives in the MoMA Archives. See also Lynes, *Good Old Modern*, 129ff.

Kaufmann as publicist: Most of the *Storagrams* under Kaufmann's presidency, along with a few of E. J.'s personal memos, survive in the store's archive at the Heinz Center today. The *Bulletin Index*'s article on Kaufmann of September 28, 1933, carried the allegation of Kaufmann's misuse of his power as an advertiser. Even today the Kaufmann stores commonly take a dozen advertising pages, sometimes even two dozen, in the *Pittsburgh Post-Gazette*.

E. J. Kaufmann's closest collaboration with the Time-Life empire came in the marketing of low-cost house prototypes by Wright and seven other architects, announced in *Life* as "Eight Houses for Modern Living" (September 26, 1938: 45–67). The architects included conservatives like Royal Barry Wills and Richard Koch, and the moderns Edward Durell Stone, Wallace Harrison, and William Wurster (Catherine Bauer's husband); *Architectural Forum* chimed in with a booster article in November. The promotion involved ten leading department stores in the country, including the May Company stores in Baltimore and Los Angeles, John Wanamaker in New York, the Emporium in San Francisco, and Carson Pirie Scott in Chicago. Readers could order house plans from any of the ten stores, but it was Kaufmann's that led the list.

In concert with a local builder, Kaufmann's erected two of the *Life* houses in Pittsburgh's Baldwin Manor subdivision, but the builder had no use for Wright, and put up houses by the traditionalists Wills and Koch instead (Cleary, *Merchant*, 32–33). Not even E. J. Kaufmann, it seems, could overcome resistance to Frank Lloyd Wright in Pittsburgh's suburbs.

The articles on La Tourelle appeared in *Country Life* 54 (July 1928): 57–60; *The Architect* 10/5 (August 1928): 611–30; *Pencil Points* 10 (August 1929): 545–48; *American Architect* 137 (June 1930): 34–35; *Architectural Record* 68 (July 1930): 47–48; and *The Western Architect* 39 (August 1930): pl. 121. Documentation on the Kaufmanns as shareholders in Pittsburgh's Aerial Surveys Inc. survives at the Heinz Center and in the Kaufmann Papers at Avery Library.

Herbert Johnson's letter to the editor, in which he denied being rich despite the luxuriousness of his new home, appeared in *Time* for January 31, 1938. The first Pittsburgh reports of Fallingwater appeared in the *Bulletin Index* of January 27, 1938, and the *Pittsburgh Press* of February 6. "Tell Us One About the Bear," *Charette* (March 1938): 1–3, was reprinted as "The Conic Dwelling; Appropriate in That Territory Commonly Known as USA, but Often Referred to by Certain Prophets as Usonia," *Federal Architect* (April 1938): 31–32, 52.

NINE: FABRICATING FALLINGWATER II: THE BUZZ THAT MADE AMERICA BUY IT

Fallingwater and its cultural background: My account of Fallingwater and the popular culture of the 1920s and '30s incorporates elements from Alex Barron's report for my Fallingwater seminar at the University of Pittsburgh in 1999. I thank John Conti for his reminder about "*Life* Goes to a Party." There is now an excellent body of studies on the culture of the 1930s. Particularly valuable to me were Robert McElvaine, *The Great Depression: America, 1929–1941* (1984, 1993); David M. Kennedy, *Freedom from Fear: The American People in Depression and War, 1929–1945* (1999); T. H. Watkins, *The Great Depression: America in the 1930s* (Boston, 1993); Frederick Louis Allen, *Only Yesterday: An Informal History of the Nineteen-Twenties* (1931), and Allen's *Since Yesterday: The Nineteen-Thirties in America* (1940); J. C. Furnas, *Stormy Weather: Crosslights on the Nineteen Thir-*

ties: *An Informal Social History of the United States, 1929–1941* (1977); and Harold Evans, *The American Century* (1998). More specific studies on the arts of the 1930s are Neal Gabler, *An Empire of Their Own: How the Jews Invented Hollywood* (1988); Edward Lucie-Smith, *Art of the 1930s: The Age of Anxiety* (1985); Rita Barnard, *The Great Depression and the Culture of Abundance: Kenneth Fearing, Nathanael West, and Mass Culture in the 1930s* (1995); and Laura Browder, *Rousing the Nation: Radical Culture in Depression America* (Amherst, Mass., 1998).

Fallingwater's cost: How much Fallingwater cost is a matter of endless interest to visitors. The definitive answer comes from E. J.'s lawyers at Reed, Smith in calculating the estate's assets in a memo of February 24, 1959. Their tabulation of $166,000 included $49,000 for the guesthouse, but excluded payment for the land (Avery).

The Depression and American society: McElvaine, *Great Depression*, xxiii–xxvi. McElvaine says of *Modern Times:* "The film is an all-out attack on, well, modern times. . . . The effects of machine industry, mass society, the unlimited pursuit of personal happiness are seen to overwhelm the 'individual,' who becomes a part of the machine."

Modern architecture now appeared nativist: Helen Searing, "International Style: The Crimson Connection," *Progressive Architecture* 63/2 (February 1982): 88–91. Other analyses of modern architecture in the 1930s in the same issue are Robert A. M. Stern, "International Style: Immediate Effects": 106–09; and Richard Guy Wilson, "International Style: The MoMA Exhibition": 92–104.

The Depression and nature: McElvaine's insight about the best-selling novels of the thirties comes from his *Depression*, 220, citing an earlier study by Michael Steiner. The origins of WPC are explored by Netting in his *Western Pennsylvania Conservancy*, 52. Roy Emerson Stryker and Nancy Wood, *In This Proud Land: America 1935–1943 as Seen in the FAS Photographs* (1973), gives a good sampling of the photographic images popularized in the years in which Fallingwater came to national attention.

The Depression and the reinterpretation of the past: The argument that the Depression made Americans rediscover their past is upheld by Alfred H. Jones, "The Search for a Usable American Past in the New Deal Era," *American Quarterly* 23 (December 1971): 710–24. H. H. Richardson emerges as a specifically American architect in Henry-Russell Hitchcock, *The Architecture of H. H. Richardson and His Times* (1936), and in James O'Gorman, *H. H. Richardson: Architectural Forms for an American Society* (Chicago, 1987). The quote from Edmund Wilson comes from his book *The Shores of Light* (McElvaine, *Depression*, 139 n). The definition of eclecticism as "design by accumulation" comes from O'Gorman, *Richardson*, 63.

Fallingwater in Hitler's shadow: Boeckel, *Visionäre*, 201–04ff reports that the Kaufmanns made Pittsburgh a home to Austrian exiles second only to New York. Wright's links to Lindbergh are documented in A. Scott Berg, *Lindbergh* (1998), 435, 451, 511.

Fallingwater and The Fountainhead: *The Journals of Ayn Rand*, ed. David Harriman (1997), 77–240, gives a basic chronology for *The Fountainhead*. Andrew Saint's *The Image of the Architect* (New Haven, 1983), 1–14, is the only work to my knowledge that takes seriously Rand's impact on the popularization of modern architecture. I base my estimate of 1934 as the year in which Rand started work on *The Fountainhead* from her letter to Wright of May 14, 1944, which states that she started the novel ten years before. My linking of *The Fountainhead* and Fallingwater goes back to my first public talk on Fallingwater, in 1986, but Donald Miller's *Architecture of Benno Janssen*, 12, independently proposed Kaufmann as a possible prototype for Gail Wynand. My thanks to Mr. Miller for stimulating encounters on this and other topics.

At the time of the MoMA show on Fallingwater, Rand lived at 66 Park Avenue, at 38th Street (communication from the Rand specialist Frederick Cookinham, December 10,

2000; verification by Katherine Hourigan, October 24, 2002). Information on Rand's retention of the *Time* issue was kindly provided by Jeff Britting, archivist at the Ayn Rand Archives (communication, December 20, 2000), who noted that the archives' inventories were still fragmentary, and much else about the writing of *The Fountainhead* may still turn up. Some of Rand's correspondence with Wright appears in *Letters of Ayn Rand*, ed. Michel S. Berliner (1995), 108–19; the detail of Wright's overcharging for the *Fountainhead* sets comes from Twombly, *Wright*, 384. The Sanborn house is described in *The Fountainhead*, 168; the Heller house on p. 124 (much is made of the fact that it sits on top of a picturesque rock, rather than facing it—surely a detail purloined from the Fallingwater story); the Wynand house on p. 583 and following. Roark's redrawing the Heller house appears on p. 126. Gail Wynand imitated E. J. Kaufmann in his acceptance of the preliminary drawings for his house without a single objection or alteration (p. 520). The fear that the Sanborn house won't stand up is reported on pp. 134 and 169.

For the plot sketch of *The Fountainhead*, see *Journals of Ayn Rand*, 166. The novel as published gives no specific date for the completion of the Wynand house (p. 573), but we can deduce the year 1937 from Roark's given age (thirty-seven) and the given year of his birth (1900). The fictive Professor Peterkin appears on p. 20 of the novel; the real John B. Peterkin in Stern, *New York 1930*, 704. The "Frink" and "Melton" buildings appear on pp. 43 and 51 of the novel. Wright spoke of Mr. Austin as his benefactor in *Autobiography*, 80–82, 106. The bored Richard Sanborn gets interested in architecture on p. 169 of the novel.

The detail of Hearst's sailing with Joseph Urban comes from David Nasaw, *The Chief: The Life of William Randolph Hearst* (2000), 285, 307–08. Wynand and Heller's expressions of affection for their architect Roark appear on pp. 135, 570, 591, 602, 603, and 607 of *The Fountainhead*; Roark's enemies in the International Style appear on pp. 473 and 474; lack of publicity for the Heller house: p. 137; Wynand tells his staff to puff Roark: pp. 590, 624. In 1946, three years after publication of *The Fountainhead*, Wright designed but did not build a house for Rand that was a near-parody of Fallingwater; two years later he designed a house called Fountainhead for Jackson, Mississippi.

Scholarly literature on both the book and the film is summarized in Merrill Schleier's "Ayn Rand and King Vidor's Film *The Fountainhead*: Architectural Modernism, the Gendered Body, and Political Ideology," *Journal of the Society of Architectural Historians* (September 2002): 310–31.

TEN: THE KAUFMANNS SHOWCASE FALLINGWATER, AND VICE VERSA

Fallingwater as futuristic but attainable: The storekeeper's creed was defined in Harris, *Merchant Princes*, 162. Harris reported Rivera's appraisal of Fallingwater (*Merchant Princes*, 105) without a source, but in 1999 he told me it came from a 1930s newspaper story. See Futagawa and Pfeiffer, *Frank Lloyd Wright*, 5:164. The history of Formica comes from von Dulken, *Inventing the 20th Century*, 40. Fallingwater's domestic technology was surveyed in Merritt Ierley, *Open House: A Guided Tour of the American Home, 1637—Present* (1999), 77; see also Ierley, *The Comforts of Home: The American House and the Evolution of Modern Convenience* (2000). E. J. cited his wish for a teletype machine in a letter to Mosher of February 10, 1937. Liliane's bidet first appears in a letter from Mosher to Wright, July 17, 1936. Liliane evidently liked it enough to order a second for the guesthouse, but for reasons unknown it never went in. The superannuated bidet showed up in E. J.'s January 25, 1940, accounting of miscellaneous expenses on the guesthouse (Avery): "Sold one bidet to Mrs. Robert Frank" for $143.55. This was for Gropius's futuristic Frank house in Pittsburgh, for which E. J. was the probable intermediary.

A clan enterprise: Interviews with I. D. Wolf Jr. and Joan Kaufmann Mendelsohn.

Getting some respect: Bulletin Index articles on Kaufmann: January 27 and November 6, 1938, also July 31, 1941; the article on Kaufmann Jr. appeared on October 27, 1938. Kaufmann is cited in Richard Breitman and Alan Kraut, *American Refugee Policy and European Jews, 1933–1945* (Bloomington, Ind., 1987), 104. The conference on the Jews of Germany was cited in Kaufmann, *Fallingwater,* 55 and in the *American Jewish Year Book,* vol. 40 (Philadelphia, 1938 [actually 1939]): 139, and vol. 41 (1939, but actually 1940): 223–24. The second report on the conference proceedings erroneously placed it in Pittsburgh, which—as we have seen—was used in the early days as Fallingwater's location.

Creation of the guesthouse: The guesthouse design was first documented in a letter of Tafel to Wright, January 12, 1938; Kaufmann to Wright, January 11 and 25 and May 31, 1938; Wright to Kaufmann, February 22, 1938. One undated plan for the guesthouse is reproduced in Cleary, *Merchant,* 101, for which Hoffmann, *Fallingwater,* 92, proposed the date of May 2. Later guesthouse plans and renderings are reproduced in Cleary, *Merchant,* 105 (a plan dated May 18, 1938) and 102–03 (an undated but corresponding perspective rendering). Masselink to Kaufmann, May 28, 1938, on the mailing of the guesthouse plans; Kaufmann to Wright, May 31 and June 16, 1938. Walter Hall's reappearance at the site was documented in the correspondence of Kaufmann to Wright, January 6 and 17, 1939, and by Hall to Wright, January 24. Wright to Kaufmann, January 26, 1939, on the mailing of the final plans. Further documentation on the guesthouse: Hall to Wright, January 30 and February 4, 1939; Wright to Hall, February 1; Kaufmann to Wright, February 2; Wright to Kaufmann, February 10. Kaufmann's promise to his daughter was recalled for me by his grandson Ted Stanford in 2000.

Fallingwater's visitors: Hoffmann, *Fallingwater,* 93, referred to Kaufmann Jr.'s visit to Gropius's famous house in Lincoln, which opened in September 1938; the new window detail drawings from Taliesin were dated October 25, 1938 (Avery). Pliny, *Epistles* V.vi.45 was quoted in translation by James Ackerman, *The Villa: Form and Ideology of Country Houses* (Princeton, 1985), 13. Ackerman's comments on Fallingwater as a villa appear in the same study on pp. 281–84. Among family friends who recall visits to Fallingwater were Maxine and William Block in the late 1940s and Richard Wechsler when the house was brand-new in 1938. A bright fifteen-year-old at the time, Wechsler was enormously taken by E. J., who persuaded his father to buy him a car. The heavenly scent of Fallingwater around Easter was recalled by Paul Mayén in 1999; Kaufmann Jr. demolished the Bear Run greenhouse around 1960 and sent it to the Hagan house at Kentuck Knob, where it survives today. Frida Kahlo's account of her amours at Fallingwater is recounted in Hayden Herrera's *Frida: A Biography of Frida Kahlo* (1983), 190–91, 233–35. My thanks to Julia Bergman of the City College of San Francisco for keeping me informed on Rivera and Kahlo research.

The Kaufmanns' stuff: Wright affirmed his clients' right to decorate as they saw fit in his *Ausgeführte Bauten und Entwürfe von Frank Lloyd Wright* (Berlin, 1910, with original supplementary English text; repr. Palos Park, Ill., 1975), n.p. Mayén's photographs appeared in the special Fallingwater number of *L'Architettura,* August 1962, and in its republication the next year in book form; Stoller's photographs were taken for a small MoMA exhibition on Fallingwater in 1963, just before Kaufmann Jr. gave the house to the Western Pennsylvania Conservancy. Haugh and Keenan's bills for removal and storage of house items date from January 1, 1956, and October 1 and 16, 1963 (Heinz). Unless otherwise noted, all references to the Kaufmanns' furnishings in and around the house come from the Fallingwater Archives. I thank the former and present curators of Fallingwater, Michele Risdal-Barnes and Cara Armstrong, for giving me access to those records, and to Becky McLean for her help in transcribing them with me. Paul Mayén generously evaluated my

1999 draft inventory of the paintings collected by the Kaufmanns from the 1920s through the 1980s.

The three projected Kaufmann essays: Kaufmann to Wright, September 9, 1940, specifies that E. J. intended to title his essay in the MoMA catalogue "To Meet—To Know—To Build—To Battle—To Love—Frank Lloyd Wright." Kaufmann Jr. promised to write on Fallingwater's furnishings, and Liliane on being a Bear Run housewife. The cute title of E. J.'s essay is utterly unlike his manner of expression, however; this suggests that Junior was handling the projected catalogue. Kathryn Smith (several communications, June 2002) intends to reconstitute the remnants of the aborted catalogue.

The Blume paintings: These are both discussed in Frank Anderson Trapp, *Peter Blume* (1987), 72, 78–83, and 98. The exhibition of *House at Falling Water* at the Southern Alleghenies Museum of Art at Loretto, Pennsylvania, was reported in the *Pittsburgh Post-Gazette* for August 28, 1999. The March 12, 1999, sales catalogue *American & European Paintings and Prints and Photography* (Skinner Gallery, Boulton, Mass.) carried the painting as lot 334, "Weekend House: A View of Fallingwater." Kaufmann paid Blume $16,000 for *The Rock* in 1948 (Heinz). My thanks to Daniel Schulman of the Art Institute of Chicago for allowing me to examine the painting, its sketches, and its documentation in detail in 1999. E. J.'s love of the painting was recalled for me in 2000 by Patricia Moorten of Palm Springs.

Rodin and Kahlo works at Fallingwater: The Rodin is documented in a letter of Ethel Clinton Appel to Joseph Johnson, January 19, 1960 (Heinz), and both it and the Marini sculptures are illustrated in Zevi and Kaufmann, *Casa sulla Cascata*, 80. Kahlo's *My Birth* and *Remembrance of an Open Wound* appear as catalogue entries 37 and 63 in *Frida Kahlo: Das Gesamtwerk*, ed. Helga Prignitz-Poda et al. (Frankfurt am Main, 1988), which cites both as paintings once owned by the Kaufmanns, but it lists *Remembrance of an Open Wound* as burned. Many paintings were lost when fire destroyed Kaufmann's country home at Garrison, New York, in 1983, but the Kahlo seems not to have been among them: Paul Mayén specifically recalled for me that it had always hung in a closet in New York. See Mayén's preface to Sotheby's *Modern Paintings and Sculpture from the Estate of the Late Edgar J. Kaufmann, Jr.* (1989). Mayén believed that Kaufmann had spontaneously given away the painting (he had donated Kahlo's *Self-Portrait with Cropped Hair* to MoMA in 1943). Nevertheless, it is hard to imagine any public institution or private collector acquiring a painting by the megafamous Kahlo and not boasting about it.

Paintings that have left Fallingwater: Compare Ethel Clinton's art inventory of January 21, 1957 (Avery), and Kaufmann's insurance policy schedule of July 11, 1960 (Heinz). In 1960 additional works were already in storage in Pittsburgh, while Victor Hammer's portrait of E. J. was captive in the Pittsburgh apartment of Grace Stoops, Kaufmann's widow.

Possessions possess: Paul Eldridge's aphorism comes from his *Maxims for a Modern Man* (1965), entry 2781. Edgar J. Kaufmann Jr., "Design, 20th-Century" is one of three related articles in the *Encyclopaedia Britannica* 7 (Chicago, 1964), 298–303. The designers Aalto, Salto, the Natzlers, Luisa Rota, Pietro Mezadona, Kaj Franck, Raymond Loewy, Paul Mayén, and Russell Wright are for the most part listed in the thirty-four-volume *Dictionary of Art* (London, 1999).

The Kaufmanns' beds and baths: E. J.'s cautionary note to Mosher is dated February 10, 1937. The chronology presented here for Liliane's missing bidet comes from Denise Miner, who kindly provided an archaeological tour of Liliane's bathroom on February 12, 2002, and a communication on February 15.

Sanitizing Fallingwater: Kaufmann Jr. referred to "the dressing room used by my father" in his *Fallingwater*, 144. WPC's *Conserve* 44/2 (March–April 2001): 12, called it Edgar Kaufmann Sr.'s dressing room/study. That E. J. hung the portraits of his grandparents at

Fallingwater occasions little surprise, since he had commissioned them himself in 1930 — evidently based on photographs—from a Viennese painter identified only as Diletz (Fallingwater Archives).

Fallingwater as Queer Space?: The subfield of architectural history called Queer Space investigates ways in which homosexuals request, or revise, spatial situations differently from straights. See Aaron Betsky, *Queer Space: Architecture and Same-Sex Desire* (1997). The most effective application of the method so far is the chapter "Philip Johnson's Glass House/Guest House as 'Gay Space' " in Alice T. Friedman, *Women and the Making of the Modern House: A Social and Architectural History* (1998), 147–55. I doubt whether Kaufmann Jr.'s reconfiguration of his space at Fallingwater lends itself to such an analysis, but some other scholar is welcome to try.

ELEVEN: THE RENAISSANCE PRINCE IN WINTER

After the war: Tafel recalled Kaufmann's offer to come to Pittsburgh in 2002. There is an oblique reference to Kaufmann's time in Washington in a letter from Wright to Kaufmann on February 6, 1943. Particulars of the sale of Kaufmann's to the May Company were provided by I. D. Wolf Jr. in 1987.

The Kaufmanns as planters: I owe the information on nonnative plants at Bear Run to Lynda Waggoner (communication, January 13, 2000). Thomas G. Clark's September 20, 1954, "Forest Land Appraisal" for Kaufmann survives in the Western Pennsylvania Conservancy Archives in Pittsburgh. My thanks to Paul Wiegman for analyzing the Arbutus and Wagon trails with me in 1999, including the anecdote about the lumbermen retaliating against E. J.

Ferncliff Peninsula: 1986 interview with Ralph Demmler, the major power in the Edgar J. Kaufmann Charitable Trust. See also Netting's *Western Pennsylvania Conservancy,* 137–38.

Proposed outbuildings at Fallingwater: Richard Cleary, "Fallingwater Was Just the Beginning: The Kaufmanns' Other Commissions for Bear Run," *Friends of Fallingwater Newsletter* 14 (1995): 1–5. Wright's drawings for the farmhouse and gatehouse complexes are discussed and several reproduced in Cleary, *Merchant,* 46–47, 116–19, 124–27, 181. Wright's farmhouse design was intended for execution in redwood, as was the home that Kaufmann Jr. built near the dairy barn around 1947. Junior's building depended on Wright's design in function, siting, materials, basic design envelope, and such features as radiant heating.

Changes inside Fallingwater: The servants' sitting room is documented in correspondence of Kaufmann to Wright, November 2, 1945, and Wright's reply of November 6 and 7, 1945. Avery Library preserves the itemized payment of $1,500 in 1946 to Hunting, Davis & Dunnell for designing a "new room"; the context makes clear that this was the servants' sitting room. My thanks to Ken Kremer for the ingenious suggestion that the value of the new room was as much structural as functional. Kaufmann Jr.'s letter to Wright on overcrowding in the dining area is undated but from context was written in December 1945; further discussion in Wright to Kaufmann, April 30, 1946, and March 18, 1947; Kaufmann to Wright, May 6, 1946, and March 13, 1947. Nine drawings for the expanded dining area and a reverse orientation to the guesthouse are listed and several reproduced in Cleary, *Merchant,* 46–47, 108–15, 181.

Kaufmann's Palm Springs house: Documentation on the Neutra house survives among Avery Library's Kaufmann Papers and among the Neutra Papers in the Charles E. Young Reference Library at UCLA; unless otherwise designated, the materials quoted here are at UCLA. Neutra's quote about not rooting his house in a soil appeared in the *Los Angeles*

Examiner for July 26, 1949. Brent and Beth Harris and their restoration landscape gardener William Kopelk kindly guided me through the Kaufmann house in 2000 and 2002. Recent studies of the house include those of Webb, *Modernism Reborn,* 162–71, and Deborah K. Dietsch, *Classic Modern: Midcentury Modern at Home* (2000), 51–57.

Neutra's Grace Miller house: Stephen Leet's *Richard Neutra's Miller House* (forthcoming) will be the definitive history of the project.

Wright sends E. J. cacti: Kaufmann asked Wright for five hundred cuttings of cholla on April 5, 1948; the reply came ten days later. The Kaufmanns' cactus gardener in Palm Springs, Patricia Moorten, recalled the incident for me in 2000, with further details from her son and successor, Clark Moorten, in 2002.

Publicizing Palm Springs: Simon Niedenthal, " 'Glamourized Houses': Neutra, Photography, and the Kaufmann House," *Journal of Architectural Education* 47/2 (November 1993): 101–12. Neutra telegraphed Henry Wright on February 22, 1947, and got his reply three days later. The release of photographs was discussed in telegrams from Kaufmann to Neutra and vice versa, both March 1, 1947.

Shulman's photographs: Dione Neutra to Kaufmann, March 6, 1947; Kaufmann to Richard Neutra, March 8, 1947. Five days later Kaufmann wrote Wright that he was finally installed in his new home. My thanks to Julius Shulman for his long and patient interviews with me in 1986 and 2000. See also Julius Shulman, *Architecture and Its Photography* (1998), 97–98. Dubbed the "house of the midcentury," the Kaufmann house was still alluring enough half a century later to be the highlight of a *New Yorker* photographic essay on Palm Springs (Kurt Anderson, "Desert Cool," February 23, 1998: 128–37); and to warrant special coverage in *House Beautiful,* April 1999; *Architectural Record* for October 1989; and *Vanity Fair* for March 1999.

Manipulating coverage of the Palm Springs house: The internal Libbey-Owens-Ford memo of March 18, 1947, was composed by an executive who signed himself L.P.J. "Bernard of Hollywood" to Kaufmann, May 22, 1947; Neutra to Kaufmann, June 15, 1947; Neutra's secretary to Henry Wright, June 24, 1947. Harry Kodinsky of Public Relations Research Services of Pittsburgh to Neutra, September 3 and 18, 1947.

"Desert Residence for Mr. and Mrs. Edgar Kaufmann" appeared in *Marg* 1/4 (Bombay, 1947): 22–30, citing the house as a "hitherto unpublished work." That was probably true of Shulman's photograph, but not of the building. Wright complained about the house to Kaufmann Jr. by letter of December 19, 1947. The reference to *Fortune*'s being about to cover the house comes in an unsigned memo to Kaufmann either from Neutra or Shulman, March 21, 1949. Ultimately, *Fortune* did not cover the house, probably because Luce or some top editor chose not to offend Wright. (*Fortune* had meanwhile covered Wright's own two houses in its August 1946 issue, 116–25.) Charles Eames to Neutra, February 5, 1947, and to Liliane Kaufmann, August 18, 1947; Bruce Goff to Neutra, March 18, 1947.

Wright's projects for Pittsburgh: Christopher Wilk, *Frank Lloyd Wright: The Kaufmann Office* (London, 1993). Wright's projects for Pittsburgh are summarized in Robert Alberts, *The Shaping of the Point: Pittsburgh's Renaissance Park* (Pittsburgh, 1980), 91–97; and in Richard Cleary, "Edgar J. Kaufmann, Frank Lloyd Wright, and the 'Pittsburgh Point Park Coney Island in Automobile Scale,' " *Journal of the Society of Architectural Historians* 52 (1993): 139–58; Cleary, *Merchant,* 53–66; and "Beyond Fallingwater: Edgar J. Kaufmann, Frank Lloyd Wright, and the Projects for Pittsburgh," *Wright Studies* (Carbondale, Ill., 2000), 2: 80–113. Ninety-three site, presentation, and detail drawings survive for the Pittsburgh Point Civic Center: Cleary, *Merchant,* 53–64, 144–61, 184–87. The conceptual link between Fallingwater and the Point Center was suggested in Smith, "Wright's Waterfall Buildings": 25.

The Kaufmann's parking garage: Sixty drawings for this project are listed in Cleary, *Merchant,* 64, 162–64, 187–89. See Kaufmann to Wright, October 13, March 29, and August 25, 1948, and September 2 and December 21, 1949; Wright to Kaufmann, December 29, 1949; and Dahlen Ritchey interview. Kaufmann to Wright, November 12, 1954, itemized the $50,000 that E. J. claimed to have paid Wright for the garage plans. The references to the parking garage project as an annex to the Carnegie Museum are ambiguous: Kaufmann described it as a garage when he wrote Wright on August 7, 1953, but his letter to Wright of August 30, 1954, leaves open the possibility that some other Wrightian structure was intended for the museum. One gets the impression that Kaufmann was jealous of the nascent Guggenheim Museum, although he played a small role in its construction: see the exchange of letters with Wright on February 23 and April 9, 19, and 24, 1954.

The Point View apartments: Cleary, *Merchant,* 64–65, 166–73, 189–93; and 1999 Gerald Lee Morosco interview.

Liliane as architectural patron: 1999 interview with Liliane's cousin and confidante Ruth Bachman.

The Kaufmanns' marital battles: Kaufmann Jr. to Wright, letter fragment dated only "Sunday" in 1951 (context suggests March); Liliane Kaufmann to Wright, March 19, 1951; Wright to Kaufmann, October 15, 1952.

Wright's Boulder House: The commission is frequently ascribed to Kaufmann Jr., but E. J.'s exchange of letters with Wright makes clear that the commission was his. In a 2000 interview the dean of Palm Springs historians, Tony Merchell, listed the Frey, Loewy, and May-Benny homes as neighbors to the Kaufmann house. Five drawings for the Boulder House survive: Cleary, *Merchant,* 48–49, 134–37, 183. Wright wrote Kaufmann on February 1, 1951, Kaufmann Jr. on the same day, and Liliane on February 9. Liliane Kaufmann to Wright, February 12, 1951; E. J. Kaufmann to Wright, same day; prospective house-builder G. C. Chamberlain to Wright, February 14; Wright to Kaufmann, March 1, 1951. The $7,500 payment to Wright for studies for a "house of the boulder-field (Palm Springs)" was cited retrospectively by Kaufmann in a letter to Wright on August 2, 1954. Liliane Kaufmann to Wright, April 11, 1951; Wright's reply, April 21.

Liliane's house on Beaver Creek: Interview with Harry Sampey, current occupant of Liliane's intended land; my thanks to Dr. Sampey for allowing me to visit his hideaway. Liliane Kaufmann to Wright, undated but by context April 1951 (Avery).

The Rhododendron Chapel: Eight drawings for the chapel survive: Cleary, *Merchant,* 49–50, 128–33, 182–83. Project correspondence: Kaufmann Jr. to Wright, September 25, 1951; E. J. Kaufmann to Wright, July 3, 1952; Wright to Kaufmann Jr., September 18 and 22, 1952; Wright to E. J. Kaufmann, September 18 and October 15, 1952.

There is no basis to a rumored connection between the chapel project and Liliane's conjectural conversion to Catholicism. In 1999 the architect Tasso Katselas recalled for me that when he apprenticed with Wright in 1952 (he quit after two days), his new boss linked Liliane's need for a chapel with her conversion, but no such conversion ever took place, and this supposed motive runs totally counter to Kaufmann Jr.'s stated rationale for the chapel. The single "conversion" document we have is a Bible that was put on Liliane's sarcophagus some time in the 1960s or 1970s, opened to the Gospel of St. Matthew. This was almost surely a loving gesture by Liliane's devoutly Catholic hairdresser, recalled by the family as "Kathy." None of Liliane's surviving family or friends ever heard of a conversion to Catholicism. Liliane's memorial service was secular and her burial was Jewish. The rumors probably have their basis in Liliane's well-known admiration for the Sisters of Mercy, with whom she worked during the war and, perhaps, from the $25,000 that the Edgar J. Kaufmann Charitable Trust donated in 1956 to Pittsburgh's Mercy Hospital in her memory (Heinz).

Liliane's death: The report of the Allegheny County coroner was read out to Donald Miller, who incorporated its detail in his article "Kaufmann's Rich Legacy: On the Store's 125th Anniversary; Reflections on the Family's Heritage," *Pittsburgh Post-Gazette* for November 10, 1996. Mr. Miller kindly amplified these details for me by communication of October 8, 2002. Other details come from Bleier and Donnelly, *Montefiore,* 88, and from interviews with Stefan Lorant; with Dr. Richard Wechsler, son of the Kaufmanns' physician, in 1999; and with the Kaufmanns' niece Joan Kaufmann Mendelsohn and their cousins James and Ruth Bachman, as above. Kaufmann Jr. regarded his mother's death as a suicide, but he was in New York at the time and had his own motivation for accusing his father of ill-treating his mother. Joan Kaufmann Mendelsohn, who organized the funeral, insisted that she had heard no rumors of suicide then or since. Dr. Alan Itskowitz and pharmacist Robert Sheer provided the pharmacological analysis of Seconal that I offer in the text, which suggests that Liliane's death resulted from carelessness rather than suicide.

Grace Stoops: Harris, *Merchant Princes,* 110–11; Ralph Demmler, *The First Century of an Institution: Reed Smith Shaw & McClay* (Pittsburgh, 1977), 169–71. Wright had plenty to say to E. J. about Grace Stoops, as he had about everything else. His letter of October 15, 1952, five weeks after Liliane's death, is one of his stranger missives. In it he advises Kaufmann to get married so that he can take care of Fallingwater better. Wright closed with the affectionate phrase "You always were too good and big to stay just a merchandise magnate," and he was among the first to offer congratulations when Stoops and Kaufmann married (telegram, September 6, 1954).

The Kaufmann tomb: Paul Mayén recalled Kaufmann Jr.'s telling him that the tomb occupied the approximate site of the proposed chapel. The Fallingwater Archives has a large drawing of June 25, 1954, for the tomb doors by the Ellison Bronze Co. of Jamestown, New York; this lists A. E. Vitaro as the tomb architect. Much documentation that once existed on the tomb is now lost—for example, a letter with sketches that Kaufmann Jr. sent his father on July 13, 1953, and notes on the participation of A. E. Vitaro in the tomb project from August 18, 1953. We learn of these items only from an October 9, 1974, inventory of two boxes of family papers from Fallingwater's director Thomas Schmidt to Kaufmann Jr. These were the papers that Kaufmann Jr. eventually donated to Avery Library—but only after removing certain documents, such as those on the tomb. Schmidt is certain Kaufmann Jr. was the effective designer of the tomb. Roy Oliver wrote Kaufmann about lighting and heating the tomb on July 10, 1954; further references to the tomb in Ethel Clinton Appel's letters to Kaufmann Jr., September 12 and October 26, 1955; February 6, July 17, September 10, October 8, and December 17, 1956; October 22, 1957; January 20 and February 26, 1958 (Fallingwater).

The Giacometti doors: Correspondence of William M. Lamond of P. Larsen Co., Pittsburgh, to M. André Suss, Suss Frères, Fondeurs, Paris, October 21 and November 2, 1954, with blueprint of tomb doors dated October 18, 1954; Ethel Clinton Appel to Kaufmann Jr., November 5 and December 2, 1957 (Fallingwater). Paul Mayén recalled that Giacometti had asked Kaufmann Jr. for scores of photographs of the trees around the tomb for use as models for the trees on his doors, but in the end he relied instead on a single scrawny tree outside his Paris studio.

"Sixty Years of Living Architecture": Twombly, *Wright,* 384; Lois Brunner, "Arthur C. Kaufmann Profile," *Philadelphia* (January 1951): 14, 15, 29, 30. Arthur C. Kaufmann to Wright, May 4, 1955; Dorothy B. (Mrs. Arthur C.) Kaufmann to Wright, July 31, 1951.

Cantilever deflection: Correspondence includes Kaufmann to Wright, May 9, 1951, September 2 and November 3, 1953; Kaufmann Jr. to Wright, September 2, 1952, and July 12, 1954; Mendel Glickman, University of Oklahoma School of Architecture, to Kaufmann,

August 25, 1954, with work specifications for the local consulting engineers Hunting, Larsen & Dunnell; Glickman to Wright, same day with similar contents.

E. J.'s decline and death: Kaufmann wrote Wright about his illness on July 30, 1951 (Avery); Kaufmann Jr. to Wright on his father's hospitalization at Lenox Hill Hospital in New York, October 7, 1952; Wright to Kaufmann, explaining Ménière's syndrome, August 2, 1954; Dahlen Ritchey interview, 1999. Kaufmann Jr. announced his father's death to Wright on April 15, 1955, with reply April 16. Kaufmann, *Fallingwater*, 60, states as a fact that Wright had seen E. J. on his deathbed, but Junior was not himself present in the house, and Kaufmann's devoted friend Patricia Moorten and her son Clark dispute the story. The *Pittsburgh Post-Gazette* for April 16, 1955, reported: "On Thursday night [just before he died] Mr. Kaufmann was in good spirits as he and his family entertained famed architect Frank Lloyd Wright," but just a few weeks later E. J.'s cousin Arthur wrote Wright to ask if this was true, in a tone that suggested it was not: Arthur C. Kaufmann to Wright, May 4, 1955.

TWELVE: EDGAR KAUFMANN JR., TRUE LORD OF FALLINGWATER

Edgar Kaufmann and Helen Frick: We know of Edgar's voting habits from the letter Joseph Johnson wrote Lloyd Skole on October 23, 1961, telling Skole that he could not visit Fallingwater on November 7, 1961, because that was election day, "and Mr. Kaufmann will definitely be in 'Fallingwater' that day to vote" (Fallingwater Archives). Details on Helen Clay Frick come from John McCarten's two-part profile in *The New Yorker* (July 15 and 22, 1939), and from talks with her great-niece and biographer Martha Sanger.

The Pittsburgh rejectionists: On William Larimer Mellon II, see Barry Paris, *Song of Haiti* (2000). Most of the other men in this grouping have entries in the *Dictionary of American National Biography* (1999), 24 vols. A tenth figure who was in many but not all respects like the other nine was H. J. "Jack" Heinz II (1908–87), who served as titular head of his family's ketchup empire even though his life passions were skiing, art collecting, amateur photography, and meddling in urban design. Heinz, as we saw earlier, maintained twelve houses.

Young Edgar: 1998 interview with Newton Chapin Jr. Kaufmann's quote appears in *The Academician,* the yearbook of Shady Side Academy (Pittsburgh, 1927), 53. Edgar wrote Victor Hammer on July 26, 1927 (Library of Congress). The Fallingwater Archives contain sheaf after sheaf of papers in English and German imploring Kaufmann Sr. to aid the Werkstätte at the time his son was living in Vienna.

Ouspensky, Gurdjieff, and Hammer: My thanks to Lynda Waggoner for informing me about Edgar's letter to Alemany and for suggesting a connection with Gurdjieff and Mrs. Wright. Before meeting Wright in 1924, Olgivanna had studied at Gurdjieff's Institute for the Harmonious Development of Man at Fontainebleau, near Paris. Her vision of the Taliesin Fellowship was based on Gurdjieff's institute, and she brought her teacher to Taliesin more than once. Edgar may well have met him there. The Fallingwater Archives still retain the envelope and photograph by which Edgar shared Hammer's portrait of his mother with W. Frank Purdy in New Canaan, Conn.; it was mailed from the Kaufmann's buying office in Palazzo Strozzi in Florence.

Edgar's five languages: Alice Goldfarb Marquis, *Alfred H. Barr Jr.: Missionary for the Modern* (1989), 190–92. Who asked Kaufmann to investigate Johnson's Nazi past is not clear: Paul Mayén said it was an official commission from MoMA, but Schulze (*Johnson,* 181–82, 238) regarded this instead as Kaufmann's personal initiative to dislodge Johnson from MoMA. Edgar recollected his time with Hammer in *Victor Hammer: An Artist's Testament* (Lexington, Ky., 1998), 15–18.

Kaufmann's account of the birth of Fallingwater: Kaufmann, "Twenty-five Years": 21; *Fallingwater,* 36; comparable accounts in Hoffmann, *Fallingwater,* 11–12, and Gill, *Many Masks,* 343. Letters from Kaufmann to Donald Hoffmann, January 14 and 21, 1974, and a third, undated but annotated by Hoffmann "rec'd Jan 16 1976" (Hoffmann files, kindly lent for my inspection by Mr. Hoffmann). Hoffmann's characterization of Edgar as "awfully cavalier with the facts" came in an interview in 1989. Frederick Gutheim cited Wright's "systematic falsification" in his "Recollections" in Tafel, *About Wright,* 216–17: "[Wright's] penchant for rewriting history . . . is not just indifference to dates and facts—including the date of his birth—but systematic falsification to make a point or overcome an opponent."

Edgar's return date from Europe: Hoffmann, *Fallingwater,* 11; Patricia Lowry, "Edgar J. Kaufmann Reflects on Fallingwater's 50 Years," *Pittsburgh Press,* October 4, 1986. The accurate date appeared in the *Pittsburgh Jewish Criterion* for July 28, 1933. My interviews with Caroline Wagner took place in 1989—my thanks to Edgar Tafel for putting us in touch. The *Champlain* left Plymouth on Wednesday, July 26, 1933, and seems to have docked in New York on Wednesday, August 2.

Radiation and Freudian therapy: Edgar's meeting with Freud is a widespread but questionable tale; nonetheless, it was vouchsafed to me in 1985 by Margaret Louchheim Meiss, a mental-health professional whose brother, Joseph Louchheim Jr., was married to Junior's cousin and great friend Aline Bernstein Louchheim Saarinen.

A lost application to Taliesin?: The report of Edgar's lost or delayed Taliesin application comes from Fallingwater guide Sue Rugg (2001 interview and communication of February 27, 2002), who gave Edgar himself as its source. Since Edgar mentioned this neither to Fallingwater's director Lynda Waggoner (communication, February 7, 2002) during the twenty-five years in which they worked together, nor to her predecessor Thomas Schmidt, with whom he was equally close, it may be one of the little jokes for which he was well known. Still, the "lost-reply" explanation for the discrepancy between 1933 and 1934 is not impossible. Edgar Tafel had never heard the story, but he thought it plausible, given the chaotic way Taliesin was administered in its early years. Longtime apprentice Cornelia Brierly told me that her older sister had petitioned Taliesin for admission in 1933 but never got an answer because Wright's then-secretary Karl Jensen threw the letter away.

Kaufmann's lost year: Cornelia Brierly was insistent in 1989 that Kaufmann had spent much time in Mexico as a painter in the circle of Diego Rivera. Since all three Kaufmanns were close to Rivera and Kahlo, Brierly's suggestion carries weight; Taliesin's archivist Bruce Brooks Pfeiffer independently told me that Kaufmann had spent a year in Mexico around 1933 or 1934. Darthea Speyer, the Paris art dealer who grew up with young Kaufmann at Bear Run, remembered "Junior went to Mexico a lot." Edgar was explicit in his loathing of his father's antics during an interview in 1986.

The mysterious Miss Adler: Kaufmann, "Twenty-five Years," and his *Fallingwater,* 36; Lisa Ronchi communication, March 25, 2001; Kaufmann referred to Zevi's publication in *Fallingwater,* 64; Hoffmann-Kaufmann correspondence, January 14 and 21, 1974, January 16, 1976. Hoffmann, *Fallingwater,* 10, smoothed over Kaufmann's evasiveness when he wrote: "In 1934, when Edgar Kaufmann, Jr., was 24 years old and back from a long stay in Europe, a friend of his in New York (a woman who worked as a secretary in an art gallery) spoke to him about [Wright's *Autobiography*] with great enthusiasm." The nonexistence of a chronologically appropriate Miss Adler was certified in interviews with Rachel Adler and Ann Yaffe Phillips at New York's Hirschl & Adler Galleries in 1993. Kaufmann refers to the E. Weyhe Gallery in *Fallingwater,* 34, but the gallery's longtime manager, Gertrude W. Dennis (communication, July 9, 1999), recalled no woman named Adler ever working there. Paul Mayén never heard of "Adler" during his thirty-six-year companionship with Edgar, either.

In contrast to the above, Lynda Waggoner (communication, August 9, 2002) recounted to me an incident years ago in which Edgar divulged that a certain Fallingwater visitor "was the woman who first gave me Wright's *Autobiography.*" But the woman in question was part of an ordinary tour group, and Edgar made his remark only after she had left. The incident strikes me as akin to the teasing that Edgar's Columbia students like Mosette Broderick experienced from time to time. The curious case of Miss Adler is certainly not yet closed, but I stick to my guns.

Son of Pittsburgh's "Marshall Field": *Frank Lloyd Wright: Letters to Apprentices,* ed. Bruce Brooks Pfeiffer (Fresno, Calif., 1982), 87. Hoffmann made clear that Edgar had refused to intercede for him at the Taliesin Archives (communication, October 15, 1991). Jensen's memo to Wright about meeting Kaufmann Jr. was undated, but the context suggests September 30, 1934.

"His father wants him to go there": Among the parents who asked Wright to take on their children as apprentices was Ernest Meyer of the *New York Post* (letter, December 12, 1938), who described his son Leonard as "intelligent, but timid; six feet tall but skinny, and needs both the hearty physical outdoor work at Taliesin, and intellectual leadership of you and your older apprentices." Likewise, on February 18, 1938, Mrs. Hylda Marks of New York asked Eugene Masselink to admit her son to the fellowship.

I thank Richard Tobias for parsing the "father wants him to go there" phrase with me in 1999. When I read the phrase to Edgar's cousins, they all interpreted it to mean that E. J. had literally forced his son to go to Taliesin. I. D. Wolf Jr. specifically recalled how happy Kaufmann Sr. had been when his son went to Taliesin, and Joan Kaufmann Mendelsohn also felt that such a scenario accorded perfectly with the characters of the players involved. Mendelsohn added that her uncle E. J. had no need of his son as an intermediary to get to Wright, and that Wright would never have accepted Edgar Jr. at Taliesin without a promise of commissions from Edgar Sr. In her *Frank Lloyd Wright,* 422, Meryle Secrest expanded on my discussion of whether it was the father or the son who first got interested in Wright. Secrest proposed that Kaufmann Sr. sent Junior to Taliesin as a scout, an advance party to secure his father's interests with Wright.

Edgar's coming to Taliesin: Wright's September 28, 1934, note to Kaufmann that "your son Edgar is a fine chap and we look forward to having him here with us" artfully hid the fact that he had not yet met Junior. The two only met around September 30, after which Wright reported back to Karl Jensen on October 5. Ethel Clinton wrote Wright on October 10 that Junior would take up residence in Spring Green on Monday, October 15. On November 3, Wright wrote E. J. about his son again, having finally gotten to know him. Kaufmann's arrival was cited in the multinewspaper column "At Taliesin" for September 27, 1934 (Henning, "At Taliesin," 81–82); his leaving appears in his *Fallingwater,* 39. Brendan Gill, "Edgar Kaufmann, Jr.: Secrets of Wright and Fallingwater," *Architectural Digest* (March 1990): 50, 54, 59, 60, 62, 64; reprinted in Gill, *New York Life,* 109–13. Gill gave me his private theory of events in 1990. The revenge that Edgar's loyalists supposedly exacted from Gill was described by Paul Mayén to Carolyn Hammer by letter of May 15, 1990 (Library of Congress). In actuality, Gill lost his job as architecture critic at *The New Yorker* because the magazine felt it needed a new voice, not because of any Kaufmann "scandal" (communication from Robert Gottlieb, July 23, 2002).

Edgar's leaving Taliesin: Wright's letter to E. J. Kaufmann about "some matter pertaining to the Junior" is dated April 27, 1935. During his long research stay at Taliesin West in the late 1980s, Wright scholar Anthony Alofsin several times heard how thoroughly Wright had humiliated Edgar. Several of the early apprentices confirmed Wright's "Whippoorwill" nickname for Edgar. The whippoorwill is a nocturnal bird that is rarely seen but incessantly heard, which seems to have been the point of Wright's cruel joke. In 1989, Wesley Peters told me: "Mr. Wright sent Junior away: he was too flamboyant, joking, didn't tie in with the general work." Donald Hoffmann interviewed Bob Mosher about the circumstances of Kaufmann's leaving around 1974, as Hoffmann told me in 1989.

Homosexuality at Taliesin: Wright alluded to those apprentices lacking in "circumspection" in his revised *Autobiography,* 429. According to Edgar Tafel, "Homosexual behavior was anathema to Wright; he could never understand it, feel for it, or condone it" (*About Wright,* 238, followed by the account of Wright's visit to a homosexual former apprentice). Gill, *Many Masks,* 459, declared: "The Wrights were at their most unyielding about transgression of sexual mores"; Secrest, *Wright,* 406, quotes apprentice John Howe on the same topic. The architect Tasso Katselas told me he quit Taliesin in 1952 because of his discomfort with the charged homosexual atmosphere there. Katheryn Smith (communication, April 12, 2002) informs me that Harold Zellman's forthcoming history of the Taliesin Fellowship will include the issue of homosexuality. The distinguished architectural historian Thomas Hines heard from several sources at Taliesin that Wright mocked Bruce Goff, the most creative of the apprentices, for his homosexuality, and only restrained himself later because of Goff's generosity in sending clients his way. This is hearsay, of course, but wholly consistent with the recollections of numerous Taliesin residents and visitors.

Edgar Kaufmann at MoMA: Edgar to Wright, January 25, 1938, and undated letter, by context probably datable to May 20, 1935. Edgar's four books on Wright were *An American Architecture* (1955), which edited various of Wright's observations into a single text; *Frank Lloyd Wright: Drawings for a Living Architecture* (1959), which two Kaufmann funds paid for; *Frank Lloyd Wright: Writings and Buildings* (1960), coedited by Ben Raeburn; and *Nine Commentaries* of 1989. A hardly unbiased glimpse of Kaufmann at MoMA is provided by the Museum of Modern Art Oral History Project. Project's interview with Philip Johnson (MoMA Archives, undated). Johnson gave credit for the "Useful Objects" concept to MoMA director Alfred Barr Jr., not to Edgar. Kaufmann wrote a long proposal to Barr on August 22, 1939, about his wish to create a permanent department of industrial design. His letterhead by then was that of Secretary of Kaufmann's Department Store (MoMA).

Edgar as a man of letters: Kaufmann's "New Directions in Design" appeared in *New Directions in Prose & Poetry 1938* (Norfolk, Conn., 1938), 157–62. Later in 1938, Kaufmann was an early visitor to the brand-new Walter Gropius house in Lincoln, Massachusetts (Kaufmann Jr. to Wright, undated letter in the period October 25–December 2, 1938). MoMA's *Guide to Modern Architecture,* 7, 97, 98, listed Kaufmann as part of its advisory Architecture Committee. Edgar described his office thus: "Walls of unfinished cork and Transite with 2 × 4's exposed alternately outside and in. Metal files act as structural element in one wall. Drawerless desk with hanging telephones; top of metal lath covered with Vinylite (elastiglass)."

Edgar in the 1940s and '50s: Kaufmann, *Fallingwater,* 36; MoMA press release "News from Good Design," undated but from context 1950. The *Pittsburgh Post-Gazette* announced Edgar's inheritance on July 16, 1953. Edgar's fights with Philip Johnson are recounted in Schulze, *Johnson,* 181–82, 238. E. J. knew René d'Harnoncourt from his war years in Washington, he told his son by letter of March 10, 1946 (Avery); Kaufmann Jr.'s duplicate IRS forms for the early 1950s are in the Fallingwater Archives. "Furnishings Post Resigned by Kaufmann," *Pittsburgh Post-Gazette,* February 12, 1955; Lynnes, *Good Old Modern,* 320.

Goldberger's "A Discerning Eye" insightfully remarked: "[Kaufmann's] stint in the world of commerce was not without its usefulness, however: throughout his life he remained fascinated by the points of intersection between serious design and the market-place, and he devoted most of his efforts at the museum to enhancing those intersec-tions." See also the same author's Kaufmann obituary in the *New York Times* for August 1, 1989.

Taking over Fallingwater: On Kaufmann Sr.'s estate, see Demmler, *Reed Smith*, 169–71. An Orphans' Court decree of May 7, 1956, gave Edgar a $652,615.65 advance on the estate. He had previously borrowed $125,000 against his inheritance from Mellon Bank (Falling-water Archives). Wilk's *Kaufmann Office* provides a full account of its move to London. Edgar's gatehouse project for Bear Run is documented in his letters to Wright of May 23 and August 2 and 10, 1955; June 9 and December 10, 1956; February 13, 1957; and by Wright to Edgar, August 6 and 13, 1955. See also Cleary, *Merchant*, 50–51, 120–23, 181–82. Edgar was confirmed as the designer of the caretaker's house by Denise Miner, whose in-laws lived there.

Management of the Bear Run Farm: All citations of Edgar's management of the Bear Run estate come from the Edgar J. Kaufmann Jr. Personal Papers in the Fallingwater Archives, plus interviews with Paul Mayén and Thomas Schmidt. On Rostow's concept of Buddenbrooks dynamics, see Hall, *Cities*, 996 n. 148.

Edgar in New York: In December 1949, Rockefeller refused Barr's request to allow the American Federation of Arts to tour his art collection, but Kaufmann, Whitney, and Philip L. Goodwin agreed (Alfred Barr Papers, MoMA). On the sale of Kaufmann's art collec-tion, see Rita Reif, "De Kooning Work Sets Record at $20.7 Million" and "Auctions," *New York Times* (November 9 and 10, 1989), and the Sotheby's catalogue to the sale. The origi-nal bill for the De Kooning, for $4,000 plus tax, is among the Kaufmann Family Papers at the Heinz Center. The minutes of the Kaufmann [Charitable] Foundation, 1958–64, at the Heinz Center carry disbursements for the Kaufmann Design Awards and for the Edgar J. Kaufmann Conference Rooms in New York. Details on the disposition of Edgar's estate were provided by Thomas M. Schmidt, Fallingwater's director when Edgar died in 1989.

Edgar and the deflected cantilevers: Edgar to Wright, September 2, 1952, and Kauf-mann, *Fallingwater*, 46, 49–51.

Giving away Fallingwater: Minutes of the Kaufmann Foundation in respect to the "Kaufmann Conservation on Bear Run," beginning July 31, 1959 (Heinz); Netting, *Western Pennsylvania Conservancy*, 23–29; Twombly, *Wright*, 418 n. 5; *New York Times*, September 7, 1963; *Architectural Record* (October 1963): 24; *Carnegie Magazine* (September, 1964): 237–41. Kaufmann was not shy in telling WPC how to run the house after he turned it over to them, according to a series of memos by Joe White, WPC's first manager at Fallingwater, beginning in 1963. The Kaufmann Foundation papers at the Heinz Center include an undated memorandum (probably 1968, by context) from Edgar alerting the foundation trustees to his unhappiness with the way WPC was handling Fallingwater. WPC had been good at maintaining the house as a tourist attraction and had been ade-quate at preparing the grounds as a nature reserve, Kaufmann said, but it had been "griev-ously remiss . . . in presenting Fallingwater to the public with shabby, grubby exteriors and filthy, decayed upholstery in the chief rooms." There was no real effort to make a Falling-water visit educational, and "[t]he present level of administrative responsibility does not properly honor my parents, nor the profound cultural values of the gifts." Construction of a visitors center at Bear Run corrected many of these problems. It was designed in 1977 by Kaufmann's friend Paul Mayén, and its half-million-dollar cost was borne by the Kauf-mann Foundation. The first center burned right after its 1979 opening, but was soon replaced by a second.

The first book on Fallingwater: Bruno Zevi, "Il Vaticinio del Riegl e la Casa sulla Cas-cata," *L'Architettura* (August 1962): 218–21, reprinted in Zevi and Kaufmann, *Casa sulla*

Cascata, 9–15. Lisa Ronchi communication, March 25, 2001. My communication on the subject with Zevi began with an exchange of telephone calls, letters, and faxes in the early fall of 1999, interrupted by his death soon after.

Edgar's later statements on Fallingwater: *The House on the Waterfall: The Story of Frank Lloyd Wright's Masterpiece* was released in a half-hour format by Pittsburgh's station WQED in 1987. Kenneth Love's hour-long *Fallingwater: A Conversation with Edgar Kaufmann, Jr.* was released in 1994 with outtakes from the original interview and other new material. Kaufmann's main printed piece on Fallingwater was his *Fallingwater: A Frank Lloyd Wright Country House* (1986), which was a slimming down of a larger book on which he had worked for years, according to Paul Mayén. I thank John Conti for generously sharing with me Kaufmann's syllabus from his course at Columbia University in the academic year 1964–65, and for his recollection that once, at least, Kaufmann refused to take credit for Fallingwater when asked about it in class (communication, February 3, 1999). Kaufmann's letter to the editor of *Time* appeared in the issue of December 25 1964. Donald Hoppen, *Seven Ages,* 106, gave his eyewitness testimony to the role played by Joe Price in convincing his father to build with Wright.

Other accounts of Fallingwater: Franklin Toker, "Master Builder: Mr. Kaufmann of Pittsburgh," in "Fallingwater: A Symposium to Honor Edgar Kaufmann, Jr., on the 50th Anniversary of the Completion of Frank Lloyd Wright's House at Bear Run, Pennsylvania," Temple Hoyne Buell Center for the Study of American Architecture, Columbia University, November 8, 1986. Letter from Edgar Kaufmann to author, February 23, 1987. Brendan Gill, "Secrets": 82, and *New York Life,* 109–13. Communication, Edgar Tafel to author, December 8, 1989. Kaufmann referred to his father in his *Fallingwater,* 34–62. Wright credited E. J. with saving the fireplace boulder (Hoffmann, *Fallingwater,* 59), but as Hoffmann noted: "Despite all the testimony to the contrary, Edgar Kaufmann, Jr., in later years grew strangely reluctant to give his father credit for the idea of leaving the boulder alone."

Edgar in his later years: Dahlen Ritchey remembered Edgar's much-improved disposition in an interview in 1998. Kaufmann Jr. to Olgivanna Wright, April 27, 1959 (Fallingwater Archives). Ethel Clinton sent $132.50 from visitor fees to the Frank Lloyd Wright Foundation on May 15, 1961. Letter, Wright to Kaufmann Sr., December 10, 1950 (Avery). Olgivanna's last visit to Fallingwater was documented in Netting, *Western Pennsylvania Conservancy,* 29, and in a 1999 interview with Gerald Lee Morosco, who knew Mrs. Wright well. Gill's observation about Edgar's always "correcting" Wright appears in his *Many Masks,* 29.

Edgar's character: "E. J. Kaufmann Jr. Is Engaged to Wed," *Pittsburgh Post-Gazette,* February 10, 1953; Edgar's closeness to Pittsburgh's African-American community was underscored in Nate Smith, "The Privilege of Being Kaufmann," *Pittsburgh Post-Gazette,* May 30, 1990, and in my 1995 interview with Gilbert Boddy Jr.

Edgar's claim to have been midwife to Fallingwater: The University of Pennsylvania's citation is dated May 18, 1987; my thanks to the university archivist for locating it for me. Hoppen, *Seven Ages,* 95; Gill, *Many Masks,* 28; Goldberger, "A Discerning Eye." O. Henry, "Mammon and the Archer," *The Complete Works of O. Henry* (1953), 1:53–58.

Edgar's death: Paul Mayén interview in 1999. Mayén died a year later.

EPILOGUE: FALLINGWATER FOR OURSELVES

Professional appraisals of Fallingwater: The accolades about Fallingwater come from *Memo,* the newsletter of the American Institute of Architects (October 1991): 6;

McCarter, *Fallingwater,* 4; Futagawa and Pfeiffer, *Frank Lloyd Wright,* 5:164; and *Architectural Record* (January 1981): 89 and (July 1991): 136–37.

Visiting famous buildings: The *Economist* for October 18, 1997, reported that 110 million Chinese had passed through Mao's mausoleum in Beijing in the twenty years since it opened in 1977; *Time Australia* (May 9, 1997) estimated that 8 million citizens visited it in 1996 alone. See also *Guinness World Records* (2000), 166; "Most Visited Historic House Museums in the United States," in *Almanac of Architecture & Design.*

Ohiopyle: The cited figures on Ohiopyle and Ohiopyle State Park come from Palmer, *Youghiogheny,* 186, and from the *Pittsburgh Post-Gazette* for June 28, 2000, which estimated that since 1970 over 3 million people have rafted the 7.5 miles downriver from Ohiopyle to Bruner Run, which is close to Fallingwater.

The meaning of Fallingwater: Walt Whitman, "Song of the Exhibition," in *Leaves of Grass* (1892; repr. New York, 1983): 161–62. Wright spoke of the architecture of democracy in *The Natural House* (1954): 58. Montgomery Schuyler's comment on the Brooklyn Bridge was cited in David McCullough, *The Great Bridge* (1972). The advertisement for Barragán's housing estate is discussed by Keith Eggener, "Towards an Organic Architecture in Mexico," in *Frank Lloyd Wright: Europe and Beyond,* ed. Anthony Alofsin (Berkeley, 1999), 166–84, at p. 183. Paul Rudolph's interpretation of Fallingwater appears in Futagawa and Rudolph, *Kaufmann House,* n.p. My closing line is a deliberate paraphrase of, and homage to, the ending of Hoffmann's *Fallingwater,* 111: "There was never any house quite like it before, and there has been none since."

Illustrations in the text are designated by the relevant page numbers; Roman numerals indicate the order of the color plates. All photographs of Fallingwater are reproduced by permission of the Western Pennsylvania Conservancy.

Wayne Andrews: 21

L'Architecte, 1931 (Willard Morgan): 177

Arizona State University Department of Archives and Manuscripts: 135 bottom

Art Institute of Chicago: VI, XIII bottom (copyright Estate of Peter Blume/Licensed by VAGA, New York, NY)

Astorino: 151 top and bottom, 191 bottom

Avery Architectural and Fine Arts Library, Columbia University in the City of New York: 101, 193 and 225 top (both Luke Swank), 304

Marlene Boyle: 3, 173, 185 top

William Boyle: 185 bottom

Butler Library, Columbia University in the City of New York: 72

Cahiers d'Art, 1929 (8–9): 24

Carnegie Library of Pittsburgh: 40 left, 45, 46, 47, 172, 235, 301 (the last three Luke Swank)

Carnegie Mellon University Architecture Archives: 66 right

Charette, March 1938: 277

Chicago Architectural Photography Co.: 16

Chicago Historical Society: ii (Bill Hedrich/Hedrich-Blessing), 133 and 338 (Hedrich-Blessing)

Harold Corsini: 135 top, 191 top, 206, 303, 350, IX, X top, XI bottom

Keith Eggener, Luis Barragán's Gardens of El Pedregal (2001): 404

Eliot Elisofon/Time Life Pictures/Getty Images: 13 (*Life,* November 9, 1942)

Herb Ferguson: II

Paintings for *Fortune* by Lucille Corcos; copyright Time Inc. All rights reserved: 49, The Kaufmann store in Fortune, 1944 color

Copyright © 2003 The Frank Lloyd Wright Foundation, Scottsdale, Ariz.: 17 top left and top right, 163 top, 339, 341, 344, 348, color of "base" plan of Fallingwater; Fallingwater color perspective

Courtesy The Frank Lloyd Wright Archives, Scottsdale, Ariz.: 125, 165

Copyright © Pedro E. Guerrero: 391

Copyright © Clyde Hare: 38

Thomas A. Heinz: 24 bottom, 29 top, III, XI

Heinz Regional History Center archives: 37; color postcard Kaufmann's 1905; color picture of Kaufmann's ground floor opening 1930;

Grant Hildebrand, The Wright Space: Pattern and Meaning in Frank Lloyd Wright's Houses (Seattle, 1991): 183

Imagepoint Pittsburgh (Will Babin): 64

Arthur Köster: 74

George Lange: 355

Claude-Nicolas LeDoux, L'Architecture Considerée sous le rapport de l'art, des moeurs, et de la législation (Paris, 1804, 1847): 144

Library of Congress, Prints and Photographs Division, Historic American Buildings Survey: 1 (HABS, PA, 26-OHPY.V, 1-2), 17 bottom left (HABS, ILL, 16-OAKPA, 3-1 [Philip Turner]), 17 bottom right (HABS, ILL, 16-CHIG, 33-3 [Cervin Robinson]), 19 top (HABS, DC, Wash, 535), 27 left (HABS, PA, 51-PHILA, 584-4), 207 (HABS, PA, 26-OHPY.V, 1-15), 227 (HABS, PA, 26-OHPY.V, 1-28)

Walter Müller-Wulckow, Deutsche Baukunst der Gegenwart; Bauten der Gemeinschaft (Leipzig, 1929): 23 (courtesy Kai Gutschow)

New York Times: 51

The New Yorker: 189 top (Ed Fisher: March 14, 1994), 279 (Robert Day: May 3, 1952)

New York City Landmarks Preservation Commission (Carl Forster): 27 right

Palmer's Pictorial Pittsburgh, 1905: Frauenheim/Kaufmann house

Bo Parker: XV

Photofest: 294

Gustav Adolf Platz, Die Baukunst der neuesten Zeit (2nd ed., Berlin, 1930): 163 bottom (courtesy Kai Gutschow)

Public Auditorium Authority of Pittsburgh (Ken Balzer): 340

Julius Shulman: 323

Julius Shulman and David Glomb: XIV

Courtesy Skinner, Inc., Boston, Mass.: XIII top (copyright Estate of Peter Blume/Licensed by VAGA, New York, NY)

Copyright © The Heirs of W. Eugene Smith/courtesy of Carnegie Museum of Art, Pittsburgh; Gift of the Carnegie Library of Pittsburgh, Lorant Collection: 354

Michael Schwarting and Frances Campani: 110

Time Life Pictures/Getty Images: 243 (Valentino Sarra: Time, January 17, 1938), 336 (Ernest Hamilton Baker: Time, August 15, 1949)

Franklin Toker: 19 bottom, 29 bottom, 40 right, 66 left, 212 (Kenneth Kremer), 225 bottom, 397, X bottom, XI top (Alex Barron), XVI (Erin Marr)

R. M. Schindler Collection, Architecture and Design Collection, University Art Museum, University of California, Santa Barbara: 176

University of Kentucky Art Museum: XII bottom

Western Pennsylvania Conservancy: 33, 55, 59, 77, 87, 93, 156 (Otto Jennings), 189 bottom, 313, 359, 361, 372, 405, I (Robert Ruschak), XII top

Every attempt has been made to give appropriate credit for the art and photography reproduced in this book. Any omissions that are pointed out will be corrected in subsequent editions.

Franklin Toker, a professor of the history of art and architecture at the University of Pittsburgh, has published books on church architecture in French Canada, the ancient cathedral of Florence (which he excavated), and the architecture and urbanism of Pittsburgh. He has won both the Porter Prize and the Hitchcock Award. Born in Montreal, he was educated at McGill University, Oberlin College, and Harvard University. A past president of the Society of Architectural Historians, Toker lives with his family in Pittsburgh. His Web site is www.franklintoker.com.

A NOTE ON THE TYPE

This book was set in Fairfield, the first typeface from the hand of the distinguished American artist and engraver Rudolph Ruzicka (1883–1978). In its structure Fairfield displays the sober and sane qualities of the master craftsman whose talent has long been dedicated to clarity. It is this trait that accounts for the trim grace and vigor, the spirited design and sensitive balance, of this original typeface.

Rudolph Ruzicka was born in Bohemia and came to America in 1894. He set up his own shop, devoted to wood engraving and printing, in New York in 1913 after a varied career working as a wood engraver, in photoengraving and banknote printing plants, and as an art director and freelance artist. He designed and illustrated many books, and was the creator of a considerable list of individual prints—wood engravings, line engravings on copper, and aquatints.

Composed by North Market Street Graphics, Lancaster, Pennsylvania

Printed and bound by Berryville Graphics, Berryville, Virginia

Designed by Iris Weinstein